RUSSIAN AND SLAVIC LITERATURE

edited by

Richard Freeborn
University of London

R. R. Milner-Gulland
University of Sussex

Charles A. Ward
University of Wisconsin-Milwaukee

1976

Slavica Publishers, Inc.

For a list of some of our other books, see the end of this book. To obtain an up-to-date catalog, with price and ordering information, write to:

Slavica Publishers, Inc.
P. O. Box 312
Cambridge, Mass. 02139

ISBN: 0-89357-038-9

Publisher's note: The three editors of this book each edited an individual section, and the three sections were combined into one book by the publisher. Each editor is responsible only for his own section. The material through page 223 was edited by Richard Freeborn; the material on pages 224 through 294 was edited by Charles A. Ward; the material from page 295 to the end was edited by R. R. Milner-Gulland.

Editor of Slavica Publishers, Inc.: Charles E. Gribble, The Ohio State University, Columbus.

Text set by Eleanor Sapp.

Printed in the United States of America by LithoCrafters, Inc., Ann Arbor, Michigan 48106.

SELECTED PAPERS IN THE HUMANITIES FROM THE

BANFF '74

INTERNATIONAL CONFERENCE

Sponsored by

The American Association for the Advancement of
Slavic Studies

The British Universities Association of Slavists

The British National Association for Soviet and
East European Studies

The Canadian Association of Slavists

General Editor

Roger E. Kanet

University of Illinois,
Urbana-Champaign

GENERAL EDITOR'S FOREWORD

Roger E. Kanet

The studies published in this volume were selected from those presented at the First International
Slavic Conference, held in Banff, Alberta, Canada,
September 4-7, 1974. The conference, which was attended by approximately 1,500 persons, was sponsored by
the American Association for the Advancement of Slavic
Studies, the British Universities Association of Slavists, the British National Association for Soviet and
East European Studies, and the Canadian Association
of Slavists. Although the sponsorship of the conference was limited to the four major English-speaking
Slavic associations, attendance and participation
were much broader and included numerous scholars from
continental Western Europe, Asia, Africa, Latin America, and Oceania. In addition, a substantial number of
scholars from the Soviet Union and Eastern Europe
participated in the deliberations of the conference.
    Among the more than 250 papers presented, a re-
latively large number has been selected for publication in two series of conference volumes. Papers in
the humanities are included in the series of books
being published by Slavica Publishers of Cambridge,
Massachusetts; those in the social sciences are appearing in the series of volumes being published by
Praeger Publishers of New York.
    As general editor of both the Slavica and Prae-
ger series of Banff publications, I wish to express
my sincere appreciation to all the individuals and
institutions that made the conference possible, including the numerous government and private organi-
zations that provided financial assistance, the members of the International Planning Committee who prepared the conference, and the participants themselves.
Finally, I wish to thank the editors of the individual volumes in the two series and the authors of the
essays for their major contributions.

PUBLICATIONS FROM THE FIRST INTERNATIONAL SLAVIC
CONFERENCE, BANFF 1974

I. Volumes in the humanities, published by Slavica
   Publishers, Cambridge, Massachusetts, 02139:

   Reconsiderations on the Russian Revolution, edited by Ralph Carter Elwood, Carleton University.

   Russian and Slavic History, edited by Don Karl
   Rowney, Bowling Green State University, and
   G. Edward Orchard, University of Lethbridge.

   Slavic Linguistics and Language Teaching, edited
   by Thomas F. Magner, The Pennsylvania State
   University.

   Russian and Slavic Literature, edited by Richard
   Freeborn, University of London, Charles A.
   Ward, University of Wisconsin-Milwaukee, and
   R. R. Milner-Gulland, University of Sussex.

II. Volumes in the social sciences, published by Prae-
    ger Publishers, Praeger Special Studies, New
    York:

    *Soviet Economic and Political Relations with the
    Developing World*, edited by Roger E. Kanet and
    Donna Bahry, University of Illinois, Urbana-
    Champaign.

    *Education and the Mass Media in the Soviet Union
    and Eastern Europe*, edited by Bohdan Harasymiw,
    University of Calgary.

    *Economic Development in the Soviet Union and
    Eastern Europe, Volume I: Reforms, Techno-
    logy and Income Distribution; Volume II:
    Sectoral Analysis*, both edited by Zbigniew M.
    Fallenbuchl, University of Windsor.

    From the Cold War to Detente, edited by Peter J.
    Potichnyj, McMaster University, and Jane P.
    Shapiro, Manhattenville College.

    *Change and Adaptation in Soviet and East European
    Politics*, edited by Jane P. Shapiro, Manhat-
    tenville College, and Peter J. Potichnyj,
    McMaster University.

Environmental Misuse in the Soviet Union, edited by Fred Singleton, University of Bradford.

Demographic Developments in Eastern Europe, edited by Leszek Kosinski, University of Alberta.

III. Additional volumes:

"Nomads and the Slavic World," a special issue of *AEMAe Archivum Eurasiae Medii Aevi,* 2(1975), edited by Tibor Halasi-Kun, Columbia University.

Russian Literature in the Age of Catherine the Great: A Collection of Essays. Oxford: Willem A. Meeuws, 1976, edited by Anthony Cross, University of East Anglia.

Commercial and Legal Problems in East-West Trade. Ottawa: Carleton University, Russian and East European Center, 1976, edited by John P. Hardt, U. S. Library of Congress.

Marxism and Religion in Eastern Europe. Dordrecht and Boston: D. Reidel, 1976, edited by Richard T. DeGeorge, University of Kansas, and James P. Scanlan, The Ohio State University.

Detente and the Conference on Security and Cooperation in Europe. Leiden: Sythoff, 1976, edited by Louis J. Mensonides, Virginia Polytechnic Institute and State University.

TABLE OF CONTENTS

RUSSIAN LITERATURE TO 1917

SLAVIC LITERATURE

RUSSIAN LITERATURE SINCE 1917

RUSSIAN LITERATURE TO 1917

Introduction

As a result of the exigencies of trans-Atlantic communication and the graver but less easily definable problem of intercontinental semantics--it took me a long time,
for example, to discover what "panels" were--the contributions to the literature panels of the Banff Conference have
no steadfastness of theme and little conspicuous related-
ness. They are the product of a desire to bring together
younger scholars in the field from both sides of the Atlantic. If there may seem to be a certain lack of unity about
the Banff contributions, there was certainly no lack of
unity, or amity, about the Conference itself. But due to
the inevitable fluidity which accompanies the preliminary
arrangements for all such international meetings, panel
chairmen changed, contributors withdrew and thematic coherence was eroded. The result is, very loosely, a series
of contributions to the study of nineteenth and early
twentieth century Russian literature which range from
Romanticism, through Psychological Realism, to examinations
of aspects of the major novels, *Anna Karenina* and *The
Brothers Karamazov*, to the Grotesque and the Occult, which
featured so prominently in the pre-revolutionary literature of this century.
Conspicuous among the contributions are detailed studies of such matters as the cross-fertilization of literary
cultures (Professor Busch's of Victor Hugo's debut in
Russia), of imagery (in Professor Golubov's study of *The
Brothers Karamazov* or Professor Ivanits's interpretation of
The Petty Demon), or of special fictive worlds, unusual
phenomena in Russian Literature (Dr. Luker's study of *Grinlandia*). Detailed critical reinterpretations are offered
by Professor Peace in his study of Gogol's *Shinel'* and by
Professor Konick in his study of *Anna Karenina*. Little-
known but important areas of criticism and religio-philo-
sophical study are explored in Dr. Little's examination of
Vyazemsky's view of Pushkin and Professor Christa's investigation of Bely's relationship with Rudolph Steiner. A
valuable survey of Russian Romantic writing is offered by
Professor Mersereau Jr and Professor Kalbouss contributes
a survey of early Symbolist drama in Russia.

A word should be said about the place of the Bely
symposium at Banff 74, organized and chaired by Professor
Belknap. It was devoted to the characteristics and the
development of Bely's prose and it provided the most coherent, scholarly and stimulating episode among the literature panels at the conference.

I would like to thank Professor John Mersereau Jr for
his aid and advice in selecting the papers for inclusion
under the heading of Russian literature, and I would like
to express my warm gratitude to all the contributors for
their patience and good nature in awaiting editorial decisions. My thanks are also due to Charles Gribble of
Slavica Publishers for offering to publish these materials
and for his courtesy in attending to the many difficulties
involved. In conclusion, I have not made it part of my
task to ensure total conformity in matters of transliteration, but I have tried wherever possible to ensure that the
text is reasonably lucid.

Richard Freeborn

P. A. VYAZEMSKY AS A CRITIC OF PUSHKIN

T. E. Little

Prince Pyotr Andreyevich Vyazemsky's (1792-1878) enthusiasm for Romanticism extended from approximately 1817
until the early thirties. Writing, in old age, of his
'youthful' polemics, he observes that Romanticism was not
properly defined then and has not been so since. Russian
critics, he asserts, were carried away by the novelty of a
phenomenon they did not understand. It was a protest
against rules and its chief attraction was novelty.[1]
Vyazemsky's comment on his younger self is trenchant but
just. The furore which broke out over Pushkin's *Ruslan
and Lyudmila*[2] proved that anything new and unfamiliar, and
at variance with Classical canons, could be dubbed 'Romantic,' and even such writers as Shakespeare, Goethe and
Schiller were considered Romantics by Vyazemsky and other
critics.[3]

Vyazemsky sums up the situation neatly, but does not
explain why an ill-defined movement should arouse the enthusiasm of so many people for so long. He wrote no theoretical study of Romanticism and his ideas on the subject
have to be gleaned by inference from notebooks, diaries
and correspondence. If at first sight his thoughts present a cheerful jumble of prejudice, dogma and useful insights, typical, in fact, of Russian criticism of the
period, certain consistent ideas can nevertheless be
singled out. Before examining them it is helpful to consider Vyazemsky's personal circumstances which have some
affinity to Pushkin's, reflecting the predicament of a
whole generation of aristocratic idealists.

In 1821 Vyazemsky was in political disgrace, and was
to remain so until 1828. He had expressed himself vehe-
mently, in letters to Alexander Turgenev, on the subject
of Russian politics and was consequently dismissed from
the Civil Service and placed under police surveillance.
The sentences passed on the Decembrists caused Vyazemsky
as much grief and indignation as Pushkin,[4] and, although
Vyazemsky was never a revolutionary, political discontent
and personal vexation doubtless fortified his desire to
make literature relevant to social and political problems
of the day. Later in the century, confronted by critics

who placed such considerations above all other yardsticks
of literary merit, Vyazemsky was to defend aesthetic standards, but during the Romantic period he was particularly
conscious of literature as a force which both reflected and
influenced society. Byron, the cult figure of Romanticism,
is invoked for this purpose as a poet who said in verse
what he might have said in prose before the House of Lords;
and any national or civic verse which contains 'lofty,'
'social' truths can, in Vyazemsky's opinion, be called
poetry.[5] In his monograph on Fonvizin (completed in 1830)
he points out that domestic and judicial abuses form the
chief inspiration behind Russian comedy which, in consequence, can be called political.[6] Significantly, therefore, in 1819, he sees the Classical-Romantic debate in
political terms, calling the Classicists despots and
pointing out that tsars were made for the people, not
people for the tsars.[7]

Paradoxically, Vyazemsky's troubled circumstances
made him see literature not only as a reflection of contemporary life, but as a means of escape from it.[8] In
1830 Vyazemsky remarks with biting irony that Russian
readers have never been afraid of boredom, and Russian
writers have taken advantage of their courage. He complains that writers concern themselves more with instruct-
ing their readers than with entertaining them,[9] and, on
another occasion, remarks that certain writers have rejected the three Classical unities and substituted the
single unity of boredom.[10] Classicism itself is condemned
as 'correct but boring,'[11] from which one may conclude that
Romanticism offered greater scope for imagination and excitement. Vyazemsky fills his letters with long, vague and
exhilarating extracts from *Childe-Harold*[12] which apparently
offered more stimulation than solemn odes, dull lyric verse
and bad imitations of French Classicism. The 'wild pecu-
liarity'[13] of Ossian doubtless appealed as much to Vyazemsky as it had done to Boswell and the young Goethe, and so,
amidst the more solemn explanations of Romanticism's popularity, one must not forget that Vyazemsky and his generation were starved of the fantastic and exotic in their own
literature, and the intoxicating qualities of Byron rather
went to their head.

Vyazemsky's enthusiasm for Romanticism was nourished
by a mixture of political restlessness, personal discontent
and a desire for intellectual and emotional stimulation.
As early as 1817 he was praising Ozerov's plays for their
departure from 'rules,' for their fullness of 'life' and

their 'movement,'[14] words which became catch phrases in
Vyazemsky's criticism as the antonyms of Classical 'stagnation' and 'lifelessness.' But amidst these vague notions
he introduced a concept which was to be of considerable importance for later criticism: *narodnost'*. In 1819 Vyazemsky conceives the word as a combination of the French
nationale and *populaire*[15] but, typically he refuses to
give it precise definition, remarking later, in 1847, that
he loves *narodnost'* as a feeling (*chuvstvo*) but not as a
system (*sistema*).[16] It is beyond empirical analysis and
resides in the deeper recesses of the human soul.[17] Other
statements imply that *narodnost'* involves the accurate
portrayal of the place and time in which the author sets
the action of his work. It takes on a socio-ethical
colouring when Vyazemsky praises both I. I. Dmitriyev and
Fonvizin for portraying vices and abuses which are specifically Russian and not foreign.[18] *Narodnost'* is Vyazemsky's attempt to remedy a defect he constantly lamented in
Russian literature: the absence of native Russian inspiration and the reliance upon imitation of foreign models.
A strict systematic definition of the term would admittedly be difficult, but Vyazemsky does not even *discuss*
the qualities which in his view constitute a particular
national ethos in literature. Inevitably vagueness leads
to triteness, when, as early as 1824 he declares that any
good Russian verse is truly Russian verse.[19] If this is
taken to its logical conclusion, the whole issue of
narodnost' and Romanticism, dissolves into a non-question,
for any 'good' literature of any age could thus be
reckoned 'Romantic,' which, in fact, Vyazemsky comes
closer to asserting when he maintains that the ancient
Classical writers were nearer to Romanticism than modern
Classicists.[20]

In common with his generation Vyazemsky adhered to
some splendid but nebulous concepts. He believed in the
inevitability of progress, the coming dawn of Universal
Enlightenment[21] and the benevolent fruits of the 'Spirit
of the Age.' Believing Romanticism to be in accord with
the 'Spirit of the Age,' and therefore bound to conquer,
his advocacy of the cause has all the brash zeal of a
prophet propounding a new vigorous faith to the weak ad-
herents of a decadent religion. 'The mind of a man knows
rest and inactivity,' he writes in 1823, 'but the mind of
humanity is always at work and always advancing.'[22] He
condemns the 'hidebound' of this world who oppose the
successes of the human mind, dubbing them 'apostates from

the Spirit of the Time' which will nevertheless stride
through them on its inexorable course.[23]   Such firm con-
victions of the inevitability of certain events indicate
Vyazemsky's implicit faith in the rule of Law, both in the
intellectual and political spheres, a respect which considerably tempered his political discontent. Certain people, in Vyazemsky's mind, were invested with the authority
to administer the invisible but ineluctable laws of intellectual progress. Catherine II, in his interpretation, was
the promoter and patron of 18th century literature, Karamzin presided over the Republic of Letters in the early part
of the 19th century. A new 'lawful' authority was needed
to sanction Romanticism. That role was filled by Alexander
Pushkin.

      Vyazemsky met the young poet in 1816, and a close
friendship followed which has formed the subject of several
studies.[24]   Vyazemsky's extensive memoir writings, together
with his correspondence, has proved a rich mine of information for Pushkin scholars. But amidst the wealth of biographical material relevant to Pushkin's life and manners,
only three complete works are devoted to literary criticism, and one of these, a foreword to *The Fountain of
Bakhchisaray* (1824),[25] is not so much a critical study of
Pushkin's poem as a piece of propaganda for Romanticism.
The two others are short reviews of *The Prisoner of the
Caucasus* (1822)[26] and *The Gypsies* (1827).[27]   Literary historians seem to have overlooked the odd fact that Vyazemsky, who is generally regarded as the critic of the Pushkin
period, wrote very little about the great man's work but
devoted more critical energy to lesser figures of another
era, such as I. I. Dmitriyev, Ozerov and Fonvizin.

      The polemic over *The Fountain of Bakhchisaray* will be
considered first, out of chronological order, for it reveals much about the intellectual and emotional background
to the Romantic debate. Vyazemsky wrote an introduction to
Pushkin's poem at the poet's request. He called it *Vmesto
predisloviya: Razgovor mezhdu izdatelem i klassikom s
Vyborgskoy storony ili Vasil'yevskogo ostrova*, being a
fictitious dialogue between a Publisher who expresses
Vyazemsky's views on Romanticism, and a Classicist who
presents the opposing view, ultimately defeated by the
superior arguments of the Publisher. He allows his Classicist just enough intelligence to make his defeat a victory for Truth rather than a prejudged outcome. The substance of the dialogue is a rehash of the arguments advanced in the controversy over *Ruslan and Lyudmila* four

years previously. A reply was published by M. Dmitriyev
in the form of a second dialogue between a Classicist and
a Publisher,[28] but ending this time in the victory of the
former. Vyazemsky replied in his turn, and the debate
dragged on tediously through a total of seven articles.[29]
Both men write in the tones of those who are in exclusive
communion with Truth and Enlightenment, vividly displaying,
at the same time, how nebulous a concept Romanticism was.
All the complexities of thought which marked the movement
in the West are reduced to issues of foreign influence,
speed of action and vagueness of plot in Romantic literature, 'graveyard' plots and idiosyncrasies of vocabulary.
Issues are clouded by the black ink of personal insult and
cheap point scoring, but even insults reflect the intellectual climate. Dmitreyev writes patronisingly of Vyazemsky's 'youthfulness' and attributes his follies to his
failure to study at University.[30] With passion for Enlightenment prevailing at the time *nevezhestvo* was as
grievous an insult then as *nekul'turnost'* is now. In the
exchanges of the time it was a common error to identify
Classicism and Romanticism with age and youth respectively.
Youth either meant the new and the good, or the upstart and
bad, depending upon age and point of view, whereas age
represented either maturity and good sense or outmoded con-
servatism. It is interesting to note, however, that
Vyazemsky was approaching 32 years of age and was hardly
in the first flush of adolescence, and Zhukovsky, considered by many Classicists to be the worst offender against
Classical prejudice, was 42. Kyukhel'beker and Katenin,
whose sentiments were similar to Dmitriyev's, were born in
1797 and 1792 respectively.

The question of foreign influence occupies a considerable portion of the debate but, after pruning away the
insults and point scoring, it is clear that Vyazemsky and
Dmitriyev held similar views and only the distorting effect of the polemic obscures the fact. Dmitriyev complains
of excessive foreign influence on Russian literature, particularly from Germany. Vyazemsky points out that Lomono-
sov, the stalwart of 18th century Classicism, has also been
heavily influenced by German forms. Dmitriyev's attempt to
deny this (purely, it seems, for the sake of argument) is
as futile as Vyazemsky's efforts to gloss over the fact he
had frequently lamented elsewhere, that Russian literature
was too imitative of foreign models. The difference of
opinion between the two antagonists is more a matter of
emphasis than of substance: Vyazemsky objected primarily

to the copying of French pseudo-Classicism; Dmitriyev objected to the imitations of Byron and the mistier German
poets; but even Vyazemsky had, on occasions, mocked
Zhukovsky's Germanophilia[31] and in his doctrine of
narodnost' had attempted to give Russian literature a
national flavour without falling, as some Classicists
were wont to do, into literary xenophobia.

Linked to the question of foreign influence is the
vexed question of Romantic vagueness. Merzlyakov had complained in 1818 that Romantic works had no plausible content, no beginning, no end, and no purpose.[32] Similar
complaints were made about *Ruslan and Lyudmila*. With all
this in mind Vyazemsky makes his Publisher, in the first
dialogue, mock Classicists who complain of 'light hints'
and 'foggy riddles' in Romantic poetry. He cites a Classical critic who could not understand what had happened
to the Caucasian girl at the conclusion of *The Prisoner of
the Caucasus*, and who consequently reproached Pushkin for
keeping the reader guessing about the girl's fate instead
of stating clearly that she had drowned herself. A Classicist, Vyazemsky observes, is not content with seeing a
building, he has to see the structural skeleton too.[33] Not
only is this a false and inappropriate analogy, for presumably the Classicists were complaining of the fragmen-
tary nature of Byronic poems and the difficulty of following an obscure plot (*The Fountain of Bakhchisaray* is, in
fact, a typical example), but Vyazemsky seems to be mocking himself. In 1822 he had complained in his review of
The Prisoner of the Caucasus that the prisoner had not
shown enough emotion at the girl's death,[34] to which Pushkin had later replied that a poet does not have to state
everything.[35] Had Vyazemsky adopted Pushkin's view point,
or was he simply playing down his own opinions for the
sake of argument with Dmitriyev? In either case, Vyazemsky was well aware of the dangers inherent in Romantic
obscurity, and, in calmer circumstances, might have conceded Dmitriyev a point.

Vyazemsky mocks the Classicists' objection to 'graveyard' themes for which they tend to blame Zhukovsky and his
translations from German and yet it was a feature of Romanticism which Vyazemsky himself regarded with, at the most,
amused tolerance.[36]

In reply to Vyazemsky's taunt that the Classicists oppose the introduction of new words into Russian, Dmitriyev
replies that they do not oppose new words, only the inappropriate combination of old words. The overcoming of what

Gukovsky has called 'semantic rationalism,' and the introduction into poetry of words which are emotive and evocative instead of being merely concretely descriptive, was
an important contribution of the Romantic movement.[37]
Nevertheless it seems that committed Romantics could be
maddeningly literal when it suited them and Classicists
could indulge in flights of Romantic fancy. Dmitriyev is
hostile, but remarkable accurate, when he describes the
Romantic tale as a combination of fast narrative and slow
action, and the Romantic hero as a man of strong passions
and cold character. Vyazemsky does not permit Dmitriyev
this incursion into Romantic paradox, although the description fits the prisoner of Pushkin's tale and precisely anticipates Hermann of *The Queen of Spades*. In
1818 Vyazemsky objects to Fonvizin's description of Paris
as a *zaraza* on the grounds that infection can rage in a
town, but the town itself cannot be described as an infection.[38] Similarly Polevoy had objected to a sighing lyre
in Pushkin's verse because only a human can sigh, not a
lyre.[39]

Despite these anomalies, in practice Vyazemsky was
firmly on the side of experiment and innovation. When,
in his notebooks, Vyazemsky defines 'Time' as the authority which will justify or reject new words,[40] he is expressing the essential difference of emphasis between the
two schools. The Romantics, believing themselves sanc-
tioned by the Spirit of the Age as vehicles of Enlightenment, were optimistic about the future and wished to expand the scope of literature to include variations of form
and a more complex expression of the human personality.
They valued good taste as much as the Classicists but had
sufficient faith in human progress to be confident that
their experiments would bear useful fruit. The Classicists, like Dmitriyev, were more cautious, and saw salvation in the established norms. Both sides had a firm
faith in 'true' literature, but Romantics believed it to
transcend rules and forms whereas Classicists thought it
to be contained within them. This polemic helped to po-
larise issues, and formed a link in a chain of thought
which led to the acceptance of new views and the departure
from a worthy but outmoded past. It was not a scholarly
conflict but the zest with which it was conducted make it
more interesting to read than debates of duller learning.

Vyazemsky's review of *The Prisoner of the Caucasus*
two years earlier is also written in a tone of brash self
assurance and raises similar questions. He welcomes

Romantic poetry while making slighting comments on adher-
ents of the 'old dynasty.' To dislike modern literature
because it has not been approved by Aristotle is, in
Vyazemsky's view, like rejecting a new species of plant
because it has not been recognised by Linnaeus. He rejects complaints about the excessive influence of foreign
writers such as Byron, Schiller and Goethe, maintaining
that Russian literature has no deep roots anyway, and is
not expressive of a powerful nation. The essence of
Vyazemsky's attachment to Romanticism is summed up in his
statement:

> Nam nuzhnyy opyty, pokusheniya; opasny nam
> ne utraty, a opasen zastoy.[41]

His observations on the poem itself constitute a
short but adequate review. He points out that the prisoner, and the plot, are vehicles for Pushkin's impressions
of a traveller; a purely descriptive poem, he thinks, can
be monotonous. Pushkin, surveying the heights of the
'poetic' Caucasus, was struck by the 'poetry of wild nature,' 'the poetry of local customs,' and, as a poet,
could not pass by in silence when everything was appealing to his imagination and emotions in a 'new,' 'strong'
tongue. Vyazemsky criticises the plot for its lack of in-
vention: the descriptive passages are entertaining but the
action is not, and Pushkin should have paid more attention
to dramatic quality. He thinks the character of the girl
is well portrayed, describing her as 'poetic' with a certain charm and absence of definition. A woman who has
loved, he continues, has fulfilled her destiny on earth
and lived in the fullest sense of the word. He hastens
to assure his readers that the verb 'love' is to be understood here in the pure, moral, and strict sense of the
word. He makes a passing reference to Classicists who
dislike a poet 'afire' and 'seething with life,' and advises Pushkin to follow the independent promptings of his
own Egeria, in full assurance that a watchful censor will
keep him within the bounds of the permitted.

It is the Prisoner about whom Vyazemsky makes his most
significant observations, considering that he is too lightly sketched, with gaps in his characterisation. Raising
the point he was to mention obliquely and self deprecat-
ingly in 1824, Vyazemsky points out that the Prisoner does
not have one grateful thought or one compassionate feeling
at the girl's death, which, Vyazemsky thinks, shows for-
getfulness on the part of the hero or the author. But,
alone among contemporary reviewers, Vyazemsky stresses the

Prisoner as a social type, with distinctive characteristics:

> A superabundance of strength, of inner life which,
> in its ambitious demands, cannot be satisfied with
> concessions to an external life which is generous
> only to the moderate desires of so called prudence.
> The inevitable result of such discord: pointless
> agitation, devouring activity directed at nothing
> substantial, hopes ever unrealised but ever aris-
> ing with new aspiration, must inevitably sow in the
> soul that ineradicable germ of boredom, morbidity,
> satiety which mark the characters of Childe Harold,
> the Prisoner of the Caucasus and all like them.[42]

Such comments are typical of Vyazemsky's critical pre-
occupations: verisimilitude of characterisation and action,
depiction of local cultures, a craving for excitement in
plot and description, the relevance of literature to contemporary life. Political references too are present,
particularly in the opening sentence: 'Captivity, it seems,
is the inspirational muse of our time,' and in the ironic
reference to the censorship.

The review has attracted unfavourable comment. Trubachov[43] points out the similarity between Vyazemsky's
comments and Pushkin's own observations in a draft letter
to N. I. Gnedich.[44] Both poet and critic complain of incomplete characterisation, an inadequate plot and the absence of dramatic tension, but even if Vyazemsky had somehow come into possession of Pushkin's observations, they
are nevertheless in accord with his own views and aesthetic standards. Belinsky, too, in his sixth article on
Pushkin, makes a rash generalisation when he writes that
critics of Pushkin's time did not understand the joy
aroused among the public by the contradictory and paradoxical hero.[45] Vyazemsky, in fact, was the only critic
among the three main reviewers[46] of the poem to define the
Prisoner as a recognisable social type, a point of view
Belinsky wholeheartedly adopts, calling the Prisoner a
geroy togo vremeni. It is possible that Belinsky mistook
Vyazemsky's comments on the incomplete characterisation of
the hero as a misunderstanding of the Prisoner's significance. In any case, censorship would have prevented
Vyazemsky from going deeper into the social and political
implications of the hero; his comments, as they stand, together with his 'political' innuendoes are bold, considering the political plight of both Pushkin and Vyazemsky,
who were in a better position than even Belinsky to under-

stand the Prisoner's situation. Vyazemsky admittedly says
little about the poem's form and structure, but Belinsky
follows his predecessor in pointing out that the plot is a
device enabling Pushkin to describe Caucasian scenery.
The trend of Belinsky's remarks follows that of Vyazemsky's
but there is an interesting divergence of opinion. In a
private letter, Vyazemsky, ever the enemy of chauvinism,
deplores Pushkin's glorification of Russian militarism in
the Caucasus, remarking that it would have been better had
he been able to praise Russia's spread of Enlightenment.[47]
Belinsky, on the other hand, speaks of the Caucasus as a
region purchased by the precious blood of Russia's sons
and the deeds of her heroes.[48]

　　Vyazemsky's review of *The Gypsies* seems more mature.
Propaganda for Romanticism is still evident but a greater
proportion of space is devoted to the poem itself. In the
preamble Vyazemsky comments on Pushkin's growing artistic
maturity and certain aspects of Pushkin's work which he
considers Romantic, particularly its novelty and excitement. Pushkin transports his readers onto a new stage:
colours and phenomena come before our gaze which arouse
unfamiliar sensations in us. As though standing before
an invisible audience of hostile Classicists, Vyazemsky
defends the episodic structure of the poem by invoking the
slogans of Romantic criticism: 'imagination' and 'feeling,' which have no need of a mathematically consecutive
narrative but can portray what they wish merely by sing-
ling out salient points. Returning to the issue raised
in the polemic over *The Fountain of Bakhchisaray*, Vyazemsky
does not consider it necessary for the poet to relate
everything. Drawing, it seems, on his memories of *The
Iliad*, he asserts that in classical antiquity armies would
besiege a town for ten years and poets would keep a journal for every day of the siege and for the activities of
each individual soldier. Romantic poetry, on the other
hand, avoids the fortress and is more concerned with the
outcome of the war. Poets no longer sing of sieges and
the capture of towns, and the hallmark of Romantic poetry
is the drive towards speedy conclusions. The 'old timers,'
Vyazemsky remarks unkindly, would attribute this to haste,
but it is, in Vyazemsky's opinion, merely a matter of pru-
dence. Heroes and heroines should be shown at decisive
moments and one takes for granted that they eat and drink
like all other sinners.

　　After this elaborate and rather facile defence of the
poem's division into descriptive, narrative and dramatic

scenes, Vyazemsky singles out other points for praise. He
enthuses over Pushkin's portrayal of the gypsies and their
environment, just as he had enthused over the picture of
tribal life in the Caucasus. Here again Vyazemsky shows
his concern for *narodnost'* in the accurate portrayal of a
cultural scene, and for emotional excitement, when he describes the 'poetic wildness' of the gypsies' customs, and
their mysterious origins. Such a tribe, he thinks belongs
to poetry and Pushkin has successfully captured the gypsies
and subjected them to his poetic imagination.

Vyazemsky praises the characterisation of the Old Gypsy
and Zemfira, pointing out the psychological versimilitude
of their portrayal as they all behave with individual idiosyncrasies of speech, movement and opinions. The scenes between Zemfira and Aleko, and the gradual development of the
plot to the climax of the murder are 'full of life, strength
and unusual accuracy'; the old man's farewell speech to
Aleko 'breathes majestic simplicity and truth, that is,
lofty poetry.'

He makes three slightly adverse comments. Like Ryleyev,
he thinks it inappropriate that Aleko should lead a dancing
bear around the country and suggests a horse as a more
suitable object of a hero's attention. He thinks it a mistake to have Zemfira die 'epigrammatically' (*umru lyubya*),
observing with what is either unnecessary pedantry or a
laudable eye for versimilitude, that there would scarcely
have been any time for her to fall out of love. The last
line of the Epilogue he considers too Greek for this context, remarking that it could have come from a Greek tragedy.

Aleko is placed firmly in a social context. Vyazemsky
assures his readers that Aleko is a prototype of the generation, a figure taken from society and put into poetry, not
vice versa. Aleko's dilemma, according to Vyazemsky, is
that he can flee from society, but not from himself, and
the essence of the poem is that Aleko cannot adapt himself
to the values of a society which has adopted him, and the
change in Aleko's pattern of life has not brought about a
corresponding change in his character. He merely brings
into his new life the same passions and torments which had
afflicted him previously, and, although he shares the work
and pleasures of his new comrades, he cannot share their
ethics.

A hidden personal and political allusion may be detected in Vyazemsky's defence of the Old Gypsy speaking
of Ovid's exile. Some critics apparently considered it
unlikely that the old Gypsy would know of Ovid, but

Vyazemsky defends the episode on the grounds that memory of
him would persist among the inhabitants of the area.   It
would be difficult to believe that Vyazemsky did not have
his tongue in cheek, for both he and Pushkin knew that Ovid
was not the last poet to be exiled there by an irate Emper-
or.

Vyazemsky rounds off his review with the wish that
Pushkin, having achieved so much will achieve yet more,
for even now he has surpassed all his contemporaries.

As a short review it presents a concise summary of,
and commentary on, plot, structure and characterisation
with comments on the work's literary affiliations.   Vyazemsky's obvious enthusiasm for the work is readily communicated to the reader.   Nevertheless it has brought disparaging comments from Trubachov[49] and, more important,
from Belinsky who, in his seventh article on Pushkin, presents a distorted and biased resumé of Vyazemsky's review.[50]   Belinsky thinks it strange that critics (i.e.,
Vyazemsky) should refer to the successful artistic progress of 'the singer of *Ruslan and Lyudmila*', but it is
hardly surprising that Vyazamsky should refer to Pushkin's first, and most controversial narrative poem, before
discussing *The Gypsies*, Pushkin's most recent and successful piece of narrative verse.   Nor is it strange, as
Belinsky seems to think, that Vyazemsky should mention
Byron's influence on Pushkin, for Byron was enjoying immense popularity and the 'dark hero' generally was setting a tremendous vogue.   Equally unjustified are Belinsky's disparaging references to Vyazemsky's comments on
the poem's structure, which was novel at the time and has
commanded the attention of later critics, among them Blagoy
who quotes Vyazemsky with approval on the subject.[51]
Belinsky's most objectionable innuendo is similar to one
in the previous article: his assertion that there is not
one word about the 'idea' of the poem in Vyazemsky's article.   But Vyazemsky's comments on Aleko as a prototype
of his generation and his difficulties in finding freedom
in a primitive society are as valid and as succint as
Belinsky's.   Belinsky mocks the idea that 'fatal' passions
control Aleko's destiny but nevertheless derides Vyazemsky's observations on the Greek ethos of the poem's conclusion.   Vyazemsky might well have sensed the inappro-
priateness of the Greek concept of tragedy in a situation
where the hero is held responsible for his own destiny.
Despite his mockery, Belinsky seems to have satisfied himself that Aleko was no innocent victim of blind fate.

From this it can be concluded that Vyazemsky was not,
in fact, a prolific author of Critical studies on Pushkin,
but the little he wrote has been unnecessarily disparaged
and underrated, despite the fact that he raised points and
queries which were taken up and developed by later critics.

In this early period Pushkin was a figurehead in the
cause of Romanticism and embodied those virtues which
Vyazemsky considered essential features of the new movement: Classical 'rules' were broken and the poet experi-
mented with new forms and linguistic innovations. He fulfilled Vyazemsky's doctrine of *narodnost'* by his seemingly
accurate portrayal of local colours and cultures, with
close attention to verisimilitude in characterisation and
plot. Moreover, Pushkin's work had strong links with the
state of Russian society and, by implication, with the political problems of the time. All this may be regarded as
foreshadowing later 'Realism' and yet, in his concept of
Romanticism, Vyazemsky also emphasised the importance of
imagination and inspiration, demanding of literature the
power to exhilarate, enchant and entertain. It is perhaps
for this that Vyazemsky should be best remembered, both as
a critic of Pushkin and as an advocate of Romanticism: he
reached a fine balance between 'Art for Art's sake' and
'Literature with Purpose' by stressing the social and political importance of literature and preserving, at the
same time, a proper regard for aesthetic values.

University of Hull
Yorks, England

NOTES

[1] P. A. Vyazemsky, *Polnoye sobraniye sochineniy*,
twelve vols., St. Pbg. 1878-1896, vol. 1, pp. 56-57.
The collected works will henceforth be designated by
the volume number in Roman figures.
[2] See V. Zelinsky, *Russkaya kriticheskaya literatura o
proizvedeniyakh A. S. Pushkina,* seven parts, part 1, M.
1887, pp. 1-86.
[3] I. p. 127.
[4] P. A. Vyazemsky, *Zapisnyye knizhki 1813-1848*, AN
SSSR, M. 1963, pp. 122-132. In 1828 Vyazemsky even expresses a desire to leave Russia and settle in Ireland,
his mother's homeland. (Vyazemsky to Alexander Turgenev,
14 November 1828, *Ostaf'yevskiy arkhiv knyazey Vyazemskikh*,
five vols, St. Pbg. 1899-1913, vol. 3, p. 183. Hence-

forth designated as OA, volume number in Roman figures.)

[5]I. p. 224 (1827).

[6]V p. 131.

[7]Vyazemsky to Alexander Turgenev, 22 November 1819, OA I, p. 359.

[8]Vyazemsky observes once in his notebooks that ink has an intoxicating quality which can give rise to drunkenness. He wonders whether many people would have remained decent people all their lives had they not tasted this fruit (VIII p. 349).

[9]V p. 22.

[10] VIII p. 395.

[11] Vyazemsky to Alexander Turgenev 22 November 1819, OA I, p. 360. In the same letter Vyazemsky wonders what could be more boring than the epic poem, particularly one which has recent history as its theme.

[12] OA I, pp. 330-332, 338.

[13] James Boswell, *The Life of Samuel Johnson LLD* (edited by Edward Malone), London 1807, p. 233.

[14] I p. 49.

[15] Vayzemsky to Alexander Turgenev, 2 November 1819, OA I, p. 357.

[16] II p. 312.

[17] I p. 130.

[18] I p. 132.

[19] I p. 176.

[20] I p. 35. This view was shared by Ryleyev. See K. Ryleyev, 'Neskol'ko mysley o poezii,' *Dekabristy* (edited by Vl. Orlov), M-L 1951, p. 558.

[21] I pp. 96-97 (1822).

[22] I p. 127 (1823).

[23] I p. 66 (1823).

[24] P. P. Vyazemsky, 'A. S. Pushkin po dokumentam ostaf'yevskogo arkhiva i lichnym vospominaniyam' *Sobraniye sochineniy 1876-1887*, St. Pbg. 1893, pp. 469-566; P. M. Bitsilli, 'Pushkin i Vyazemsky, k voprosu ob istochnikakh pushkinskogo tvorchestva,' *Godishnik na sofiyskiy universitet*, istoriko-filologicheskiy fakul'tet, book 55, Sofia 1939, pp. 1-52; I. N. Rozanov, 'Knyaz' Vyazemsky i Pushkin (k voprosu o literaturnykh vliyaniyakh), *Besedy* I, M. 1915, pp. 57-76; N. Barsukov, 'Knyaz' P. A. Vyazemsky i Pushkin,' *Starina i novizna*, vol. 8, St. Pbg. 1904, pp. 1-55; P. B. Struve, 'Dukh i slovo Pushkina,' *Belgradskiy pushkinskiy sbornik*, Belgrade 1937, pp. 265-342. Günther Wytrzens, Pjotr Andreevič Vyazemskij, Vienna 1961, pp. 129-153; M. I. Gillel'son, P. A.

Vyazemsky, *Zhizn' i tvorchestvo*, L. 1969, passim.

[25] A. S. Pushkin, *Bakhchisarayskiy fontan*, St. Pbg. 1824, pp. 1-20; I pp. 167-173.

[26] *Syn otechestva*, part 82, no. 49, St. Pbg. 1822, pp. 115-126; I pp. 73-78.

[27] *Moskovskiy telegraf*, part 15, section 1, M. 1827, pp. 111-122; I pp. 313-320.

[28] *Vestnik Yevropy*, no. 5, M. 1824, pp. 47-62.

[29] Reprinted in V. Zelinsky, op. cit., part 1, pp. 137-171, with a slight aberration in the chronological order and the omission of one article by Dmitriyev, "Vozrazheniye na razbor vtorogo razbora,' *Vestnik Yevropy*, no. 8, M. 1824, pp. 271-301.

[30] *Vestnik Yevropy*, no. 5, M. 1824, pp. 47, 58.

[31] Vyazemsky to D. N. Bludov, 11 February 1817, OA V part 1, p. 108. Vyazemsky to Zhukovsky, 24 March 1819, *Russkaya starina*, vol. 112, St. Pbg. 1902, p. 202.

[32] Quoted by N. I. Mordovchenko, *Russkaya kritika pervoy chetverti XIX veka*, AN SSSR, M-L 1959, p. 155.

[33] I p. 172.

[34] I p. 77.

[35] A. S. Pushkin, *Polnoye sobraniye sochineniy*, ten vols, M. 1962-66, vol. 10, p. 56. Designated henceforth as Pushkin, volume number.

[36] See Vyazemsky's description of a visit to a ruined monastery, OA V, part I, p. 71, and his humorous reference to Zhukovsky's horror ballads, P. A. Vyazemsky, *Stikhotvoreniya*, L. 1958, p. 78.

[37] G. Gukovsky, *Pushkin i russkiye romantiki*, M. 1965, p. 89.

[38] Vyazemsky to A. F. Voyeykov, 27 July 1818, *Russkaya starina*, vol. 76, St. Pbg. 1892, p. 654.

[39] V. Zelinsky, op. cit., part 2, p. 16.

[40] P. A. Vyazemsky, *Zapisnyye knizhki 1812-1848*, AN SSSR, M. 1963, p. 26.

[41] I p. 75.

[42] I p. 76.

[43] S. S. Trubachov, *Pushkin v russkoy kritike*, St. Pbg. 1889, p. 56.

[44] Draft letter from Pushkin to Gnedich, 29 April 1822, Pushkin, 10, pp. 649-50.

[45] V. G. Belinsky, *Polnoye sobraniye sochineniy*, AN SSSR, thirteen vols, M. 1940-1952, vol. 7, p. 375. Designated hereafter as Belinsky and volume number.

[46] The two others were P. A. Pletnyov, *Sochineniya i pis'ma*, three vols, vol. 1, St. Pbg. 1885, pp. 68-81, and

M. Pogodin, V. Zelinsky, op. cit., part 1, pp. 105-19.

[47] Vyazemsky to Turgenev, September 1822, OA II, pp. 274-75.

[48] Belinsky 7, p. 373.

[49] S. S. Trubachov, op. cit., p. 118.

[50] Belinsky 7, pp. 385-86 (1844). 'Turn the pages of periodicals of the time,' writes Belinsky, 'and you will read what was written in them about *The Gypsies*: you will be surprised that it was possible to say so little about so much! There you will find mentioned only Byron, the gypsy tribe, the impropriety of the dancing-bear profession, the successful development of the *singer of Ruslan and Lyudmila*, surprise at the really surprising individual parts of the poem, attacks on the seemingly Greek line *I ot sudeb zashchity net* . . . and much more in this vein, but not a word, not a hint about the idea of the poem!

[51] D. D. Blagoy, *Masterstvo Pushkina*, M. 1955, pp. 110-11.

VICTOR HUGO'S NARRATIVE PROSE DEBUT IN RUSSIA

Robert L. Busch

In Russian literary circles of the very late 1820s
and early 1830s Victor Hugo was associated not only with
the triumph of Romanticism but also with the hegemony of
freneticist elements within it. These elements were derived from the poetics of the so-called *école frénétique*,
a strong current within French literature of the 1820s.

This current, itself the progeny of the English Gothic
and German Sturm and Drang traditions, placed great emphasis on arousing horror and/or terror in the reader. In
characterization its works stressed the dark "satanic" side
of human nature and its potential for crime and the breaking of various taboos. Stylistically, the lexicon and
phraseology of freneticist works often reveal the author-
narrator's concern for conveying heightened emotion and
suffering, and violent human transgressions were commonly
represented grapically with an abundance of naturalistic
detail. Setting, both natural and physical, is used to
instil dread in the reader. To this end dark sinister
castles and monasteries, subterranean vaults and passage-
ways, dungeons, graveyards, and nocturnal storms are frequently encountered in the works of the "école frénétique."

Works from this current as well as its English and
German predecessors had been widely translated into Russian
prior to 1830. Although their frequent translation attests
to their popularity with the general reader,[1] they found
little favor among Russian critics. This was especially
so in the 1820s when Byronic narrative poems and historical novels by Scott held sway over the tastes of most
critics and literary sophisticates. The situation was to
change at the turn of the decade however when major French
literary talents emerged and incorporated freneticism into
their works. In addition to Hugo, writers such as Honoré
de Balzac, Paul Lacroix, Eugène Sue, Jules Janin[2] and
others managed to get freneticist literature to be taken
seriously at the highest levels of the Russian readership.
Russian men of letters often referred to these writers
collectively as *iunaia Frantsiia* (less often as *iunaia
slovesnost'*), terms used to designate the new French contingent known as *la jeune France*. However the incorpora-

tion of freneticism into the works of the aforementioned
authors was so great that the Russian terms for *école
frénétique* (neistovaia shkola and neistovaia slovesnost')
were then and still are used in criticism and literary
scholarship to denote the French contingent.[3] Its titular
head was Victor Hugo, who achieved great prominence in
Russia of the early 1830s.

To the domain of freneticist narrative prose Hugo and
his fellow writers brought more than just talent. There
were certain innovations or modifications which served to
raise freneticist fiction above the level of the penny
dreadful with which so many Russians had disparagingly
associated it.

One can outline the most significant modifications of
traditional freneticism manifest in the works of *iunaia
Frantsiia*. One notes the exploitation of sharp tonal contrasts. These involve the intermixing and/or juxtaposition
of the horrific and the humorous, of the tragic and the
comic, of the sublime and the grotesque (the latter being
associated with that which is ugly or bizarrely distorted).
Victor Hugo's literary practice as well as his famous programmatic preface to *Cromwell* provided great impetus for
the use of these contrastive effects.[4] Tonal contrasts
were achieved in part through the abundant use of irony--
sometimes in author-narrator utterances at the expense of
a given character, sometimes in the gruesome fate of a
given character. Occasionally, this might be achieved by
depicting vice triumphant, as per Pushkin's *Evgenii Onegin*,
Chapter Three, stanza twelve:

> A nynche vse umy v tumane
> Moral' na nas navodit son,
> Porok liubezen i v romane,
> I tam uzh torzhestvuet on.[5]

The *absolute* triumph of vice was actually rather uncommon
in the literature of the major representatives of *iunaia
Frantsiia*. However so, must one add, was the triumph of
virtue. And certainly the author-narrator figures were
far less likely to make condemnatory statements about
their errant characters than was previously the case.
Furthermore, these characters were apt to be unrepentant.
Somewhat paradoxically, given increased author-narrator
detachment vis-à-vis character, one notes an increase in
tendentiousness with respect to social ills. A glaring
illustration of this trend can be made by comparing Hugo's
Le dernier jour d'un condamné (1829) with *Claude Gueux*
(1834). Both are directed against capital punishment.

In the first case, the point is implicit, in the second, stridently explicit.[6] A concern about social ills implies an interest in current affairs. Thus one notes, especially in works by Janin and Balzac, a movement away from exotic historically distanced settings toward contemporary or roughly contemporary urban settings. In 1830 the abolition of censorship in France opened the gates to increased tendentiousness. It also allowed authors a free hand in the extremely graphic depiction of freneticist subject matter. Thus previous canons of "good taste" gave way to extreme naturalism, the limits of which resided essentially in a given author's own sense of what was proprietous and aesthetically worthy.[7]

As V. V. Vinogradov pointed out on a number of occasions, freneticism in the works of members of *iunaia Frantsiia* caused considerable shock and consternation in Russian literary circles. Indeed according to Vinogradov the popular works of *iunaia Frantsiia* were instrumental in challenging the "old poetics" within the Russian literary context, poetics based on "good taste" and "embellished nature." Thus in *Evoliutsiia russkogo naturalizma* and in other studies of the 1920s Vinogradov sought to substantiate the role of freneticist poetics in the early formation of Gogol's talent, in the development of the Russian naturalist school, and in the establishment of a dominant "freneticist school" in original Russian literature of the early 1830s.[8]

There can be no doubt that the narrative prose writings of "*iunaia Frantsiia*" posed a challenge to entrenched attitudes toward literature and there can be no doubt that its works had some impact on original Russian literature of the period. These works posed not only a strictly literary-aesthetic but also a social challenge. For in becoming increasingly contemporaneous and relevant to social issues, such literature tended to infringe upon a domain traditionally reserved to government officials and policy makers. Not only jurisdiction was involved of course, but also the very nature of the ideas that were either construably or directly propounded in the French works.

From the brief introduction to *iunaia Frantsiia*'s poetics, it follows that many of its works would not measure up to the strictures imposed upon literature in Russia, namely that it display "good intentionedness" (*blagonamerennost'*) and thus not be blasphemous, immoral or incendiary. Certainly the tsarist censorship of the period found the narrative prose works of Victor Hugo to be lacking in this respect. Among the leading representatives of *iunaia Frantsiia* Victor Hugo was the most liberal in a literary-political sense. His assertion that romanticism was liberalism in literature, his fondness for depicting popular revolts and his calling into question the humaneness of his country's laws all made of him a suspicious figure insofar as tsarism was concerned.

During the period with which this study deals Victor Hugo wrote five major narrative prose works. *Claude Gueux*, the novella *à thèse*, was not translated into Russian, but did make the list of officially forbidden books in nineteenth-century Russia. From the remaining four works, five translations were prepared. Only two of them were published. *Bug-Jargal* (1820-26) was twice translated but refused publication by the censorship, once in 1831 and again in 1832. The huge novel, *Notre-Dame de Paris* (1830-31) was also translated in its entirety and refused publication.[9] *Han d'Icelande* (1823), another lengthy and archly freneticist novel, was *apparently* published in 1833.[10] The first narrative prose work by Victor Hugo to be published in Russia was his short novel *Le dernier jour d'un condamné*. This work, along with *Notre-Dame de Paris*, contributed greatly to establishing Hugo in Russia as a foremost writer of narrative prose. The work was first translated partially in 1829 and completely in 1830. It was thus instrumental in drawing widespread attention to the freneticist works of *iunaia Frantsiia*, a role it shared with Jules Janin's notorious and highly controversial novel *L'âne mort et la femme guillotinée*, which first appeared in a Russian translation early in 1831.

Given the fact that Hugo's other major prose works were denied wide readership and were generally published in Russian only in fragments, it was indeed the timing and the merit of *Le dernier jour* . . . which largely accounted for its author's impact on the Russian literary context. For certainly, in the domain of narrative prose, Hugo fared extremely poorly on a quantitative basis insofar as the number of translations of his works is concerned. If from 1829-1835 one totals the number of translations involving the works of Janin, Balzac, Dumas, Lacroix and Sue, Hugo's will account for only eight out of over one hundred titles. Moreover, Hugo's were excerpted in all but two instances, whereas this was generally not the case for his fellow writers.[11] In spite of this relatively poor quantitative showing, Hugo's name became synonymous with the new freneticist fiction, and one often encounters references to

his *Le dernier jour* . . . as a work that embodied the horrific poetics of *iunaia Frantsiia*. And this was essentially true. As the title suggests, the work deals with the
dilemma of a man sentenced to death. The time is the second half of the 1820s. It is the narrator himself who records his mental torture during not just "the last day,"
but more exactly the last days prior to his rendezvous with
the guillotine. Time is increasingly compressed as the inevitable end draws closer, the anguish increasing as the
narrator passes from the relative bliss of uncertainty surrounding the outcome of an appeal to the absolute knowledge
of the day and time of his execution. Increasingly he
comes to experience a spiritual wasteland in which he is
alone against all others in his confrontation with death.
In its episodes, composition, setting and style, the work
is indeed eminently freneticist. Further testimony to this
can be evidenced in Bestuzhev-Marlinskii's enthusiastic
praise for the work and its author in a letter to N. A.
Polevoi dated May 18, 1833.

> Pered Giugo ia nits . . . eto uzh ne dar, a genii
> vo ves' rost. Da Giugo na plechakh svoikh vynosit
> v goru vsiu Frantsuzskuiu slovestnost' i topchet
> v griaz' vse ostal'noe i vsekh nas, pisak . . .
> Kstati, *Poslednii don' osuzhdennogo*--uzhasnaia
> prelest'! Eto vdokhnuto temnitsei, pisano
> slezami, pechatano gil'otinoi . . . Puskai
> zhmutsia krashenye guby i tabachnye nosy, chitaia
> etu knigu . . . puskai podsmeivaiutsia nad neiu
> kromeshnye zhurnalisty--im bol'no dazhe i slyshat'
> ob etom, kakovo zhe vynosit' eto! . . .[12]

Additionally, in this connection, one can cite N. A.
Polevoi's reference to the work as one that embodied the
dubious poetics of naked truth:

> Skol'ko slov, nichego ne poiasniaiushchikh!
> Tak mozhno opredelit' i *Poslednii den' pri-*
> *govorennogo k smerti* Giugo, i *Mertvogo osla,*
> Zhanena, i dazhe *Zapiski Samsona*, palacha.
> Nash vek liubit naguju istinu: no dostoinstvo-
> li eto v esteticheskom smysle?[13]

The privately expressed reaction to *Le dernier jour* . . .
and to Hugo's prose in general was more complimentary than
that expressed in published criticism.[14] Extensive articles devoted to Hugo's works were extremely rare, and in
the only such one devoted to his narrative prose, *Le*
dernier jour . . . was characteristically found lacking by
the reviewer, N. A. Polevoi, who expressed dissatisfaction

with all of Hugo's novels written prior to *Notre-Dame de Paris*.[15] Still, published Russian criticism did, like Marlinskii, note the psychological depth achieved by Hugo, a depth in its degree and force unlike anything in Hugo's early prose. It was this depth which was doubtless responsible for F. M. Dostoevskii's esteeming the work a "masterpiece," the most lifelike and truthful work ever written by its author.[16]

In its short review of the Russian edition of *Le dernier jour . . .*, the *Moskovskii telegraf* noted Hugo's fusion of artistry and psychological penetration in treating his subject:

> Nel'zia, vprochem, ne soznat'sia, chto v etom
> uzhasnom bezobraznom sochinenii, est' mnogo
> myslei poeticheskikh. Gugo [sic] kak anatom
> razobral vse oshchushcheniia cheloveka,
> obrechennogo k smerti. Kartina strashnaia i
> nepriiatnaia! . . .[17]

In his article "O russkoi povesti i povestiakh Gogolia," Belinskii too paid tribute to Hugo's convincing rendering of pre-death torment:

> Giugo nikogda ne byl osuzhden na smertnuiu
> kazn', no kakaia uzhasnaia, razdiraiushchaia
> istina v ego *Poslednem dne osuzhdennogo!*[18]

The reviewer for the *Severnaia pchela* also brought out the preeminence of the work's psychological aspect for the Russian reader as opposed to its humanitarian aim, which was alleged to be pertinent only to France:

> Kniga, o perevode koei izveshchaem nashikh
> chitatelei, prinadlezhit ne k prevoskhodneishim
> ego tvoreniiam, no obratila na sebia vnimanie
> vazhnost'iu svoei nravstvennoi i politicheskoi
> tseli. Vprochem, tsel' siia sushchestvuet
> tol'ko dlia Frantsii, gde smertnaia kazn' ves'ma
> obyknovennaia. U nas zhe kartina siia imeet odno
> psikhologicheskoe dostoinstvo.[19]

Whether relevant or not to Russia the socio-political, ideational aspect of the novel was noted in addition to its psychological aspect not only in the above review but also in the previously mentioned review that appeared in the *Moskovskii telegraf*. Consequently, Vinogradov's characterization of the Russian reception of the work is somewhat misleading:

> Dlia literatury 30-kh godov v nem [v litera-
> turnom tsikle R.L.B.] sushchestvenny byli etapy
> "smertnichestva": temnitsa s ee fizicheskimi

istiazaniami, s ee uzhasom predsmertnykh tomlenii
i eshafot. No oni ponimalis' men'she vsego, kak
novaia khudozhestvenno-idealogicheskaia konstruk-
tsiia, kak novye formy tematiki sotsial'nogo
protesta ili kak svoeobraznaia psikho-metafizi-
cheskaia kontseptsiia smertnoi kazni. Iz *Le
dernier jour* V. Giugo izvlekalis' lish' obshchaia
fabul'naia skhema, v kotoruiu teper' i upiralos'
vsiakoe "neistovoe" izobrazhenie osuzhdeniia
predsmertnykh tomlenii prestupnika v temnitse.[20]

Prior to its complete translation in 1830 *Le dernier
jour* . . . was first made available to Russians in excerpts
in three issues of Semen Egorovich Raich's journal *Galateia*
for 1829.[21] Certainly, were the Russian reader of this
time to have been left solely at the mercy of this incomplete translation of Hugo's work, Vinogradov's characterization of the Russian perception of the work would be
plausible. For indeed the attention to plot and certain
spectacular scenes within the work were dominant in the
Galateia translation. This was true in spite of the fact
that an editor's note, which was used to motivate the excerpting of an "imperfect" work, stressed its *psychological*
importance:

> Dolzhno soznat'sia, chto nekotorye chasti sei
> mrachnoi kartiny otdelany s bol'shim iskustvom
> [sic], khotia tseloe i ne iz"iato ot nedostatkov.
> Vprochem, sochinenie sie imeet neot"emlemuiu
> vazhnost' v psikhologicheskom otnoshenii i
> rassmatrivaemoe s sei tochki zreniia, ono daet
> vysokoe poniatie o talante i nabiliudatel'nosti
> Avtora. Reshaias' pomestit' iz nego neskol'ko
> otryvkov, my nadeemsia dostavit' tem udovol'stvie
> chitateliam.[22]

Given this stress on the psychological profundity of Hugo's
work, Raich's selection and rendition of the material from
the work were infelicitous. Without designating which
chapters were being presented, *Galateia* translated in the
following order Chapters 2, 8, 9, 11, 13*, 16*, 30*, 23*,
32, 40, 43, 48, and 49. The specially marked chapters were
abridged. Roughly two-thirds of the total translated material involves the depiction of external events which have
independent "story interest," i.e., the chaining of the
convicts (Chapter Thirteen), the argotic song (Chapter
Sixteen), and the meeting with the jolly recidivist who
recites the story of his life, which is also soon to be
ended by the guillotine (Chapter Twenty-Three). It would

be incorrect to suggest that these chapters do not have any
psychological relevance, for all are perceived and related
by the narrator. Nevertheless, they do not represent the
direct product of his own tortured psyche as he tries to
face up to the significance of what lies before him. Chapters Sixteen and Twenty-Three are recorded by the narrator
but originally narrated by others. Chapter Thirteen *is* the
direct product of the condemned man's own perception. However, the significance for his own condition of the narrated event involving the chaining of the convicts comes in
at the end. There it is incidental, albeit important.
However, until then all attention and interest were concentrated upon the spectacle involving the convicts.

      With respect to the argotic song of Chapter Sixteen
one observes something similar, especially since the
Galateia translation omits the preceding portion of the
chapter in which the condemned man sets the mood by relating his moral and physical depression in the stifling atmosphere of Bicêtre.

      The chapter concerning the meeting with the jovial
recidivist to some degree includes within it the contrastive principle on which it was based. Therein the condemned man's anguish is reaching new heights just a few
hours before his execution. Concomitantly he finds himself a captive audience for the merry banter of a grotesque
highwayman and cutthroat who manages to "con" him out of
his jacket. However, the contrastive effect of this scene
in relation to the narrator's mental state is dependent
upon its being perceived in relation to the preceding chapters. These convey the mounting despair of the condemned
who has suddenly learned that morning that his execution is
scheduled for the afternoon. The *Galateia* version does
provide some of this contrast by placing Chapter Thirty
before Chapter Twenty-Three. However, Chapter Thirty,
which shows the condemned in desperate need of a compassionate spiritual confessor rather than the automaton provided by the state, appeared at the end of issue No. 18 of
Galateia. Consequently, Chapter Twenty-Three led off the
final set of excerpts in issue No. 19. Thus one must assume that for many readers the wanted contrastive effect
was lost.

      The handling of stylistic detail in the *Galateia* ver-
sion roughly parallels its handling of composition. The
approach was extremely free. In addition to the deletion
of whole paragraphs, one finds skipping and paraphrasing.
Paraphrase is particularly evident in Chapters Thirteen,

Sixteen and Twenty-Three.

The rendition of Chapter Sixteen includes the text of
the song of the fifteen-year-old girl whose beautiful
voice, but "hideous lyrics," the narrator hears from within his cell. As mentioned, this song is full of argot
which was undoubtedly incomprehensible to Hugo's French
reader of 1829. Consequently, the author-narrator provided a textually integrated summary translation following
the song. However, the *Galateia* version does not present
the song itself in verse form but paraphrases it with the
aid of the narrator's paraphrase. But then there ensues a
translation of the narrator's paraphrase, which is essentially a duplication of what has just preceded. Within the
translated paraphrase itself there is still more watered-
down paraphrase. Thus

> Cette femme qui court à Versailles avec un placet
> et cette Majesté qui s'indigne et menace le
> coupable de lui faire danser *la danse où il n'y a*
> *pas de plancher*.

is rendered as:

> . . . zhena idet v Versal' i podaet Koroliu
> pros'bu, no on otvergaet ee i podpisyvaet
> smertnyi prigovor.[23]

In the recidivist's tale of murder on the highway, he
states:

> On prenait l'argent, on laissait aller au hasard
> la bête ou la voiture, et l'on enterrait l'homme
> sous un arbre, en ayant soin que les pieds ne
> sortissent pas; et puis on dansait sur la fosse,
> pour que la terre ne parût pas fraichement
> remuée.

Galateia rendered this as:

> . . . den'gi otymali, loshchadei puskali na voliu,
> a tela zaryvali pod kakim-nibud' derevom i
> utaptyvali zemliu nogami, chtoby bylo nezametno.[24]

In Chapter XLVIII, as the condemned is carted trembling to
the place of execution, the priest accompanying him asks
if he is shuddering from the cold. In the original his reply includes both direct discourse and reported thought:

> - Oui, ai je repondu.
> Helas! pas seulement de froid.

In *Galateia* this was rendered completely by direct discourse:

> -Ia drozhu ne ot odnogo kholoda.[25]

In general, the *Galateia* version does not give a
thorough, let alone subtle, conveyance of the emotions of
the condemned. There is almost no attention whatsoever to

the macabre setting which conditions the mood of the narrator. One must consider that any serialized reproduction of
a novella like Hugo's *Le dernier jour* . . . would weaken
its overall effect which results from a concentrated, well-
knit body of scenes revealing the progressive mental undo-
ing of a man prior to his physical extermination. However,
Galateia contributed to an imperfect acquaintance with
Hugo's work not only by serializing it, but by serializing
only parts of it. These were selected and rendered in such
a way as to illustrate inadequately the psychological aspect which had been advanced as particularly praiseworthy
in the editor's note previously cited herein.

Fortunately, acquaintance with Hugo's novella was not
to depend solely on the *Galateia* excerpts. Early in 1830,
shortly after the appearance of the excerpts, a complete
translation of *Le dernier jour* . . . was published. While
not flawless, this translation was, on the whole, an extremely thorough, accurate and faithful rendition of the
original. While absolute errors are extremely rare, it is
possible to note occasional alterations or omissions which
lessen the force of the original. For example:

> C'est un spectacle qu'on embrasse plus aisément
> d'un coup d'oeil, c'est plus tôt vu. C'est tout
> *aussi beau et plus commode.* Rien ne vous dis-
> trait. Il n'y a qu'un homme, et sur cet homme
> seul autant de misère que sur tous les forçats
> à la fois. *Seulement, cela est moins éparpillé;*
> *c'est une liqueur concentrée, bien plus*
> *savoureuse.*
> Zrelische prigovorennogo k smerti legche okinut'
> odnim vzgliadom, ono skoro okanchivaetsia, i na
> onoe *udobno smotret'.* Tut ne razvlekaetes' vy
> nichem. Pered vami odin chelovek, i emu odnomu
> takaia zhe mera bedstvii, kak vsem kolodnikam
> vmeste, *tol'ko muki sii soedineny v odnu tochku.*[26]

Here the narrator's sarcasm is diminished and the idea of
an execution as both a spectacle and a treat designed for
mass consumption is far less forcefully expressed.

Similarly, the shocking quality of the original is
somewhat diminished as a result of imprecision:

> Dautun, celui qui a coupé son frère en quartiers,
> et qui allait la nuit dans Paris jetant la tête
> *dans une fontaine*, et le tronc dans un égout.
> Dotiun razchetveril svoego brata, i noch'iu
> brosil golovu *v ruchei*, a tulovishche v
> stochnuiu iamu.[27]

One encounters approximate translations, most notably in
Chapters Sixteen and Twenty-Three where argot figures so
prominently. Here, as in the *Galateia* version, the translator relies on glosses in the original and only occasionally attempts to come up with Russian equivalents for the
French thieves' jargon:

- Qui êtes vous? lui ai-je dit enfin.
- Drôle de demande! a-t-il répondu. Un friauche.
- Un friauche! Qu'est-ce que cela veut dire?
  Cette question a redoublé sa gaité.
- Cela veut dire, s'est-il écrié au milieu d'un
  éclat de rire, que le taule jouera au panier avec
  ma sorbonne dans six semaines, comme il va faire
  avec ta tronche dans six heures. - Ha! ha! il
  paraît que tu comprends maintenant.
- Kto ty? skazal ia emu nakonets.
- Smeshnyi [sic] vopros! otvechal on. Kusok miasa.
- Kusok miasa! Chto eto znachit? Vopros sei
  umnozhil ego veselost!.
- Eto znachit, vskrichal on, zakhokhotav gromko,
  chto palach budet igrat' moeiu golovoi cherez
  shest' nedel', tochno tak kak s tvoeiu cherez
  shest' chasov. A! A! teper' vidno ty ponjal.[28]

Although there are signals in the text which indicate the
tone of the recidivist's remarks and subsequent narration,
these lack the zest and intrinsic humor of the original.
Consequently they do not bring out in full measure the
contrastive use of comedy and tragedy which Hugo exploited.

In the unexcerpted translation, the argotic song is
translated as a song. It is, however, fully comprehensible
and requires no glosses for the Russian reader. Thereby,
contrary to the *Galateia* version, the ensuing paraphrase
does not stand out as gratuitous since it is clearly intended to provide the narrator's reaction to the song as
such.

The censorship was probably responsible for a number
of approximate translations or omissions. However, evidence
of this is not without contradictions and inconsistencies.
In the prefatory "Une comédie apropos d'une tragédie," one
finds unscathed the appeal to the Charter and the liberty
of the press as a defense of the book's right to exist in
spite of its seditiousness. From Chapter Six the narrator's humanitarian aim, which serves to motivate the recording of his pre-death travail, is adequately rendered:

Ne posluzhat li sii zamechaniia iznemogaiushchego
uma, sie bespreryvnoe umnozhenie stradanii, sei

rod myslennogo sozertsaniia rasstaiushchegosia s
zhizniiu urokami dlia tekh, kotorye delaiut
prigovor? Mozhet byt' chtenie sie ostepenit ikh
ruki na drugoi sluchai, kogda dolzhno budet
takzhe klast' mysliashchuiu golovu, golovu
cheloveka, na tak nazyvaemye imi vesy pravosudiia.[29]
Nevertheless, in this same chapter one can note that tht
translator was not allowed to include an explicit condemnation of laws which allow capital punishment:

Qu'est-ce que la douleur physique près de la
douleur morale!
Horreur et pitié des lois faites ainsi!
Chto bol' fizicheskaia v sravnenii so nravstvennoi?
Uzhasno![30]

What one finds consistently deleted in the full-length
translation are all construably dubious or vain references
to royalty. Thus, "Vous serez seul dans votre loge, comme
le roi" is rendered: "Vy budete v svoei lozhe odni."[31] From
the argotic song, the last stanza relating the King's determination to reject a petition and hang the thief is left
out. Only in the ensuing paraphrase is it suggested that
the matter ends poorly for the thief. Thus, "Cette femme
qui court a Versailles avec un placet, et cette majesté
qui s'indigne et menace le coupable de lui faire danser *la
danse ou il n'y a pas de plancher*" is rendered: "Prikhod
zheny k Koroliu s chelobitneiu, negodovanie Korolia!"[32]

What is striking here is that the earlier *Galateia*
version had made the king's reaction unmistakable. There
are other significant instances where the *Galateia* rendition included construably objectionable material which was
either left out or made presentable in the full-length
version. For example, the condemned man's thoughts concerning the king from whom he is desperately hoping to
receive a pardon are greatly altered:

Il y a dans cette même ville, à cette même heure,
et pas bien loin d'ici, dans un autre palais, un
homme qui a aussi des gardes à toutes ses portes,
un homme unique comme toi dans le peuple, avec
cette différence qu'il est aussi haut que tu es
bas. Sa vie entière, minute par minute, n'est
que gloire, grandeur, délices, enivrement. Tout
est autour de lui amour, respect, vénération.
Les voix les plus hautes deviennent basses en
lui parlant et les fronts les plus fiers ploient.
Il n'a que de la soie et de l'or sous les yeux.
A cette heure, il tient quelque conseil de

ministres où tous sont de son avis; ou bien songe
à la chasse de demain, au bal de ce soir, sûr que
la fête viendra à l'heure, et laissant à d'autres
le travail de ses plaisirs. Eh bien! cet homme
est de chair et d'os comme toi![33]

In the unexcerpted version anything that might be prejudi-
cial to the concept of royalty was removed--probably by
the censor:

V sem zhe gorode, v sei samyi chas, nedaleko
otsiuda, v drugikh palatakh, est' chelovek,
kotorogo vsia zhizn', iz minuty v minutu, est
slava, velichie, naslazhdenie, upoenie. Vse
vokrug ego liubov', pochtenie, predannost'. V
prisutstvii ego, golos samyi gromkii stanovitsia
tikhim, i chelo samoe gordoe prekloniaetsia.[34]

Galateia, for all practical purposes, translated the original completely:

V etom samom gorode, v etot chas, i nedaleko
otsiuda, v drugom dome nakhoditsia chelovek,
kotoryi takzhe imeet strazhu u vsekh dverei,
chelovek, kotoryi odin stoit v narode, kak ty,
s toiu tol'ko raznitseiu, chto on stoit tak
vysoko, a ty tak nizko. Vsia ego zhizn'
bezpreryvnaia tsep' chestei, velichiia,
udovol'stvii; vse vokrug nego ispolneno
liubov'iu, pochteniem, uvazheniem; samye
gromkie golosa stanoviatsia tikhimi, kogda
govoriat s nim; samye gordye liudi prekloniaiut
pred nim svoiu golovu. Vzory ego vezde
vstrechaiut tol'ko shelk i zoloto. On teper',
v etu minutu, prisutstvuet v sovete ministrov,
i vse soglasny s ego mneniem; dumaet li on ob
okhote na zavtrashnii den', ili o bale v
nyneshnii vecher, on predstavliaet drugim
zabotit'sia o svoikh uveselenliakh. I etot
chelovek sostavlen iz takogo zhe tela i krovi,
kak ty . . . .[35]

In spite of these severe cuts in the otherwise complete translation, careful analysis of it reveals it to be
quite good as translations went during the period in question. The reviewer for the *Moskovskii telegraf*, while ill
disposed toward the work, found the translation excellent:

Nedostatkov sego sochineniia nevozmozhno
ischislit'; no dolzhno skazat', chto russkii
perevod ego ochen' khorosh.[36]

Clearly the inconsistent cuts involving free-thinking

passages can be accounted for by the vagaries of Russian
censorship during the period. In general, such inconsistencies are ascribable to time, place and personalities.
With respect to the latter two, Moscow, *Galateia*'s place
of publication, was known to be more liberal than Petersburg, where the complete translation was published. Individual censors were known to be extremely cautious or
carefree, harsh or benevolent. Indeed benevolence was
carried to the point of not even reading the material
passed for publication in the case of Sergei Nikolaevich
Glinka's role as censor for the *Moskovskii telegraf*, a
fact that understandably caused its publishers no little
consternation.[37]

     Taken together, both of the translations examined
herein illustrate not only the vagaries of the censorship
but also those of translation practice as a whole during
the period. Quite apart from "incendiary" material the
individual markers of an author's style, including the
stylistic features of freneticism were often subject to
deletion and alteration. This was especially so in the
case of the *Galateia* excerpts, and could be extensively
documented in the case of translations involving other
authors associated with *iunaia Frantsiia*. There had been
a long Russian tradition of "free translation" or adapta-
tion, and this factor together with censorship and the
strictures of previous literary norms made the writings
of *iunaia Frantsiia* highly subject to modification.
Testimony to this is provided by Irina Aleksandrovna
Lileeva in her introductory article to a Russian bibliography devoted to Balzac:

     Chitatel' 30-40-kh godov znakomilsia s Bal'zakom,
     k solzhaleniiu, kak pravilo, po ves'ma plokhim
     perevodam. Na stranitsakh zhurnalov vystupal
     tselyi otriad perevodchikov, kotorye ili
     voobshche ne podpisyvali svoi perevody ili zhe
     skryvalis' pod psevdonimami i initsialami.
     Podavliaiushchee bol'shinstvo perevodchikov
     videli svoiu zadachu lish' v tom, chtoby peredat'
     siuzhet proizvedeniia, inogda dazhe priblizitel'no,
     i uzh ni v koem sluchae ne zabotias' ob
     osobennostiakh stilia ili iazyka pisatelia.
     Besuslovno byli i iskliucheniia . . . .[38]

     Clearly the full-length translation of Hugo's *Le
dernier jour* . . . was an "exception" to the situation
both as described by Lileeva, and as evidenced in *Galateia*'s rendition. In other translations of Hugo's

narrative prose, fidelity to the text of the original was
much greater, although, as has been seen, excerpting was
consistently an obstacle to widespread acquaintance with
his works in this mode. To be sure the majority of Russia's literary sophisticates could bypass censorship restrictions by reading Hugo in the original. This fact is
attested to by A. V. Nikitenko in his diary wherein he
notes that S. S. Uvarov, the Minister of National Education, was wrong in ruling against the publication of *Notre-
Dame de Paris*.

> Ministr polagaet, chto nam eshche rano chitat'
> takie knigi, zabyvaia pri etom, chto Viktora
> Giugo i bez togo chitaiut v podlinnike vse te,
> dlia kogo on schitaet eto chtenie opasnym.[39]

In spite of the ability of some Russian readers to cir-
cumvent censorship by reading French works in the original,
the question of translation does not lose its significance.
Through translation, the prose works of *iunaia Frantsiia*
could achieve a greater penetration of the Russian literary context and therefore were potentially able to have a
wider impact on Russian prose at a key period in its development. The question of what was translated and how it was
translated is important for the assessment of the literary
ties between France and Russia for this time. Although
this area of inquiry was greatly enriched by the efforts
of V. V. Vinogradov and a number of other prominent Soviet
literary scholars, its investigation is still incomplete.

University of Alberta
Edmonton, Alberta

NOTES

[1] For evidence of this see Apollon Aleksandrovich
Grigor'ev, *My Literary and Moral Wanderings*, trans. by
Ralph E. Matlaw (New York: Dutton, 1962), pp. 92-125.
    [2] On the now forgotten Jules Janin and Russian litera-
ture see Viktor Vladimirovich Vinogradov's *Evoliutsiia
russkogo naturalizma: Gogol' i Dostoevskii* (Leningrad:
Academia, 1929), especially the essay "Romanticheskii
naturalizm (Zhiul' Zhanen i Gogol')," pp. 153-205; also
Boris Georgievich Reizov's "K istorii romanticheskogo
urbanizma: 'Ispoved' Zhiulia Zhanena i 'Otets Gorio'
Bal'zaka," in the book: *Iz istorii russkikh literaturnykh
otnoshenii XVIII-XX vekov* (Moscow-Leningrad: Izdatel'stvo
Akademii Nauk, 1959), pp. 132-40.

[3]As testimony to the resurgence of a hitherto briefly quiescent freneticism at the turn of the decade one can cite the following criticism of Jules Janin's notorious novel *L'âne mort et la femme guillotinée:* "Je ne suis ni prude ni béguele, et je sais m'accommoder de l'horreur quand il faut; mais ce que je ne puis souffrir, c'est que l'horreur qui autrefois dans les livres n'étais jamais que l'épisode, aujourd'hui fasse le fond et le suget même; c'était une exception, aujourd'hui c'est une règle; elle faisait des pages, à cette heure elle fait des livres," *Journal des débats* 22 août (1829). Cf. ibid., 8 janvier (1833), Philarète Chasles' bitter laments over the freneticist hegemony of the early 1830s; also see Pierre-Georges Castex' article "Frenésie romantique," in Dumont, Francis, ed., *Les petits romantiques français* ([Liguge?]: *Cahiers du Sud*, 1949), pp. 29-46.

[4]In the preface Hugo gave formulaic expression to such effects: "Nous voici parvenus à la sommité poétique des temps modernes. Shakespeare, c'est le Drame, et le drame, qui fond sous un même souffle le grotesque et le sublime, le terrible et le bouffon, la tragédie et la comédie, le drame est le caractère propre de la troisième époque de la poésie, de la littérature actuelle." Victor Hugo, *Oeuvres dramatiques complètes, oeuvres critiques complètes*, réunies et présentées par Francis Bouvet (Paris: J. J. Pauvert, 1963), p. 143. Crucial passages from the preface involving contrastive effects appeared in Nikolai Alekseevich Polevoi's *Moskovskii Telegraf*, XLI, No. 19 (1832), pp. 310-14. Russians commonly associated these with Hugo much earlier. For example, Nikolai Ivanovich Nadezhdin's doctoral dissertation of 1830, *De origine natura et fatis Poëseos, quae Romantica audit*, contained sallies against the poetics propounded in Hugo's preface.

[5]Aleksandr Sergeevich Pushkin, *Polnoe sobranie sochinenii v desiati tomax* (Moscow: Izdatel'stvo Akademii Nauk, 1962-66), Vol. V, p. 60. Cf. the following rather exaggerated charges of immorality directed at "*iunaia Frantsiia*," and specifically at Sue, Janin and Bal'zac: Pochti na kazhdoi stranitse vstrechaesh' v nikh pokhvaly ubiistvu i glubochaishie beznravtvennosti, i eto, kazhetsia, edinstvennaia filosofskaia cel' tvortsov etikh sochinenii. "Mnenie izvestnogo angliiskogo zhurnala, *Edinburgh Review*, o nyneshnei frantsuzskoi slovesnosti," *Biblioteka dlia chteniia*, I (1834), pp. 57-58.

[6]So much so that Osip Senkovskii referred to *Claude Gueux* as a dissertation. The increased social commitment

in French literature of the period explains the furor
caused by Théophile Gautier's preface to *Mademoiselle
de Maupin* (1835-1836), in which he argued against the
preoccupation of his fellow writers with utilitarian and
ethical aims.

[7]For more detailed accounts of freneticist literature
and its manifestation in the works of *iunaia Frantsiia* and
Russian literature of the early 1830s, see the author's
article "N. A. Polevoj's *Moskovskij Telegraf* and the critical debate over "Junaja Francija," in *The Canadian Revue
of Comparative Literature*, Vol. I, No. 2 (1974), pp. 123-
37; also Vinogradov's "O literaturnoi tsiklizatsii . . . ,"
in *Evoliutsiia russkogo naturalizma*, especially pp. 109-14

[8]See for example, "Romanticheskii naturalism . . . ,"
p. 156, and also *Etiudy o stile Gogolia* (Leningrad: Academia, 1926), pp. 38-39, where Vinogradov speaks of the
"enthronement" (*votsarenie*) of Russian freneticism in connection with its French counterpart. Vinogradov's claim
is overstated. Although a "freneticization" of Russian
literature did occur, it was lesser in degree and scope
than Vinogradov suggested. The developmental tie with the
latter naturalist school is largely based upon freneticist
depictive techniques, commonly expressed during the period
by such terms as raw nature or the bare truth (*golaia
natura, golaia istina*) and subsumed by the reference to
freneticism as that "dirty type of literature" (*griaznyi
rod literatury*). For additional information on French-
Russian literary ties during this period, see Mikhail
Pavlovich Alekseev, "Viktor Giugo i ego russkie znakomstva," Sergei Nikolaevich Durlynin, "Aleksandr Diuma--
otets i Rossiia," and Leonid Petrovich Grossman, "Bal'zak
v Rossii," in *Literaturnoe nasledstvo* (Moscow: Zhurnal'no-
gazetnoe ob"edinenie, 1937), Vols. XXXI-XXXII, pp. 777-92,
491-562 and 150-372, respectively; also Boris Viktorovich
Tomashevskii, *Pushkin i Frantsiia* (Leningrad: Sovetskii
pisatel', 1960).

[9]In *Evoliutsiia russkogo naturalizma*, p. 300,
Vinogradov erroneously suggests that *Notre-Dame de Paris*
was published in translation. For additional information
on Victor Hugo and the tsarist censorship see Ieramiia
Iakovlevich Aizenshtok, "Frantsuzskie pisateli v otsenkakh
tsarskoi tsenzury," in *Literaturnoe nasledstvo*, Vols.
XXXIII-XXXIV, pp. 787-94.

[10]The qualifier "apparently" is used because, given
Hugo's renown, the work was strangely ignored by Russian
critics. Only a single brief critical mention of the work

was to be found in Russian periodical literature, *Biblioteka dlia chteniia*, I, otd. vi (1834), p. 47. The translation by one Esipov could not be located in several of
the foremost libraries of the U.S.S.R.: Gosudarstvennaia
Biblioteka imeni V. I. Lenina, Gosudarstvennaia Publich-
naia Biblioteka im. M. E. Saltykova-Shchedrina, and
Vsesoiuznaia Gosudarstvennaia Biblioteka Inostrannoi Literatury: a number of excerpts from *Bug-Jargal* and *Notre-
Dame de Paris* were published in the early 1830s. From
Bug-Jargal, Chapters XXXII-XXXV, pp. 273-76 and 281-84,
appeared in *Literaturnaia gazeta*, Nos. 34-35 (1831); from
Notre-Dame de Paris: Chapter I, Book III, "Notre-Dame" as
"Parizhskii Sobor Bogoroditsy," *Teleskop*, VII (1832), pp.
133-47; Chapter II, Book V, "Ceci tuera cela" as "Zod-
chestvo i knigopechatanie," *Moskovskii telegraf*, LIII,
No. 13 (1833), pp. 3-34; Chapter V, Book X, "Le retrait
où dit ses heures monsieur Louis de France," as "Otryvok
iz novogo romana Viktora Giugo," ibid., XL, No.s 14, 15
(1831), pp. 181-213 and 334-57, respectively; and Chapters
II and III, Book VI, "Le trou aux rats" and "Histoire
d'une galette au levain de maïs," as "Dve glavy iz *Notre-
Dame de Paris*," in *Syn otechestva*, CLVI (1831), pp. 193-
211 and 257-80, respectively. For additional biblio-
graphical information concerning translations of Hugo's
works, see Iurii Ivanovich Danilin, *Bibliografiia russkikh
perevodov Viktora Giugo* (Moscow: Vsesoiuznaia Gosudarstvennaia Biblioteka Inostrannoi Literatury, 1953).

[11] See the author's N. A. Polevoj's "*Moskovskij telegraf* . . . ," p. 129, for a breakdown of sixty-five translations by these authors appearing between 1831-1835 in
major Russian periodicals (*Teleskop, Syn otechestva,
Moskovskii telegraf, Severnaia pchela, Biblioteka dlia
chteniia, Literaturnaia gazeta*, and *Russkii invalid*. In
addition to Hugo's censorship problems, a factor contributing to his being excerpted so much might have been the
length of his works. The other writers mentioned wrote
many shorter works which figured prominently in the number
of translations which appeared in periodicals. Nevertheless, voluminous works were occasionally serialized--
Balzac's *L'histoire des treize* and *Père Goriot*, the latter
on two occasions.

[12] Aleksandr Aleksandrovich Bestuzhev-Marlinskii,
Sochineniia v dvukh tomakh (Moscow: izdatel'stvo
khudozhestvennoi literatury, 1958), Vol. II, pp. 650-51.

[13] *Moskovskii telegraf*, XLI, No. 20 (1831), p. 534.

[14] See for example, Alekseev, "Viktor Giugo i ego

russkie znakomstva," pp. 788-91; cf. also Pushkin's reference to *Le dernier jour* . . . in a letter to V. F.
Viazemskaia: "Vous avez raison de trouver l'*Ane* délcieux.
C'est un des oeuvrages les plus marquants du moment. On
l'attribue à V. Hugo-- j'y vois plus de talent que dans le
dernier jour ou il y en a beaucoup." Pushkin, Vol. X, p.
284. This can be contrasted with published critical statements attributed to Pushkin, which censure the type of
material selected by Hugo for his novella: "my kinulis' na
plutovskie priznaniia politseiskogo shpiona i na poias-
neniia onykh kleimennogo katorzhnika. Zhurnaly napolnilis'
vypiskami iz Vidoka. Poet Giugo ne postydilsia v nem
iskat' vdokhnovenii *dlia romana, ispolnennogo ognia i
griazi.*" Ibid., Vol. IX, p. 105. The quotation origi-
nated in Pushkin's short article "O zapiskakh Samsona,"
from *Literaturnaia gazeta*, No. 5 (1830).

[15] See "O romanakh Viktora Giugo, i voobshche o
noveishikh romanakh," *Moskovskii telegraf*, No. 3 (1832),
p. 376. This article was spread over three issues of
Polevoi's journal, Nos. 1, 2, and 3, pp. 85-104, 211-38,
370-90.

[16] See Dostoevskii's introduction to "Krotkaia" (1876).
If Vinogradov was correct, Dostoevskii may have been acknowledging an "old debt" to Hugo. In addition to compositional and thematic ties between Hugo's work and
Dostoevskii's mature fiction, Vinogradov found the image
of the seemingly moribund hag who appears to the condemned prisoner in his nightmare (Chapter Forty-Two), to
have been integrated by Dostoevskii in Raskol'nikov's
dream of his victim Alena Ivanovna and in the Kirillov
suicide scene in *Besy*. See "Iz biografii odnogo
'neistovogo' proizvedeniia (*Poslednii den' prigovorennogo
k smerti*)," in *Evoliutsiia russkogo naturalizma*, pp. 127-
52.

[17] *Moskovskii telegraf*, XXXII, No. 8 (1830), p. 513.

[18] Vissarion Grigor'evich Belinskii, *Polnoe sobranie
sochinenii* (Moscow: Izdatel'stvo Akademii Nauk), Vol. I,
p. 279.

[19] *Severnaia pchela*, No. 50 (1830).

[20] See "Iz biografii odnogo neistovogo proizvedeniia"
in *Evoliutsiia russkogo naturalizma*, p. 132. Vinogradov
goes on further to note that neither the compositional
form of Hugo's "confessional" work, nor its emphasis on
the evolution of the hero's psychological state, nor the
position of the author-figure vis-à-vis the narrator were
canonized within the freneticist cycle of the 1830s. In

this respect one must agree with him.

[21] See Nos. 17-19, pp. 3-15, 62-79, and 137-63, respectively.

[22] *Galateia*, IV, No. 17 (1829), pp. 3-4.

[23] Victor Hugo, *Romans* (Paris: Éditions du Seuil, 1963), p. 225, and *Galateia*, IV, No. 18 (1829), p. 73, respectively.

[24] Ibid., p. 230, and No. 19, p. 141, respectively.

[25] Ibid., p. 239, and p. 160, respectively.

[26] Victor Hugo, *Romans*, p. 227, and *Poslednii den' prigovorennogo k smerti* (Saint Petersburg: Tipografiia Imperatorskogo Vospitatel'nogo Doma, 1830), p. 90. Emphasis added.

[27] Ibid., pp. 220-21, and p. 52, respectively.

[28] Ibid., p. 229, and pp. 100-101, respectively. Cf. this same passage in Natalia Grigor'evna Kasatkina's modern translation from 1953:

-Kto vy takoi? nakonets sprosil ia.
-Vot tak vopros! otvetil on. -Kak kto? Ispechennyi!
-Ispechennyi! Chto èto znachit?
Ot moego voprosa on zakhokhotal eshche pushche.
-Eto znachit, chto kat skosit moiu sorbonnu cherez
 shest' nedel', kak tvoiu churku cherez shest'
 chasov, - otvetil on skvoz' smekh.
-Ege! Vidno, smeknul! Viktor Giugo, *Sobranie sochinenii v desiati tomakh* (Moskva: Izdatel'stvo "Pravda," 1972), Vol. I, pp. 156-57.

[29] Victor Hugo, *Poslednii den' prigovorennogo k smerti*, p. 40. As pointed out earlier, Hugo's humanitarian aim is essentially intrinsic to the novella. He made this aim unmistakably explicit in an extensive preface to a later edition of the work in 1832.

[30] Victor Hugo, *Romans, op. cit.,* and *Poslednii den' prigovorennogo k smerti*, p. 219, and p. 41, respectively.

[31] Ibid., p. 221, and p. 56, respectively.

[32] Ibid., p. 225, and p. 77, respectively.

[33] Ibid., p. 235. The preceding lines refer to an imaginary voice "at the narrator's ear" and thus the direct discourse which is missing in the Russian.

[34] Victor Hugo, *Poslednii den' prigovorennogo k smerti*, p. 140.

[35] *Galateia*, IV, No. 19 (1829), pp. 148-49. Cf. a passage from the episode in Chapter Thirteen in which the prisoners temporarily transform their brutal enchainment into a festive occasion: "*La societé avait beau être là, représentée par les geôliers* et les curieux épouvantés,

le crime la narguait en face, et de ce châtiment horrible
faisait une fête de famille"; unexcerpted version: Ne
smotria na prisutstvie tiuremshchikov i ostrashennykh
zhitelei, zavlechennykh liubopytstvom, prestuplenie,
preziralo ikh iavno, delalo iz sego uzhasnogo nakazaniia
semeinyi prazdnik; *Galateia*: Tshchetno stoilo pred nimi
pravosudie v osobe ikh strazhei, tshchetno grazhdanskoe
obshchestvo iavlialos' pred nimi v osobe liubopytnykh
Parizhan; prestuplenie nasmekhalos nad nimi iavno i
obrashchalo nakazanie v semeistvennyi prazdnik. Victor
Hugo, *Romans, op. cit.*, p. 222; *Poslednii den' prigovorennogo k smerti*, p. 60; and *Galateia*, IV, No. 18 (1829),
p. 67, respectively.

[36] *Moskovskii telegraf*, XXXII, No. 8 (1830), p. 513.

[37] For more on tsarist censorship, see Mikhail Kon-
stantinovich Lemke, *Nikolaevskie zhandarmy i literatura
1826-1855 gg. po podlinnym delam tret'ego otdeleniia
sobtv. E. I. Velichestva*, 2nd ed. (St. Petersburg: S. V.
Bunin, 1908). Also Vadim Erazmovich Vatsuro and Maksim
Isaakovich Gillel'son, *Skvoz' "umstvennye plotiny"--iz
istorii knigi i pressy pushkinskoi pory* (Moscow:
Izdatel'stvo "Kniga," 1972).

[38] Anastasiia Vladimirovna Paevskaia and V. T.
Danchenko, *Onore de Bal'zak--bibliografiia russkikh
perevodov i kriticheskoi literatury na russkom iazyke
1830-1964* (Mowcow: Izdatel'stvo "Kniga," 1965), p. 11.
Cf. Belinskii's indignation over the translater's failure
to render the richness and psychological penetration of
Balzac's style in a review devoted to the appearance in
Russian of *La Vendetta* and "Gobseck," *Molva*, III, No. 26
(1832), p. 101; also B. G. Reizov, *Bal'zak--sbornik
statei* (Leningrad: Izdatel'stvo Leningradskogo Universi-
teta, 1966), for a study of two nearly simultaneous
translations of Balzac's *Père Goriot*, the one displaying
extreme license, the other great fidelity. The translations of Jules Janin's *L'âne mort et la femme guillotinée*
and Bal'zac's tale "*Le doigt de Dieu*" (ultimately incorporated in *La femme de trente ans*) offer further outstanding examples of translational inadequacy of a kind referred to by Lileeva.

[39] See Aizenshtok, "Frantsuzskie pisateli, v otsenkakh
tsarskoi tsenzury," p. 788. Cf. the earlier cited reference by Pushkin to Janin's *L'âne mort* . . ., long before
its appearance in a Russian translation.

THE CHORUS AND SPEAR CARRIERS OF RUSSIAN ROMANTIC FICTION

John Mersereau, Jr.

Let me "realize" the metaphor of my title. Imagine an opera company composed of Russian Romantic fiction writers. Top billing is reserved for the tenor, Lermontov, the baritone, Pushkin, and the basso, Gogol. Everyone else sings in the chorus or is relegated to carrying a spear. My judgment may be harsh, but I have auditioned widely, a task which has been largely dull, sometimes hilarious, and occasionally unexpectedly rewarding. Now it is true, to be fair, that an author such as Prince V. F. Odoevsky was good enough at least part of the time to take a leading role, especially when compared with Gogol in poor form (e.g., *The Portrait*). Marlinsky, the loudest voice in the chorus, tried to sing arias, but even a hoarse Pushkin always sounded better. Weldman had potential, but he paid little attention to the score and sang largely for his own amusement. If the public had selected the soloists, doubtless Faddey Bulgarin would have been center stage, for he was a favorite of the balcony. But in my own company of Russian Romantic fictionists he has been relegated mostly to spear carrying, for his voice was uneven and unpredictable. Alas, there were no Russian *divas* to match the performances of Pushkin, Lermontov and Gogol.

Well, let us not flog the metaphor. Before proceeding further we must resolve a question basic to my subject: that is, what is meant by Romantic fiction, and is there any justification in categorizing such apparently disparate authors as Pushkin and Marlinsky as Romantic fictionists?

First, with a measure of arbitrariness, which I acknowledge, I have defined the Romantic period in Russian fiction as roughly 1815-1840.[1] Obviously there were precursors and there were *epigoni*. Still, within the limits of these dates there are certain norms of composition with respect to genres, structure, means and manner of narration, hierarchy of plot-setting-character, and literary language which justify an assertion that such a thing as Romantic fiction existed in Russia at this time. Therefore, despite the fact that there are many areas of striking dissimilarity between the works of Marlinsky and

Pushkin, and despite the evidence that much of Pushkin's fiction was in fact a parody of Romantic clichés, their fiction was created in conformity to or tension against a certain system of prevalent norms--that is, the norms which represent the common denominators of much of what was written during this period. Of course no system of norms is static, since literature is constantly in flux. There was, in fact, a great deal of hybridization of genres during the Romantic period, a sign of healthy ferment signaling evolution.

The norms unifying Russian Romantic fiction are perhaps best understood when contrasted with norms operative during the period of Realist fiction:

1. The fictional world is represented through metaphoric means (as opposed to Realism's representation through metonymic means).[2]

2. The dominant narrative mode is telling (as opposed to Realism's means of showing). That is, a narrator primarily recounts events rather than presenting dramatic scenes of the events themselves.

3. Primacy of plot and setting (as opposed to Realism's primacy of character, with emphasis upon psychologization).

4. In Romantic fiction there is evidence of an author-narrator voice, with frequent intrustions into the action by this voice (as opposed to the absence of authorial voice in Realist fiction).

5. Romantic fictionists seemed quite concerned with providing a motivation or justification for their stories, that is, to explain the genesis of their tales, thus the framed structure where an anecdote is related by one of a group of raconteurs, a form found in *Belkin Tales*, *Evenings on a Farm Near Dikanka*, Odoevsky's *Motley Tales*, etc. On the other hand, Realists were concerned with motivating the inner details of their fiction.

6. The psychology of Romantic characters was often completely arbitrary; this arose partly because characters had to be subordinated to intrigue. Realists present characters whose psychological condition is motivated and consistent.

7. Romantic fictionists were concerned with the exotic in all forms, and this was manifested by bizarre situations, unlikely characters, and unusual settings, both temporal and spatial. Realists tended to deal with mundane contemporary experience.

8. The implausible or even the supernatural were quite
    permissible in Romantic fiction, whereas Realist fic-
    tion is usually bound by rules of probability and
    totally excludes the supernatural.

Now, whatever might be said about Pushkin having been
a Classicist or an early Realist, or about Gogol having
been the father of critical Realism, it is clear that they
were operating more in accordance with these norms of Romanticism than those of Realism. Parody of Romantic
clichés, or a concern with motivated psychology, as in
Pushkin's case, and dirty details, as in Gogol's, do not
make Realists of them. The case of Lermontov is more complex, for his fiction exemplifies the evolution from Romanticism to Realism. His unfinished historical novel
Vadim is simply a nightmarish collage of the most colorful Romantic clichés. His society tale, *Princess
Ligovskaya*, also unfinished, reveals a definite effort to
psychologize his protagonist, using methods which later
became canonical for Realism; still, the work definitely
belongs to Romantic fiction. With *A Hero of Our Times*,
Lermontov continued to utilize Romantic genres, namely
travel notes, intensified anecdote, physiological sketch,
society tale, and confession, Romantic characters, and not
a little of traditional Romantic style. Still, he combined
these in such a way as to focus primarily upon the psychological makeup of his protagonist, with the plot at the
service of characterization and dramatic representation
(showing) tending to displace the method of telling.
Lermontov's complex structure was hardly suitable for
imitation by other would-be Realists, but he still must
be credited with creating the first modern novel of psychological Realism in Russian fiction. *A Hero of Our Times*
is, accordingly, a sort of literary mule, neither a horse
nor a jackass and incapable of reproducing, but having the
strength to plow the first furrow and delivering an impressive kick.

Now, what about the chorus and the spear carriers,
the justly and the unjustly forgotton fictionists of Russia's Romantic Period? I will take them more or less as
they appeared on the literary scene and try to give some
idea of the nature of their art and their contribution, if
any, to the evolution of Romantic fiction towards Realism.

For this group, the title of "Mr. Russian Romantic
Fiction" must go to Alexander Bestuzhev, better known by
his pseudonym Marlinsky. He was a Romantic writer who
lived an exemplary romantic life: officer, Decembrist

conspirator, political prisoner, common soldier, finally an
officer in the Caucasian army, only to disappear in 1837
during a Russian landing at Adler on the Black Sea coast.
Since he was only 40 at the time, since only 137 years have
passed since his disappearance, and given the reputation of
the Caucasus for the longevity of its inhabitants, Marlinsky is probably still alive in some remote *aul* at the age
of 177, working on a sequel to *Amalat Bek*, his story of the
tragic fate of a Caucasian mountaineer who was caught between the grindstones of his native culture and religion
and that of his Russian captors and would-be benefactors.
I would expect his sequel to be much like the former work,
because Marlinsky did not display much development in the
course of his literary career, and although he tended towards longer forms of fiction in his post-Decembrist period, his style remained largely unchanged. *Marlinism* or
Marlinskyism are the terms used to refer to his tumid and
grandiloquent style, which is heavy with epithet, striking
metaphors, and a very pronounced overlay of authorial comment. With respect to this last quality, Marlinsky was
really unconscionable, probably taking his cue from
Laurence Sterne, the most egregious of all whimsical narrators. Digressiveness is one of Marlinsky's hallmarks,
and his digressions range from brief aphoristic comments
on man and life in general, a feature typical of Romantic
fiction, to a digression embracing an entire chapter, as
for example, chapter two of *The Test* (Ispytanie), an un-
related genre painting of the Petersburg food market.

It is easy to fault Marlinsky for his stylistic excesses, his wooden characters with their arbitrary motivations, his regression to Sentimentalist locutions whenever his characters became emotionally involved, and his
everlasting moralizing. On the other hand, his contributions must also be recognized. His travel notes, *A Journey to Revel* (Puteshestvie v Revel'), published in 1821,
is an engaging and lively account of actual travel interwoven with rather fascinating information on the past of
Livonia. Then his cycle of historical tales set in Eston-
ia and Latvia provided amusement for a generation of Russian readers whose tastes favored neo-Gothic excesses.
Perhaps they also inspired Wilhelm Küchelbecker to attempt
his *Ado* (1825), a Livonian myth notable for its ponderous-
ness and faulty socio-historical content. *Roman and Olga*,
published in 1823, a historical tale of Novgorod in the
good old days (when the Teutonic Knights knew their place),
set a standard which was hardly bettered by the Russian

imitators of Walter Scott who swarmed forth at the turn of
the thirties. Finally, Marlinsky was one of the first to
develop the society tale, and his *A Novel in Seven Letters*
(Roman v semi pis'makh) (1825), *The Test* (Ispytanie)
(1830), and *The Frigate "Hope"* (Fregat "Nadezhda") (1834)
established patterns of plot, character types, and treatment (a critical depiction of the *haut monde*) which were
imitated by many practitioners of this genre in the thirties and forties.

Tales of the supernatural had a brief vogue in the
later twenties, but one must emphasize that most authors
who wrote in this genre treated the supernatural satiri-
cally—that is, they exposed the supernatural content as
a dream or hallucination—or if the supernatural were
treated as an actual phenomenon, it was shown to be de-
classé, comic, or capable of being defeated by righteous
morals. Alexey Perovsky, who employed the pseudonym
Antoni Pogorelsky, was one of the first to adapt E. T.
A. Hoffmann's *Maerchen* technique to Russian types with his
charming *The Lafertov District Poppyseed Cake Vendor*
(Lafertovskaia Makovnitsa), 1825. Here an evil witch,
whose chin and nose bang noisily together whenever she is
angry, conspires with her demonic cat to achieve the fe-
line's wedding to her innocent niece. One of the more
amusing scenes occurs when the cat, masquerading as a
titular counsellor, Aristarchus Faleleyich Purrkin (Murly-
kin), leaves the girl's house sedately but then runs for
his life when a neighborhood dog penetrates his disguise.

Most have heard of Perovsky's *The Smolny Institute
Graduate* (Monastyrka), a work appearing in 1830, which revealed considerable potential in its first volume. What
was unusually promising about this novel in volume one was
the effort to get inside the head of the protagonist,
Anyuta, to show the complexity of her mental states, to
reveal an evolution of attitudes. To accomplish this, the
author provided letters, exterior observers, a dream sequence, but in the second volume (1833) the emphasis on
psychologization was largely abandoned as the story fo-
cused upon the tribulations caused Anyuta by her villain-
ous guardian, Klim Sidorovich Dyundik, the ultimate
poshlyak. Dyundik, who was probably Chichikov's uncle,
is a schemer outclassed only by his beloved spouse, Marfa
Petrovna, who dies from apoplexy when she is thwarted in
her plot to marry Anyuta to her queer nephew. Her dutiful
husband, with her at the end, reports that her last words
were "Goodbye, my dear!," but other witnesses unanimously

assert that she said, "Scram, you idiot!" (Otvazhish',
durak!)

In 1831 and 1832 readers of the literary almanac
Northern Flowers (Severnye Tsvety) encountered two unusual
stories, *Beethoven's Last Quartet* (Poslednii kvartet Beet-
govena) and *Opere del Cavaliere Giambattista Piranesi*.
Both were signed with the cryptic letters, soft-sign, hard
sign, short ee (miakii znak, tverdyi znak, i kratkoe),
which stood for the last letters in the name of Prince
Vladimir Odoevsky. Odoevsky was a close friend of Pushkin
and Delvig and a sometime contributor to their publications. In the pre-Decembrist era Odoevsky, who was a
trained Schellingist, had been a member of the Moscow
Lovers of Wisdom Society (Ljubomudry) and with Wilhelm
Küchelbecker had edited *Mnemosyne* (Mnemozina), the almanac-
journal which was oriented toward German idealistic philosophy.

Odoevsky wrote a number of *Künstlernovellen*, stories
whose protagonists were artists of one sort or another,
painters, musicians, or persons of unusual talent and sensitivity. One of the basic themes of this genre was "an artist's life is not a happy one," particularly so because a
Philistine public sees the artist at best as an artisan and
at worst as a starving fool. Odoevsky's *Künstlernovellen*
underscored the sublimity of the artist's calling, while
stressing that his fate was to be ignored and misunderstood. More than a little of E. T. A. Hoffmann's ideology
finds its reflection in Odoevsky's treatment of the artist.

I do not want to convey the impression that Odoevsky
was a sort of Russian Hoffmann. That would be unfair to a
writer who produced a number of stories outside the normal
genres of Romantic fiction. This is true even of his
Künstlernovellen mentioned before, for they lack the usual
society tale format. A number of Odoevsky's short stories
have delightful titles, such as *Why it is Dangerous for
Young Ladies to Promenade on Nevsky Prospect* (Pochemu
opasno molodym devushkam guliat' po Nevskomu Prospektu),
the point of which is that individuality is lost once a
young woman succumbs to the blandishments of the Petersburg
dresshops, or *The Fairy Tale of a Corpse Whose Owner Was
Unknown* (Skazka o mertvetse, neizvestno komu prinadlez-
hashchem), a satire on bureaucrats and ignorance. Odoevsky's satirical bent found more conventional expression in
two society tales, both fairly well known--if seldom read--
and both of less artistic value or originality than many of
his lesser known works. These caustic satires are *Princess*

Mimi (Kniazhna Mimi) and *Princess Zizi* (Kniazhna Zizi),
which reveal the *beau monde* to be a vipers' pit of intrigue and calumny. Odoevsky takes pains in *Princess Mimi*
to provide motivation for his vicious heroine, a spinster
who compensates for her lack of a husband--thus she has no
social clout--by keeping her acquaintances in mortal terror
of her evil tongue.

Following the example of Pushkin's Belkin or Gogol's
Red Panko--or was it Washington Irving's *Tales of My Grandfather?*--Odoevsky presented a series of short stories narrated by Iriney Gomozeyko under the collective title *Motley
Tales* (Pestrye rasskazy) (1833). A number of these stories
were modified in 1844 when this author published his *Russian Nights* (Russkie Nochi), a series of tales integrated
by the philosophical discussions of its narrator-commenta-
tors. Incidentally, Odoevsky insisted that the structure
of this work occurred to him before he became aware of
Hoffmann's *Serapion Brothers*. The main narrator of *Russian
Nights* is Faust, and this fact coupled with Odoevsky's general interest in first causes and encyclopaedic knowledge,
gained for him the sobriquet of the Russian Faust.

If Odoevsky was the Russian Faust, then Alexey Weldman can be called the Russian Puck. Incidentally, if my
pedantry can be pardoned, he was not of German origin, as
is often assumed, but a descendant of the Swedish Weldmans,
and judging from his brand of humor, he must have been of
Danish-Swedish extraction. If there is one dominant feature of his fiction, it is his unrestrained wit, which
finds expression in parody, pun and unconscionable play
with reader expectations. This quality is evident in his
first important work, *The Wanderer* (Strannik), published
in 1831, a facetious variant of the travelogue, which combined an imaginary journey occurring in the narrator's
study with an account of a real journey several years
earlier. This charming work is a Russian salad, or perhaps Smorgasbord, of genre descriptions of seedy Bessara-
bian towns--Jassy and Kishinyov--serious and facetious
digressions, caricatures, parodistic poetry and whimsical
interruptions. He has a map of Europe on his desk and
carelessly knocks over a glass of water:

> Do you see? . . . Oh, what carelessness! . . .
> What a terrible flood in Spain and France! . . .
> That's what comes of setting a glass of water on
> the map! . . . but who would ever have thought I
> would knock it off the Pyrenees with my elbow?

Weldman retired from the army as a Lt. Colonel in

1831, and the next decade saw a prodigious flow of historical novels, fantastic tales and short stories. To mention
just a few, *The Manuscript of Martin Zadeka* (Rukopis'
Martyna Zadeki) (1833), *Kaschey the Deathless* (Kashchei
bessmertnyi) (1833), *Sleepwalker* (Lunatik), (1836), *Alexander of Macedonia, Son of Philip* (Aleksandr Filippovich
Makedonskii) (1836), *Cavalry Captain Chernoknizhnikov, or
Moscow in 1812* (Rotmistr Chernoknizhnikov, ili Moskva v
1812 g.) (1837).

   Sleepwalker is typical of this author, revealing his
genuine inventiveness and unusual precociousness and at the
same time his inability to "put it all together." The novel has two parts, and this division is not casual: in the
first part we meet the hero, Aurelius, a Moscow youth so
devoted to the sciences that he is oblivious to the fact
that the French are invading the city. The disjointed
quality of the narrative and the leitmotif of the moon
emphasize the hero's totally unreal perception of the
world. While sleepwalking or in a trance, Aurelius sees
the face of a beautiful woman, Lydia, and this becomes an
ideal vision which he cherishes through the course of subsequent adversities, including capture by the French. Captivity, rubbing shoulders with real Russian patriots,
brings about a transformation in Aurelius, and in part two
he functions on the level of reality, even becoming the
leader of a group of guerrillas which decimate the retreat-
ing French. In Weldman's descriptions of the chaotic atmosphere pervading Moscow as the French arrived, in the
vivid scenes of partisan attacks, and in his emphasis on
the patriotism and sacrifice of the common soldier, this
author anticipated *War and Peace*. Tolstoy must certainly
have read and remembered *Sleepwalker*, a claim which may be
even more categoric when one looks at the character of
Evgenia, the younger sister of Aurelius' companion-in-arms
Beloselsky: like Natasha Rostova, she is the dynamic spirit of the Beloselsky household, in love with life, with
her military brother, and sight unseen, with Aurelius, who
is brought to their estate to convalesce. Evgenia is as
spontaneous as Natasha, hopping, laughing, singing, playing tricks on her family, yet having her serious, inner
life as well. This characterization represents a real advance in the delineation of the female personality, which
even in 1837 was often just an arbitrary clustering of various virtues.

   Alas, the plot is basically rather silly: just as
Aurelius proposes to Lydia, whom he has rediscovered after

the war, his father discloses that it was Lydia's father who had run off with his wife years before; thus, Lydia and Aurelius are semi-siblings. Lydia ends up marrying Belo-selsky and Aurelius goes to Paris (which is described as a combination of Sodom and Gomorrah) to pine. There is some indication that ultimately he returned to Russia and the charming Evgenia--the more fool if he didn't.

Typical of Weldman's whimsicality is his society tale, *Erotida* (1835), whose heroine has been raised by her widower father as if she had been a son destined for the dragoons. The story is composed of Romantic clichés, lin-guistic, situational, etc., intensified to the point of absurdity. Weldman's readers, conditioned by Marlinsky, Polevoy, or others, must have been constantly deceived by this tale, which, in Gogolian fashion, sets off towards an apparent goal but ends in a blind alley or somewhere in the opposite direction.

A lieutenant stationed in a remote backwater falls in love with Erotida, but they must part. Several years later he meets a young widow in Carlsbad and becomes infatuated. Meanwhile a mysterious young officer also arrives and forces himself upon the lieutenant. Suspecting that the young officer has designs on Erotida, the lieutenant chal-lenges him: they fight, the young officer turns out to be Erotida herself (she had been testing the lieutenant's sincerity). But then, rather than tear his hair from grief and vexation, the lieutenant indifferently dumps the corpse of his beloved in the river and takes off. *Finita la com-media*, to the bewilderment of most readers.

Thus far we have treated only members of our chorus of Romantic fictionalists, so for a change of quality let us look at one of the spear carriers--in fact, this particular author, A. A. Pavlov, could hardly even grasp his spear properly. In 1836, he published his *Kasimov Tales and Legends* (Kasimovskie povesti i predaniia), in whose preface he quite properly begged his readers' indulgence:

> This is my first attempt, the first work of a
> young imagination, and therefore I ask that my
> Readers not be severe judges. . . . If fate al-
> lows me to live to a ripe old age, with what
> pleasure will I then open my composition, writ-
> ten in the 17th year of my life.

History has not recorded whether Mr. Pavlov reached ripe old age, but if he did, it is probable that his pleasure in reading his juvenile composition was somewhat less than anticipated.

The first "legend," entitled *Amin*, is a so-called
Eastern tale, a trivial moralistic story about three Mos-
lem brothers and what each does with his inheritance. The
youngest, true to his father's deathbed admonition, follows Mohammed's law, and predictably he remains prosperous
while his unfaithful brothers suffer death and penury.

The story *Pigich* begins promisingly enough with the
introduction of the legendary Kasimov bandit Pigich, a
hideous villain who lives in a remote swamp with his gigantic and grotesque sister-in-law. This unsavory twosome travels about in a cart pulled by a shaggy bear. The
exuberance of the youthful author is evident from the following description of the title figure:

> The gaffer was more than fifty years old. His
> fact was sprinkled with ulcerous, reddish pim-
> ples, which came together on his nose in one
> putrid spot. . . . His stature was the smallest.
> His back was ornamented as with a camel, by two
> humps. From his knees his legs went in oppo-
> site directions, and they seemed momentarily
> ready to break under the weight of his body.
> His arms were disproportionately long, and
> three fingers on each of his hands did not bend.

Then follow a number of lurid scenes, but justice triumphs
when the shaggy bear perishes in a *banzai* attack against
the police, the monstrous sister is axed to death, and
Pigich seized and executed. A. A. Pavlov's other tales
are more somber and much duller.

Nikolay Polevoy's efforts as editor of *The Moscow
Telegraph*, one of the most energetic of those periodicals
supporting the Romantic movement in Russia, merit him an
honorary membership in the chorus, but actually as a fictionist he was essentially a spear carrier. After Odoevsky, Polevoy was one of the first to exploit the theme of
the artist in conflict with society, and his *The Artist*
(Zhivopisets), which appeared in 1833, rather set the formula for the *Künstlernovelle*. The protagonist, Arcady, is
a clerk's son with artistic talent, and owing to this he
gains a toehold in society. However, lack of recognition
as an artist and unrequited love lead to his total disil-
lusionment, and he retreats to Italy where he dies.

A much more ambitious work by Polevoy appeared in
1834, *Abbaddonna* (*sic*), a novel in four volumes incorpor-
ating elements of the physiological sketch, the "psychological" novel, the novel of manners and the *Künstlerroman*.
The setting is a German principality in the early 19th cen-

tury, and our hero is the impoverished poet Wilhelm Reich-
enbach. Through the intercession of Eleanora, an actress
of bad reputation but good connections--she is the mistress
of the director of the state theatre--Wilhelm's drama is
staged, and he becomes an overnight success. The naive
Wilhelm also becomes ensnared by the love-stricken Eleanora, who more or less seduces the young poet away from
his betrothed, the bourgeois Henrietta Schultz. After a
long series of intrigues and accidents too tedious to re-
count, Wilhelm is finally brought back to his senses when
his mother reads him passages of Klopstock's _Messiah_:
Abdiel saves the fallen angel Abaddon, but perishes for
his pains.

Polevoy is at times an amusing satirist, and his
gibes, directed both at the _haut monde_ and the _bourgeoisie_,
are effective. His exposé of the triviality of certain men
of letters is also well done.

Another spear carrier, who is known at least in footnotes, is A. V. Timofeev, author of "The Artist" (_Khudo-
zhnik_) (1834). Timofeev's name is mentioned in most discussions of the popularity of the _Künstlerroman_, though it
appears that very few commentators have actually read his
novel, since no one ever provides any artistic evaluation.
It is dull beyond belief, the form being that of a first-
person _apologia_ typical of the Romantic version of the so-
called "psychological novel." The narrator, whose name is
Ivan, a fact revealed only in volume three, is the illegit-
imate son of an estate owner and a serf, a born loser whose
modicum of artistic talent does secure for him an education
and training. But he is a fish out of water, neither serf
nor gentry, and he ends up disenchanted and perhaps even
mad. Among his woes, in addition to dire poverty and the
lack of appreciation of his vast canvases of Prometheus and
so on, is the circumstance that he is in love with his
half-sister. To add insult to injury, his drunken mother
shows up inopportunely to embarrass him in front of his
high class friends.

Even if one accepts the possibility of such a person
as this protagonist, he elicits little sympathy, since his
confession is one long whimper about his life, interspersed
with inane digressions of a quasi-philosophical nature. He
is long-winded, tedious, and almost proud of his misery.
Ultimately the reader is exhausted and repelled. Presumably, Mr. Timofeev did not intend that sort of reaction.

Writers like Timofeev and Polevoy are easy to fault,
and particularly this is so from the perspective of a

century and a half. Still, I do not think it is unfair to
assert that they really did nothing to advance the art of
fiction or to make the prose literary language a more
flexible vehicle. If their works did indeed provide
amusement to their contemporaries, well and good, but
when compared with·innovators such as Odoevsky and Somov,
the Polevoys and Timofeevs must be ranked much lower.

A literary figure of the Romantic era who deserves to
be better known is Mikhail Pogodin, historian, professor,
and editor of *The Moscow Herald*. His particular achievement was the depiction of the life of the lower classes,
particularly merchants, whose speech characteristics he
sought to reproduce.

Pogodin is often mentioned for his *The Black Affliction* (Chernaia nemoch'), appearing in 1829, the tragic
biography of Gavrilo, the son of a Moscow merchant, who
aspires to knowledge of the Good, the True, and the
Beautiful. His father, a typical *samodur*, insists the
boy follow the age-old merchant patterns of living, and
when he arbitrarily arranges his son's wedding, the dis-
traught Gavrilo drowns himself. The details of merchant
life are interesting, but this sociological content hardly compensates for what is essentially an undramatic and
rather sentimentalized story. A recommended work is his
The Deacon-Wizard (Djachek-Koldun), a very funny tale of
a glib bellringer who persuades an impoverished sexton to
connive with him by pretending to have second sight. They
succeed famously for a while, being handsomely rewarded by
their gullible clients, but they are finally exposed and
punished by the ecclesiastical authorities. The comic exterior of this tale screens a strong content of social
protest, for although the central figures are engaged in
gulling the public, they are essentially harmless, whereas
their gentry "marks" are shown to be vicious and dishonest.

Most Romantic authors made at least one attempt at an
epistolary novel or novelette. Pogodin's *Sokolnitsky Park*
(Sokolnitskii sad) (1832), is one of the best. B. B. and
Luisa write to their correspondents about their chance
meeting and developing friendship, while Vsevolod and
Katinka read between the lines and expose the incipient
love affair by return mail. Katinka, in fact, analyzes
Luisa's letters line by line to prove to Luisa that she
can't hide her love for B. B. The story ends happily with
B. B. winning Luisa from the grasp of an older man whom
her uncle was forcing her to marry, and the misogynist

Vsevolod becomes sufficiently softened to marry the perceptive Katinka.

Epistolary novels are often just a series of effusive and sentimental letters; on the contrary, Pogodin's *Sokolnitsky Park* provides individualized and restrained letters, especially those of B. B., which persuasively chronicle the development of his affection for Luisa. There are, it is true, some "achs" and some tears, which seem to be a regression; one must remember, a century and a half ago a youth experiencing first love, and moreover one steeped in Romanticism, quite realistically could have been expected to give vent to some emotional enthusiasm.

Faddey Bulgarin was one of the most popular authors of the Romantic period, but he is remembered today because of his dirty tricks on Pushkin and his endeavors to monopolize the Petersburg periodical market. What is generally overlooked is that Bulgarin did not become a pariah until the end of the twenties, and this person who is now constantly thought of as a police spy, renegade Pole, informant, pathological liar, etc., all of which he was, had been a contributor to all issues of the Decembrist almanac *Polar Star* and that the first parts of Griboedov's *Woe from Wit* were published by Bulgarin in his own almanac, *A Russian Thalia*.

In the latter twenties Bulgarin published three historical tales in various numbers of Delvig's *Northern Flowers*, and these works provide a sufficient sample to determine that at best he was a mediocre writer. His *The Ruins of Almodavar* (Razvaliny al'modavarskie) is a highly sentimentalized tale of a pitiful Spanish girl who goes mad when her fiancé is murdered by marauding French soldiers. The story is framed by travel notes which briefly relate how the narrator, a Pole serving in Napoleon's invasion force (as Bulgarin himself had served), found himself in Almodavar and narrowly escaped death when the crazed girl mistook him for the slayer of her fiancé. The tragic tale itself is told to the officer by his Spanish guide.

The Fall of Wenden (Padenie Vendena) concerns the seige of that Livonian city by the forces of Ivan the Terrible. Bulgarin derives his tale from Karamzin's *History of the Russian State*, but unlike Karamzin, who deplores the ruthlessness of Ivan's pacification of Livonia, Bulgarin paints Ivan as a wise and kind victor, one who is even capable of forgiving the town's defender, Boysman, who chose to blow up the castle's powder magazine and perish in a *Götterdämmerung* rather than fall into Ivan's clutches. The love story woven into this distortion of history is inconsequential and vapid.

But Bulgarin's real claim to fame was not the idealized historical tale, nor yet the full and pedantic Eastern tale, to which genre he also contributed, but rather the picaresque novel, in particular *Ivan Vyzhigin*, a four volume chain of adventures stretching from ByeloRussia to the Kirghiz steppes and from Petersburg to Venice. In his introduction, Bulgarin attempts to defuse any and all criticism *avant la lettre*, stressing the long tradition in Russian literature of satire as a moral force and noting that his hero is not idealized, being like all mortals innately good but sometimes weak. Bulgarin then indulges himself with gross misrepresentation, claiming that this is the first original Russian novel of its kind: "I dare to assert that I imitated no one, copied no one, and wrote that which was conceived in my mind alone." Well, *Ivan Vyzhigin* is not the first original Russian novel of its kind, and with little effort one can see its direct heritage from Chulkov's *The Pretty Cook* (Prigozhaia povarikha), Narezhny's *A Russian Gil Blas* (1814), or his work of 1824, *The Two Ivans, or a Passion for Litigation* (Dva Ivana, ili Strast' k tiazhbam). Pokrovsky has conclusively demonstrated even circumstantial similarities between *Ivan Vyzhigin* and Bishop Krasicki's *Pan Podstoli*, published in Warsaw in 1778.[3]

I suppose in days when amusement was hard to come by that *Ivan Vyzhigin* had its virtues, but it is a penitential chore to read it today. The characters are totally lifeless and even unsympathetic, their adventures improbable. Despite the wide spatial range of the work, the action moves very slowly, principally because Bulgarin stuffs this story with all kinds of peripheral information, interpolated tales, etc. The section dealing with Ivan's enslavement by the Kirghiz nomads provides extensive details about the native habits and includes a long digression by the nomad leader in which he recounts his life in Petersburg, an experience which left him appalled at the baseness of Russian society.

We are told that *Ivan Vyzhigin* was very popular reading among the middle and lower classes, and this may well have been true, since the satirical javelins are directed primarily at the upper classes. The moral certitudes professed by the narrator suggest a bourgeois mentality as his alter ego. The emphasis on the profitability of virtue is no more appealing than in Richardson's *Pamela*.

Mention of Samuel Richardson's practical morality brings to mind his Russian counterpart, Dmitri Begichev (1786-1855), whose family chronicle, *The Kholmsky Family* (Semeistvo Kholmskikh), appeared in three parts in 1832 and was subsequently expanded by an additional three parts, the final one being published in 1841. Mr. Begichev must be categorized as a spear carrier, and a timid one at that: his name did not appear on any of the first three volumes, since, as he explained in his unsigned introduction, he was afraid of what the critics might say. Begichev's anxiety about critical response even finds expression in his chronicle, where the domestic felicity of one of the Kholmsky daughters is ruined when her poet husband is crucified by the critics.

This family history involves over one hundred characters and essentially concerns the trials and tribulations of a widow who seeks favorable marriages for her four daughters and only son. Interwoven with this are biographies of their acquaintances, depiction of the typical activities of gentry families, description of the manners of provincial households. Marital problems occupy the author's special attention, because, as he states in his introduction, "in married life one must pay unceasing attention to his own actions, not to discount the slightest trifles, which, seeming insignificant nothings, sometimes have dire consequences."

Of the four sisters, Begichev has appointed Sophia as his *raisonneur*, an exemplar of decorum and strategy, while her sister Elizaveta is the specimen of a thoughtlessly outspoken bride. Elizaveta foolishly marries the rich Prince Radmirsky, only to find that he is incredibly stingy and still dominated by his malicious mother. Sophia moves to loosen the covetous prince's pursestrings by coaching Elizaveta on how to manoeuvre her reluctant spouse into doing what she wants. My own reaction is that Elizaveta's brutally frank approach is more honest, especially when dealing with a fatheaded *poshlyak* like the prince, who is really concerned only with horses and appearances.

Begichev's story is heavily sociological and his description of the interiors of gentry homes suggest comparison with those of Turgenev, whose interiors not only provide social commentary on a period but also a psychological commentary on the person who chose the decorations. Is it only accidental that Prince Radmirsky's country estate is called Nikolskoe, the same as that of Mme. Odintsova in

Fathers and Children?

Irrespective of his practical ethics, Begichev deserves some credit for choosing as his subject the life and loves of the provincial gentry, with emphasis upon the way they actually lived, rather than following the easier path of satirical distortion. This early example of the family chronicle is interesting--up to a point--and justifies our remembering the nervous Mr. Begichev. Apparently the critics did not pillory him as feared, and thus he was encouraged to reappear in 1840 with not only *Olga, or the Russian Gentry's Way of Life at the Beginning of the Present Century,* in four parts, but also *Provincial Scenes.*

If there were timid spear carriers, such as Begichev, and inept ones, such as A. A. Pavlov, there were also exhibitionists, who rushed to center stage and shook their spears with violent animation. In this group are found the Russian diciples of *L'Ecôle frênêtique,* or Young France, as the critics came to call it. Crime and terror were their playthings, and no deed too extreme to shock them. The early Marlinsky of the Livonian historical tales has qualities of *L'Ecôle frênêtique,* but it is uncertain whether these came from France or directly from the Gothic tradition, which culminated in 1820 with Charles Maturin's *Melmoth the Wanderer.*

I am indebted, if that is the right word, to Professor Robert Busch for providing me with a volume by Peter Mashkov entitled *Tales and Dreams* (Povesti i mechty), published in 1833. Here we have the most violent and ghastly acts carried out by incredible characters whose motivations defy the imagination, and who, along with the narrator, speak in clichés of petrified Sentimentalism.

The print of freneticism's deformed paw is clearly evident in Mashkov's *Perfidy* (Verolomstvo), a combination of epistolary and omniscient narration which comprise a tale of betrayal and vengeance set in a remote peninsula of gloomy, grey and ominous Finland. The quality of the story does not justify my including a summary of the plot, but without it the reader will really have no comprehension of the "frenetic" nature of Mashkov's fiction. Briefly: the young, handsome and wealthy Sugrobov, miserable over betrayal by his fickle wife, has retreated to Finland and become a recluse. However, one day by chance, he saves Antonia, a pretty neighbor just returned from an institute, from pursuit by a malicious snake. Sugrobov is attracted by the girl, but reluctant to risk another betrayal; she is instantly infatuated. Then a

certain Adolf appears at Sugrobov's house and demands
10,000 roubles or he will commit suicide on the spot.
It appears he is being blackmailed by a hideous wizard
named Martin, who had observed Adolf accidentally kill
his rival for the affections of the comely Amalia. Sugrobov provides the funds, Martin is bought off, and Adolf
and Amalia are wed, but she dies within two weeks. At the
funeral, Adolf "withdrew his unbreathing friend from the
coffin, covered her icy lips with flaming kisses," etc.
Adolf and Sugrobov then become inseparable until Sugrobov
marries Zemfira, a gypsy girl of fifteen who catches his
fancy. Antonia, naturally, is plunged into despair. One
night Sugrobov overhears Adolf and Martin plotting his
death, but he is able to bribe the greedy Martin to kill
Adolf instead. The corpse of Adolf, who had secretly been
Zemfira's lover, is taken to a pavilion where Zemfira
awaits the news of her widowhood. But instead Sugrobov
appears and presents her with the bloody remains of Adolf.
The final scene is, as they used to say, "worthy of the
brush of a Rembrandt or Salvatore Rosa." Zemfira seizes
Martin's daggar, stabs herself and dies on Adolf's corpse.
Sugrobov now promises the wizard 40,000 roubles if he
will open his veins, a deal too profitable for the rapa-
cious wizard to ignore. As Sugrobov dies, the now insane
Antonia appears and imagines it is their wedding day. The
pavilion catches fire, and Antonia perishes with her imaginary bridegroom.

Mashkov's freneticism is never more evident than in
The Frightful Marriage, An Event from the 17th Century
(Uzhasny brak, sobytie XVII veka), published in 1835. Here
we have Lorenzo, an embittered Spanish nobleman, who
"thirsted for blood and whose firm hand was tireless in
spilling it." When he falls in love with the seventeen
year old Isabella, Lorenzo himself violates the sacred oath
he has imposed on his band of cutthroats to avoid all contact with women. The brigands refuse to execute him, as he
orders them to do, but rather sentence him to marry Isabella and slay her within a month. Lorenzo weds the girl,
and on the thirtieth day learns, to his horror, that he is
to become a father. But duty before everything:

> A second blow follows the first, and the Spanish
> girl's head, severed from the torso, fell on the
> floor with open eyes . . . the tongue muttered
> several mute sounds and several violent spasms
> racked the nerves of the decapitated woman . . .
> one of her hands struck Lorenzo on the breast.

For what it is worth, this story is better than
Mashkov's earlier tales, for he avoids his ponderous
nature descriptions and usual overt sententiousness.
One might compare this story with another tale featuring
the bloodthirsty outcast-hero of noble origins, beheading, and violence for its own sake: this was the historical novel *Vadim*, the work of an eighteen year old cadet
at the Guards' School in Petersburg, Mikhail Lermontov.
But Lermontov began where Mashkov ended.

The historical novel had, indeed, a vigorous exploitation in Russia following the publication in 1829 of
Mikhail Zagoskin's *Yuri Miloslavsky, or the Russians in
1612* (Jurij Miloslavskii, ili Russkie v 1612 godu). Besides knowing Scott directly, or in French translation,
and having access to the continental army of his imitators, Russian authors had their own strong tradition of
historical fiction. The Russian historical tale led back
to the turn of the century with Karamzin and Zhukovsky,
and the genre enjoyed a revival after 1823, when Marlinsky's *Roman and Olga* provided what might be called a "new
look" in historical fiction. But it was Zagoskin who pop-
ularized the novel à *la* Scott, and many Romantic fictionists tried their pens at some narrative with a historical
setting. The best of all was Pushkin's *The Captain's
Daughter* (Kapitanskaia dochka) (1836); Gogol's *Taras Bulba*
(1835) had its admirers; Lermontov wisely left his *Vadim*
(1831-1833?) unfinished. The rest of the historical novelists must all be considered spear carriers. Among these,
one might note a few of the better known works, such as
Ivan Lazhechnikov's *The Last Novik* (Poslednii Novik)
(1831) and *The Ice Palace* (Ledianoj dom) (1835), Konstantin Masalsky's *The Palace Guard* (Strel'tsy) (1832)
and *The Black Box* (Chernii iashchik) (1833), Peter Zotov's
Leonid (1832), and Bulgarin's *Dmitry the Pretender* (Dmi-
trii samozvanets) (1830). But there were dozens of other
authors, probably properly forgotten, who published historical novels in the thirties, mostly in one edition
only, and in small numbers, thus eventually to disappear
totally and forever.

I want to discuss only one rather unique historical
fictionist whose unusual subject matter and adequate talent merit his being remembered: Ivan Kalashnikov, an un-
ashamed imitator of Scott, the chronicler of the life of
Siberian merchants. In the preface to his *The Daughter
of the Merchant Zholobov, A Novel Drawn from Irkutsk
Legends* (Doch' kuptsa Zholobova. Roman izvelchennii iz

irkutskikh predanii), published in 1831, he stated his purpose was to acquaint his readers with an area "which until
the present time is a little known and almost fairy tale
country. Recently, in one of our better newspapers it was
written that in Irkutsk people ride on dogs. If that is
the way people think who are engaged in scholarship, what
can one expect of the rest?"

The Daughter of the Merchant Zholobov moves like mo-
lasses in Siberia, with lengthy circumstantial details of
Irkutsk merchant life. As a novel, it only gets underway
at the end of the first volume when, following the Scot-
tian formula, the two lovers have been separated by the
forces of evil. The horizon then expands to Lake Baikal,
we attend the Autumn festival of the native Buryats, whose
shaman slaughters dozens of animals to the gods of nature,
we have combat between man and bear, man and man, etc.
Kalashnikov is actually more reminiscent of Fenimore Cooper
than of Scott, having a similar romantic emphasis on the
grandeur of nature, native customs, and the heroic exploits
of those spreading the "blessings" of civilization.

Kalashnikov, who was at pains to assure his readers
that those in Irkutsk did not ride dogs, was also at pains
to pursuade his readers that the death of the villian in
the novel--by spontaneous combustion--was not improbable:
"Spontaneous combustion of the human body is a most unusual event, but nonetheless does occur in nature. It results from the use of internal and even external alcoholic
substances. The body burns without any external flame
having touched it." For what it is worth, Dickens and
Gogol also have recourse to this phenomenon of involuntary internal incineration.

Kalashnikov's next novel, *The Kamchatka Girl* (Kam-
chadalka), (1833), has an even more exotic setting and
takes place in the late 1700s, when the natives of the
Kamchatka peninsula still retained their aboriginal customs. Kalashnikov does not idealize this life at all, but
rather, in almost freneticist style, emphasizes its cruelty
and suffering. For lovers of grotesque horror, I recommend
the scene of the drunken Eskimo's suicide, which takes
place before the indifferent eyes of his family.

The ethnographic interests evidenced in Kalashnikov's
novels also found an early expression in the works of
Vladimir Dal, who probably deserves a place in the chorus
for having introduced into Russian literature a wide range
of characters from the lower social classes. Dal placed
special emphasis upon the speech characteristics of his

protagonists, and in this he helped legitimize the use of
dialect, jargon, sub-standard speech for literary purposes.
Dal's initial recognition came with the publication in 1832
of his *Russian Fairy Tales* (Russkie skazki), but two years
earlier he had published in *The Moscow Telegraph* a variant
of travel notes entitled *The Gypsy Girl* (Tsyganka), derived
from his personal observations of gypsy life when traveling
in Bessarabia. In the course of the thirties Dal published
four volumes of *True Stories and Fairy Tales* (Byli i nebyl-
itsy), but his real popularity came in the forties with his
ethnographic sketches and physiological sketches. The latter have earned him a prominent place in the ranks of the
Natural School, that Janus-faced manifestation which embodied qualities of both Romanticism and Realism.

In 1835, a new voice was heard in the chorus, that of
Nikolay Pavlov, whose *Three Tales* (Tri povesti) appeared
that year as a separate volume. Two of these stories in
particular merit attention, *The Name Day Party* (Imeniny)
and *Yataghan* (Iatagan), both embodying vigorous social protest. The former is a *Künstlernovelle* whose protagonist is
a serf musician. Pavlov himself had been born a serf, freed
while a child, trained as an actor, and later had graduated
from the University of Moscow and taken a position in the
judiciary system. Although his wit and personality established a place for him in society, his origins did qualify
him as an advocate for the oppressed and as a critic of social abuse. His musician (a cousin to Timofeev's artist?)
has received an education and circulates easily in society.
Then he falls in love with a gentry girl, Alexandrina, and
has to tell her that he is a serf. When his benefactor-mas-
ter loses him at cards, the musician is so humiliated that
he runs away. After various incidents, he is made a soldier and through the heroism of desperation wins honors and
promotions. Returning home as an officer, he stops at a
country inn, where he is befriended by a stranger, to whom
he tells life story. The stranger invites him to attend
his wife's name day party, and, you guessed it, the wife
turns out to be Alexandrina. There is a duel, and apparently the serf-musician-officer is eliminated.

I will not linger on this story, which is complicated
by having numerous narrators (whose voices are indistinguishable) and whose effectiveness is weakened by the use
of coincidence and eavesdropping to advance the plot.
There is, however, some evidence of Pavlov's concern with
motivating the psychological condition of his main character, and in this respect the story moves away from the arbitrary emotional states of typical Romantic fiction.

Yataghan, whose title refers to a Turkish sabre with curved blade, is far more sophisticated. Here Pavlov demonstrates a continuing concern with human motivations while exploring the psychological factors which affect social relationships. In so doing he is no Tolstoy, but he must be credited with moving significantly in that direction. Pavlov presents long passages of inner thought, he reveals emotional conditions by exterior gentures, he psychologizes by describing the private quarters of various characters. Alas, he is not able to individualize his characters to the degree that we can really sympathize with them; rather they remain somewhat abstract, embodying just a few distinctive features: the dashing young guards' officer, Bronin, the adjutant whose ridiculous sense of honor costs him his life, and the parvenu colonel who aspires to the material comfort and prestige of a country gentleman.

The story is suspenseful and strangely powerful, perhaps because Pavlov avoids the overexaggeration so typical of this period. The action takes place in a provincial garrison town, whose first citizens are a widower prince and his pretty princess daughter. The tragic conclusion is foreshadowed by the colonel's insistence that the yataghan is an unseemly gift for Bronin's doting mother to give to her newly promoted son. But the real cause of the tragedy is not the weapon but the false values which motivate all the characters, pride which has become monstrous in its ability to overwhelm mind and actions.

Although still somewhat under the thumb of the Marlinsky tradition, which is evident in the overdrawn metaphors, the digressiveness, the address to readers and characters, the occasional flights of grandiloquent declaration, Pavlov's independence is asserted in the unexpected understatement pervading the story. The duel between Bronin and the adjutant is not described, the scene of the colonel's assassination is kept under tight control, and the execution of Bronin is remarkable for its laconicism and graphic suggestiveness:

> After a certain time that same batallion which
> had followed the colonel's coffin was lined up
> on the drill field for another matter. In front
> of the ranks stood five officers. Among them
> one was without arms, in non-regulation dress.
> They saluted. The batallion adjutant read an
> order. The command was given, "Line up in two
> ranks, ground your arms." Fresh cut rods were

quickly distributed to the ranks. Some soldiers
grasped them expertly and swung them smartly
through the air, and, bantering with their comrades, said under their breath, "You have to
walk the green street."
The drums rolled, and they led him to this
street . . .
Several officers turned away . . .
Behind the ranks the doctor walked up and down,
and nearby a cart was waiting . . .

I would like to conclude with mention of another member of the chorus, one who has remained largely unheard
from owing to the louder, though not necessarily finer,
voices of his contemporaries. This is Orest Somov, an
author whom I have sought to resurrect from the oblivion
of an occasional footnote by my articles,[4] and, hopefully,
he will become better known with the publication of his
selected prose in Russian by *Michigan Slavic Materials*.
He has often been regarded merely as a "Ukrainian writer"
because of his concern for the folklore and traditions of
his native Little Russia. In fact, he contributed considerably to the evolution of fiction in the twenties and
early thirties.

In his treatment of peasant types, he anticipated
Turgenev. Somov preceded Dal in the creation of Russian
fairy tales, and not *vice versa* as is often stated. In
utilizing Ukrainian *byt* and types for fictional purposes,
he suggested a similar path for Gogol, whom, incidentally,
he encouraged as a novice writer. He was the first to
create a fully developed *skaz* tale, *Monster* (Kikimora),
appearing in 1830. His society tale of 1827, *The Holy
Fool* (Iurodivy), paralleled Marlinsky's efforts in that
genre, and his sketch in that story of the holy fool was
one of the first domestic physiological sketches, again
before Dal. Somov's problem was that perhaps he tried for
too much, he reached too high, so that when he stumbled
the result was particularly noticeable. In a social satire such as *A Novel in Two Letters* (Roman v dvukh pis'-
makh), he was right on the threshold of critical Realism,
utilizing many devices which later became canonical for
that mode, but his regressions to the language of early
Romanticism calls attention to itself in that context and
destroys the illusion of reality.

Let me provide one example of Somov's art, the story
Matchmaking (Svatovstvo), published in *Northern Flowers for
1832*. Subtitled "From the Memoirs of an Old Man About His

Youth," it is presented in a quasi-skaz manner, full of the features characteristic of oral narration. The story opens with a one-sided dialogue, the narrator asking questions on behalf of his readers and then providing the answers (shades of *Notes from Underground*):

> Maybe, gentlemen, you are surprised, you are look-
> ing at one another and whispering among your-
> selves: 'Who,' you say, 'is talking to us? And
> what's the use of one stranger irritating other
> strangers, and why should the inhabitant of a
> provincial hamlet speak with those who live in
> the capital and torment our ears, which are ac-
> customed to choice expressions and involved
> greetings?' Permit me, gentlemen, to report
> everything about myself that is necessary. I
> remind you only that I myself was a learned
> person, and if it had not been for the damned
> school holidays, then it might have been that
> I would never have lost my knowledge of Latin.

The protagonist, Demid Kalistratovich Slostyona, is one of the first of a line of tragi-comic petty civil servants in Russian fiction, buffeted by misfortune, misunderstood, frustrated, and withal charitable and meek. The pathos of their circumstance is that fate does not recompense them for their generosity and good deeds. Demid's plight is that his girl is "married out from under him" to a callous officer, who shortly abandons his bride to poverty and consumption. Demid supports her faithfully, and ultimately mourns her passing and his own solitariness. While the tale does have real comedy in some early scenes where Demid chronicles his gaffes in society, it closes on a sad note:

> As for me, I no longer think of marriage. My
> first dreams of happiness have vanished like
> smoke, and now I while away my time as an old,
> kinless bachelor. I go to work, I strictly ob-
> serve my oath of office, and I bear indiffer-
> ently the complaints of my fellow workers, whose
> opinions differ from mine. In the evening I
> read whatever God provides and write my memoirs
> from boredom. I don't know whether they will
> interest you, dear sirs, as much as me. In any
> case, I wish you happiness.

Somov was in the grave by the spring of 1833 at the age of 40. Since he had been experimental, since he had been moving in the direction of what was to become Realism,

one may assume that had he lived longer he would have continued to progress and might ultimately have established
the name for himself which his originality and persever-
ance merited.

Of course, the list of spear carriers might be considerably expanded, and I suppose it was uncharitable of
me to exclude such talents, albeit modest, as I. I.
Panaev, writer of numerous society tales, the Countess
E. P. Rostopchina, who also contributed to that genre,
Osip Senkovsky (Józef-Julian Sękowski), author of humor-
less Eastern tales and sometimes amusing pieces over his
pseudonym of Baron Brambeus, Nikolay Grech, author of an
interminable picaresque-morality novel entitled *The Woman
in Black* (Chernaia zhenshchina) and Vasily Ushakov, who
enjoyed modest success in the thirties. There are also
many more historical novelists capable of bearing spears.
However, none of these writers really advanced the art of
prose fiction, either with respect to genre development
or the broadening of the prose literary language.

It should become evident, following this presentation of the chorus and spear carriers of Russian Romantic
fiction, that Pushkin, Lermontov and Gogol really were
outstanding and deserving of separate billing. At the
same time, their eminence notwithstanding, they are linked
to the prose tradition of their contemporaries, and their
own art was inevitably affected by that contact. They
might struggle against the norms of Romanticism, parody
its clichés, mock its excesses, but they could never
stretch the norms too far, or they would have bewildered
their readers. Willy-nilly, they were obliged to sing
against the background of the chorus and endure the hum-
ming of the spear carriers.

*University of Michigan
Ann Arbor, Michigan*

NOTES

[1]My "period" or "historical" concept of Romanticism
is a development of argumentation advanced by René Wellek
in *Concepts of Criticism* (New Haven and London: Yale University Press, 1963). See my "Normative Distinctions of
Russian Romanticism and Realism," *American Contributions
to the Seventh International Congress of Slavists, Warsaw,
1973* (The Hague, Mouton & Co., 1973), Vol. II, 394-417. I
reject the so-called "typological" concept of Romanticism,

which suggests that a "system of characteristics" can be
formulated for Romanticism outside the boundaries of the
early 19th century. See A. A. Gadzhiev, "Romantizm kak
iavlenie tipologicheskoe," *Voprosy romantizma* (Kazan:
1972), Vyp. V, 23-35. Romanticism limited to 1815-1840
is a sufficiently grotesque monster without expanding its
profile into other centuries. Romantic *elements* can, of
course, exist outside Romanticism, but the movement considered as a system of norms is early 19th century.

[2]This is discussed in Roman Jakobson, "The Metaphoric and Metonymic Poles," *Fundamentals of Language*
(The Hague: Mouton & Co., 1956), 77-78.

[3]It is clear from this "genealogy" that *Ivan Vyzhigin*
is really not within the canon of Romantic fiction. It
merits attention, however, owing to its unusual popularity
and as a link of sorts between Narezhny and Gogol's *Dead
Souls*, the ultimate mutation of the didactic picaresque
novel.

[4]"Orest Somov: An Introduction," *The Slavonic and
East European Review* (June, 1965), XLIII, No. 101, pp.
354-370; "Orest Somov and the Illusion of Reality," *American Contributions to the Sixth International Congress of
Slavists* ('s-Gravenhage: Mouton & Co., 1968), Vol. II, pp.
307-331. *Selected Prose of Orest Somov* (in Russian), with
introduction by John Mersereau, Jr., *Michigan Slavic Publications* (1975).

GOGOL AND PSYCHOLOGICAL REALISM: SHINEL'

Richard Peace

'We have all come out of Gogol's *Overcoat*' is one of
those clichés about Russian literature which still persists, in spite of the near apocryphal nature of the original utterance;[1] in spite of the fact that Akakii Akakievich
is by no means the first portrait of the 'little man' in
Russian literature; above all in spite of the fact that the
attribution of this remark to Dostoevsky casts *Shinel'* as
the forerunner of the Russian psychological novel and of
'realism in a higher sense.' Yet the cliché persists precisely because it has a truth of its own. Rozanov in attacking the idea could only invert it, and even then he
conceded its validity on a superficial level at least:

> The view that all our literature derives from
> Gogol is well known. It would be more correct
> to say that the whole of our literature was the
> negation of Gogol, a struggle against him. It
> can be seen to derive from him only if one looks
> at external phenomena, if one compares the de-
> vices used in the artistic process, the forms
> and concrete objects.[2]

The challenge of this 'external view' of Gogol was
taken up by B. M. Eikhenbaum. In his iconoclastic essay
'Kak sdelana *Shinel'* Gogolia' he attacked those critics
who reduced the whole 'maze of concatenations' (*labirint
stseplenii*) to one mere idea: the 'secondary layer' of the
pathetic, and ridiculed those 'naive readers,' who saw in
the description of Petrovich and his surroundings what they
took to be 'realism': the description of *byt*. In Gogol, he
tells us, the plot line (*siuzhet*) has only superficial
meaning; Gogol's characters are 'petrified poses'
(*okamenevshie pozy*):

> The real dynamic force of his works, and by the
> same token of their composition too, inheres in
> the construction of a narrated tale (*skaz*), it
> is in language play. His characters are petri-
> fied poses. Over them all, in the guise of a
> producer and the real hero, there reigns the
> spirit of the artist himself enjoying himself
> in play.[3]

Thus Eikhenbaum not only challenges the realism of Gogol's
art, he also denies psychology to his characters.[4] At
first sight there is much to recommend such a view, yet
ultimately it is unsatisfying. There is one quality above
all which marks literature off from the other arts, a
quality which is its very essence--meaning. To look at
Shinel' as 'language play' is an interesting first step,
but the literary critic must then go further and ask what
meaning emerges from this language play. Eikhenbaum's own
answer: a comic effect--the grotesque, refers merely to the
surface level of the story; it treats 'devices' as ends in
themselves. Yet to present everything as surface is to
'out-Gogol-Gogol' who loves to pretend that all is 'surface'; and this, the most important of Gogol's *priemy*--
his central device--has been largely ignored by the Formalists. It is no longer adequate to ask *how* Gogol's overcoat was made, we must seek to find out *why*.

Eikhenbaum attempts to shift the psychological interest of the story from its chief protagonist, Akakii
Akakievich, to the 'producer' figure, and it would be
futile to deny that (from Rudyi Pan'ko on) one of Gogol's
favourite devices is to filter his stories through the distorting consciousness of an inept narrator. Yet the fact
has then to be explained why it was the 'petrified pose'
Akakii Akakievich which made such an impact on the reading
public and on Russian literature itself, and not Eikhenbaum's 'real hero'--the spirit of the author manifesting
itself in the shadowy and elusive narrator figure.

In many ways Akakii Akakievich is a typical Gogolian
hero--a psychological nonentity placed in a world of grotesque reality. This lopsided harnessing of psychological
simplicity to material complexity is a constant feature of
Gogol's writing, be it Pirogóv in *Nevskii Prospekt* or
Chichikov in *Mertvye dushi*. Often there are clear indications that the bizarre physical world, in which the 'psychological primitive' lives and has his being, has a
strange correspondence with the character himself, whether
it be one of mimicry (*Sobakevich*) or ironical inversion
(*Starosvetskie pomeshchiki*).[5] When, however, this grotesque outer world loses all semblance of reality and
plunges unequivocally into the fantastic, the reader becomes disturbingly aware that real psychological depths
can be glimpsed through this now almost transparent device
of the ambient 'reality' (e.g., *Vii, Nos, Ivan Fedorovich
Shpon'ka i ego tetushka*).

In Gogol the typical psychological nonentity sits

like a 'dead soul' in the middle of a cocoon of complexity, which is composed not merely of a bizarre ambient
'reality,' but also of the author's style with its cluttered periods and narrative devices. The Formalists admire the intricacy of this cocoon, but they refuse to see
its function, its protective purpose. Nevertheless many
of Gogol's characters exhibit a strange paradox: they are
creatures apparently without psychology, who contrive to
exhibit psychological problems and if we are to understand
this, the cocoon must not be dissociated from its occupant
as the Formalists seem to wish.

Critics of the nineteenth century (and all followers
of Belinsky) saw that the cocoon had a deeper purpose, and
they identified its content as social criticism. In challenging this assumption the Formalists sounded a welcome
and imaginative new note.[6] It cannot be denied, however,
that social criticism is implied in Gogol's treatment of
the police (in particular his laughter at the inept *budochniki*). Veneration of rank and the insolence of authority (the significant person) are presented with implied
censure. Yet the authorities in Akakii Akakievich's own
department are not responsible for his plight. The director gives him a much higher bonus than he had expected
when he so needs the money for his coat. Afterwards the
assistant chief clerk invites him to a party, partly in
honour of his coat. Nor can it be argued that the civil
service has turned him into the automoton that he undoubtedly is. We learn that he had once been given more
interesting work but had proved incapable of it. Even more
significantly the whole of his formative years are bridged
by a verbal formula which suggests that he was born to be
exactly what he is:

> The child was christened. At which he began to
> cry and he pulled such a face as though he sensed
> beforehand that he would be a titular councillor.
> (142)

Almost immediately after this we find him already long established in the office as a copy clerk:

> . . . so that later people became convinced that
> he had obviously been born into the world ready
> made, in a uniform and with a bald patch on his
> head. (143)

His christening seems to pre-ordain his profession and his
profession seems to have been entered on at birth.

If the other clerks poke fun at him they do little
more than the narrator himself, for in spite of his

strictures on those writers who mock titular councillors,
he nevertheless constantly presents his own hero as a
figure of fun with a neck that reminds him of a toy
plaster-kitten, and the strange ability always to find
himself under a window when rubbish is being thrown out.

Moreover the poverty of Akakii Akakievich, which is
the corner stone for any social interpretation of the
work, cannot be taken at its face value: it is always presented with hyperbole. In the first place Akakii Akakievich is by no means at the bottom of the hierarchy of
ranks—he is in the ninth grade (there were another five
grades below his). Other titular councillors in Gogol do
not appear to be in such financial straits. Poprishchin
(*Zapiski sumasshedshego*) goes to the theatre, reads
Severnaya pchela, orders a new uniform. Nor in *Shinel'*
itself is poverty stressed in the lives of the other minor
civil servants, their leisure time is full of theatre going, card-playing, tea-drinking. Indeed all their various
activities are used as a contrasting device to set off the
absolute lack of any outside activity on the part of
Akakii Akakievich himself:[7]

> Even during those hours when the grey sky of St.
> Petersburg grows completely dim, and all civil
> service folk have eaten and dined, each in his
> own way according to the salary he receives and
> his own particular whim, when everything is at
> rest after the scraping of departmental pens and
> flurry of their own and other people's necessary
> business and all that an indefatigable person
> willingly takes upon himself, more even than is
> necessary, when the civil servants rush off to
> devote the time which remains to enjoyment; a more
> spirited one will head for the theatre, another
> into the street allotting his time to the examina-
> tion of various hats, another will go to a party
> to waste it in compliments to some pretty girl,
> the star of a small civil servants' circle; another,
> and this happens most frequently of all, will go
> simply to see a colleague living on a third or
> second floor in two small rooms with a hall or a
> kitchen, with one or two pretensions to fashion, a
> lamp or some other such thing, which has cost many
> sacrifices, the foregoing of dinners and outings;
> in short, even at that time, when all civil ser-
> vants are scattered in the small apartments of
> their friends playing *shturmovoy* whist, sipping tea

from glasses along with cheap rusks, inhaling
smoke from long pipes, and, as the cards are
being dealt, relating some piece of gossip re-
tailed from higher society, something which a
Russian can never do without in any circumstances,
or even when there is nothing to talk about, re-
telling the eternal anecdote about the commandant, who was informed that the tail of the horse
of the Falconet monument had been fractured,--in
short, even at a time when everyone strove to
enjoy himself, Akakii Akakievich did not surrender himself to any diversion. (146)

This enormous sentence, constructed on the Gogolian formulae words *dazhe* and *slovom* is a verbal sledgehammer brought
to bear on the tiny nut of Akakii Akakievich--it is one of
the narrator's 'strong effects' (*sil'nye effekty*), the
sort of 'strong effect' to which the incoherent Akakii
Akakievich will be subjected by others throughout the
further course of the story.

But the reader himself is also on the anvil: he becomes so dazed under the assault of this sentence that he
can easily be persuaded that such phrases as: 'each in his
own way according to the salary he receives' and 'some
other such thing, which has cost many sacrifices, the
foregoing of dinners and outings' are stressing the central
issue of poverty, whereas the real burden of the passage is
the richness and variety of the lives of other civil servants when compared with the lack of activity of Akakii
Akakievich himself.

A comparable device is to be seen in the figure of the
assistant chief clerk, who, if Akakii Akakievich seems incredibly poor, seems by contrast to be exaggeratedly afflu-
ent. He is, after all, only the assistant chief clerk yet
he not only lives in the better part of St. Petersburg, but
occupies the best part of the house--the first floor. He
has servants, appears to be able to throw a lavish party
without any difficulty and invites guests whose coats have
beaver-fur collars and velvet lapels.

Akakii Akakievich has absolutely no social life, he
has no dependents, is over fifty and has been in the department for longer than anyone can remember, yet he appears to be unable to afford something as essential as a
proper coat to keep out the St. Petersburg frost.

It is not as though he is incompetent in monetary affairs. For every rouble which he spends he always puts
half a copeck away in a money box. By this means he has

already accumulated half the sum necessary for his new coat
--forty roubles. According to Akakii Akakievich's system
of saving this must represent a total of eight thousand
roubles which he has spent 'in the course of several
years,' so that, as he receives four hundred roubles per
year, it represents twenty years' salary (the actual period of saving might not be as long as this, since we know
that he gets bonuses from the director).

He is expecting a bonus for the holiday, but it is
allotted in advance for other clothing:

> It was necessary to get some new trousers, to
> pay the bootmaker an old debt for vamping old
> tops, and he also had to order three shirts
> from the seamstress, and a couple of items of
> the underwear which it is unseemly to mention
> by name in print. (153)

The coyness of the comic tone suggests that this is
not to be taken at its face value, and indeed after his
death none of this other clothing is mentioned:

> They did not seal his room, nor any of his
> things, because in the first place there were
> no heirs, and in the second place, very little
> inheritance had been left, to be precise--a
> bunch of goose quills, a quire of white offi-
> cial paper, three pairs of socks, two or three
> buttons which had dropped off his trousers, and
> the dressing gown,[8] already well known to the
> reader. (168)

Yet the boots and the underclothing had earlier figured
prominently in his economies, for he had resolved:

> when walking along the streets, to step on the
> stones and paving as lightly and carefully as
> possible, almost on tiptoe, so that by these
> means he would not wear out his soles quickly,
> to give his undergarments to be washed by the
> laundress as seldom as possible, and in order
> to prevent them getting too dirty from wear,
> to take them off every time he came home, and
> wear only a fustian dressing gown (*khalat*),
> which was very ancient, and had been spared even
> by time itself. (154)

All this is grotesque: the poverty of Akakii Akakievich is
not credible in real terms. If all the titular councillors of Tsar Nicholas I were so inexplicably indigent,
he would never have had a civil service.[9] Yet although
the material poverty of Akakii Akakievich is open to

question, what is not in doubt is his spiritual poverty: it
is not Akakii Akakievich's lack of material resources which
is striking, but the paucity of his spiritual resources.
Gogol, once more is here employing his central device: the
external world reflects an inner world: in Akakii Akakievich's outward indigence we have a metaphor of his inner
poverty.[10]

Akakii Akakievich's inner world is completely obsessive. He has only one passion--the copying out of words:

> There, in this copying he was aware of a world
> of his own which was pleasant and full of
> variety. (144)

Passion is not too strong a word for his one obsession:

> One could scarcely find a man who lived so much
> in his job. It is not enough to say that he
> worked with zeal; no, he worked with love. (144)

His love of writing is not merely a job; his leisure
hours, spent at home, are devoted to his one great passion.
Even when walking about the streets he is incapable of
thinking about anything else (once again the behaviour of
other civil servants is used as a contrasting device):

> But if Akakii Akakievich looked at anything,
> then everywhere he saw his own clear lines,
> written in an even hand, and only if a horse's
> muzzle sprang out of nowhere, lodged itself
> on his shoulder and blew out through its nos-
> trils a whole wind on to his cheek--only then
> would he notice that he was not in the middle
> of a line, but rather in the middle of the
> street. (145)

This day-dream quality associated with Akakii Akakievich's
copying is suggestive of 'writing' of a different order.
Our hero might almost be a writer in a more fundamental
sense--a man obsessed by words like Gogol himself.[11] But
Akakii Akakievich's imagination is caught not by the content and significance of words, but by their outward form,
their most palpable material expression. Even in his inner world surface has ousted content.

Akakii Akakievich's obsession with words is understandable: communication is his central problem. When he
is given a job which entails the alteration and the use of
words rather than merely copying them, he is at a complete
loss. In daily life too, communication is difficult because of his lack of words:

> It must be explained that Akakii Akakievich ex-
> pressed himself for the most part in prepositions,

> adverbs, and ultimately in particles which had
> absolutely no meaning (*znachenie*) whatsoever. If,
> indeed, it were a very difficult matter, he even
> had the habit of leaving his phrases unfinished,
> so that very frequently he would begin his utter-
> ance with the words: "It, indeed, is absolutely,
> and that." and then there was just nothing else
> at all, and he himself would have forgotten, be-
> lieving that he had already said everything. (149)

Akakii Akakievich not only lacks words himself he is at the
mercy of the words of others, even of the rhetorical effects of Petrovich the one-eyed tailor, who, we are told:

> . . . was very fond of powerful effects. He
> liked in some way or other, suddenly to take
> people completely aback, and then look side-
> ways to see what sort of face the bewildered
> person would pull at such words. (151)

The 'powerful effect' of Petrovich, the price he quotes for
a new coat, is the device of hyperbole. It challenges the
indigence of Akakii Akakievich on both its levels.

In all Akakii Akakievich's obsessive copying of words,
what he seeks to make his own is not *beauty of style* but
communication with someone unknown or someone important.

> . . . he would purposely take a copy for him-
> self, for his own pleasure, particularly if
> the document was distinguished, not by the
> beauty of its style, but by the fact that it
> was addressed to some new or important person.
> (146-7)

When, however, in real life he tries to communicate with a
'new and important person' (the general to whom he is ad-
vised to turn for help), he is a second time devastated by
words:

> But the significant person, pleased by the
> fact that the effect had even surpassed all
> expectations, and completely intoxicated by
> the thought that a word from him could even
> deprive a man of his senses, looked sideways
> at his friend to find out how he looked on the
> matter. (167)

Here the interview with the general seems consciously to be
likened to the earlier visit to the tailor:[12] both love *effekty* and both look sideways to see what reaction there is to
their words. But the interview with Petrovich ends: '. . .
and Akakii Akakievich went out completelyannihilated after
such words.' The 'annihilation' is no longer metaphorical,

after the words of the general, Akakii Akakievich takes to
his bed and dies.

The scene with Petrovich prefigures the later inter-
view with the general in more ways than one. Thus Akakii
Akakievich almost loses his senses under the first of
Petrovich's verbal 'effects':

> At the word "new" everything went misty before
> Akakii Akakievich's eyes, and every single
> thing in the room became all jumbled in front
> of him. All that he saw clearly was the gen-
> eral, with the face gummed over with paper, on
> the lid of Petrovich's snuff-box. (151)

The snuff-box general with his obliterated face, who so
swamps Akakii Akakievich's consciousness after he has heard
the significant word of Petrovich, seems to find embodied
expression in the real life general who is always referred
to as the 'significant person' (i.e., *znachitel'noye litso*
--literally 'significant face') and whose word 'could even
deprive a man of his senses.'

It would therefore appear that the general is the
personification of significance (in both senses: meaning
and importance) and it is this which overwhelms the 'in-
significance' of Akakii Akakievich. But the general is
presented with great irony. The narrator, in introducing
him indulges in extended word-play on the significance of
'significant' and 'insignificant.' To illustrate his point
he tells an anecdote about a civil servant of the same rank
as Akakii Akakievich (titular councillor), who through outward show, tried to give himself greater significance. Immediately after this there is a description of the 'methods' of the significant person, from which the reader
senses that he too suffers from a verbal poverty not unlike that of Akakii Akakievich himself:

> The methods (*priemy*) and habits of the *signifi-
> cant person* were imposing and grand but laconic
> (*nemnogoslozhnyi*). The chief basis of his sys-
> tem was sternness "sternness, sternness and
> sternness" he used to say and on the last word
> he would usually look significantly into the
> face of the person to whom he was speaking. (164)

There is an apparent play on words here (*znachitel'noye
litso*, in italics; and *smotrel znachitel'no v litso*). In
fact the general is nothing more than yet another facade--
a 'significant face,' a snuff-box general. His usual way
of addressing subordinates consists of three phrases: 'How
dare you?'; 'Do you know to whom you are speaking?; Do

you know who it is who stands before you?'   It is not so
much *what* he says as *how* he says it which makes its effect.
Thus he first addresses Akakii Akakievich:

> . . . in a firm, abrupt voice, which he had pur-
> posely practised beforehand, alone in his room
> before the mirror, a week before he had received
> his present post and the rank of general.[13]   (166)

The whole irony of Akakii Akakievich's fate is that he
falls victim to one who is also a 'copier of words.'

   Akakii Akakievich's obsession with the outer form of
words, with their well-executed graphic clothing, is a mark
of his desire to be master of them, and at the same time it
is a sad comment on his inability to capture their content.
He is thus a character in a well-known Gogolian mould,
caught between the 'visible laughter' of the outer surface
and the 'unseen tears' of the inner world. Yet there is
one person with whom he does appear to be able to communicate. On collecting his wits in the street after his first
visit to Petrovich we are told that he:

> . . . began to converse with himself not jerkily
> any more, but reasonably, and frankly as though
> with a sensible friend, with whom one could have
> a chat about something intimate and near to one's
> heart.   (152)

Communication which is difficult with others seems easy
with himself—the one friend he has. Nevertheless there is
another 'friend' who comes into his life; a friend who significantly has his own outward form—his new overcoat.

   He must endure privations if he is to gain it; he must
go without food. Eating for him, previously, was the act
of an insentient creature (he only realised that it was
time to stop when he saw that his stomach had swelled) but
now the idea of the coat represents a new 'spiritual' sustenance:

> He even trained himself to go without food in
> the evenings, but on the other hand he had spir-
> itual food (*on pitalsia dukhovno*) for he bore in
> his thoughts the eternal idea of the future coat.
> From that time on it was as though his very ex-
> istence had become somehow fuller, as though he
> had got married, as though some other person were
> present alongside him, as though he were not
> alone, as though some congenial life-long lady
> friend (*priiatnaia podruga zhizni*) had agreed to
> go together with him along life's way—and this
> lady friend was none other than that very over-

coat with its thick padding and strong lining
which would not wear out. (154)

The 'eternal titular councillor' has found his mate,
not in the 'eternal feminine,' but in the 'eternal idea' of
his new coat. A man without content has fallen in love
with his new façade.

The effect the coat has on his personality is remarkable:

> He became somehow livelier (i.e., *zhivee* = more
> alive), even firmer in character, like a man who
> had determined and set himself a goal. Doubt
> and indecision, in a word all wavering and vague
> traits, disappeared of their own accord from his
> face and his behaviour. From time to time fire
> showed in his eyes, and the most daring and bold
> thoughts flashed through his mind: "should I not
> really put marten on the collar?" (154-5)

The entertaining of 'the most daring and bold thoughts' in
respect of the coat seems to be carrying on the sexual motif, and certainly the coat has replaced his old love:

> Once, when copying a document, he nearly even
> made a mistake, so that he exclaimed "ugh" al-
> most audibly and crossed himself. (155)

When he has enough money to buy the material[14] for his
coat: 'his heart usually quite quiet, began to beat'; and
the day on which the coat was actually brought to him is
given almost ceremonial importance by one of the narrator's
verbal formulae:

> It was . . . it is difficult to say on what
> precise day, but probably on the most solemn
> of days in Akakii Akakievich's life, that
> Petrovich finally brought the coat. (156)

This most solemn (*samyi torzhestvenneishii*) of days in the
life of Akakii Akakievich might almost be a wedding. Certainly the festive occasion is linked to an awakening of
feeling:

> In the meantime, Akakii Akakievich went along
> in the most festive disposition of all his feel-
> ings (*v samom prazdnichnom raspolozhenii vsekh
> chuvstv*) (157)

and this new outward form has even brought him 'inner happiness' (*vnutrennee udovol'stvie*).

This sense of a special occasion is carried on in the
treatment Akakii Akakievich receives at the office. It is
suggested that he should throw a party that evening so that
his colleagues can drink to the coat (*vsprysnut'*). Akakii

Akakievich is only saved from further embarrassment by the
intervention of the assistant chief clerk who invites
everybody round to his apartment instead, as it so happens
that the day is his name's day.

> The whole of that day was for Akakii
> Akakievich just like the greatest solemn
> festival. He returned home in the happiest
> frame of mind. (158.

His whole way of life appears to be changing:

> He dined cheerfully and after dinner he did
> not write anything, not a document, but just
> lay like a sybarite on the bed, until it got
> dark. (158)

He then puts on his overcoat and sets out for the party.
The section which follows is one of the key sections of
the story.

> The narrator again loses his memory when he wishes to
give the precise location in St. Petersburg of the apartment of the assistant chief clerk (it does not matter that
he has not bothered to tell us where Akakii Akakievich
lives nor where he works). The problem of where the assistant chief clerk lives however, is solved by one of the
narrator's verbal formulae:

> What is at least sure is that the civil servant
> lived in the better part of town, therefore not
> all near to Akakii Akakievich. (158)

--a formula which seeks to emphasise the social distance
between two worlds. But the distance is also psychological; the physical landmarks of the route, as the narrator
confesses by way of excuse, are all confused in his head:

> . . . and everything that there is in St. Peters-
> burg, all the streets and the houses have so be-
> come fused and jumbled in one's head that it is
> difficult to get anything out of there in a de-
> cent form. (158)

Certainly, there seems to be a parallel between what is
going on in the streets of St. Petersburg and what is going
on in another head--that of Akakii Akakievich. His movement into greater life is not merely a physical progression, it reflects a process going on within Akakii Akakievich himself. Once more we have an example of Gogol's
central device; the outer world is a metaphor for the inner:

> At first Akakii Akakievich had to pass through
> several desolate streets with feeble lighting,
> but the more he drew near to the apartment of

> the civil servant, the livelier the streets be-
> came, the more populated, more powerfully il-
> luminated. (158)

His progress is from desolation to life, from darkness to
light; and now the former automoton, who never used to notice anything in the street, seems to have his eyes open
for the first time: 'he looked at all this as though it
were something new.'

An even more amazing awakening seems to be taking
place:

> He stopped with curiosity before the lighted
> window of a shop to look at a picture in which
> a beautiful woman was depicted, who was throw-
> ing off her shoe, and thus exposing her whole
> leg, and not a bad one at that, and behind her
> back a man with side whiskers, and a beautiful
> goatee beard below his lip, had stuck his head
> through the doorway from another room. Akakii
> Akakievich shook his head from side to side,
> grinned, and then went on his way. Why did he
> grin? Was it because he had encountered a
> thing that was completely unknown to him, but
> about which each one of us has retained some
> sort of sixth sense (*chut'e*), or like many other
> civil servants, did he think the following:
> "Well those French. If they take a fancy to
> something like that, then it is, indeed, just as
> it were. . . ." But perhaps he did not even
> think that--it is after all impossible to get
> inside the soul of another man and find out
> everything that he thinks.[15]   (158-9)

Thus the narrator figure disclaims all attempt at psychological analysis. Yet his own speculations, before his
assertion that it is impossible to get inside another man,
not only call attention to Akakii Akakievich's state of
mind, they suggest his ambiguity of response in an evocative way.

A similarly effective denial of psychological insight
occurs after the loss of the coat when he has returned home
and gone to bed:

> . . . and how he spent the night there may be
> judged by those who are capable to any extent
> of imagining the situation of another man. (162)

Gogol in rejecting any possibility of getting inside his
characters is not abandoning the attempt to portray their
psychology. He merely proceeds by different means. Akakii

Akakievich wears his new overcoat like a different frame of
mind; his brand-new outward form is his new self. At the
same time the overcoat also has for him associations of a
new relationship, a 'life-long lady-friend,' so that when
in his progress through the 'streets' of St. Petersburg he
encounters sexual titillation, perhaps for the first time,
his reactions are ambiguous, but not as ambiguous as the
narrator would have us believe.

   Naive ambiguity is a constant feature of the narrative
technique. Eikhenbaum has called attention to the puns in
Shinel', and has interpreted them on a surface level as a
device contributing to the humour.[16]   Admittedly the puns
do communicate a waywardness and playfulness of tone to the
narrative, yet their contribution is not so much to the
humour of the story as to the external presentation of the
inner world of the central character, a man who is himself
obsessed by the outward forms of words, their graphic con-
tours, only because their real content and function eludes
him. The pun is precisely this: a word taken at face value
which nevertheless has a hidden content beneath its deceptive surface. *Shinel'* is indeed an edifice of words but
the verbal play has more meaning than is at first apparent
and the relationship between façade and interior is not
only the central 'device' of *Shinel'*, it is the architec-
tural principle which informs its shape.

   There is a great deal of verbal play at the opening of
the story, up to that point which Eikhenbaum calls the end
of 'the first act of *Shinel'*' (i.e., the whole of the introductory section ending with the play on the word
sovetnik).

   In introducing Akakii Akakievich the narrator places
exaggerated importance on the naming of his hero,[17] whereas, as we have seen, his formative years are merely bridged
by a verbal formula. All this suggests that his name is
far more important than his life in determining his character. In particular the origin of the surname is treated
with naive seriousness:

   The civil servant's name was Bashmachkin. From
   the very name itself one can see that at some
   time it had been derived from a shoe; but when,
   at what particular time and in what way it was
   derived from a shoe - nothing of this is known.
   Both his father and his grandfather, and even
   his brother-in-law, all Bashmachkins through
   and through, used to walk about in boots changing the soles only three times a year. (142)

The whole of this explanation is patently absurd, if taken
at its surface meaning; yet, on another level, it suggests
a whole train of semantic ambiguities which are picked up
and developed later in the story, in such a way as to reveal the psychological problems of Akakii Akakievich himself.

In the first place the verb 'derived' is taken quite
literally (the all important qualification 'word' which
ought to precede 'shoe' is omitted), so that our hero's
name appears to have come directly from an article of
footwear--a shoe; just as later it will be suggested that
he has almost got married to an article of clothing--an
overcoat. The hero through his surname is thus directly
identified with a mere casing of the human body, and one
moreover, which in Russian, has associations of oppression
and subjection.[18]

The narrator compounds the absurdity by asserting that
all Akakii Akakievich's family wore boots (i.e., a masculine form of footwear as opposed to the more feminine
'*bashmak*'), and gives the irrelevant information that they
had the soles replaced only three times a year (the saving
of his soles will later figure prominently in Akakii
Akakievich's economies needed to acquire the coat). The
list of Akakii Akakievich's relatives, who, according to
the narrator, are all genuine Bashmachkins (*i vse
sovershenno Bashmachkiny*) includes a 'brother-in-law' (*i
dazhe shurin*) despite the fact that, as this is a relationship by marriage, he could not possibly be a genuine Bashmachkin as the narrator claims. Yet the inclusion of this
brother-in-law is absurd in an even more profound sense.
Russian relationships by marriage are very precise, and
shurin can only mean 'one's wife's brother.' For Akakii
Akakievich to have a '*shurin*,' he must also have a wife,
but a wife is no more in evidence than these other relatives with whom he is here credited. Akakii Akakievich is
completely alone. This little verbal puzzle, therefore,
tangles the 'shoe' from which his name is derived, with
the relatives from whom he is actually derived (his father
and his grandfather) and ties them in with a figure to whom
he can only be related by a sexual bond (the brother-in-
law).

The theme of the wife who is non-existent but implied,
appears again when the narrator gives examples of his
'downtrodden' existence: the teasing to which he is subjected at the office:
They would relate, right in front of him,

> various stories concocted about him. They said
> about his landlady, an old woman seventy years
> old, that she beat him, and they would ask him
> when their wedding would be. They would scat-
> ter paper on his head calling it snow. (143)

The motif of the 'shoe' is prominent in the picture which
stirs a vague sexual awakening in Akakii Akakievich, and
the detail seems intentional, for virtually the same picture is described at the end of *Nos*, but without the mention of a shoe.[19]   At a later stage a shoe will also link
this picture with his landlady. The 'shoe,' from which his
outward identification (his name) is derived, suggests a
latent sexual motif in much the same way as does that other
item of apparel, his other outward form, the overcoat.

Akakii Akakievich's progress through St. Petersburg
may be interpreted as a journey in self-exploration: It is
certainly a progress towards light. He moves away from his
own badly lit part of the city, past the lighted window
with its erotic picture to the apartment of the civil servant who has invited him; 'the assistant chief clerk lived
in great style;[20] there was a lantern shining on the stair-
case.'   (159)

The fact that Akakii Akakievich is at first overawed
is again suggested by Gogol's external method of psychological portrayal. Akakii Akakievich is reduced to the
status of an object among other objects:

> On entering the hall Akakii Akakievich saw on
> the floor a whole row of galoshes. Among them
> in the middle of the room stood a samovar, nois-
> ily emitting clouds of steam. On the wall hung
> nothing but overcoats and capes, among which
> there were several which even had beaver collars
> or velvet lapels. (159)

It seems significant that he is confronted with footwear
and overcoats. The only thing which appears to have life
in this ante-room is another inanimate object—the samovar.
Real life, once more, it seems, is going on elsewhere:

> On the other side of the wall noise and talk
> could be heard, which suddenly became clear and
> resonant, when the door opened and a servant
> came out with a tray ranged with empty glasses,
> cream jugs and a basket of rusks. The civil
> servants had obviously been gathered here a
> long time and had all drunk a first glass of
> tea.   (159)

But the occasion has been held partly to honour Akakii

Akakievich's new coat. He is accepted by this society, and
his overcoat is rapturously admired, even though there are
better ones hanging up in the hall.

>   Then of course everybody dropped him and his
>   coat and turned, as is the custom to the tables
>   intended for whist. (160)

After all Akakii Akakievich is not really at home in these
surroundings. He tries to creep away, but is made to stay
for supper and two festive glasses of champagne. It is
after midnight when he escapes. He finds his coat, 'which,
not without regret, he perceived was lying on the floor'
(160). He carefully shakes it, and goes down to a still
lighted street. Here, sexual promptings (inexplicable to
the narrator) once more well up within him:

>   Akakii Akakievich went along in a gay mood, and
>   for some unknown reason he was even almost on
>   the point of running up behind some lady or
>   other, who went past like lightning, and every
>   part of whose body was full of unusual movement.
>   But, however, he stopped at once and went on as
>   before very slowly, amazed himself at this un-
>   accountable burst of speed. (160-1)

His progress now, however, is away from light and conviv-
iality towards the dark, shuttered emptiness of his own
quarter:

>   It was still light in the street. One or two
>   small shops, those permanent clubs for servants
>   and all sorts of people, were open, and others
>   which were closed showed, nevertheless, a long
>   stream of light the whole length of the door
>   jamb, a sign that they were not yet deprived of
>   company, and that, probably, maids or servants
>   were still finishing off their talk and gossip,
>   and plunging their masters into perplexity as
>   to their whereabouts. (160)

Thus even the humblest members of society have life in this
area of the city, but two sentences later (after the incident with the woman) there is another passage which stands
out in sharp contrast.

>   Soon there stretched before him those desolate
>   streets, which even during the day are not so
>   cheerful, and all the more is this so in the
>   evening. Now they had become even more hushed
>   and deserted. There began to be fewer lamps.
>   Less oil, it seemed, was allocated here. From
>   here on there were timber houses and fences; not

a soul anywhere. The only thing that glistened
was the snow in the streets, and the low slum-
bering hovels with their closed shutters looked
gloomy and black. (161)

On his outward journey he had been *looking* for the first
time in his life. Now, as he crosses a dark square, where
a light seems 'at the world's end' and 'it is as though
there is a sea around him,' our explorer closes his eyes--
and is robbed of his overcoat by men with moustaches. Thus
he is brutally deprived of the promise of a fuller life
offered to him so briefly and so tenuously.

He goes home to his landlady and the details of his
return seem to refurbish in ironical terms the elements of
the picture in the lighted window which had earlier aroused
such strange stirrings within him:

The old lady, the landlady of his apartment,
hearing the terrible knocking at the door, hur-
riedly jumped out of bed and with a shoe on
only one foot, ran to open the door, holding
her nightshirt to her chest out of modesty. (162)

The landlady, as we know, has already been associated with
the marital state of Akakii Akakievich by the clerks at the
office, who teased him about marrying her and scattered
'snow' on his head. Now, when he comes back covered in
real snow, his landlady, like the woman in the picture,
confronts him with 'a shoe on one foot' and the hint of
sexual titillation (holding her nightshirt to her chest,
out of modesty'). But the 'man at the door' is not the
dandy with the side whiskers and beautiful beard, it is the
dishevelled Akakii Akakievich, with what little hair he
has in complete disarray.[21]

So Akakii Akakievich is thrown back on his seventy-
year old landlady, by the 'light' of whose candle he used
to work in the evenings (after first having taken off his
underwear to economise on laundry!). On her advice he
goes to the police, but the district superintendent seems
to think that the loss of the coat is in some way connected
with its owner's dissolute life:

The district superintendent received the story
of the theft of the coat somehow in an exceeding-
ly strange way. Instead of turning his attention
to the main point of the matter, he began to question Akakii Akakievich why it was that he was returning home so late, and hadn't he called in and
been in some disorderly house or other? (163)

Here, as elsewhere in the story, the significance of the

coat is interpreted not in terms of the obvious but in terms of a suggested sexual theme. This even seems to be hinted on his death bed; for he keeps asking his landlady to drag a coat-thief out from under his blanket.

We have seen that in the opening section of *Shinel'* verbal play is an important device for establishing motifs which are to be developed in the central section of the story, now in the final section, the ghost sequence, verbal play has a similar function. There is a recurring pun on the concepts of 'dead' and 'alive.' The police (*budochniki*) are ordered to apprehend the '*dead man* dead or alive.' One of them apparently succeeds, but loses the ghost because he pauses to take snuff of a quality 'which even a dead man couldn't stand,' and so from that time on the police 'got so frightened of dead men, that they were even fearful of arresting the living.' Finally there is an 'apparition' at the end of the story, who when challenged by a policeman, shows him a huge fist 'such as you would not find on the living.'

All this seems like humour directed at the police who throughout the story have shown themselves to be particularly inept, but there is also a serious intention behind the word-play. The ghost is first introduced as 'a dead man in the form of a civil servant' (*mertvets v vide chinovnika*). Later he is simply referred to as the 'dead man--civil servant' (*chinovnik mertvets*). The verbal play on 'dead and alive' is therefore a motif pointing to the artistic function of the story's fantastic ending; it raises the whole question of '*chinovnik-mertvets.*'

When he was alive, Akakii Akakievich was in reality more like a 'civil servant in the form of a dead man.' The promise of an awakening into life, flimsy though it may have been was cruelly taken from him by men with moustaches. When he has died he returns as a 'dead man in the form of a civil servant' to avenge himself, and by one of those ironies in which the story abounds, he proves to be more effective as a dead man, than he was when alive.

It is typical of Gogol that this inversion to which the central character is subjected, should also be reflected in the treatment of his ambient 'reality.' When earlier Akakii Akakievich was going through the streets of St. Petersburg, the narrator was insistent that everything in the city was so muddled in his head that he could not remember names; now, when his hero appears as a ghost, he is very meticulous about giving the precise location of each appearance. In the first instance a real man was going

through a spiritual city: in the second a spirit man is
haunting a concrete and actual city.

It is only after the ghost has robbed the 'significant person' of his overcoat that this unquiet spirit is
finally laid, and the whole incident is presented with the
same ironic parallelism of detail which has been noted
elsewhere in the story.

The significant person, having just learned of the
death of Akakii Akakievich, goes to a party to cheer himself up (Akakii Akakievich had been to a party before he
lost his coat). Here (like Akakii Akakievich before him)
he has two glasses of champagne. He feels in a gayer mood,
and just as Akakii Akakievich had then, for some unknown
reason, wanted to chase after a woman in the street, so
the significant person now entertains thoughts of an amorous nature:

> The champagne put him in a mood for special
> measures; that is he decided not to go home
> yet, but to call on a certain lady of his ac-
> quaintance, Karolina Ivanovna, a lady who ap-
> peared to be of German extraction, and for whom
> he felt an entirely friendly relationship. (171)

Here, as in the earlier incident with Akakii Akakievich,
the narrator shows himself to be naively uncomprehending
about the sexual motivation of his characters.

Whereas Akakii Akakievich had been making the first
tentative gestures in the direction of life, the general
has grasped it firmly. In the first place he took an active part in the evening gathering as a man among equals.
On leaving the party he is going to a real mistress, moreover, unlike Akakii Akakievich, he also has a family:

> But the significant person, although he was
> quite content with the family affection he
> received at home, considered it fitting to
> have a lady friend in another part of town
> for friendly relationships. This lady friend
> was not a whit better or younger than his wife.
> But such problems do exist in the world, and
> it is not for us to judge them.[22]   (172)

It seems poetic justice that the ghost should rob this 'man
of substance' of his greatcoat at this precise moment. The
effect is cathartic: the ghost is laid, and the general
himself becomes a much better person.

The story ends with yet another ironic twist. Another
ghost is seen and it is believed to be the ghost of Akakii
Akakievich, but it is really an 'apparition,' and when

challenged by a particularly inept policeman, it threatens
him with a fist not unlike that of the man who stole Akakii
Akakievich's overcoat in the first place, and showed him a
fist 'the size of a civil servant's head.' The policeman
leaves the apparition alone.

> The apparition, was however much taller and wore
> really enormous moustaches, and turning its steps,
> as it seemed, towards the Obukhov Bridge, it
> completely disappeared in the darkness of the
> night.   (174)

Even Akakii Akakievich's credibility as a ghost, it seems,
is being challenged by those men with moustaches and the
whole story ends on a note of darkness.[23]

What relationship does this strange tale have to psychological realism? In the first place the story is presented (though not consistently) through the mouth of a
less than intelligent narrator, who seems to be the very
antithesis of the 'omniscient author' able to get inside
all his characters: the central device of Tolstoi's psychological realism. Yet the rational dissection of thought
processes should not be confused with the realistic presentation of psychology. Indeed the artificiality of the
device is revealed in *Anna Karenina*, when the author gets
inside the mind of a dog and shows it to be more intelligent than human beings.[24]

Dostoevsky, another master of psychological realism,
also likes to make use of a narrator who is not fully
aware of all the facts. Such a figure is used (though
again not consistently) in *Besy*, where Dostoevsky is faced
with the same problem as Gogol in *Shinel'*: The presentation of a central character (Stavrogin) who is a spiritual
void. Here, as with Akakii Akakievich, the technique of
speculation and innuendo is not only far more effective
than an omniscient analysis of motive, it also shows greater psychological realism: 'It is, after all, impossible to
get inside the soul of another man and find out everything
he thinks.'

In facing up to the demands of this kind of psychological 'realism,' Gogol resorts to a purely external
method of portraying the inner world, which is 'psychological' realism (in another sense): his way of making the
psychological world 'real' is to make the real world 'psychological.' Gogol is not alone in using this technique,
but there is perhaps no other author in Russian literature
who employs it so exclusively. In Dostoevsky's *Zapiski iz
podpol'ia*, when the hero refers to St. Petersburg as 'the

most abstract the most contrived city on the earth's globe,'[25] there is a strong suggestion that he is viewing it as a mental landscape, but far more explicit is the identification of his own living quarters, 'the underground,' with a psychological state.

For Tolstoi a journey of spiritual and sexual awakening is not reflected in an urban setting, but in nature. In *Voina i mir* Prince Andrei sees his own inner state reflected in the oak tree which he passes both on his way to see the Rostovs and on his journey back again, but as is usual in Tolstoi this is made explicit.[26]

Chekhov began as a humorist very much in the mould of Gogol. His story *Smert' chinovnika* is little more than a reworking of *Shinel'* which concentrates on bizarre pathos and humour, but the mature work of Chekhov constantly treats the psychological problem which lies at the heart of *Shinel'*--the inability to communicate. Moreover Chekhov's well-known use of mood and atmosphere is really only a sophisticated and subtle development of the relationship between the psychology of a character and his ambient reality which we find in Gogol.

In Goncharov's novel *Oblomov* we find an article of clothing, a dressing gown, used as a constant motif indicating the psychological state of the hero. However, unlike Akakii Akakievich, Oblomov is offered a relationship with a real woman, Ol'ga Il'inskaia. Through her he experiences a spiritual awakening, and she ousts the 'dressing gown' from his consciousness. He becomes a different man. Unfortunately he is unable to live up to the demands of a real woman. He allows her to be taken from him by the 'man of action,' Stolz, whilst he sinks back to his dressing gown and the solace of his landlady.

Verbal play on Bashmachkin's name is an important feature of *Shinel'*; it sets up verbal associations which link him with women. Oblomov himself has a name, Il'ia Il'ich, not unlike that of Akakii Akakievich (i.e., the patronymic echoes the christian name), moreover it is a name which links him with the woman in his life--Il'inskaia. Oblomov's surname, too, has its own connotations. *Oblomok* means 'broken off bit.' He is 'a broken off bit of the past'--*oblomok proshlogo*. Playing with the names of his characters is a favourite device of Dostoevsky. Thus Razumikhin in *Prestuplenie i nakazanie* has a name derived from *razum* ('reason') but he is variously called Vrazumikhin (*vrazumit'* = 'to knock sense into') and Rassudkin (rassudok = 'reason'). It has often been pointed out that by giving his hero in *Bednye liudi* the surname Devushkin (*devushka* = 'girl'), Dostoevsky is consciously rewriting *Shinel'* by striving to humanise the theme. Such an idea supports Rozanov's contention that Russian literature is a struggle against Gogol rather than a development from him. Dostoevsky 'rewrote' *Shinel'* yet again in his story *Vechnyi muzh*. Here a minor civil servant Trustosky (the name suggests 'coward') with a Gogolian christian name and patronymic, Pavel Pavlovich, is identified as a husband under his wife's shoe (*muzh pod bashmakom*). She has been unfaithful to him, and he gains his revenge on Velchaninov (the man who has 'robbed' him of his wife and family) by haunting him. He does not do this literally like Akakii Akakievich, but shadows Velchaninov in the streets, and tries to frighten him in bed at night by ghostly behaviour. In the ghost sequence at the end of *Shinel'* Gogol had identified the need of the 'little man' to be revenged on those to whom he feels inferior. Dostoevsky, however, in taking up Gogol, has seen this problem differently. In *Shinel'* the ghost was a ghost; in *Vechnyi muzh* the 'hauntings' are the 'little man' playing at being a ghost. It is by play-acting like this (krivlianie) that the 'little man' in Dostoevsky always seeks to get his revenge; it is a constant element in the mature Dostoevsky's portrayal of downtrodden characters. The ambivalence that this sets up is no longer the Gogolian one 'dead or alive' it is 'victim' or 'tryant' (i.e., *'khishchnyi tip'*, *'smirnyi tip'*).[28]

   Tolstoi is perhaps furthest of all away from Gogol, and in his story about the inner poverty of a civil servant, *Smert' Ivana Il'icha* Gogol's procedures are inverted. Thus it is not his lack of material possessions which reflects the inner poverty of Ivan Il'ich, quite the reverse --it is his material wealth, his attachment to things. Riding home after a dispiriting visit to the doctor, the mood of Ivan Il'ich is reflected in the mood of the street, but it is not Gogol's method of making the outside world point inwards, Tolstoi makes it clear that it is rather Ivan Il'ich who is projecting his mood on to the street:

   Everything on the streets seemed to Ivan
   Il'ich to be sad, the cab drivers were sad,
   the houses were sad, the passers-by, the shops
   were sad.[29]   (49-50)

The paradox of the story is that the more death overwhelms him physically, the more alive does he become spiritually-- the more he becomes aware. This awakening of consciousness

is presented, as with Akakii Akakievich as a progress towards light. The light which disappears from his eyes
(physical death) Ivan Il'ich finds in death (spiritual
life) in the light at the end of the tunnel,[30] so that,
oddly, like Akakii Akakievich, he seems more alive in
death than he had been in life.

    Whether one sees the main stream of Russian prose
fiction as stemming directly from *Shinel'*, or whether, on
the other hand, one agrees with Rozanov that those who
followed Gogol were struggling against him (and these two
viewpoints are not irreconcilable) it is nevertheless beyond dispute that this strange tale of a civil servant and
his coat has had a profound effect on Russian literature.
Such an impact cannot be attributed merely to its being a
collection of stylistic devices. The devices are there,
beyond all doubt, but their function is the indirect projection of character: their contribution is towards that
non-rational approach to the portrayal of psychology,
which is the great underlying strength of Russian psychological realism.

NOTES

[1]For a discussion of this see: F. C. Driessen, *Gogol
As a Short-Story Writer: A Study of His Technique of Com-
position* (translated from the Dutch by I. F. Finlay), The
Hague, Mouton, 1965, p. 185 (note 4).

    [2]V. V. Rozanov, *Legenda o Velikom Inkvizitore*, Munich,
Fink, 1970 (Reprint of St. Petersburg 1906 edition), p. 15.

    [3]B. M. Eikhenbaum, "Kak sdelana *Shinel'* Gogolia,"
Skvoz' literaturu, 'S-Gravenhage, Mouton, 1962, p. 177.

    [4]This idea is widely accepted. See Rozanov, *Legenda*,
p. 21; N. Berdiaev, *Russkaya ideia*, Paris, YMCA, 1946, p.
83. In a more recent study we read: 'In *The Overcoat* the
subconscious is also important but relatively superficial.
The depiction of the hero, Akakij Akakievic, despite its
justifiable fame is without psychological depth. His importance as a character depends primarily on his symbolic
meaning rather than on the state of his inner life. Contentment does not breed the conflicts which incubate the
subconscious.' (L. J. Kent, *The Subconscious in Gogol'
and Dostoevskij, and Its Antecedents*, The Hague-Paris,
Mouton, 1969, p. 84.) I would argue that the 'contentment'

of Akakii Akakievich is deceptive (as is also that of Ivan
Shpon'ka, Khoma Brut, Major Kovalev) and agree with Driessen that: '. . . no-one who knows Gogol somewhat will
doubt that he is a masterful psychologist, of a completely
different type to Dostoeyevsky however.' Driessen, *Gogol*,
p. 195.

[5]Sobakevich appears to Chichikov to have no soul, or
if he has, it is hidden, like that of the immortal Koshchei,
behind the mountains. Yet every object in his house seems
to mirror his personality: '. . . in short every object,
every chair, seemed to say: I too am Sobakevich, or I too
am very like Sobakevich.' N. V. Gogol, *Polnoe sobranie
sochinenii*, Izdatel'stvo Akademii Nauk, SSSR, 1940-52,
vol. VI, p. 96.

In *Starosvetskie pomeshchiki* the sterility of the old
couple is set against the inexplicable fertility of their
Ukrainian estate.

[6]At the beginning of *Shinel'* the narrator himself
would seem to lend weight to the Formalists' view. The
opening is a verbal arabesque which advances the narrative
not a whit; it ends where it began: 'V odnom departamente
. . . odnim departamentom.' Moreover in the course of
this verbal flight the idea of the social interpretation
of literary works is mocked in the anecdote about the
kapitan ispravnik. See: N. V. Gogol, *Poln. sob.*, vol.
III, p. 141 (in the text all references to *Shinel'* are to
this volume, and the pages will merely appear as numbers
in brackets).

[7]In *Nevskii Prospekt* Gogol gives reasons other than
poverty to explain why titular councillors stay at home:
'Young provincial registrators, provincial and college
secretaries stroll about a long time; but old college
registrators, titular and court councillors for the most
part stay at home, either because they are married people,
or because the German cooks who live with them give them
good food.' *Poln. sob.*, Vol. III, p. 15.

Senkovsky has Baron Brambeus (at the beginning of his
"Poeticheskoe puteshestvie po belomu svetu") complain
about the amusements of the people in the tenth class
('razvlechennia ego slishkom vialy') and he fears that
everyone else will become titular councillors, whilst he
is left behind in the tenth class. O. I. Senkovsky,
Fantasticheskie puteshestviia Barona Brambeusa, St. Petersburg, Pliusher, 1835, p. 4. The difficult social position
of the titular councillor sprang from the fact that it
marked an important career threshold: beyond it hereditary

nobility was conferred as of right. Unlike Akakii Akakievich, however, there is another titular councillor mentioned in Shinel' who tries to assert the social position
of the ninth grade:

> They even say that when some titular councillor
> or other was put in charge of a separate small
> office, he immediately screened off for himself
> a room of his own, calling it an "audience cham-
> ber," and at the door he placed attendants with
> red collars and braid, who would get hold of the
> handle of the door, and open it for every cal-
> ler, even though there was scarcely room in the
> audience chamber for a normal sized desk. (164)

[8]The 'dressing gown' (*kapot*) refers to his old thread-
bare coat, it is not the real dressing gown (*khalat*) mentioned during his regime of economies.

[9]The inspirational source for *Shinel'* (according to
P. V. Annenkov) is in itself instructive. The original
anecdote concerned a civil servant who saved up to buy a
sporting gun and then lost it. Whereas Gogol's hero endures great privations in order to afford, not a luxury
for his recreation, but an absolute necessity of life.
P. V. Annenkov, *Vospominaniia i kriticheskie ocherki*, St.
Petersburg, 1877, vol. I, pp. 188-189.

[10] In Gogol's treatment of Akakii Akakievich it is almost as though he is exploiting an ambiguity of meaning,
which he had already suggested in *Nevskii Prospekt*:

> Do you think that this gentleman who is
> strolling along in an extremely well made
> little coat is very rich? Nothing of the
> sort: he consists entirely of his little
> coat. *Poln. sob*. vol. III, p. 45.

Here the question is apparently posed in terms of the
wearer's wealth, but the comment: '*on ves' sosotoit iz
svoego siurtuchka*' suggests something far more fundamental
than lack of material resources.

[11] It is true that in *Nevskii Prospekt* Gogol writes:

> But the old college secretaries, titular and
> court councillors walk quickly with their heads
> bowed, they cannot be bothered with examining the
> passers by; they have not yet fully wrenched them-
> selves away from their cares; there is a jumble in
> their heads and a whole archive of business begun
> and not ended; for a long time the document box
> or the fat face of the director of the office
> appears before their eyes instead of a shop

sign. *Poln. sob.* vol. III, p. 14.
Nevertheless, the obsession of Akakii Akakievich is the
very process of writing itself, and *Shinel'* dates from
1842, the time of Gogol's new plans to develop a positive
message for his *'Poema,' Mertvye dushi*. The second version of *Portret* also dates from this time, and critics
have pointed to the relevance of his new conception of
this work to the artistic theories Gogol was bringing to
bear on *Mertvye dushi* itself. (See: *Poln. sob.* vol.
III, p. 667).
Russian uses the same verb *'pisat'* both for 'to paint' and
'to write,' and in painting (the artistic process examined
in *Portret*) the problem of façade versus content is even
more acute. Thus the narrator in the second version of
Portret is told by his saintly father:
> Examine and study every single thing you see,
> subject it to your brush, *but in everything be*
> *able to find an inner sense*, and most of all
> try to grasp the lofty secret of creation.
> *Poln. sob.* vol. III, p. 135 (italics mine).

In a letter to A. Smirnova (24th December 1844) Gogol
writes of his earlier stories:
> It is quite true that you will find in them
> little bits of my mental and psychical state
> of those days, but without my personal con-
> fession, no one will ever notice or see them.
> *Poln. sob.* vol. XII, p. 419.

Vybrannye mesta iz perepiski s druz'iami was Gogol's attempt (ill-fated, as it turned out) to reveal the content of his life and work, and here he writes in the third
letter on the subject of *Mertvye dushi*: 'all my latest
works are the history of my own soul.' *Sob. soch.* vol.
VIII, p. 292.

It may well be that *Shinel'*, that strange story of
the search for content through façade, derives its compelling power from the fact that it is a reflection of a
personal and artistic crisis. experienced by the author
himself.

[12] Cf. Driessen, *Gogol*, pp. 206-207.

[13] In *Vybrannye mesta* Gogol advocates that such a re-
hearsal of lines should be adopted by a priest. *Poln.
sob.* Vol. VIII, p. 327. Gogol's crisis over 'content' is
perhaps that his positive message is uncomfortably like
his negative one. Thus the acquisitiveness of Chichikov
is refurbished in Kostanzhoglo (*'vsiakaia drian' daet
dokhod'*). *Poln. sob.* vol. VII, p. 68.

[14] In *Ivan Shpon'ka i ego tetushka* the hero dreams that
a wife is some sort of material which can be made up into a
coat (*siurtuk*). *Poln. sob.* Vol. I, p. 307.

[15] The penetration of the inner self was something of
which Gogol was wary in life as in art. Thus in reply to
a correspondent about the problem-fraught second part of
Mertvye dushi he uses almost identical words: 'zalez ty
razve v moiu golovu?'. *Poln. sob.* vol. VIII, p. 296.

[16] Eikhenbaum, *Skvoz' literaturu*, p. 172.

[17] For a discussion of the implications of the hero's
christian name see Driessen, *Gogol*, p. 194.

[18] Cf. *'byt' pod bashmakom u kogo-nibud'*.

[19] '. . . and a lithographed picture depicting a young
woman adjusting her stocking, and a dandy looking at her
from behind a tree, who had a cut-away waistcoat and a
small beard--a picture which had been hanging in the same
place for more than ten years.' *Poln. sob.* vol. III, p.
72.

In *Nevskii Prospekt* we read that at dusk '. . . there
would look out from low shop windows those prints which do
not dare to show themselves at daytime.' *Poln. sob.* vol.
III, p. 14.

[20] Literally: 'on a big foot' (*zhil na bol'shuiu nogu*).

[21] See also Driessen, *Gogol*, p. 194.

[22] The family affection with which the significant person is 'quite content' consists merely of the kissing of
hands, and Gogol describes this in a purely ritualistic
way which seems to deprive it of any emotional content:

> Two sons, one of whom served in the office,
> and a nice looking sixteen year old daughter,
> with a slightly hooked but nice little nose,
> would come and kiss his hand every day, saying
> "Bonjour, papa." His wife, a lady of fresh
> complexion and not really bad looking even,
> would allow him to kiss her hand and turning
> it round the other way would kiss his hand.
> (171-72).

[23] Originally Gogol had this apparition with moustaches
making not for the Obukhov Bridge but for the Semenovskii
Barracks (See *Poln. sob.* vol. III, p. 686). As this implied that the apparition was a soldier, it was changed
apparently for reasons of censorship. The sexual theme of
soldiers' moustaches is hinted at earlier in the description of Petrovich's wife:

> . . . but she could not boast of beauty, it
> seemed; at least only guards soldiers would

peep under her mob cap, twitching their moustaches and emitting a special sort of voice. (148)
(Cf. also *Koliaska, Poln. sob.* vol. III, p. 178)
[24] L. N. Tolstoi, *Polnoe sobranie sochinenii*, Moscow.
G.I.KH.L., 1928-58, vol. XIX, p. 168.

In *Zapiski sumasshedshego* Gogol penetrates the minds
of dogs as a device illustrating the madness of the hero.
But he also gets inside the mind of one of Chichikov's
horses (*Poln. sob.* vol. VI, p. 59).

[25] F. M. Dostoevsky, *Sobranie sochinenii*, G.I.KH.L.,
Moscow, 1956, vol. IV, p. 136.

[26] L. N. Tolstoi, *Poln. sob.* vol. 10, pp. 153-4; 156-7.

[27] Stolz speculates what the marriage of Olga and
Oblomov might have been like:

Marriage was only a form and not content, a
means and not an end. It would have served
as a broad but immutable frame for visits, receiving guests, meals and evenings of empty
chatter.

I. I. Goncharov, *Sobranie sochinenni*, Moscow, G.I.KH.L.,
1959, vol. IV, p. 389.

[28] F. M. Dostoevsky, *Sob. soch.*, vol. IV, p. 501 (see
also note on p. 609).

[29] L. N. Tolstoi, *Poln. sob.*, vol. 26, p. 85.

[30] L. N. Tolstoi, *Poln. sob.*, vol. 26, pp. 112-113.

TOLSTOY'S UNDERGROUND WOMAN: A STUDY OF
ANNA KARENINA

Willis Konick

In Moscow, Karenin, who has gone to seek a divorce, pursue bureaucratic intrigue and escape his intolerable family situation, receives a telegram from Anna. She claims to be dying, and asks that he return and forgive her. Harsh and pitiless, Karenin reckons that to pardon would be sham, but to ignore her plea, and face the remote likelihood of her death, might disturb his future calm. He resolves to return to Petersburg, frankly wishing for her death, appalled to learn she has successfully given birth to a daughter, and lives on in fever and crisis. But when he is brought to her, a sudden witness to her tears, her need to punish that "other woman" who tempted her to indifference, cruelty, his mood changes; in the presence of the weeping and penitent Vronsky, Karenin gives way to his inherent faculty for deep, unequivocal response, reclines his head in the bend of Anna's arm, and forgives unceasingly, unrestrictedly, not only forgives Anna's sin but, at Anna's request, draws Vronsky to him, grasps the hand of the adulterer, and forgives him as well. It is a scene of great emotional power, one of the most striking in *Anna Karenina* and one which long remains in the reader's memory. I particularly remember this scene as I saw it many years back during a theatrical presentation of the novel at the Moscow Art Theatre. The production, which limited itself to Anna's story alone, was unfortunately false in most respects, false to the spirit of the novel, full of actors striking empty poses and reciting empty speeches. But as I watched and fidgeted I kept hoping that the scene of childbirth, the scene of Anna's near death would work; it was so naturally dramatic, so full of emotional meaning, that even the bad acting and prevailing disposition to melodrama could not entirely rob it of life. And true enough, when it came, the actors, as if sensing a dramatic peak had arrived, attempted some degree of restraint. There was Anna, writhing on her bed, speaking that great speech on forgiveness, and Karenin seated next to her, his head bent, and Vronsky behind them, covering his face with his hands. Everything proceeded

exactly as it had in the novel, yet strangely enough I
found it not moving but repulsive, embarrassing, worse
than all the distortions that had preceded it. I left
the theatre in a sour mood, and attributed my disappointment to the difficulties involved in adapting so complex
a work for the stage.

Years later, while teaching the novel, I reread the
scene and fall into that same sour temper I recall so vividly from my evening in the theatre. Might Tolstoy, in
some measure, have intended to arouse precisely this mood?
Does this magnificent and climactic scene of forgiveness
and self-discovery, this artistically subtle reversal of
roles, as a commanding and sympathetic Karenin faces a
subdued Vronsky, turn into a parody of absolution? But
Karenin's pardon is certainly genuine: Tolstoy has long
prepared us for his susceptibility to tears; we already
know that he teeters on the brink of an abyss, and now he
has simply fallen in, to discover greater spiritual resources than we might have guessed. And Vronsky's defeat
is entirely plausible; he himself recognizes that Karenin's adoption of Christian forgiveness transforms the dull
cuckold and disarms the sophisticate. Might the source of
our annoyance, our vague misgivings, be Anna herself? It
is she who, however innocently, inspires tenderness in one
man and mortification in the other. When Karenin first
enters it is she who gazes upon him with new affection and
declares: "I am still the same. But there is another
woman in me, I'm afraid of her: it was she who fell in
love with that man, and I tried to hate you, and I could
not forget the self that had once been. I'm not that woman. Now I'm my real self, all myself. I'm dying now, I
know I am; you ask him. I feel it already. . . . I only
want one thing--for you to forgive me, forgive me completely!" Despite her fears, Karenin instantly relents;
she puts her arms around him, raises her eyes "defiantly"
and states: "'there, I knew he would be like that! Now
good-bye everyone, goodbye! . . .'" The doctor calms her,
she rests more quietly and speaks again:

> 'Remember one thing: that I only wanted your
> forgiveness, nothing more. . . Why doesn't he
> come? she cried, turning to Vronsky at the door.
> 'Come in, come in! Give him your hand.'

Vronsky approached the side of the bed and,
seeing Anna, buried his face in his hands again.

> 'Uncover your face! Look at him! He is a
> saint,' she said. 'Yes, yes, uncover your face!'

she cried angrily. 'Alexei Alexandrovich, uncover his face! I want to see him.'
         Karenin took Vronsky's hands and drew them
away from his face, terrible with its look of
agony and shame.
         'Give him your hand. Forgive him.'
         Karenin held out his hand, not attempt to
restrain the tears that streamed down his cheeks.
         'Thank God, thank God!' she cried, 'now
everything is ready. I will just stretch my legs
a little. There, that's nice. . . Oh, God, oh
God, when will it end? Give me some morphia!
Doctor, give me morphia! Oh God, oh God!'
         And she began tossing about in the bed.
         (pp. 438-39)[1]

All kinds of unpleasant thoughts occur as one reads these
lines. One can well understand Anna's suffering and fear
--she is terribly ill, after all--but she does rather expertly prepare for her own death, laying down conditions,
extracting promises, setting her affairs in proper order
("now everything is ready"). There is something of the
stage-manager about her, as she compels the two men to
perform her bidding. And while the moralist might applaud
Anna's decision to condemn that "other woman," to defy the
adulteress, one might also expect more sympathy for Vronsky. Most curiously, she tells Karenin she wishes only
one thing, his forgiveness, and then, grown calm, she discovers that she wants yet another thing, that Karenin forgive Vronsky as well, that Vronsky be brought from his hiding place and exposed to shame he can only erase by suicide. In this sense the scene prefigures her own actual
death, and Vronsky's living suicide that follows.
         Is such cruelly manipulative behavior born of Anna's
present terror and anxiety, or is it fashioned from some
earlier paradigm, which then remains reasonably constant
throughout the novel? Is Anna the drowning man who grasps
that death is only moments away and wildly flounders for
support, or is she that figure on the ledge, poised high
above the street, tensely observing the gathering audience
below and the dismayed faces thrust from windows above,
silently attending to the counsel of pastor and police,
waiting until the anxiety of the crowd equals his own
dread? The answer to this question will surely provide
some definition of Anna's character. And since such def-
initions are already numerous--and contradictory--it
might be well to pause at this point and summarize them.

    As in all situations which aggravate man's natural
opposition to his neighbor, there are hawks and doves on
the question of Anna. The hard line is best expressed by
M. S. Gromeka, whose long essay (or series of essays) on
the novel appeared less than a decade after its publication. Gromeka finds much to pity in Anna and Vronsky and
more to censure: in trying to legitimize their adulterous
union they break the ineffable law of man's nature, and
prepare their own destruction. As for Anna, she is simply a woman of fierce and criminal passion, who sacrifices her family, her social position and finally her own
life in the name of love.[2] Gromeka's outlook has remained a minority position, and the vast majority of commentators upon the novel prefer to view Anna as victim
rather than felon. B. Eikhenbaum, in his study of Tolstoy
in the '70s, compares Anna to the heroine of Ostrovsky's
The Storm, and claims that "The further the novel approaches its conclusion, the more enigmatic Anna's guilt
becomes. Anna is transformed from criminal to victim,
and the natural question arises: why the epigraph 'Vengeance is mine, and I shall repay.'"[3] V. Shklovskii enthusiastically states that "Anna Karenina stands in the
novel separately from all others, above all others, because she loves as one really loves."[4] John Bayley (in
Tolstoy and the Novel) considers Anna neither "selfish"
nor "vindictive" by nature, and suggests that she and
Vronsky might still have made a go of it, had it not been
for her terrible "sense of isolation."[5] In his recent
critical introduction to Tolstoy's works R. F. Christian
speaks of the "warmth and sincerity" of Anna's character,
of Tolstoy's own battle against "his rational urge to condemn her for breaking the rules."[6] Undoubtedly there are
moments in the novel which would seem to support the widespread suspicion that Tolstoy, despite his harsh epigraph,
succumbed to the charm and vivacity of his heroine. Even
the childbirth scene could accommodate this vision of Anna,
had Tolstoy excluded Anna's peremptory stage directions.
We might then rest quietly with Garbo's Anna, with Vivien
Leigh's Anna, with the Moscow Art Theatre's Anna, with an
Anna ravished by Vronsky, wasted by her husband, undone by
her society, ruined by all those unable to respond to her
full and passionate love. This Anna is ultimately compelled, out of her own desperation, to do their work and
destroy herself: again, the drowning man rather than that
figure poised, waiting, high on the ledge.
    The contradictions intrinsic to such an interpretation

of Anna are many. Could an author as careful, as deliberate as Tolstoy, grow so fuzzy about a heroine whose proper
likeness occupied him through many drafts of the novel?
And what of those grave inconsistencies in Anna's own behavior? She herself is aware of some of them, though blind
to others, and when they grow too clamorous, too burdensome,
she screws up her eyes and pushes them away from herself.
Why does she so wildly veer from pole to pole like some
crazed magnet? Is this merely characteristic of Anna late
in the novel, when she truly does begin to see double,
when her sense of her own identity grows so tenuous that
the image she sights in the mirror no longer bears intimate
connection to her own consciousness, when, trance-like, she
raises her own hand to her lips and kisses it, as she might
touch, caress the hand of another? Or does such curious
behavior make its appearance much earlier in the novel?
Certainly Anna arouses countless questions from the beginning, and at least three aspects of her nature become explicit shortly after we first meet her in Moscow. There
is the alluring, vivacious figure who steps off the train
and promptly enchants Vronsky, with all that "suppressed
animation" darting "between her sparkling eyes and the
slight smile curving her red lips (p. 74)." There is Anna
the peacemaker who, through honest affection for both parties, brings the warring Dolly and Stiva together again.
And there is Anna at the ball, more charming than ever,
whom Kitty views from that vast distance born of competi-
tion and despair: "Yes, there is something strange, dia-
bolical, and enchanting about her (p. 97)." Which of these
three provides the source of future pain and doubt and
passion, or do all three play a role? And why does Anna,
out of all the young men she has met and will meet, select
an officer so blank and typical, so handsomely cardboard
as Vronsky? She herself, upon her return to Petersburg,
cannot imagine anything between them, until that unac-
countable excitement and vitality returns, to stretch her
nerves "like strings around pegs," to cause her to see
real objects as hazy, dislocated, transformed, a phenomenon she finds not terrifying but "rather pleasant (pp.
116-17)." Later, lying in the darkness and thinking of
Vronsky, she will seem to see the very brightness of her
own eyes (p. 164). Is there something dangerous as well
as attractive in her new-found vivacity? We understand
why she is displeased by her first sight of Karenin, after
her return to Petersburg, with his ungainly walk, his pro-
truding ears, his swollen veins, his habit of cracking his

knuckles. But why does she find her son, whom she loves
so unreservedly, also disappointing? "Just as her husband
had done, her son produced on Anna a feeling akin to disappointment. In imagination she had pictured him nicer
than he actually was. She had to descend to reality in
order to enjoy him as he was (pp. 122-23)." And why, later
in the novel, when her passion for Vronsky rules her
thoughts, must she invest him with greater appeal than he
seems to possess? "She laid her hands on his shoulders,
and gave him a long, searching look, her eyes full of love.
She was studying his face, making up for the time she had
not seen him, comparing, as she did every time they met,
the picture of him in her imagination (incomparably superior, impossible in reality) with him as he actually was
(p. 382)." Once she takes Vronsky as her lover, does she
wholly despise her husband? Is she entirely accurate when
she characterizes their previous years together as sham?
We know she must now record each defect in him "because of
the great wrong she was doing him (p. 207)." But we also
know some kind of understanding must have once existed
between them, perhaps a rather enviable one, for Karenin
immediately perceives her new "impenetrable armor of
falsehood," and recalls, not years of barren indifference,
but a reservoir of mutual trust: "But for him, knowing
her, knowing that when he was five minutes late in going
to bed she would remark on it and ask the reason--who
knew that she always immediately told him all her joys,
pleasures, and sorrows--for him her reluctance now to
notice his state of mind or say a word about herself
signified a great deal. He saw that the depths of her
soul, always before open to him, were now closed against
him (p. 162)." Moreover Anna's recurrent dream, after
what I shall call the "seduction scene," when she and
Vronsky destroy the "first stage" of their love and commence their affair, is one in which both husband and lover
play a significant part. "She dreamed that she was the
wife of both of them and that both lavished their caresses
on her. Alexei Alexandrovich was weeping, kissing her
hands, and saying, 'How happy we are now!' and Alexei
Vronsky was there too, and he, too, was her husband. And
she was marvelling that this had once seemed impossible to
her, and she would explain to them, laughing, that it was
ever so much simpler this way and that now both of them were
contented and happy. But this dream weighed on her like
a nightmare and she awoke from it in terror (p. 166)."
This wish-fulfilling dream, by the way, which assumes the

proportions of nightmare in moments of wakefulness, will
be realized in that very childbirth scene I spoke of earlier, as husband and lover gather at her bed, and Anna orders
the conduct of the two Aleksei's.

     More questions arise. Why, after the seduction scene
I refer to above, does Anna rather ominously warn Vronsky:
"Everything is over. . . I have nothing but you left. Remember that (p. 166)." At this point any number of options
still exist: she has not told her husband of her affair,
and she certainly does not intend to relinquish her son.
Or does she already begin to squeeze life of its alterna-
tives, until she will be left only with raw, naked choice?
And why later, at the scene of childbirth, does she also
command Karenin to remember she wanted only his forgiveness, nothing more? Why does she swear at several points
in the novel that she will never abandon her son and then,
at the end of Part IV, leave in headlong flight, with
hardly a thought to the boy? Why, during the childbirth
scene, does she condemn that "other woman," who led her to
love Vronsky and then despise Karenin for his charity,
find him a "loathsome presence (p. 450)"? How might one
explain her curious behavior toward Vronsky after her
visit to her son, in Part V of the novel? First she seems
to forget him entirely, then she experiences a new wave of
love for him, and then, just as abruptly, she resolves to
punish and hate him, to go to the opera and expose herself
to public humiliation. Why do we find this mature, experienced and sophisticated woman, reunited with her son,
"crying in the same thin childlike way as he. . . (p.
566)"? And why, earlier in the novel, when she receives
her husband's letter, sternly prohibitive but promising
truce, when she feels she will not know "freedom in love,"
does she weep "unrestrainedly, as children weep when they
are punished (p. 316)"? Why, after the depth of understanding she reveals to Dolly in Moscow, her acceptance
of error, of occasional deflection from one's best and
natural path, does she continually find herself in the
unenviable position of loving two beings at once? If we
are to believe the testimony of her dream, her yearning
for husband and lover, she remains firmly wed to Karenin
even after she and Vronsky commence their affair. And
when the break with her husband arrives, she finds herself torn between equal passion for Vronsky and for her
son. As she confesses to Dolly: "I love these two beings
only, and the one excludes the other. I cannot have them
both; yet that is my one need. And since I can't have

that I don't care about the rest. Nothing matters, nothing, nothing! (pp. 671-72)." Is it mere circumstance which
visits such despair upon this woman, or does some pattern
emerge, some terrifying need to embrace hopeless opposition? And, finally, why do we know so little of her former life, compared to all the other characters, who seem
admirably ready to absorb their past and probe their future? Of her years with Karenin there are only hints, and
of her life before that, her adolescence, even less. Only
late in the novel, in a rare reflective moment, does Anna
glimpse herself as a girl of seventeen, and ask "Was that
really me, the girl with the red hands? (p. 790)" Such
curious omissions led one critic to comment shrewdly: "To
the very end Anna is a wonderful woman whose early history
has never been fully explained."[8]

Is there some context which might bear the weight of
these incongruities, might explain such strangely incon-
stant behavior? There seems to lurk here some imperative
need to make immoderate and imprudent requests of self and
others, but it appears locked to equal fear of such demands. One hesitates to define this as the response of
an unhappily neurotic woman; such labels customarily precede the dismissal of the character from the work of art,
from one's field of vision. Yet in the terms of the
writings of at least one psychoanalyst, a number of statements on the neurotic personality so conform to elements
in Anna's character, that I must at least tentatively offer them here, in partial support of my hypothesis. The
writer is Karen Horney, the book is *The Neurotic Personality of Our Time*, a thorough but not complex application
of post-Freudian psychoanalytic theory, easily accessible
to the layman and written with a minimum of jargon. In
brief and compelling terms, Horney describes the neurotic
condition as an "insidiously increasing, all-pervading
feeling of being lonely and helpless in a hostile world,"[9]
as a thirst for two contrary rewards: affection, and power
and control.[10] She understands that this need for affection can be easily misconstrued, and that all of us who
have hoped for a little more love and warmth in life need
not post ourselves at the analyst's door. "The difference," she cautions, "between love and the neurotic need
for affection lies in the fact that in love the feeling
of affection is primary, whereas in the case of the neurotic the primary feeling is the need for reassurance, and the
illusion of loving is only secondary."[11] Since Anna speaks
of love constantly, until Vronsky, late in the novel, begs

her to find a synonym, we might be on interesting ground
here. Even more pertinent to Anna's nature is Horney's
explanation of what she calls the need for unconditional
love: "The neurotic wish for unconditional love . . . is
much more comprehensive than the normal one, and in its
extreme form it is impossible of fulfillment. It is a
demand for love, literally without any condition or any
reserve . . . a wish to be loved regardless of any provocative behavior."[12]   I hope to use these quotes from
Horney to create some key, some structure which may guide
us through those inconsistencies I spoke of earlier. But
if the psychoanalytic mood seems gloomy or pretentious,
one may merely think of Anna as a person who comes to deal
in absolutes: unconditional demends, total fears, extrem-
ities of power and subservience, an unusual figure for
Tolstoy at this stage of his career. Indeed, she might
well be called Tolstoy's underground woman, not because
Tolstoy shares theme or style with Dostoevsky, but because
Anna, like the underground man, is the prime subversive
force in the novel, inciting and alarming all others.

Quite early in the novel, much earlier than we might
expect, we are offered Anna's own vision of a "cold and
hostile" world. It is the morning after the races, the
morning after she has told Karenin of her adulterous union
with Vronsky, and has experienced the brief elation of
telling the truth. Diconsolately she walks about the ter-
race of her summer home and ponders her future:

'Can it be that they won't forgive me, won't understand how none of it could be helped?' she
said to herself.

Standing still and looking at the tops of
the aspen-trees waving in the wind, with their
rain-washed leaves glistening brightly in the
cold sunshine, she knew that they would not
forgive her, that everything and everybody
would be merciless to her now as was this sky,
these green trees. And again she felt that
duality in her soul. (pp. 312-13)

In marked contrast to such despair, to the imminent birth
of a duality which forges each emotion, each human trait
to its opposite, joy to hopelessness, self-confidence to
perplexity, we have the Anna, much earlier on, who con-
vinces Dolly to follow her first and best impulse, to return to her husband. Dolly has posed the fateful question, whether Anna might be equally forgiving of a husband's indiscretion. Anna replies:

'I do not know, I cannot tell. . . . Yes, I
can,' said Anna, after a moment's consideration;
and, capturing in her thought the situation and
weighing it on her own inner scale (*uloviv
mysl'iu polozhenie i svesiv ego na vnutrennikh
vesakh*), she added: 'Yes, I can, I can, I can.
Yes, I should forgive. I would not be the same,
no; but I should forgive, and forgive as utterly
as if it had never happened, had never happened
at all.' (p. 85)[13]

Could anything be more different than these two visions of
Anna? Anna with Dolly is unquestionably Anna at her best,
Anna as we shall seldom see her again, giving of herself,
responding to others honestly and openly, but with a dutiful and necessary caution (not detachment). She still retains that happy facility for drawing back not in hesita-
tion but in thought, so that she might gauge the demands
of experience against her own inherent strength. For Anna
staring at the aspen trees the inner scale has vanished;
there are no decisions to be made, nothing against which
to reckon one's strength; one can only acknowledge weakness
and await defeat. How then was that inner scale abandoned
--how and why? How could such a poised, confident woman
lose the power to decide, the right to hope?

Certainly a partial answer to this question must lie
in her "illicit" love, the union with Vronsky which forms
shortly after her meeting with Dolly, and in her subsequent
guilt and doubt, her quarrels with her husband, her concern
for her son. With Seriozha as admonitory compass, Anna
and Vronsky sail off into deep and troubled waters, Vronsky
an experienced but not always attentive navigator, Anna an
overwrought and queasy passenger. But must adulterous love
bear such grievous consequences? Unlike Gromeka, Tolstoy
does not yet seem in a mood to condemn; he keeps his distance and his equanimity, and permits Anna to make her
choice. Obviously the earnest and moral Anna cannot enter
into an affair with the easy abandon and good humor of
Princess Betsy, but she can, with her good sense, her "inner scale" weigh her awakened passion for Vronsky, her
loyalty to her husband, her deep affection for her son,
and find each possesses considerable density, and manifest,
though not equal, value. It will not make the conflict of
loyalties any easier, and it will not erase her sense of
guilt, but it will help her to make some necessary distinctions. At Princess Betsy's party, after her return to
Petersburg, she seems almost ready to do so. The discus-

sion is of love, various opinions are expressed, and
Vronsky, now in pursuit, waits breathlessly for Anna's
own response. Pausing for a moment she answers: "I think
. . . that if there are as many minds as there are heads,
then there are as many kinds of love as there are hearts
(p. 154)." A sensible, intelligent position, and one Anna
never returns to again; the more fully she enters into
liason with Vronsky, the more eagerly she embraces a new,
dangerous and far more radical definition of love.

    We catch a glimpse of this spectacular metamorphosis
at the ball in Moscow, and it is Kitty who first senses
the change in Anna. This assured and gracious woman grows
suddenly intoxicated, as Kitty once was, with the spirit
of the ball and the stimulation of conquest. It is not
Anna alone whom Kitty observes, however, and her shock is
far greater when she witnesses the transformation in
Vronsky:

> Every time he spoke to Anna, her eyes lit up
> joyously and a smile of happiness parted her
> red lips. She seemed to be making an effort to
> restrain these signs of joy but in spite of her-
> self they appeared on her face. 'But what of
> him?' Kitty looked at him and was filled with
> dread. What was so plainly mirrored in Anna's
> face, she saw in him. What had become of his
> usually quiet, firm manner and tranquil, care-
> free expression? Now, every time he turned to-
> wards Anna, he bowed his head a little, as if he
> wanted to fall at her feet in adoration, and his
> eyes held only submission and fear. 'I would
> not offend you,' his every look seemed to say.
> 'I only want to save myself but I do not know
> how.' The expression on his face was one Kitty
> had never seen before. (pp. 95-96)

The key to why Anna falls so abruptly in love with Vronsky,
and precisely Vronsky, lies in that "look of adoration."
She will recall it as she leaves for Petersburg on the
train, and all the remembered excitement of the ball will
return; she will contemplate it regularly as he pursues
her about St. Petersburg. Nor will that adoration ever
waver much, not until late in the novel when Vronsky, grown
impatient with idolatry and surfeit with her beauty, will
fret and sulk like any ordinary husband. Though he is very
much the aggressor at the early stages of their affair,
and generously possesses all those attractively masculine
traits Karenin sorely lacks, he is, in his manly way,

genuinely submissive when it counts, and yields to Anna's
emotions on the occasion of every serious crisis—and there
are many of them. He is unaccountably ready to share her
tears (see pp. 339-40). He immediately responds to her
injunction that he come to her home, though he knows her
husband has forbidden his presence there, that their accidental meeting will precipitate a new crisis (as it does).
Again and again her feelings are promptly communicated to
him; he acts as litmus paper for every threat to her own
well-being: "In her presence he had no will of his own:
without knowing the grounds for her distress, he already
felt himself involuntarily infected by it (p. 337)." Such
ready sympathy is powerfully appealing, of course, but for
Anna it is bad medicine; Vronsky's adoration, right there
at the ball, sparks that need in Anna for unconditional
love, and once it has been awakened she can never go fully
back to the woman she was before. Something stirs within
her that has clearly lain dormant, unrecognized for years,
perhaps all her life; once provoked it will increasingly
demand its own special nourishment, it will seek to order
its own affairs. Vronsky's worshipful gaze and her own
vitality will lead her to that point where she loses mastery of herself, where her intelligence no longer works,
where she can only gaze at the aspen trees and reflect on
human malice.

    I do not think such a sudden metamorphosis implausi-
ble, though its consequences for Anna are extreme. Who has
not felt at least mild exhilaration when invested with new
power: a love declared, a reward granted? At such moments
our inner scales plunge precipitately to one side, and we
experience an agreeable imbalance, just compensation for
the neglect or indifference of others. Anna's response,
however, is of a slightly different order; she is not only
stimulated by the ball, by the attractive man with whom
she dances and by the promise of submissiveness he offers,
but she is also stirred by that twin imperative of which
Horney speaks: the craving for affection and the craving
for power and control. Newly alive, reborn in the very
sparkle of her eyes, the only love now worthy of the name
must rise from some source beyond her, and flow unceasingly
and exclusively in her direction. Like the child who observes that, by tears, by naughtiness, by some childishly
shrewd threat, some half-contrived, half-real accident, he
may bring his parents to him, he may arouse their maximum
love or attention, so Anna increasingly relies on tears and
threats and scenes half-staged, half-real to draw forth the

fullest response from Vronsky and, on occasion, from her
husband. She herself will respond with all the sparkle
and vivacity of the child, those short bursts of warmth
and affection that make the child lovable. But, like the
child, she also fears the very weapons she uses: tears may
become the prelude to real suffering and remorse, and the
accident, begun in artifice, may end in real hurt. And
there is another fear more profound: that the parent will
not respond, that the demand may prove too great, and the
bedroom door will remain closed, the child will be left to
weep alone with his cut, celebrating his loneliness in a
thin, childish wail, like the cry Anna joins to her son's.
Anna, returning home from Princess Betsy's gathering with
Vronsky, after her impressive conclusion that there are as
many loves as hearts, warns Vronsky that he had best not
speak so easily of love, that the word means too much to
her, and we surmise that those words spoken at Princess
Betsy's spring from a different Anna, and that love, in
her new sense, will require the totality of a Vronsky, or
a Karenin, or a Seriozha. And as she consumes more she
gives correspondingly less; her greed grows too great and
her essential generosity of spirit, glimpsed in that scene
with Dolly at the beginning of the novel, and her reason,
which she can never entirely abandon, tell her she asks
much and grants nothing in return. Her passion, her need
to be placated, her ventures, often brilliantly successful,
into managing the deeds of others are accompanied by spurts
of self-hatred--"I am a bad woman, a wicked woman." She
feels increasingly inadequate to the awesome task she has
set for herself; to conceal, beneath affection's countenance, a quest for consummate power. But attempts to think
through her dilemma grow too painful, and she must increasingly fling herself into new action. Even when she imagines herself most wholly the slave to others, there lies,
quiescent, an unborn threat. Thus her "Remember that" to
Vronsky, during the seduction scene, is not so much cau-
tionary, a reminder of his new responsibilities, as a half-
challenge, later to emerge in repeated challenges that he
prove his love. Thus, in the childbirth scene, she asks
her husband for just one thing--that he forgive her--and
then, when that request has been granted, she is inspired
to another, like the child who, having exacted one promise,
tries the game anew. But once she gains Karenin's forgive-
ness--and no gift could be more totally unconditional--she
loathes him for that very love, she is physically repulsed
by his presence, she must escape at any cost, escape from

her demand and his compliance. And there is yet another
demand she must fulfill, a burden equally heavy: that she
create beauty wherever she goes, her own beauty particularly, and that all ugliness, all disfigurement must be shut
out. In Europe, where conditions are ideal, she turns her
full attention upon Vronsky, creates an island of beauty,
submerges, with unexpected ease, all consciousness of husband and son. After her return to Russia, with one marriage dissolved and another impossible, she will play the
role of wanton society expects, but she will also needless-
ly coquette, so that she may test the force, the reliabil-
ity of her beauty. Her need for beauty is insensate.
Even before the break with Karenin, the visions in her head
can only rarely be met in reality: Vronsky perceived must
be raised to the level of the Vronsky of her imagination,
while her son, whom she so fully, so physically loves,
disappoints her expectations when she returns to Petersburg. But the figure of Karenin, as she meets him at the
train, arouses not pity but repugnance: he is ugly and
must be shut out. The effort to make life totally beautiful, like the effort to love and be loved unconditionally,
causes her to miss something rather essential to life: the
pain, compromise and occasional ugliness through which one
may perceive a new and deeper joy. It is Kitty at the ball
in Moscow, at the moment of Anna's rebirth, who recognizes
that it is cruelty which heightens her enchantment, for
Kitty is Anna's first victim: when Anna is born something
in Kitty dies. And because all this rises from Moscow,
where Anna is both mother and babe, where Vronsky is both
father and servant, where Kitty is anxious midwife, it is
quite natural, quite fitting that Anna is not provided
with a past.

But Anna is not only a woman without a past; she is a
woman with very little *sense* of the past. The study of
history is an occupation totally foreign to her; all her
needs can be compressed into a single moment, but the moment can never be repeated. Through the microscope we observe the path of the amoeba. A mere blob, a species of
microscopic jelly, it strikes forth for food, edging closer
to its quarry. Systematically it flows outward, grasps the
particle to itself, alters its shape to accommodate its
victim and then moves on, one being again, though not precisely in the form we observed earlier. Each time it
chooses to annex more food, it must also form its new self.
Anna perceives experience in much this way: each moment is
not only an opportunity to grasp for the totality of the

other, to love or to be loved absolutely, it also *expresses
the totality of all experience with the other and the totality of all knowledge of self.* Whatever came before has
little bearing upon the present: all deeds, both good and
bad, slip into nothingness as new deeds are perpetrated;
all memories, both joyful and melancholy, pass into oblivion as the next crisis arrives. Time's succession take
on the character of slides replacing one another on a
screen, slides which our host has neglected to place in
any particular order, so that we soon abandon any hope of
discerning a harmony in what we see, and find our continuity in the mere sequence of brilliant images upon the
screen, and in the moment of darkness which precedes them.
When Karenin returns to Petersburg, to the wife he hoped
might die, Anna triumphantly heralds the death of the woman
who once loved Vronsky. But all memory of Vronsky seems
dead too; until it is time for him to come forward and receive Karenin's forgiveness he is ignored. Later, as the
novel draws to its conclusion, it counts for little that
Vronsky has stuck by Anna with dogged faithfulness; each
new meeting demands a renewal of their vows, however false
such renewal seems to Vronsky. Prior evidence cannot ap-
pease Anna's doubts; the testimony of the moment must be
judged solely on its own merits. A brilliant example of
the manner in which Anna isolates herself from the past
occurs in the scene which follows Anna's meeting with her
son, after her return from Europe. Anna fails to tell
Vronsky of her intention to visit Seriozha, for she knows
that he will not react as she does, that he lacks the
strength of emotion she requires, the ability to fix upon
the instant as singular, confined, divorced from all
others. "Her suffering was the more poignant that she had
to bear it in solitude. She could not and would not share
it with Vronsky. She knew that to him, though he was the
primary cause of her distress, the question of seeing her
son would seem a matter of very little account. She knew
that he would never be capable of appreciating all the
depth of her anguish, and that his cool tone if the subject were mentioned would make her hate him. And she
dreaded that more than anything else in the world and so
she concealed from him everything related to her son (p.
560)." (Yet Vronsky cannot help noticing that something
oppresses her and, cast into his own isolation, concerns
himself with her new mood.) The meeting with her son calls
forth the worst and best in Anna: she tells Seriozha what
is required, that he must love the father with whom he

remains, but she cannot hide her hatred, her sense of com-
petition for Seriozha's attention and regard when she
catches sight of Karenin himself. Returning to her hotel
room, more shattered by the meeting than she had expected,
she tries to conquer her loneliness. She first turns to
Vronsky's child, her daughter, but there is no satisfaction there: little Annie remains perpetually at a distance
from her mother; she is indigestible, she cannot be wholly
absorbed, so that Anna, through her, may assume a new self.
Instead Anna chooses to compare Seriozha at that age to her
second child, not to revive the past but to reaffirm the
despair, the bitterness of the present. Rummaging through
her photographs she suddenly and quite unexpectedly comes
across a likeness of Vronsky. Though heretofore she has
forgotten his presence, his very existence, his image now
looms forth to blot out the past. Initially, however, it
is a photograph of her son she seeks to extricate.

> Her deft little hands, whose slender white fin-
> gers moved with a peculiar nervous energy that
> day, pulled at the corner of the photograph, but
> the photograph had caught somewhere, and she
> could not get it out. There was no paper-knife
> on the table, and so, pulling out the photograph
> that was next to it (it was one of Vronsky taken
> in Rome in a round hat and long hair), she used
> it to push out her son's photograph. 'Yes, there
> he is!' she said, glancing at the portrait of
> Vronsky and suddenly remembering that he was the
> cause of her present misery. She had not once
> thought of him all the morning. But now, coming
> all at once upon that manly, noble face, so famil-
> iar and so dear to her, she felt an unexpected
> surge of love for him.
>   'But where is he? How is it he leaves me
> alone in my misery?' she thought suddenly with a
> feeling of reproach, forgetting that she herself
> had kept from him everything concerning her son.
> She sent a message asking him to come to her im-
> mediately, and sat waiting with beating heart, re-
> hearsing to herself the words in which she would
> tell him all about it, and the expressions of
> love with which he would comfort her. The servant
> returned with the answer that he had a visitor
> with him but that he would come immediately, and
> that he asked whether he might bring Prince
> Yashvin, who had just arrive in Petersburg. 'He's

not coming alone, and he hasn't seen me since
dinner yesterday,' she thought. 'He'll be coming with Yashvin, so that I shan't be able to
tell him everything.' And all at once a strange
idea crossed her mind: what if he had ceased to
love her? (pp. 567-68)

The slides flash rapidly and abruptly upon the screen, they
unnerve us by their brightness, their disorder; even the
arbitrary moments of darkness form no respite, for we know
they deceive us, throw us off guard, so that we may be
even more shaken by new emotion, new shock. All the love
Anna has felt for her son thrusts itself upon Vronsky, but
no good will be derived from this "unexpected surge." She
must commit to his care the full strength of her affection,
but he is not there, and it seems unlikely, once he has
arrived, that he will be in a proper mood to receive the
gift she offers. And so--new image blazing upon the screen
--love shifts to reproach, almost to hatred, but--yet another flash of light and brilliant slide--hatred is inad-
missable, it causes one to doubt not the force of one's own
love, but the love of the other. Torn by despair, by fear,
by the wavering conviction she has lost her beauty, she
goes to the opera, endures public humiliation, and thereby
earns the right to demand she be loved unconditionally.

The curious face time bears, in Anna's portion of the
novel, accounts for the many cycles and repetitions that
come to dominate her life. Against the three major events
of the first part of the novel--Anna's joy in Moscow, the
seduction scene and the childbirth scene, which she regards
as mere prelude to her death--we may place Anna's new joy
in Europe, another seduction scene, this time between Anna
and her son, and, of course, Anna's opportunity to again
manage her own death. Moreover the final scene of Part
IV, in which Vronsky returns to Anna's home for one last
visit, in which he and Anna unexpectedly decide to flee to
Europe, contains all components of the Vronsky-Anna relationship (see pp. 460-61): their passion; Vronsky's easy
reassurances (now that he has expunged his guilt through
attempted suicide his composure returns); their tendency
to regard their love as exclusive, permanent, when it has
not been such in the past and will be less so in the future; their capacity for communicating emotion to one another; their refusal to deal seriously with matters which
threaten later discord; their unusual willingness to sacrifice too much--Anna abandons her son, because she now
lives totally in Vronsky, while Vronsky gives up his post

in Tashkent; Anna's self-pity, her inclination to use death
for dramatic effect; their conspiracy to ignore rather than
despise Karenin. By the end of the novel, as Anna is drawn
inexorably toward the train, toward personal disaster and a
new roster of victims--Vronsky, Karenin, to some extent her
son--the pattern is so clear it warrants little comment.
Indeed, in the final pages of Part VII Anna fully recognizes the pattern herself, but she can do nothing to dis-
lodge its inexorable force. As she turns her blinding
searchlight upon her own affairs, she grimly perceives that
she is dissatisfied, and there is no further way the hated
and urgent thirst for absolute love, first awakened at the
ball in Moscow, can now be appeased. Bayley, in *Tolstoy
and the Novel*, feels Anna still holds doom in abeyance,
remains alive to the possibility of reconciliation, renewed love, because he sees her successive moods as linked
rather than separate; he does not recognize they are slides
which flicker on and off the screen, ever more rapidly, and
thus misconstrues the compulsive nature of her quest. No
matter; *she* knows the pattern cannot be broken:

> 'My love grows more and more passionate and self-
> ish, while his is dying, and that is why we are
> drifting apart' she went on musing. 'And there's
> no help for it. He is all in all to me, and I
> demand that he should give himself more and more
> entirely up to me. And he wants to get farther
> and farther away from me. . . . He says I am in-
> sanely jealous; but it is not true. I am not
> jealous, but unsatisfied. . .' (p. 796)

No character in a novel, from first draft to final
copy, was ever more transformed than Anna Karenina. Here
she is as Tolstoy first imagines her:

> . . . she was unattractie, with a low forehead, a
> short, almost snub nose, and she was too fat. She
> was so fat that if she had been a little more so,
> she would have been deformed. If it had not been
> for her thick black lashes, adorning her gray eyes,
> her thick black hair, beautifying her forehead, if
> it had not been for the harmony of her figure, the
> grace of her movements, like her brother's, and
> her tiny hands and feet, she would have been ugly.
> But, despite the unattractiveness of her face,
> there was something in the good-natured smile on
> her lips that made one like her.[14]

From the very beginning Tolstoy struggles with the problem
of properly conveying to his reader that his heroine is

both attractive and unpleasant. The idea of physical un-
attractiveness, near obesity, a low brow and snub nose,
does not work satisfactorily, for it too obscures the appeal of her smile and her grace. And what will snare the
shallow Vronsky we meet in the early chapters of the work?
He is not accustomed to searching for deeper beauty beneath a repellent exterior. But once Tolstoy makes Anna
beautiful, must we assume he then falls in love with his
heroine, loses his way and starts anew? Might he not
merely take those less sympathetic qualities he wishes to
suggest and place them on a psychological rather than a
physical plane (a step of great importance for the novel's
development)? There is still much "one can like" in the
final version of Anna: her beauty, her wit, that strength
of character which long holds her private devils at bay.
Because I have tried to show how dominant the unpleasant
side of her nature is, and how early in the novel it appears, I do not mean to neglect those more familiar aspects of her character which inevitably call forth the
reader's sympathy. She is in every sense unique. Or, to
use the adjective Soviet critics most often apply to her,
she is a "nezuariadnaia zhenshchina," an "exceptional woman." Yet such a strongly individual temperament is something Tolstoy comes increasingly to distrust, as he moves
toward his late period. Soon all traits of character
which foster self-distinction will be condemned, but even
now being unique can become a very mixed blessing: it
breathes new life, new force into Anna at the ball in
Moscow, and then burdens her with more vitality, more
power than she can handle; it takes the finest product
her class can engender, a truly beautiful and intelligent
woman, and guides her to self-destruction. Early in the
novel, as Anna searches for Vronsky to inform him she has
confessed the truth to her husband, she finds herself at
Princess Betsy's, in the company of women who are also
carrying on affairs. Betsy, noting her anxiety, warns her
she is becoming too serious, urges her to avert her gaze
from the "tragic side" of life. Anna's response is significant:

>   'How I wish I knew other people as I know
>   myself!' said Anna gravely and thoughtfully.
>   'Am I worse than others, or better? Worse, I
>   think.' (p. 321)

How much in character Anna remains! It would never occur
to her to ask--am I the same?

*University of Washington
Seattle, Washington*

NOTES

[1]All quotes taken from L. N. Tolstoy, *Anna Karenin*, translated by Rosemary Edmonds, Baltimore: Penguin Books, 1954.

[2]See M. S. Gromeka, "Poslednie proizvedeniia L. N. Tolstogo," *Russkaia mysl'*, kn. II (February, 1883), pp. 214-265.

[3]B. Eikhenbaum, *Lev Tolstoi, semidesiatye gody*, Leningrad: Sovetskii pisatel', 1960, p. 202.

[4]V. Shklovskii, *Zametki o proze russkikh klassikov*, Moscow: Sovetskii pisatel', 1953, p. 282.

[5]John Bayley, *Tolstoy and the Novel*, London: Chatto and Windus, 1966, p. 227.

[6]R. F. Christian, *Tolstoy: A Critical Introduction*, Cambridge: Cambridge University Press, 1969, pp. 178-79.

[7]A far more subtle version of Anna as victim appears in R. P. Blackmur's *Eleven Essays on the European Novel* (New York: Harcourt, Brace and World, 1964). For Blackmur Anna shares her misfortune with all the other major figures in the novel: they cannot "keep pace" with one another. In this instance, Vronsky cannot "keep pace" with Anna and so destroys her. Naturally the horse-race scene, and the death of Vronsky's mare Frou-Frou, her back broken by his "dreadful, unforgivable blunder," figures largely in such an interpretation as ready symbol of Anna's fate. However tempting such an approach may be (Blackmur is not the first to conjoin Anna and Frou-Frou), what then is one to do with Part VII, where Vronsky clearly stands at the sidelines, now a spectator at the race, wringing his hands now in rage, now in impotent despair, as Anna hurtles down the course, prepared to destroy herself? Moreover, while in the earliest version of the horse-race scene Anna and Vronsky play their roles simultaneously (Anna, then Tat'iana, stands at the course rather than in the stands; she herself runs up to the wounded Vronsky, fallen from his horse "Tiny" or "Tania," so that we may not miss the connection), in the final version of the scene Anna's hysteria and Vronsky's grief are deliberately separated by the author, so that we are really given two variants of the race, separated by several chapters in which we pick up Karenin and bring him on the scene: one from Anna's point of view and one from Vronsky's. The full significance of the horse-race is not lost on Vronsky, but it is not Anna he mourns, however remotely, but Frou-Frou and his own grievous error. Suddenly Vronsky steps into new

maturity: he realizes that life contains irretrievable errors, and that he can make them: "for the first time in his
life he knew the bitterest kind of misfortune--misfortune
beyond remedy, caused by his own fault (P. 218)." Ironically this is the same Vronsky who, a few chapters earlier,
when Anna confessed her pregnancy, reassured her with
Stiva Oblonsky's favorite phrase: "There is a way out of
every situation (p. 206)."

[8]Percy Lubbock, *The Craft of Fiction*, New York: Viking
Press, 1957, p. 246.

[9]Karen Horney, *The Neurotic Personality of Our Time*,
New York: W. W. Norton and Co., 1937, p. 89.

[10] Ibid., p. 105.

[11] Ibid., p. 109.

[12] Ibid., pp. 130-31.

[13] L. N. Tolstoi, *Sobranie sochinenii v dvadtsati tomakh,*
Moscow: Gosudarstvennoe izdatel'stvo khudozhestvennoi literatury, 1963, Vol. 8, p. 87. I have altered the English
translation, in this instance, to conform more closely to
the original.

[14] L. N. Tolstoi, *Polnoe sobranie sochinenii* (Jubilee
edition), Vol. 20, Moscow: Gosudarstvennoe izdatel'stvo
"Khudozhestvennaia literatura," 1939, p. 18. ". . . ona
nekrasivaia s nizkim lbom, korotkim, pochti vzdernutym
nosom i slishkom tolstaia. Tolstaia tak, chto eshche
nemnogo, i ona stala by urodliva. Esli by tol'ko ne
ogromnye chernye resnitsky, ukrashavshie ee serye glaza,
chernye ogromnye volosa, krasivshie lob, i ne stroinost'
stana i gratsioznost' dvizhenii, kak u brata, i kroshechnye
ruchki i nozhki, ona byla by durna. No, nesmotria na
nekrasivost' litsa, bylo chto-to v dobrodushii ulybki
krasnykh gub, tak chto ona mogla nravit'sia."

RELIGIOUS IMAGERY IN THE STRUCTURE OF
THE BROTHERS KARAMAZOV

Alexander Golubov

1.

The refutation of Ivan Karamazov's "Legend of the
Grand Inquisitor," which, in a letter to Liubimov (May 10,
1879), Dostoevsky called "the culminating point [*kul'-
minatsionnaia tochka*] of the novel,[1] was to have been contained in Book VI of the novel: "My hero's blasphemy will
be triumphantly refuted in the next number [of *Russkii
Vestnik*] for which I am working now with fear, trembling
and reverence."[2] After working on Book VI, "The Russian
Monk," throughout June and July of 1879, Dostoevsky mailed
it to Liubimov from Ems, and in the accompanying letter
commented:

> I myself feel that I have not succeeded in ex-
> pressing even one-tenth part of what I wanted.
> I look, however, upon this sixth book as *the
> culminating point* [*kul'minatsionnaia tochka*]
> *of my novel* [emphasis mine]. . . . Though I
> too am fully in accord with these same ideas
> which he [Zosima] expressed, however, if I
> personally expressed them *myself*, then I would
> have expressed them in a different form and
> different language; but he could not express
> himself in a different language, or in a dif-
> ferent form than that which I have given him.
> Otherwise I would not have created an artistic
> character.[3]

A rather curious situation thus presents itself:
either there are, as Nathan Rosen has argued, not one but
two culminating points in the novel,[4] or else, having
written "The Russian Monk," Dostoevsky no longer considered Book V significant enough to be a "culminating point."
In either case, however, as Rosen has observed, because
of their structural placement, the two culminating points
"do not culminate in anything except the main action of
the novel."[5] The significant implication of this argument is that the refutation of the Grand Inquisitor is
contained not only in the section entitled "The Russian

Monk," but, in fact, in the novel itself, indeed, "in a
different form and in different language." Direct support
for this conclusion comes from Dostoevsky himself, who
made the following notation in his notebook in reference
to the Grand Inquisitor: "[My critics] did not even dream
of such a strong denial of God . . . to which *the whole
novel* [Dostoevsky's emphasis] serves as an answer."[6]

Dostoevsky himself, then, considered the arguments
proposed by the Grand Inquisitor to be refuted. But what
is the nature of this refutation? In a letter dated June
9, 1879, Pobedonostsev suggested to Dostoevsky that proof
of faith must be non-intellectual:

> What madness [*bezumie*] to ask: *Prove* your
> faith to me. One should say: *Show* me your
> faith. It [faith] is encompassed not in an
> abstract formula, but in *the living image
> of a living man and a living deed* [emphasis
> mine]--the image of God.[7]

Several indirect notations in Dostoevsky's notebook further
point to his plan for a "meta-logical," non-Euclidian refutation:

> All of Christ's ideas are refutable by the
> human mind and seem impossible to carry out.
>
> Moral ideas do exist. They grow out of re-
> ligious feeling, but can never be justified
> by logic alone.[8]

Finally, there is direct epistolary evidence offered by
Dostoevsky himself. Having submitted "The Russian Monk"
to Liubimov, Dostoevsky wrote to Pobedonostsev from Ems
(August 24, 1879) that the refutation of the ideas presented by Ivan through the Grand Inquisitor

> is not direct, not point by point to the
> theses that were expressed earlier, . . .
> *but is only implied* [emphasis here and below
> mine]. Here something is presented directly
> opposed to the world-outlook expressed above,
> but again, it is presented *not point by point,*
> but, so to speak, *in an artistic picture.*[9]

Thus the primary refutation of the "legend of the
Grand Inquisitor" is, in Pobedonostsev's terms, indeed,
"a living picture of a living man and a living deed":
the hagiographical portrait--*zhitie*--of Starets Zosima.
But the ultimate refutation lies in the living images of
the people who lead their lives in the framework of the

novel. "The frame of 'The Russian Monk,' with the pale
sketch of Zosima erased or to be covered over as in a
palimpsest, is now to be filled with a vivid picture: the
destinies of the Karamazov brothers."[10] Significantly,
the destinies of the whole Karamazov family are drawn in
terms of religious and liturgical imagery that has its
direct roots in the religious account of the life of a
priest-monk.

2.

In 1854, in a letter to Mme. N. D. Fonvizin, the wife
of the exiled Decembrist I. A. Fonvizin, Dostoevsky wrote:
"If anyone were to prove to me that Christ is outside of
Truth, and if Truth *really did* exclude Christ, I should
prefer to remain with Christ rather than with Truth."[11]
These curious words, echoed many years later in a conversation between Shatov and Stavrogin in the novel *Besy*
(*The Possessed*), and still later in Dostoevsky's last
notebook, serve to point to the profound affinity that
bound Dostoevsky to the person of Christ throughout the
author's life. "It is not like a boy that I believe in
Christ and confess Him [*Ego ispoveduiu*]," Dostoevsky remarked in his notebook toward the end of his life, "it is
through a *great furnace of doubt* that my *hosanna* has
come."[12] And it is precisely through the illuminating
prism of these words that Dostoevsky's creation of the
iconographic figure of Starets Zosima should be viewed.
One should keep in mind that Zosima is, first of all,
an *ieroskhimonakh*, that is, a monk at the third and final
stage of the Orthodox monastic ladder, who at the same
time is a *priest*.[13] Zosima's *priesthood* is a fact of immense significance in relation to his function in the
novel. In general, priesthood in the Orthodox Church is
endowed with a mystical and sacramental, rather than a
simple teaching function. One of the episcopal prayers
addressed to Christ and recited during the ordination of
an Orthodox priest lists, among five main priestly functions, two that see the priest as directly continuing
Christ's ministry on earth: "to proclaim the Gospel of
Your [Christ's] Kingdom" and "to renew Your people through
the baptismal fount of the second birth [*vozobnovliati
liud Tvoi cherez kupel' vtorogo rozhdeniia*]."[14] In its
priestly aspect, then, compounded by his monastic vows of
poverty, chastity and obedience, Zosima's whole life becomes, as it were, the direct continuation of Christ's
own life in the world, and thus a living spatial extension

of the Gospel into contemporary surroundings.

An analogous interpretation of this function of
Zosima can be found in the novel itself. In the third
section of "The Russian Monk," entitled "From the Conversations and Teachings of Starets Zosima," we are given the
thoughts of Zosima himself on this subject:

> How many meek and humble monks there are, yearn-
> ing for solitude and fervent prayer in peace.
> . . . And how surprised men would be if I were
> to say that from these meek monks, who yearn for
> solitary prayer, the salvation of Russia will
> come perhaps once more. For they are in truth
> made ready in peace and quiet 'for the day and
> the hour, for the month and the year.' Mean-
> while, in their solitude, they keep the image
> of Christ fair and undefiled, in the purity of
> God's truth, from the times of the Fathers of
> old, the Apostles and the martyrs. And when
> the time comes they will show it to the creeds
> of the world. That is a great thought. That
> star will rise out of the East.[15]

It is not surprising therefore, in view of what has
been said, that the imagery of the Gospels permeates not
only the structure of the section entitled "The Russian
Monk," but branches out into the remaining portions of
the novel.

A significant part of the "The Russian Monk" is, as
Dostoevsky's narrator remarks, "the last conversation
[*posledniaia beseda*] of Zosima with the guests who visited
him on the last day of his life (298)." Alyosha's *zhitie*
of Zosima is placed into a direct relationship with this
final gathering as its extension and embellishment: "This
last conversation . . . has been preserved in writing.
Alexey Fyodorovich Karamazov wrote it down from memory,
some time after the death of the starets (298)." And
though, the narrator warns the reader, in Alyosha's account "Father Zosima's talk goes on without interruption,
as though he told his life to his friends in the form of a
story (298)," there really were interruptions. Casually
the narrator mentions the fact that Zosima's conversation
was interrupted "once or twice by Father Paissy's reading
from the Gospel," and by other incidents. Mention of the
Gospel at this particular point is, it appears, quite
significant: one gets the sense that the conversation and
the reading are somehow profoundly related. This becomes

an antiphonal process of sorts, where the conversation
thematically echoes the Gospel, and the Gospel becomes an
"icon" of the conversation. We are not told what it is
specifically that Father Paissy reads, and at this point
it really does not matter. The distinct impression one
gets, however, is that symbolically the conversation and
the reading, supposedly occurring on two different planes
of meaning, actually merge into one. Linear time, for all
practical purposes, disappears into simultaneity. *"It is
a mystery* [emphasis mine]," Dostoevsky comments, wherein
"the passing earthly show and eternal verity are brought
together. . . . In the face of the earthly truth, the
eternal truth is accomplished" (304). This fusion of two
points of linear time is important, inasmuch as it appears
at other critical junctures in the novel, as we shall note
below.

The motif of the "last conversation," when juxtaposed
with the Gospel, immediately suggests a parallel motif of
the Last Supper, which was followed by Christ's "farewell
discourse" with the Apostles and by the so-called High-
Priestly Prayer. Indeed, a side-by-side comparison of
Zosima's "last conversation" with the relevant section in
the Gospel according to John, the only evangelist to record this discourse, yields a number of significant parallels, directly implying deliberate efforts to this end on
the part of Dostoevsky.

Christ's Farewell Discourse with the Apostles occupies a central place in the Christology of the New Testament: Christ here "no longer addresses the world; from now
on, He speaks to His disciples, and beyond the cross mani-
fests himself only to the disciples."[16] In much the same
way, it can be said that Zosima's "last conversation" occupies a central part of Book VI, "The Russian Monk." In
much the same way as Christ in the "Last Discourse" of
John's Gospel, Zosima addresses a most intimate and exclusive gathering of "friends and admirers," and beyond the
grave, appears in a vision only to his closest disciple,
Alyosha Karamazov.

Christ's Discourse can be divided into several broad
themes: The New Commandment (John 13: 33-35 and 15: 9-13);
Christ as the Way (John 14: 1-14); The Testament of Peace
(John 14: 27); Hate of the world directed at the disciples
(John 15: 18-27 and 16: 1-4); Joyful meeting after death
and resurrection (John 16: 16-22) and the High-Priestly
Prayer (John 17: 1-26). All of these themes find a direct
thematic parallel in Book VI, "The Russian Monk," and in
Book VII, "Alyosha."

All four evangelists agree that the "new commandment"
of love directed at one's fellow man was the central issue
of Christ's moral teaching:

> Little children, yet a little while I am with
> you. You will seek me; and as I said to the
> Jews, so now I say to you, where I am going
> you cannot come. A new commandment I give to
> you, that you love one another. By this all
> men will know that you are my disciples, if
> you love for one another (John 13: 33-35; cf.
> also Matt. 22: 36-40; Mark 12: 28-31; and Luke
> 10: 25-28).[17]

The commandment of love is also central to the teaching of
Zosima, although Dostoevsky now expands this commandment
to include not only one's fellow man, but all of creation:

> Love a man even in his sin, for that is the
> semblance of Divine Love and is the highest
> love on earth. Love all God's creation, the
> whole and every grain of sand in it. . . .
> If you love everything, you will begin to com-
> prehend it better every day. And you will at
> lost come to love the whole world with an all-
> embracing love (334).

Recapitulating His earthly ministry, Christ pointed to Himself as the way to the Father and to ultimate salvation,
concluding with the Testament of Peace:

> Let not your hearts be troubled; believe in
> God, believe also in me. . . . I am the way,
> and the truth, and the life; no one comes to
> the Father but by me; . . . Truly, truly I
> say to you, he who believes in me will also
> do the works that I do; and greater works
> than these will he do, because I go to the
> Father. . . . I will not leave you desolate;
> I will come to you. Yet a little while, and
> the world will see me no more. . . . Peace I
> leave with you, my peace I give to you (John
> 14: *passim*).

The same structural and thematic motifs (death premonition,
father-children relationship, continuation of the Christian
ministry by the disciples) resound in Zosima's recapitula-
tion of his own life and in his teaching that Christ is the
way to Russia's salvation. Appropriately, Zosima also includes a "testament of peace":

My life is ending, I know that well, but
every day that is left me I feel how my
earthly life is in touch with a new, infinite,
unknown but approaching life. . . . One who
does not believe in God will not believe in
God's people. He who believes in God's people will see His Holiness too, even though he
had not believed in it till then. Only the
people and their future spiritual power will
convert our atheists, who have torn themselves away from their native soil. And what
is the use of Christ's words, unless we set
an example? . . . Lord, send peace and light
to They people (304-08, *passim*).

An important part of Christ's Last Discourse is His
prophecy that His followers would be subjected to persecution by the world:

If the world hates you, know that it has hated
me before it hated you. If you were out of
the world, the world would love its own; but
because you are not of the world, but I chose
you out of the world, therefore the world hates
you (John 15: 18-19).

This idea of the persecution of the "chosen ones" by the
"world" is reiterated by Zosima from the point of view of
a fulfilled prophecy, with the same emphasis on the concept of being *in* the world, but not *of* it:

In the enlightened world the word [monk] is
nowadays pronounced by some people with a
jeer, and by others it is used as a term of
abuse, and this contempt for the monk is growing. It is true, alas, it is true, that there
are many sluggards, gluttons, profligates, and
insolent beggars among monks. Educated people
point to *these*: 'You are idlers, useless members of society, you live on the labour of
others, you are shameless beggars'. . . .

. . . .

The monk is reproached for his solitude, 'You
have secluded yourself within the walls of the
monastery for your own salvation, and have forgotten the brotherly service of humanity!' But
we shall see who will be most zealous in the
cause of brotherly love. For it is not we, but
they, who are in isolation, though they don't

> see that. Of old, leaders of the people came
> from among us, and why should they not again?
> The same meek and humble ascetics will rise
> up and go out to work for the great cause (327
> and 339)

Zosima tells Alyosha much the same thing, though with a
slightly different emphasis that in no way negates what
came previously:

> This is what I think of you, you will go
> forth from these walls, but will live like
> a monk in the world. You will have many ene-
> mies, but even your foes will love you. Love
> will bring many misfortunes to you, but you
> will find your happiness in them, and will
> bless life and will make others bless it--
> which is what matters most (297).

The structural and thematic relationship between the
ideas of John's Gospel and Book VI of *The Brothers
Karamazov* is quite evident at this point. This relationship can now be expanded so as to encompass other sections
of the novel.

By the end of Book VI, two different worlds, as it
were, have opened up to the reader: the iconographic,
spiritual world of Zosima and the monastery, and the deeply sensuous, materialistic and passionate world of the
Karamazov family. In the structure of the novel it is,
of course, Zosima who becomes the intermediary bridge
linking the two worlds, neither of which *alone* can sus-
tain true life.

3.

The direct connection between Zosima and two of the
Karamazov brothers--Alyosha and Mitya--has been suffici-
ently well established in Dostoevsky scholarship. But in-
vestigations into the respective relationships linking
Zosima and Fyodor Pavlovich on one hand, and Zosima and
Ivan on the other, have only skimmed the surface. And yet,
profound direct connections are, in fact, forged by
Dostoevsky's use of religious imagery and allusion.

In the very beginning of Book II, "An Inappropriate
Gathering," the whole Karamazov family, together with
Miusov and the seminarian Rakitin, minus Mitya, who joins
the group much later, gather in the cell of Starets
Zosima. "The pretext for this gathering was a false one,"
Dostoevsky's narrator remarks. "It was at this time that

the discord between Dmitri and his father Fyodor Pavlovich
on the grounds of inheritance and the division of material
wealth seemed at its acutest stage, and their relationship
had become insufferably strained" (28). In agreeing to
the meeting, Zosima smilingly, though unwillingly, replied,
"Who has made me a judge over them?" (29). This reply is,
as was noted by V. E. Vetlovskaia,[18] a thinly disguised
reference to the almost identical words of Christ in Luke
12: 13-21:

> One of the multitude said to him, "Teacher,
> bid my brother divide the inheritance with
> me." But he said to him, "Man, who made me
> a judge or divider over you?" And he said to
> them, "Take heed, and beware of all
> covetousness; for a man's life does not con-
> sist in the abundance of his possessions."
> And he told them a parable, saying, "The
> land of a rich man brought forth plentifully;
> and he thought to himself, 'What shall I do,
> for I have nowhere to store my crops?' and
> he said, 'I will do this: I will pull down
> my barns, and build larger ones; and there
> I will store all my grain and goods. And I
> will say to my soul, Soul, you have ample
> goods laid up for many years; take your ease,
> eat, drink and be merry.' But God said to
> him, 'Fool! This night your soul is required
> of you; and the things that you have prepared,
> whose will they be?' So is he who lays up
> treasure for himself, and is not rich toward
> God."

When taken in the context of the original cause for the
meeting--an argument over inheritance between Fyodor
Pavlovich and Mitya--and, later, the Grand Inquisitor's
rebuke of Christ for His rejection of the temptation by
bread, Dostoevsky's use of the Gospel parable is indeed
significant.

During the gathering, Fedor Pavlovich, acting the role
of the buffoon, dropped on his knees and "aped" the Gospel narrative: "Teacher! . . . what must I do to *inherit*
[emphasis mine] eternal life?" (28; cf. Matt. 19: 16-26;
Mark 10: 17-27; and Luke 18: 18-27). Here, however, the
significance of Zosima's reply lies not in what he *does*
say, but rather in what he *does not* say: the omission is
so very evident as to hardly be one of pure chance.
Fyodor Pavlovich thus sets himself up, as it were, for

the re-enactment of the parable. As Vetlovskaia quite
correctly points out:

> On the day preceding the fateful night [of his
> murder], as if concerned with the closest con-
> formity to the . . . parable, . . . Fyodor
> Pavlovich increasingly continues to worry about
> increasing his wealth to his lowly ends. Ask-
> ing Ivan to stop on business in Chermashnya, he
> says, among other things: "Just think: eight
> and eleven--a difference of three thousand.
> It's as if I found these three thousand. . . ."
> But during the same night Fyodor Pavlovich is
> murdered. The uselessness and "foolishness"
> of all his efforts directed at gaining and se-
> curing worldly, material well-being becomes
> evident, and the tragic end of the hero acquires
> . . . the guise of a just reward to his soul
> for wanting to "eat, drink and be merry,"
> gathering "treasure for himself" and forget-
> ting God. Thus, a most important moment of
> the novel, when placed in relationship to an
> evangelic parable, is explained in full accord-
> ance with it.[19]

This is not to suggest, of course, that at some point or
other the plot of the novel should always be interpreted
so as to strictly conform to the intended meaning of the
parable, or be in any way limited by it. This would be an
unwarranted oversimplification. There is, in fact, a closer, more essential relationship between Zosima and Fyodor
Pavlovich: their respective position as *father*--the first
spiritual,[20] the second almost purely physical and biolog-
ical--*vis à vis* the three sons. Dostoevsky's use of the
parable in Luke 12 thus not only does not stand apart in
meaning and significance, but rather serves to reinforce
and underscore the more essential relationship, and at the
same time to create a certain inner tension between the
more abstract "ideological syndromes" that these two men
represent. Furthermore, the allusion to the parable
places the two "ideological syndromes" in direct perspective with the basic elements of Christian teaching, and
also serves as an additional bridging element which connects the deaths of the two fathers to those of Markel and
Il'iusha.

The "inappropriate gathering" is also important in
another aspect. Immediately after the episode wherein
Fyodor Pavlovich "apes" the evangelical truth-seeker,

Dostoevsky establishes a close tie between Zosima and Ivan
--also a "seeker of truth," in the nineteenth-century
fashion.

Ever since the days of Rozanov down to the late
Philip Rahv, Dostoevsky criticism has tended, by and
large, to view Ivan as the polar opposite of Alyosha.
According to this position, Ivan is seen as respectfully
returning to God his entry ticket to paradise while spir-
itually merging with the Grand Inquisitor.

The grounds for such an interpretation of Ivan's
role are more than shaky, based as they are on essentially
incomplete evidence. Indeed, Ivan is brought by the
author to the doorstep of death and to an intellectual
and spiritual crisis of enormous magnitude--and then
strangely abandoned. And thus the hasty reader, quickly
jumping to the wrong conclusions, bases himself on what is
largely circumstantial evidence to assign Ivan a fate
which a close textual reading of the novel does not truly
allow.

We will recall that during the moments when the
gathering is awaiting Zosima's arrival, Ivan and Father
Paissy have a long conversation about a journal article
on Church-State relationships and ecclesiastical courts:
an article only "quite recently" published by Ivan. Without going into the details of Ivan's argument, let us look
at its two most important implications.

First, it accurately foreshadows the later appearance
in the novel of the "Legend of the Grand Inquisitor."
Here, however, in contrast to the position taken in the
Legend, Ivan *rejects* the third temptation by bread, siding
in this instance with Father Paissy and Zosima, and thus
explicitly refuting the Grand Inquisitor's argument.[21]

Second, in his view of the function of ecclesiastical
courts, Ivan comes to the conclusion that the Church, instead of the process of excommunication, must "completely
and honestly adopt the idea of the regeneration of man,
his reformation and salvation" (63).

Unfortunately, Dostoevsky did not bring Ivan past his
spiritual and intellectual death to ultimate regeneration,
reformation and salvation. But the internal evidence offered by Ivan's discussion with Father Paissy, the journal
article (which actually is written *after* the "Legend of
the Grand Inquisitor"), and, later, the devil's broad hint
to Ivan (in the latter's nightmare) that his path may ultimately bring him to the gates of a monastery,[22] suggests
that Ivan, too, would have undergone the process of Chris-

tian redemption and freely embraced Christ.

This conjecture is supported further by Ivan's conversation with Zosima. Almost at the conclusion of the "inappropriate gathering" in Zosima's cell, a rather curious dialogue ensues between Zosima and Ivan:

> "The question [of immortality] is still fretting your heart, and not answered. But the *martyr* [emphasis here and below mine] likes sometimes to divert himself with his despair, as it were, driven to it by despair itself. Meanwhile, in your *despair*, you, too, divert yourself with magazine articles and discussions in society, though you don't believe your own arguments, and with an *aching heart* mock them inwardly. . . . That question you have not answered, and it is your great grief, for it clamors for an answer."
>
> "But can it be answered by me? Answered in the affirmative?" Ivan went on *strangely*, still looking at the starets with the same *inexplicable* smile.
>
> "If it can't be answered in the affirmative, it can never be answered in the negative. You know that that is the peculiarity of your heart, and all its *suffering* is due to it. But thank the *Creator who has given you a lofty heart capable of such suffering;* 'of thinking and seeking higher things, for our dwelling is in the heavens.' God grant that your heart will attain the answer on earth, and *may God bless your way*" (70).

Zosima thus points out an important thing: that Ivan's mental striving is of a positive, religious nature, at the one and the same time a gift of God and a cross to be borne by Ivan throughout his earthly life. Zosima's words: "of thinking and seeking *higher things, for our dwelling is in the heavens*" are given by Dostoevsky as a citation from a Church-Slavonic text: "*gornaia mudrstvovati i gornikh iskati, nashe bo zhitel'stvo na nebesekh est'*. As far as I have been able to determine, these words represent a synthesis of the teaching contained in two Pauline epistles, Colossians 3: 1-2 and Philippians 3: 20. In their Church-Slavonic version, the two texts, taken in their broader context and placed side-by-side, would read as follows: *Ashche ubo voskresnuste so Khristom, vyshnikh ishchite, idezhe est' Khristos odesnuiu*

Boga sedia: Gorniaia mudrstvuite, a ne zemnaia (Col. 3: 1-
2). And, continuing in Philippians: *nashe bo zhitel'stvo
na nebesekh est', otonuduzhe i Spasitelia zhdem, Gospoda
nashego Iisusa Khrista* (Phil. 3: 20). The respective
rendering of the two texts according to the Revised Standard Version would read as follows: "If then you have been
raised [resurrected] with Christ, seek the things that are
above, where Christ is, seated at the right hand of God.
Set your minds on the things that are above, not the things
that are on earth." "But our commonwealth is in heaven,
and from it we await a Saviour, [our] Lord Jesus Christ."

In the context of the expanded quotation, Ivan becomes, in a certain sense, one of the "initiated"--believ-
ers in the resurrection of Christ--to whom the original
Pauline epistles were addressed. Thus Dostoevsky not only
underscores the basic ontological unity of Zosima and Ivan,
but establishes Ivan's membership in the "Church," in the
fundamental meaning of the word as the "fellowship of
humanity in Christ."

As if underscoring the meaning of his words and the
fact of God's own blessing of Ivan's path through life,
Zosima gives Ivan the *priestly* blessing:[23]

> The starets raised his hand and would have
> made the sign of the cross over Ivan from
> where he stood. But the latter rose from
> his seat, went up to him, received his bless-
> ing, and, having kissed his [Zosima's] hand,
> went back to his place in silence. His face
> looked *firm and earnest* [emphasis here and
> below mine]. This action and all the preced-
> ing conversation, which was *so surprising*
> from Ivan, *impressed everyone by its strange-
> ness and a certain solemnity*, so that all were
> silent for a moment (70).

Clearly, something of utmost significance had transpired
at that moment between Zosima and Ivan: something that was
freely accepted by Ivan, impressed everyone in the room,
and was emphasized by a period of silence. The importance
of this incident is underscored several pages later, when,
also in a mysterious fashion, Zosima bows to the ground :
front of Dmitri.

We thus see that the destinies of the Karamazov fami
find a common denominator in their interaction with Zosim
during the latter's life. But even as Christ's earthly
ministry was consummated in His death and resurrection and

subsequent appearance to the disciples, thus, too, Zosima's
message was fulfilled in his death and appearance to
Alyosha in the Cana of Galilee incident in Book VII.

In the Christian tradition, the marriage feast at
Cana has the significance of being the scene of the first
miracle performed by Christ in His earthly ministry. But
in a larger sense, Christ's transformation of water into
wine at the marriage supper in Cana, when seen in the context of the whole, acquires an additional dimension of
significance as a mystical prelude to the transformation
of wine into the Blood of the New Covenant at the Last
Supper which immediately preceded the betrayal and crucifixion.

The marriage feast was a standard metaphor in the
Judaic theological tradition of the Old Testament. In
this tradition, the House of Israel was seen as the Virgin
Bride awaiting the coming of her Bridegroom--the Messiah.
In much the same sense, this metaphor later entered the
Christian tradition. The Bridegroom/Bride relationship
between the Messiah and the House of Israel was now understood as being the representation of the relationship
between Christ and His Church. The coming of the eschatological Kingdom of God is thus portrayed in the Gospels
as the messianic nuptials (John 3: 28-29; Matt. 22: 1-14;
Luke 22: 16-18), where Christ appears not only as the midnight bridegroom, but also as the New Wine (Mark 2: 22).

Dostoevsky stands wholly within Christian tradition,
therefore, when he merges the wedding feast at Cana with
the symbolic messianic wedding feast in Alyosha's dream
in Book VII. Here again, one must pay particular attention to the disappearance of linear time: the reality and
time of Alyosha's dream is at once the reality of Zosima's
death, Zosima's resurrection, and the Cana incident in the
Gospel. Moreover, we should stress also the basic significance of the dream: *revelatio per somnium*, revelation and
religious guidance received via the dream mechanism, is a
standard religious device not only in the Judaeo-Christian
tradition, but in the more primitive religions as well.
It is in this light that we should view Alyosha's dream:

But what's this, what's this? Why is the
room growing wider? . . . Ah, yes. . .   It's
the marriage, the wedding. . .   Yes, of course.
Here are the guests, here sits the young couple,
the merry crowd and. . .   Where is the wise
governor of the feast? But who is this? Who?
Again the walls are receding. . . who is getting

up from the great table? What! He here, too?
But he's in the coffin. . . but he's here
too. He has stood up, he sees me, he is coming here. . . . God!"

Yes, he came up to him, to him, he, the
joyful, thin little old man, with tiny
wrinkles on his face, joyful and laughing
softly. . . .

"We are rejoicing, . . . we are drinking
the new wine, the wine of new, great glad-
ness" (379).

The symbolism of Cana in this episode thus occurs simultaneously on two planes. For Zosima, it is the fulfillment of his work and the arrival of the Kingdom of Christ,
the transformation of the "water of earthly life" into
the wine of a new immortal existence. For Alyosha, however, the meaning of Cana remains on an essentially different plane: though the "water" of his life is also symbolically given a new dimension of meaning, i.e., transformed into "wine," it is also the beginning of his own
ascent of Golgotha, where the wine of life would further
be transformed into the blood of suffering. And indeed,
after seeing the vision, Alyosha leaves the monastery to
follow the road that Zosima had once ordained for him.

But there is yet another important wedding supper in
the structure of *The Brothers Karamazov*: the "midnight
bridegroom" is Mitya, and the locale is shifted to Mokroe.
Significantly, this episode occurs at the same time that
Alyosha is having his own vision of Cana, and thus, by
artistic parallelism, it is placed in a direct relationship to it: "it was the very night, and perhaps the very
hour, in which Alyosha fell on the earth, and rapturously
swore to love it for ever and ever" (433).

It should be stressed that this second wedding supper
occurs amidst resounding religious echoes of Christ's torments preceding His betrayal, Crucifixion, and Descent
into Hell. The prelude to this second symbolic "wedding
feast" is a religious folk legend of the Harrowing of
Hell, recounted to Mitya by his driver Andrei:

You see, sir, when the Son of God was nailed
on the cross and died, He went straight down
to Hell from the Cross, and set free all sinners that were in agony. And Hell groaned, because he thought that sinners would not come to
him again. And God said to him, 'Groan not, O
Hell, for to you shall come from here all the

mighty of the earth, the rulers, the chief
judges, and the rich men, and you shall be
filled up as you have been in all the ages,
till I come again.' Those were the very
words, sir (436).

Andrei's narration of this legend is followed directly by
Mitya's prayer, in which we hear motifs not only of
Christ's own prayer on the Mount of Olives (cf. Matt. 26:
38-39; Mark 14: 33-36), but also of the Orthodox Euchar-
istic canon:

Lord, receive me, with all my lawlessness,
and do not condemn me. Let me pass by Thy
judgement . . . do not condemn me, for I
love Thee, O Lord. I am a wretch, but I
love Thee. If Thou sendest me to hell, I
shall love Thee there, and from there I shall
cry out that I love Thee for ever and ever.
. . . But let me love to the end, here and
now, to the end, for just five hours till
the first hot ray of Thy light (437).

And again we hear the motifs of the Mount of Olives prayer
during the wedding supper itself:

O God! restore to life the man I knocked
down at the fence! Let this fearful cup
pass from me! Lord, thou hast wrought mir-
acles for such sinners as I. . . (462).

And the supper ends with the arrest of the innocent one:
Mitya is charged with the murder of his father, Fyodor
Pavlovich. Thus, in a succession of religious symbols,
the central Christian mystery of the Eucharist is symbolically reenacted, and Alyosha's vision of Cana acquires
again a tragic significance in its tie to the Last Supper: here the wine of life once more is to be transformed
into the blood of redemption.

Mitya's ascent of Golgotha, both in the fact that it
is freely chosen, and in its implication of the Christian
redemption, has an overwhelming religious meaning. This
appears clearly in yet another mystical dream, this time
seen by Mitya after his arrest. This dream aptly continues the stream of religious imagery of Eucharist, Passion and Resurrection that began with Andrei's narration
of the legend of Christ's descent into hell and concluded
with Mitya's arrest.

We will recall that immediately prior to his arrest
Dmitri had promised to love Grushen'ka even in Siberia,

though at that moment "Siberia" appeared only as a vague
premonition of "the cup." Mitya's promise was itself the
result of a dream--Grushen'ka's dream--that was rooted in,
but at the same time transcended the bounds of time and
space:

> "Why Siberia? Never mind, Siberia if you
> like. I don't care . . . we'll work . . .
> there's snow in Siberia. . . . I love driv-
> ing in the snow . . . and must have bells.
> . . . Do you hear, there's a bell ringing?
> . . .
>
>   There had certainly been the sound of a
> bell in the distance, but the ringing had
> ceased. . . .
> . . . .
>
>   "What's the matter? Was I asleep? Yes
> . . . a bell. . . I've been asleep and dreamt
> I was driving over the snow with bells, and
> I dozed. I was with someone I loved, with
> you. And far, far away. . . . I was cold,
> and the snow glistened. . . . You know how
> the snow glistens at night when the moon
> shines. It was *as though I was not on earth*
> [emphasis mine]" (468).

After his arrest, Mitya has an analogous "unearthly" dream.
Mitya's dream is, as the narrator tells us, "a strange
dream, utterly out of keeping with the place and the time"
(537),[24] and yet profoundly related both to Grushen'ka's
dream and to the circumstances of his own arrest:

> He was driving somewhere in the steppes . . .
> and a peasant was driving him in a cart with
> a pair of horses, through snow and sleet. He
> was cold, it was early in November, and the
> snow was falling in big wet flakes, melting
> as soon as it touched the earth. . . . There
> were peasant women drawn up along the road, a
> lot of women, . . . all thin and wan, with
> their faces a sort of brownish color, especi-
> ally one at the edge, a tall bony woman, who
> looked forty, but might have been only twenty,
> with a long thin face. And in her arms a
> little baby was crying. And her breasts
> seemed so dried up that there was not a drop
> of milk in them. And the child cried and
> cried, and held out its bare little arms,

with its little fists blue from the cold.

"Why are they crying? Why are they
crying?" Mitya asked, as they dashed gaily
by.

"It's the babe," answered the driver,
"the babe is weeping."

And Mitya was struck by his saying, in
his peasant way, "the babe [*dityo*]," . . .
there seemed more pity in it.

"But why is it weeping?" Mitya persisted
stupidly, "why are its little arms bare? Why
don't they wrap it up?"

. . . .

"Tell me why it is those poor mothers
stand there? Why are the people poor? Why
is the babe poor? Why is the steppe barren?"
. . .

. . . .

And he felt that a passion of pity, such as he
had never known before, was rising in his
heart, that he wanted to cry, that he wanted
to do something for them, so that the babe would
weep no more . . . and his heart glowed, and he
struggled forward towards the light, and he
longed to live, . . . to go on and on, towards
the new, beckoning light, and to hasten, hasten,
now, at once! (537-38).

Thus Mitya's own Mount of Olives prayer for "love to the
end, . . . till the first hot ray of Thy light" resulted
in his vision of "a new light, as of joy" (538), and ultimately this vision had the same religious and mystical
quality as the vision experienced by Alyosha after his
Cana dream.[25]   Later, in prison, Mitya himself was to explain the mystical significance of the dream to Alyosha:

"Brother, these last two months I've found
in myself a new man, a new man *has been resurrected* [*voskres*; emphasis here and below mine]
in me. He was imprisoned in me, but would
never have revealed himself [*iavilsia*] but for
this thunder from Heaven. I am afraid! And
what do I care if I spend twenty years in the
mines . . . ? I am not afraid of that--it's
something else that I fear now: that the *resurrected man* might leave me [*chtoby ne otoshel ot
menia voskresshii chelovek*]. Even there, in the

mines, under the earth, right next to myself,
I may find a human heart in another convict
and murderer, and I may make friends with him,
for even there one can live and love and suffer. One can *regenerate and resurrect*
[*vozrodit' i voskresit'*] in that convict a
frozen heart, . . . and at last break out
[*vybit'*] from the dark depths [from the cave,
iz vertepa] into the light a lofty soul, a
suffering consciousness, *regenerate* an angel,
resurrect a hero! There are so many of them,
hundreds of them, and we are all to blame for
them. Why was it that I dreamt of that 'babe'
at such a moment? 'Why is the babe so poor?'
That was a prophecy [*prorochestvo*] to me at
that moment. It's for the 'babe' that I'm going. Because we are all responsible for all.
For all the babes, for there are big children
as well as little children. All are 'babes.'
I go for all, because someone must go for all.
I didn't kill father, but I've got to go. I
accept it. . . . Oh yes, we shall be in chains
and there will be no freedom, but then, in our
great sorrow, we shall rise again to joy,
without which man cannot live nor God exist,
for God gives joy: it's His privilege--a grand
one. . . . If they drive God from the earth,
we shall meet Him underground. . . . And then
we, underground men [*podpol'nye cheloveki*] will
from the bowels of the earth sing a tragic
hymn to God, with Whom is joy! Hail to God
and His joy! I love Him!" (627-28).[26]

Dostoevsky's constant allusion to the Resurrection, in its
juxtaposition with the motifs of hell and damnation and
the underground, which were already present in Andrei's
folk legend of Christ's harrowing of hell is, I believe,
quite transparent in its symbolism. In this respect, too,
one might go a step further and suggest yet another dimension of meaning to Mitya's "babe."

One of Dostoevsky's favorite works of art was
Raphael's *Sistine Madonna*, a reproduction of which hung
over the sofa on which he died. The painting depicts a
young girl of about twenty, holding a child in her arms.
Four figures behold the Virgin--a bishop, a martyr, and
two angels. The Child's lips are firmly pressed together
and His hair is matted on His forehead as, deep in thought,

he beholds a frightening vision, perhaps of Golgotha. It
is not inconceivable, therefore, that Mitya's acceptance
of suffering "for the babe" is acceptance of suffering for
Christ as Child, as He is depicted not only on the *Sistine
Mandonna*, but throughout Russian iconography as well.
Mitya's road to Siberia thus becomes, by extension, both
symbolically and ontologically, Christ's own path to
Golgotha.

4.

In conclusion, one can make a rather general observation: it is through a regular, structured succession of
religious motifs and images that Dostoevsky refutes the
Grand Inquisitor, drawing an "artistic picture" of a situation that directly opposes the central propositions of
the Grand Inquisitor's argument. The Grand Inquisitor
bases his argument on a rebuke to Christ for not depriving
mankind of freedom:

> "Instead of taking possession of men's freedom,
> You increased it, and burdened the spiritual
> Kingdom of mankind with its sufferings forever.
> You desired man's free love, that he should
> follow you freely. . . . Man must hereafter
> with free heart decide for himself what is good
> and what is evil, having only Your image before
> him as a guide" (264).

The consequences of this, the Grand Inquisitor projects,
would be man's ultimate rejection of Christ:

> "Did you not know that he would at last re-
> ject even Your image and Your truth, if he is
> weighed down with the fearful burden of free
> choice? They will cry aloud at last that the
> truth is not in You. . . ." (264).

But the Grand Inquisitor was wrong, Dostoevsky claims.
Throughout the novel, the successive movements of the three
Karamazov brothers, which are mirrored by the movements of
the secondary characters, lead them to a free acceptance of
the author's thesis: that even in suffering, in hell itself,
men will continue to make their choice freely, and that
choice will inevitably lead to Christ as the Way.
This is the refutation offered by Zosima, once an army
officer, now of his own volition a priest-monk. This is
the refutation made by Zosima's brother Markel. And this
is also the refutation made, or to be made, by the

Karamazov brothers, who freely ascend their own private
Golgothas to suffer, each in his own way, "for the Babe."

Wheaton College
Norton, Massachusetts

NOTES

[1] F. M. Dostoevskii, *Pis'ma*, ed. A. S. Dolinin (Moscow
1928-59), IV, No. 660, 53. The English text here and below
is given according to Michael A. Minihan's translation of
Konstantin Mochul'sky, *Dostoevsky: His Life and Work*
(Princeton: Princeton University Press, 1967), pp. 584-89.

[2] Loc. cit.

[3] *Pis'ma*, IV, No. 685, 91.

[4] Nathan Rosen, "Style and Structure in *The Brothers
Karamazov:* The Grand Inquisitor and The Russian Monk,"
Russian Literature Triquarterly, I, No. 1(1971), 352- and
354. My interpretation of Dostoevsky leans rather heavily
on insights gained from my association with Professor Rosen
during my graduate study under his tutelage. In particular, this paper owes much in basic conceptual formulations
to the above-cited article on the relationship of the Book
of Job to the structure of *The Brothers Karamazov*.

[5] Ibid., p. 352.

[6] N. N. Strakhov, *Biografiia, pis'ma i zametki iz
zapisnoi knizhki F. M. Dostoevskogo* (St Petersburg, 1883),
p. 375.

[7] *Literaturnoe nasledstvo*, XV (Moscow, 1934), 137.

[8] *Literaturnoe nasledstvo*, Vol. LXXXIII (Moscow,
1971), *Neizdannyi Dostoevskii: Zapisnye knizhki i tetradi
1860-1881 gg.*, pp. 676, 695, *et passim*.

[9] *Pis'ma*, IV, No. 694, 109.

[10] Rosen, "Style and Structure," p. 361.

[11] *Pis'ma*, I, No. 61, 142.

[12] *Literaturnoe nasledstvo*, LXXXIII, 696.

[13] The three progressive stages of the Eastern Orthodox
monastic ladder are, in their Russian terminology: *riasofor,
malaia skhima*, and *velikaia skhima*. The vows of the latter
usually, though not always, involve those of silence
[*bezmolvie*] and solitude [*zatvor*]. In Church practice,
comparatively few monks reach the stage of *velikaia skhima*,
as Zosima did. Zosima's monastic rank is implicit in the
name *ieroskhimonakh*: priest-monks at the stage of *malaia
skhima* are termed *ieromonakh*. Dostoevsky mentions the fact
that Zosima is an *ieroskhimonakh* at least twice in the
novel. First, this term appears in the title of Section

Two, Book Six: "*Iz zhitiia v Boze prestavivshegosia ieroskhimonakha startsa Zosimy* . . . ." Again, the term appears in the first sentence of Section One, Book Seven: "Telo usopshego ieroskhimonakha startsa Zosimy. . . ."

[14] Arkhiepiskop Ioann [Shakhovskoi], "Filosofiia pravoslavnogo pastyrstva," *List'ia dreva: Opyt pravo-slavnogo dukhovedeniia* (New York: Ichthys, 1964), p. 38.

[15] Fyodor Dostoevsky, *The Brothers Karamazov*, trans. Constance Garnett (New York: Modern Library Giant, n.d.), p. 328. Subsequent references to this novel are given according to this translation, and appear in the body of the paper in parentheses. In several instances I have revised Garnett's translation for the sake of clarity and to correct errors of implicit or explicit meaning.

[16] James C. Plastaras, *The Witness of John: A Study of Johannine Theology* (New York: Bruce, 1972), p. 151.

[17] Citations from the New Testament here and elsewhere are given according to *The Holy Bible: Revised Standard Version* [*The Oxford Annotated Bible*], Herbert G. May and Bruce M. Metzger, eds. (New York: Oxford University Press, 1962).

[18] V. E. Vetlovskaia, "Simvolika chisel v 'Brat'iakh Karamazovykh,' *Trudy otdela drevnerusskoi literatury*, Vol. XXVI (Leningrad, 1971), *Drevnerusskaia literatura i russ-kaia kul'tura XVIII-XX vv.*, p. 146.

[19] Ibid., p. 147.

[20] In Eastern Orthodox church practice, the institution of *dukhovnyi otets*--spiritual father--is an essential one. The *dukhovnyi otets* is spiritual guide and confessor, having the power to grant absolution for confessed sins.

[21] The relationship between Ivan's article and the Legend of the Grand Inquisitor merits further study in a separate monograph. Indeed, though Ivan relates the "Legend" to Alyosha *after* the article is printed, Dostoevsky tells us that it was conceived by Ivan about a year *before*.

[22] The Devil tells Ivan: "I lead you to belief and disbelief by turns, and I have my motive in it. . . . I shall sow in you only a tiny grain of faith and it will grow into an oak tree--and such an oak tree that, sitting on it, you will long to enter the ranks of the 'hermits of the wilderness and women-saints,' for that is what you secretly wish for very, very much. You shall eat locusts, you shall wander [*potashchishsia*] into the wilderness to save your soul!" (684). This hint retains its intrinsic meaning regardless of whether the reader here considers the devil as

an externalization of Ivan's subconscious, or as an entity
having an objective and separate existence apart from Ivan.

[23] In Orthodox church practice the priest's blessing
is endowed with overwhelming significance. The blessing
hand itself becomes a symbolic spatial anagram of Christ:
the fingers are folded in such a way as to form the letters *IC XC*, i.e., the name "Jesus Christ." In the light
of this, Zosima's blessing of Ivan is particularly significant.

[24] Throughout the incident at Mokroe and in relation
to Alyosha's vision of Cana, Dostoevsky places a special
emphasis on the factor of time. Thus, he specifically
mentions the "ninth hour," the "third hour," and "five
hours till the first hot ray of . . . light," i.e., midnight. The significance of these particular hours is,
again, religious: the third hour is the time of Pilate's
judgment of Christ and His sufferings in the praetorium;
ninth--His death on the cross; twelfth--His Resurrection.
The twelfth hour is also the hour of the 'midnight bridegroom," i.e., the consummation of history and the coming
of the eschatological Kingdom of God.

[25] One should point out the prevalence of light imagery
in the two visions. Dostoevsky here employs a standard
liturgical metaphor of the Church. In the main hymn
(*tropar'*) of the feast of Christmas, for example, Christ
is referred to as "*svet razuma* (light of wisdom)" and
"*solntse pravdy* (the sun of truth)"; in the hymn of the
minor *introit* of the Vesper service, Christ is termed
"*svete tikhii sviatyia slavy* . . . *Otsa nebesnago* (peaceful light of the holy glory . . . of the heavenly Father)"
and "*svet vechernii* (evening light)"; the prayer of the
First Hour reads, in part: "*Khriste, svete istinnyi,
prosveshchaiaii i osviashchaiaii vsiakogo cheloveka
griadushchego v mir* (O Christ, true light, who enlightens
and sanctifies every man who comes into the world). . . ."

[26] In the context of Dostoevsky's language and imagery
in this passage, and in the light of what has been said in
the preceding footnote (q.v.), a significant, and, I think,
very fruitful comparison may be made with the *kondak* of the
feast of Theophany: "*Iavilsia esi dnes' vselennei, i svet
Tvoi, Gospodi, znamenasia na nas, v razume poiushchikh
Tia: prishel esi i iavilsia esi, Svet Nepristupnyi*" (Today Thou hast appeared to the universe, and Thy light, O
Lord, has shown upon us, who with understanding praise
Thee: Thou hast come and revealed Thyself, O Light unap-
proachable [*The Divine Liturgy of St. John Chrysostom,*

with appendices (New York: Russian Orthodox Greek Catholic
Church of America, 1967), p. 177]).   Christ's epiphany
was also accompanied by the thunderous voice of God the
Father: cf. Matt. 3:17; Mark 1:11; and Luke 3:22.

THE GROTESQUE IN FEDOR SOLOGUB'S NOVEL
THE PETTY DEMON

Linda J. Ivanits

F. K. Sologub's classic novel *The Petty Demon* (*Melkii bes*), written between 1892 and 1902 and first published in book form in 1907, is one of the most powerful depictions of petty evil in Russian literature. This depiction is achieved largely through the presentation of the protagonist, the insane provincial school teacher Peredonov, who is in D. S. Mirsky's opinion "one of the most terrible figures ever created by a poet."[1] In the course of the development of the action, which is concentrated primarily around Peredonov's quest for a promotion and the attempts of various townspeople to marry him, a vast number of characters comprising an entire cross section of a provincial town is introduced. The society presented is immersed in triviality and is without intellectual interests or guiding ideas. The townspeople spend their time spreading gossip, playing cards, and drinking; petty acts of spite form the basis of normal relationships. Only children seem somewhat free of the moral stagnation of the novel's provincial town.

This picture of rural Russia led a number of Sologub's contemporaries to acclaim *The Petty Demon* as an accurate representation of rural Russian conditions during the political reaction following the assassination of Alexander II, and hence an essentially realistic work. Soviet criticism has generally followed in accepting this evaluation.[2] However, alongside the presentation of everyday life (*byt*) in the novel one can find elements of the fantastic. Peredonov's best friend Volodin is uncomfortably ram-like; the townswoman Vershina is cast in the image of a proverbial witch--thin, black, and wizened. Perhaps the most obvious element of fantasy in the novel is the presence of the *nedotykomka*, a haunting gray spirit which torments Peredonov. And, even though Peredonov's insanity may provide a plausible explanation for improbable creatures and events, nevertheless the suggestion remains that Sologub's provincial town is not typical and that it may in fact resemble an inferno more truly than actual conditions in rural Russia.

Clearly one of the basic problems to be faced in treating *The Petty Demon* is the relationship between provincial *byt* and the fantastic. This relationship has caused a certain amount of confusion among critics. In addition to those who consider the novel realistic because of its apparent indictment of provincial conditions, there are those who maintain that the novel is totally lacking in realism. One critic suggests that Sologub is in no way true to reality because the creatures populating this world are closer to evil chimeras than to human beings; another, remarking that the novel suffers terribly from lack of verisimilitude, notes that in the final analysis the only thing the novel really depicts is the hostile attitude of its author to the world. A few critics, mainly Symbolists, felt that the novel accurately presented reality precisely because in it aspects of the everyday world are combined with the supernatural.[3]

This paper is essentially a study of the relationship between *byt* and the fantastic in *The Petty Demon*. The very title of the novel hints at a possible relationship: that the pettiness and vulgarity of daily life--*poshlost'*--are a mask of the demonic. The cosmos of the novel, appearing initially to be a typical provincial society, slips almost imperceptibly into an inferno. The artistic method through which *poshlost'* is integrated with the demonic is the grotesque.

A few words should be said about the concept of the grotesque underlying this study. Recently the grotesque has been described both as the trivial perceived as demonic and as the demonic made trivial--understandings which certainly pertain to *The Petty Demon*.[4] This definition seems accurate with the qualification that in literature as well as in painting and sculpture the combination of the trivial and the demonic takes a highly visual form. The grotesque is a particular distortion of the usual representation of man, and as such it implies a play with the concept of what it is to be human. This distortion is frequently achieved through a combination of elements from the animal, plant, spirit, and mechanical worlds with human elements. Often bodily confines are violated and extended to ludicrous or obscene proportions. In the case of non-human creatures the form is humanized, yet remains lacking in genuine humanity. In the grotesque object the trivial and the obscene yield to the uncanny and vice versa so that it produces an uncomfortably estranging effect perhaps best described as simultaneously ridiculous and sinister.[5]

The above understanding seems to apply to such figures as Gothic gargoyles, the strange creatures of Hieron-
ymous Bosch's hell, Pieter Bruegel's illustrated proverbs,
Jacques Callot's sketches for the Commedia dell'Arte, and
many of the paintings and sketches of Francisco Goya—all
of whom are generally accepted as grotesque.[6] A few other
aspects of the grotesque might be noted. A particular
type of motion which is gestic and apparently unmotivated
and which tends to turn back on itself is peculiar to the
grotesque figure. Senseless, impromptu acts of spite,
obscenity, and scandalmongering are common activities, and
they imply abrupt directionless motion. The dance of
death, consisting of jerky hops and strange contortions,
has been called the archetypal grotesque motion.[7] Insanity is a frequent motif accompanying the presentation of
grotesque creatures because it provides a cover for irrational behavior.

A particular type of scenery which conveys the feeling of a defined space and is at the same time cluttered
and colorful is characteristic of the grotesque. Parties
and masquerades are frequent settings because they provide
an element of artificiality and estrangement. If the grotesque object is placed outdoors, then nature tends to
come alive and acquire a hostile mien. Language is a significant factor in the presentation of grotesque characters. Words tend to lose their value as a means of exchanging ideas, and they often acquire a magical significance. A character's language, like his motion, tends to
be abrupt and illogical. Often in a literary work the
creation of the grotesque is accompanied by an uneven narrative style which draws attention to the vocal texture by
employing such devices as verbal nonsense and cacophony.[8]

The Petty Demon contains an entire roster of grotesque
characters. Although the paucity of artistic detail in the
novel has been noted,[9] nevertheless, enough information is
given to enable the reader to formulate a visual image of
each personage. Three primary means of rendering the characters grotesque are used: (1) the exaggeration and repetition of one or two salient physical features, (2) metaphor,
and (3) literary allusion. The effect is that the characters are not rendered so overwhelmingly unhuman as to be
totally fantastic; each character remains a part of provincial *byt*, yet at the same time his essential humanity is
called into question and he is given an identity within a
demonology.

The Characters

The major character and focal point of *The Petty Demon*
is the paranoid schoolmaster Ardal'on Borisovich Peredonov.
He was modeled on a teacher whom Sologub knew personally
when he taught in the provinces, and this prototype, like
the character generated from him, was to Sologub the very
incarnation of *poshlost'*.[10]   Peredonov is banal, vulgar,
and sadistic in his treatment of students. He is obsessed
by the desire to be promoted to the position of inspector
of public schools, and much of his activity revolves around
proving his loyalty to the regime and Church and defending
himself from possible slander.   Because of his university education and high rank in the
civil service, Peredonov is considered a good match, and a
number of intrigues are concerned with trying to capture
him in marriage. His mistress Varvara finally succeeds in
winning him through two forged letters from a certain
Princess Volchanskaia which promise him the inspectorship
if he marries her. As Peredonov's insanity increases, he
suspects that his best friend Volodin wants to kill him,
marry Varvara, and assume the inspectorship. The novel
ends when Peredonov cuts Volodin's throat.
    Peredonov's is the most elaborate portrait in *The
Petty Demon*, and it is possible to form a rather precise
visual image of him. Basically he is drawn from the outside in, through externals which serve both to create a
pictorial image of him and to reflect the status of his
soul. His face is ruddy, sleepy, and generaly indifferent. He has small, puffy eyes framed in gold-rimmed
glasses; his eyes are expressionless and as his insanity
increases they become vacant "like the eyes of a dead
man."[11] He has chestnut brown hair which is thinning,
and he is gaining weight around the middle--suggestions
that he is approaching middle age. To avoid catching cold,
Peredonov wears an overcoat, even in warm weather. His
tendency to encase himself in an overcoat indicates a fear
of his surroundings, and thus points to his paranoia. The
indifference and lack of emotion in his face and eyes suggest that he is somehow lifeless.
    Even more important than his physical delineation in
rendering Peredonov grotesque are the comparisons used in
his presentation. In the course of the novel he is likened to a corpse, a puppet, a pig, and a devil. The metaphor of the walking corpse (*khodiachii trup*) is the logical culmination of a visual representation stressing lack

of emotion and lifelessness. The comparison of Peredonov
to a puppet serves to mechanize him; the suggestion is
that someone other than he is in control of his movements.
Significantly, this comparison is used of him when he is
engaged in a hysterical, awkward dance, which may be considered a dance of death (257).

Peredonov is called a pig several times. Varvara is
the first person in the novel to call him a pig; it is her
response to his spitting in her face. Possibly the most
striking comparison of Peredonov to a pig is in the form
of a pun on the word "piatachek," which means both "five-
kopeck piece" and "pig snout" in Russian. Peredonov and
his friend Rutilov are talking:

"You, Ardal'on Borisych, will never be a
bull, because you're a downright pig."
"You're lying!" said Peredonov sullenly.
"No, I'm not lying, and I can prove it,"
said Rutilov maliciously.
"Prove it," demanded Peredonov. . . .
"Ardal'on Borisych, do you have a five-
kopeck piece (*piatachek*)?"
"I have, but I won't give it to you,"
Peredonov answered angrily.
Rutilov broke into a laugh
"If you have a pig snout (*piatachek*),
then how come you're not a pig?" he shouted
joyfully.
Peredonov grabbed his nose in terror.
"You're lying, what sort of pig snout
(*piatachek*) do I have? I have a human mug
(*chelovech'ia kharia*) (60-61).

This pun serves not only to liken Peredonov to a pig, but
it also reveals the terror and bewitching power which words
carry in the cosmos of *The Petty Demon*.[12] Peredonov must
grab his nose to make sure it is in fact human. Ironically, when he answers Rutilov that he does not have a pig
snout (*piatachek*), he uses a word that can mean both human
mug (*chelovech'ia kharia*) and pig snout (*svinaia kharia*).
The implication is that he may be a pig after all.

While the metaphor of the pig points directly to
Peredonov's vulgarity, that of the devil suggests the
demonic side of his personality. Significantly, in folk
belief, after the black cat, the pig is the most frequent
animal form which the devil assumes.[13] In literary tradition too the pig is a common embodiment of the devil; no
doubt the most well-known instance of this in Russian

literature is the pig which wallows in the puddle in the
middle of Mirgorod. Rutilov calls Peredonov a devil several times as Peredonov successively refuses to marry each
of his three sisters. On one of these occasions he calls
him a devil in eyeglasses, thus adding a human and comic
touch to the traditional image of the devil. Another significant instance in which Peredonov is called a devil occurs just prior to his murder of Volodin. Peredonov,
Varvara, and Volodin are at Peredonov's apartment drinking
vodka; Varvara repeats the common saying "Husband and wife
make one devil" (*Muzh da zhena--odna satana*, 382). It
seems that Peredonov's demon-nature grows during the course
of the novel: he is now no longer a common devil (*chert,
bes*) but rather the "prince of darkness" (*Satana*).[14]

The comparisons used in Peredonov's depiction dehumanize him by pointing to his deadness and by suggesting that
he has another, non-human essence--that of a pig/demon.
The presence of bodily hungers--appetite--in the place of
emotion and feeling tends to further dehumanize Peredonov.
Vodka is perhaps the most obvious sign of appetite in *The
Petty Demon*. A staple of Peredonov and his friends, it
runs through the novel as a leitmotif accompanying
Peredonov on his visits, present at his parties, and
present too at the slaying of Volodin. As Peredonov's
paranoia grows, his intake of vodka increases until, towards the end of the novel, he begins to appear at the
gimnaziia drunk. Varvara excuses Peredonov's strange (insane) behavior as drunkenness, and this causes her no
worry. Vodka and cards are the only means Peredonov has
of entertaining his friends, an indication of the meager-
ness of his imagination. Both vodka and card-playing have
a particular significance in folk superstition: one of the
devil's most common human hosts is a drunk, and one of the
most frequent forms of entertainment among devils is card-
playing.[15]

As is frequent in the creation of the grotesque object, the motif of the buffoon is combined with that of
the demon in Peredonov's characterization. This is most
evident in the ridiculous yet sinister antics in which he
engages. For example, on his wedding day Peredonov red-
dens his cheeks with Varvara's rouge, paints "P's" on his
chest, stomach, elbows, and various other places, attempts
to wear one of Varvara's corsets, and, finally, tries to
have his hair cut in an imaginary "Spanish style"--all to
distinguish himself from Volodin. The comic element in
Peredonov's buffoonery is diminished by the error in con-

ceptual thinking which underlies it. His paranoia is by
now so acute that he believes Volodin will "crawl under
his skin" and assume his (corporal) identity, his wife,
and the inspectorship. This series of antics is uncanny
because it illustrates the magic power which words have
acquired for Peredonov. A statement which originally was
a general formulation of the fear that Volodin wanted to
marry Varvara and become the inspector--"Perhaps he's
even thinking of marrying Varvara and crawling under my
skin, (71)"--has become for Peredonov a literal possibility.

Peredonov's motion is significant. He moves suddenly, without any apparent motivation, as if he were responding to stimuli rather than reflecting on situations.
On two occasions in the novel he engages in a dance of
death. The same abruptness and lack of transition is
evident in his language. His speech usually consists of
short units, often only one or two words. Although his
language is vulgar, it tends to be grammatically correct
--in contrast to that of Varvara and Volodin. As a rule
Peredonov does not initiate conversation, but rather re-
acts to someone else's words; and there is a notable absence of formal greetings and the usual politenesses of
social convention in his speech. He tends to use sub-
standard words in place of the standard lexicon; for
"face" (*litso*) he substitutes "mug" and "snout" (*kharia,
rozha, rylo, morda*). He uses a colloquial form of the
verb "to lie" (*vrat'* instead of *lgat'*), and he refers to
persons with whom he is on more or less equal terms by a
debasing diminutive form of their names ("Var'ka" rather
than "Varvara," "Pavlushka" rather than "Pavel").[16]

For Peredonov language is a means of fulfilling bodily needs, of abusing, of spreading gossip, of charming,
and of countercharming; words have lost their value as a
means of exchanging ideas and opinions. Yet, although
language loses its primary communicative function, it
nevertheless acquires magical powers for Peredonov. He
is almost mesmerized into marrying a Rutilov girl by
Rutilov's rapid, persuasive, albeit illogical, speech:

> "You just wait by the gate," convincingly
> said Rutilov, "and I'll bring out whichever
> one you like. Listen, I'll prove it to you.
> Is it true that twice two is four, yes or no?"
>   "Yes," answered Peredonov.
>   "Well, since twice two is four, it follows

that you should marry my sister."
    Peredonov was struck. "Yes, that's true,"
he thought, "of course twice two is four."
And he looked with respect at the sober-looking
Rutilov. "I'll have to get married. Can't
argue with him." (49)[17]

Once he decides not to marry a Rutilov girl, Peredonov
feels he must recite a countercharm to overcome the spell
of Rutilov's "logic":

Chur-churashki, churki-balvashki, buki-
bukashki, vedi-tarakashki. Chur menia,
chur menia. Chur, chur, chur. Chur,
perechur, raschur.(59)[18]

The settings in which Peredonov is placed tend to
take on his sullenness and seem to be an extension of his
personality. Hints are given that his apartment is dirty
and smelly; it is certainly stuffy, since to avoid drafts
Peredonov refuses to open the window. Nature particularly
mirrors Peredonov's inner state. He is often pictured
alone going to and from places. Streets, trees, grass,
physical surroundings, and especially the weather take on
his moods and reflect his boredom, anguish, and fear. As
Peredonov's paranoia increases and he becomes deader,
nature comes alive and seems hostile to him:

Sadness wearied Peredonov all the way.
Everything looked at him hostilely, everything was permeated with threatening signs.
The heavens frowned. The wind blew straight
at him and was sighing about something. The
trees did not want to give shade--they kept
it for themselves. But the dust rose up in
the form of a long, half-transparent gray
serpent. Why is the sun hiding behind a
cloud--could it be spying? (285)

It is possible to see in Peredonov a continuation of
the tradition in Russian literature which deals with the
government official (*chinovnik*). Peredonov is a distant
relative of such "little men" as Gogol's Akakii Akakievich
and Dostoevskii's Makar Devushkin even though his rank in
the civil service is much higher. He is also related to
Gogol's Poprishchin and Dostoevskii's Goliadkin, both of
whom are, like him, insane. Above all, however, he is
related to Chekhov's Belikov of "A Man in the Case"
("Chelovek v futliare") to whom there is a direct reference in the novel. Both are teachers in a *gimnaziia*:

Peredonov teaches Russian literature; Belikov teaches
Greek. Certain similarities are evident in their physical
delineations. Like Peredonov, Belikov encases himself in
an overcoat even in warm weather. Both are drawn through
an emphasis on deadness. In Belikov's case, the motif of
the corpse, suggested in his tendency to shut himself off
from his surroundings, is realized in his death: he seems
fully at home in his coffin.[19] Most of all Peredonov and
Belikov are connected by the status of their souls. Both
are morose, joyless creatures who infect everything around
them with their atmosphere of fear and suspicion.

  Peredonov's pictorial delineation, achieved through a
combination of human, animal, mechanical, and demonic
traits, is the first of many such creations in *The Petty
Demon*. The two persons closest to Peredonov, Varvara and
Volodin, are also genuinely grotesque. Varvara's physical
representation is achieved through a juxtaposition of contradictions. She has a wrinkled face on which there is a
sullen, spiteful expression, but which nevertheless preserves traces of former beauty. The joining together of
objects from different realms, frequent in the creation of
the grotesque object, in Varvara takes the form of a combination of the lewdness and vulgarity of a prostitute
with the gentle beauty of a Greek goddess:

> She quickly undressed, and smirking impu-
> dently showed Peredonov her slightly painted,
> slender, beautiful and supple body.
>   Although Varvara was staggering from
> drunkenness and her face would call forth
> repulsion in any normal person with its
> flabby, lewd expression, her body was
> beautiful, like the body of a gentle nymph
> with the head of a withered harlot attached
> to it by the power of some despicable spell.
> (72)

The motifs of mechanization and of the mask are also
present in Varvara's characterization. The high heels she
wears cause her walk to be jerky, approaching the waddle
of a duck; she is so heavily powdered and rouged that her
blushing cannot be seen. In Varvara's creation there is a
certain identity of mask and face: the vulgarity which
powder and rouge seem to suggest is painted on top of the
lewdness which accompanies her decaying beauty. For the
social visits she makes after her marriage, Varvara dons
a new hat which is abundantly covered with flowers in all
colors. Thus another element, this time from the plant

world, is added to the motley amalgamation which comprises
her visual image.

Hints are given that Varvara has a witch-like nature.
Peredonov senses that she has the power to charm him. He
is alarmed because she cooks from a black book, a suggestion of sorcery, and he fears that she has the ability to
cast a spell on him with cards. Indeed, Varvara, like the
rest of the novel's society, believes in black magic. She
is able to recognize her crony Grushina's ability at sorcery, and she immediately suspects sorcery when a hat which
Peredonov left in his former apartment is returned (46,
251).

The only person in the novel who sincerely likes
Peredonov is Volodin, yet Volodin is the person from whom
Peredonov suspects the brunt of the attack against him, and
in the end he becomes Peredonov's only victim. Volodin's
physical creation is based on the motif of metamorphosis;
he is, as his name implies, amazingly like a ram. In fact,
as the initial and final descriptions of him suggest, he is
more a humanized sheep than a dehumanized person:

> A bleating sound like a sheep's voice was heard
> in the hall. . . .
> In walked Pavel Vasil'evich Volodin, with a
> loud, cheerful laugh, a young man totally like
> a sheep in face and manners: curly-headed like
> a sheep, bulging and vacant eyes--everything
> just like a sheep--a stupid young man. (25)

And after Peredonov cuts his throat:

> Volodin kept bleating and attempting to grab
> his throat with his hands. . . . Suddenly he
> grew deathly pale and toppled onto Peredonov.
> An intermittent squeal was heard, as though
> he were choking, and--quiet. (383)

Volodin's bestial stupidity is especially reflected in
his language. Even within a society that has lost its ability to communicate, Volodin's speech stands out as absurd.
It is totally insipid and devoid of meaning; he uses an excessive number of endearing diminutives, which add a sugary
touch to his expression, and he frequently misuses words.
For example, just after he is introduced in the novel, he
cries out like a jack-in-the-box:

> "Ardal'on Borisych, dear friend!" . . .
> "You're at home drinking a little coffee, so
> here am I--so here I am."

("Ardal'on Borisych, druzhishche!" . . .
"ty doma, kofeek raspivaesh', a vot i ia, tut
kak tut, 25.)

An especially incongruous touch is added to Volodin's
depiction by Peredonov's attempt to marry him to Nadezhda
Adamenko. She is an attractive, intelligent girl who has
no part in the day to day affairs of the town. Rather,
she spends her time lying on a couch reading books--a suggestion perhaps of the sentimental heroine. As a couple
they are a complete mismatch, both visually and intellectually. The costume Volodin grafts on his ram-like frame
when he is courting Nadezhda renders him additionally ludicrous: he wears a tight-fitting frock coat, a freshly
starched shirt, a gaudy necktie, and his woolly hair is
pasted down with pomade and scented.

The two widows Vershina and Grushina play a significant role in Peredonov's fate. Vershina wants to marry
Peredonov to her ward, an awkward Polish girl named Marta,
and she therefore beckons him into her house whenever he
passes. Grushina is Varvara's confidante in her attempts
to marry Peredonov, and it is she who does the actual
forging of the letters. But Vershina is also involved in
the ruse of the letters. She instills suspicion into
Peredonov about the authenticity of the first one, thus
causing Varvara to have Grushina forge a second; moreover,
at the end of the novel she tells Peredonov outright that
the second letter was a forgery and thus directly precipitates the murder of Volodin.

Vershina is an obvious witch. She is a small, thin,
prematurely wizened woman with black eyes and brows, a
dark complexion, and dark yellow teeth, and she always
dresses in black. Her gestures are smooth, almost imper-
ceptible, her smile is crooked, and her tone of voice
monotonous. Vershina is a chain smoker, and she should be
visualized with puffs of smoke rising in front of her.
Vershina's garden is an important part of her characterization; it is lush and vibrant with color, and it is chaotic. This garden and the gray house within it form the
only setting for the many meetings between Peredonov and
her, for, unlike most of Peredonov's other friends, she
never visits him at his home. During these meetings he is
in her territory, an enchanted realm, and the implication
is that he is also under her spell.

While Vershina is depicted in black, gray is used for
Grushina, and dust rather than smoke becomes her characterizing motif:

> Mar'ia Osipovna Grushina, a young widow,
> had a somehow prematurely faded appearance.
> She was thin, and her dry skin was all covered
> with wrinkles which were small and seemingly
> filled with dust. Her face was not devoid of
> pleasantness, but her teeth were dirty and
> black. Her hands were thin, and her fingernails
> were long and clawlike, and under her nails was
> dirt. At a quick glance, she not only appeared
> very dirty, but she gave the impression that
> she never washed, but was only beaten out along
> with the clothes she wore. One would think
> that if she were struck several times with a
> carpet-beater, a column of dust would rise to
> the very heavens. Her clothing hung on her
> with rumpled creases as though it had just been
> taken from a bundle which had been lying
> crumpled up for a long time. . . . Her conver-
> sations were for the most part immodest, and
> she habitually attached herself to men hoping
> to find a husband. There was always some un-
> married official occupying a room at her
> house. (42)

Grushina's pictorial representation emphasizes her dirtiness, and this is supported by her corresponding vulgarity, the immodesty of her conversation, and the general
depravity of her life. Her house is slovenly, and her
walls are decorated with poorly-drawn pictures of naked
women. This house, like Vershina's house and garden, is
an important locus of action in the novel. It is here
that the forgery takes place and that Peredonov, during
a party, makes his final decision to marry Varvara.

Certain parallels in the depictions of Vershina and
Grushina are evident. Their names are phonetically similar, and each is drawn through the use of color (black-
gray) and a corresponding motif (smoke-dust).[20] It seems,
however, that Vershina's witch nature is more striking.
Significantly, except for the business of finding Marta a
husband, she scarcely seems to be a part of the provincial *byt* of the novel; she belongs almost wholly to the
supernatural. It is likely that Grushina is also a witch;
she is a known fortune-teller. Nevertheless, this witch
nature is hidden under layers of dirt, and her involvement
in the petty affairs of the town serves to ingrain her in
the *byt* of the novel. In a sense, Vershina and Grushina
may be considered two aspects of a total grotesque

personality: the demonic predominates in Vershina, but
poshlost' is more obvious in Grushina.

The most unusual and the most seemingly mismatched of
the potential fiancees for the dull-witted, gloomy
Peredonov are the three lively, attractive, intelligent
Rutilov sisters. Even so, the possibility of a match between Peredonov and the Rutilov girls is to be taken seriously within the world of *The Petty Demon*. It is repeated many times that the girls are attractive, gay, and
lively: Dar'ia, the oldest, is the tallest and the most
slender; Liudmila is the quickest to laugh; and Valeriia,
the youngest, is the smallest and the most frail, and she
is slightly envious of her older sisters who seem heartier
and more sure of themselves. The Rutilov girls are not
drawn through an emphasis on significant physical features,
and the actual visual image which emerges is rather vague.

The sisters are characterized rather by secondary effects such as the foods they eat, the atmosphere they
create about them, and, especially, by literary and folk
allusions. The Rutilov home is an example of impeccable
neatness and care; it is dust-free, pleasant-smelling,
colorful--the very opposite of the Peredonov and Grushina
households. The sisters' home conveys the appearance that
those who live there belong to the best circles of local
society and are in every way proper. But the foods they
eat--fruits, nuts, halvah, and imported liqueurs--suggest
something unusual.

The Rutilov girls are introduced into the novel
through a curious scene. Their brother--so he thinks--has
persuaded Peredonov to marry one of them, but Peredonov
has a condition: he demands that each of the sisters tell
him how she will please him. Peredonov, alone and fearful,
is standing in the darkness of the Rutilov garden waiting
for the sisters to give their answers. And, they come in
the order of age:

> Dar'ia: I will bake very tasty pancakes for
> you, hot ones--only don't choke on
> them!
>
> Liudmila: And I will walk about the town each
> morning to gather all the gossip and
> then relate it to you. It'll be
> great fun!
>
> Valeriia: And I won't tell you for anything how
> I'll please you--guess yourself. (54)

The answers provide a comic touch because, with their references to appetite (pancakes), scandal, and eroticism (Valeriia's vague hint), they play directly to the *posh-lost'* and coarseness in Peredonov. More importantly, this scene is a clear parody on the opening lines of Pushkin's fairy tale "Tsar Saltan" ("Skazka o Tsare Saltane. . ."):

> Beneath a window three fair maidens
> Were spinning late one evening.
> "If I should be the tsaritza,"
> Says the first maiden.
> "Then for the whole Christian world
> I would prepare a banquet."
> "If I should be the tsaritza,"
> Says her sister,
> "Then for the entire world,
> I alone would weave the linen."
> "If I should be the tsaritza,"
> Spake the third sister,
> "For the Lord-Tsar,
> I would bear a *bogatyr'*."[21]

Perhaps the most obvious significance of this parody is that it casts the three Rutilov sisters into the roles of remoldings of the "fair maiden" (*krasna devitsa*) of the Russian fairy tale. This, combined with the actual lack of pictorial detail in their characterizations, suggests that perhaps they are best visualized as the perfect, but nondescript beauties of Russian folk art. Peredonov, by implication, becomes a parody of the tsar—and in a weirdly perverted way, his ability to choose from almost any of the young girls in town makes him a local autocrat. Of course, in Peredonov the color and splendor of the fairy-tale world have degenerated to *poshlost'*—appetite, scandal, and vulgar eroticism. Moreover, if the comparison between the scenes in *The Petty Demon* and "Tsar Saltan" can be sustained, there is the additional hint that at least the two older sisters may have evil powers; in the fairy tale the tsar marries the youngest, and the others, who become the palace cook and the palace weaver, work toward her destruction.

The suggestion that the fairy-tale beauty of the Rutilov sisters may conceal a sinister nature is borne out by the comparison of the sisters to witches. Peredonov calls them witches immediately after refusing to marry them. Moreover, in their frenzied drinking, singing, and dancing they are likened to witches celebrating their Sabbath:

The sisters were young and beautiful, and
their voices rang out loudly and wildly--the
witches on bald mountain would have envied
them their dance. (181)

Liudmila attains an identity of her own apart from
her sisters in her relationship to Sasha Pyl'nikov, the
fourteen-year-old schoolboy with whom she falls in love.
The exotically sensuous games of the young couple run
counterpoint to the coarse relationship between Peredonov
and Varvara. In addition to the metaphor of the witch,
certain other comparisons play a vital role in Liudmila's
presentation: she is also compared to a water nymph
(*rusalka*) and to a devil (*chert*).

In Russian folklore the *rusalka* is a water nymph,
often descended from an unbaptized child, who appeared
naked, with loose, flowing hair, and who often enticed
her victim to drown himself or tickled him to death.[22]
Liudmila is first called a *rusalka* by Sasha after she overcomes him in a mock wrestling match. Later, Liudmila
compares herself to a *rusalka* and, at the same time,
frankly admits to being a pagan:

"I love beauty. I am a pagan, a sinner. I
ought to have been born in ancient Athens.
I love flowers, perfumes, bright clothes,
the naked body. They say there is a soul.
I don't know; I haven't seen it. But what
is it to me! Let me die completely like a
rusalka; let me melt away like a cloud under
the sun. I love the body--strong, agile,
naked, which can experience pleasure."
   "And can also suffer," said Sasha softly.
   "And suffer, and that is good," whispered
Liudmila passionately. "There is sweetness
even in pain, if you can feel the body and
see its nakedness and bodily beauty." (323)

Sasha, prompted by this speech, asks Liudmila why she goes
to church if she is a pagan, and Liudmila's reply places
Christian worship on the plane of physical experience:

"Well," she said, "it's necessary to pray,
to weep, to light candles, to give, to remember. And I love it all--the candles, the icon
lamps, the incense, the chasubles, the sing-
ing--if the singers are good--and the icons
with their settings and ribbons. Yes, all of
that is so beautiful. And I also love . . .

Him . . . you know, the Crucified. . ."
"You know, I dream of Him sometimes--He
is on the cross, and there are little drops
of blood on his body." (324-25)

The above passages not only elaborate on the sensuous-
ness of Liudmila's love of beauty; they also reveal the joy
she finds in pain and thereby point to her sadistic tendencies. Some of her actions also reveal this: she pinches
Sasha's cheeks until it hurts because she enjoys the red
spots; she pulls his ear; and she makes him kiss her knees,
during which she has an expression of "triumphant cruelty
on her face" (216, 213, 318). Furthermore, she has an
erotic-sadistic dream in which she takes pleasure in watching Sasha whipped (182). Such sadism suggests that, aside
from the clear aesthetic differences, Liudmila may in fact
be very much like Peredonov, who enjoys seeing his students
whipped. But, perhaps the strongest link binding Liudmila
to Peredonov is the metaphor of the devil. She is called
a devil specifically in her relationship to Sasha. Liudmila is waiting for Sasha who does not come; she is dis-
turbed:

> "What makes you cry and grieve over a young-
> ster?" said Dar'ia. "One might say that the
> devil has bound himself to an infant."
> "Who is this devil?" cried Liudmila passion-
> ately, and she blushed crimson all over.
> "Why, you dearie," Dar'ia replied. "It's
> nothing that you're young, but only. . ."
> Dar'ia did not finish but whistled pierc-
> ingly.
> "Stupidities," said Liudmila in a strangely
> ringing voice.
> A weird and cruel smile illumined her face
> through her tears like a brightly shining ray
> at sundown through the last outpouring of a
> sluggish rain. (218-19)

It is significant that Dar'ia recognizes Liudmila's
devil nature. Of all the sisters, she may be the most advanced in the occult. She is the one who drinks, sings
chastushki, and dances the most wildly. The piercing
loudness of her voice is macabre--like that of a corpse:
"If a corpse were taken out of the grave so that it could
sing all the time, it would sing in this fashion" (179).
When Dar'ia dances, her eyes remain motionless "like the
dead moon in its orbit" (181). This suggestion of deadness is sustained in the description of how she kisses

Sasha--"loudly, but indifferently, as though he were a board" (206). The motif of the corpse and the comparison of the witch dehumanize Dar'ia and render her grotesque.

It appears that all the sisters have witch-like natures, although in varying degrees. The oldest Dar'ia is the most advanced, then Liudmila, and finally Valeriia, who, younger and weaker than her sisters, is not so fully developed. Perhaps it is in view of their identity within the novel's demonology, and not in view of their attractiveness and seeming propriety, that the sisters should be understood as serious candidates for marriage with Peredonov.

Sasha is introduced into *The Petty Demon* through a rumor which Grushina tells Varvara of a boy posing as a girl in the *gimnaziia* in order to snare Peredonov and find a husband. Thus, although a connection is not explicitly made, it appears that Sasha too is introduced as a possible bride for Peredonov (139-43). He is one of the few genuinely likeable creatures in the novel, yet even he has a dual nature. The motif of metamorphosis is basic to Sasha's characterization. His physical delineation turns on his attactiveness and his resemblance to a girl. He is about fourteen, slender, dark, and he has a high, broad chest; his skin is yellowish in hue, even, and soft. He has black, mysteriously sad eyes and long, blue-black lashes; his face is smooth, with no evidence of a beard, and it is pale. He has rosy cheeks, and he frequently blushes; his hair is dark-brown and short. The smoothness of his skin, his rosy cheeks and blushing, and his high chest cause him to be taken for a girl, and at the same time it is these traits which are the source of his sensuous appeal for Liudmila.

Both Peredonov's and Liudmila's initial visits to Sasha are prompted by a desire to find out if he is in fact a girl. The rumor that he is a girl, circulated throughout the *gimnaziia* by Peredonov, causes the headmaster to have Sasha examined by a physician. Although this examination reveals that Sasha is a boy, it in no way excludes the possibility of metamorphosis: Sasha may be both a boy and a girl. His name suggests this: he is almost always called "Sasha," a diminutive form of both "Aleksandr" and "Aleksandra." Significantly, the erotic games in which Sasha and Liudmila engage play on the questionable status of his sex: Liudmila delights in dressing Sasha in her own clothing. Moreover, she and her sisters collaborate in sending Sasha to the town masquerade dressed as a girl--a geisha.

Even after Sasha is examined, Peredonov continues to be obsessed with the possibility that he is a girl:

> Was he really a boy? Or, perhaps there were
> two of them--brother and sister--but you can't
> tell who's there. Or perhaps he even knows
> how to change himself from a boy to a girl.
> (331)

The ambiguous nature of Sasha's sex seems to be connected with the metaphor of the werewolf. Varvara calls him a werewolf almost as soon as she hears about him (*chistyi oboroten'*, 42).[23] Within a few pages Peredonov's cat is also called a werewolf (146), and in a dream which Peredonov subsequently has, Sasha and the cat collaborate to entice him in a werewolf-like fashion:

> Peredonov dreamed a foul and terrifying dream:
> Pyl'nikov came and stood in the doorway and
> beckoned and smiled. It was as if someone
> drew Peredonov to him, and Pyl'nikov led him
> along dark and dirty streets, and the cat ran
> alongside, and its green pupils glimmered. . .
> (230)

Perhaps more than any other physical feature, Sasha's mysteriously sad eyes allude to his primordial nature:

> Kokovkina [Sasha's landlady] came to comfort
> Sasha. Sasha was sitting sorrowfully by the
> window looking at the starry sky. His black
> eyes were now peaceful and strangely sad.
> Kokovkina silently stroked him on the head.
> (155)

At one point in the novel, Sasha's landlady surprises the couple at Liudmila's and finds Sasha dressed as a girl. After this, Sasha is forbidden to visit Liudmila. Thus, for the fittings for the geisha costume and for the masquerade itself, Sasha must escape through the window of his room at night. These nocturnal ventures which he makes for the purpose of "appearing to be a girl" (a geisha) suggest metamorphosis and contain a hint of his werewolf-like nature. One of the many puns which Liudmila makes when they are together alludes to this:

> "Now who wants to be sprayed?" Liudmila asked,
> and she took a bottle of perfume in her hands
> and looked inquisitively and craftily at
> Sasha.
>   "I want to," repeated Sasha.

"You want to? You bay? There it is! Bay!"
gaily teased Liudmila. (208)[24]

In Russian the words punned on are "who wants" and "who
bays" (*kto zhelaet* and *kto zhe laet*).

Even Sasha, the most appealing creature in the novel,
has an identity within the demonology of *The Petty Demon*.
The werewolf, however, has a particular significance in
Sologub's art; it often stands as a symbol of a wistful,
nostalgic longing for a primeval existence and an escape
from everyday reality (especially *poshlost'*).[25] It is
meaningful that Sasha's nostalgia should reveal itself
particularly after a visit from Peredonov, the novel's
prime embodiment of *poshlost'*.

In addition to the above characters, most of whom
play fairly major roles in Peredonov's life, the novel
consists of a vast number of minor characters. Most of
these characters are also grotesque, and many have obvious
identities within a demonology. For example, Peredonov's
landlady Ershova is one of the most striking examples of
a witch in the novel. She is an old, dirty, and disheveled
woman with a flushed face. She is habitually drunk and
smells of vodka. Ershova practices sorcery: it is she who
has a spell cast on Peredonov's old hat, and she returns
Peredonov's cat with rattles on its tail. As the town
ruffians, the Avdeev boys are responsible for the execution of much of the foul play in the novel: for example,
they tar Marta's gates, break Peredonov's windows, and
throw litter into Peredonov's carriage after his wedding.
It is said of them that they seem to spring from the
earth and be swallowed up by it, a suggestion that they
are best understood as evil spirits (251).

After the reception of the first forged letter,
Peredonov resolves to visit a number of the town functionaries to ward off slander which might prevent him
from receiving the inspectorship. Peredonov's visits
are a clear echo of the series of visits which Gogol's
Chichikov makes to various landowners to buy up deceased
serfs. In both cases the visits serve as a device for
introducing new characters into the novels, thus filling
out the depiction of provincial society. Both Peredonov
and Chichikov are eager to insure themselves of higher
positions on the social ladder, and both plan to do it
through marriage. Peredonov thinks if he marries Varvara
he will receive the patronage of Princess Volchanskaia.
Chichikov thinks that once he has purchased dead serfs he
will appear rich enough to marry a wealthy heiress. In

both cases the purpose of the visits is a mockery of reality: Chichikov's serfs are legally alive but actually
dead; Peredonov defends himself from slander which, at
this point at least, exists only in his imagination.

The official whom Peredonov visits are rendered grotesque mainly through the exaggeration of certain features
and through the complementary presentations of their
houses. Here the grotesque serves not so much to render
them members of a demonology as to suggest that they per-
sonify certain weaknesses. Again a comparison may be
made between these officials and the landowners whom
Chichikov visits, who are also grotesque: Manilov personifies effusive, honeyed sentimentalism; Sobakievich is
the embodiment of crude, sub-human beastliness; Pliushkin
is the archetypal miser.

Skuchaev ("Mr. Bored"), the mayor of the novel's
town, is a tall, stout man with closely-cut black hair,
crafty black eyes, and plump little fingers. During his
conversation with Peredonov his eyes become dull and he
takes on the mien of a foolish old man. His house is an
extension of his personality: the first floor is preten-
tiously austere, but the children's rooms are cosily
pleasant; it smells of freshly waxed floors mingled with
the faint order of food. Skuchaev seem to embody the
dullness and boredom of provincial life. Even his common
features and his plump fingers suggest stagnation.

The merchant Tishkov ("Mr. Quiet") who arrives towards the end of Peredonov's visit itensifies the general
impression of boredom and stagnation. Tishkov talks incessantly in rhyme, and his creation is based on the grotesque motif of the automaton:

> It was all the same to Tishkov whether people
> listened to him or not; he couldn't help grab-
> bing at strange words for the sake of rhyme and
> he acted with the steadiness of a cleverly de-
> vised annoyance machine. Looking at his quick,
> precise movements, it was possible to think that
> this was not a living person, that he already
> died or never lived, and that he saw nothing in
> the living world and could hear nothing besides
> his deadly resounding words. (109-10)

The district attorney Avinovitskii is drawn through
an emphasis on his frightening appearance: his bluish-
black beard is so large that he appears thin behind it,
and he has a threatening, shouting manner. He greets

Peredonov with, "Do you have a confession? Did you kill somebody? Did you start a fire? Did you rob the mail?" (113). Avinovitskii's house also has an angry, evil look which frightens Peredonov and causes him to recite a countercharm before entering. It is gray with a high-pitched roof sloping down to windows which touch the ground. The entry gates are higher than the house itself, and behind them a dog growls at passers-by. Avinovitskii is best understood as a personification of terror. He is a bullying, small-town power holder.

The marshall of the nobility Veriga is a retired cavalry officer whose aspiration is to be the governor of a province. The motif of mechanization is suggested in his presentation: he holds himself erect, and rumor has it that he wears a corset. Veriga's face is clean-shaven and uniformly crimson; his head is shaved with the closest cutting clippers to minimize his bald spot. His eyes are gray and amiable, yet cold. Veriga's house is reminiscent of a villa in Pavlosk or Tsarskoe Selo, where wealthy Petersburg aristocrats spent their summers. Veriga's meticulous attention to his appearance and his *comme il faut* appearance point to his desire for promotion. He is a more intelligent and more sophisticated Peredonov at a higher stage in his climb up the social ladder.

The visual delineation of the representative of the district land council Kirillov turns on a union of incongruous parts and mechanization. He is so slender and boyish that he resembles a child with a glued-on beard; his facial expression is alternatively grave and childishly naive. His eyes are alert and have a slight gleam in them, but they stare straight ahead as though they are somehow not alive: "It was as if someone had taken the living soul out of him, and in its place inserted an unliving but dexterous mechanism" (129). Kirillov's house points to his affected concern for the public good and his preoccupation with agricultural matters. Many of the effects in the house are intended to remind one of the simple, peasant life: a chair with arms made of axe handles, an inkstand shaped like a horeshoe, an ash tray resembling a peasant's bast shoe. The study is dusty, with boxes full of papers and cases of books on agriculture and education. The living room contains drawings of farm machinery, and the hall is full of samples of various grains and of the coarse bread used during years of famine. Everything in this house--the chair, the inkstand, the ash tray, the chaos of books, papers, models, and grain samples, and,

most of all, the busy but inanimate hustle and bustle of
Kirillov himself--indicates that the idea of social good
has been reduced to triviality. Kirillov is perhaps best
understood as a particular embodiment of *poshlost'*.

The chief of police Min'chukov has lips that are
bright-red and thick, a bulbous nose, and a zealous but
stupid expression on his face. He stoops slightly, and
his fingers hang down like rakes. There is a feeling of
clutteredness and frenzy about Min'chukov's house: the
ceilings are low, the furniture is pressed close together;
the courtyard is littered, and carts covered with matting
are standing around. People are constantly flitting in and
out bringing and leaving things. The indication is that
Min'chukov takes bribes. He is probably intended as a
personification of greed.

In addition to dehumanized provincial types, *The Petty
Demon* contains a number of grotesque characters whose creations proceed not from the usual image of man, but rather
from the non-human world. In these characters the grotesque is achieved largely through humanization. These
bizarre creatures include card-figures, Peredonov's cat,
Princess Volchanskaia, and, most importantly, the
nedotykomka.

Playing cards are signs of the meager values of the
society of the novel--of *poshlost'*, and they are implements of magic used in spell-casting and fortune-telling.
As Peredonov becomes increasingly paranoid, cards become
objects of terror for him. He imagines that they are spying on him, and he cuts out their eyes to prevent this.
Later, in his delusions, cards assume human forms: the
eights become werewolfish students; a jack who made him
lose a game turns up as the postman (256).

Unlike the usual black famulus of witches and sor-
cerers, Peredonov's cat is white, fat, and ugly. In the
course of the novel, Peredonov comes to fear that the cat
has the power to bewitch him. At one point he suspects
that the cat may have denounced him to the authorities:

> Peredonov thought that the cat might have
> gone to the police in order to purr out
> everything that it knew about Peredonov,
> about where he went at night, and why--it
> would reveal everything, yes, and even meow
> things that never happened. Trouble! (242)

As was the case with the card figures, the motif of

metamorphosis is used in the cat's presentation. Peredonov
recognizes him in an unfamiliar guest at his wedding:

> Among the guests there was one with a red
> moustache whom Peredonov didn't even know.
> He looked unusually like the cat. Had their
> cat turned himself into a person? It wasn't
> for nothing that this young man was continu-
> ally sniffing--he hadn't forgotten his cat
> habits. (287)

The alleged author of the letters promising Peredonov
the inspectorship is the wealthy Petersburg aristocrat
Princess Volchanskaia. The Princess never actually appears in the novel, but as his paranoia grows, Peredonov
suspects that she is near-by watching him. Her visual
creation is based on the reiteration of her extreme age
and on her assuming the form of the queen of spades. When
notification of his promotion does not arrive, Peredonov
begins to fabricate stories about the Princess and then to
believe his own fabrications. He says that formerly he
was her lover, even though she was very ugly, and that now
she wants him to love her again. In these stories the
Princess assumes the image of a traditional witch:

> The Princess, in Peredonov's imagination, grew
> more decrepit day by day and became more hor-
> rible: yellow, wrinkled, hunchbacked, fang-
> toothed, evil. . . .
> "She's two hundred years old," said
> Peredonov, and strangely and wistfully
> looked in front of him. "And she wants me
> to make love to her again. Until then she
> doesn't want to give me the position." (336)

The most important image in the presentation of Princess Volchanskaia is that of the queen of spades because it
provides a clear reference to Pushkin's tale "The Queen of
Spades. It is possible to observe a close parallel in the
plots of the two works. In "The Queen of Spades" the protagonist Germann relies on an old Countess to reveal a
mysterious secret whereby he may win a fortune at cards.
This thought becomes an obsession with him, and his entire
fate is placed in the hands of the old woman. The vehicle
through which he hopes to obtain an audience with the
Countess is her poor-relative ward Lizaveta, and he courts
her to this purpose. In *The Petty Demon* Peredonov is obsessed with his inspectorship just as Germann is with his
secret of the cards; and he relies on the Princess, who is

Varvara's patron, to obtain it for him. Varvara is the
novel's counterpart to Lizaveta, although she contrasts
sharply with the young ward in her lewdness.

The image of the old Countess of "The Queen of Spades"
provides a clear visual referent for a grotesque image of
Princess Volchanskaia. The following succession of images
is given of the Countess: (1) a young, beautiful, but
frivolous woman of the 1770's; (2) an ancient, hideous
woman of the 1830's who is trying to preserve her long
faded beauty; (3) a corpse; (4) an apparition; and (5) the
queen of spades.[26] The most basic image is that of her as
an old woman trying to preserve the habits and dress of her
youth. A clear grotesque image of the Countess is created
based on the incongruity between her puffy, decrepit flesh
and the various adornments she grafts on to make herself
look younger: a powdered wig, rouge, extravagant dresses,
and, an element from the floral world, roses. An additionally estranging factor is provided by the knowledge
that these accessories are sixty years out of fashion.

There is a suggestion that the Countess, like the
Princess, may have a witch-like nature. The last thing
Germann calls her before drawing the pistol in order to
force her to tell him the secret is "old witch."[27] But
the Countess does not reveal her secret while she is
alive. This leads to another parallel between the Countess and the Princess. Even though Princess Volchanskaia
never appears corporally in *The Petty Demon*, she exercises an overwhelmingly destructive influence on
Peredonov's fate. His belief that she has turned against
him leads him into a deeper terror and suspicion of others
which ultimately culminates in the murder of Volodin and
his collapse into total senselessness. Similarly, it is
not as a living woman, but as a corpse, an apparition, and
as the queen of spades that the Countess has her most
powerful influence on Germann's fate. She squints at him
and mocks him from her casket causing him to faint. Later
that night, she appears to him at his apartment and reveals the sequence of cards by which he can win his for-
tune--three, seven, ace. But, on the final day of the
gambling, instead of drawing an ace, he draws the queen
of spades:

> At this moment it seemed to him that the queen
> of spades squinted at him and smiled wrily.
> An unusual resemblance struck him. . .
> "The old woman!" he shouted in horror.[28]

Germann loses everything and goes out of his mind; Peredonov murders Volodin and then collapses into complete insanity the day after he is told that the letters were
false.

Though the grotesqueness of Princess Volchanskaia
depends largely on a play with the form of a decaying
human figure, it seems probable that the referent for
her pictorial creation is to be found in literature and
not in visual reality. The similarities in plot between
"The Queen of Spades" and *The Petty Demon*, the image of a
decaying old witch-like woman, and, above all, the metaphor of the queen of spades suggest that Princess Volchanskaia is a literary reincarnation of Pushkin's old
Countess.

The most important of the non-human creatures in *The
Petty Demon* is the *nedotykomka*, a gray spirit which appears in the midst of the incense during the blessing of
Peredonov's new apartment and torments him from this
point to the murder of Volodin. The name "nedotykomka"
literally means "not-quite-pokeable-female-creature," and
it points to the spirit's elusiveness. In contrast to
all the previously discussed characters, the *nedotykomka*'s
pictorial delineation is not the product of the distortion of a familiar form. It is "faceless," a creature of
"undefined outlines" (156). Therefore, it is difficult to
visualize the spirit, although not entirely impossible.
An abundance of perceptual criteria are used in the
spirit's delineation: it is smelly, noisy, and extremely
active. These traits perhaps indicate that the *nedotykoma*
is primarily a presence to be felt, and only secondarily
a creature to be visualized.

The spirit is gray, and the repetition of this color
suggests that it is to be understood as a characterizing
epithet. Other attributives reinforce its grayness and
point to the sense in which it is to be understood: it is
"dirty" and "dusty" (286, 308). Undoubtedly a primary
function of the color gray is to join the *nedotykomka* and
Peredonov to each other; it is indicative of the boredom,
squalor, and *poshlost'* of his existence. But, as a color,
gray conveys a feeling of drabness--colorlessness--rather
than of pigmentation. This essentially visual trait probably serves a mainly psychological purpose: it links the
spirit to Peredonov's soul.

One of the most highly sensual traits used in the depiction of the *nedotykomka* is smell. The spirit is called

"stinking" (*voniuchaia*, 308). Although smell provides an
obvious feeling of the spirit's presence, the use of this
particular word, which is vulgar and highly characteristic
of Peredonov, suggests that it may be a way in which he
perceives it rather than an actual attribute of the creature. This is another means of relating the *nedotykomka*
to Peredonov's soul and to his apartment, which is also
foul smelling and which in its way is a mirror of his soul.

     Sound and motion are other essential ingredients in
the creation of the *nedotykomka*. The spirit constantly
laughs and jeers at Peredonov, and it is this mockery more
than anything else which instills horror into him and
drives him to such acts as chopping the table under which
it is sitting (310). The *nedotykomka* moves incessantly;
characteristic motions are quivering, fidgeting, rolling
about on the floor, and jumping about. Both the tremendous noise which the spirit makes and its quivering,
whirling movements connect it with Peredonov's psychic
state. They provide a clear index of the restlessness
and agitation in his soul. These traits also suggest a
possibility for visualizing the *nedotykomka*.

     Although in *The Petty Demon* the *nedotykomka* does not
smile (image), but always laughs (sound), it is only a
brief step to imagine the visual representation of this
laughter as a taunting smile, a smirk, or a leer. In
fact, the spirit can perhaps best be pictured as a leer
implanted on a small, amorphous grayish mass which is continually whirling about Peredonov, yet which is impossible
to touch or approach. If this is correct, then the leer
adds a human element to the delineation of the *nedotykomka*
and renders it grotesque.[29] Moreover, the spirit's motion
may be considered a continual dance of death.

     Peredonov is the only one of the characters in the
novel who sees the *nedotykomka*, and he, of course, is insane. Yet, while there can be no doubt that the
nedotykomka reflects Peredonov's soul and is symptomatic
of his insanity, there are reasons for believing that it
has a broader meaning that would be possible if it were
merely the extension of a madman's consciousness. Rather,
it is integral to the total vision of the world both in
The Petty Demon and in Sologub's work in general. This is
suggested first of all by the spirit's presence outside
the novel; the *nedotykomka* is the subject of an earlier
lyric.[30] However, the most convincing evidence that the
spirit is a reality existing beyond Peredonov's consciousness is not so much its appearance outside the novel

as the particular way in which it is presented in the novel
itself. Although only Peredonov sees it, nevertheless, the
nedotykomka is never presented totally through his vision.
Unlike the other fantasy creatures, the spirit never occurs
in a dream; and, furthermore, it is never presented through
interior monologue, which would bring the reader directly
into Peredonov's consciousness without the obvious presence of the narrative voice. Rather, the *nedotykomka* is
always presented as a statement of fact within the narration, and this signifies that the narrator shares in the
vision of the spirit.

It is important to consider the particular nature of
the novel's narrator. In *The Petty Demon* there is minimal
distance between the implied author and the narrator who
retains almost absolute control over the telling of the
story. Moreover, it seems that the testimony of this
narrator-implied author is to be considered true and his
judgment is valid; he is, in Wayne Booth's terminology,
reliable. [31] When the *nedotykomku* is first introduced, the
narrator's voice is totally predominant. The passage is
highly poetic, and the language is totally uncharacteris-
tic of the vulgar, dull-witted Peredonov:

> An amazing creature of indefinite features ran
> out from somewhere--a small, gray, lively,
> nimble *nedotykomka*. It chuckled, and quivered,
> and whirled around Peredonov. But when he
> stretched out his hand toward it, it quickly
> slipped away, ran behind the door or under
> the dresser, and, after a minute appeared
> again, and quivered, and teased--gray, faceless,
> nimble. (156)

Although the spirit's presence is always narrated, in later
passages the device of narrated perception is often in
evidence. [32] Through the use of modal words, often characteristic of Peredonov, and of the present tense, the
reader is able to enter into Peredonov's experiencing consciousness:

> The *nedotykomka* ran about under the chairs and
> in the corners and squealed. It was dirty,
> smelly, repulsive, and terrifying. It was
> already clear that it was hostile to Peredonov,
> and that it had come especially for him, and
> that formerly it hadn't existed anywhere. It
> was created--and bewitched. And, to be sure,
> it lived for his terror and destruction,

magical, many-shaped--it pursued him, deceived
him, laughed at him--now rolling about on the
floor, now pretending to be a rag, a ribbon,
a branch, a cloud, a dog, a column of dust
on the street, and everywhere it ran after
Peredonov, it exhausted him and wearied him with
its jerky dance. If only someone would deliver him with some word or sweep it away.
But there are no friends here, no one will
come to save him, he must outwit it himself
before it destroys him, the spiteful creature. (308-9)

The import of the narrator's voice in the presentation of the spirit is that the *nedotykomka* can be considered an objective reality of the cosmos of *The Petty Demon*,
and not just the hallucination of a madman. The *nedotykomka* is perhaps best understood as a symbolization of
evil. The creature's eerie laughter hints at a diabolic
nature, and the attributive "faceless" (*bezlikaia*) applied to the spirit on its first appearance may link it
to the devil who is also faceless. The appearance of
the *nedotykomka* under various guises also connects it to
the devil; according to folk belief the devil can assume
many forms of which the dog is very common. The guise
of the column of dust is additionally significant: according to the folk, devils stir up such columns when they
dance.[33] Particularly meaningful in suggesting the spirit's devil nature is the guise of the serpent which it
assumes at the masquerade. As the form of the devil in
the Biblical myth of the Fall, this guise connects the
spirit with primordial evil. Yet, while the *nedotykomka*
is no doubt a manifestation of the evil which pervades and
rules the cosmos of *The Petty Demon*, it should not be understood as a grandiose symbol of the denial of God and
his creation. Rather, the spirit embodies petty evil--
poshlost' and spite raised to cosmic dimensions. The
grayness, dirtiness, and dustiness of the spirit point
clearly to this.

A recent critic has suggested that the real import of
the *nedotykomka* is that it signals Peredonov's contact with
another reality.[34] His vision of the spirit can in fact be
understood as a sort of self-transcendence. He is initiated into a truth beyond himself and beyond the limits of
visual reality--for the other characters do not see it.
Of all the characters in *The Petty Demon*, Peredonov seems
the most total in his devotion to petty evil. If, as an

embodiment of this evil, the *nedotykomka* can be considered
his "god," then, in religious terms, Peredonov is a fully
integrated man. He has perhaps reached a stage of "trans-
figuration," albeit in a negative sense; his vision of
this dirty, gray spirit can possibly be considered the con-
verse of the vision of light of Orthodox mysticism.[35]

Most of the characters of *The Petty Demon* are grotesque. The starting point for their visual creations is
usually the normal form of a human being, an animal, or
an object. The grotesque is then achieved through dehu-
manization or humanization. It is necessary to bear in
mind the highly pictorial quality of the novel. Perhaps
so little attention has been paid to this aspect in the
past because of the major roles which metaphor and literary and folk allusion play in creating the visual images
of the characters.[36] The use of such "indirect" means of
physical description serves a particular function: at the
same time that it suggests a non-human essence, it leaves
the character rooted in *byt*. The existence of the more
fantastic characters is rendered plausible by Peredonov's
insanity.

Possibly the most basic motif used in the delineation of the strange creatures of *The Petty Demon* is that
of the mask. It is implicit in their dual natures: in
most cases, a human identity veils a perhaps truer identity within a demonology. It is significant that the idea
of the mask was basic to Sologub's conception of art. He
believed that the purpose of art is to remove appearances
--masks (*lichiny*) and to reveal the true Countenance of
things (*Lik*).[37] In *The Petty Demon* the tension between
appearances and reality is obvious not only in the depictions of the individual characters, but in the presentation of the cosmos as a whole.

The Cosmos

The aggregate of dual-natured creatures in *The Petty
Demon* presents a picture of an utterly bizarre society,
and the physical environment in which these strange characters are placed intensifies this impression. A few of
the more important places of action in the novel might be
noted: Peredonov's stifling, dirty apartment and Grushina's dusty house; the unpaved dusty and muddy streets
of a provincial town; Vershina's lush, enchanged garden;
a billiard hall filled with smoke; the pleasant home of

the Rutilov girls; a splendidly colorful seventeenth-cen-
tury Russian church. These settings are too lush and too
disparate to be characteristic of a normal, drab Russian
provincial town. Rather, this is typical scenery for the
grotesque. The visual world of people and places which
emerges is an amalgamation of the ugly and the beautiful,
the everyday and the exotic, the vulgar and the supernatural.

     The activities of the town as a whole are significant
in suggesting the true nature of the cosmos. Scandalmongering is a basic preoccupation of this society, and
it is also a sign of *poshlost'* and spitefulness. Rumor
has it that Veriga wears a corset; Grushina and Rutilov
taunt Peredonov with stories that his students drink,
smoke, and chase girls; Peredonov's visits to the town
functionaries are prompted by fear of scandal, and the
content of the conversations during these visits is largely
gossip. Probably the most significant rumors in the novel
are those concerned with Sasha. He is introduced through
a story that he is a girl. This rumor prompts Peredonov
to visit Sasha and then to report the scandal to the headmaster and to spread the story throughout the *gimnaziia*.
Liudmila, who is loved in the town for her charming, lively
way of relating gossip, hears this rumor, and, curious, she
goes to visit Sasha. Preposterous as it may seem, this
rumor contains a glimmer of truth: Sasha's characterization
turns on the suggestion that he has the ability to change
himself into a girl. Later in the novel, Peredonov spreads
a rumor that Sasha has been perverted by Liudmila. Grushina and Varvara write letters of this to the headmaster,
and he, upset, resolves to investigate the truth of the
situation. Liudmila, however, enchants him into believing
an outright lie--that her relationships with Sasha is perfectly innocent. Although Peredonov is telling the truth,
he is vulgar, coarse, and obviously insane; Liudmila is
believed because she is attractive, sweet-smelling, and
well dressed. Rumor thus serves as a means of confusing
appearance and reality. Moreover, in the strange world of
the novel, the most unbelievable tales seem to contain a
hint of truth.

     Although a sense of stagnation and inertia pervades
the atmosphere of *The Petty Demon*, the pace of the action
is frenzied. Much of the hustle and bustle is centered
around getting people married. Most obvious are the attempts to catch Peredonov, but, in addition to this,
Peredonov hopes to find Volodin a wife, and Grushina and

Vershina are looking for husbands. The desire to marry is
not prompted by any feeling between the couple involved,
but by an apparently rootless conviction that one simply
should be married. Many petty abuses are connected with
the business of marriage: Volodin is persuaded to have
Marta's gates tarred because he was rejected as her fi-
ance; Vershina tells Peredonov of the forgery largely because her plan to marry him to Marta failed; Grushina arranges for litter to be thrown into the carriage of the
newly-wed Peredonovs. Marriage is, of course, a legitimate
human concern, and, moreover, the wedding ceremony serves
as an excellent reflection of a society's customs--an embodiment of *byt*. Yet, within folk superstition, weddings
are among the most basic activities of witches and de-
mons.[38]   It is probable that in the world of the novel,
byt is a sham, and the rage to marry is in reality devilry.
     The question of motivation is important. The sense of
motion out-of-control conveyed by rumor and the instinc-
tiveness of the desire to marry are indications that reflective, rational behavior is somehow absent from the
cosmos of the novel. Yet, at least an appearance of
cause-and-effect motivation can be found in *The Petty Demon*. At the outset, the basic intrigue unfolds as a conflict between Peredonov's quest for a promotion and the
attempts of various townspeople to marry him. Such events
as Peredonov's visits to the town functionaries, his attempts to find Volodin a wife, his frequent attendance in
church, as well as Varvara's arranging for the forgery of
the letters, and Vershina's maneuvers to get Peredonov
into her garden all fit into the development of this intrigue and are thus provided with a seemingly clear motivation. It is true that these events are at times accompanied by other, seemingly unmotivated acts such as
Peredonov's molesting his cat, teasing his students, and,
especially, malicious town gossip--all of which seem to
originate in pure spite. But, at least for the first
part of the novel, this secondary strain is subordinate
to and integrated within the mainline development of
Peredonov's quest and the attempts to marry him. It is
possible to say that the image of the cosmos which emerges
in this part of the novel is one in which there exists a
certain logic to human behavior.
     However, about the time of the appearance of the
nedotykomka, the uninterrupted, sequential development of
this intrigue is broken, and many small episodes having
very little to do with Peredonov's quest for a promotion

or the attempts to marry him are introduced. Just prior
to the spirit's appearance an incident in which Peredonov
steals a pound of raisins and blames it on his servant is
related; Sasha is introduced and Peredonov visits his
lodgings. Just after the *nedotykomka*'s appearance the
narration shifts to the story of the tarring of Marta's
gates and then to Peredonov's meeting with the headmaster
of the *gimnaziia*. Now too the erotic affair between Sasha
and Liudmila gets underway. In a word, the narration becomes fragmented, and events are neither a development of
the main intrigue nor are they provided a clear motivation. The rational ordering of the world of *The Petty
Demon* is revealed as an illusion; chaos, within which
the *nedotykomka* has its existence, replaces cosmos.

The motif of insanity, which often accompanies the
presentation of the grotesque, plays a significant role
in *The Petty Demon*. Peredonov suffers from paranoid
schizophrenia, and his affliction is portrayed with a
clinical accuracy. He lives in suspicion and fear of
both people and objects, and his most specific fear is
that he will be poisoned. In taking measures to defend
himself, Peredonov displays an amazing degree of activity.
Serious aberrations in conceptual thinking are evident in
Peredonov's portrayal, and these are perhaps best reflected
in his language: words are lost as a means of exchanging
ideas. Rather, they are a means of abusing and fulfilling
bodily needs; eventually words take on a literalness and
acquire magical properties. Medically speaking, the central event in Peredonov's insanity is the appearance of
the *nedotykomka*; this signals the point at which he enters
into a fantasy world and begins to have hallucinations.[39]
The accuracy of Sologub's depiction of paranoia caused one
of his contemporaries to cite the novel as an example of
new, psychological rather than sociological, realism.[40]
However, it seems that, like *byt* and motivation, psychological verisimilitude is another mask of the novel. It
provides a protective veil and an acceptable explanation
for preposterous behavior and fantasy creatures. This is
most strongly suggested by the objectivity of the *nedotykomka*: the spirit is to be understood as a fact of the
world of the novel and a creature which transcends
Peredonov's consciousness—and not as a projection of his
fantasy. The indication is that Peredonov's insanity
grants him a vision of the truth that the world is chaotic,
hostile, destructive, and hence evil.

The true face of the cosmos of *The Petty Demon* is

revealed at the masquerade. Most of the weird creatures
whom the reader has met one by one in the course of the
novel are now gathered together under one roof. The masquerade includes the motif of insanity in two ways: it
suggests that the entire town is insane, more like a mad-
house than provincial Russia, and it removes the protective veil of "insanity" from what Peredonov perceives and
reveals that his vision of the cosmos is accurate. A conflict of appearance and reality is evident in the very
announcement of the masquerade. Rumors circulate that the
prizes will be a cow for the best female costume and a
bicycle for the best male costume. But, as soon as the
townspeople have become enthusiastic about the prizes, it
is discovered that in reality only a fan and an album
will be given. Even so, almost the entire town turns
out for the event. The possible gaiety and festivity of
the occasion is dampened from the beginning by the knowledge that the hall seems a little dirty and the crowd is
already slightly drunk: *poshlost'* has invaded the realm
of the exotic.

Some of the costumes should be noted. Varvara does
not labor over hers; she wears a mask with a stupid face,
rouges her elbows, puts on an apron, and goes as a cook
"straight from the stove" (347). This slovenly outfit is
similar to her usual dress; she thus goes as herself,
though slightly costumed. Grushina chooses to dress as
the goddess Diana. Her costume is immodest, but it has
many folds in which she can hide the sweets she steals for
her children. The scantiness of this costume reveals that
she has flea bites on her body. She is her vulgar, inde-
cent self, and, significantly, her costume is interpre-
tated not as Diana the goddess, but as Dianka, the dog.
The Rutilov girls do not fuss over their costumes: Dar'ia
goes as a Turkish woman, Liudmila as a gypsy, and Valeriia
as a Spanish dancer. They dress exotically, but not out-
landishly, and in this sense, they too are themselves.
Sasha, of course, goes as a geisha, and the import of this
costume is that it plays on the ambiguous status of his
sex.

Neither Volodin nor Peredonov wears a costume. Volodin displays his ram-like, bestial nature by stomping
wildly and by tearing ferociously at Sasha when the crowd
attacks him. Peredonov has no need of a costume; he has
achieved an inverted sort of integration in his devotion
to petty, spiteful evil, and in him mask and face are one.
It is at the masquerade that the *nedotykomka* too is finally

attired in its true garb: the evil serpent.

In all individual instances the costumes worn (or not
worn) tend to reveal the identity of the character rather
than to hide it. This is also true of the crowd as a
whole: it is drunk, vulgar, spiteful, and bestial. This
bestiality, to the point of mania, is revealed especially
in a savage attack on Sasha after he receives the prize
for the best female costume:

> The geisha rushed towards the doors, but
> they would not let her through. Malicious
> shouts were heard in the excited crowd around
> her:
> "Make her take off her mask!"
> "Off with the mask!"
> "Catch her! Hold her!"
> "Tear it off her!"
> "Take away her fan!". . .
> The geisha fought back desperately. A wild
> brawl began. They smashed the fan, tore it
> up, threw it on the floor, and trampled it.
> The crowd with the geisha at its center
> tossed violently about the hall, sweeping on-
> lookers from their feet. Neither the Rutilovs
> nor the stewards could get to the geisha.
> The geisha, nimble and strong, screamed pierc-
> ingly, scratched, and bit. She firmly held
> her mask on, now with her right, now with her
> left hand. (362)

After Sasha had been carried out of the hall, the
final event in the revelation of the true nature of the
town occurs. Peredonov, prompted by the *nedotykomka* in
the form of a serpent, sets fire to the clubhouse. The
townsfolk have gathered together, their bestial and
demonic natures have been revealed, and, with Peredonov's
arson, the suspicion that this is an inferno becomes a
visual reality. The masquerade is now vested in its mask
--fire, which is really its face.

The world of *The Petty Demon* is visually close to
that of Bosch's hell and Bruegel's proverbs. It is a
world in which petty, spiteful evil pervades the atmosphere
and swallows up the characters. The *nedotykomka* is the
ruler of this world, and Peredonov is the spirit's faithful servant. But, he is only the first of many lesser
servants, for the entire cosmos of the novel is populated

with petty, spiteful beasts, witches, and devils. The
artistic means through which *poshlost'* and the demonic
are integrated in these creatures is the grotesque.

In *The Petty Demon* one can see a continuation of the
tradition in Russian literature which perceives evil as
petty; Peredonov may legitimately be considered a relative of both Chichikov and Smerdiakov. It is also possible to see in the novel an inversion of attempts in
Russian and world literature to depict the totally good
man. In this sense, a recent critic's understanding of
Peredonov a fin de siecle redoing of Don Quixote is justified.[41] But, there is no reason why this comparison
cannot be extended to include other saintly figures.
Peredonov's can also be understood as an inversion of
Dostoevskii's Myshkin. Sologub seems to be attempting to
depict the totally evil man and the totally evil society.
In the final analysis, it may be possible to understand
the novel as a reversal of the Christian myth of redemption in which Peredonov is an inversion of Sologub's conception of Christ.

The Pennsylvania State University
University Park, Pennsylvania

NOTES

[1]D. S. Mirsky, *A History of Russian Literature*, New
York: Alfred A. Knopf, 1960, p. 444.

[2]Respectively, Petr Kogan, *Ocherki po istorii noveishei
russkoi literatury*, Moskva: 1911, Vol. III, pp. 105-08, and
B. V. Mikhailovskii, *Russkaia literatura XX veka*, Moskva:
1939, p. 284.

[3]Respectively, Iurii M. Steklov, "O tvorchestve
Fedora Sologuba," *Literaturnyi raopad*, Vol. TT, S. Peterburg: 1909, p. 165; A. E. Red'ko, "Fedor Sologub v bytovykh
proizvedeniiakh i v tvorimykh legendakh," *Russkoe bogat-
stvo*, Vol. II, no. 2 (1909), p. 81; and Andrei Belyi,
"Dalai-lama iz Sapozhka," *Vesy*, No. III (1908), p. 63.

[4]Respectively, Victor Erlich, *Gogol*, New Haven: Yale
Univ. Press, 1962, p. 5, and Lee Byron Jennings, *The
Ludicrous Demon: Aspects of the grotesque in German Post-
Romantic Prose*, Berkeley and Los Angeles: Univ. of Cali-
fornia Press, 1963, p. 17. In general, Jennings very
closely approximateswhat this study understands as the
definition of the grotesque.

[5]Jennings (*The Ludicrous Demon. . . ,*p. 10) says that
the grotesque object is perceived as simultaneously ludicrous and fearsome.

[6]Wolfgang Kayser, *The Grotesque in Art and Literature*, New York: McGraw Hill, 1963, pp. 32-33, 181, suggests that the grotesque effect in Bosch may be weakened because his paintings seem to contain a symbology that is decipherable within the usual Christian framework. Kayser postulates a vision of cosmic absurdity as a condition for the grotesque.

[7]Jennings, *The Ludicrous Demon*, p. 20.

[8]Ludmila Foster defines the literary grotesque totally in terms of a style which "employs the devices of distortion and shift to create an effect of absurdity or estrangement," "The Grotesque: A Method of Analysis," *Zagadnienia rodzajów literackich*, Vol. IX, no. 1, Lódź, 1966, p. 81. She also suggests that in *The Petty Demon* the grotesque effect is weakened by the absence of this style. "A Configuration of the Non-Absolute: The Structure and Nature of the Grotesque," *Zagadnienia rodzajów literackich*, Vol. IX, no. 2, Lódź, 1967, p. 39.

[9]Galina Selegen', *Prakhitraia viaz'*, Washington: Victor Kamkin, 1968, p. 139.

[10]A. A. Izmailov, "F. Sologub o svoikh proizvedeniiakh," *Birzhevye vedomosti* (Oct. 16, 1906), p. 3. B. Iu. Ulanovskaia maintains that the model for Peredonov was a certain Ivan Ivanovich Strakhov who taught with Sologub in the Velikie Luki district in the late 1880's. Ulanovskaia also appears to have located prototypes for Varvara and Volodin, "O prototipakh romana F. Sologuba *Melkii bes*," *Russkaia literatura*, Vol. XII, no. 3, 1969, pp. 181-84.

[11]F. K. Sologub, *Melkii bes*, in *Sobranie sochinenii*, Vol. VI, S. Peterburg: Shipovnik, 1909-14. All subsequent quotations from *The Petty Demon* will be from this edition and will be indicated by page number in the text.

[12]A. E. Red'ko, "Fedor Sologub. . .," p. 78, makes much of this pun. He suggests that in the long history of the pun on "piatachek" this is the first time the element of horror has been added.

[13]S. V. Maksimov, *Nechistaia sila--Nevedomaia sila*, in *Sobranie sochinenii*, Vol. XVIII, S. Peterburg: Prosveshchenie, 1908-13, p. 11.

[14]Ibid., p. 12.

[15]Ibid., p. 8.

[16]Selegen, *Prekhitraia viaz*, pp. 147-76, discusses the language of *The Petty Demon* at length.

[17]This alludes to and parodies the well-known passage in which Dostoeviskii's underground man defies the

laws of logic and mathematics. *Polnoe sobranie sochinenii*, 6th ed., Vol. III, S. Peterburg, 1904, pp. 322-23.

[18]Vladimir I. Dal', *Tolkovyi slovar' zhivogo veliko-russkogo iazyka*, Vol. IV, S. Peterburg, Moskva, 1914, p. 1380. The word *chur* indicates a limit. In a charm it perhaps signifies a line beyond which evil spirits cannot cross.

[19]A. P. Chekhov, *Polnoe sobranie sochinenni i pisem*, Moskva: Gos. Izd. Khudozh. Lit., 1944, Vol. IX, pp. 253-57.

[20]The names "Vershina" and "Grushina" are interesting. The word "vershina" denotes a "summit" and the phonetically similar verb "vershit'" is commonly used in the sense of "to sway destiny" (*vershit' sud'bami*). Her name thus suggests that she may be the major witch of the novel, and it points to the influence which she has on Peredonov's destiny. Grushina's name is from the Russian word for pear, and it adds a comic touch to her delineation.

[21]A. S. Pushkin, *Polnoe sobranie sochinenni v desiati tomakh*, Vol. IV, Moskva: AN SSSR, 1963, p. 429.

[22]Dal', *Tolkovyi slovar'*, Vol. III, p. 1744.

[23]The word "oboroten'" is not an exact equivalent of the English "werewolf." Rather, it has a broader meaning and signifies a creature that has the ability to change from a human nature into an animal or plant nature at will. See Maximov, *Nechistaia sila*, p. 118.

[24]Maximov lists reports of similar punning on the part of *rusalki*, *Nechistaia sila*, p. 118.

[25]See, for example, Sologub, "Belaia sobaka," *Sob. soch.*, Vol. VII, pp. 11-18.

[26]Pushkin, *Polnoe sobranie*. . ., Vol. VI, pp. 319-56.

[27]Ibid., p. 341.

[28]Ibid., p. 355.

[29]Mikhail Bakhtin maintains that the mouth is most significant in creating a grotesque image of the body, *Rabelais and His World*, Cambridge: M.I.T. Press, 1968, p. 316.

[30]Sologub, "Nedotykomka seraia. . .," *Sob. soch.*, Vol. V, p. 14.

[31]Wayne C. Booth, *The Rhetoric of Fiction*, Chicago: University of Chicago Press, 1968, pp. 169-209.

[32]Ronald J. Lethcoe, "Narrated Speech and Consciousness," Unpublished dissertation, University of Wisconsin, 1969.

[33]Maksimov, *Nechistaia sila*, . . ., p. 8.

[34]F. D. Reeve, *The Russian Novel*, New York, 1966, p. 315.

[35] Anon., *Orthodox Spirituality*, London: S.P.C.K., 1968, pp. 96-97.

[36] Selegen' has a good discussion of the role of color in characterization, *Prekhitraia viaz'*, pp. 136-40.

[37] Sologub, "Edinyi put' L'va Tolstogo," *Sob. soch.*, Vol. X, p. 196.

[38] Maksimov, *Nechistaia sila*, . . ., p. 8.

[39] Sologub's depiction of paranoia is in accord with the following: Sigmund Freud, "On the Mechanism of Paranoia," *General Psychological Theory*, New York, 1963, pp. 29-49; Carl G. Jung, *The Psychogenesis of Mental Disease* in *The Collected Works of C. G. Jung*, Vol. III, New York, 1960; and Jacob Kasanin, ed., *Language and Thought in Schizophrenia*, New York, 1944.

[40] Kogan, *Ocherki* . . ., p. 106.

[41] Andrew Field, "Translator's Preface," in F. Sologub, *The Petty Demon*, Bloomington: Indiana University Press, 1970.

THE BIRTH OF MODERN RUSSIAN DRAMA

George Kalbouss

Russian symbolism has been more than adequately credited with giving a rebirth to Russian poetry. Few persons
are aware, however, that the symbolists also contributed
to the birth of a modern Russian drama and that their
theories in drama existed far in advance of those of western theoreticians. This paper attempts to chronicle the
very first attempts of the symbolists to establish a new
drama in Russia, in the period 1890–1917.

The Symbolists were very much aware of the fact that
a new drama was evolving in western Europe and that its
philosophical premises closely paralleled their own. The
credit for bringing this theater to the attention of the
Russians belongs particularly to Dmitri Merezhkovsky and
Nikolai Minsky (Vilenkin) who, together with several other
literary critics, began to question the aesthetic values
of the 19th century Russian theater which stressed a star-
system and pseudo-realistic dramaturgy.[1] D.D.K., writing
in the progressive *Severny vestnik* (*Northern Messenger*),
in 1894 wrote:

> Our poor native Russian theater during the
> last few years has witnessed quite a few [stag-
> ing] attempts. Just about every year people
> undertake to uplift its artistic level. Trying
> something to this end are literary-dramatists,
> venerated actors, and theater buffs "who know
> the stage"--but with no results.

> Let us hope that the Russian theater may
> have a better fate in the future. May the
> [young] at least inhale the aroma of artistic
> truth from the stage, and may [future attempts
> at drama] not be formed from the same cliches
> whose lack of meaning is very obvious.[2]

D.D.K. and similar critics continue their attacks on the
status quo of theater throughout the 1890s. In the subsequent issue of *Northern Messenger* D.D.K. reviewed four
plays with titles typical of what was found in the indi-
ces of the journals of the time: Karpov's *Rai zemnoi*

(Heaven on Earth), Aleksandrov's *Sporny vopros* (A Point of
Disagreement), V. Krylov's and V. Velichko's *Pervaya mukha*
(The First Fly), and Suvorin's *On v otstavke* (He's Retired).
   The complaints of these few critics first found support by Konstantin Stanislavsky who through his bold staging methods and new acting techniques seriously challenged
the values of the old star-system and traditional acting
conventions. Stanislavsky thus should be credited with
creating a climate which would freely consider a theater of
symbolism. Moreover, Stanislavsky who is now much better
known for his realistic productions was initially interested in also staging in a theater of symbolists in what he
termed "the fantastic."[3] In *My Life in Art*, he recalls:

> The fantastic on the stage is an old pas-
> sion of mine. If there is beautiful fantasy
> in a play, I confess that I am ready to pro-
> duce it for the sake of the fantasy.[4]

   In the 1890s a few of such "fantastic" productions
included Hauptmann's *The Assumption of Hannele* (1896) and
The Sunken Bell (1898). When he realized that he was
overextended in his production of realistic plays and that
he could not devote enough time to non-realistic drama, he
then created a separate studio in the 1900s, his *Teatr-
studiya* (Theater Studio) for experimentation with stage
symbolism, and this studio played a significant part in
the development of Meyerhold's career. He brought both
Gordon Craig and Isadora Duncan to Russia, and his commitment to symbolist drama may be testified by the fact that
he made Maeterlinck's *Blue Bird* his theater's tenth anni-
versary performance. Contemporaneous with Stanislavsky, a
number of dramas written in the "new" style, both Russian
and western European, began to appear in the *Northern Messenger* and the newly-created theatrical journal *Artist*.
   The critic Ivan Ivanov can be credited with introducing Maeterlinck to the Russians. Ivanov's critical theories stand very close to the world-view posited by the
first Russian symbolists: that the universe is dual in
nature, that the "real" world is actually a reflection of
another "ideal" world and that existence is at best illusion. In his article on *Midsummer Night's Dream* in 1889,
Ivanov interpreted the play as an allegory which related
phenomenal existence to a reality available only to the
very gifted. A poet was needed to discover the essence
of reality, and this need was to become one of the most
important themes in Russian symbolist playwriting:

But not all mortals are given the power to
ascend to the world of ideas, far from it!
People languish in a deep cellar often for all
of their lives. Above them shines the sun of
truth, the world of ideas glistens, but the
people cannot see this world. . . . Yet at
least the chosen are brought out of this world
of illusions by a godly power and by means of
stubborn thought and long-suffering experience
they are brought into the kingdom of ideas.
. . .[5]

In 1892, writing in the journal *Mir Bozhy* (God's
World), Ivanov echoed Nietzsche, with whose *Birth of Tragedy* he was no doubt familiar, and called for a theater to
"awaken the mind and give joy to the senses,"[6] a theater
which would look for its sources to the Dionysian and medieval mystery plays rather than to the realistic drama.
    The first original plays written in Russian in this
new spirit were by Merezhkovsky and Minsky. These overly
wordy works are strongly dependent on the new European and
represent the first significant departure from the *byt*-
play and the one-act anecdote-play in the 1890s.
    Ten years earlier, in 1880, Minsky had written a short
mystery-play" in rhymed verse, *Solntse* (The Sun), the plot
of which concerns a debate about the place of good and
evil in God's act of creation. The play is a closet drama
deriving its only dynamism from the dialogue. The language is in the traditional high style.

Один из демонов: Тебе ль, Господь, родник твори-
                                    мых сил,
                Тебе ль просить у разума совета?
                Ты разума мудрее, ты силен,
                Ты поразил Хаос рукой могучей..[7]

    (One of the Demons: Is it for Thee, O Lord, the
                        source of creative powers
                        Is it for Thee to ask advice
                        of reason?
                        Thou art wiser than reason,
                        thou art mighty
                        Thou hast triumphed over Chaos
                        with a mighty hand).

    The religious and mystical mystery-play overtones of
The Sun already capture much of the spirit of later symbolist drama. The play presents an admixture of a concern for

the eternal and a flavoring of mysticism in which the traditionally religious and the poetic are intertwined by
means of highly stylized and intentionally artificial dialogue. Minsky's second play, *Osada Tulchina* (The Siege of
Tulchin), in blank verse, dramatizes the persecution of the
Jews under Bogdan Khmelnitsky and while containing little
to commend itself as a symbolic drama, nevertheless is the
first in a number of historical dramas written by the symbolists.[8]

Merezhkovsky wrote his first drama, *Vozvraschenie k
prirode* (Return to Nature) in 1887.[9] Using the premise of
Calderon's *Life is a Dream*, that the world is merely an illusion of consciousness and that nothing is real, the play
fits well into the Symbolist world-view. The lines of
Silvio, the play's main character, anticipate a number of
yet-to-be-written poems of Russian symbolism:

> Быть может призраки -- и леса
> И звезд таинственные хоры --
> Весь мир -- создание мечты
> И все величие вселенной
> Над вечной бездной пустоты
> Лишь отблеск радуги мгновенной...[10]

(Perhaps the woods and mysterious
Choirs of stars are illusions,
The world is the creation of dreams,
And vastness of the universe which is suspended
Over the abyss of eternal emptiness
Is but the reflection of a momentary rainbow.)

This drama also contains many of the essential episodes and relationships between characters which were later
to appear in other plays. The play presents the basic symbolist concept of reality, that of the existence of two
separate worlds, with man standing on the one troubled with
suffering, evil, and discord and reaching somewhat futilely
for the other. This concept is framed in a legend with its
overtones of mystery. As with Minsky's play *The Sun*, the
verse dialogue is written in an elevated, bookish tone.

Western writers have always provided inspiration to
the Russians and Merezhkovsky looks to a number of them for
a justification of the symbolist world-view in drama. In
order to discover the symbolic within the real, one must,
first of all, turn away from the realistic traditions of
19th century drama and look to earlier periods. In an
article on Calderon, Merezhkovsky writes:

No nineteenth-century writer had either ex-
ceeded or even equalled either the Greek trage-
dians or the English and Spanish playwrights of
the XVI and XVII centuries in depicting great
passions or the tragic will. . . .[11]

To Merezhkovsky, the strength of Calderon's, Shakespeare's and Aeschylus's drama, lies in the ability of
their main characters to involve the audience in a kind of
transformational elation (*vostorg*), which would arouse
within the spectators a "capacity to desire" (*umet'
zhelat'*), an idea later posited by Artaud and many other
more recent dramatists.

It is thus logical to Merezhkovsky that Calderon's
dramas as well as those of the Greeks have religious foundations, and that they employ many liturgical conventions
and devices. Religious rituals provide dramatists with a
wealth of readily available and easily understood word and
picture symbols which transcend reality. Thus, to them
early drama is richer than that of the 19th century. Symbols and not realistic situations created the bond between
spectator and actor:

> Symbols--these are the philosophical and
> artistic language of Catholicism. The deepest
> mysteries of religion were opened to the be-
> lievers through symbols. Almost all of the
> liturgy consists of them, they adorn churches
> and are used as the materials for religious
> art. Calderon's mystery [*Bowing to the Cross*]
> has not yet separated itself from religion and
> has taken on the symbolic language of Catholi-
> cism, the same way Greek tragedy has taken on
> the language of mythology from the cult of poly-
> theism.[12]

Merezhkovsky does not take the final step, however,
and suggest that contemporary mystery-plays with contem-
pory and understood symbols replace the medieval ones--as
did Bely and Bryusov later; nevertheless he strongly advocates the use of symbols in drama as well as the importance of writers such as Calderon whose world now "anticipates our contemporary philosophical inclinations."

In 1892, Merezhkovsky published his first of many
translations of the classics, Aeschylus' *Prometheus Bound*.
Also, following Minsky's example of *The Sun*, he wrote a
brief Christian mystery, *Khristos i dusha chelovecheskaya*
(Christ and Man's Soul), based upon a play by the medieval

Italian playwright, Giacapone da Todi. The drama's theme
is again that of the dual worlds, with the soul of man desiring to escape from the suffering of reality and enter
into the serenity of heaven. The only means of escape is
through Death. The Image of Death-the Consoler, Death-the-
Redeemer was to become widespread in much of Russian symbolism. The proof of the beneficence of Death is, of
course, seen in Death's link to Love in the Story of Christ,
particularly in the works of Gippius and Sologub. The
play's last lines are:

Душа: Я плакать буду вечно
        За мир Он пролил кровь,
        Любил так бесконечно
        И умер за любовь!
        В любви -- какая сила!
        Любовь, о для чего
        Безумная, убила
        Ты Бога моего?[13]

(Soul: I will cry eternally
        He shed his blood for the world,
        He loved it so endlessly,
        And died for his love!. . .
        There is such power in love! . . .
        O love, why did you,
        O mad one, kill
        My God?)

    Merezhkovsky and Minsky were developing their first
ideas on symbolic drama at a time when Henrik Ibsen's popularity was gaining both with the reading and the theater-
going public. By 1883, his *Doll's House* had already been
translated into Russian under the title of *Nora*[14] and had
proved to be extremely popular with the readers. In 1891
two more of his dramas were published in Russian, *Doktor
Shtokman* (Enemy of the People) and *Ellida* (Woman from the
Sea).[15] The significance of Ibsen at this time cannot be
underrated; both the practitioners of theatrical realism
and the new symbolists found his plays illustrative of
their positions. In dramas such as *Shtokmann* and *Ellida* one
could find both *byt* and transcendent thought, both dramatic events and symbolic relationships. Ibsen's influence
remained extremely strong on the Russian symbolists, particularly from his more realistic plays, and both Merezhkovsky and Minsky saw Ibsen as the significant force in
the creation of a new drama.

The year following the publication of *Shtokman* and
Ellida, Minsky wrote a series of articles, "Genrikh Ibsen
i ego p'esy iz sovremennoi zhizni" ("Henrik Ibsen and his
plays drawn from contemporary life") which later became a
book. To Minsky, Ibsen was able to view reality in many
new and exciting ways:

> Such an author must have seen his duty not
> only in producing strong impressions but also
> in creating according to non-realistic tech-
> niques. [16]

Ibsen is not an imitator of reality but its interpreter; out of mundane, everyday situations he is able to evoke
the universal problems of man. *Enemy of the People* is an
excellent example of such mastery because the play depicts
a microcosm of all mankind in a small Norwegian town.
Rather than begin with a real person, Minsky states ap-
provingly, Doctor Stockmann is "a function, a mathematical
entity, a possibility."[17]   Ibsen then imposes the reality
of small-town Norway onto the abstraction and thus we see
the ideal and the real structure of the dramatic conflict
of the play. The conflict of the ideal on the plane of
the real was to form the basis for a large number of later
symbolist dramas.

Ibsen was attractive to Minsky and Merezhkovsky also
because his plays assert the individuality of women. [18]
Minsky lauded Ibsen's efforts to assert the independence,
moral integrity and humanity of women, and welcomes him
to the group of Russian writers, notably Tolstoy and
Dostoevsky who, as far as Minsky was concerned, had already long accepted the fact that a woman was as much an
individual entity as a man. Minsky's admiration for Ib
sen's women is reflected through his own Nora heroine in
the play *Al'ma* in 1900; other Noras were soon to appear in
the plays of Merezhkovsky, Sologub, Gippius and Chulkov.

Ibsen was also enthusiastically received by A.
Volynsky, the editor of *Northern Messenger*. In a lengthy
study of Ibsen's recently translated play *Master Builder*
(Stroitel' Sol'ness) in 1893, Volynsky proclaimed the play
as one of "genius in terms of idea and completely outstanding in technique."[19]   As with Merezhkovsky and Minsky,
Volynsky saw Ibsen as a writer able to reveal a hidden
world out of the everyday.

> After the drama's heroine's final speeches,
> the reader's thoughts soar somewhere far away,
> to the clouds, liberated from the anguish of

ordinary existence; they are joyously carried
away to the radiant poetic vision created by
the remarkable artist's powers.[20]

Symbols unite the two worlds, plot with character,
thought with action:

> . . . the entire story relies upon poetic
> allegory, symbolistic allusions, on pyscho-
> logical and philosophical ideas hidden beneath
> the external happenings of the drama. . . .[21]

Merezhkovsky's first play in a contemporary setting
Groza proshla (The Storm Has Passed) is patterned directly
on *Doll's House*. Slightly embellished with a few images
popular in the "decadent" spirit of the new symbolist
poetry, the plot is nevertheless faithful to the Ibsen
play. Elena, the wife of a prominent publisher, Kalinovsky,
once obtained money to pay to save his health by committing
adultery with an artist, a fact which he does not discover
for many years. When he discovers the truth, his righte-
ousness is stronger than his love and he rejects Elena.
Later, he and Elena are reconciled. The "decadent" spirit
in *The Storm Has Passed* is seen in the themes of adultery
and death. Unlike Nora whose "crime" was at best a legal
misdemeanor, Elena obtains her money from the artist
Palitsyn with whom she committed adultery; i.e., she is
a *de facto* prostitute. Palitsyn, her erstwhile lover, in
turn, is a "decadent" of the new generation, seeing his
main life-relationship with Death; it is due to the fact
that both Palitsyn and Elena think about Death that they
are brought together as kindred souls:

> *Elena:* Death . . . Do you frequently think
> about it?
> *Palitsyn:* Sometimes I believe that it is all
> I think about, and nothing else.
> *Elena (lively):* Yes, yes . . . Isn't that the
> truth? I'm the same way. . .
> Only I don't tell anyone about
> it.
> *Palitsyn:* You don't need to, the others won't
> understand.[22]

The death-equals-beauty idea emerges when Palitsyn decides to concentrate on art rather than on death.

In the figure of Elena, Merezhkovsky also creates the
first emancipated woman whose image will be seen in many
forthcoming plays written by the symbolists. Elena is not

only a Nora, she also possesses some of the characteristics of Hedda Gabbler; she is as Nora the woman striving to free herself from the traditions of a male-dominated society, but as Hedda she is the woman concerned with the transcendent meaning of a life which always culminates in death. Even though she is reconciled with Kalinovsky, her true love remains the painter Palitsyn with whom she had intercourse in both the physical and intellectual sense.

Eliminating the stage devices of confidantes in *Doll's House*, Morezhkovsky concentrates the action on the triangle of Elena-Kalinovsky-Palitsyn. By doing this, however, Merezhkovsky is forced to abandon a number of possibilities for lively dialogue; by using a smaller number of characters the dialogue is less varied and the play is consequently less interesting. This was a weakness of Merezhkovsky's dramas in general.

Another weakness is the play's happy ending with the reconciliation between Elena and Kalinovsky who promise to rebuild their lives. The ending is not well motivated out of the incidents in the plot.

The significance of Merezhkovsky's play is that it represents the first of many which can be termed contemporary-symbolic, that is, presenting a transcendent message in a realistic setting. The story of a woman trying to liberate herself from her husband is on the primary level; on a deeper level the play discusses the meaning of life and life as it is in reality, and on a social level it touches on the transcedent questions of the meaning of death and beauty. Merezhkovsky merely presents the deeper themes, though, and does not fully explore them.

In much of Ibsen symbolism is hidden beneath the images of the every-day life. It was in the plays of Maurice Maeterlinck that the symbolists first found symbolism overtly presented. Maeterlinck's first works translated into Russian appeared in 1893, a poem without a title, and a tale, "Seven Princesses" (Sem' Printses); neither was accompanied with any explanation as to who the author was.[23]

In 1894, Maeterlinck's *L'Intruse* was published in *Artist* under the title of *Vtirushka*. In the same year this play was staged at the Moscow Okhotnichy klub (Moscow Hunting Club).[24]

The strength of Maeterlinck's dramas lay in the fact that they centered in a *taina* (mystery), which is the essence of religious theater:

The mystery--this is the true content of
art; the series of inexplicable feelings, the
mysterious echo of all of man's existence in
images, in sounds--this is the single goal of
the poet.[25]

Strindberg was introduced in Russia by *Grafinya Yuliya*
(Miss Julie), much to the displeasure of the more traditional critics. V. Cheshikhin, in his review of the play,
wrote:

. . . the works of the symbolists will not
arouse good, kind feelings in the spectator's
hearts; the symbolists are not concerned with
the intellectual and spiritual side of man.[26]

Nevertheless, others, including the venerated Boborykin, saw great value in Strindberg's works and called *Miss
Julie* one of the "brightest attempts at innovation on the
Scandinavian stage." At the same time, Boborykin urged
new Russian dramatists to remain faithful to the Russian
realistic stage tradition.[27] As with Ibsen, it was the
symbol-in-reality of Strindberg's works that appealed to
the symbolists.

In 1894 Merezhkovsky published the Symbolists' first
large treatise on dramatic theory, "Neo-romantizm v drame"
(Neo-romanticism in drama). In this work, Merezhkovsky
discusses the contributions of writers such as Ibsen,
Maeterlinck, Hauptmann, Beaubourg to the creation of a
new theater. At the same time, Merezhkovsky identified
three terms which later became the cornerstones of Russian
symbolist drama: *volya* (will), *taina* (mystery) and *skazka*
(fairy-tale). It was the presence of these three concepts
in the drama that rendered it as essential theater.

In his discussion on will, Merezhkovsky observes that
the plot of a drama is constructed inversely to that of a
novel. The characters in novels use their wills to determine their fates. Conversely, in the drama characters'
fates are determined at the beginning of the play, and the
characters' wills fight a losing battle. "The essence of
drama" he writes, "is the battle of a conscious will with
obstacles,"[28] as for instance, in Greek drama. Nineteenth-century realistic drama is thus an aberration, because its characters determine their own destinies; in
this respect, it is closer to the definition of a novel
than to the definition of theater. The new drama must

return to the classic tradition and present the human will
in conflict with mysterious outside forces such as Fate in
the Greek tragedies. But this is a new Fate, for the new
drama is more horrible than that of the ancients because
it is found internally, within the subjective self, rather
than externally, on some lofty Olympus:

> The objective of the new tragedy consists in
> portraying horror and the greatness of this *in-*
> *ternal fate* which every person carries in his
> heart from the day of his birth to his demise.
> . . . The tragedy of the future must bring
> something completely different, it must ex-
> plore the power of Fate. . . . The drama must
> . . . strive to penetrate into the very sources
> of any kind of suffering, any kind of evil,
> even if it lies beyond the boundaries of
> earthly reality.[29]

Unfortunately, Merezhkovsky states, this kind of dramatic creation has not yet been made in analyzing Maeterlinck, Merezhkovsky observes (as Maeterlinck had once
done) that the Belgian's plays are better read than seen.[30]
The *skazka* (fairy-tale) element in the new drama provides its enchantment and magical quality. To Merezhkovsky,
the best examples of *skazka* were found in the plays of
Gerhard Hauptmann. Merezhkovsky felt the best of Hauptmann
were his realistic plays, such as *The Weavers*. Nevertheless, Hauptmann also attempts to bring in folkloric,
ethereal and lyrical elements of his culture into many
of his plays. Thus Hauptmann's dramas are both realistic
and yet symbolic, through the use of certain folk elements.
The *taina* (mystery), of course, evolves out of the
fact that this internal fate is not fully comprehended.
The internal force becomes an "other" character in the
presentation, one whose presence is felt by characters
and spectators alike. This "other" character thus becomes
as present in the new drama as various Gods were in ancient liturgies.
In his summation, Merezhkovsky agrees with the western critics of neo-romantic drama that it is basically a
drama of rejection, the rejection of the bourgeois ethic
as well as the liberal ideas of the French revolution.
The lack of a positive philosophical idea in the new drama
is its inherent weakness and thus, as Merezhkovsky sees
it, prevents it from much future development.[31] Merezhkovsky's conclusion suggests a reason for the popularity of

the *realistic* Ibsen and the *realistic* Strindberg with the
early Symbolists. Merezhkovsky, while calling himself a
symbolist, was still too much a positivist to reject
wholesale the presentation of reality and strong characters and conflicts in the early works of the Scandina-
vians.

Besides the attempts of Minsky and Merezhkovsky, few
other symbolist dramas were written before 1900.
Barantsevich claims he wrote an allegory on "Everyman"
theme in 1895, which is very much similar to Andreyev's
Life of Man, but was published only in 1907.[32]   Boris
Glagolin claims to have advocated the theater of enchantment in 1897-8, in a journal of 30 copies entitled
Nastroenie (Mood), but complains that Bely and Bryusov
were receiving all the credit. However, we have only
their statements, their journals have completely disappeared.[33]   Only two dramas of the modernist typ? appeared
in print after 1897, both being "closet" drama:. P. Ryabov's *Dar Nochi* (Gift of Night) is an allegory presenting
a typical crisis of symbolism, namely, a husband (Asty),
and wife (Faina), are tired of life in the real world and
look for escape in the ideal world:

Астий: Мы заперты, прикованы!.. И только мысль,
       одна лишь мысль способна вылетать из
       круга... А этот круг -- земля -- со
       всем, что есть на ней, с морями, го-
       рами, со всем живущим.[34]

       (Asty: We're locked in, chained in!. . . Only
       thought is capable of lifting us out of
       this circle. . . . And this circle is the
       earth, with everything that exists in it,
       with seas, mountains, with everything
       living.)

Escape finally does come as the allegory of Night appears and takes the two away from the impending (and horrible) dawn.

Gift of Night is a typical example of the kind of
brief play which was to be written throughout the Silver
Age as a sort of contemporary poetic mystery play, in imitation of the works of the symbolists. It is perhaps one
or several of these plays that Chekhov satirizes in *The
Seagull*.

Minsky's next short play, *Kholodnye slova* (Cold Words)
presents a brief episode in which a modern poet is asked by

a family Man to tell his children a Christmas story. The
only story the Poet knows is one he had seen in a prophet-
ic dream, entitled, "Polyarnaya skazka" (Polar Tale) which
ends with the Tsar' Polyusa (King of the Pole), telling
the poet in a vision,

> ... Мои лобзания смертельны,
> Усни, остынь, забудь, прости![35]

(My kisses are deadly,
Sleep, become cool, foreget, forgive!)

The message is too deep for the Family Man who decides
that Christmas messages for children must be simple and
therefore shallower:

> Семянин: Вам нужды нет в моей указке
>   Но жаль, вас дети не поймут.[36]

(Family Man: You don't have what is necessary
            in my request
            Too bad; the children won't under-
            stand you.)

The conclusion anticipates that of many future symbolist
dramas: the poet is simply incapable of communciating his
vision to the layman.

In 1896 Minsky also published his second historical
play *Smert' Kaya Grakha* (The Death of Caius Gracchus)[37] in
a collection of his poetry.

Thus, primarily through the activities of Minsky and
Merezhkovsky, as well as those of their colleagues in the
Northern Messenger and *Artist,* the new western European
theater, with all of its symbolic and neo-romantic under-
currents, was exposed to the Russian theater enthusiast.
The dramas of Ibsen, Maeterlinck, Hauptmann and others
were interpreted in the light of how they modernized drama
and how they employed the symbolic. A new vocabulary of
drama terms was formed and an emphasis was placed on the
involvement and participation of the spectator in the en-
actment of the play.

In the ensuing decade, many of the conceptions formulated in the 1890s by Minsky and Merezhkovsky were to
become refined and expanded; nevertheless, much of the
credit for the establishment of the theoretical and actual
playwriting foundations for Russian symbolist drama belongs to these two authors.

The Ohio State University
Columbus, Ohio

NOTES

[1] V. Charsky, "Khudozhestvenny teatr," *Krizis teatra* (Moscow: Problemy iskusstva, 1908), 126-56. This article describes in greater detail the problems of the theater in the 1890s and discusses the meaning of Stanislavsky's reforms.

[2] D.D.K. "Teatr (Tekuschy repertuar)," *Severny vestnik*, 1894, No. 1 II, 71.

[3] Later in his life, the outspoken (against Stanislavsky) Evreinov fully recognized Stanislavsky's contributions in N. Evreinov, *Istoriya russkogo teatra* (New York: Chekhov, 1955), 311-361.

[4] Constantin Stanislavsky, *My Life in Art*, trans. J. J. Robbins (New York: Meridian, 1963), 40.

[5] Iv. Ivanov, "Son v letnyuyu noch," *Artist*, 1889, No. 1, 72.

[6] Iv. Ivanov, "Ideinaya kritika dramy i stseny," *Mir Bozhy*, 1892, part I, 1.

[7] N. Minsky, *Solntse, Vestnik Evropy*, 1880, No. 5, 236.

[8] Many of the other European symbolist playwrights also enjoyed the historical play format.

[9] D. Merezhkovsky, *Sil'vio (Vozvraschenie k prirode)*, *Severny vestnik*, 1890, No. 2, 69-90; No. 3, 68-81; No. 4, 45-69; No. 5, 57-75. Text quoted from Merezhkovsky, *Polnoe sobranie sochineny, XXIII, op. cit.*, 236.

[10] Ibid., 236. Calderon had already been introduced to the Russians earlier, and had been translated by Ostrovsky.

[11] D. Merezhkovsky, "Kalderon v svoei drame, "Poklonenie krestu," *Trud*, 1891, No. 24, p. 652.

[12] Eskhil, *Skovanny Prometey*, perevod. Dm. Merezhkovskogo, *Vestnik Evropy*, 1891, No. 1.

[13] Dm. Merezhkovsky, "Khristos i dusha chelovecheskaya," *Sbornik 'Nivy'*, 1892, No. 5, p. 16.

[14] G. Ibsen, *Nora*, perevod Veinberg (St. Petersburg, 1883).

[15] G. Ibsen, *Doktor Shtokman*, perevod N. Mirovich, *Artist*, 1891, No. 15, *Ellida*, perevod V. M. Spasskaya, *Artist*, No. 16.

[16] N. Minsky, "Genrikh Ibsen i ego p'esy iz sovremennoi zhizni," *Severny vestnik*, 1892, No. 9, 77.

[17] Ibid., 95.

[18] Ibid., 82.

[19] A. Volynsky, "Literaturnye zametki," *Severny vestnik*, 1893, No. 5, II, 110.

[20] Ibid.

[21] Ibid., 110-11.

[22] D. Merezhkovsky, *Groza proshla, Trud*, 1893 (Jan.),
122.

[23] M. Meterlink, "Stixotvorenie," per Ladyzhinsky, *Mir
bozhy*, 1893, No. 3, p. 33. "Sem'printses. Skazka," per
G. Z. *Severny vestnik*, 1893, No. 4, pp. 189-208.

[24] Meterlink, Vtirushka, per E. N. Kletnev, *Artist*,
1894, No. 28. "Okhotnichy klub. Vtirushka Meterlinka,"
Artist, 1894, No. 37, pp. 196-7. B. I. Rostotsky, "Moder-
izm v teatre," *Russkaya Khudozhestvennaya kul'tura kontsa
XIX - nachala XX veka*, I (Moscow: Nauka, 1968), p. 179.

[25] Ibid.

[26] V. Cheshikhin, "Dramy Strindberga," *Artist*, 1894,
No. 38. Strindberg was first introduced in an article ---,
"Dramaturg-khimik," *Mir bozhy*, 1893, No. 2, p. 252.

[27] A. Boborykin, "Literaturny teatr," *Artist*, 1894,
No. 34, 25.

[28] D. Merezhkovsky, "Neo-romantizm v drame," *Vestnik
inostrannoi literatury*, 1894, No. 11, 101.

[29] Ibid., p. 105.

[30] Ibid., p. 106.

[31] Ibid., pp. 119-120.

[32] Kaz. Barantsevich. "Iz Mraka," *Probuzhdenie*, 1907
(June 9), No. 28, pp. 428-31.

[33] Boris Glagolin, "Vs. Meierkhol'du," *Zhurnal Teatra
Literaturno-khudozhestvennogo obshchestva*, 1907-8, No. 3
and 4, 77.

[34] P. Ryabov, *Dar nochi. Teatral*, 1897, No. 30, 87.

[35] N. Minsky, *Kholodnye slova, Severny vestnik*, 1896,
No. 1, 7.

[36] Ibid., p. 7.

[37] N. Minsky, *Smert' Kaya Grakha* in *Stikhotvoreniya*,
izd. 3-e (St. Petersburg, 1896).

ALEXANDER GRIN'S *GRINLANDIA*

Nicholas J. L. Luker

I

"An utter exotic not only in Soviet literature but in
Russian literature as a whole"--so the American critic
Bernard Guerney has aptly described Alexander Grin.[1] Indeed, Grin (born Grinevsky in 1880), is one of the most
curious and intriguing figures of Russian letters. To
this day bizarre and colourful legends still surround his
name: that he did forced labour in Siberia for the brutal
murder of his first wife; that he consorted with revolutionary bomb-throwers, stunt-men, wrestlers and sword-
swallowers; and that he was a highly dangerous, sea-far-
ing desperado who had killed an English captain in the
Indian Ocean off Africa, had stolen his victim's sea-chest
full of manuscripts and that little by little he was publishing them as his own, translating them masterfully into
Russian while carefully concealing the fact that he knew
English. Grin's real biography only served to bolster such
eccentric rumours: youthful wanderings as a Gorkian *bosyak*
in the Crimea where he took on every conceivable casual
job, from stevedore to professional beggar; then revolutionary work in illegal propaganda for the Socialist Revolutionary Party which brought him first imprisonment and
then exile, first in Siberia and later in Archangel Province; there followed riotous times in the haunts of Petersburg's bohemia during the early years of the First World
War, when Grin gambled and drank in the company of the
foremost literati of the day, amongst them Andreyev,
Kuprin and Mirolyubov; next came service in the Red Army
and near-death from typhus in Petrograd after 1917; and
finally Grin's strange exodus to the south, his beloved
Crimea, where he severed most links with his friends and
acquaintances in the north, and where he spent the last
decade of his life, to die forgotten and unsung in the
summer of 1932. A colourful biography in anyone's book.
　　Looked upon during most of his writer's career as no
more than a gifted plagiarist of Western writers of adventure like Bret Harte, Mayne Reid and Fenimore Cooper (some
critics even styled him the "Russian Edgar Allan Poe"),

rarely admitted to the pages of the "thick" Russian journals during his lifetime, and in the late Stalin period
after his death vilified as a "rootless cosmopolitan" hostile to the Soviet regime, Alexander Grin is today one of
the most popular writers in the Soviet Union. Most editions of his works are collector's items, and when a volume of memoirs about him appeared in 1972,[2] fights broke
out in Moscow and Leningrad bookshops amongst Grino-
maniacs eager to secure the fast-disappearing copies for
themselves. Recent years have shown an extraordinary interest in Grin on the part of biographers and critics, in
the West as well as in the Soviet Union,[3] a phenomenon
which is a direct reversal of the position in the late
1940s and early 1950s, before Stalin's demise, when Grin
was officially proscribed in the press and his works removed from library shelves in Russia.

What this article aims to examine is only one element
of Grin's work, but one which is fundamental to an understanding and appreciation of him and which is largely responsible for the strange magic which his name holds for
so many Russian readers, young and old alike. That element is *Grinlandia*. Grin's imaginary, exotic setting of
Grinlandia is traditionally associated with his romantic
fiction, and it is this colourful sub-continent of his own
dreaming which, more than anything else, has helped to
create the curiously attractive yet elusive aura of "for-
eignness" around his name. A ghost which I wish to lay
here is that Grin himself gave the name *Grinlandia* to his
devised setting. Far from it: the term was first coined
by the critic Zelinsky in 1934,[4] two years after Grin's
death, and since then has become widely used.

II

Grin quite deliberately made it impossible to locate
his imagined country on the globe. Nevertheless, many
early commentators on his work were mystified and naively
tried to define its geographical position, believing it to
be no more than a skilfully masked representation of some
actual country. As the critic Frid wrote in 1926 in his
review of Grin's *sbornik The Gladiators*: "Almost always the
action takes place somewhere in the West--in a country
which sometimes resembles England or France, and sometimes
a forgotten republic of South America--but yet it takes
place in none of these countries."[5] If *Grinlandia* is to be
placed somewhere on the globe (and this certainly makes it

easier to visualise the location of his works), then the
best region would seem to be South-East Asia, southern
Indochina or northern Indonesia, perhaps. However, it must
be said that Grin's writing is almost totally devoid of any
definite Oriental flavour, and the inhabitants of *Grinlandia* are undeniably European. The only very approximate geographical co-ordinate we are given is the information that
the Grinlandian towns of Liss and Zurbagan are regular
ports of call for ships travelling between Europe and
Australia.[6]

A detailed examination of the way *Grinlandia* evolved
in its creator's mind over the years lies outside the scope
of this paper. Suffice it to say that that evolution was
gradual, and only towards the end of Grin's life in the
late 1920s did it become an elaborate sub-continent complete with its own towns, topography and indented coastline. While the setting of the early romantic tale *Reno
Island* (1909) is simply a tropical island set in a geographical vacuum—"there were no names for this world,"[7]
Grin notes—*The Lanfier Colony* which followed it in 1910
takes place more precisely on a peninsula, and although
the continent behind that peninsula is not specified by
Grin, the reader learns that "the [sea] route to Europe
lies some hundred miles further south."[8] In the much later
works, the novels *The Golden Chain*[9] of 1925 and *The Road
to Nowhere*[10] of 1930 (Grin's last completed novel), we
find a composite and detailed picture of a fully developed
Grinlandia with her own roads and railways, shops and
theatres, hotels and prisons.

Grinlandia has her own invented towns with their curious European-sounding names: Liss, Kasset, Zurbagan,
Dagon, Poket, San-Riol', Gel'-G'yu, Gerton, Takhenbak.
The action of each of Grin's six novels and of most of the
tales of his mature years is situated at an identifiable
point in this devised setting, either alongside or over-
lapping that of the others. Thus the novel *She Who Runs
on the Waves* (1928)[11] begins in Liss and takes us by sea
to Gel'-G'yu, *The Golden Chain* opens in Liss and closes
not far away, on Cape Garden, while *The Road to Nowhere*
unfolds in Poket and carries us to Liss before bringing
us back to Poket again at the close.

An odd thing about the actual development of *Grinlandia* as a setting is this: while many of Grin's early
realistic tales, such as *To Italy* (1906),[12] *The Third
Floor* (1908)[13] and *The Window in the Forest* (1909),[14] are
devoid of *precise* geographical location (though this may

usually be inferred as either Europe or Russia), some of
his first romantic stories written at the same time contain elements both of the real world and of the emergent
imaginary setting shown side by side, as if Grin were
evaluating each before deciding which to settle on. Finding himself alone in an unnamed tropical environment, the
sailor hero of *Reno Island* recalls both the society of men
so repellent to him in the actual world which he has just
left, and the dreary, dismal woods of his homeland, which
one can construe as Russia. In *The Lanfier Colony* the
hero's imagination takes him back "to the titanic cities
of the north,"[15] despite the fact that on his anonymous
peninsula he is now separated from that reality by "thousands of miles of distance."[16] The new, exotic environment
of South America for which Shil'derov, the hero of *The
Distant Journey* (1913),[17] prepares to quit his native provincial Russian town exists to begin with only in his
imagination, side by side with the oppressive reality of
his accustomed surroundings. This same curious duality of
real and unreal is evident in the opening paragraph of another tale, *The Hunting of Marbrun* (1915), where the narrator cries: "Moscow! Heart of Russia! I recalled your
golden cupolas, your crooked alleys, your black caps and
white aprons, as I sat in the railway carriage, speeding
towards Zurbagan!"[18] Very soon in this tale, however, we
see the exotic and the imaginary supersede the mundane and
the real, as the hero nears *Grinlandia*: "I recalled you,
Moscow, and immediately forgot you, for the landscape I
observed from the carriage window was exotic down to the
last stone; one had to learn this landscape just like the
mysterious script of the Orient!"[19]

Thus *Grinlandia* can, it seems, be reached by train, as
here (though characters very rarely enter the country by
rail), or by ship, the usual method of transport, as is
demonstrated by the many vessels which call at Liss and
Zurbagan *en route* from Europe to Australia and the South
Pacific. The escape of both heroes of Grin's first two
romantic tales, *Reno Island* and *The Lanfier Colony*, from
the real world into Grin's imagined one, is effected by
sea. By geographically linking in this way, albeit tenuously, his devised land with the actual world, Grin lends
to his *Grinlandia* a greater degree of verisimilitude.

Yet however imaginary *Grinlandia* and her towns, the
real world beyond her confines still preserves its identity, and most of Grin's mature works contain precise
references to specific geographical locations in the

actual world. The drunken sea-pilot of the tale *The Navigator of the "Four Winds"* (1909)[20] refers to Havana, Lisbon, Valparaiso and Shanghai; the hero of *She Who Runs on the Waves* revels in the names of their home ports painted on the sterns of ships riding at anchor in Liss, those "exciting words . . .'Sydney' . . .'London' . . .'Amsterdam' . . .'Toulon'";[21] the address of a character in the story *The Heart of the Wilderness* (1923) is given as "2, Flag Street, Melbourne";[22] while the criminal hero of the tale *René* (1925) has escaped, we are told, "from the gigantic international gaols of Paris, London and New York."[23]

But however scrupulous Grin is in asserting the continued existence of the real world beyond the bounds of his imagined setting, details of actual geography are never permitted to approach too close to the shores of *Grinlandia* and threaten her special geographical immunity. In the tale *The Return* (1924), for example, the ship on which the hero is a stoker sails from Hamburg to Calais, but then continues its voyage "under a foreign flag to the port of Prest."[24] The reader who glibly assumes Grin to have simply substituted Prest for the French Atlantic port of Brest is rapidly discomfited, for he soon finds that Grin's Prest lies full in the tropics. By moving from the real ports of Hamburg and Calais to his devised one of Prest, Grin not only isolates himself geographically from the actual world, but also secures maximum immunity from his reader's associations with it.

This is not to say, however, that precise geographical data drawn from the real world never penetrate into *Grinlandia*, but when they do so, it is only in an indirect and formal way. Thus the girl Consuelo of *The Road to Nowhere* is described as being of Spanish descent; Davenant, the hero of the same novel, is cared for by a doctor of the Red Cross hospital in Poket; Captain Eskiros of the tale *Ships in Liss* (1922)[25] is a native of Colombia; and the sculptor of the statue in Gel'-G'yu of the legendary marine phantom of the novel *She Who Runs on the Waves* learnt his art in Florence. But such details are never obtrusive and are valuable to Grin only in that they lend verisimilitude to a setting which is otherwise wholly fictional. Much more important than such fleeting and token references to the real world within Grin's imagined setting is his wide and frequent use of place names from all over the globe, particularly in the context of the sea and ocean voyages. It is the strongly evocative quality

of these far-away places with their alluring, magic names,
from the Philippines to Port Stanley, from Zanzibar to
Peru, and from the Klondike to New Guinea, which goes so
far in creating the peculiarly exotic and strangely foreign flavour so characteristic of Grin's best work.

Where then did Grin find the extraordinarily vivid
descriptive elements--both topographical and climatic--
which when compounded created his *Grinlandia*? In South-
east Asia perhaps? He was never there. In Egypt, the
only foreign country he ever visited? Hardly, for its
landscapes are most unlike those of his devised setting.
The paradoxical answer is that Grin found those descriptive elements within his native Russia. From his first
wanderings there as a youth in the late 1890s, Grin fell
in love with the southern Crimea, with its brilliant sunshine, blue sea, whitewashed houses, little winding streets
and colourful population. In the eyes of this youth from
grey Vyatka, the very epitome of sunless provincial Russia, the Crimea was dazzlingly exotic. Recalling with
nostalgia the view of the coast seen from the Black Sea,
Grin writes in his unfinished *Autobiographical Tale* (1931):
"All the coastal landscape of the Caucasus and the Crimea
produced an extremely strong impression upon me."[26]
Rather like the Crimea which Grin knew, *Grinlandia* is a
region of coastal towns and fairly mountainous and relatively unpopulated hinterland. Grin often openly admitted that features of the coast he loved were assimilated
into his work. In the same *Autobiographical Tale* he writes
of Sevastopol: "Subsequently some traits of Sevastopol entered into *my* towns; Liss, Zurbagan, Gel'-G'yu and Gerton."[27] Behind the programmatic description of Liss in
the tale *Ships in Liss* can be glimpsed picturesque Black
Sea ports like Yalta, Sevastopol or Feodosia which Grin
knew and loved. The description is given here at length
because it is the best and most typical of all Grin's
pictures of towns and their harbours in *Grinlandia*:

> There is no port more disarrayed and wonderful
> than Liss, except, of course, Zurbagan. The in-
> ternational, polyglot town is distinctly reminis-
> cent of a vagrant who has at last decided to
> plunge into the thickets of a settled life. The
> houses are set at random amidst vague allusions
> to streets, but there could be no streets in the
> true sense of the word in Liss, for the town
> sprang up upon fragments of rocks and hills,

linked by steps, bridges and spiralling narrow
little paths. All this is heaped up with dense,
thick tropical greenery, in whose fan-shaped
shadows flash the child-like, fiery eyes of
women. Yellow stone, blue shadow, picturesque
fissures in the old walls; somewhere in a
knoll-shaped yard stands an enormous boat
being repaired by a barefoot, taciturn fellow
smoking a pipe; the sound of singing far off
and its echo in the ravine; a market on piles,
under awnings and huge umbrellas; the glint of
a weapon, bright clothing, the fragrance of
flowers and greenery which evokes a muffled
yearning, as in a dream, for romance and as-
signations; the harbour, grubby like a young
chimney-sweep; furled sails, their slumber,
and then the winged morning, the green water,
rocks, and the ocean's expanse; and at night the
magnetic fire of the stars, and boats full of
laughing voices--this is Liss.[28]

While traits of actual Crimean geography very often
provide the basis not only for the ports of Grin's imagined coastline but also for the whole climatic and topographical complexion of his devised setting, smaller
elements of reality, also drawn from his own experience
in the Crimea, are to be found transposed into the environment of *Grinlandia* and used as part of the apparatus of adventure on which his plots so often rely. Of
these smaller elements, the smuggling motif is perhaps the
most obvious. Smuggling of the kind so central to the
plots of the novels *She Who Runs on the Waves* and *The Road
to Nowhere* was a traditional profession in Odessan folklore. Another secondary motif is that of the port
tavern and its *habitués*--one of Grin's favourite locales--
which is of prime importance, for example, in *Ships in
Liss* and in the early chapters of *The Road to Nowhere*.

There are of course very many still less obvious elements of Grin's imaginary world which have their origin in
reality. The statue of the Duke of Richelieu in Odessa
would seem to be reflected in the name Duke given to Grin's
hero in the tale *Captain Duke* (1915),[29] while the scenes
during the digging of the tunnel to free the hero in *The
Road to Nowhere* are probably closely based on Grin's own
experiences in Sevastopol gaol where he spent almost two
years from 1903 till 1905. It is tempting to search for
further instances of this kind in Grin's writing, but

Kovsky[30] has rightly warned against the current tendency
to treat Grin's imaginary setting as some "codified" form
of reality in the way that Vikhrov, for example, has
done.[31] As Kovsky points out, the fact that the towns
and landscapes of *Grinlandia* were greatly inspired by the
Crimea does not make Grin's fictitious setting into a
real one.

III

A second ghost which I wish to lay here is that *Grinlandia* was intended as a Utopia where both Grin and his
characters could escape the pressures and discomforts of
reality. Several Soviet critics of Grin, notably Vazhdayev[32] and Tarasenkov[33] in the late Stalin period, have
made crudely sociological capital at Grin's expense over
this point. Accusing Grin of bourgeois idealism and aggressive reaction, they saw his *Grinlandia* as no more than
an idealised cosmopolitan paradise, a cunning literary
smoke-screen behind which bourgeois tradition and social
inequality could live on undisturbed. Another charge
levelled at Grin by Vazhdayev in particular is that *Grinlandia* is a *capitalist* Utopia. This is a manifest error
on the critic's part, for Grin makes no attempt to conceal
the defects of capitalism in his imaginary setting, and indeed often exaggerates them so as to provide a motive for
his heroes' actions in defence of morality and justice.
The best instance of this is the novel *The Road to Nowhere*,
where the hero clashes with the massed opposition of a
bribed judiciary and venal governors, and is well-nigh
destroyed by them. Exactly like the real world beyond
her shores, *Grinlandia* has her men of influence, power
and evil: autocratic and reactionary government ministers,
wealthy and unscrupulous shipping magnates, cruel confidence tricksters and vicious thugs. But the majority of
such characters emerge as a direct contrast to Grin's
favourite heroes, whose prime virtues are generosity and
selflessness. As the kind doctor says to the hero of *She
Who Runs on the Waves* as they talk of the hard-headed
shipowner, Braun: ". . . he's a man of business, of profit,
far removed from you and me. . . ."[34]
As money has the same power and influence in *Grinlandia* as in the real world, Grin's heroes, engaged as
they are not in the mundane and trivial but in the extraordinary and significant, must have enough of it to guarantee them complete freedom of action and independence from
others. But whilst the source of the wealth of many

secondary characters in Grin's tales and novels is often
specified (quite often it derives from dishonesty), the
source of the financial independence of primary characters
is referred to only in the most nebulous of terms, if at
all. In the earliest romantic tales no reference is made
to the reasons for the heroes' apparently complete financial independence. In "*She*" (1908),[35] for example, we are
not told how the hero's protracted travels through Europe
in search of his beloved are financed, while in *The Lanfier
Colony* no clue is given as to the hero's material position
before he discovers gold on the peninsula. In his first
novels, written in the early 1920s, Grin does supply more
precise details of his heroes' wealth. The hero Grey's
grand gesture in the finale of *Scarlet Sails* (1923)[36] is
possible in the degree of its beneficence only because of
the great fortune deriving from his wealthy aristocratic
background. The plot of Grin's third novel, *The Golden
Chain* (1925), pivots on the priceless golden anchor chain
discovered by Ganuver, and wealth and its unfortunate consequences provide the fundamental theme of the work. But
in the later novels Grin simply declines to reveal the
source of his primary characters' substance altogether.
As Kovsky has indicated, such is the case, for example,
with Thomas Harvey, the monied hero of *She Who Runs on the
Waves*.[37] His financial affairs are, Grin tells us, in the
hands of his attorney, the shadowy Lerkh, who throughout
the novel is no more than a background name frequently repeated by the hero in connection with matters of finance:
"Pending the arrival of money, about which I had written to
Lerkh. . ."[38]; "Lerkh replied, as was his habit, by sending
a hundred pounds. . . ."[39] (note that *Grinlandia*'s currency
is sterling). Such references and other equally vague allusions like ". . . I [Harvey] had won a legal dispute
which had brought me several thousand. . .",[40] are of
course totally nominal and essentially meaningless, serving merely to provide a pseudo-realistic background for the
hero's unrestricted activities.

While often the financial circumstances of Grin's
heroes may be defined at least in the very vaguest of
terms, their occupations and professions are either not
stated at all or described in a way which in essence supplies no factual information of any substance. In this
respect Grin quite deliberately avoids showing his hand.
The precise occupation of both Drood, the hero of Grin's
second novel *The Shining World*,[41] and Harvey, of *She Who
Runs on the Waves*, remains a complete mystery. We see
these characters only in the roles assigned them by their

creator, and at the end of each novel they dissolve back into the limbo from which they first so unaccountably emerged. As the government minister says of Drood: "Who he is—we don't know. His aims are unknown to us."[42] When Sandy, the adolescent and partly autobiographical hero of *The Golden Chain*, asks the mysterious Dyurok "Who are you?", the latter replies simply: "Nothing! Nothing! . . . I'm a chess player."[43] In the tale *The Blue Cascade of Telluri* (1912), the hero Reg's reply to the heroine Isotta's question "And what is your occupation?", is less evasive but more mysterious than Dyurok's: "I do everything which others retreat from because they are lacking in quickwittedness, audacity or imagination. I am the second soul of people."[44] Just as to define in too great detail the material circumstances of Grin's heroes would make their links with the real world too patent and so reduce the value of their imaginary environment, so the clear statement of their occupations would, by way of association in the reader, damage the curious social independence enjoyed by *Grinlandia* and her people.

For the same reasons the main heroes of Grin's novels and romantic tales are of indeterminate nationality. Grey and Assol' (*Scarlet Sails*), Drood and Tavi (*The Shining World*), Sandy, Molly and Ganuver (*The Golden Chain*), Harvey, Daisy and Biche (*She Who Runs on the Waves*), Jessy and Morgiana in the novel of that title (1929),[45] and Davenant and Galeran (*The Road to Nowhere*), are all citizens of *Grinlandia* and have no *direct* links with any countries of the real world. But this invented nationality has a somewhat exclusive quality and Grin's heroes do not always wear it passively. When questioned by the colonist Gupi (in *The Lanfier Colony*) who has watched him row ashore from a Dutch sailing ship: "The captain is a kinsman of yours, perhaps?", the hero, Gorn, rejects Gupi's suggestion that he might be Dutch, and then refuses pointedly to elaborate:

> Gorn: "The Captain is a Dutchman, and for that reason he could hardly be my kinsman."
> Gupi: "But what is your name?"
> Gorn: "Gorn."[46]

Curiously, however, this imagined nationality of an imagined land does not necessarily extend to the secondary characters in *Grinlandia*. For instance, in connection with the old tradition of the carnival in Gel'-G'yu in *She Who Runs on the Waves*, we read that Italians and French

formerly made up a large proportion of the colony's population. The girl Consuelo of *The Road to Nowhere* is not
only described as of Spanish stock, but at the age of ten
was sent to a *pension* in Spain for seven years, before returning to Gerton.

Much has been said by critics--unfortunately all too
often in a superficial and denigratory way--about the extent of Grin's indebtedness to the Western literary tradition of the adventure genre, to the novels of Rider Hag-
gard, Bret Harte, Mayne Reid, Fenimore Cooper, Robert Louis
Stevenson and others which Grin is known to have read vora-
ciously in his youth. Again, an investigation of this very
intriguing and complex aspect of Grin's work is not the immediate object of this article. It is enough to say that the
strict linear division of characters into "white" and
"black," "good" and "bad," is an accepted convention of the
adventure genre as practised by the above authors and by
others like them, and it is a convention which Grin utilises in his own way in his romantic fiction. But this very
functional and schematic system of delineation does not
mean that Grin's *primary* characters possess insufficiently
elaborate individuality or inner psychology, a failing frequently found in the Western writers of adventure so often
wrongly regarded as Grin's masters. In fact, it is the
psychology and behaviour of his heroes and not their social
role which most interests Grin, and this feature of his
work represents a conscious extension of, if not a deliberate departure from, the traditional priorities of the typical adventure story. But his *secondary* characters, whilst
still subject to the same schematism applied to their primary fellows, are important to Grin in exactly the opposite
way; their role is broadly social rather than psychological, and they undergo comparatively little, if any, examination of their inner condition at the author's hands.

Thus, paradoxically, while the primary characters represent a departure from the tradition of the adventure
genre proper, the secondary ones show a return to it.
These are the colourful and often bizarre romantic figures
who populate the towns and ports of their romantic *Grinlandia*, and they are just as indispensable to the creation
of that picturesque land as are the graceful ships at anchor in Liss or the mysterious taverns in Zurbagan. As
characters they are the stock-in-trade of the standard adventure tale, and their various occupations predispose them
to the exotic and the *romanesque*: smugglers and sea-dogs,
explorers and inventors, ships' pilots and hunters. Such

are the four bantering captains, Duke, Estamp, Renior
and Chinchar, who greet the pilot Bitt-Boy in *Ships in
Liss*; such are Dyurok and Estamp, the solid and fearless
mariners who sail away to adventure with young Sandy in
The Golden Chain; Astarot, the brave and selfless hunter
in *The Rifleman from Zurbagan* (1913);[47] the bold smugglers Petvek, Utlender, Getrakh and Tergens who with the
hero Davenant fight the customs officers in *The Road to
Nowhere*, and scores of characters like them.

IV

As I have attempted to show, the deliberate isolation
of Grin's imagined setting from the actual world prevents
associations with that world from encroaching upon *Grinlandia* and damaging the curious geographical immunity which
she enjoys. Just as one cannot situate *Grinlandia* geographically on the globe, so it is impossible to place the
novels and stories set there in any definite chronological
context or historical epoch. By contrast, many of Grin's
early realistic tales, especially those of his SR cycle,
can be set with reasonable accuracy against the political
backcloth of Russia during the first ten or fifteen years
of this century. In addition, though dates are sometimes
not specified in several of Grin's short tales of the First
World War, it is usually impossible to mistake what war he
intends. But in most of his romantic tales and in all his
novels, where the location is *Grinlandia*, the dates and
temporal indications Grin gives are so deliberately haphazard that they hinder rather than help his reader's efforts to determine the work's place in time. This, I
think, is a particularly intriguing feature of *Grinlandia*.
For example: the inscription on the statue of Frezi Grant
in *She Who Runs on the Waves* is dated as December 5th,
1909,[48] but this detail is of no help in defining the precise temporal context of the whole novel. Likewise, in
the tale *The White Sphere* (1924), the notice referred to
in the opening paragraph states that the auction hall in
question was founded in 1868,[49] but this information does
not tell us *when* the action of the story takes place. In
his last novel Grin weaves a more complex web of chronological detail. Consuelo is said to have returned to the
town of Gerton at the age of seventeen, after spending
seven years in Spain, shortly before the annual festival
on June 9th to celebrate the arrival of the ship *Minerva*
in Gerton roads on that date in 1803.[50] But Grin is very

careful not to say exactly *when* Consuelo herself arrived
back in Gerton from Spain—a piece of information which
would define the action of the novel much more precisely
in time. In *Scarlet Sails* the casks of ancient wine in
the Grey family cellars were brought there by an ancestor
of the hero's in 1793 from Lisbon.[51] Again, the detail
enables us to do no more than set the tale imprecisely
somewhere in the 125 years between that date and the writing of the work late in the second decade of this century.
The Golden Chain contains a rather more intriguing example
of Grinian chronology. The buccaneer's priceless golden
anchor chain was, we are told, forged on April 6th, 1777,
and then lay under water for 140 years before being discovered by Ganuver, whom it made a millionaire.[52] Is it
perhaps only coincidence that this chronology means that
Ganuver's find occurred precisely in 1917?

Only very occasionally does Grin give precise indications of time, and then they refer not to details within
the narrative but to the whole action of the novel. Thus
the epilogue of *The Golden Chain* is set in 1915, while the
action of *The Road to Nowhere* unfolds, the author tells us,
some twenty years before the work is written.[53] Grin also
sometimes follows a convention of the adventure tale by using the deliberately imprecise temporal formula "In 189—"[54]
(*The Golden Chain*), a device which lends authenticity to
the narrative.

Yet for all their apparent plausibility, Grin's dates
and chronological details, like his geography, are pure in-
vention and essentially have no real bearing upon his narrative. But they do enable him to punctuate his fiction
with a degree of temporal verisimilitude and to create that
indefinably "historical" atmosphere which surrounds *Grinlandia* and her people.

It is strange, however, that whenever Grin does appear to attempt to give some general temporal basis, however indistinct, to his writing by references to chronology, however unsystematic they are, any "stabilising" effect briefly achieved in this way is rapidly destroyed by
the elements composing the overall social and economic appearance of his *Grinlandia*. These elements are drawn from
the most varied historical epochs and Grin does not hesi-
tate to include together details which are chronologically
quite inconsistent with each other. Thus the sailing ships
of *Scarlet Sails*, *She Who Runs on the Waves* and *Ships in
Liss* co-exist with the modern liners and steamers of *The
Voice of the Siren* (1927)[55] and *The Return*, and with the

submarine of *The Destroyer* (1919).[56] Along the streets and
roads of *Grinlandia* travel the elegant carriages of *A Personal Technique* (1926)[57] and *The Road to Nowhere,* and the
sleek cars of *Jessy and Morgiana* and *The Grey Automobile*
(1925).[58] Grin's hero may hitch-hike if he cannot afford
the train fare (*The Road to Nowhere*), or hire a horse
(*The Rifleman from Zurbagan*). He may call in at a dilapi-
dated port tavern (*Ships in Liss*) or put up at a smart town
hotel (*The Shining World*).

Yet when we examine it more closely, Grin's juxtaposition of elements derived from very different epochs is not
as haphazard as may at first seem. *Grinlandia* is a predominantly archaic country and its creator is sometimes
openly hostile towards features of the modern world, like
the car (*The Grey Automobile*) or the aeroplane (*The Compe-
tition in Liss*) (1921).[59] In the tale *Ships in Liss* Grin
clearly admits his liking for people who, as he puts it,
recall old snuff-boxes, polished by time and filled with
secret poetry: "There are people who remind one of an old-
fashioned snuff-box. Picking up such a thing, one gazes
at it in fecund reverie. It is a whole generation, and we
are foreign to it."[60] He goes on to define the poetic type
of person for whom he feels so much sympathy, and the list
of his preferences is a programmatic statement of many of
the temporally dissonant elements of *Grinlandia*, the old
contrasted with the new:

> Such a person will prefer horses to a railway
> carriage; a candle to an electric light bulb;
> a girl's fluffy plaits to her intricate coif-
> fure smelling of burning and musk; a rose to
> a chrysanthemum; a lumbering sailing vessel
> with its lofty mass of white sails . . . to
> a toy-like, neatly pretty steamship.[61]

It is not only many of Grin's people who possess this
poetically archaic quality. Liss, that most attractively
poetic of all his ports, belongs decidedly not to the modern but to the antique world. As Grin remarks coyly in
Ships in Liss: "We shall not analyse the reasons why Liss
was and is a port of call exclusively for sailing ships.
These reasons are of a geographic and hydrographic kind."[62]
The real reasons, of course, are not those to which Grin
alludes at all. They are of a purely literary and personal
kind. He must preserve the romantic, old-world aura of his
favourite imaginary port, and to have inelegant and obtrusive steamships call there would strike a discordant note.

Many characters and objects in Grin's romantic works
belong to the archaic world of old snuff-boxes: his garru-
lous captains and weather-beaten pilots; his fairy tale-
like eccentrics, such as Bil'der in *Captain Duke* and Egl'
in *Scarlet Sails*; his graceful sailing ships like the *She
Who Runs on the Waves*; his quaint taverns with their odd
names "The Prickly Pillow" and "Drive Away Your Sorrow";[63]
and his imposing ancient castles, like that of Grey in
Scarlet Sails. Such details create a deliberately decorative reflection of olden days, somewhat reminiscent of
Hans Andersen and Stevenson, and contribute to that elusively "historical" essence which pervades Grin's best
romantic works.

Grinlandia is thus compounded of the elements of two
worlds which are temporally quite distinct from each other.
The first and by far the more important is exotic, antique,
romantically stylised; the second, much less elaborate, is
overtly and frequently extravagantly modern. By giving
details from varied epochs in his writing or indeed in one
and the same work which he frequently does, Grin aims to
upset his reader's ideas of time and so escape the temporal
associations he naturally forms when presented with a
chronologically consistent picture of a specific historical
period. It is important to note here that though Grin's
work has an undeniable generally antique flavour, it is
never specifically historical or documentary like that of
Western authors such as Cooper, Mérimée and Stevenson,
whom he was so often said to resemble.

V

No examination of *Grinlandia* would be complete without
a brief mention of the sub-tropical sea which laps her
shores. A traditional constituent of the work of many
writers of the adventure genre, the sea is the most important single element in Grin's fictional setting. To the
imaginative youth from drab, landlocked Vyatka the sea and
its romance held out the best promise of excitement, variety, exoticism and adventure, and to the creative writer
it provided the elemental environment where his robust
heroes could most effectively show their mettle. Speaking
of Grey, his hero in *Scarlet Sails*, Grin reveals evoca-
tively the special features which make a life at sea so
alluring:

> No profession, except this one, could so suc-
> cessfully combine in one whole all the treasures

of life. . . . Danger, risk, the might of nature, the glimmer of a distant land, the miracle of the unknown, fleeting love shining with
meetings and partings; the fascinating restless
succession of encounters, faces, events; the
infinite variety of life, whilst high in the
heavens shines first the Southern Cross, then
the Great Bear, as all the continents pass before your watchful eyes. . . .[64]

The ocean provides the backdrop for many of Grin's
best tales, among them *Ships in Liss, Captain Duke, Reno
Island, The Voice of the Siren* and *The Return,* and for all
his novels except *The Shining World* and *Jessy and Morgiana.*
Much of the romantic attraction of the ocean around *Grinlandia* lies in the fact that, like the colourful flags of
the many ships upon it, it is international. The mere
mention of the distant places which are to be reached
across it is enough to arouse in both Grin and his reader
that poignantly romantic yearning felt by the hero of *She
Who Runs on the Waves* as he gazes in reverie at the ships
anchored along the jetty in Liss: ". . . in the shadows of
the huge sterns looming over the quay I made out the exciting words, those tokens of the *Unrealised* [*Nesbyvsheesia*]:
'Sydney,' 'London,' 'Amsterdam,' 'Toulon' . . ."[65]

Rarely is the sea in Grin a passive constituent of his
narrative. More often it plays an active and even decisive
role in his plots. In the tale *Captain Duke* it provides
the stimulus for the hero's change of heart and for his return to his former beloved seafaring life; in *The Voice of
the Siren* the ocean's boundless promise, reverberating in
the blare of a great liner's siren, brings back strength to
the young hero's paralysed legs; and in *The Return* the sea
is the agent of the hero's spiritual transformation, carrying him from his native Norway south to the tropics and
back home again to die in new, full awareness of the infinite variety of experience present in life. In *Scarlet
Sails* the ocean is not only the whole *raison d'être* of the
hero, but also the purveyor of the heroine's miraculous
happiness. Sometimes, however, Grin's ocean is a hostile
force, not a kindly agent, in his heroes' destinies.
Whilst in *Scarlet Sails* it avenges the evil done by the
shopkeeper Menners by drowning him in a furious storm, in
The Death of Romelink (1910)[66] it brings the hero's death
in a shipwreck as retribution for his spiritual bankruptcy.

The French critic Claude Frioux--one of the handful of
Western commentators on Grin's work--makes the interesting

point that Grin is a poet of the port rather than of the
open sea, because the former setting, with all its bustle
and variety, offers him greater literary scope:

> Grin préfère le port à la mer, car le léger
> recul, cette frange d'émoi, d'attente ou de
> souvenir qui borde le départ ou la genèse de
> l'événement révèle de façon plus libre et plus
> insinuante tout ce qu'apporte à la sensibilité
> l'épisode aventureux.[67]

Grin exploits the potential of the port as a setting in
such tales as *The Port Commandant* (1933)[68] and *Ships in
Liss*, and in the third chapter of *She Who Runs on the
Waves* he describes the permanent, mysterious charm of
the harbour:

> . . . a harbour is always full of promise; its
> world is filled with undiscovered meaning, to
> be found in the pyramids of bales lowered from
> the gigantic cranes, or scattered amongst the
> masts, or hemmed in beside the quays by the
> iron flanks of vessels, where in the deep cre-
> vasses between the tightly ranged decks there
> lies silently in shadow, like a closed book,
> the green water of the sea. Not knowing whether
> to soar upwards or sink back, clouds of smoke
> swirl from the huge funnels; tense and checked
> by chains stands the might of the propellers,
> of which a single movement is enough for the
> still water under the stern to burst up like
> a rising knoll.[69]

In his preference for the harbour, Grin differs markedly
from authors of maritime Anglo-Saxon adventure literature,
like Conrad and Poe, whose setting is so often the high
seas.

VI

I have touched in this article on the link between
Western writers of adventure and the apparatus of Grin's
romantic fiction. Grin's use of many of the established
conventions of the adventure genre, notably its predilec-
tion for exoticism, intrigue and sharply differentiated
character types, is quite deliberate. But while such conventions are responsible for many features of *Grinlandia*
and for the kinds of event that take place in her, it would

be quite wrong to assume that Grin himself was unaware of
the limitations and shortcomings inherent in those conventions. Unfortunately, this error has been made by the
overwhelming majority of commentators who have pointed to
the similarities between Grin's work and that of Western
writers of adventure. Indeed, as if giving voice to his
own reservations about the adventure genre which in so
many ways he admired, there were occasions, especially
towards the end of his career, when Grin exposed in his
writing the exaggerated romance and stylised exoticism
lent by the adventure genre to "foreign" settings and characters. In one of the last tales he ever wrote, *The 'Stone
Pillar' Ranch* (first published in 1961),[70] Grin attempts
to put exoticism in its proper perspective by pointing to
the fact that the exotic is by no means a defined or static
concept applicable only to certain areas of the globe.
Where it is to be found, he insists, depends not on the
dictates of time-honoured literary convention but simply on
the geographical region with which a given individual is
familiar. Exoticism, he infers, is therefore merely a
question of relativity. In this late story his heroine
Areta, a native of the Argentine pampas, is as eager to
visit exotic (to her) Europe as his hero, an old English
clerk from Plymouth, is to witness at first hand the life
of the South American gauchos of which he has dreamed for
decades. What Grin appears to be doing here is to define
the literary ingredient broadly dubbed "the exotic" and to
strip it of superficial glamour. To him the exotic is not
simply a literary seasoning but something significant in
its own right, in the geographical or ethnographical sense.
But what is exotic to Grin's readers is simply part of the
everyday setting to his characters. Just as the girl Areta
finds nothing exotic in her native pampas, so the heroes of
Grinlandia see nothing exotic in the region in which they
live. They are not imported by their creator into his
imagined country to wonder open-mouthed at its splendours,
but are true natives of that region and know no other. It
is only his European or Russian environment which makes the
reader feel that Grin's devised country is exotic. Would
not his technique of *dépaysement* make less impression perhaps upon a native of, say, Australasia or of the Pacific
seaboard of South America?
       Whilst it is true that in several shorter and earlier
works, written before 1917, such as *From a Detective's
Notebook* (1912),[71] *Taboo* (1913),[72] and *The Hunting of a
Hooligan* (1915),[73] Grin does parody aspects of the adven-

ture genre, in his longer romantic tales and novels which
demand greater elaboration of setting, character and atmosphere, he utilises many of the conventions of that genre
as a fully serious foundation on which to base the moral
and ethical structure of his thought. His *romanesque* adventures and intrigues, his delineation of character into
stereotyped categories of "white" and "black," the traditionally Manicheistic struggle between the forces of good
and evil, and the sea and its romance—all these are standard elements of the work of dozens of Western authors of
adventure which so fascinated Grin in his youth, and which
helped to create *Grinlandia* and her people.

Two broad features of *Grinlandia* are of prime importance to the effective communication of Grin's ethical message: her imagined geography, which affords Grin locational
freedom, and her confused or non-existent chronology, which
affords him temporal freedom. Grin's unusualness *vis-à-vis*
the adventure genre lies in the fact that he develops both
these features to an extent not found in the adventure
authors proper whom he was so often wrongly said to resemble very closely.

* * * * * *

Conventional though many of the elements which Grin
assimilated from the adventure genre may be, the use he
makes of them is original. This is true of the quaintly
antique and poetic quality of so many of his settings, but
more particularly so of his Grinlandian heroes. While outwardly they may appear stereotyped, inwardly they are complex, sensitive and infinitely human, and it is upon them
that the more important but less obvious second level of
meaning in Grin's work relies. His object in lavishing so
much descriptive care upon his imaginary environment of
Grinlandia was merely an intricate means to a very simple
end: to create a stable and plausible backcloth for the
events of his plots. As Frioux puts it: "Grin ne veut pas
dépayser, mais acclimater dans le pays du rêve."[74] It is
this extraordinary plausibility of *Grinlandia*, achieved at
the cost of immense effort and scrupulous care, which makes
Grin's romanticism not ephemeral and intangible but strangely realistic and palpable. Yet having said all this about
the setting of Grin's own dreaming, it is important to remember that it is the ethical problems of all men as examined in *Grinlandia*, and not her imaginary geographical location and inconsistent chronology which most concern Grin.

Asked once why he deliberately avoided precise geography
for his setting and orthodox names for his characters, Grin
replied simply: "I do not think that your attitude to, let
us say, Hamlet, would change if you were told that he was
not a Dane but, say, an inhabitant of New Zealand."[75]

NOTES

[1]B. G. Guerney, *An Anthology of Russian Literature in
the Soviet Period*, New York, 1960, p. 387.
  [2]*Vospominaniya ob Aleksandre Grine*, ed. Vl. Sandler,
Leningrad, 1972.
  [3]See, for example, the following books: Kovsky, V.,
Romanticheskiy mir Aleksandra Grina, Moscow, 1969; Mik-
hailova, L., *Aleksandr Grin*, Moscow, 1972; Prokhorov, Ye.,
Aleksandr Grin, Moscow, 1970; Luker, N. J. L., *Alexander
Grin*, Letchworth, England, 1973. And the following arti-
cles: Rossel's, Vl., "Dorevolyutsionnaya proza Grina," in
A. S. Grin, *Sobraniye sochineniy v shesti tomakh*, Moscow,
1965, Vol. I, pp. 445-53; Rossel's, Vl., "A. Grin. Iz
neizdannogo i zabytogo," *Literaturnoye nasledstvo*, No. 74,
Moscow, 1965, pp. 628-48; Rossel's, Vl., "A. S. Grin,"
Istoriya russkoy sovetskoy literatury, Tom I, 1917-29,
Moscow, 1967, pp. 370-91; Sandler, Vl., "Shol po zemle
mechtatel'," foreword to A. S. Grin, *Dzhessi i Morgiana*,
Leningrad, 1966, pp. 3-20; Sandler, Vl., "O cheloveke i
pisatele," foreword to A. S. Grin, *Belyy shar*, Moscow,
1966, pp. 3-25; Sandler, Vl., "Chetyre goda za Grinom,"
Al'manakh *Prometey*, Vol. V, Moscow, 1968, pp. 190-207;
Vikhrov, V., "Rytsar mechty," foreword to A. S. Grin, *Sob.
soch. v shesti tomakh*, Moscow, 1965, Vol. I, pp. 3-36.
And in French: Castaing, P., "Le thème du conflit chez
Aleksandr Grin," *Cahiers du Monde Russe et Soviétique*,
Vol. XII-3, July-September, 1971, pp. 217-46; Croisé, J.,
"Alexandre Grine et l'Irréel," *La Revue des Deux Mondes*,
December, 1959, pp. 707-11; Frioux, C., "Alexandre Grin,"
Revue des Etudes Slaves, Vol. 38, 1961, pp. 81-7; Frioux,
C., "Sur deux romans d'Aleksandr Grin," *Cahiers du Monde
Russe et Soviétique*, Vol. III-4, October-December, 1962,
pp. 546-63.
  [4]Zelinsky, K., "Grin," *Krasnaya nov'*, No. 4, 1934, p.
200.

[5]Frid, Ya., "A. Grin, *Gladiatory*," *Novyy mir*, No. 1, 1926, pp. 187-8.

[6]See Claude Frioux's admirable "map," an attempt to give some specific geographical location to Grin's major works, in his article above, "Sur deux romans d'Aleksandr Grin," p. 559.

[7]*Sobraniye sochineniy v shesti tomakh*, Moscow ("Pravda"), 1965, Vol. I, p. 255. This is by far the best and most representative selection of Grin's prose work. The abbreviation Sob. soch. will be used henceforth in references to this edition. All translations from the original Russian are my own. Other recent collections of Grin's work are: *Fandango*, Simferopol' (Izd-vo "Krym"), 1966; *Dzhessi i Morgiana*, Leningrad ("Lenizdat"), 1966; *Belyy shar*, Moscow ("Molodaya gvardiya"), 1966; and *Izbrannoye*, Simferopol', (Izd-vo "Krym"), 1969.

[8]Sob. soch., I, 317.

[9]Sob. soch., IV, 3-126.

[10] Sob. soch., VI, 3-228. See my article on this novel in *New Zealand Slavonic Journal*, No. 11, 1973, pp. 51-75.

[11] Sob. soch., V, 3-183.

[12] Sob. soch., I, 37-46.

[13] Sob. soch., I, 170-9.

[14] A. Grin, *Dzhessi i Morgiana*, op. cit., pp. 294-8.

[15] Sob. soch., I, 320.

[16] Ibid.

[17] Sob. soch., II, 317-32.

[18] Sob. soch., III, 305.

[19] Ibid.

[20] Sob. soch., I, 278-83.

[21] Sob. soch., V, 6.

[22] Sob. soch., IV, 334.

[23] Sob. soch., V, 321.

[24] Sob. soch., V, 287.

[25] Sob. soch., IV, 243-62.

[26] Sob. soch., VI, 271.

[27] Sob. soch., VI, 347. One recent commentator is more precise, seeing Sevastopol in Zurbagan, Feodosia in Gel'-G'yu, and Odessa in Liss. (See Pirozhkov, A., "Strana Grinlandiya," *Knizhnoye obozreniye*, No. 34, 1970, p. 12.)

[28] Sob. soch., IV, 244.

[29] Sob. soch., III, 336-55.

[30] Kovsky, V., *Romanticheskiy mir Aleksandra Grina*, Moscow, 1969, p. 170.

[31] See Vikhrov, V., "Rytsar mechty," Sob. soch., I, 15-16, 27.

[32] Vazhdayev, V., "Propovednik kosmopolitizma. Nechistyy smysl 'chistogo iskusstva' A. Grina," *Novyy mir*, No. 1, 1950, pp. 257-72.

[33] Tarasenkov, A., "O natsional 'nykh traditsiyakh i burzhuaznom kosmopolitizme," *Znamya*, No. 1, 1950, pp. 152-64.

[34] Sob. soch., V, 28.

[35] Sob. soch., I, 158-70.

[36] Sob. soch., III, 3-66. Grin's most famous work.

[37] See Kovsky, op. cit., p. 112.

[38] Sob. soch., V, 6.

[39] Sob. soch., V, 7.

[40] Sob. soch., V, 172.

[41] Sob. soch., III, 66-215.

[42] Sob. soch., III, 99.

[43] Sob. soch., IV, 46.

[44] Sob. soch., II, 108.

[45] In *Dzhessi i Morgiana*, Leningrad, 1966, pp. 372-491.

[46] Sob. soch., I, 318.

[47] Sob. soch., II, 372-405.

[48] Sob. soch., V, 109.

[49] Sob. soch., IV, 275.

[50] Sob. soch., VI, 108.

[51] Sob. soch., III, 21.

[52] Sob. soch., IV, 39.

[53] Sob. soch., VI, 3.

[54] Sob. soch., II, 376.

[55] In *Belyy shar*, Leningrad, 1966, pp. 81-6.

[56] Sob. soch., IV, 262-8.

[57] Sob. soch., V, 409-14.

[58] Sob. soch., V, 183-219.

[59] Sob. soch., III, 432-8.

[60] Sob. soch., IV, 243.

[61] Sob. soch., IV, 243-4.

[62] Sob. soch., IV, 245.

[63] See Sob. soch., IV, 244.

[64] Sob. soch., III, 27.

[65] Sob. soch., V, 6.

[66] Sob. soch., II, 3-11.

[67] Frioux, C., "Alexandre Grin," *Revue des Etudes Slaves*, Vol. 38, Paris, 1961, p. 84.

[68] Sob. soch., VI, 362-71.

[69] Sob. soch., V, 7.

[70] In *Fandango*, Simferopol', 1966, pp. 412-520.

[71] In *Dzhessi i Morgiana*, op. cit., pp. 212-4.

[72] *Argus*, No. 7, 1913, pp. 51-60.

[73] *Argus*, No. 6, 1915, pp. 23-30.

[74] Frioux, C., op. cit. (note 6), p. 560.

[75] Verzhbitsky, N., "Svetlaya dusha," *Nash sovremennik*, No. 8, 1964, p. 104.

ANDREY BELY'S CONNECTIONS WITH EUROPEAN OCCULTISM

Boris Christa

Andrey Bely's connections with European, that is to
say with West-European, occultism exercised a profound influence on his work and through him on the work of other
symbolists, especially on Blok. They have not to date been
studied in depth. References abound in the literature
about Bely, but many of the statements are misleading and
a lot of them are manifestly wrong.

An interest in all aspects of the occult is an important common denominator uniting the writers and poets of
the Russian symbolist movement in all its phases. As the
movement matured the focal point of occult interests
shifted from early infatuation of the decadents with the
black arts, demonology, satanism and the like to an all-
absorbing quest for metaphysical enlightenment that led the
later symbolists to embark on the study of the occult wisdom of classical Greece and Rome, Eastern mysticism and
finally the teachings of contemporary European occultists.

Bely with his powerful intellect and strong orphic
urge saw himself as the ideological leader of his literary
generation and felt it incumbent upon himself to discover
new dimensions of spiritual experience. Of all the symbolists he was the most intrepid explorer of occult world-
conceptions and philosophical systems. From 1912 onwards
he became an ardent devotee of the occult science of anthroposophy and of its founder, the Austrian teacher and
academic, Rudolf Steiner. It seems ironic that Bely, neo-
Slavophile as he was, should come to be so strongly influenced by Western occultism. The metaphysical themes and
motifs that occur in the early part of his work, up to and
including the *Silver Dove*, are predominantly indigenous in
inspiration, stemming from Tyutchev, Solovyov and Russian
sectarianism. However, in Bely's works beginning with
Pepel' (Ashes) the focal point of metaphysical interest
shifts from the transcendental symbol of the Sophia to the
emblematic image of the risen Christ. This fact provides
some explanation for Bely's enthusiasm for the teachings
of Rudolf Steiner. His interest was stimulated by the fact
that Steiner's anthroposophy is centered on the figure of
Christ, moreover it also allocates a particularly signifi-

cant messianic role to the Russian people in the future evolution of mankind.

     After a series of occult portents and fateful coinci-
dences, Bely met Steiner personally in Cologne in May 1912[1]
and during the next four years he embarked, together with
his wife Asya Turgenev, on an intensive course of transcendental meditation, spiritual discipline and self-develop-
ment under Steiner's guidance. It was a passionate interest and absorbing study. The depth of Bely's attachment to
anthroposophy is evidenced by innumerable passages in his
work of the ensuing period. There is no doubt in his mind
regarding "a rhythmic progression" towards spiritual insight which he formulates as "music, reason, philosophy,
anthroposophy, wisdom."[2] Much of his writing becomes a
record of this progressive, upward path of inner development.

     The works which Bely wrote during this period, such as
the poetic cycle *Zvezda (The Star)*, the narrative poem
Khristos voskres (Christ Has Risen), the novels *Kotik
Letaev (Kitten Letaev)*, *Kreshchenny Kitaets (The Christened
Chinaman)*, *Zapiski chudaka (Notes of an Eccentric)* and
others abound in images, themes and motifs that are based
on his reading of occult literature or are suggested by his
experiences as a would-be initiate. A knowledge of the
occult background sheds a great deal of light on these
works and elucidates the impact they made on Bely's contemporaries. There seems little doubt, for instance, that
the puzzling image of Christ heading the revolutionary
rabble in Blok's *Dvedantsat' (The Twelve)* is derived directly from one of the 'occult' poems in Bely's *Zvezda
(The Star)*,[3] which has a similar image and which was copied
by Blok into his diary some days before he wrote his own
poem.[4]

     In his own career as an occultist, Bely found that en-
lightenment did not come to him as easily as he had hoped
and expected. In 1916, after living for nearly two years
at Steiner's anthroposophical centre at Dornach and en-
countering considerable frustration in his endeavours to
gain spiritual vision, Bely took the opportunity of his
call-up to return to Russia. There he was presently over-
taken by the revolution and spending five years in extremely difficult conditions, frequently in states of profound
inner stress and later in conditions of great physical
hardship, he did not leave Russia again until the end of
1921. When eventually he arrived in Germany a further blow
awaited him. His wife, Asya, refused to return to him,

while Rudolf Steiner declined to sponsor his return to
Switzerland to rejoin the inner circle of initiates at
Dornach. This rejection was a traumatic experience for
Bely who vented his feelings in a cycle of anguished poems.

The problem of Bely's subsequent relation to Steiner's
occultism has given rise to a good deal of speculation and,
it would seem, misapprehension. This is due particularly
to the very biased interpretation offered by Mochulsky,[5]
who claims that after 1922 Bely became totally disillu-
sioned and broke permanently with Steiner and with anthroposophy. His judgments are evidently founded on very limited evidence. They are based on the testimony of *Posle
razluki* and on the memoirs of Khodasevich, Tsvetaeva,
Berberova and others who witnessed Bely's emotional outbursts against Steiner and his occult teachings. To get
a more balanced view of the situation it is essential to
have a close look at all the evidence and especially at
Bely's writing on occultism of the period, which seems to
have been largely ignored by his biographers to date.

In reaching the conclusion that Bely in 1922 made a
complete break with Steiner and his occultism, Mochulsky
and others in his wake failed to appreciate a basic feature of Bely's life and works. They disregard the somewhat paradoxical fact that he actually combined his emotional instability and ambivalence with notable intellectual steadfastness. This is a point well taken by J. D.
Ellsworth in his literary profile of Andrey Bely published
in 1972.[6] While Bely's attitude towards people showed
violent change, his world conception remained basically un-
altered throughout his career.

It must be granted, however, that there are moments
when it is easy to be mislead regarding Bely's true position. Like Dostoevsky before him, Bely is capable of putting the case 'contra' with persuasive power and with considerable venom. But this does not mean that he has necessarily abandoned the views under attack. In this connection, it is essential to bear in mind that the provocative
challenging and temporary 'debunking' of cherished beliefs,
the technique sometimes described as 'metaphysical irony,'
was a feature of the symbolist literary idiom. It is especially typical of the young Bely but it persists also in
his later work. Seen in this context, the whole episode of
the contradictory attitudes towards Steiner and his occultism which Bely expressed in the period 1922-3 is completely characteristic and also very revealing. A full understanding of it gives a key to many of the themes and ideas

of his later work.

Bely in 1922 was in a state of extreme emotional tur-
moil. According to Nina Berberova he was "like a beast
wounded unto death, and all means to hurt others seemed to
him legitimate when he himself had been so hurt. To alleviate the pain all blows were permitted."[7] It seems understandable that he should be prompted above all to take revenge on those that had hurt him, namely his former occultist friends. Bely at this stage was concerned not only
that these friends should be aware of his animosity towards
Steiner and the anthroposophists, but he wanted to hurt
them as much as he could in the eyes of the world. Bely
was a totally dedicated writer. His pen was not only means
of livelihood, it also was his weapon.

The pain, frustration and desire for vengeance, which
Bely felt after the parting of ways with Asya, who spent
the remainder of his life in Dornach, find literary expression in his last cycle of verse *Posle razluki (After the
Parting)*. Strikingly novel in form, but embued with genuine poetic inspiration, these poems which mark the end of
Bely's career as a 'lyricist,' express feelings of bitter
resentment towards Asya and Rudolf Steiner. In them he
takes up again and again the theme of lament for long years
wasted on occult searchings. All is now lost--past ideals
have disappeared and in the course of the 'special years'
that lie behind, the poet has lost even his personal identity and his soul.[8]

The longest of the poems is called *Malen'ky balagan na
malen'koi planete 'zemlya'* (A little puppet-show on the
little planet 'Earth'). The choice of title, with its
clear allusion to Blok's *Balaganchik (The Puppet-show)*,
makes clear the satiric intent. This poem, which according to the sub-title is "to be yelled without interruption
through the air-vent of a Berlin window"[9] combines a shriek
of pain with a stream of hysterical abuse. Images of Bely's
past life are evoked with nostalgic fervour and contrasted
with his present despair. Responsible for it all is Asya
with her hypocritical assumption of spiritual superiority
that "perverts the spirit of life"[10] and "spins an evil
circle of high-flown falsehoods around herself."[11] Even
worse is the twice cursed 'devil' that has come between
them to separate them forever.[12] The identification of
this 'devil' with Dr. Steiner his former spiritual guide
and mentor seems clear. Bely in his usual uninhibited fashion vents his spleen until in the final lines of the poem
his window slams shut, the tirade is finished. It is worth

noting and quite characteristic of his ambivalence that
Bely unsparingly directs his outbursts also against himself. He hates everyone including himself and he asks for
nothing except oblivion.

Bely was not content to confine his literary attacks
on occultism and on his former occultist friends to poetry
but, although he does so in a disguised and indirect way,
he also enters the polemical arena against them. In the
first issue of the journal *Beseda* of which Bely, together
with Gorky and Khodasevich, was joint editor, there appears an article entitled 'Anthroposophy--translation of
a manuscript.'[13] The author of this, Dr. Hans Leisegang,
is described as a 'Dozent' of the University of Leipzig.
There is an editorial footnote which says:

> Owing to a happy combination of circum-
> stances the author of this article had the
> opportunity to make use of materials not pub-
> licly available, and accessible only to mem-
> bers of the anthroposophical society--moreover
> not to all of them. Significant excerpts from
> the so-called "lecture-cycles" are here made
> public for the first time.[14]

The article begins with a sketch of Steiner's life and
a history of theosophy and anthroposophy and then goes on
to a critical exposition of the teachings of Steiner including its most occult and, to an outsider, alienating aspects and finishes with a bitingly hostile account of the
current state of the occult movement and of what the author
calls anthroposophical propaganda. In effect then, the
article is a demonstrative act of betrayal. The teachings
of the occult movement of which Bely has been a dedicated
and prominent member are revealed to all and sundry and
the movement itself is presented as being essentially
fraudulent and promoted for financial gain. The article
thus expresses in an organised, literary way similar doubts
and criticisms concerning Rudolf Steiner and his 'occult
science' as those with which Bely had been orally bela-
bouring his emigré friends in Berlin in 1922.

It is obvious that the publication of this vitupera-
tive attack on Steiner and his school was directly sponsored by Bely. Since he was one of the editors and the
only one with specialist knowledge in the field of occultism, it would be unthinkable that such an article could
have been published in *Beseda* without at the very least,
his knowledge and consent. Furthermore, the position of
the article in the journal seems significant. It follows

directly after an article on the Russian intelligentsia in Berlin written by Bely. So it is almost as though
there is a Bely section of the journal and that the article
is part of it.

    The circumstances of how the author of the manuscript,
a promising German academic, who later occupied chairs of
philosophy at Jena and Berlin, should have come to entrust
his manuscript to the editors of an obscure Russian emigré
journal for translation and publication, remain obscure and
somewhat puzzling. There seems to be however little doubt
that Bely took a hand in the production and presentation of
the Leisegang article. In fact, it seems more than likely
that Bely himself translated and possibly re-worked the
manuscript. There are also several scathing footnotes
signed 'The Editor' which underline points of attack made
in the body of the text.

    There are some valid arguments that point to Bely as
the translator and perhaps even co-author of the Leisegang
article. It contains some innuendoes that are rather reminiscent of the polemical style of Bely's attacks on
Chulkov and the mystical anarchists in *Vesy* inspired by
the frustrations of his rejection by Luybov' Blok. There
is also a good deal in the content and structure of this
article that seems to indicate Bely's authorial participation. The factual part of the article follows very closely
the outline of the leading ideas of Steiner's teaching giv-
en in Chapter 18 of Bely's book *Rudolf Steiner i Goethe v
mirovozzrenii sovremennosti (Rudolf Steiner and Goethe - A
Contemporary View).* [15] Bely had of course given many lectures during the period 1919-21 on European occultism at
the Volfil Institute in Petrograd and he was very used to
talking about this topic. The exposition of the subject in
the Leisegang article is certainly very smooth and sure and
does not read at all like a translation. Moreover, the
writer appears to be thoroughly familiar with the Russian
translations of Steiner's work--much more familiar than
with the German of the original titles which are quoted on
some occasions, presumably because they had not been translated into Russian.

    It certainly seems strange that whereas the author of
the article was a German and it had ostensibly first been
written in German, yet in the citations of German titles
there are a number of elementary spelling mistakes. For
instance *Seele* is spelt *Seelle*, *Welt* is spelt *Wellt*, etc.
It is inconceivable that such mistakes could have been
made by a German academic and so it must be regarded as

certain that Leisegang relied heavily on his Russian editor
and certainly did not, or probably could not, proof-read
his article in its Russian form. These mistakes in the
German could however well have been made by Bely whose German according to the testimony of various people was never
very good.[16]

If then we accept Bely's sponsorship and authorial
participation in the article it gives us concrete proof of
the assertion made by Berberova that in his frenzied days
in Berlin in 1922 Bely derived some perverse satisfaction
from, as she puts it, demonstrating to his friends "the
ruins of the once beautiful building of his anthroposophical beliefs."[17]

Furthermore, if we accept the obvious conclusion that
Bely sponsored, translated and possibly re-wrote the
Leisegang article in its Russian version, this would demonstrate strikingly both his capacity for great vindic-
tiveness if hurt, and also for indulging in double-dealing.
On the other hand, there are some important reservations
that preclude the acceptance of the article as conclusive
evidence that Bely ultimately rejected Steiner and his occultism.

From internal evidence, it seems clear that the
Leisegang article was in fact prepared some time before it
was published, i.e., late in 1922 or in the early 1923. It
was printed in the first issue of a new magazine and it is,
of course, quite usual for the material of an opening number to be ready some time before it appears in print. I am
suggesting that by the time the first issue of *Beseda*, containing the article, was published, Bely's hostility towards Steiner was ebbing. It is certainly significant that
he did not make any polemical attacks under his own name.
In fact, it would seem that quite early in 1923 Bely, the
'lost sheep' as Gippius once described him during these
years,[18] was beginning to return to the fold of anthroposophical endeavour.

In the New Year of 1923, there occurred an event of
catastrophic significance for European occultism. The main
temple-like building of the anthroposophical headquarters
at Dornach caught fire and burnt to the ground. The destruction of the magnificently carved, huge, wooden
'Johannesbau,' in the building of which Bely and Asya had
participated with such enthusiasm in the years before
1914-16, must have made a strong impact on him. It is
probably not even unduly fanciful to suggest that he may
have felt in some mystic way a sense of guilt. In 1922,

during his periods of despair and hatred towards Asya and
towards Rudolf Steiner, he must undoubtedly at moments have
wished disaster upon them as fervently as, for instance,
Dostoevsky ever wished death upon his father. And as with
Dostoevsky after his malevolent wish was fulfilled, the
catastrophe left its residual mark of guilt and remorse.

At all events, early in 1923 Bely once again takes up
his contacts with the anthroposophists. He comes now increasingly under the influence of Klavdiya Vasilyeva, a
dedicated follower of Steiner with whom he subsequently
returned to Russia and who became his second wife. He
finds the time to contribute an article on 'Die Anthroposophie und Russland' to the leading occultist journal
Die Drei,[19] and in May of that year he once again attends
an anthroposophical congress in Stuttgart, staying at the
home of Dr. Unger, one of the leaders of Steiner's movement
in Germany.

On this occasion he once again met Asya, now under
much happier auspices, and also had a final meeting with
Rudolf Steiner. According to Asya's evidence this occasion brought a complete reconciliation and she reports him
as saying that Steiner had now given him enough to last
him for the remainder of his life.[20]

These matters seem to leave little doubt that Bely's
early biographers were quite mistaken in their assumption
that Bely in 1922 made a complete break with Steiner and
with his style of occultism. If any doubts remain regarding Bely's position they must, however, surely be resolved
by reference to a further article which Bely wrote in
Beseda in 1923 and which seems to have escaped their attention altogether. The article has the title 'Anthro-
posofiya i Doktor Gans Leisegang' (Anthroposophy and Dr.
Hans Leisegang). Written a few weeks before his return
to Russia it represents a public profession of faith and
an act of atonement. Bely now recants all his public and
private attacks on Steiner's occultism by coming to his
defence against the earlier attacks of Leisegang.

One cannot, however, help being conscious of a certain feeling of constraint in the tone of. this article.
Bely's polemical writing is usually full of personalised
venom, but this is quite lacking here. The tension is
about as great as that engendered by a man playing chess
against himself. For obvious reasons he deals very be-
nignly with his opponent, but deftly presents the other
side of the argument and gives a completely positive account of Steiner's work and his occult movement. Consid-

ering how soon before his final departure from Berlin this
article was written, particular attention should, however,
be paid to its concluding lines. There, after demonstratively stressing that he is writing while sober and of
sound mind, as though he were composing his last will and
testament, Bely declares that he has studied Steiner's work
for twelve years, has heard him deliver no less than four
hundred open and closed lectures and that he continues to
be his pupil and a member of the Anthroposophical Society
and all the allegations against Steiner of the Leisegang
article are wrong and unfounded.

Yet even in spite of this unequivocal profession of
faith shortly before his return to Russia, given Bely's
previously noted extreme ambivalence, some reservations
and doubts remain. Probably the most revealing insight
into his complex and divided nature can realy be obtained
from *Zapiski chudaka (Notes of an Eccentric)*,[21] the most
personal and undisguised of all his books especially with
reference to his experiences as an occultist. In this two-
volume collection of autobiographical episodes and sketches, Bely describes his experiences while at Dornach, where
he lived at close quarters with Rudolf Steiner, and on his
way back to Russia. It is written in the first person
singular and some of his experiences as a disciple of
anthroposophy are narrated with great warmth and sympathy.
But this book also has a paranoic, satirical and bitter
vein and, although it is clearly a self-portrait, it is
revealing that Bely identifies the hero as a kind of dis-
illusioned double of himself with the pseudonym of Leonid
Ledyanoy.[22]

This gives an important clue since the conflicting
aspects of Boris Bugaev's personality[23] could well be
linked symbolically with his chosen pseudonyms--Andrey
Bely and Leonid Ledyanoy. The Bely part of the writer
struggled constantly and often desperately for wisdom and
self-perfection and aspired to the role of a spiritual
leader and mentor. It seems clear that as he left to return to Russia in 1923 these spiritual aspirations were
once again identified with the teachings of Steiner's occultism, and anthroposophical themes and motifs can be
traced in many of the works of his last years.[24]

On the other hand, the cynical and icily cerebral side
of the Bugaev character, associated with the Ledyanoy
pseudonym, continued to exist in spite of attempts at
permanent sublimation. It too, continues to be in evidence in the writing of the last years, especially in the

satirical aspects of the last novels and of his memoirs.
     In the final analysis, it would seem that under the
steadying influence of Klavdiya Vasilyeva, Bely's view of
the world became more consistently stable and serene during his last years. There seems no doubt that the influence on him of Steiner's 'occult science' continued to be
very strong. We learn that he spent a good deal of his
time on studies based on the scientific methods advocated
by Steiner and derived from Goethe, which combine detailed
observation with a meditative approach. He was, like
Goethe intensely interested in colour and built up collections of stones and leaves displaying wide ranges of
natural colour shades. He also planned and worked a great
deal on a 'history of the development of self-awareness'
which still remains unpublished. All this provides ample
evidence that even during his last oppressive years in
Stalin's Russia, Bely remained true to himself. So, in
conclusion and in summary it may be definitely asserted
that he did not ever forsake either his interests in the
occult or his commitment to Rudolf Steiner's anthroposophy.
If we are prepared to take any extrinsic critical approach
to Bely's work it is of considerable relevance to bear this
in mind.

University of Queensland

NOTES

[1]A. Bely, 'Iz vospominaniy,' *Beseda*, 2, 1923, pp. 83-
127.

[2]A. Bely, *Putevyya zametki*, Berlin, 1922, Vol. 1, p.
26.

[3]'Rodine,' *Stikhotvoreniya*, Moscow, 1966, p. 381.

[4]A. Blok, *Dnevniki*, Leningrad, 1928, Vol. 2, p. 94.

[5]K. Mochulsky, *Andrey Bely*, Paris, 1955, Chap. 9,
pp. 233-257.

[6]J. D. Elsworth, *Andrey Bely*, London, 1972, p. 113.

[7]N. Berberova, *The Italics are Mine*, New York, 1969,
p. 159.

[8]A. Bely, *Posle razluki*, Berlin, 1922, p. 64.

[9]Ibid., p. 65.

[10]Ibid., p. 72.

[11]Ibid., p. 79.

[12]Ibid., p. 81.

[13]H. Leisegang, 'Antroposofiya,' *Beseda*, 1, 1923, pp.
237-263.

[14] Ibid., p. 237.

[15] A. Bely, *Rudolf Steiner i Goethe v mirovozzrenii sovremennosti*, Moscow, 1916.

[16] This was confirmed by Bely's first wife, Asya Turgenieff-Bugaeff, in a personal interview with the author of this article.

[17] Berberova, op. cit., p. 164.

[18] Z. Gippius, *Zinyaya kniga*, Belgrade, 1926, p. 211.

[19] A. Bely, 'Die Anthroposophie und Russland,' *Die Drei*, Stuttgart, 1923, No. 4/5.

[20] A. Turgenieff, *Erinnerungen an Rudolf Steiner*, Stuttgart, 1973, p. 12.

[21] A. Bely, *Zapiski chudaka*, 2 Vols., Berlin, 1922.

[22] Ibid. See: 'Vmesto predisloviya,' p. 10.

[23] 'Andrey Bely' was, of course, a pseudonym. The writer's real name was Boris Bugaev.

[24] See: Holthusen, j., 'Andrey Belyj und Rudolf Steiner,' *Festschrift fur Max Vasmer*, Berlin, 1956.

THE POETRY OF BRUTALITY : ANDRZEJ BURSA
AND RAFAŁ WOJACZEK

Bogdan Czaykowski

A book should serve as
the axe for the frozen
sea within us.
--Kafka

Gwałt niech się gwałtem
odciska.
--Mickiewicz

I

Jak oddać zapach w poezji . . .
na pewno nie przez proste nazwanie
ale cały wiersz musi pachnieć
i rym
i rytm
muszą mieć temperatury miodowej polany
a każdy przeskok rytmiczny
coś z powiewu róży
przerzuconej nad ogrodem

rozmawialiśmy w jak najlepszej symbiozie
aż do chwili gdy powiedziałem
„wynieś proszę to wiadro
bo potwornie tu śmierdzi szczyną"

możliwe że to było nietaktowne
ale już nie mogłem wytrzymać/[1]

[How to convey scent in poetry . . ./certainly not
through simple naming/scent must permeate the whole/both
rhyme/and rhythm/must have the temperature of a honey
grove/each rhythmical leap/resemble the swaying of a rose/
poised over a trellis
we conversed in an atmosphere of the best symbiosis/
until I said:/'please take this bucket out/the stench of
piss is intolerable'
maybe this was tactless/but I couldn't stand it any
longer. (translation by Adam Czerniawski)]

The poem, entitled "Dyskurs z poetą," is by Andrzej Bursa (b. 1932) and it is dated 1957, the year of Bursa's sudden death, at the age of twenty-five. At the time, and until 1968, it was widely believed that Bursa had committed suicide.[2]

Bursa's writings[3]--he wrote a macabre novel and short plays in addition to poetry--were unusual even in the post-war Polish context, where one of the leading poetic developments was the poetry of Tadeusz Różewicz, often described by critics as "stark," "naked," and "harsh." Yet Różewicz's poetry has seldom been called "brutal" or "violent," epithets which recur whenever Bursa's poetry is discussed.[4] Bursa's manner should be also sharply distinguished from the poetry of the so-called *turpiści*, poets like Stanisław Grochowiak, who explore the stylistic possibilities of ugliness, and whose poetry has little of the direct aggressiveness of tone, uncompromising frankness and sarcasm, so characteristic of Bursa.[5]

It would seem, then, that if there is a justification for such terms as "the poetry of brutality" or "the poetry of violence," it must be sought in qualities that are not merely anti-aesthetic. But before going on to a more detailed discussion of the poetry of Bursa and Wojaczek, I should like to place it in a wider context.

II

Perhaps one of the earliest uses in the twentieth century of the word "brutal" in connection with poetry occurs in the short preface that J. M. Synge wrote in 1908 to his *Poems*. The passage reads: "Even if we grant that exalted poetry can be kept successful by itself, the strong things of life are needed in poetry also, to show that what is exalted or tender is not made by feeble blood. It may almost be said that before verse can be human again it must learn to be brutal."[6]

Synge's desire that "the timber of poetry" have strong roots "among the clay and worms," although evident in some of his poems, did not result in the "brutalization" of his poetry. On his own admission he had written most of the poems included in his volume before the views quoted above "had come into his head." It is in his plays that we admire the "savage, salty tang" of his peculiar Anglo-Irish idiom, and enter into a world "crammed with violence and energy."[7] Yet Synge's formulation is of interest. It documents an early reaction in this century to the aesthetic

movement, and is a reminder of the deeply ingrained suspicion that there is a natural opposition and hiatus between
"poetic expression" and the "truthfulness of experience,"
that precisely because "the poet nothing affirmeth, and
therefore never lies," he does lie by making poetry out of
reality, i.e., by transforming reality into aesthetically
structured fiction.

This view, that poetry is a "beautiful lie," although
common and persistent, must be contrasted with claims that
are made from time to time that at least not all poetry--
and for "poetry" we may read here "literature"--is "dishonest" by its very nature. To take one instance of such
claims, we may turn to T.S. Eliot. In his essay on Blake,
Eliot has pointed to the poet's ". . . peculiar honesty,
which in a world too frightened to be honest, is peculiarly
terrifying. It is an honesty against which the whole world
conspires, because it is unpleasant." He added that such
unpleasantness "is found (not everywhere) in Homer and
Aeschylus and Dante and Villon . . . and Shakespeare and
. . . in Montaigne and in Spinoza."[8]

A similar point was recently made by one of the representatives of the "poetry of violence," the British poet
Ted Hughes:

> The role of this word "violence" in modern
> criticism is very tricky and not always easy to
> follow. . . . One common use of it I fancy oc-
> curs where the reviewer type of critic is
> thinking of his audience. . . . When my Aunt
> calls my verse "horrible and violent" I know
> what she means. . . . What she has is an idea
> of what poetry ought to be . . . a very
> vague idea, since it's based on an almost total
> ignorance of what poetry has been written. . . .
> If one were to answer the exam question:
> Who are the poets of violence? you wouldn't get
> far if you began with Thom Gunn. . . . No, you'd
> have to begin with Homer, Aeschylus, Sophocles,
> Euripides, etc., author of Job, the various
> epics . . . Dante, Shakespeare, Blake. When
> is violence "violence" and when is it great
> poetry? Can the critic distinguish? . . .[9]

That, of course, depends on the critic. But Hughes is
undoubtedly right to ask whether there is anything distinctive in the so-called "poetry of violence" or "poetry
of brutality" to justify the use of these terms. Can we

speak of a distinct trend or type of poetry within the modern movement of anti-poetry that differs both from the
merely anti-aesthetic as well as from the "unpleasantness"
of the great poets of the past? In short, is it possible
to substantiate by way of literary analysis what are often
merely impressionistic statements of literary critics?

What is obvious is the seeming inability of critics to
dispense with the term "violence," its synonyms and cog-
nates, when speaking about a large body of contemporary
poetry, the poetry of Ginsberg, Lowell, Plath, Gunn, Hughes,
Berryman, MacBeth--to name only a few of the American and
British representatives of this trend.

The criteria used in classifying poems as "brutal" or
"violent" are often thematic and ideological, although one
finds also examples of a more formal and stylistic approach. Thus, the critics speak of the "relation of the
violence of the poem to the violence of the world," of
"ethical militancy," "active hostility," "wild release of
psychic energy," "aggression on sensibility," or "the
vandalism of anti-poetry." A critic says of Ted Hughes
that his poetry's "bloodymindedness is the reflex of recent history" and that his "Nature is Nazi, not Words-
worthian."

At the same time we find observations concerning the
speaking voice of the poems, their versification, imagery
and language, but even here the statements are often metaphorical and impressionistic. Typical examples are: "deliberate brutality of the speaking voice," "brutal frankness," "violence takes the form of near-violation of formal
stanzaic, metrical and syntactical equilibrium," "the poem
assaults its own margins," "a plethora of kinaesthetic ad-
jectives and images," "one has the sense of the poems as
projectiles, constructed out of the scrap and refuse of
history and hurled with a kind of contempt," "fierce, critical style," "pathological violence of language," "sadistic
imagery," or "brutal unlanguage." Such phrases are evocative and evaluative rather than analytical, although they
can often be validated. [10]

What follows is an attempt to go beyond such critical
idiom, and to identify more precisely the poetic and linguistic features that give rise to the impressionistic reactions. However, I do not wish to deny the fact that
when we try to validate our reactions to poetry in a more
analytical and objective way, it is the original reaction,
whether individual or inter-subjective, that often guides
our attempts, for ultimately poetry is what makes a number

of linguistic fact function qualitatively, as an object of
sensibility activating our imagination and sense of values.

III

   Let me now return to Bursa's "Dyskurs z poetą."
Broadly speaking, the poem utilizes the opposition between
"the high" and "the low," not in order to ennoble "the
low," but to ridicule and discredit "the high." The manner in which "the high" is discredited may be called
"brutal."
   Let us note, to begin with, that the form of the poem
is by no means uncontrolled; on the contrary, although it
is written in "free verse," the poem is highly structured,
its structure resembling that of a sonnet, with a tripar-
tite division into the equivalent of an octave (the first
nine lines), followed by a quatrain and a closing couplet.
The three parts correspond to the three movements of the
poem's argument, which is presented as a situation (this
recalls the typical procedure of C. K. Norwid, in such
poems as "Sfinks," "Fatum," or "Mistycyzm"). Thus, to
clarify the poem's structure we must analyze the interaction between the dramatic and the stylistic layers of
the poem.
   The poem begins with a voice speaking, and at first
it is not clear whether the voice is that of the "I" of
the poem, or of the "poet." The opening line is both a
statement of the theme of the "discourse" and an indicator
of the conversational situation (it "carries on," so that
we enter the conversation *in medias res*). Throughout the
"octave" no indication is given of how we should read the
opinions expressed. Moreover, an informed reader would
easily recognize, in the views expressed, elements of modernist poetics, for instance, of Mallarmé's dictum "Nommer
un objet c'est supprimer les trois quarts de la jouissance
de poème . . .," or Tadeusz Peiper's "Proza nazywa, poezja
pseudonimuje." The style of the "octave" is perhaps a
little precious, but initially it does not give the impression of parody, and the reader accepts it as a poetic
statement in a recognizable convention, the subject matter
and diction belonging to the "high" type of discourse.
Thus, there is no warning of the sudden shift in tone, diction, and taste that follows.
   The quatrain clarifies a number of things about the
octave, and carries the argument a step further. The first
line gives a slight hint of irony ("w symbiozie"); the

second is stylistically neutral, but it introduces the "I"
of the poem, thus differentiating the speakers and identi-
fying the opinions expressed in the octave as those of the
"poet." The next two lines are the climax of the poem:
they are a climax dramatically, by bringing the conversation to a head, stylistically (there is contrastive tone
and diction), and conceptually, since "zapach" is named
directly. Thus the effect of the two lines results from
the combined impact of the situational, stylistic and conceptual elements.

In itself, the naming of the offensive smell is not
inappropriate, although more neutral terms could have been
used, but by contrast it is "brutal" in its disregard of
the sensibilities of the "poet," and its frankness and
abruptness. Not only is the poetic spell broken, but the
"octave" is now marked as ironic and parodic. It is now
the first voice (the voice of the "poet") that appears, by
a sudden reversal, inappropriate in the context of the
situation, for it is surely no less incongruous and tactless to talk about the conveying in poetry of the scent of
a rose in a room where the stench of urine is intolerable
than to say that it stinks when someone is talking about
the scent of roses. It would appear that there is an in-
sensitivity peculiar to the refined sensibility, which
even an intolerable situation cannot deflect from the pursuit of refinement and beauty.

The closing couplet transfers us to the plane of social convention, which parallels the convention of poetry,
or, to be more precise, of the poetry of suggestion. The
ironically apologetic tone of the lines reinforces the effect of the statement made in the quatrain (by emphasizing
its tactlessness) and justifies it: "I couldn't stand it
any longer." The tactless, brutal reaction is grounded in
the undeniable authenticity of a simple biological fact,
and it is difficult to argue with such basic reactions.
But the line is also meaningful in another way, for it refers also to the "poet's" discourse on how to convey scent
in poetry, so that once again the situational and the conceptual elements are drawn together. Bursa's poem "contains within itself the reason why it is so and not otherwise," and the reason, although of the lowest order, is,
at the same time, incontrovertible: "I couldn't stand it
any longer."

IV

In "Dyskurs z poetą," the "high" and the "low" are
brought into collision within the confines of the poem.
But this is not a necessary prerequisite for achieving the
effect of shock or brutality, since even the most permis-
sive society has its taboos and values. A number of
Bursa's poems achieve such effects without actually embodying the contrast between the "high" and the "low"; the
"high" remains outside the poem as its implied context,
whether it is the context of culture in general, or morals,
aesthetic values, or high-minded lies. This does not mean
that stylistic effects do not play a role, but it does mean
that there is no direct clash of style and diction within
the poem. In such poems the contrast is rather between the
style and the content, or between recognizable stylistic or
formal conventions and their deliberate "misuse."

A typical example is Bursa's prose-poem "Ze sposobów
znęcania się nad gośćmi niskiego wzrostu" (On Ways of Tormenting Short Guys).[11] An almost impersonal voice, characterized mainly by the occasional use of slang, gives directions on how to torment short men physically and morally. Apart from the word "kurdupel," which is vulgar and
contemptuous, and several colloquial phrases, the diction
is not particularly expressive. In fact, the entire piece
is prosaic and matter-of-fact, resembling in style the im-
personality of cooking recipes, do-it-yourself kits, or
game descriptions. In spite of a few touches of sadistic
glee the professional tone dominates throughout. The intent of the poem is to shock not through a display of
sadistic emotions, but by its treatment of sadism as a
subject for professional advice. This violation of the
code of humanity is rendered more shocking by the fact that
the directions are given not in the infinitive form (in
Polish a typical procedure in this type of discourse), but
in the imperative mood: "wywołaj go," "odbierz mu ją,"
"chwyć go za kołnierz," "potrzymaj nad ogniem," "daj
prztyczka w nos," "uderz w twarz," "wal." Given the subject-matter, the effect of cold-blooded brutality is thus
achieved by a combination of what may be called "objectivization" and the use of the imperative mood--a clear
enough instance of the deliberate perversion of stylistic
and formal conventions. It would be enough to rewrite the
passage in the indicative mood or to change the crucial
verbs into the infinitive form, to defuse the effect; the
description would still be unpleasant (or grotesque), but

it wouldn't be as shocking. In itself, of course, the imperative mood is neither brutal nor gentle; it is its function within the poem that gives it its force.[12]

The device of objectivization has a particular usefulness for Bursa's type of poetry precisely because it excludes value judgments, imposing an alien style or structure upon a subject-matter that calls for a humanistic
treatment. This procedure can strongly offend our sensibility, since it is directed in the largest terms against
our sense of "what is appropriate," as when we call certain
acts committed by man "inhuman," that is, at variance with
man's moral and intellectual standards. Such inappropri-
ateness occurs in a number of Bursa's poems. A good example is the poem "Z zabaw i gier dziecięcych" (Nursery
Toys and Games), where the structure of a game is imposed
upon moral matters:

> When everything becomes a bore
> get yourself a little old man and an angel
> this is how you play:
> trip the old man up so he falls on his face in
>   the gutter
> the angel hangs his head sadly
> give the old man a sixpence
> the angel lifts his head
> take a stone and smash the old man's glasses
> the angel hangs his head sadly
> offer the old man your seat in the tram
> the angel lifts his head
> empty a chamber-pot over the old man's head
> the angel hangs his head sadly
> say to the old man "God bless"
> the angel lifts his head
> and so on
> then go to sleep
> an angel will appear in your dreams
> or a devil
> angel--you win
> devil--you lose
> if you dream of nothing nothing at all
> --a draw[13]

[Gdy ci się wszystko znudzi/spraw sobie aniołka i
staruszka/gra się tak:/podstawisz staruszkowi nogę że
wyrżnie mordą o bruk/aniołek spuszcza główkę/dasz
staruszkowi 5 groszy/aniołek podnosi główkę/stłuczesz
staruszkowi kamieniem okulary/aniołek spuszcza główkę/
ustąpisz staruszkowi miejsca w tramwaju/aniołek podnosi

główkę/wylejesz staruszkowi na głowę nocnik/aniołek
spuszcza główkę/powiesz staruszkowi „szczęść Boże"/aniołek
podnosi główkę/i tak dalej/potem idź spać/przyśni ci się
aniołek albo diabełek/jak aniołek wygrałeś/jak diabełek
przegrałeś/jak ci się nic nie przyśni/ r e m i s]

The crucial phrase in the poem is the line: "this is
how you play," the implication being that ethics is no more
than a game (R. D. Laing's little book, *Knots*, is full of
such games, some of which can be read almost as poems of
alienation). Viewing life as a game is characteristic of
Bursa's attitude in general and occurs as a theme in several of his poems, such as "Szachy" (Chess), "Obrona
żebractwa" (Defence of Beggardom), "Przecież znasz
wszystkie moje chwyty" (Sure, You Know All My Tricks),
"Rzeźnia" (Slaughterhouse). Moreover, the idea of the
game, however serious, seems to underlie most of his poems.

Another variant of the device of objectivization is
found in such poems as "Pantofelek" (Slipper Animalcule)
and "Syllogizm prostacki" (A Vulgar Syllogism), *viz*., the
style and form of logical argument. Here, however, the
function of the device is different: it is treated in both
poems precisely as a mere device, and juxtaposed with the
authenticity of subjectivism. In addition, the first of
the two poems is an interesting example of seemingly gratuitous verbal aggression:

Dzieci są milsze od dorosłych
zwierzęta są milsze od dzieci
mówisz że rozumując w ten sposób
muszę dojść do twierdzenia
że najmilszy jest pierwotniak pantofelek

no to co

milszy mi jest pantofelek
od ciebie ty skurwysynie[14]

[Children are nicer than adults/animals are nicer than
children/you say that reasoning in this way/I must reach
the conclusion/that the nicest of all is the protozoan
slipper animalcule

so

I prefer the slipper animalcule/to you you sonofabitch (translation by A. Busza and B. Czaykowski)]

The last line comes as a shock not only because it
contains an obscenity (a common Polish expletive), but also because it seems addressed directly to the reader. It
is tempting to work out the strictly logical side of the

arguments in the poem, but such an effort would be futile
and irrelevant. In "Pantofelek" Bursa plays with logical
structure in order to dismiss it. His appeal is to authen-
tic experience: it is obvious--even when expressed in a
hyperbolic manner--that some human beings are worse than
animals, and anyone who tries to use (or misuse) logic in
order to deny this truth places himself in the category of
hypocrites and liars. Bursa's short poem has a "logic" of
its own.

The first part of the poem "Syllogizm prostacki" presents two "syllogisms" whose conclusions are obviously absurd:

> You will not get anything nice for free
> sunset is free
> therefore it is not beautiful
> but in order to puke in the loo of a first-class
>   joint
> you've got to pay for a drink
> ergo
> the loo of a dance hall is beautiful
> and a sunset is not

Having led us thus far, the author now gains our sympathy and approval:

> but I say this is rubbish

However, we have reclaimed him into the realm of culture
prematurely, for we are in for a second shock:

> I've seen a sunset
> and a night-club loo
>
> there is not much difference[15]

> [Za darmo nie dostaniesz nic ładnego/zachód słońca
> jest za darmo/a więc nie jest piękny/ale żeby rzygać w
> klozecie lokalu prima sorta/trzeba zapłacić za wódkę/ergo/
> klozet w tancbudzie jest piękny/a zachód słońca nie
>   a ja wam powiem że bujda
>   widziałem zachód słońca/i wychodek w nocnym lokalu
>   nie zajduję specjalnej różnicy.]

The poem is a calculated affront to refined sensibility and
provokes negative reactions.

If "Pantofelek" may be said to have a logic of its own,
and "Syllogizm prostacki" is no more than an outrageous
joke, relying on the impudent opposition to the apparent
objectivity of good taste of one man's opinion, the un-

titled poem "Jaki miły i mądry facet" ends in release of
extreme verbal hostility without any apparent justification, other than the hatred of anything that is "cultured":

> Jaki miły i mądry facet
> naprawdę mądry
> nie z tych przemądrzałych
> obieżyświat
> co to z niejednego pieca chleb jadł
> wyrozumiały i uprzejmy
> cała anatomia jego twarzy
> zdradzała lekki wysiłek
> ust:
>
>   by mądrzej i grzeczniej do mnie mówić
>
> oczu:
>
>   by uważniej i uprzejmiej mnie sluchać
>
> taaak...
> naprawdę nie mogłem nie napluć mu w mordę[16]

[What a nice and wise guy/really wise/not one of those
too-clever-by-half/he's been around/he's sniffed more than
one pot/understanding and obliging/the whole anatomy of his
face/betrayed a slight/effort/of the lips:/to talk to me
ever so wisely and politely/of the eyes:/to listen to me
ever so carefully and obligingly
        yes Sir/I really couldn't resist spitting in his face.
(translation by A. Busza and B. Czaykowski)]

To sympathize with the point of view of this poem we
have to make certain far-reaching assumptions about human
society and culture (assumptions which have been made by
the entire counterculture movement). None of Bursa's poems
articulates these assumptions in full, but as we read them,
poem after poem, we begin to piece together a point of view
and a *persona* that contribute to the effects of brutality
and shock while giving the individual poems their consistency and justification.

The poems I have discussed so far contain several aspects of the *persona* of Bursa's brutal poetry: uncompromising frankness, aggressiveness, sadism, cynicism, vulgarity,
sarcasm, impudence; elsewhere we find moral nihilism, pessimism, bitterness, irresponsibility, blasphemy, touches of
masochism, hooliganism, arrogance, etc. There are, in
fact, several poems which define the *persona* directly,
while others deal with the conditions and causes of the
brutalization of Bursa's idiom and imagination. To the

former group belong such poems as "Dziewictwo" (Virginity),
"Sobota" (Saturday), "Pochwała władz miejskich" (In Praise
of Municipal Authorities), "Ostatni promyk nadziei" (The
Last Ray of Hope). The latter group includes "Nauka
chodzenia" (Learning to Walk), "Kopniaki" (Kicks),
"Katownie" (Houses of Torture), "Zażalenie" (Complaint),
"Dobry psychiatra" (A Good Psychiatrist), "Malarstwo
obłąkanego" (Madman's Painting).

Of the former group, "Dziewictwo" consciously evokes
the *persona* of the *poète maudit*, while giving it an original ironic twist:

Minąłem salę błękitna gdzie pili wino
i szmaragdową gdzie poker szedł
minąłemsalę żołtą gdzie palili opium
i herbaciarnię gdzie żuli peyotl
wstąpiłem też do kabiny purpurowej
zaciemnionej jak trumna
o przeznaczeniu odrażającym i rozkosznym

dopiero po północy
uznawszy że jestem wystarczająco nasycony kolorami
odważyłem się wyjść na ulicę

cóż kiedy i tak
lilijna biel mojej duszyczki
zwróciła uwagę policjanta[17]

[I passed the blue room where they were drinking wine/
and the emerald room where poker rolled/I passed the yellow
room where they were smoking opium/and the tea-room where
they chewed peyotl/I also stepped into the scarlet chamber/
darkened like a coffin/set for a horrible and delicious
purpose

only after midnight/deciding that I was sufficiently
soaked in colors/did I dare to go out into the street

but in vain/since my lily-white soul/still caught the
eye of a policeman.
(translated by A. Busza and B. Czaykowski).]

All in all, the *persona* of Bursa's brutal poetry bor-
rows various traits from the hooligan, the rebel, the *en-
fant terrible* and the *poète maudit*. The poet does not
spare ingenuity (or the reader's sensibility) in making
his poetic "I" odious, exasperating and insultingly frank.
There is no need here to go into the autobiographical aspect of Bursa's poetic "I"; it is sufficient to say that
when his poetry is taken in its totality, including the
early lyrical poems, the longer poem "Luiza" and "St.

Joseph" (his only portrait of a positive hero), there emerges at a deeper level a not unattractive authorial personality.

> Of all Catholic saints
> I like Saint Joseph best
> he was no masochist
> or some other queer
> but a professional
> always with that axe
> without the axe he must have felt
> his arm was crippled
> and though it came hard to him
> he brought up the Brat
> which he knew
> was not his son
> but God's
> or somebody else's
> and when they were running away from the police
> ....
> he carried the Child
> and the heaviest basket[18]

[Ze wszystkich świętych katolickich/najbardziej lubię
świętego Józefa/bo to nie był żaden masochista/ani inny
zboczeniec/tylko fachowiec/zawsze z tą siekierą/bez
siekiery chyba się czuł/jakby miał ramię kalekie/i chociaż
ciężko mu było/wychowywał Dzieciaka/o którym wiedział/że
nie był jego synem/tylko Boga/albo kogo innego/a jak
uciekali przed policją/ . . ./niósł Dziecko/i najcięższy
koszyk.]

But the crucial point is that the negative *persona*
functions as a vital element in the technique of shock, and
that it is invested with a high degree of autobiographical
verisimilitude.

What gives this *persona* its deepest and most offensive dimension is its acute nihilism and the extent of its
bitter hostility. It is enough to list some of the titles
of Bursa's poems to make the point: "Faith," "Hope,"
"Love," "It's Difficult to Make Friends," "In Praise of
Municipal Authorities," "Dictator," "Pedagogics," "Virginity," "A Funeral Speech," "A Good Psychiatrist," "Morn-
in the Park"--each of these poems is an attempt to offend
aesthetic and moral sense, each is a debunking or unmask-
ing of high ideals and supposedly cherished values, and
each presses home the conviction that "higher" culture is
only a cover for the grossness of reality. Moreover, these

assaults on sensibility are conducted in poetic form (for these are poems) and by a poet, and isn't it the poet's function to humanize the world, or at least to create beauty?

The causes and conditions of the brutalization of Bursa's poetry are implicit in most of his poems, but several speak of them more directly. Very revealing in this respect is the poem called "Malarstwo obłąkanego," and especially the lines:

> Rozmawiają ze mną uprzejmie
> Aha teraz ze mną rozmawiają uprzejmie
> . . . .
> Ja jestem zrobiony z krwi kości skóry i włosów
> a byłem manekinem guzikiem automatu numerem
> > w kartotece[19]

[They are talking to me nicely/Yes they are now talking to me nicely/ . . ./I am made of blood bone skin and hair/And I was a mannequin a machine button a number in a file (translation by A. Busza and B. Czaykowski).]

In "Luiza," the process of maturation is presented as a progressive brutalization of the young sensibility which faces "the terrible consequences of a dead prospect." The poem "Nauka chodzenia" (Learning to Walk) creates a minor myth of gratuitous cruelty and violence:

> Tyle miałem trudności
> z przezwyciężeniem prawa ciążenia
> myślałem że jak wreszcie stanę na nogach
> uchylą przede mną czoła
> a oni w mordę
> nie wiem co jest
> usiłuję po bohatersku zachować pionową postawę
> i nic nie rozumiem
> "głupiś" mówią mi życzliwi (najgorszy gatunek
> > łajdaków)
> „w życiu trzeba się czołgać czołgać"
> więc kładę sie na płask
> z tyłkiem anielsko-głupio wypiętym w górę
> i próbuję
> od sandałka do kamaszka
> od buciczka do trzewiczka
> uczę się chodzić po świecie.[20]

[I had so much trouble/overcoming the law of gravity/ I thought that when at last/I stood on my feet/they'd raise their hats to me/instead/I get a kick in the face/

what's up/ heroically I try to remain upright/and I can't
figure it out/"you're a fool" say the well-wishers/(the
worst kind of bastards)/"in life you must crawl crawl'/so
I lie down/with my backside angelically-stupid sticking
up/ and try/ from sandal to slipper/from shoe to sneaker/
learning to walk in the world. (translation by A. Busza
and B. Czaykowski)]

Jerzy Kwiatkowski writes that Bursa creates in his
poems "a myth of gratuitous universal hatred."[21]   But this
is only one aspect of Bursa's world. The reality of his
poetry is brutal in all its aspects; even death cannot be
trusted to bring relief from suffering and malice:

Inaczej wyobrażałem sobie śmierć
wierzyłem naiwnie
że szczytowy orgazm przerażenia
wytrąci mnie wreszcie ze strefy bólu

Tymczasem wszystko czuję
          widzę wszystko
pozostając na prawach trupa
          bez możliwości jęku
                    drgnięcia
                    poruszenia się[22]

[I imagined death differently/I believed naively/that
the final orgasm of terror/would at last wrest me from the
zone of pain
But so far I feel everything/I see everything/enjoy-
ing the status of a corpse/and unable to utter a cry/to
jerk/to move]

In concrete, historical and biographical terms, Bursa's
world is the world of memories of the war, of Stalinism and
tempered totalitarianism, the world of a young man who,
having been fed the "wooden bread" of propaganda and in-
doctrination, leaves behind the dreams and illusions of
childhood and early adolescence (beautifully evoked in some
of Bursa's lyrical poems), and enters manhood. It is a
world not unlike that of Rimbaud's "Les poètes de sept ans,"
only modernized and less directly personal. It is precisely the heightening of intellectual and emotional sensitivity to existential problems characteristic of the period of
maturation, exacerbated by a particularly oppressive social
and political reality, that explains the range and intensity of Bursa's verbal aggression.

I don't believe in the impossible
Nothing is impossible in this world

which consists of
hee! hee! hee!
of tiny whirling specks
which so far
hee! hee! hee!
nobody has seen[23]

[Nie wierzę tylko w niemożliwe/Wszystko jest możliwe
na tym świecie/składającym się/hiii... hiii/z wirujących
punkcików/których jeszcze/hiii...hiii/nikt nie widział.]

And since nothing is impossible in this world, Bursa
tells in one of his poems how a certain Doctor C., "a rich
man and a miracle marker," started collecting legless boys,
collected twenty-two of them, divided them into two teams
of eleven each and taught them to play soccer.[24]

V

Rafał Wojaczek was born in 1945 and died in 1971, apparently by committing suicide. He published two volumes
of poems during his lifetime, *Sezon* (*Season*, 1969), and
Inna bajka (*A Different Fable*, 1970); two other volumes,
containing a number of new poems, appeared posthumously:
Którego nie było (*He Who Was Not*, 1972) and *Nie skończona
krucjata* (*The Unfinished Crusade*, 1972). He was considered by his admirers the first truly worthy successor of
Bursa, and some have called him a "Polish Rimbaud." Both
these opinions obviously need to be qualified. However,
just as there was something Rimbaudian in Wojaczek's tal-
ent--in its precociousness, intensity of vision, and
stylistic virtuosity--so his uncompromising frankness and
the savage flouting of taboos recall Bursa. And yet, in
spite of its imagery of violence, its vulgar diction and
obscenities, Wojaczek's poetry has also been called sentimental.[25]

Bursa's aggressiveness was the result of "outraged
innocence." Behind his nihilistic mask, it has been argued, Bursa was a Romantic, or at least a moralist. The
anger and scorn that runs through his poetry is the *saeva
indignatio* of a satirist.[26] Although his earliest poems
are narrowly personal in theme and lyrical in character,
their lyricism is that of a strong personality attracted
to classical forms or to Brechtian dryness. But what
needs to be stressed especially is the fact that the form
of Bursa's poems of brutality is strictly functional, and
that its function is to shock. Form is not meant, nor in
fact allowed, to serve aesthetic ends.

Wojaczek's poems, on the other hand, have a formal and stylistic finish that attracts attention, or at least blunts and often alleviates their brutal impact. With few exceptions, his poems deal with strictly personal feelings and obsessions, such as the fear of, and fascination with, death (in this respect he reminds one of Sylvia Plath), sexual hunger and the violence of sex, loneliness, the sense of unfreedom and existential despair. Their tone, despite the brutal effects, is lyrical, and they are frequently expressed in the form of lullabies, ballads, songs, and incantations.

Bursa's language is colloquial and rhetorical, he seldom uses rhyme or stanzaic patterns, his form is "internal." Wojaczek's poetry employs rhyme and assonance, and a variety of stanzaic forms. He uses metrical patterns skilfully, alternating between melodiousness and roughness. And he knows how to walk the tightrope between brutality and artistic virtuosity. Jerzy Kwiatkowski, while confessing that he finds many of Wojaczek's poems revolting, called him nevertheless "one of the foremost poets of his generation."[27]

Wojaczek's view of the role of the poet is presented in a brilliantly perverse manner in his poem "Babylon":

Who walks on the naked body of a woman with boots on
You answer: the poet
Scum
his own death's pimp who's always rhyming her with
                                                    laughter

Is he such a good salesman that he can live off her
You answer: he has just to stick out
his holy arse through the window
and the mob will run and kiss off his pimples, when
                                              he lets them

So what are you doing beside me
You answer: am I not
attractive and feminine enough for you
Then put on your spurs and stab me breathless[28]

[Któż to chodzi z butami po nagim ciele kobiecym/
Odpowiadasz: poeta/Gnój/alfons swej śmierci co ją rymuje
wciąż ze śmiechem
     Czy tak dobrze sprzedaje że może z niej żyć/
Odpowiadasz: wystarczy że wystawi w oknie/święty tylek a
lud/zbiegnie się scałowywać, gdy da, pryszcze
     Więc nie rozumiem co ty robisz przy mnie/Odpowiadasz:

czy ci się/nie podobam czy mało jestem ci kobieca/Ach,
załóż jeszcze ostrogi i kłuj aż mi braknie tchu]

This procedure of expressing non-erotic themes in sexual terms occurs in many of his poems, sometimes to a degree that even Freudians would consider exaggerated. The
characterization of the poet as "his own death's pimp,"
"salesman," and the giver of climactic experience, recalls
the concern of poets, at least since the Romantic period,
with the parasitic nature of the poet's function, and the
moral justification of art. "Am I not attractive and
feminine enough for you," a voice asks, and then urges:
"Then put on your spurs and stab me breathless." In
Wojaczek's poetry violence and brutality become one more
source of aesthetic pleasure, and it is possible to
speak, in his case, of a kind of aestheticism of violence.

In contrast to Bursa, the principal locus of brutal
effects in Wojaczek's poetry is the diction and imagery,
and not the sphere of actions, attitudes and linguistic
gestures of the *persona*. Wojaczek's poetic "I" is mainly
lyrical, vulnerable, and not free of self-pity; and while
he is often the hero of his poems (in one of them he calls
himself "that sonofabitch Rafał Wojaczek"), his actions
are described rather than dramatized. The "I" has no recognizable voice, distinct from the general tone of his
poems. Lacking a pronounced dramatic character, his poetry negates the "high" by means of an extreme form of
reductionism, bringing everything down to the level of
the most basic physiological and psychological processes:
it speaks of love in terms of sex, of sex in terms of sado-
masochistic violence, of higher aspirations in terms of
physical hunger and lust.

Since, however, this reductionism extends also to the
"I" of his poems, the effect of brutality is reinforced by
the scandalizing exhibitionism with which the poetic "I"
reveals its neurotic characteristics. Thus one may speak
with justification of his poems' "brutal frankness" in the
sense in which this phrase has been used of the so-called
"confessional" American and British poets.[29] The reduc-
tionist image of the lyrical "I," apparently rooted in real
enough psychological problems (which were diagnosed as a
case of *personalitas inadequata*),[30] is especially shocking
in those of his poems which are written in the naked style
of anti-poetry. A good example is the poem "Mit rodzinny"
(Family Myth):

This is a sausage
my edible mother

there she hangs on a metal hook
smelling of the chimney

and she is cheap
in fact she never bargained
she was considerate and knew her place
. . . .
Now I am hungry
and my mother hangs

so I stare at the shop-window
dribbling
sperm and saliva

soon I'll stop dithering
go in and ask
for that one

That is a sausage
my edible mother
and this my childish hunger[31]

[To jest kiełbasa/To jest moja matka jadalna
Ona wisi na niklowym haku/i pachnie kominem
Ona jest tania zresztą nigdy się nie drożyła/była
wyrozumiała i znała możliwości
. . . . . .
Więc wpatruję się w wystawę/i czuję/jak mi cieknie/
ślina i sperma
Wiem za chwilę już nie będę się wahał/wejdę i
poproszę/tę właśnie
To jest kiełbasa/To jest moja matka jadalna/A to jest
mój głód dziecinny]

The poem is not only repulsive in its imagery, and
shocking in diction, but it is also outrageous in its almost literal identification of a human being with a con-
sumable object: a sausage. Both the object of desire and
the desiring subject are reduced to a level where they
cease to be recognizably human. The "family myth" becomes
both infantile and brutish, and the poetic form does nothing to alleviate this effect.

"Mit rodzinny" is one of Wojaczek's earlier poems (it
is dated 1965). In his later work the naked style is seldom used on its own, and the tendency is towards a brilliant display of formal and stylistic virtuosity, as in
the poem "Dwoje" (Twosome):

Choć się nie znają jeszcze znają się zawczasu.
   Obrzydzeni zarówno
   lecz ciało samo stręczy.
Jej włosy które plączą się z niskim obłokiem
   gdy mówi: nasram
   na sławę poety.

Niebo już wie czym będzie kiedy ich zastanie
   razem: śmierć na Księżycu
   --z jelit wyjdą im glisty.
Wreszcie każde z nich będzie po sobie wspomnieniem
   --dwa wirujące
   pioruny kuliste. [32]

[Although not yet acquainted they already know each
other/Disgusted equally/but the body itself panders./Her
hair which tangles with a low cloud/when she says: I will
shit/on the glory of poets.

Heaven already knows what it will be when it finds
them/together: death on the Moon/--worms will crawl out
of their bowels./In the end each will be a memory after
the other/--two whirling/balls of fire.

(translation by A. Busza and B. Czaykowski)]

It is a typical Wojaczek poem: it speaks of love,
death and poetry; it combines vulgar diction and revolting imagery with intricate poetic form, and ends in a
brilliant image that underscores the iconicity of the
poem's stanzaic pattern: two "spherical" stanzas, the
second of which closes with a highly effective rhyme.
Its baroque poetics is unmistakable.

The baroque style provided Wojaczek with a perfect
model, fully realized in Polish poetic tradition (to mention only Jan Andrzej Morsztyn, Stanisław Herakliusz
Lubomirski, and Daniel Naborowski), of fusing discordant,
jarring elements into dazzling poetic form. Yet, as is
obvious from his poem "Babylon," the pursuit of virtuosity
of style and form, and in fact the very concept of poetry,
carried for Wojaczek strong implications of inauthenticity
and fraud. His poetic development occurred at a time when
the majority of postwar Polish poets, whether of the generation of Stanisław Grochowiak (b. 1934), Ernest Bryll and
Jarosław Marek Rymkiewicz, or of Mieczysław Stanclik (b.
1944) and Zenon Maciej Bordowicz, could be justifiably accused of an excessive indulgence in stylization and verbal
play. Różewicz's and Brusa's forceful emphasis on the
"truth of poetry" was accepted by Wojaczek as a moral imperative which he interpreted for his own generation--the

generation of poets who had not experienced war, and for
whom Stalinism was at the most a childhood nightmare--in
an almost masochistic fashion:

> Salt into our wounds, a cartload of salt
> lest anyone say he doesn't smart
>
> Sand into our eyes, a whole Sinai of sand
> lest anyone say that he is not blind
>
> Hunger for our bellies, dry slices of hunger
> lest anyone say he doesn't feel hunger
>
> A boot in our crotch, a thousand kicks
> lest anyone be in a mood to breed
>
> A knout on our heads or a hundred sticks
> lest anyone say that he can still think
>
> fear into our hearts, a mass of sheer dread
> lest anyone say he is not afraid
>
> And lead into the lungs or a noose on the neck
> lest anyone say that he is not dead[33]

[Sól w nasze rany, cały wagon soli/By nie powiedział
kto, że go nie boli
    Piach w nasze oczy, cały Synaj piasku/By nie
powiedział kto, że widzi jasno
    Głód w nasze trzewia, suche kromki głodu/By nie
powiedział kto, że nie wie, co głód
    But w nasze krocza, kopniaków choć tysiąc/By nie
powiedział kto, że spłodził by co
    Knut w nasze głowy, sto pałek umyślnych/By nie
powiedział kto, że sobie myśli
    Strach w nasze serca, tyle grozy gestej/By nie
powiedział kto, że nie zna lęku
    I salwę w płuca czy też sznur na szyje/By nie
powiedział kto, że jeszcze żyje]

The poem, entitled "Apocalypsis cum figuris," is at
first sight paradoxical: on the one hand, it asserts, although indirectly and ironically, that life is horrible;
on the other, it is a prayer for a life of even greater
horror. The paradox, however, becomes less puzzling if we
recall Kafka's statement that "a book should serve as the
axe for the frozen sea within us," and that Wojaczek is not
alone in believing, as he does in this poem, in the salu-
tary value of brutal shock.
    It is, then, hardly surprising that he should try to

go beyond the baroque style, one of whose characteristics
is its ability to dazzle even by means of horror. Hence a
number of Wojaczek's poems read like attempts to brutalize
the baroque style by saturating it with unpleasantness to
the point where it ceases to give its peculiar kind of
aesthetic pleasure:

> Piersi przekłute drutem do robótek
> Ma moja żona I ciągle jej rad
> I wciąż jej krwawe ciało wielbi kat
> Kuchennym nożem biodra grubo struże
>
> I parzy stopy i opala łydki
> Wyłuskał jabłka z kolan Żyły z ud
> I na widelec ponawijał kiszki
>
> I szuka dalej Wymacawszy odkrył
> Kość ogonową i odrąbał ją
> I nożyczkami do naskórków srom
> Wypreparował i wyłupił oczy
>
> I przez maszynkę do mielenia mięsa
> Przepuszcza oba pośladki i krew
> Wiadomo po co rozciera na szkle
> I każdy włos jej na czworo rozszczepia
>
> Bo ciągle wierzy że przecież odnajdzie
> Takim cierpliwym oprawcą któż by
> Inny jak tylko poeta mógł być
> Znam go Nazywa się Rafał Wojaczek[34]

The imagery of the poem is utterly revolting. But the
morbid sado-masochistic operations which the poet is per-
forming on the body of his wife have the semblance of a
scientific quest for some kind of ultimate truth. Moreover, it is the extreme dedication to the art of torment
and self-torment that distinguishes the poet, whose function is here equated with that of the executioner and the
torturer. Wojaczek was as proud of his professionalism as
Bursa, who wrote of St. Joseph:

> he was no masochist
> or some other queer
> but a professional
> always with that axe
> . . . .
> and when they were running away from the police
> . . . .
> he carried the Child
> and the heaviest basket

For Bursa violence was principally a form of action, but for Wojaczek it was the inner condition of man. For both of them human reality is brutal, and poetry has to be true to reality.

VI

I have suggested that one of the principal means by which Bursa achieves the effect of brutality is the aggressive negation of the "high" by the "low," explicit or implicit, on the plane of style, structure, and the more specifically mimetic plane of action, situation, speaker, voice; and that a similar negation occurs in Wojaczek's poetry, where it consists in the reduction of the human psyche to cruel and neurotic animality.

No doubt, the distinction between the "high" and the "low" is largely conventional, but it is a convention that reflects the very *differentia* of man's condition, his social status which gives rise to culture. The distinction runs through theories of poetry from Aristotle to Northrop Frye: the former laid the groundwork for its formulation in terms of genre and style, when he suggested that literature may portray life as better than it is, worse than it is, or as it is; the latter redefined it in the categories of the "high mimetic" and the "low mimetic." [35] But ultimately it is rooted in the more basic distinction between "animal condition" and "human condition," between brute and man.

Thus, the generic meaning of brutal is clear: it refers to all that which deliberately or unconsciously obliterates the distance between man and animal. All the other senses of brutality follow from this basic one, and are rooted in it. They include, according to Webster: ". . . grossly ruthless, devoid of mercy or compassion, cruel and cold-blooded, harsh and severe, unpleasant to a degree that is nearly unbearable, unpleasantly accurate and incisive . . . " as well as stressing ". . . sensuality, coarse cruelty, or crude grossness, always without the alleviation of normal human moderation, reticence, sympathy, mercy, or consideration of others." [36]

In poetry, the qualifying phrase of Webster's: "without the alleviation of normal human moderation," etc., is crucial. Cyprian Norwid, whose observations on literature contain a wealth of insights, asked in his "Milczenie": "Czy śpiącego można przebudzić *grzecznie*?" and answered:

Podobno, że nie: gdyby albowiem budziło się go
upadkiem na twarz najlżejszego listka róży,
jeszcze byłoby to tylko bardzo wykwintnie albo
poetycko pomyślanym, lecz nie byloby *grzecznie*,
bo końcem końców, trzeba śpiącemu przerwać
snowania myśli jego—i to przerwać doraźnie,
nie powoli, lecz nagle, przenosząc go jednym
ruchem w rzeczywistość i oczywistość inną. Nie
można przeto z jednej oczywistości przerzucać
nikogo w drugą sposobem grzecznym, i pewne
brutalstwo nierozłącznym zdawa się być od roboty
takowej. [37]

The key phrases are: "nie można przeto z oczywistości
jednej przerzucać nikogo w drugą sposobem grzecznym, i
pewne brutalstwo nierozłącznym zdawa się od roboty takowej."
The poetry of brutality makes use of this mechanism, it attempts to transfer the reader from the "high" level of culture and humanity to the "low" level of brute reality without alleviating or moderating this passage by means of poetic form or humour. It differs from the grotesque by refusing to subsume the harshly clashing elements under a
higher form of aesthetic structure. In the poetry of
brutality the principles of *discordia concors* and *catharsis*
do not apply.

University of British Columbia
Vancouver, Canada

NOTES

[1]A. Bursa, *Utwory wierszem i prozą* (Cracow: Wydawnictwo Literackie, 1969), p. 111.
   [2]Cf. B. Czaykowski, "Poezja gwałtowna: Andrzej Bursa,
1932-1957," *Tematy*, 31-32 (1969), 306-309.
   [3]The edition *Utwory wierszem i prozą* contains almost
all of Bursa's poems, the novel *Zabicie ciotki* (*Killing the
Aunt*), several short prose pieces, the short plays
"Zwierzęta hrabiego Cagliostro" (Count Cagliostro's Animals) and "Żakeria czyli Męczeństwo wiejskiego proboszcza"
(Jacquerie or The Martyrdom of a Village Vicar), and a selection of articles.
   [4]Cf. Jerzy Kwiatkowski, *Klucze do wyobraźni* (Warsaw:
Państwowy Instytut Wydawniczy, 1964), pp. 174-188; B.
Czaykowski, op. cit.; Stanisław Stanuch, introduction to
Utwory wierszem i prozą; Stanisław Barańczak, *Ironia i
harmonia* (Warsaw: Czytelnik, 1973), pp. 75-91.

[5] A closer parallel to Brusa's manner of writing is found in the "brutal prose" of Tadeusz Borowski, Marek Hłasko and Marek Nowakowski.

[6] J. M. Synge, *Plays, Poems and Prose* (London: Dent, 1964), p. 219.

[7] M. MacLiammóir, Introduction to Synge, op. cit., p. vii.

[8] T. S. Eliot, *Selected Prose* (Harmondsworth: Penguin Books, 1963), pp. 159-160.

[9] Ted Hughes, Interview by Egbert Faas, *London Magazine*, No. 1 (1971), pp. 5, 7.

[10] See the following publications: Robert Conquest, *New Lines II* (London: MacMillan, 1963); M. L. Rosenthal, *The New Poets* (New York: Oxford University Press, 1967); A. Alvarez, *Beyond All This Fiddle* (London: Allen Lane, 1968); Charles Newman (ed.), *The Art of Sylvia Plath* (Bloomington: Indiana University Press, 1970); Martin Dodsworth, ed., *The Survival of Poetry* (London: Faber, 1970); Jonathan Raban, *The Society of the Poem* (London: Harrap, 1971).

[11] A. Bursa, p. 155.

[12] Cf. R. Wellek's statement: "No single stylistic device, I believe is invariable: it is always changed by its particular context. . . . often the most commonplace, the most normal, linguistic elements are the constituents of literary structure. A literary stylistics will concentrate on the aesthetic purpose of every linguistic device, the way it serves a totality, and will beware of the atomism and isolation which is the pitfall of much stylistic analysis." In T. A. Sebeok, ed., *Style in Language* (Cambridge, Mass.: M.I.T., 1964), pp. 417-418. Cf. also Z. Folejewski, "Czy czasownik jest źródłem energii w funkcji poetyckiej?", *Studia Filozoficzne*, 1974:5, p. 114.

[13] A. Bursa, p. 123. Translation by Jan Darowski in Celina Wieniewska, ed., *Polish Writing Today* (Harmondsworth: Penguin Books, 1967), pp. 104-105.

[14] A. Bursa, p. 124.

[15] Translation by A. Czerniawski, in C. Wieniewska, pp. 103-104.

[16] A. Bursa, p. 98.

[17] A. Bursa, p. 115.

[18] A. Bursa, p. 126. Translation by Adam Czerniawski, in C. Wieniewska, p. 103.

[19] A. Bursa, p. 67.

[20] A. Bursa, p. 96.

[21] Jerzy Kwiatkowski, p. 180.

[22] A. Bursa, p. 88.

[23] A. Bursa, pp. 81-82.   Translation by Jan Darowski, in C. Wieniewska, p. 109.

[24] A. Bursa, p. 85.

[25] Stanisław Barańczak, *Nieufni i zadufani* (Wrocław: Ossolineum, 1971), pp. 144-145.

[26] Cf. B. Czaykowski, pp. 308-309, 321-322.

[27] Jerzy Kwiatkowski, *Twórczość*, No. 7 (1974), p. 139.

[28] Rafał Wojaczek, *Twórczość*, No. 8 (1971), pp. 6-7.

[29] Cf. M. K. Rosenthal, chapters II and III, *passim*.

[30] Jerzy Kwiatkowski, pp. 138-42.

[31] R. Wojaczek, *Sezon* (Cracow: Wydawnictwo Literackie, 1969), p. 17.   Translation by A. Busza and B. Czaykowski.

[32] R. Wojaczek, *Nie Skończona krucjata* (Cracow: Wydawnictwo Literackie, 1972), p. 52.

[33] R. Wojaczek, *Odra*, No. 10 (1970), p. 26.   Translation by A. Busza and B. Czaykowski.

[34] R. Wojaczek, *Nie skończona krucjata*, p. 31.

[35] N. Frye, *Anatomy of Criticism* (Princeton: Princeton University Press, 1957), *passim*.

[36] Webster's *Third New International Dictionary of the English Language* (Springfield, Mass.: G. & C. Merriam Co., 1965), p. 286.

[37] C. K. Norwid, *Pisma wszystkie* (ed. J. W. Gomulicki; Warsaw: Państwowy Instytut Wydawniczy, 1971), p. 221.

THE CHANGING ROLES OF CZECH LITERARY CRITICISM OVER THE PAST TWENTY-FIVE YEARS

Igor Hájek

[This paper surveys the main changes in Czech literary criticism over the past quarter of the century. While academic criticism is not disregarded, the accent is on criticism appearing in the literary press. The term is thus used in a broad sense and incorporates criticism proper as well as what is usually called "serious book reviewing"; in other words, materials of the *T.L.S.* or *New York Review* type. A particular feature of the time and area examined is that a considerable amount of criticism was published in the form of afterwords or introductions to books of fiction and poetry. Due to the role it played in its time, this "applied criticism" is also taken into account.]

> No literature can successfully carry out its task without having an opportunity for free expression. It can be influenced neither by party or class theses nor by state officialdom. Every kind of official art and offical literature becomes distasteful overnight and immediately loses its appeal.
>   (Edward Beneš, Speech at the Congress of Czech Writers, June, 1946.)[1]

> I assign great importance to your Congress. I believe that it marks the first phase of the post-May /1945/ post-February /1948/ transformation of our literature and all culture, the phase of searching for new attitudes, new ways, a new orientation. . . . The phase of clarification has been completed by your decision to establish a new, ideological organization associating literary forces, which sees its main task in an active, creative participation in the building of a better tomorrow in our country, in the education of a new, socialist man.
>   (Klement Gottwald, Message to the 1st Congress

of the Union of Czechoslovak Writers, March,
1949.)[2]

Though less than three years separate these two quotations, they in fact mark two eras. Beneš's attitude was
that of a liberal democrat: literature should not be directly involved in politics, and an exchange of ideas
should take place without hindrance or restrictions placed
on it by a ruling ideology. Indeed, the very notion of a
ruling ideology must have been alien to Beneš and to those
who sympathized with his view. The attitude he expresses
more or less reflects the situation which prevailed between
1945 and 1948. Ideas, trends and philosophies existed side
by side or clashed freely, the most conspicuous among them
being a native Czech version of existentialism[3] and a renewed Marxist stream, which had been present in Czech literature since before World War II. Some critics sought
continuity with pre-war literature, others stressed the
need for literature to assume new functions. Yet criticism remained within the customary limits of interpretation and evaluation without imposing on literature the
standards of one obligatory model.

As late as in the spring of 1948, when the communist
party had established itself as the ruling power in society, several groups of young writers presented programmes
for literature which differed widely, though agreeing on
a "positive and active attitude of literature to socialism."[4] However, even a Marxist historian of Czech literature had to admit that "this broad basis of young creative
activity soon lost the opportunity for further development."[5] The tenet that a variety of views on the role of
literature in social life was unacceptable was first voiced
in a speech by Klement Gottwald at the Congress on National
Culture in April, 1948, in which he emphasized the educational role of literature and called for the "nationaliza-
tion of culture."[6] But it was left to the first congress
of the now institutionalized Czechoslovak Writers' Union in
1949 to interdict all literary concepts which were in any
way at odds with the then prevailing interpretation of socialist realism, a doctrine formulated by A. A. Zhdanov in
September, 1946, in his criticism of the Soviet magazines
Zvezda and *Leningrad*. The programme for Czech literature
devised at the congress meant in fact a wholesale adoption
of Zhdanov's pronouncements.

Obviously the new situation implied a great change in
the position of the literary critic: he was made the

custodian of ideological purity. His work, far from paralleling that of the writer or poet, was given a place of new
importance in the literary process, becoming directly involved in it, indeed part of it. Like the trade unions,
the critics, too, became the "transmission lever" of Party
policy. Criticism was now an instrument of guidance--at
times gentle and inconspicuous, but more often harsh, even
destructive--with the critic representing the official view
of the Party, or, to be more precise, of the Ideological
Department of its Central Committee. He was thus endowed
not only with influence, but also with a certain amount of
political power (and social prestige) which even his most
habitually devastating Western colleague could not match.[7]

The 1st Congress of the Writers' Union was followed in
January 1950 by a working conference at which the chief
party ideologist, Ladislav Štoll, reviewed the past thirty
years of Czech poetry. In his long speech, later published
in book form, he rejected most of modern Czech poetry of
the years between the wars (generally considered to be one
of the finest periods of Czech literature), and extolled
the communist poet S. K. Neumann as "the backbone of the
development of Czech poetry over the past half-century."[8]
He had also kind words for Jiří Wolker, who had remained a
"proletarian poet" until his early death at 24 in 1924,
but it was Neumann who emerged as the paragon, because
"having surmounted a thousand confusions, errors and prej-
udices, he attained that inner certainty and unity which
is to be envied not only by his fellow poets, but also by
the younger generation--that is, the realization that *truth
is the weapon of the modern working class and that the
working class is the weapon of truth.* Hence his close and
wholehearted allegiance to the newly-born socialist world,
to the working class, to the communist party, to the Soviet Union, to Lenin and Stalin."[9]

Closeness to party line was one of Štoll's main criteria of literary excellence. Speaking for instance of
Nezval's surrealist period, he pointed out that "a reactionary tendency" could be detected in his work, evident
"in his emotional requisites such as dice, cards, planets,
forebodings, in the entire Freudian concept of subjectivism
in his poetry, in his 'philosophy' of fear, in the theory
that the creative process is involuntary." Despite all
that, Štoll had felt sure that "this was not the essential
element of Nezval's poetry, that the source of his crea-
tiveness [held] one of the vital requirements for healthy
poetry, namely, a joyful life of the senses, historical

optimism, undoubted intellectual power, love for the people, a positive attitude to the Soviet land, consciousness
of the historical mission of the working class."[10]

Štoll directed his most scathing criticism against the
work of František Halas, an introspective neo-baroque poet
(and, incidentally, a communist) recently deceased, who had
a profound influence on the younger generation. He was
presented as the arch-fiend and a corrupter of youth.
"Therefore it is necessary to ask oneself," Štoll said,
"how it is possible that Halas's poetry is still acclaimed
by some critics even in the communist press as the peak of
Czech poetry, and by some young poets, especially such as
Hořec and Kundera, who demonstratively acknowledge Halas
as their teacher."[11]   As a result of this rhetorical question Halas became a non-person.

Štoll's speech set out a guideline for Czech criticism
in the early 1950s. One of the first manifestations of its
new role as a means of the application of a normative
aesthetic was the campaign (this, too, being a fairly new
concept) which followed the publication of Jaroslav Seifert's book "The Song of Viktorka" (*Píseň o Viktorce*) in
the spring of 1950. There are suggestions that in the
background there may have been other reasons for the attack
than the mere fact that in both its subject matter and
tenor the book differed radically from the then preferred
model. However, in the absence of published memoirs and
reminiscences dealing with this event, the assumption cannot be proved. What we do know is that Seifert had been
viewed with distrust by some communist artists and poli-
ticians since his early abandonment of the "proletarian
poetry" movement in the mid-twenties,[12] and that he could
not have endeared himself to the Party in the 1930s with
poems such as "In Lenin's Mausoleum."[13]

"The Song of Viktorka" itself had nothing to do with
politics. Based on an episode and bearing the name of a
character from the novel "Granny" (*Babička*) by the most
revered of Czech nineteenth-century writers, Božena
Němcová, it was in fact a cycle of poems in which all
the sweet sadness of Seifert's poetry, both the passionate
enjoyment of life and the mournful acceptance of the passing of time, could be found. It was not the kind of poetry which could be tolerated at a time when poets were expected to sing the glories of factory chimneys belching
black smoke and see them as symbols of a happy future for
all.

The task of launching a full-scale Zhdanovian attack

on Seifert, the consequences of which were to be felt
throughout Czech literature and criticism for years to
come, was taken on by another poet, Ivan Skála, in *Tvorba*.[14]
Skála's criticism, if it can be called that, was typical of
its kind, though perhaps more vicious than any other. It
combined some rather facile observations of a literary nature with a grotesquely perverted interpretation of the
meaning of the work as well as with the formulation of
standards which set up an obligatory model of art, binding
on all writers and poets. In other words, the critic did
not base his approach on the work examined; instead he
started from premises which were frequently of an extra-
literary character.

Backed by the authority of the party--*Tvorba* was the
official cultural weekly of the Central Committee--Skála's
judgment concerned more than Seifert's alleged sins. He
accused the poet, for instance, of "sinking over deeper
into his subjectivism, his apolitical attitude, refusing
to recognize the educational role of art and focusing his
attention not on reality, but on the glittering fragments
which he extracts from it, thereby also depriving them of
their connection with life." If we replace the negative
with the positive, this turns out to be just another summary of the tenets of socialist realism. The area from
which the poet should draw his themes, too, was suggested
in a similar way by the critic: ". . . Seifert does not see
the joy of our working man, he does not see his heroism,
his optimism, he does not see the marvelous new qualities
budding in our people, nor the grand and happy prospect for
the morrow." Most dangerous seemed to be the heresy of subjectivism, for if an author did succumb to the temptation
of allowing personal feelings to colour his views, he
risked that these would be absurdly generalized and turned
against him. Skála's criticism continued: "For us today
life has a scent it never had before. For us today the
flowers give scent which once reached us only over the
fences of rich men's gardens. Seifert sings: 'The scent of
the rosemary has lost its scent today. For Seifert time
rushes quickly. He complains: 'What is life? Tears and
commotion and haste.' Such is the picture of the world
today as he has presented it to us. . . ."

Nearly a quarter of a century later this kind of criticism, besides sounding slightly comical, would perhaps be
ascribed to sheer misunderstanding. We consider it obvious
that the waning "scent of the rosemary," far from being a
symbol of the poet's longing after the old capitalist

order, was just a sorrowful admission of approaching old age.[15] In those days, however, this was taken seriously-- so seriously that for the next four years a great Czech poet could not publish another book.

The tone set by Štoll dominated Czech criticism throughout the first half of the 1950s. Though it would do injustice to Czech critics to say that all of them adopted his extreme hard line, the difference was mostly only one of degree. Writers were in the unenviable posi- tion of having to cope with the endless stream of demands placed on them by critics obsessed with the formulation of an ideal of the new novel, the new poetry, the new drama. Individual vision was castigated in the name of collectiv- ism; originality in the name of comprehensibility and re- alism; tragic endings in the name of historical optimism of the working class. At the same time the constant neces- sity to watch against the alien "bourgeois cosmopolitanism" fostered a parochial outlook. A considerable section of pre-war Czech literature was still out of bounds, and Karel Čapek could be published again only after a Russian critic, S. V. Nikol'skii, had rehabilitated him in a monograph (published in Czech in 1952).[16] The injustice done to older Czech literature, in particular to those works of the pre-war period rejected as "bourgeois," began to be felt strongly, and after Nikol'skii, in the mid-1950s, there were attempts to rehabilitate more authors and more individual works, and to present a fresh view of the Czech avantgarde of the 1930s so forcefully condemned by Štoll. These efforts paved the way for publication of books which had been under an interdict since 1948.

The role which literary criticism assumed here was one which could perhaps be described as "justification," and it was most remarkably successful in connection with the publication of foreign writers in Czech translation. While we have been so far following the development of Czech criticism in relation to Czech literature, a small digression may be in place here to remind ourselves how "justification" of previously forbidden writings worked in the case of foreign literature. In the early 1950s the same standards of acceptability were applied to foreign authors as were imposed on Czech writers. This meant that the field was narrowed to classics (Shakespeare, Dickens) and a handful of contemporary "progressive" writers (Fast, Aldridge). Nor was it only Western literature which was subject to this strict selection--it concerned some

"dubious" Soviet authors as well (Babel'). The image presented of modern Western writing (and in particular British
and American literature) was very similar to that which can
be found in Howard Fast's essay "Literature and Reality."
In fact, Fast's booklet, which portrayed American literature as a "cultural dung heap of reaction" with Franz Kafka
sitting very near the top of it,[17] was translated into
Czech and served for quite a time as a prime source of information and guidance. While in his homeland Fast's
critical view was obviously one of many and could not as-
pire to be considered the definitive view, once introduced
into the Czech situation it became the final judgment,
like Štoll's verdict on Czech poetry.

     The only way to rectify the situation, induced perhaps
inadvertently by Fast, but very purposefully by his Czech
followers and disciples, was to present a different critical view of the condemned authors, based, however, on the
same, i.e. ,Marxist, premises. By the mid-1950s there
had emerged a new generation of well-educated young critics
and writers, well-versed in Marxism, who were ready and
willing to undertake this task. The process of rehabilitation and "justification" usually started with the appearance of a critical essay which examined in depth an author
or a particular work which had until then been branded
"bourgeois" or "decadent." The essay would shed new light
on the work and emphasize its positive side, as seen from
a Marxist viewpoint. This would more often than not arouse
the publisher's interest and the author of the essay would
be invited to write an internal reader's report, justifying
why this or that book should be published; or rather, why
its publication would not harm the interests of a socialist
society. The book would then be published with a thorough
and informative preface or afterword, usually written by
the author of the original essay. The reviews were written
by other people, but by then the rehabilitation was more or
less complete.[18]

     The same tactic (though this may not be the right
word: it was rather a slow and painful effort to re-estab-
lish common sense) was followed, with some modifications,
in relation to Czech literature, both older and contemporary. The process was accelerated by the events in 1956.
The Second Congress of the Writer's Union which took place
shortly after the XXth Congress of the Communist Party of
the Soviet Union, was very different in tone from that held
in 1949. At this Congress, Czech writers took a stand
which brought about the first important clash with the

party leadership. In respect to the development of Czech criticism, this stand reaffirmed and gave support to the effort to widen the limits of "acceptability." Also at this Congress the decision was adopted by the Writers' Union to launch new literary magazines. This simple fact marked the end of institutionalized criticism, as room was now provided for unofficial views (namely in the new magazines *Květen* and *Plamen*).

Yet it was not all smooth sailing and there were setbacks. Representatives of the old normative critique were once more called to action after the publication of Josef Škvorecký's novel "The Cowards" (*Zbabělci*), which appeared at the beginning of 1958 (to be withdrawn from bookshops and banned two weeks after publication), and again it was the Party cultural weekly *Tvorba* which led the attack and started a campaign, almost exactly eight years after the campaign against Seifert. Once again, the author became for a time a non-person.

This *cause célèbre* has been described before, and an account of the affair was given by the author himself,[19] so we shall not repeat the story here. Also, rather than quoting the simplistic invectives of the campaign, let us see what a Czech critic had to say about it in 1964, on the occasion of a new edition of the book:

> So the misunderstanding about *The Cowards* stemmed from an inability to read a piece of modern writing of some degree of complexity which diverges from the established model of realistic prose, from an inability to grasp the meaning overlying the structure of uncommented episodes. And, of course, there was the fact that Škvorecký was already, at that time, staking everything on one card and refusing to plump for the golden mean which would have saved him unpleasantness, but would also have robbed his first novel of its chief virtue - the attack on outworn novelpatterns, the attempt to inject the fresh blood of new methods into the sclerotic prose form which had evolved after 1948, the challenging of the idea that the old-time realistic narrative style was the one and only orthodox socialist style.

And further: "The hysterical campaign against the book retarded and complicated the advance, but did not halt it."

He also added that the novel would "continue to serve for a
long time yet as a voice of conscience for socialist literary critics."[20]

Though the word "conscience" was very much in the air
then, this seems to have been the first time it was used in
connection with literary criticism, and it meant a new kind
of commitment. No longer was the critic committed to a
narrow dogma, requiring the same from the author; they were
now both engaged in a search. One hesitates to give a name
to the object of the search, as it was so diversified and
had so many facets, but it was certainly no coincidence
that the words "life," "human," and "existence" occurred so
often at that time. It is in fact difficult to define the
particular role of Czech literary criticism in the early
1960s. It became part of the general intellectual effort
of the time, which culminated in the Prague Spring of
1968.[21] As within the limits of censorship all social
sciences engaged in some sort of critique, literary criticism seemed even a little overshadowed by them. Nonetheless, it was the critical reevaluation of a literary figure
and his work which speeded up the process--the conference
on Franz Kafka in Liblice in May 1963.

The Kafka conference was perhaps the last occasion
when critical discussion of literary affairs had to stand
in for a debate of an overt socio-political nature. Until
that point, this, too, had been one of the roles of Czech
literary criticism, which explains why it had enjoyed so
much general interest and prestige. Even the man in the
street was eager to find out what the critics would say,
how they would react to a new novel or a book of verse, as
long as he could draw political conclusions from their reactions.

In this sense criticism had lost many of its narrowly
political aspects by the mid-1960s. Having freed itself
from imposed tasks and from its duty, in turn, to impose
rigid standards of a partly extra-literary character on
others, it could pay more attention to literature itself.
Earlier, when there was little new literature of any worth,
great debates on the role and function of criticism had
been conducted in the pages of literary journals and in
special symposia. Now the new critical approaches of the
1960s coincided with a burgeoning of Czech literature (and
culture in general), the like of which had seldom been
seen before. A series of polemics and discussions in the
weekly journal of the Writers' Union, *Literární noviny*,
helped to air new ideas, to revise old dogmatic attitudes,

to define criticism's position both in and towards literature, and to assert the critic's identity. In 1964 it was
the discussion on the poetry of the 1930s and 1950s; in
1965 a discussion on the role of the critic followed a
symposium on criticism; in 1966 the subject of the discussion was prose.

The increasing number of translations from world literature enhanced the awareness of the comparative unity of
literary development. Native traditions were re-examined
and foreign trends observed, and in at least one case it
was found that a connection could be established between
the two: the pre-war Prague structuralist school, after a
long banishment, was returning home via France. The impression was one of passionate pursuit of contemporary
critical thinking, of criticism anxious to contribute with
finely honed instruments to the achievement of the new
task which Czech literature had spontaneously set itself:
to provide insight into the human soul rather than help to
manipulate it.

The heritage of the pre-war avantgarde was claimed and
defended against its chief detractor.[22]   And, for example,
how different now was the picture of Halas from that which
Štoll had presented of him:

> In the poetry of Halas we have an individually-
> conceived modelling of human existence in dan-
> ger, constantly dislocated from the sense and
> the fullness of things but, despite all the
> absurdity and the tragedy, always impelled in-
> wards, to itself, to the stillness and primor-
> dial waters. It is a modelling which accords
> with the most penetrating sociological and
> philosophical analyses of the world today.
> Modern man is deprived of his intimate and
> individual world, he is subjected, in the words
> of Herbert Marcuse, to total desublimation,
> forced--by abundance, too--on to the one-dimen-
> sional plane of all-powerful technology and
> manipulation. Man stands to lose his inner
> sense, his metaphysical roots, his fate. Halas
> has experienced this growing alienism and fu-
> tility in several important directions and to
> the utmost limits.[23]

It may be obvious from this extract that Czech criticism was growing philosophical, perhaps too philosophical
some would say. But this was only natural after the long

rule of a rigid, dogmatic ideology which assumed to have a
ready-made answer to everything. After all, the same process was taking place in literature itself, and critics
were faced with a new, complex prose and poetry, which was
very different from that sclerotic writing of the 1950s.
This is how a critic took up the challenge presented by
one of the younger authors:

> While in no way invalidating the axiom that,
> essentially, art socializes the reader's in-
> dividuality, because it offers to the separ-
> ate and finite individual the enjoyment of
> that which he could possess, although he does
> not and will not achieve it, namely, "the full-
> ness of humanity," Linhartová obeys the rules
> of the game in a quite unusual manner. Far
> from augmenting man with anything external to
> him, she returns to him something which should
> belong to his inner being but, as things are,
> is missing; the aim is to achieve something
> which, while in the same order as "the full-
> ness of humanity," is both more particular and
> more elementary, that is, *the fullness of
> man*." The phrase still retains, for us, mem-
> ories of the strongly sensual accent imparted
> to it by our interwar avantgarde and the nar-
> rower significance attributed to it by the
> poetists, and even more by Nezval. Linhart-
> ová, however, imparts another meaning, more
> intellectual and abstract, that of *liberating
> and constituting being*. [24]

As their profession was coming into its own, the critics
could at last devote their attention to aspects of literature which previously had been either taken for granted or
considered too esoteric. After the rule of the cliché had
come to an end, it was only natural to turn attention to
language. Here is what another critic had to say about the
same author: "Even intent on precision, Linhartová notices
the inability to name, the inadequacy of language; but
being a maximalist, she is not content that our narrative
is not happening, that it has happened. Meaningful speech,
to her mind, should say what is to come; that is, speech as
a project and the project as a singular type of reality,
not explaining, but preceding the material realization.
This maximalist approach is applicable only apart from the
everyday and the given; it can succeed only in work based

on abstraction. It applies, for instance, to the artistic
language, where Věra Linhartová is in her element. She
restores to language its logic and precision; she regener-
ates poetic definition, emphasizing that notion and noti-
fying have a common root."[25]

This phase of critical activity came gradually to an
end in the period of the so-called normalization after
1968. The closing of virtually all literary journals and
magazines and the banning of most of the better known
critics put an end for a time to literary criticism. Views
expressed in the two journals where literary criticism can
be found (*Tvorba* and *Literární měsíčník*), were at first
marked by the necessity to denigrate the literary achievements of the previous period. A new, politically motivated
critical look at Milan Kundera, for instance, claimed that
"evidently all he wanted from this book [*The Joke*], too,
was success. And this time it came off as never before.
But he was inaccurate in estimating the time scale of the
success. With the ebbing of the waves of crisis threatening our society, a crisis which this novel helped, in its
way, both to voice and to encourage, we are left with what
Kundera actually wrote, stripped of everything projected
into it by mass psychosis. Then it becomes increasingly
clear where the author overestimated his powers."[26] At
present there is a tendency to avoid both the "leftist"
and "rightist" mistakes with the result that criticism
lacks both the vicious force of the Stalinists and the
intellectual brilliance of the so-called revisionists:
mediocrity has become the order of the day.

One cannot resist the temptation to end with a note
on a new role found for the method of "justification."
During the post-1968 "normalization" hundreds of books
were black-listed, stopped at the printers, or withheld
in the warehouses pending the decision of whether they
should be pulped or not. Among them was a two-volume
symposium devoted to Otakar Březina (1868-1929), a mystic
who won a mention in one of J. D. Salinger's short stories, but who had always been a headache even for liberal
Marxist criticism. A quotation from a monograph which
just managed to get published in 1970 will help to explain
it:

> He has suffered at the hands of those who have
> given undue weight to the mystical element in
> his verse, and of those who, being opposed to
> mysticism, have failed to find another key to

interpreting his symbolism. That Otakar Březina
was, for a time, actually placed almost outside
the logical sequence of Czech writing was not
solely a consequence of the undue emphasis laid
in a certain period on the realistic trend in
literature. It was also due to our failure to
delve deeper into the sources of spiritual life
in the last century and in earlier periods of
our literary history. While we talked about
tradition, our understanding was not always
correct. And so, from the contention that a
worker might not perhaps understand Březina's
verses, we drew hasty conclusions of a kind
quite undeserved by one of the greatest figures in Czech and world poetry of the turn of
the century.[27]

Times had changed again, however, and the publishers
of the two volumes were faced with the possibility that the
book would be pulped, particularly as the symposium was so
obviously in celebration of the long neglected poet. To
save it, they used the time-honoured ploy of "justification" and commissioned an introduction which was attached
in the form of a separate pamphlet to the two volumes.
Only this time the method was put in reverse: instead of
praising the poet, the introduction disavowed him: "His
art is deeply embedded in the soil which was able to nurture what are, indeed, splendid images of universal harmony and reconciliation. But these are not the stuff of
our reality, which is why they bore no fruit and why they
cannot bear fruit to nourish us. Such fruit will flourish
--and the logic of world art shows us this--where the decadence of Březina's soil is overcome, as was the case
with Gor'kii, Mayakovskii, Neumann, and also with Nezval.
And in this respect Březina's work points only halfway, and
that, it seems, is undoubtedly the least feasible of
paths."[28] This is the most peculiar role that Czech literary criticism has yet found itself in, but however in-
glorious it was, it helped to save the book.

University of Lancaster
England

NOTES

[1] *Projev Dr. Edvarda Beneše na sjezdu českých spisovatelů* (Prague: Syndikát českých spisovatelů, 1946), p. 18.

[2] Klement Gottwald, *Spisy XV* (Prague: Státní nakladatelství politické literatury, 1961), p. 203.

[3] It developed during the Second World War as an indigenous movement and it was only after the war that its relationship with French existentialism could be fully realized.

[4] František Buriánek, *Česká literatura 20. století* (Prague: Orbis, 1968), p. 256.

[5] Ibid.

[6] Klement Gottwald, *Spisy XIV* (Prague: Státní nakladatelství politické literatury, 1958), pp. 376–377.

[7] The Party's official view has less effect on academic criticism and critical research conducted mainly in the opulent institutes of a university or at the Academy of Sciences, where quick and timely reaction to everyday needs of ideology is difficult. But, though to some extent protected from the requirement to render service at short notice, the academic critic cannot hope to enjoy the influence and occasional fame (or notoriety) of his prompter colleagues unless he is able to combine both types of work. Still, his work is not entirely devoid of risk: many an academic career has been ruined by fluctuating ideological guidelines or by the results of a long and painful research appearing at a politically inopportune moment.

[8] Ladislav Štoll, *Třicet let bojů za českou socialistickou poesii* (Praque: Orbis, 1950), p. 17.

[9] Ibid.

[10] Ibid., p. 99. Closer examination reveals that Štoll's approach to individual poets depended to a remarkable degree on their attitude to the Soviet purges and trials in the 1930s and to Stalin. "It is symptomatic," he stressed for instance, "that not a single one of these poets—neither Hora, nor Seifert, nor Halas—found a word of verse for Stalin" (p. 83). In his eyes this was sufficient reason for condemnation.

[11] Ibid., p. 111.

[12] This period is described e.g., in Alfred French, *The Poets of Prague* (London: Oxford University Press, 1969), pp. 8–28.

[13] In the poem *V Leninově mausoleu* Seifert describes how the dead Lenin is awakened by the sound of shots and think-

ing that the revolution is in danger he wants to go to its
help. The guard, however, knows that the shots come from
the Lubianka prison, where executions are in progress, and
tells Lenin: "Sleep, comrade, and be rather grateful / for
your fame: / today one better be quiet here, / mind one's
own business." (*Básnický kalendář let 1918-1938* [Prague:
Kmen, 1938], pp. 147-148.)

[14] At the 2nd Writers' Congress in 1956, the poet
František Hrubín, himself a victim of such methods, tried
to exonerate Skála, saying that "he had not realized somebody put his hand on the trigger of a guillotine" (quoted
from personal recollection). Skála's subsequent behaviour
and recent career do not at all suggest that he had been an
innocent pawn in a political game.

[15] In Czech folk poetry, rosemary is the symbol of love.

[16] For a brief summary of Nikol'skii's essay see
Milada Součková, *A Literary Satellite* (Chicago and London:
The University of Chicago Press, 1970), p. 53.

[17] Howard Fast, *Literature and Reality* (New York: International Publishers, 1950), p. 9.

[18] Modern American literature was in this way almost
single-handedly rehabilitated by Josef Škvorecký in his
multiple role of critic, essayist, and publishers' editor.
His "justifications" were collected in *O nich - o nás*
(Hradec Králove: Kruh, 1968). Škvorecký also described
the technique in episodes in his novels *Lvíče* and *Mirákl*.
Perhaps the ultimate in "justification" was the conference
on Franz Kafka in 1963 which took place while most of his
work was still unavailable.

[19] Josef Škvorecký, *All the Bright Young Men and Women*
(Toronto: Peter Martin Associates Ltd., 1971), pp. 57-58.

[20] Milan Jungmann, *Literární noviny*, 41 (1964).

[21] For the role played by culture, see Chapter 5 in
Vladimir V. Kusin, *The Intellectual Origins of the Prague
Spring* (Cambridge: Cambridge University Press, 1971).

[22] A polemic between Štoll and some critics ran through
several issues of *Literární noviny* in 1966, occasioned by
his new book, *O tvar a strukturu ve slovesném umění*. It
was stopped by the Ideological Department of the Central
Committee.

[23] Zdeněk Kožmín, *Host do domu*, 17 (1969), p. 17.

[24] Jiří Opelík, *Nenáviděné řemeslo* (Prague: Československý spisovatel, 1969), p. 148.

[25] Vladimír Karfík, *Orientace*, 6 (1968), p. 87.

[26] Jiří Hájek, *Konfrontace* (Prague: Československý
spisovatel, 1972), p. 88.

[27] Josef Zika, *Otakar Březina* (Prague: Melantrich, 1970), p. 7.

[28] Josef Veselý, Introduction to *Stavba ve výši - Symfonie bratrských hlasů* (Brno: Blok, 1970), p. 7.

B. PRUS' *THE DOLL*: AN IRONIC NOVEL

Jerzy R. Krzyzanowski

> "Sophisticated irony merely
> states, and lets the reader
> add the ironic tone himself."
> Northrop Frye, *Anatomy of
> Criticism*

I

In one of his most celebrated statements concerning
the purpose of art, Joseph Conrad once wrote that "a work
of art that aspires, however humbly, to the condition of
art should be defined as a single-minded attempt to render
the highest kind of justice to the visible universe, by
bringing to light the truth, manifold and one, underlying
its every aspect."[1] A noble task indeed, and to the extent
that literary criticism is a kind of art, the same principle should apply to its purposes and standards as well.
But works of art must be available and known in order for
critics to attempt to render justice to them, and many
valuable works have been ignored only because they have
not been translated into an easily accessible language.

The recent first English publication of *The Doll* by
Bolesław Prus provides us with an opportunity to rediscover
a literary masterpiece of the Polish nineteenth-century
novel. Eighty-two years after its original publication in
1890, *The Doll* comes to the English-speaking readers and
must either win their approval as a major part of nineteenth-century fiction, or fall into oblivion as have many
other novels of that time. It is the purpose of this paper
to make an attempt at rendering justice to the novel's
artistic values, particularly by emphasizing its irony, a
basic structural device on which the whole novel hinges.

The history of *The Doll*'s reception is itself somewhat
ironic, and a brief survey of its fate will add to our understanding of the problems a critic of Prus' fiction faces
even today. Originally serialized in a Warsaw newspaper,
Kurjer Codzienny, in 1887-1889, *The Doll* [*Lalka*] began to
draw criticism even before it appeared in a book form.
T. T. Jeż accused it of being tendentious, Piotr

Chmielowski tried to prove that its composition was faulty, while Józef Kotarbiński compared it to "a rich park established without any plan, without harmony between the groups of trees," etc.[2] Most critics credited Prus with great talent and congratulated him on his first major novel, despite certain weaknesses in its composition. The first major attack against *The Doll* was launched by Aleksander Świętochowski, the most influential personality in the Positivist movement of the 1880s. He took to task the characters in *The Doll*:

> Let us imagine a small gallery of beautiful
> sculptures which, by some accident, got busted
> and which someone not very well acquainted
> with their forms put together again partly by
> instinct, thus exchanging many parts of their
> bodies. Let us imagine, then, that after
> such a restoration Hercules has received
> Adonis' head, Venus with a head of Diana,
> Cupido with the legs of little Bacchus--and
> then we will have a picture of *The Doll*, and
> partly of all major novels of its author.[3]

The controversy about the novel's value and its drawbacks persisted for years, and it is only in most recent times that its place in Polish literature has been at last firmly established. As the noted Polish critic, Kazimierz Wyka, stated:

> If a novel could possess its own normative
> aesthetics, and if such an aesthetics was to
> be written based on a selected Polish novel,
> all that would be needed would be *The Doll*,
> I believe, . . . for in that particular novel
> it is its form which is best balanced and
> therefore the most invisible, seemingly the
> most obvious--so obvious because it is not
> sufficient in any of its parts.[4]

The Doll has received extensive attention on the part of Modern Polish critics. There are at least five major monographic studies devoted entirely to it, while scores of articles, papers, and polemics about it appear in Polish academic journals virtually every year.[5] While *The Doll* continues to be a vital issue in Polish criticism, its reception abroad has been negligible until very recently, mostly for the lack of available foreign translations. Natalia Modzelewska's Russian translation of 1948 has been

re-published at least twice, in editions of Prus' selected
writings in 1955 and 1961. The German translation appeared
in 1954, followed by the French translation of 1964 in the
series "Collection UNESCO d'oeuvres representatives."
David Welsh's English translation appeared in 1972.[6]

    The Doll's delayed appearance in translation was not
the case of oversight, for as soon as *The Doll* was originally published, a Polish critic Adam Bełcikowski announced it in his yearly review of Polish literature in
the London *Atheneum*: "The *Puppet* is certainly one of the
most remarkable additions made of recent years to our imaginative literature, and is quite the most notable work produced in the last twelve months."[7] In France an interesting essay, including some vital critical remarks on *The
Doll*, was published by Ch. Chéret in *La Revue* in 1902,[8] but
bad timing prevented it from arousing interest since France
was just recovering from "l'invasion étrangère dans la littérature française," as a French critic Henri Bordeaux
called it.[9] Maria Kosko, whose study on the French reception of Sienkiewicz's *Quo vadis?* provides excellent insight
into the literary polemics of that period, concludes that
the nationalist crisis was over by February, 1902,[10] and
the ground for yet another foreign novel for the French
readers had to be prepared anew. The translators from
Polish were painfully aware of the situation. In a letter
to Prus, Bronisław Kozakiewicz, who had just completed his
translation of Prus' historical novel *The Pharao*, wrote on
April 17, 1902: "I have to wait though until May 15 before
I let it go, since the French reading public is a little
bit tired with translations. Besides, the public has to
be prepared with a few articles which will be published in
Le Matin and *Écho de Paris*. . . . Starting April 20 I am
beginning a journalistic campaign on *The Pharao*; I have
nice promises and great hope."[11]

    These and similar reasons must have contributed to the
fact that *The Doll*, too, received a rather limited reception abroad, even during the next decades. But the problems concerning it seem to lie deeper. After all, *The
Pharao* and many of Prus' short stories enjoyed numerous
foreign translations since the 1880s.[12] Was *The Doll*, of
which Manfred Kridl wrote that "without exaggeration one
may say that it is the most distinguished novel produced
in Poland up to that time and the finest novel of its period,"[13] either too Polish, too provincial, or too topical?
Why didn't it capture the attention of foreign critics when
for so many years it remained a classic in its own country?

The answer seems to be fairly simple: it is not the
fault of the novel but of the critics who failed to recognize its artistic merits. Polish critics concentrated
mainly on either the ideological or social significance of
the novel, while most of the foreign critics presented Prus
as a novelist in general and comparative terms. For example, in his monographic study of *The Doll*, Zygmunt
Szweykowski devoted twenty-eight out of the total three-
hundred-and-sixty pages to the problems of composition and
literary devices of the text. He devoted the rest of his
study to biographical, historical, and ideological problems. [14] Among the articles written in languages other than
Polish, the majority deals with such comparative topics as
Turgenev and Prus, Prus and Gončarov, Prus and Spielhagen,
etc. [15] The study of Prus' characters, written by Jerzy
Pietrkiewicz in 1960, did not sound an encouraging note:
"The heroes of his major novels are in fact portraits of
failure, and theirs is an all-embracing kind of failure
which involves the collapse of successful plans, material
and spiritual losses, and in two cases the loss of life at
the end of the story." [16]

Now that we finally have the English text of *The Doll*
available, the time has come to render critical justice to
that novel, and, following Conrad's inspiration, "to bring
to light the truth, manifold and one, underlying its every
aspect."

II

As we stated earlier, irony is a basic structural device in *The Doll*. Interestingly enough, no critic has ever
paid sufficient attention to its major role in the novel,
although quite a few have mentioned Prus' ironic mood casually while elaborating at some length on his humor. It is
necessary to define in what sense the term irony will be
used here since there exist major discrepancies among the
literary theoreticians concerning its precise definition.
Indeed, even J. A. K. Thomson, one of the pioneers of modern literary studies and the author of a historical study
on irony and its origins, remarked at the very beginning of
his work that "irony, which is a criticism of life, is as
hard to define as poetry." [17] Since that time, of course,
the tools of literary research have been sharpened thanks
to many ingenious and sophisticated studies written by
American Neo-critics as well as the Russian Formalists, but
differences of opinion persist. For Cleanth Brooks irony

is "a general term for the kind of qualifications which the
various elements in a context receive from the context"[18];
Boris Tomaševskij considers it merely a rhetorical trope
when he refers to "the use of words in a sense contradictory to their meaning," a phenomenon "belonging to the
phenomena born by metonymy."[19]   A different attitude is
represented by a Polish scholar, Julian Krzyżanowski, according to whom irony is a part of the comic in general, a
result of a negative, complicated, and speculative reaction
of a writer, a psychological attitude rather than merely a
literary device in a text.[20]   One must settle on a definition which may encompass those diversified views and opinions.   Such a definition was offered by Northrop Frye in
his *Anatomy of Criticism*, where he stated that "when we try
to isolate the ironic as such, we find it seems to be simply the attitude of the poet as such, a dispassionate construction of a literary form, with all assertive elements,
implied or expressed, eliminated."[21]   And Sonia Gotman, who
based her essay on irony in Čexov's fiction on Frye's assertion, adds that "irony may have a dispassionate front,
but when we penetrate it we grasp the ironist's real attitude."[22]   This amended definition works very well indeed in
analysing Prus' fiction in general, and *The Doll* in particular.

     In order to grasp the full meaning of the irony in
Prus' attitude and literary technique, we must go back to
the beginning of his literary career.   Somewhat like Chekhov, Prus started as a humoristic columnist in 1872, and
for almost forty years contributed regularly to the Warsaw
newspapers in the form of his weekly "chronicles."   Collected today, these "chronicles" comprise twenty impressive
volumes.[23]   From the beginning, the author's goal was two-
fold--to criticize and to amuse.   Prus was writing in the
repressive political climate of the 1870s and the following decades, combatting the overpowering presence of Russian censorship on the one hand, and the negative attitudes
of some Polish circles toward the Positivist movement on
the other.   Humor alone could not suffice to combat those
two forces, and Prus instinctively chose to develop a protective shield of irony behind which he could hide his real
concern for the welfare of the nation, whose very existence
was threatened after the 1863 national uprising.   Furthermore, at the beginning of his journalistic career Prus
joined the staff of a satirical weekly *Mucha*, and soon was
appointed its editor-in-chief.   In that position he mas-
tered the art of satire, which grew directly from his

ironic attitude toward some social problems he chastised
in his early writings. His journalistic techniques of
irony and satire carried over into his fiction, which he
began writing in 1874. His early stories, written before
1881, were often little different from his weekly newspaper column, displaying his humoristic attitude combined
with didactic goals. As the Polish critic Janina
Kulczycka-Saloni notes:

> Those who see in Prus a humoristic writer
> above all make a mistake, generalizing some
> insignificant cases from the first (but not
> very first) years of his creative work. Prus
> did not begin with humoristic stories. His
> first writings in *Opiekun domowy* are above
> all social, and his *Listy ze starego obozu*,
> besides some humoristic coloring, have clearly
> didactic goals; the very fact that the first
> outlines of his short stories were interwoven
> in the text to support the author's practical
> philosophy indicates what attitude Prus had
> toward his writing, and what role didacticism
> played in them. [24]

A detailed critical discussion of that early period
resulting in such well-known short stories as *Michałko*
(1880), *Antek* (1881), *The Waist Coat* (1882) as well as a
short novel *The Outpost* (1886) would exceed the limits set
forth for this paper; suffice it to say they all represent
a practical authorial workshop of a writer whose talent,
interest, and ambitions moved him closer and closer to the
crucial test of creating a major contemporary novel about
all those problems which moved him deeply. That novel,
originally intended to be titled "Three Generations," [25]
came down to us as *The Doll*.

The first installment of the novel appeared in *Kurjer
Codzienny* on September 29, 1887, and it ran with some interruptions till May 24, 1889. It was brought out in book
form by Gebethner and Wolff at the beginning of 1890, and
almost instantly stirred an animated critical discussion
which still continues. [26]

III

The time and setting of *The Doll* are clearly defined.
The novel encompasses the period between March, 1878, and
October, 1879, with some extensive flashbacks to the 1840s.

Most of the action takes place in Warsaw, with one long
excursion to Paris, and some short trips to the Polish
countryside. The description of life then, both based on,
and substantiated by the evidence from contemporary Warsaw newspapers, together with some detailed references to
certain streets, buildings, and locations in Warsaw,[27]
prompted most critics to consider *The Doll* a perfect example of "the nineteenth-century realism at its best," as
Czesław Miłosz puts it.[28]   And Jan Kott, whose perceptive
studies in French literature established him as a major
critic of the nineteenth-century realistic fiction, went
even further in stating that "the place occupied by *The
Doll* in Polish literature can be only compared with the
area covered by Balzac and Flaubert on the map of French
literature."[29]   But the opening paragraph of the novel does
more than just provide a realistic time and setting of the
action; it sets out the ironic mood which will prevail
throughout the novel and become a decisive structural element in it:

> Early in 1878, when the political world was con-
> cerned with the treaty of San Stefano, the
> election of a new Pope, and the chances of a
> European war, Warsaw businessmen and the in-
> telligentsia who frequented a certain spot at
> the Cracow Boulevard were no less keenly inter-
> ested in the future of the haberdashery firm
> of J. Mincel and S. Wokulski.[30]

The ironic contrast of the political events of world-
wide importance, and the petty gossip of the Warsaw busi-
nessmen and "the intelligentsia of a certain part of
Krakowskie Przedmieście," as the original Polish text
reads,[31] is emphasized by the narrator's qualifying remark
about their being "no less keenly interested" in the private affairs of Mr. Wokulski. That contrast is developed
in the paragraphs which follow, as Prus juxtaposes the
names of Bismarck and MacMahon with those of Mincel and
Wokulski, particularly with the latter, his business, and
eventually his background. The narrator is not satirizing
anyone in particular, but by contrasting the events of
note in the world to the narrow interests of his characters, he exposes the pettiness of the provincial world of
Warsaw, into which he will eventually introduce Wokulski
as the protagonist of the novel. As Stanisław Eile, whose
penetrating study centers on the narrator's role in *The
Doll*, pointed out: "Any reader of *The Doll* who is sensitive

to the position of the narrator versus the narrated story must be struck by the fact that the narrator's ideological-cognitive posture vacillates between a position of a reporter who registers the novelistic facts, and that of an interpreter who sometimes becomes a moralist."[32]

As the plot of the novel unfolds we see Wokulski through the eyes of his old friend Rzecki. We learn more about him from the impressions he makes on Izabela Łęcka, the aristocratic girl he is in love with, than from his own actions. Since his presentation differs depending on which character is viewing him, the question of Wokulski's real identity arises. Is he treated as ironically as the rest of the characters in *The Doll* because of his love for the girl of higher social standing and because of his frustrations? Or is he a tragic hero whose unfulfilled ambitions bring him to the brink of his final destruction? Perhaps a comparison with another literary hero of our time will bring him closer to the American reader and answer that question. Quoting one of Wokulski's exclamations, "How can I draw her attention to myself if not with money,"[33] a Polish critic Adam Kaska remarks: "No, that motto does not come from a novel by Fitzgerald. I have taken it from another book, well known to a Polish reader. Yes, so speaks Wokulski in Prus' *The Doll*. One could pick up more of similar quotations, and make some kind of a literary puzzle: Gatsby or Wokulski? The answer would not always be easy."[34]

Indeed, despite the differences between the 1870s in Poland, and the 1920s in the United States, Wokulski and Gatsby belong to the same breed of men driven to their ultimate destruction by a foolish love with a girl socially superior and morally inferior to the protagonist. And if *The Great Gatsby* "represents the irony of American history and corruption of the American dream," as John Henry Raleigh pointed out, for Fitzgerald "has run in his characteristic changes, doubling and re-doubling ironies,"[35] the same, *mutatis mutandis*, is true of *The Doll* and its unhappy hero. Gatsby's celebrated remark on Daisy: "Her voice is full of money,"[36] could as well apply to Izabela Łęcka. The ironic mood of the American novel may very well serve those American readers who would like to investigate Prus' novelistic technique used some forty years earlier.

The irony in *The Doll* is of three kinds. In some few instances it is explicit to the point of becoming satirical or even grotesque. More often, however, it is implicit but

ever present, making the novel structurally coherent.
There is also a subtle verbal irony which is lost in translation. Selected examples of these types of irony will be
dealt with subsequently in this paper. The first kind is
particularly evident in chapters presenting the aristoc-
racy, a very special world Wokulski wants to enter in order
to marry Izabela. Her father, Mr. Łęcki, lives not only on
borrowed time but on borrowed money as well. Virtually all
his friends, the princes, the counts, the barons, resemble
a gallery of caricatures whom Prus describes with an ironic
detachment expressed not so much by the narrator's comments
as by the contrast of their idle and superficial lives with
Wokulski's driving energy. And yet it is Wokulski who is
barred from that enchanted world of the upper class because
he is just a businessman who does not belong in the aristocratic circles. This represents an ironic theme in itself,
and since it forms the novel's main plot, the role of irony
becomes quite obvious.

It is worth noting that this type of irony eventually
turns into satire and grotesque in the second half of the
novel. Beginning with Chapter 31 of the English edition,
characteristically titled "Ladies and women," Prus not only
introduces some new characters who do not play any significant role, thereby stressing the superficiality of the social life of the upper classes, but gives them proper names
of mocking quality. And so we meet Miss Pantarkiewicz
(Guinea Hen), Mrs. de Gins Upadalska (Fallen-down), Mrs. de
Fertelski Wywrotnicka (Upside-down), Prince Kielbik (Gud-
geon, also Fuzzy-minded), Count Sledziński (Herring), etc.
Whereas in his previous novel, *The Outpost*, the name of the
protagonist, Ślimak (Snail) indicated some qualities in his
character, this time the mocking names just serve a satirical purpose.

Such overdrawn satire prompted some critics to compare
Prus' novelistic technique with that of Dickens or even
Prus' contemporary caricaturist, Franciszek Kostrzewski,
whose pictures of Warsaw characters were quite popular at
that time. That type of criticism, launched by Świętochowski, resulted in the novelist's angry reply in his well-
known article *Słówko o krytyce pozytywnej*, a masterpiece of
ironic polemics in itself. Nonetheless, this type of criticism was repeated by Karol W. Zawodziński as recently as
1946.[38]

The second type of irony is much more intricate and
subtle, for it is only implied in most cases. This could
account for its absence in critical discussions of the nov-

el, but it certainly deserves more attention than the obvious manifestations of the novelist's satirical vein.   It
must be noted here that some of Prus' ironic attitude was
noted by his contemporary critics who grasped its general
tone and the author's philosophy. Kazimierz Ehrenberg, a
Polish journalist and critic, commented as early as 1890
on a Latin inscription inscribed on Wokulski's alleged
grave in the ruins of an old castle, *Non omnis moriar*: "Is
this irony? Or is it a reproach that so it will be forever, that there always will be people among us who will
nostalgically repeat the enchanted words of the Romantic
seers in order to blame them for their own mistortunes?"[39]

Only seventy years later Prus' subtle irony was understood in a much broader and more literary sense by a French
author of the introduction to *La Poupée*, Jean Fabre, who
noted "the main value of the irony" in the novel as opposed
to rather insignificant events depicted in it.[40]   The early
critics, preoccupied with the novel's ideological message,
missed the point almost completely. They did not notice
that Wokulski's downfall, more ironic than tragic since it
was brought about not only by social injustice but by his
own folly, represented an ironic twist in itself. In fact
the novel is so deeply saturated with "doubled and re-
doubled ironies" that merely quoting them would result in
quoting pages after pages almost *in extenso*. Let us therefore point out just the most interesting examples, leaving
to the careful reader the pleasure of adding the ironic
tone, as Northrop Frye advises.

We can grasp some of Prus' ironic technique beginning
with the title of the novel, for the novelist's claim that
it derives from the law-suit between the baroness Krzeszow-
ska and Mrs. Stawska about an alledgedly stolen doll cannot
be taken seriously.[41] It is, of course, Izabela, "the society doll," to whom it refers, although she obviously is
the object of Wokulski's passion rather than the subject of
the novel as well. After Wokulski's ambiguous disappear-
ance--we do not know whether he committed suicide or so-
bered up and went to Paris to become a scientist--Dr. Szuman mourns Rzecki's death, and asks the fateful question:
"Who will be left here in the end?" "I shall," comes an
instant reply pronounced simultaneously by Szlangbaum, a
Jewish inheritor of Wokulski's fortune, and Maruszewicz, a
petty swindler. "There will be no lack of men," adds
councilor Węgrowicz, a silly gossip who, incidentally, had
appeared in the opening scene of the novel and did not play
any role throughout.[43] This trio, representing all the

pettiness and baseness in the Polish society, is an ironic
parallel to Wokulski's firm belief in "the earth, the simple man, and God,"[44] as the only hope for himself and for
the nation.

It has often been noted that a group of chapters generally entitled "the memoirs of an old clerk" provide not
only the *Vorgeschichte* of the actual story, but also introduce a much needed relief from the tensions in Wokulski's
personal affairs.[45] Rzecki's memoir uses a special kind of
auto-irony with which, as Henryk Markiewicz pointed out, he
"consciously creates his own ridiculousness, with a comical
exaggeration describing his behavior and psychical reactions, and gives his own statements a parodistic style."[46]
It is Rzecki, the old clerk and a faithful friend of Wokulski, who at the beginning of the novel sets in motion a
display of mechanical toys, and at the end of it repeats
the show, this time, however, with thoughts which sum up
the novelist's attitude toward the characters and events
depicted in the novel: "And, as he watched the movements
of the inanimate objects, he repeated for the thousandth
time: 'Puppets! . . . All puppets! They think they are doing as they choose but they only do what the springs command, blind as they are!'"[47]

An additional bitter ironic twist is provided by the
fact that even at that very last moment of his sad happiness Rzecki is being watched by a new clerk since the owner of the store suspects him of stealing after more than
twenty-five years of faithful service.

Rzecki's memoir provides the novel with humor, an important element otherwise largely missing in Wokulski's
story. Rzecki's encounters with the students renting an
apartment in Wokulski's house, his conversations with his
associates and friends, his constant suspicions concerning
Wokulski's alleged involvement in politics—all these factors make Rzecki and his memoir an integral part of the
novel. Initially misunderstood by the critics who thought
it a nuisance in the novel's construction,[48] it received
its due appreciation only from modern critics who, like Ch.
Chéret in 1902, noted that "nothing is more amusing than
his Napoleonic ideas of the Romantic and liberal kind expressed in front of his subordinates, one of whom is a socialist, another one an anti-Semite, and still another one
a *je menfichiste*."[49]

To complete this survey of ironic devices used in *The
Doll*, we ought to mention a third type of irony, the subtle
verbal irony unfortunately often lost in translation. As

an excellent example we may take Prus' handling of a very
delicate Jewish question which grows in importance as the
novel progresses. In a scene at the court, when Rzecki
describes the public attending the proceedings, he notices
"the Jews who, as I was later informed, are the most patient of all audiences at the court cases."[50]   In the
original Polish version of the novel the Jews are referred
to as "Żydki"[51] instead of grammatically correct "Żydzi,"
and even Dr. Szuman, who is Jewish himself, speaks of them
as "te Żydziaki"[52] instead of as "ci Żydzi," substituting
non-virile and diminutive forms often encountered in spok-
en Polish to indicate either ironic, or at least contemptuous, attitude of the speaker. In this way, through his
characters, Prus disclosed his attitude toward the so-called "Jewish question" which caused him much trouble from
the beginning of his literary career. (Accusations against
him ranged from rampant anti-Semitism to charges that he
was a Jew in disguise, not Aleksander Głowacki [which was
his real name], but "a young Jew, Ajzik Głowasser.")[53]

Another example is perhaps even more telling since under the verbal irony there is the disclosure of a tension
seemingly created by a misunderstanding, but in fact by
hyper-sensibility of a Jew who knows he cannot be accepted
by his Polish associates in spite of his wealth. When Mr.
Szlangbaum takes over Wokulski's business he notices a
certain coolness of his employees who "would jump into the
fire" for Wokulski. In the ensuing heated exchange of
words, one of the clerks, Lisiecki, asks Szlangbaum:

> "And do you know, sir, why we'd jump into
> the fire for Wokulski?"
> "Because he has more money," Szlangbaum
> replied.
> "No, sir. Because he has something you
> haven't got, and never will have," said
> Lisiecki, striking himself on the chest.
> Szlangbaum went as red as a vampire:
> "What is it?" he cried. "What haven't I got?
> We cannot work together, Mr. Lisiecki. . . .
> You insult my religion!"[54]

For the benefit of the American reader it must be explained here that only the Jews in Poland were circumcised,
and Lisiecki's reference was understood by Szlangbaum as a
direct hint to that fact which was generally considered
derogatory. That type of poignant irony is much more so-
phistocated than Prus' sarcastic remarks on the aristoc-
racy.

Taking into consideration the various forms of irony
discussed above we may ask whether Prus used his irony as
an intentionally employed, carefully thought out literary
device, or just as a manifestation of his general attitude
toward certain social problems. Recently published documents will help answer these questions. It has been known
for years that since 1886 the novelist kept special notes
on his aesthetic and literary theories. The existence of
those materials, presumably lost, was first hinted at by
Feliks Araszkiewicz in 1925.[55] Nine years later Zygmunt
Szweykowski corrected that assumption and published some
fragments of those notes,[56] but only in 1963 Stefan Melkowski researched those materials and used eleven notebooks
out of the existing twenty one in his study on Prus' aesthetics and literary composition.[57] Leaving aside Prus'
general literary theories, which to a great extent follow
the poetics of the nineteenth-century novel, the most
specific remarks concerning the problem in question can be
found in the following note:

> Composition ideas: 1. Next to A put contrast
> and antithesis. E.g. a decent man next to a
> scoundrel, a thinker next to an artist and a
> hero. 2. Next to a large feature or phenom-
> enon put a small one. E.g., someone very
> wise has a missing finger; a man threatened
> with bankruptcy has lost his hat; or a man
> lucky in love has just torn his dress. 3.
> Next to + virtues put + small vices, and next
> to + vices-- + vitures. E.g., a very brave
> man stutters, a thief loves birds, etc. 4.
> Real and fantastic /metaphysical/ charac-
> ters.[58]

Although irony as a literary device is not mentioned
in the fragments published by Melkowski, the method of
using contrast obviously creates tensions implied in
irony. Melkowski seems to be correct in concluding that
"the means serving the composition of a literary work play
a subservient role to its ideology. They are only definite 'devices' by which the author communicates his
thoughts and emotions to his readers."[59] But Prus must
have been well aware of the role of those devices. As
another Polish critic, Edward Pieścikowski, demonstrated
analyzing Prus' next major novel, *Emancypantki*, the novelist purged the last version of the novel of such authorial
comments in the narration as "indeed," "of course," "really," "in fact," etc.,[60] thereby creating a distance between

the reader and the fictious character, obviously an ironic device. Thus we may conclude that Prus' ironic attitude toward certain philosophical and social problems resulted in his conscious use of literary devices which from the literary point of view made his novels, and especially *The Doll*, structurally sound and coherent.

We have tried here to underscore some artistic aspects of *The Doll* so far generally overlooked by the critics, and, at the same time, to introduce one of the major Polish nineteenth-century novels to foreign readers who may not have a chance to read it. If we succeeded, that kind of rendering justice to a work of art Joseph Conrad was speaking of has been accomplished.

> *The Ohio State University*
> *Columbus, Ohio*

NOTES

[1]Joseph Conrad, "Preface" to *The Nigger of the "Narcisus"* (London: The Gresham Publishing Co., 1925), vii.

[2]Henryk Markiewicz, *"Lalka" Bolesława Prusa* (Warszawa: Czytelnik, 1967), p. 178.

[3]Ibid., p. 184.

[4]Kazimierz Wyka. *Pogranicze powieści* (Kraków: Wydawnictwo M. Kot, 1948), p. 42.

[5]Zygmunt Szweykowski, *"Lalka" Bolesława Prusa* (Warszawa: Gebthner i Wolff, 1927); Jan Kott, *O "Lalce" Bolesława Prusa* (Warszawa: Książka i Wiedza, 1950); Henryk Markiewicz, *Prus i Żeromski* (Warszawa: Państwowy Instytut Wydawniczy, 1964); Ludwik B. Grzeniewski, *Warszawa w "Lalce" Prusa* (Warszawa: Państwowy Instytut Wydawniczy, 1965); Stanisław Eile, "Dialektyka 'Lalki' Bolesława Prusa," *Pamiętnik Literacki*, LXIV (1973), 1, 3-51. See also a bibliography in Janina Kulczycka-Saloni, "Bolesław Prus," *Literatura polska w okresie realizmu i naturalizmu*, Obraz literatury polskiej XIX i XX wieku, No. 2 (Warszawa: Państwowe Wydawnictwo Naukowe, 1966), pp. 189-200.

[6]Bolesław Prus, *The Doll*, tr. by David Welsh (New York: Twayne Publishers, 1972).

[7]Adam Bełcikowski, "The Review of Continental Literature," *Atheneum*, July 5, 1890, No. 3271, 24.

[8]Ch. Chéret, "Alexandre Glowacki /Boleslav Prus/", *La Revue*, XLII (1902), 204-223.

[9]Henri Bordeaux, "L'invasion étrangère dans la littérature française," *Le Correspondent*, December 25, 1901.

[10] Maria Kosko, *Un"best-seller" 1900. Quo vadis?*
(Paris: Libraire José Corti, 1960), p. 114.

[11] Quoted in Krystyna Tokarzówna and Stanisław Fita, *Bolesław Prus, 1847-1912. Kalendarz życia i twórczości* (Warszawa: Państowy Instytut Wydawniczy, 1969), p. 581.

[12] Janina Kulczycka-Saloni, *Nowelistyka Bolesława Prusa* (Warszawa: Czytelnik, 1969), pp. 243-250.

[13] Manfred Kridl, *A Survey of Polish Literature and Culture* ('S-Gravenhage: Mouton and Co., 1956), p. 365.

[14] Zygmunt Szweykowski, *"Lalka" Bolesława Prusa*, pp. 301-29.

[15] Zbigniew Folejewski, "Turgenev and Prus," *The Slavonic and East European Review*, XIX (1950-51), 132-38; Mieczysław Giergielewicz, "Prus and Gončarov," *American Contributions to the Fifth International Congress of Slavists, Sofia, 1963* (Hague: Mouton and Co., 1963), 129-46; Jadwiga Maurer, "Bolesław Prus und Friedrich Spielhagen. Zur Problematik der romantischen Liebe in 'Lalka" und in 'Reih und Glied'," *Der Welt der Slaven*, 3-4 (1960), 340-46. The Polish bibliography (see note 5 above) also lists numerous studies on Prus and Balzac, Prus and Daudet, Prus and Musset, Prus and Dickens, etc.

[16] Jerzy Pietrkiewicz, "Justified Failure in the Novels of Bolesław Prus," *The Slavonic and East European Review*, XXXIX (1960), 95-107.

[17] J.A.K. Thomson, *Irony: A Historical Introduction* (Cambridge, Mass.: Harvard University Press, 1927), p. 2.

[18] Cleanth Brooks, *The Well Wrought Urn* (New York: Reynal and Hitchcock, 1947), p. 191.

[19] Boris Tomaševskij, *Teorija literatury* (Moskva: Gosudarstvennoe Izdatel'stvo, 1928), p. 41. For a comparative study of similarities and differences between those two schools of criticism see Ewa M. Thompson, *Russian Formalism and Anglo-American New Criticism* (The Hague: Mouton and Co., 1971).

[20] Julian Krzyżanowski, *Nauka o literaturze* (Wrocław: Ossolineum, 1969), p. 202.

[21] Northrop Frye, *Anatomy of Criticism* (Princeton: Princeton University Press, 1973), pp. 40-41.

[22] Sonia Gotman, "The Role of Irony in Čexov's Fiction," *Slavic and East European Journal*, XVI (1972), No. 3, 297.

[23] Bolesław Prus, *Kroniki*, oprac. Z. Szweykowski (Warszawa: Państwowy Instytut Wydawniczy, 1953-1970), 20 vols.

[24] *Nowelistyka Bolesława Prusa*, p. 206.

[25] Markiewicz, p. 88.

[26] For a selection of criticism see Markiewicz, pp. 153-310.

[27] Ludwik B. Grzeniewski, op. cit.; see also "Inna zabawa 'Lalką'" in Markiewicz, pp. 134-48.

[28] Czesław Miłosz, *The History of Polish Literature* (New York: Macmillan, 1969), p. 298. See also David Welsh, "'Realism' in Prus' *Lalka*," *The Polish Review*, IX (1963), No. 3, 33-38.

[29] Jan Kott, p. 67.

[30] *The Doll*, p. 1.

[31] David Welsh, who translated the novel into English, admits several omissions and mistakes in the English text of the novel. (David Welsh, "Ayesha, Aspasia and Isabella," *American Contributions to the Seventh International Congress of Slavists, Warsaw, August 21-27, 1973*, [The Hague: Mouton and Co., 1973], p. 560.

[32] Eile, p. 3.

[33] *The Doll*, p. 91.

[34] Adam Kaska, "Posłowie" to the Polish translation of The Great Gatsby by F. Scott Fitzgerald (*Wielki Gatsby*, [Warszawa: Czytelnik, 1962], p. 235.)

[35] John Henry Raleigh, "F. Scott Fitzgerald's *The Great Gatsby*," in *F. Scott Fitzgerald. A Collection of Critical Essays*, Arthur Mizener, ed. (Englewood Cliffs, N.J.: Prentice-Hall, 1963), p. 99.

[36] F. Scott Fitzgerald, *The Great Gatsby* (New York: Charles Scribner's Sons, 1953), p. 91.

[37] Originally published in *Kurjer Codzienny*, Nos. 308-316 (1890), reprinted in Bolesław Prus, *Pisma* (Warszawa: Państwowy Instytut Wydawniczy, 1950), XXIX, 163-212.

[38] Karol Wiktor Zawodziński, *Opowieści o powieści* (Kraków: Wydawnictwo Literackie, 1963), p. 164.

[39] Markiewicz, p. 194.

[40] Ibid., p. 306.

[41] Ibid., pp. 87-88.

[43] *The Doll*, p. 701.

[44] Ibid., p. 608.

[45] Kridl, p. 368.

[46] Markiewicz, *Prus i Żeromski*, pp. 60-61.

[47] *The Doll*, pp. 697-98.

[48] E.g., see a review by Piotr Chmielowski, reprinted in Markiewicz, *"Lalka" Bolesława Prusa*, p. 173.

[49] Ch. Chéret, p. 221.

[50] *The Doll*, p. 514.

[51] Bolesław Prus, *Lalka* (Warszawa: Państwowy Instytut Wydawniczy, 1973), vol. II, p. 238.

[52] Ibid., p. 412.

[53] Krystyna Tokarzówna and Stanisław Fita, p. 209.

[54] *The Doll*, p. 612.

[55] Feliks Araszkiewicz, "Rekopis Bolesława Prusa o kompozycji," *Pamiętnik Literacki* (1925-26), 633-650.

[56] Zygmunt Szweykowski, "Z puścizny po Prusie," *Ruch Literacki* (1934), No. 10, 313ff.

[57] Stefan Melkowski, *Poglądy estetyczne i działalność krytyczno-literacka Bolesława Prusa* (Warszawa: Państowy Instytut Wydawniczy, 1963). For a detailed list of Prus' notes, see Tokarzówna and Fita, p. 777.

[58] Melkowski, pp. 105-106.

[59] Ibid., p. 109.

[60] Edward Pieścikowski, *Emancypantki Bolesława Prusa* (Warszawa: Państwowy Instytut Wydawniczy, 1970), p. 109.

STYLISTIC ELEMENTS IN NJEGOŠ'S *GORSKI VIJENAC* AND MAŽURANIĆ'S *SMRT SMAIL-AGE ČENGIGĆA*

Charles A. Ward

In the history of Serbian and Croatian literature two works stand out above all the rest--Ivan Mažuranić's epic narrative *Smrt Smail-age Čengiǵa* (*Smail-aga Čengić's Death*, 1845) and Petar Petrović Njegoš's dramatic epic *Gorski vijenac* (*The Mountain Wreath*, 1847). Though written by authors from entirely different cultural, social, and educational backgrounds, these two works have many elements in common. Mažuranić (born 1814) and Njegoš (born 1813) knew first hand the struggles of captive Slavs against foreign tyranny. Their natural desire for freedom for their people was reinforced when they discovered in Western romantic literature themes of rebellion and struggle against oppression, with the great emphasis on the unique genius of each nation. In deciding their mode of expression both authors turned to their national verse forms, the South Slavic oral tradition, which had narrated the struggle of Slav with Turk for hundreds of years. Yet both authors stamped this verse form with their individual literary genius and their own aesthetically conceived views of the events they described. Mažuranić told of the death of Smail-aga Čengic, Turkish ruler of part of Hercegovina, who was killed in 1840 by a Montenegrin raiding party. Njegoš's work, set in the seventeenth century, presents the deliberations of a Montenegrin bishop authorizing the killing of Turkish converts who, by their presence, threatened the survival of Serbian orthodoxy and culture.

It is the combination of striking similarities and marked differences between these two poems which makes a joint examination of them so rewarding. Both are vitally concerned with the struggle of Christian against Turk, of good against evil. Both express a conception of Fate or inevitable necessity which leads to the culminating events; both draw on the oral tradition for the basic verse form; both celebrate the folk and their traditional life disrupted by oppressors; and both use images and metaphors drawn from nature in describing the struggles.

The differences between the works are as important and significant as the similarities. The authors' differ-

ing poetic conceptions are reflected in their verbal style,
their approach to the materials, and the structure of the
poems. In generalized, simplified, terms Mažuranić is describing a series of actions which illustrate his view of
destiny and the fate of tyrants. He is concerned with the
sequence of actions and their consequences, not their
causes. One act leads inevitably to others, until they
culminate in Čengić's death. In presenting this inexorable chain of occurrences, Mažuranić is concerned with the
action and reaction of events, with what physically happens
to Čengić.

Njegoš, on the contrary, is concerned with the discussions and decisions which lead to an action. He is absorbed by the causes that lead to the decision to liquidate the Turkish converts. His interest thus turns to the
inner world of emotions and personalities and to the historical circumstances which have contributed to the conflict of ideas. The action, when it comes, is an anti-
climax, a physical signal to mark the resolution of the inner struggle. It is a lyric and dramatic presentation as
opposed to Mažuranić's more classical, epical approach.
These fundamentally different poetic conceptions require
different structuring of the stylistic elements by which
they are expressed.

Mažuranić presents the conflicts in the first fifteen
lines of his poem. Beginning *in media res*, he at once
shows Čengić ordering the torture of the Montenegrin captives and mentions the possibility of retaliation. He has
Čengić order the senseless execution of his advisor Durak,
whose son Novica then turns against Čengić and defects to
the Montenegrins. In these first lines Čengić likewise reveals his pride and his compulsion to act brutally to show
that he is not afraid of others. These conflicts between
Čengić and the Christians, between Čengić and his own ad-
visors, and between Čengić and himself are shown in action;
we do not see any of the characters thinking about their
reasons for doing what they do. Even when Čengić feels
some inner twinge of fear or apprehension (ll. 65-76),
Mažuranić is purposely vague in explaining what it is and
gives us no insight into Čengić's thoughts. Čengić sum-
marily kills the captives and Durak, and this action causes
other actions.

Next we see Novica traveling, but only when he arrives
in Cetinje do we discover that he is defecting to the Montenegrins to seek aid in revenging himself on Čengić. The
Montenegrin raiding party then gathers by itself, without

anyone even calling for assembly. Action leads to action
inexorably, inevitably, as Mažuranić studiously avoids presenting characters deliberating over courses of action.
Statements by Novica and the old priest are declarations
of confidence and resolution; Fate leads them on and they
play the roles assigned. The poem is largely narrative,
presenting the action as fact, and there is little dialogue which would give greater scope to the play of ideas.

Mažuranić has managed to combine romantic narrative
poetry, epic, and themes of classical tragedy. To bolster
the epic content, Mažuranić makes Čengić a much more evil
person than historical accounts record. Čengić must be
raised to the level of an absolute evil with which Christianity is locked in mortal struggle. Yet like the protagonists of Greek drama, Čengić has committed a crime
against society and cannot escape his fate. In Mažuranić's
view, Čengić's is the fate of all tyrants, to eventually
meet their doom. Because of the broader implications of
the story and the classical sparseness of the style, the
exact historical details about the characters are not important. The fact that Čengić did not live in the town
Mažuranić mentions, and that Novica could not have gone
through villages in the order presented in the poem did
not really matter to Mažuranić, for the important fact was
that Čengić was a tyrant and Novica was turning against
him. In terms of the poetic conception, the main consideration is not that Mažuranić had made Novica, a Montenegrin in real life, into a Turk, but that the Novica in
the poem merged his desire for personal revenge with the
general will of the whole people, and thereby fulfilled
the destiny ordained by fate.

Njegoš's approach is quite the opposite of Mažuranić's.
After a dedication to Karadjordje, the father of Serbian
freedom, Njegoš presents bishop Danilo's magnificent mono-
log which contains the basic conflicts of *Gorski vijenac*:
the historical conflict of the Serbs with the Turks, to
whom they had lost their freedom, and against whom they
had vowed continuing resistance; the conflict of Orthodox
Montenegrins and Montenegrins converted to Islam, whom
Danilo sees destroying Montenegro from the inside; and
Danilo's inner conflict, whether or not to authorize killing these converts to preserve the country. The poem develops as a series of conversations between characters in
a pseudo-dramatic form. The tension and drama of the poem
come from these discussions, the interaction of competing
ideas. The action--the fighting itself--plays almost no

role. The conflicts of the characters' ideas are heightened by a series of scenes of Montenegrin life--wedding pro-
cessions and songs, abduction of brides, fortune telling,
and so on--where these traditional activities are in some
way upset by the presence or participation of the converted
Turks.

The image of fate suggested in *Gorski vijenac* differs
from Mažuranić's immutable fate which, presented in a context stripped of detail and specific personalities, makes a
statement about the destiny of all tyrants. Njegoš is concerned not so much with Fate as such, but with the fate of
a particular country in particular historic circumstances.
Serbia's fate is to struggle with the evil which descended
in 1389 at Kosovo when the state was defeated by the Turks.
The Turkish empire cannot be defeated, but the domestic
Turks as representatives of Turkish evil must be stopped
before they adulterate, and thereby destroy, Serbdom. To
further emphasize the national essence of his story, Njegoš
chose only actual characters from Montenegrin history. He
then presents three stages of the struggle for freedom--
the battle of Kosovo of 1389, which is constantly hovering
in the background of the dialogues; the massacre of the
Turkish converts, which is the subject of the poem; and the
freeing of Serbia by Karadjordje in the early nineteenth
century, mentioned in the dedication of the poem.

While the actual massacre does not seem to have taken
place historically, it is the only possible outcome of the
themes and arguments which Njegoš presents. Any other outcome would have signified the doom of Serbdom. In describing Čengić's death, Mažuranić changed the circumstances of
an actual event to make it suit his purposes. Njegoš presented the actual circumstances of seventeenth century
Montenegro, but invented the massacre as the necessary outcome of the line of reasoning he employed. In Mažuranić
the people were an anonymous mass acting out the Fate ordained from above. Njegoš introduces the people directly
into the dialogues in the *kolo*, a kind of folk chorus com-
menting on their history and on what should be done. It is
they who blame the current misfortunes on the Serbs themselves, on the "velikaši" who had betrayed Serbian integrity. Mažuranić saw the Turks only as senseless tyrants
over innocents ("Što je raja kriva?," 1. 504). Milija in
Gorski vijenac accepts the verdict of the *kolo*, that lax-
ity in Serbian leaders has contributed to the problem of
the country. He uses this verdict of the people as a reason for action. The "velikaši" made the wrong decisions

once, after Kosovo. Now the present-day chieftains gathered at Lovćen have another chance to clear themselves with
the historical verdict of the people:

Čujte li kolo kako pjeva,
Ka je ona pjesna izvedena?
Iz glave je cijela naroda!
I imaju razlog Crnogorci
Da nas dići prokletu gomilu . . . (11. 291-95).

(Do you hear what the kolo sings,
As it set forth that song?
It is from the head of the whole nation!
And the Montenegrins have a reason
To raise an accursed pile on us . . .)

In the dialectic of the poem, the kolo's comments become a
call for action. The evil is there and must be destroyed.
But bishop Danilo sees both sides and suffers at the
thought of what he must do. Njegoš goes further and gives
the converted Turks the opportunity to speak, and in some
cases to call for reconciliation. The presentation of
both views as well as the lack of action and Danilo's
loneliness and despair in reaching his decision keep this
work from being an epic. In Mažuranić things are cleaner
cut; it is pure epic without fuzzy edges: Čengić is evil,
his evil actions bring an active response. There is nothing for the characters to think about or discuss.

This contrast of the two poetic conceptions, of fate-
oriented epic and painful lyric deliberation leading to
action, is reflected not only in the thematic considerations of the representative poems, but in the stylistic
traits of each author, in choice and use of metaphor, in
the way nature and natural images are used, in the way
characters are presented, described, and developed.

Mažuranić uses images from nature to differentiate
Turks and Christians in relation to God's world. The epic
structure requires the greatest differentiation of the opposing forces, and Mažuranić uses as many details as possible to heighten the contrast. He shows the Turks at
odds with natural life, bringing death, destruction, and
perversion. Gacko field was beautiful until the Turks
came:

Gacka polje, lijepo ti si,
Kad u tebi glada nema,
Ljuta glada i nevolje ljute!
Al te jadno danas pritisnuli

krvni momci i oružje svijetlo,
Bojni konji, bijeli čadorovi,
Teška gvožđa i fakale grozne. (11. 478-84)

(Gacko field, lovely you are,
When there is no hunger on you,
Fierce hunger and fierce distress!
But on you today, wretched one, crowded
Gloody lads and shining arms,
Battle horses, white tents,
Heavy irons and horrible fetters.)

The Turks' actions are a perversion of peasants' farming
life; their horses are cavalry chargers, not plowhorses;
their implements the tools of torture. They drag the rayah
by their horses' tails (1. 492) making a monstrous harrow
of live bodies (1. 580). Earlier they used oxen to draw
captives onto torture stakes (11. 21-25). The Turkish tax
collectors come from the four points of the compass.
There is no exit for the rayah, no relief from their travail. In a lyrical moment the narration comments on this
displacement of the rayah from their natural life:

Stvorac višnjih pticam nebo dade,
Tiha duplja i žuđena gnijezda:
Ribam vode i pučine morske,
Stan od stakla, nek se po njem šire:
A zvijerinju livade i gore,
Hladne špilje i zelene luge;
Jadnoj raji? ne dade ni kore
Suha hljeba, da je suzam kvasi.
Al' što velju? dade nebo dobro
No je nesit sve već Turčin pobrō. (622-631)

(The great creator gave to birds the heavens,
Quiet hollows and desired nests;
To fish the waters and the sea's abyss,
A home of glass in which to propogate;
And for the beasts, the meadows and mountains,
Cold caverns and green groves;
To the wretched Rayah? not even a
Crust of dry bread to moisten with its tears.
But what am I saying? The good heavens gave,
But the insatiable Turk has taken all away.)

The Turks do not live and prosper like other inhabitants of
God's world; they are robbers and torturers. They are not
even healthy, but are afflicted by filth and decay (11.
505-6).

Mažuranić uses images from nature to present the
Christians in as favorable a light as possible. Sympathy
has been aroused for the rayah by their birthright which
the Turks rudely stole. The Montenegrins and their land
are one ("This land gave you birth," 1. 334). They and
their land are one when they gather to raid Čengić's camp:

> . . . proz mrak scijeniš,
> Studen kamen prima život,
> Drhće, gamzi, diže glavu
> Iz tvrdoga stanca snažnu
> Pest pomalja, nogu krepku,
> I proz mrazne živce vruća,
> Rek' bi, krvce vri mu rijeka. (217-223)

> (Through the darkness you think
> That the cold stone receives life,
> Trembles, crawls, raises its head,
> That from the hard stone stick out
> A strong fist, a sturdy foot,
> And through the icy veins there flows,
> It seems, a hot river of blood.)

Land and people are one; God made the land, and its people
will win over the ungodly tyrant. The elements are favorable to the Christians. The priest who appears in the
morning is accompanied by the sun and is characterized as
the "bellwether" of their flock. Darkness hides their
first assembly and their approach to Čengić's camp. Their
attack is accompanied by a storm, to emphasize their one-
ness with nature and their role as the instrument of fate.

Mažuranić thus uses nature to reinforce this basic opposition of evil Turkish oppressor and innocent subjugated
Christian. Identified with nature, the Christians are the
hard rock of Montenegro on which the Turkish monster dulls
its teeth (1. 372); they are pastoral nature which has been
outraged by the Turks; and they are the storm of retribution sent by God to punish the tyrant. For the most part
these are "one-to-one" comparisons, where the Christians
are described positively as part of nature, and the Turks
are inimical to natural life. The comparisons have no
secondary, allegorical implications.

Njegoš uses nature somewhat differently in *Gorski
vijenac*, for his style is expressive, not declarative. His
images reinforce ideas and refer to themes in the poem. He
uses images from nature as symbols or allegories of the
Turkish-Christian conflict, or as portents of such conflicts to come. Characters in *Gorski vijenac* also use

nature for analogies to provide reasons and justifications
for action. Toward the beginning of the poem Draško wanted
to kill a coocoo bird (1. 182) but was reprimanded because
coocoos were thought to be the daughters of Prince Lazar
who, because of their mourning for their father and Serbia
after the defeat of Kosovo, turned into coocoo birds. By
introducing this scene Njegoš simultaneously presents a
Montenegrin folk belief and points to Serbia's unhappy history, and more specifically to Serbia's defeat at Kosovo.
Kosovo broaches the problem of what to do about the converted Turks. The coocoo thus has nothing really to do
with nature, but suggests the themes which dominate the
poem.

 Birds reappear as a portent of the coming strife and
as a symbol of Turkish-Christian conflict as two cocks are
shown fighting. The Serb Rogan wants the weaker to win,
while the Turk Skender-aga thinks it only natural that the
more powerful should prevail. This brings to focus a
dilemma first mentioned by Danilo--does might make right,
and can a weak country justify attack on the forces of a
stronger oppressor?

 Some young Montenegrins capture partridges which appear on Mt. Lovćen on Christmas Eve. The assembled crowd
demands that these birds be released, saying that they had
fled up the mountain to escape Turkish oppression. This is
a projection of their own position, and nature becomes a
mirror in which they see their own misfortunes reflected.
Sometimes Njegoš manipulates nature to provide the necessary image. Near the beginning of the poem, on the heights
of Lovćen, Obrad sees two bolts of lightning intersect to
form a cross. He comments on this never-before seen event
and takes it as a sign that God will help the Serbs.

 Radonja's speech on the heights of Lovćen is entirely
allegorical. The clouds pile up all around with lightning
and thunder below, while he sits above warming in the sun.
All surrounding areas are oppressed alike by the cloud, but
the mountain top remains sunny and free. A similar allegory of clouds is found in the *kolo*'s last appearance:

  Bješe oblak sunce uhvatio,
  Bješe goru tama pritisnula . . . (2622-2623)

  (A cloud had seized the sun,
  A darkness had oppressed the mountain . . .)

Here the clouds and darkness are not only Turkish occupation but the eclipse of Serbian spirit, the loss of spirit

and hope which was finally revived by the massacre of the
Turkish renegades. Three stages of cloud imagery can
clearly be distinguished: Mažuranić's "Oblak krije zvijezde
jasne," 1. 232, where a real cloud hides the stars so the
raiding party can assemble unseen. In Radonja's speech on
Lovćen, the existence of the clouds is probable, but his
description of them is allegorical. In the final *kolo* the
cloud is totally allegorical, having no natural context at
all.

Many examples of nature imagery are found in Abbot
Stefan's speeches in *Gorski vijenac*:

> Sve priroda snabd'jeva oružjem
> Protiv neke neobuzdne sile,
> Protiv nužde, protiv nedovoljstva;
> Ostro osje odbranjuje klasje,
> Tranje ružu brani očupati . . . (2301-5)

> (All nature is provided with weapons
> Against some unfettered power,
> Against want, against dissatisfaction;
> A sharp sting defends the wasp,
> Thorns protect the rose from being picked . . .)

The observation of natural defenses in nature leads to the
analogy with man. Nature has provided all creation with
defenses, so that evil does not conquer. So, too, the
people are the defenders of church and tribe. Nature thus
becomes the model for action, and the justification of the
massacre of the Turkish converts. In a later speech Stefan
returns to the struggles found in nature:

> Sv'jet je ovaj tiran tiraninu
> A kamoli duši blagorodnoj!
> On je sostav paklene nesloge;
> U nj ratuje duša sa tijelom,
> U nj ratuje more s bregovima . . . (11. 2499-2503)

> (This world is a tyrant to tyrants
> Not to mention to a noble soul.
> It is a mixture of hellish disharmonies,
> In it soul struggles with body,
> In it the sea struggles with the shores . . .)

The model for violence is thus found in nature.

In numerous other places Njegoš uses images from nature in allegorical fashion. Mićunović, speaking of the
young Montenegrins' readiness to do battle, resorts at
once to analogy:

Tek što vučad za majkom pomile
Igrajuć se strašno zube svoje
Već umiju pod grlom ostriti;
Tek sokolu prvo perje nikne,
On ne može više mirovati,
Nego svoje razmeće gnijezdo,
Grabeć' slamku jednu i po jednu
S njom put neba bježi cijučući (11. 116-24)

(As soon as the wolf cubs crawl after the mother
Playing frighteningly with their teeth
They already know how to sharpen under the throat;
As soon as the falcon's first feathers appear,
He can no longer sit still
But picks apart his nest,
Grabbing one straw after another
Rushes with it to the sky, chirping.)

Skender-aga uses a similar device to an opposite end, telling the bishop, "Staro drvo slomi, ne ispravi," 1. 801 (You break an old tree, you can't mend it), meaning Christian faith in Montenegro, which should not give way to long-ascendent Islam.

Scattered metaphoric allegories based on nature occur throughout. Selim-pasha is making an inspection tour:

Da pregledam u mladeži zube,
Da se ruža u trn ne izgubi,
Da ne gine biser u bunište (11. 1089-91)

(To look at the youths' teeth,
That a rose is not lost in the thorns,
That a pearl is not lost in the trash.)

The images have meaning on several levels. The pasha views the sultan's subjects as cattle, or horses, to be examined before acquisition. The youths, presumably, are girls for the harem and boys for the janissary troops. The image can be viewed from either side's standpoint--the Montenegrins seeing the bloom of their youths being stolen from them, the best stock from which the resistance to Turks would come. The Turks see the girls as pretty faces to please the sultan, and want to be sure not to miss any. *Gorski vijenac* abounds in such images, but these are sufficient to provide a contrast to Mažuranić's usage.

One of the more obvious differences between *Smrt Smail-age Čengića* and *Gorski vijenac* is in the presentation and use of characters. Most of Njegoš's characters are determined by the ideas they express--they are their ideas. All represent slightly different approaches to the problem of Turk and Montenegrin, to the problem of Serbdom's fate. The positions range the full spectrum, from Vuk Mićunović's refined heroism and insistent call for battle, to Danilo's careful weighing of both sides. Mićunović's seriousness is offset by Knez Janko's jokes and by Vuk Mandušić's more human, less fanatic heroism. Danilo's cautious reasoning and concern for the state is matched by Abbot Stefan's concern for higher religious law. The Turks have their range of opinions, from the haughty superiority of Hamza of Nikšić to the religious ecstacies of Mustaj Kadi. The Turks cannot accept Danilo's insistence on one religion for Montenegro, and eloquent pleas for mutual co-existence are made by Skender-aga (11. 964-72) and Ferat Začir (11. 1016-22). These divergent views are argued back and forth, and slowly and inexorably the range of options narrows as various clashes and reports of troubles with the converted Turks give concrete evidence and embodiment to the fears Danilo expressed in the opening monologue, that the domestic Turks would destroy Serbdom from within.

In contrast, *Smrt Smail-age Čengića* is almost devoid of characters. Since man is subject to a higher fate, and his freedom of choice is limited, interest turns to action rather than deliberation. Čengić as the central character is most fully presented, but is one-sided, a representative of absolute evil, with no redeeming features. Various of his retainers are mentioned. Novica represents the principles of vengeance, but his personality is effaced by the anonymity of the raiding party. A few other Turks are named, but are subservient to their master. The Christians do not even have names. The rayah is a tortured mass of captive subjects of the sultan who gain a certain nobility through their helpless suffering. The Montenegrins in the raiding party are also nameless. They are a hundred men moving as one. In their unity they represent the instrument of fate bringing doom to Čengić. Fate moves inexorably through the poem as Čengić is drawn to his fate by provoking retaliation, by his anger at not collecting the tribute, by his shame at blinding one of his own men by accident, and by his final raving at fate which reveals his tent's location to the raiding party, which just as inexorably had assembled, taken their vows, and moved unerring through the dark and threatening night. The effacing of the characters perfectly reflects Mažuranić's decision to use Čengić's death as the pretext for a statement

of fate in general, just as Njegoš's many individual characters reflect the dialectical nature of his poem.

The types of comparisons outlined here are only an
introduction to some ways of comparing these two works,
with the goal of revealing more clearly by contrast the
specific differences, as well as the nature of the virtues, of these masterpieces.

University of Wisconsin-Milwaukee
Milwaukee, Wisconsin

INTRODUCTION

This is a selection of papers delivered at the major recent international conference of Slavists held at Banff, Alberta—the most ambitious such conference, in fact, yet to have taken place in the West. The volume's origin has important consequences both for its overall shape and for the nature of the individual contributions. A chance element naturally enters into the range of subjects covered, since participants at the Conference chose their own topics; on the other hand the organization of the programme into thematically-orientated panels provided common reference points for contributors, with the result that the material presented in this volume falls naturally into certain basic categories. The contents of our volume, then, will appear less "shaped" than would be the case if the collection had resulted from initial editorial direction as to subject-matter: but it has, we hope, the merit of representing a more spontaneous choice of topics, that in their variety reflect the problems in Russian and East European literature of most vital concern to scholars working the mid-1970s.

The papers themselves, intended for oral delivery and subsequent discussion at the Conference panels, will probably strike the reader as being generally more concise and (if one dare say it) more attractively and accessibly presented than many he will have encountered in typical scholarly publications. Though some have been revised or amplified since the Conference, reediting that would have impaired the freshness—in some cases the tendentiousness—of the points the authors make has not been encouraged; the value of this volume should lie at least partially in the degree to which it expresses the spirit of inquiry and the opening up of new ground characteristic of the Banff conference.

Our contributors' emphases and manners of approach are, I believe, significantly different from what might have been expected had a similar conference been held one or two decades ago. The familiar "hero" and "villain" figures of conventional literary historians—Eastern or Western—make little appearance; instead we encounter the often more interesting writers (Khlebnikov, Shklovsky, Grin, the *Oberiuty*, the *derevenshchiki*, etc.) whom they had overshadowed. One "classic" novel, *The Quiet Don* (recently of course the subject of much discussion and speculation) is illuminated in a way that casts an original light on its moral and literary qualities. Several papers discuss issues of literary theory that have merited reexamination: "modernism" and parody, the relationship between Formalism and Marxism, the functional structure of the typical socialist-realist novel; contributors have characteristically taken a cool and balanced attitude towards Soviet culture, neither ignoring its deficiencies nor denying the validity of its achievements.

Contributions to the general Soviet Literature panels at the Banff conference constitute our first group of papers. Two more limited topics discussed at special panels are the subject of our second and third sections. One is the work of the poet Mandelshtam in the light of his widow's remarkable memoirs: this gave rise to a lively session at Banff, with several unscripted and controversial interventions from the floor. The other is the contemporary school of "village writers," whose work is the most stimulating phenomenon in Soviet prose writing today. It is to be hoped that the three papers concentrating on major figures of this tendency will be seen as constituting a uniquely valuable aspect of the volume, since the few scholarly publications on the subject at the time of writing have been scattered and haphazard; for the first time Western readers have a chance to acquire a detailed and comprehensive view of their work in its literary and social context.

R. R. Milner-Gulland
Reader in Russian Studies
University of Sussex, England

KHLEBNIKOV AND $3^6 + 3^6$

R. D. B. Thomson

In November, 1921 Khlebnikov wrote a group of poems[1] that are sometimes called a "triptych of revolution." Soviet critics consider that the group consists of the following poems: *Noch' pered Sovetami*, *Prachka* and *Nastoiashchee*.[2] Vladimir Markov, however, has argued that *Prachka* and *Nastoiashchee* "are almost indistinguishable, as they are really two versions of the same project," and he suggests that *Nochnoi obysk* should be included in the trilogy, while admitting that there are "objections to his classification."[3] The object of this essay is to substantiate this suggestion, and to show that the poems *Noch' pered Sovetami*, *Nastoiashchee*, and *Nochnoi obysk* do form a "triptych": that each of the poems gains from being read in the context of the others, and that they are united, by their setting (above all the theme of "night" and the chronological progression implied by the titles), their imagery, and the argument that finally unfolds at the end of *Nochnoi obysk*.

An important clue is given by the mysterious epigraph at the head of *Nochnoi obysk*, $3^6 + 3^6$. Commentators have usually repeated in some bewilderment the conjecture of Petr Miturich (who married Khlebnikov's favourite sister, Vera) that the number (1458) represents the number of heartbeats (about 18 minutes) between the two deaths in the poem, the execution of the White youth, and the immolation of the Red sailors, or (which is much the same thing) the time required to read the poem.[4] Both suggestions are untenable: the action of the poem involves several discussions, a prolonged assault on a piano, and a meal, which can hardly be fitted into 18 minutes; an oral reading of the poem requires about 40 minutes.

The real significance of the epigraph is that Khlebnikov associated the powers of three with a reversal of historical events and trends: "Particularly characteristic for two opposed points in time is the formula $3^a + 3^a$ or $3^n + 3^m$, or in simpler form 3^n.[5] Such a formula links an event and a counter-event in time." There are certain unresolved problems in this formulation. It might be expected that if the formula 3^n links event and counter-event, then the formula $3^a + 3^a$ should link event, counter-event and counter-counter-event, but Khlebnikov did not consider this possibility. Another complication is caused by the fact that the number of days in Khlebnikov's 3^6 (729) is almost exactly the same as the number of days in two years (730); thus $3^6 + 3^6$ in days is equivalent to 2 + 2 or 2 X 2 or 2^2 in years. Now 2 and its various powers are for Khlebnikov associated with the reinforcement of a historical event or trend. Thus the same historical formula can be viewed in two different ways: as a reversal if the time is measured in days, and as an intensification if the unit of measurement is the year. In 1921-2 Khlebnikov regarded the day as the basic unit of time, but the inconsistencies are reflected in the ambiguity of the poem itself.

In the light of all this the fact that Khlebnikov dated these poems, a practice which he followed on only a handful of other occasions (as Khlebnikov students know to their cost), acquires special significance. It would seem clear that the epigraph refers to something that has happened in the past, and that has been reversed at the time of *Nochnoi obysk*. Elsewhere indeed Khlebnikov refers to 1921 as "povorotnyi god."[6] Khlebnikov could not be speculating about the future here, because he did not know which of the infinite number of the powers of three would be relevant; it must then refer to the past,namely to some event in November, 1917. Fortunately (since this month contained a disproportionate number of historical events), Khlebnikov has left us a clear indication in the first fragment of his *Doski sud'by* (a work devoted to the elaboration of his numerological and historical theories). Among the patterns of events characterising three and its powers Khlebnikov lists the following: "Tsarist debts acknowledged by Soviet Russia 6/xi 1921, $3^6 + 3^6$ = 1458 days after the beginning of Soviet power 10/xi 1917, when they were reduced to nil."[7] Later on in the same article and with slightly different dates, 1/xi 1917 (perhaps a misprint for 10/xi?) and 7/xi (1921, Khlebnikov repeated the claim: "Shift to the right, negotiations on the acknowledgement of Russia's debts."[8] Khlebnikov has allowed for the leap year and the change to the Gregorian calendar; the slight discrepancy (if "one" is a misprint for "ten") can be resolved by recognising that in the former case both the terminal dates are included, in the latter only one of them.

It is noteworthy too that Khlebnikov's imagery in *Nochnoi obysk* shows several similarities to that found in

his writings on the numerology of history. In *Doski sud'by*
he used the following image to characterise the properties
of the powers of 3: "The event makes a turn of two right
angles and gives a negative refraction of time. The midnight of an event becomes its midday and reveals the harmonious movement of the clock of humanity, ticking with the
blazing explosions of the capitals of states."[9] And so the
trilogy is set during a night which is turned into day by
the shots and arson of the final pages. This climax is introduced by one of the sailors lighting his cigarette from
the ikon-lamp. When Khlebnikov revised this passage for
inclusion into his "super-tale" *Zangezi* he introduced the
image of the "matches of fate" (*spichki sud'by*) for this
sacrilegious act and so strengthened the link between the
cigarette and the final fire, only implied in *Nochnoi
obysk* by the phrase:

Курится?
Петух![10]

In *Zangezi* this section is followed by one devoted to
Khlebnikov's theories of the periodic tables of history,
and particularly the significance of the powers of three.
    The general thrust of the epigraph is thus clear
enough, namely, a belief that the original impulse of the
October Revolution had been counteracted by the recognition of the foreign debts incurred by Imperial Russia.
This concern was shared by many of Khlebnikov's Futurist
colleagues at the time. In his "Rosta windows" Maiakovskii
tried to justify this switch in policy, but despite his
orthodox explanations, his own misgivings are clearly apparent.[11]
    The indignation of the Futurists was particularly in-
tense because of their curious, but widespread brand of
Marxism. While accepting the historical inevitability of
the Revolution and the inauguration of a new age, they were
acutely conscious of the subversive power of the past, and
particularly its culture, whether as manifested in its arts
and sciences or its habits of thought and behaviour.[12] It
is the question of the relationship of the culture of the
new age to that of the past that lies behind Khlebnikov's
revolutionary trilogy.
    The cycle, then, and particularly *Nochnoi obysk*, is
about the apparent reversal of the revolutionary impulse,
and the imagery and form consistently illustrate this
theme. Each poem of the trilogy contains a clash between
representatives of the old order and the new. In *Noch'*

pered Sovetami and *Nastoiashchee* the Lady and the Grand
Prince[13] respectively open and close the poems; the central part of each poem is given to the people. Their sense
of injustice and impotent hatred in the first poem ex-
plodes in the second and becomes the dominant element in
the third. In *Nochnoi obysk*, however, it is the revolutionary sailors who introduce and end the poem, while the
central part depicts their dealings with the middleclass
family.

     An even greater symmetry governs the design of the
whole trilogy. The Lady's nurse, and later spokesman for
the insulted and injured peasantry, is introduced at the
beginning of the cycle, in *Noch' pered Sovetami*, as
"zloveshchee videnie." Khlebnikov's original version of
Nochnoi obysk ended with the line "Starukha, zloveshchaia
Starukha!" Most commentators have identified the second
old woman with the mother of the executed White youth, but
in view of this symmetry between the beginning and end of
the cycle (striking enough even if one discounts the echo
of "zloveshchee" as a discarded variant) it is likely that
she is to be interpreted as a symbolic figure of retribution. Khlebnikov had already done just this in the short
poem "Aziia," where Asia is depicted as a "povitukha -
miatezhei starukha" (the old midwife of revolts) turning
the pages of a book, in which the "execution of Tsars is
an angry exclamation-mark."[14] Thus the figure of retribution actually turns against the revolutionaries in the
closing lines of the poem.

     The image of the ikon also undergoes a similar devel-
opment. It appears in the opening scene of *Noch' pered
Sovetami* and is associated with both the Lady and the
nurse, and so with the culture of the past, now under sentence. The image does not appear in *Nastoiashchee*, but
section 17 of *Prachka* is devoted to the imaginary and real
gods of Tsarist oppression. In *Nochnoi obysk* a shot is
fired at the ikon, and the figure of Christ is subjected
to various theomachian challenges. But the god who has
hitherto been treated with such contempt is finally allowed
to answer back; and the fire that breaks out is the divine
response to their sacrilege.

     It is worth noting too the image of blue eyes that
occurs in *Noch' pered Sovetami*. The nurse has blue eyes,[15]
as do her grandmother[16] and her father.[17] This colour is
associated with the sea, and so with the Revolution. (The
association of revolutionaries and particularly Chekists
with steel-blue eyes was later to become a cliche in the

works of Boris Pil'niak and Vsevolod Ivanov). But in
Nochnoi obysk, the colour blue is also associated with
God. One of the sailors has an image of Christ tattooed
on his chest in "blue gunpowder - a custom of the seas."[18]
The ikon depicts Christ with blue eyes[19] - even this conventionally revolutionary image has been taken away from
the revolutionaries and given to God.

The dominating image of the whole triptych is that of
the hounds hunting the hare; it is in this image that the
central theme of retribution is explored. In *Noch' pered
Sovetami* the hounds are identified with the landowners; the
bulk of the narrative consists of the nurse telling how her
grandmother was compelled to suckle one of the landowner's
hounds together with her own son. (Khlebnikov's word-play
on "shchenochek"/"synochek"[20] emphasises this equation, and
later the grandmother becomes a "shchepka" from feeding the
"shchenok").[21] The peasants take the side of the hare in
their master's hunting expeditions. But throughout the
poem there are hints at a reversal of this situation. The
young boy (the nurse's father) strangles his master's favourite hound and is flogged for it almost to death.[22]
This story is framed by the nurse's warnings and threats
to the lady that she will be hanged on the next day. The
word *dobycha* (prey) applied to the lady appears twice in
the opening lines. Both these episodes foreshadow the uprising of the people against their oppressors. In *Prachka*
this reversal seems to be complete: the workers are compared to puppies[23] while old St. Petersburg, which the
workers are ambushing with a firebrand, is compared to a
hare. This image does not appear in *Nastoiashchee*, however, perhaps because Khlebnikov had thought of another way
of treating the image in the final part of his trilogy.

At the beginning of *Nochnoi obysk* the Red sailors enter looking for their prey, "white beasts" (the colour indicates not only the Whites but also the fact that the
hares are white in *Noch' pered Sovetami*).[24] But in the
crucial piano-smashing episode this image is again reversed. It is worth quoting this episode in some detail,
because Khlebnikov deliberately emphasizes it.

> Кто играет из братвы?
> - А это можем...
> Как бахнем ложем...
> Аль прикладом...
> Глянь, братва,
> Топай сюда,
> И рокот будет и гром и пение...

И жалоба,
Как будто тихо
Скулит под забором щенок,
Щенок забытый всеми.
И пушек грохот грозный вдруг подымается,
И чей-то хохот, чей-то смех подводный и
Столпились. Струнный говор,   /русалочий.
Струнный хохот, тихий смех.
- Прикладом бах! [25]

In this passage Khlebnikov passes almost imperceptibly from
the direct speech of his characters to a third-person narrative - presumably at the line: "I zhaloba." Suddenly a
new set of associations is presented, utterly different
from the coarse speech, violent actions and general cacophony of the whole cycle up to this point. But these elements return and the piano is thrown out of the window
("etot iashchik, gde voet tsutsik"[26] as one of the sailors
comments scornfully).

        If the above passage had stopped at the comparison of
the piano to a puppy and had then continued with the piano-
smashing, then *Nochnoi obysk* would have added little to the
theme of crude revenge (rather than retribution) as it is
found in the other poems of the cycle; the piano, as an image of bourgeois life is common in early Soviet literature,
and as such it makes an appearance in *Prachka*. But at this
point the frightened puppy ceases to be an object of simple
hatred and irresistible power; it is associated once again
with the old world and its culture, but it is now treated
as a victim and linked to the image of a *rusalka*, evocative
of a totally different set of values for Khlebnikov. It is
this reinterpretation of the "shchenok"/"tsutsik" image
that gives the trilogy much of its power and ambiguity. As
Nochnoi obysk unfolds, the presence of new supernatural
forces makes itself felt more and more strongly. Just as
the piano does not tamely give up the ghost, but laughs
elusively, like a *rusalka*, so too the reproachful eyes of
Christ in the ikon survive the sailor's bullet, and recall
to the sailor too a "*rusalka* with cloudy, powerful eyes."[27]

        Both these images are closely linked with the central
episode in the poem, the execution of the White boy. He
laughs and asks to be shot in the forehead:

        - Даешь в лоб, что-ли? [28]

His request is granted, and his last words are:

- Прощай дурак! Спасибо
  За твой выстрел.[29]

His acceptance of death and his insolent courage (they are
echoed later by his sister, but she is spared), make a deep
impression on the sailors, and one of them continues to reflect on it:

Подлец! смеется после смерти![30]

and later, in a monologue, he goes over the events leading
up to the execution three times;[31] he becomes increasingly
aware of the wanton destructiveness of his actions, and of
the reproach in the eyes of the ikon. But he too refuses
to submit: he challenges God as the White boy had challenged him:

- Даешь в лоб что-ли?
  Даешь мне в лоб, Бог девичий,
  Ведь те же семь зарядов у тебя.
  С большими синими глазами?
  И я скажу спасибо
  За письма и привет.
  - Море! Море!
  [...]
  Хочу убитым пасть на месте,
  Чтоб пал огонь смертельный
  Из красного угла.-
  Оттуда бы темнело дуло
  Чтобы сказать ему - дурак!
  Перед лицом конца.
  Как этот мальчик крикнул мне,
  Смеясь беспечно
  В упор обойме смерти.
  Я в жизнь его ворвался и убил,
  Как темное ночное божество.
  Но побежден его был звонким смехом,
  Где стекла юности звенели.
  Теперь я Бога победить хочу
  Веселым смехом той же силы,
  Хоть мрачно мне
  Сейчас и тяжко. И трудно мне.[32]

In the final lines he seems to have achieved his ambition.
He sees the fire break out, and coolly assumes the pose he
has sought:

Горим! Спасите! Дым!
А я доволен и спокоен,
Стою, кручу усы и все как надо.

Спаситель! Ты дурак![33]

but somehow the gesture seems of "dubious value" as Vladimir Markov has suggested.[34]   It is partly that the atmosphere of the two passages is quite different. In the first
case the tone is foolhardily heroic, in the second it is
grim and fatalistic. What had been instinctive and natural
for the White boy is achieved by the Red sailor through
will-power and deliberate emulation, and the contrast between the sudden heroism of the boy and the obsessive ambition of the old sailor serves still further to weaken the
impact of the second death. Thus the verbal repetitions
serve to suggest the differences rather than the similarities between them.

   But why should the Reds wish to emulate the values of
the Whites anyway? The symbols of the old regime, the
ikon, the piano, the people themselves, have been ruthlessly smashed throughout the trilogy; they have no value,
utilitarian, cultural or sentimental, for the new order.
How then is the reader to interpret this scene? Is it a
sellout of revolutionary ideals (equivalent to the acknowledgement of the international debts of Imperial Russia)? -
or a recognition of the excesses of the revolution condemned to "repeat the mistakes of its predecessors" and
its failure to acquire the old values (hence the divine
"retribution," and the restoration of the Tsarist God)?
In a word, how free is the Bolshevik Revolution of its
past? Here the "recognition of Tsarist debts" acquires a
more complex meaning. The past is not simply a set of ob-
ligations which are not binding on the revolution; it is
also a set of values, moral, aesthetic and spiritual which
are admirable. Can the Revolution acquire the latter
without the former?

   On the one hand there is a marked shift from the
straightforward acceptance of the Revolution in *Noch'
pered Sovetami* and *Nastoiashchee* to the complexities of
Nochnoi obysk; but on the other it is simplistic to assume that Khlebnikov simply switched his loyalties in the
course of the trilogy. He had little sympathy for the
culture of the past. He signed the notorious manifesto
"Poshchechina obshchestvennomu vkusu" (1912) which advocated "dumping Pushkin, Dostoievskii, Tolstoi, etc., etc.,
from the steamship of modernity."[35]   And it may well have
been Khlebnikov who gave Maiakovskii the idea of retorting
to Merezhkovskii's "Griadushchii Kham" (The Coming Ham,
1906) with the witty rhyme "Prishedshii sam" (Arrived in

Person).[36] In 1922 Khlebnikov took up the idea again in a
short poem, "Priznanie" in which he pointed to the "fateful" coincidence that the first letters of his and Mayakovsky's surnames provided the consonants for "Kham."[37]

To clarify the complexities of Khlebnikov's attitude
to the past it may be helpful here to make a few comparisons with two of Blok's most famous works, *Dvenadtsat'* and
Vozmezdie. The similarities between *Dvenadtsat'* and
Nochnoi obysk have often been remarked, but never analysed in detail. Vladimir Markov has pointed to the similarity between Khlebnikov's "Ubiitsy sviatye" and Blok's
"Sviataia zloba" and a number of other verbal parallels;[38]
but the most striking resemblance – the image of Christ –
seems never to have been discussed. In Blok's poem the Red
soldiers glimpse the figure through the snowstorm and shoot
at it. But despite their rejection of Him, despite their
barbarities and blasphemies, Christ takes up the red flag
at their head.[39] He identifies Himself with the revolutionaries whether they will or not. In Khlebnikov the
motif seems to be echoed by the sailor who has a Christ
tattooed on his chest in gunpowder. But at the end of his
poem the blasphemy and sacrilege seem to have been finally
rejected. God has detached Himself from the revolutionaries.

These differences would seem to spring largely from a
fundamental difference in handling symbols. Blok was prone
to regard the past as a symbolic foreshadowing of the present[40] (much as medieval theologians felt that every event
in the Old Testament was a prefiguration of some incident
in the life of Jesus). He did not see Christ primarily as
a historical or religious figure, but as a symbol, the only
conceivably adequate symbol for the new revolution, social,
moral and spiritual that he sensed. The actual qualities
and traditional associations of Christ were irrelevant to
his purpose, and in some cases even at odds with it (e.g.,
his comments on the Christ in *Dvenadtsat'* "I myself sometimes hate this effeminate figure").[41] The tone of this
poem is predominantly harsh, sarcastic, cacophonous and
blasphemous. Only in the final lines does he introduce
images of beauty and purity, gentleness and unearthly
mystery, to prepare the appearance of Christ:

>   ...Так идут державным шагом –
>   Позади – голодный пес,
>   Впереди – с кровавым флагом,
>   И за вьюгой невидим,
>   И от пули невредим,

Нежной поступью надвьюжной,
Снежной россыпью жемчужной,
  В белом венчике из роз -
Впереди - Исус Христос. [42]

For Blok the hostility of the Red Guards to Christ is unimportant: men are, and always have been, unaware of the
real forces directing their affairs.

In *Nochnoi obysk*, however, the traditional associations of Christ are strongly emphasised, and Khlebnikov
introduces the themes of mystery and beauty much earlier,
some four pages before the end:

Глаза предрассветной синевы
И вещие и тихие
И строги и прекрасны,
И нежные несказанной речью,
И тихо смотрят вниз
Укорной тайной,
На нас, на всю ватагу
Убийц святых,
На нашу пьянку
Убийц святых. [43]

This appeal to the values of beauty and pity prepares the
reader more thoroughly for the final scene, and it indicates the fundamental difference between the two poems.
Khlebnikov is interested in the moral dilemma of the Revolution; Blok is oblivious of it. Blok's poem ends in ecstasy; Khlebnikov's in an unsolved mystery. As Markov has
said, the ethos of the two poems is "completely different."[44]

The resemblances to *Vozmezdie*, on the other hand are
much more substantial, and help to show what the poem is
saying. Blok's title means "retribution" in a double
sense: first of all the sense of divine recompense for individual or collective faults. It is in this sense that it
is generally understood, though it is unclear how this
theme fits into what we know about the poem. In Blok this
motif is often associated with the Don Juan theme as in
"Shagi Komandora." It does not seem to have been remarked
that one element of the Don Juan story can be found in
Nochnoi obysk - the challenge by the villain-hero to a
supernatural being. Compare the Red sailor's challenge to
the ikon:

- Даешь в лоб что-ли?
Даешь мне в лоб, Бог девичий,

Ведь те же семь зарядов у тебя.
С большими синими глазами?
И я скажу спасибо
За письма и привет.
- Море! Море!
Он согласен!
Он взмахнул ресницами,
Как птица крыльями.[45]

with Don Juan's invitation to the statue. Of course in
Khlebnikov the erotic overtones that usually accompany
this theme are absent.

There is, however, a deeper meaning in Blok's title,
inherent in the epigraph, taken from Ibsen's *The Master-
Builder*, "Youth is retribution."[46] In this interpretation
each generation brings its own retribution to its predecessors. Retribution is a never-ending process.[47] In July
1919, eighteen months after completing *Dvenadtsat'*, Blok
described his intentions in *Vozmezdie* thus:

> Its plan presented itself to me in the form
> of concentric circles, which became narrower and
> narrower, and the very smallest circle, com-
> pressed to the limit, begins to live its own
> independent life, to expand and displace its
> surroundings, and, in its turn to react upon
> the circumference.[48]

This scheme is then translated into terms of the changing
relationship between the individual and his environment,
from the rampant individualism of the nineteenth century
to a new collectivism and back again:

> Individual scions of every family develop
> to their allotted limits, and are then swal-
> lowed by the surrounding world environment
> [...] The world maelstrom sucks almost the
> whole man into its vortex; hardly any trace
> remains of the individual personality, and if
> it continues to exist, it becomes unrecogniz-
> able, mutilated. Man was but has ceased to be,
> only the flabby, grubby flesh and the smoulder-
> ing little soul remain. But the seed has been
> sown, and in the following firstborn something
> new and obstinate begins to act on the surround-
> ing world; in this way a family that has ex-
> perienced the retribution of history, the en-
> vironment, and the age, begins in its turn to

exact retribution [...] What next? I do not
know, and never have done; I can only say that
this whole conception arose under the pressure
of my constantly growing hatred for the various theories of progress.[49]

Accordingly the vast scheme of *Vozmezdie* was to end with an
epilogue depicting a child fathered by the hero "on a
passionate and sinful night in the womb of some quiet and
feminine daughter of a forgotten people."[50]

Because of Blok's professed "hatred for the various
theories of progress" this scheme appears to treat history
as a process of continuing meaningless oscillation between
two poles, but it is more likely that Blok intended some
kind of higher synthesis to emerge from this dialectical
process. In any case the difference from the Apocalyptic
finality of *Dvenadtsat'* is obvious. Throughout 1918 and
1919 Blok gradually withdrew from that extreme position.
The article "Katilina" (April–May 1918) marks a transi-
tional stage in that it still regards the Revolution as an
Apocalyptic event, but now places it at some unspecified
time in the future. Such later documents as the unsent
letter to Maiakovskii of December 1918 and the article
"Krushenie gumanizma" prepare the main points made in the
Vozmezdie preface, written in July, 1919.

These ideas are similar to those of Khlebnikov's trilogy. In both the ebb and flow of history obey their own
laws, regardless of human concepts of justice and culture.
But where Blok still needs the prospect of a "synthesis" to
give some humanly intelligible meaning and direction to the
historical process, for Khlebnikov history moves in an in-
scrutable, though not totally incomprehensible way. His
theory of the "periodic tables" of history may not seem so
different from Blok's "retribution," but he finds room in
it for the expression of individual freedom (is there any
in Blok's two great poems?), and the moral and logical
dilemmas of his theme are not sacrificed to any metaphysical dogma.

On a deeper level the structure of Khlebnikov's trilogy, the epigraph $3^6 + 3^6$, and the subtle balance of the
narration in *Nochnoi obysk*, raise, without claiming to resolve, one of the most fascinating issues of Soviet aesthetics: the attitude of the new society to the culture of
the old. Can one acquire the values and achievements of
the past without being contaminated by its less desirable
characteristics? It is fitting that it should have been a
Futurist and not a Marxist who gave this theme its first

and profoundest expression in Soviet literature.

University of Toronto
Toronto, Ontario, Canada

NOTES

[1] *Noch' pered Sovetami* was not given a date in *Sobranie proizvedenii Velimira Khlebnikova* in 5 vols, Moscow, 1928-33 (Stepanov, in fact, suggested 1920), but later editions give 1 Nov., 1921. *Prachka* is also dated 1 Nov., 1921. *Nastoiaschee* was originally assigned to "7/II - 11/II - 1921," evidently a misreading of November (eleventh month) as February (second month) due to a confusion between Roman and Arabic numerals, which has been corrected in later editions. *Nochnoi obysk* is also dated 7 Nov. - 11 Nov. 1921.

In the present paper quotations will be taken from the five-volume *Sobranie proizvedenii*, 1928-33, reprinted as *Sobranie sochinenii* in 4 books, ed. Vladimir Markov, Munich, 1968-72. Book I contains vols. I and II of the Stepanov edition, Book II - vols. III and IV; Book III contains Stepanov's vol. V, with some additional material of particular relevance to this essay. Hereafter this edition will be abbreviated as *SS*, Vols. I-V.

[2] V. Khlebnikov, *Izbrannye stikhotvoreniia*, ed. N. Stepanov, Moscow, 1936, p. 64.

[3] Vladimir Markov, *The Longer Poems of Velimir Khlebnikov*, Berkeley, 1962, p. 167.

[4] *SS*, Vol. I, p. 325. Khlebnikov usually took 81 heartbeats to the minute in his calculations, and he was particularly impressed to discover that a German infantryman was required to take 81 paces to the minute. Elsewhere, however, he distinguished between a man's heartbeat (70 to the minute) and a woman's (81). But Khlebnikov was only concerned in these calculations to relate the heartbeat to the day, which remained the chief basis for all his historical calculations.

[5] *SS*, Vol. V, p. 474.

[6] *SS*, Vol. IV, p. 149.

[7] *SS*, Vol. V, p. 476. Despite Khlebnikov's dating it appears that this action was taken by the Soviet Government at the end of October, 1921. (See *Izvestiia*, 29 Oct. 1921).

[8] *SS*, Vol. V, p. 483.

[9] Ibid., p. 477.

[10] *SS*, Vol. I, p. 267 and Vol. III, p. 347. The
"matches of fate" image occurs elsewhere in Khlebnikov's
late works. See "Kak stado ovets mirno dremlet ..." (*SS*,
Vol. III, p. 180) and "Kto on, Voronikhin stoletii ..."
(*SS*, Vol. V, p. 103).

[11] V. V. Maiakovskii, "Priznali dolg," *Polnoe sobranie
sochinenii* in 13 vols, Moscow 1955-60 (hereafter *PSS*),
Vol. III, p. 429. It may be noted that once recognition
had been granted, the Soviet government repudiated its commitment to repay these debts, at the Genoa Conference of
April, 1922. Maiakovskii's poem "Moia rech' na Genuezskoi
konferentsii" (*PSS*, Vol. IV, p. 27) was written to celebrate the occasion. The same reaction can be detected in
Aseev's "Liricheskoe otstuplenie," (1924):

>   Знаю я:
>   мы долгов не платим
>   И платить не будем.
>   Но под этим истлевшим платьем
>   Как пройти мне к людям?

(N. Aseev, *Sobranie sochinenii* in 5 vols, Moscow, 1963-4,
Vol. I, p. 395. "I know that we are not paying and never
will pay these debts, but beneath this thread-bare clothing, how am I to get through to people?").

[12] For an elaboration of this idea see my article
"Mayakovsky and his Time Imagery," *Slavonic and East European Review*, No. 111, April 1970, pp. 181-200.

[13] Markov suggests that this figure may have been based
on the Grand Prince Konstantin, a popular and prolific
poet, who wrote under the psendonym K.R. (op. cit., p.
227). Here too the old order is inextricably associated
with the old culture.

[14] *SS*, Vol. III, p. 122.

[15] Ibid., p. 217.

[16] *SS*, Vol. I, p. 220.

[17] Ibid., p. 224.

[18] Ibid., p. 268.

[19] Ibid., p. 270.

[20] Ibid., p. 224.

[21] Ibid., p. 228.

[22] Ibid., p. 230. Vladimir Markov assumes that the
boys dies, and so wonders when he had time to father the
nurse (op. cit., p. 169); in the poem, however, we are
told only that he develops consumption and looks worse
than many who are laid in the grave.

[23] *SS*, Vol. III, p. 232.
[24] *SS*, Vol. I, p. 221.
[25] Ibid., p. 261.
[26] Ibid., p. 262.
[27] Ibid., p. 272. The "rusalka" image is one of the most commonly found in Khlebnikov. It is invariably associated with positive values, aesthetic and spiritual, and contrasted with the materialism and cruelty of this world. Compare in this connection "Poet," 1919 (*SS*, Vol. I, pp. 153-9) and "Nad glukhonemoi otchiznoi: 'Ne ubei!" (*SS*, Vol. III, p. 57).
[28] *SS*, Vol. I, p. 255. The phrase "Daesh' ..." becomes a leitmotif of retribution, and it is regularly answered by "Daem ..." (the sailors) or "Daet ..." (the ikon or God). It is used again with the same associations in *Zangezi*:　Если в пальцах запрятался нож,
　　　А зрачки открывала настежью месть -
　　　Это время завыло: даешь,
　　　А судьба отвечала послушная: есть.

(*SS*, Vol. III, p. 354)

[29] Ibid., p. 256.
[30] Ibid., p. 257.
[31] Ibid., pp. 265-6.
[32] Ibid., pp. 269, 271.
[33] Ibid., p. 273.
[34] Vladimir Markov, op. cit., p. 181.
[35] Quoted from V. Maiakovskii, *PSS*, Vol. XIII, p. 245.
[36] Maiakovskii's speech with this title was given on 24 March, 1913. Khlebnikov's first usage of the phrase occurs in "Neizdannaia stat'ia" (*SS*, Vol. V, p. 187), which can be dated only approximately to 1913-14; he used the phrase again in "Razgovor Olega i Kazimira" (Ibid., p. 194), an article based on the same material. Presumably the phrase was current among the Futurists at the time, but we know that at the end of his life Khlebnikov accused several of his Futurist colleagues (notably Maiakovskii and Aseev) of plagiarising his ideas. See "Kruchenykh" (*SS*, Vol. V, p. 400).
[37] *SS*, Vol. III, p. 293.
[38] V. Markov, op. cit., p. 183.
[39] This possibly controversial interpretation is based not so much on the text of the poem as on Blok's comments in his diary for 10 March, 1918 that "... Christ is with the Red Guards. One can hardly dispute this truth, perfectly plain for people who have read the Gospel and thought

about it" (*Sobranie sochinenii* in 8 vols., Moscow-Leningrad, 1960-63, hereafter Blok, *SS*, Vol. VII, p. 330).

[40] For example in his use of Kulikovo as a symbolic presage of the revolt of the Russian people against the intelligentsia he was not interested in any specific parallels or resemblances. Khlebnikov, on the other hand, had a more "allegorical" outlook; he was particularly interested in the trivia, the insignificant details that accompanied historical events on their various appearances. These differences reflect essential differences in their outlooks. Blok was an Apocalyptic, who believed that he was living at the end of history, that the events of his time gave a new meaning to the whole of preceding history. Khlebnikov was well aware that history would continue after him, as can be seen from his predictions of historical events in the future.

[41] Blok, *SS*, Vol. VII, p. 330.

[42] Ibid., Vol. III, p. 359.

[43] V. Khlebnikov, *SS*, Vol. I, p. 269.

[44] V. Markov, op. cit., p. 183.

[45] V. Khlebnikov, *SS*, Vol. I, p. 269.

[46] Blok, *SS*, Vol. III, p. 295.

[47] In view of the two-way nature of this concept of retribution it may be noted that Khlebnikov's Red sailor is called Starshoi (senior) while the White victim is characterized by his youth and especially his "youthful laughter" (*SS*, Vol. I, p. 271).

[48] Blok, *SS*, Vol. III, p. 297.

[49] Ibid., pp. 297, 298.

[50] Ibid., p. 299. This idea anticipates in some respects the appearance of the orphan Tania Zhivago at the end of Pasternak's novel.

GRANDSONS OF KOZMA PRUTKOV: REFLECTIONS ON ZABOLOTSKY, OLEYNIKOV AND THEIR CIRCLE

R. R. Milner-Gulland

For choosing what may seem a rather puzzling or whimsical title for this paper I have two basic motives: one, as it were, long-term, and one that prompted me in a more limited but immediate way. More than ten years ago, when I first became interested in the early work of the poet Nikolay Zabolotsky--which was incidentally extremely hard to obtain, since very little of it had been republished in East or West until 1965[1]--several questions and suspicions began (at first subconsciously) to formulate themselves in my mind. The work itself was alluring: witty, grotesque, phantasmagorical and obscure by turns, and in general the fleeting mentions it had received in the then standard books on Soviet Russian literature hardly managed to suggest quite how odd and disturbing it was. They quickly and conveniently pigeonholed Zabolotsky as a late Futurist, without going far towards explaining how such a phenomenon could arise in apparent cultural isolation. Worse than that, they failed to account for--or indeed adequately to describe--the poetry itself, with its curious intentional naivetés, its Pushkinian or Derzhavinian passages, its apparently chaotic fragmentation through which nevertheless shimmered more than a hint of unified and deeper purpose. As the only writer of a full-length study of Zabolotsky in English puts it, in his early work "the tone is never allowed to stabilize."[2] This disturbing aesthetic quality seemed to have literary implications which were worth following up; when (not without difficulty) I managed to do so I discovered that there was a whole area of Soviet Russian literature, culture, philosophy and aesthetic thought whose existence in the 1920s-30s, though touched on in a few Soviet published sources, remained quite unknown in the West, and involved many significant figures besides Zabolotsky himself. It was startling, for example, to find that the editors of the 1965 American edition of Zabolotsky's work showed no inkling in some 150 pages of commentary of the existence of formally-established literary group (known as OBERIU) to which the young Zabolotsky belonged and whose

manifesto of 1928 he indeed prepared.[3]   In the last decade
this field has begun to be opened up by a number of scholars in Russia, Eastern Europe and the West,[4] and in a short
paper I shall not attempt to duplicate work already done by
trying to outline its complexities and sketch all the personalities who have emerged from the shadows.   Instead I
shall concentrate on one important but little-investigated
area of it, and in so doing introduce the work of one of
Zabolotsky's most interesting close colleagues, who has
never yet, so far as I know, achieved more than passing
mention in Western scholarly literature.   Examination of
this writer helps to explain, or set in context, some of
the odder qualities of Zabolotsky's work.

        Now for the second and more recent impulse towards the
theme of this paper.   Kozma Prutkov needs no description or
explanation of mine for anybody who knows nineteenth century Russian literature.[5] He is surely the most loved and
admired "invented" writer in any literature, going far beyond the original "mystification" his creators foisted upon
an appreciative public, developing not only a wide range of
performance (over poetry, prose and plays) but an astonish-
ingly persuasive "personality." His "works" are the greatest Russian parodies, but readers have felt they are somehow more than *just* parodies.   There now exists an admirable
short study of Prutkov in English,[6] and it was when I was
reading the section on his predecessors (quite numerous)
and successors (rather few) that the desirability of adding
a footnote to the history of the Prutkovian tradition in
Russian literature was brought home to me.   Dr. Monter,
rightly brushing aside the "obvious imitators" of Prutkov
in the later 19th century, considers that his true heritage
"can be found in the lighter moments of highly serious
writers, Dostoevsky and Solov'ev," but that generally
speaking "Prutkov as a parodic literary figure remains
without heirs."[7] True, she adds what looks like a rather
hasty footnote telling us that "Prutkov's later successors
in the late 1920s were the Oberjuty"--precisely the group
mentioned above, whose Declaration was largely composed by
Zabolotsky--and directing us to George Gibian's book
Russia's Lost Literature of the Absurd.[8] This, however,
is only the beginning of the story, and the indication
could mislead rather than enlighten the curious reader.
For Gibian's book is basically concerned with a different
side of the *Oberiu* phenomenon, whereas the "modern Kozma
Prutkov"--there indeed was such a writer--was not actually

a member of this group, though linked with it in some significant ways.

The writer in question was Nikolay Makarovich
Oleynikov (1898-1938 or perhaps 1942), a figure who will
not be found in anthologies or standard histories of literature, though there is a brief entry under his name in the
Soviet *Short Literary Encyclopedia*.[9] Until about 1960 his
very existence, let alone his work, had been almost completely forgotten in the USSR, whereas in the West he had
never been known at all. But since then he has joined that
significant category of "rediscoveries" who, as anyone who
has worked in the field will doubtless recognize, give a
good deal of the interest and surprise to our study of
Soviet literature. While still "underpublished," with much
of their material passing from hand to hand in faded type-
scripts, they have become names to conjure with--memoirists
continually allude to them, bits and pieces of their work
appear in periodicals such as the indispensable *Den'
poezii*, they can indeed become the over-cherished possession of a coterie--but a comprehensive view of the work is
generally hard for the outsider to obtain, for despite
their post-Stalin total or partial rehabilitation they are
still not fully acceptable writers from the point of view
of some "official" Soviet circles. Zabolotsky himself came
into such a category until recently, and all his brilliant
and varied literary associates of the '20s-'30s, with the
exception of the playwright Yevgeny Shvarts, continue to do
so. It takes some persistence and detective work for the
non-Russian to get to know such writers, but usually it
will be found that the groundwork for their investigation
has already been done by Soviet scholars; and I believe it
is important we in the West should attempt to carry this
further, if only because our whole concept of Soviet culture may be considerably altered and enriched if we do so.
There is also something rather ignominious when Western
scholarship stumbles along, several years behindhand, in
the wake of rediscoveries the Russians themselves have
made, but are not yet in a position fully to exploit.
Both sides can and ought to help the other.

Oleynikov, then, has become a figure frequently mentioned, from time to time republished, but seldom discussed
or properly assessed as a writer. The references to him in
memoirs are nearly always vivid and anecdotal; it would
appear that in the brief space of little over a decade in

which he made his mark in Leningrad literary life he left
an indelible impression on those who came into contact with
him.[10] In short, he was an original, and in a manner perhaps rare in Soviet cultural life: a brillant, biting,
sometimes destructive wit, perpetrator of absurd or anarchic practical jokes, master of verbal repartee. The locale for this activity heightened unexpectedness:
Oleynikov's place of employment was the Children's Literature Section of the State Publishing House (GIZ, subsequently DETGIZ), where he worked nominally under Samuil
Marshak as editor of magazines and writer of poems and
stories for children; he usually employed the pseudonym
"Makar Svirepiy"--which incidentally sounds parodistic on
such early Soviet pseudonyms as Mikhail Golodny, Demyan
Bedny, etc. Oleynikov had been brought to GIZ by the
playwright Shvarts, who discovered him in his native Donbass on an extended visit he paid there in 1923. Already
Oleynikov, a man of tempestuous energy, had broken violent-
ly with his prosperous, White-sympathizing Cossack family,
had fought in the Civil War and become a Bolshevik party
member, and had (totally without experience) set up a
couple of journals, *Kochegarka* and *Zaboy*. He was already
a practical joker, but his jokes often had purpose as well
as crazy phantasy: to get to Petrograd he equipped himself
with an official *spravka* from his *selsovet*, reading:

"Сим удостоверяется, что гр. Олейников Нико-
лай Макарович действительно красивый. Дана
для поступления в Академию художеств."

He had of course assured the chairman of the local council
that only beautiful people were accepted into the Academy.
Once installed in the *Dom knigi*, Oleynikov sharpened his
wits against his "best friend and bosom enemy" Shvarts,
while together they constructed more or less benign mysti-
fications, both for their own amusement and for the benefit
of impressionable visitors. Typical was the dialogue between Shvarts and Oleynikov when they introduced themselves
to the young writer Igor Bakhterev at a somewhat eccentric
poetry evening, early in 1927:[11]

"Перед вами Козьма Прутков - сказал один.
- Евгений Львович любит преувеличения. Я
внук Козьмы Петровича, но по прямой линии -
поддержал шутку другой."

That meeting, of course, partially provided the title for
my paper, and is in some ways a crucial event in the later
history of Russian experimentalist, "modernist" literature;
but before we look further at its consequences let us
briefly examine Oleynikov's poems and his claims for kinship (or even, as other writers have testified, spiritual
self-identification) with the great Kozma Prutkov.

Insofar as it is possible to reassemble the heritage
of Oleynikov, it seems that about 50-60 "adult" poems—as
distinct from his considerable output for children—have
survived.[12]   Only three were printed in his lifetime, in
the inauspicious year 1934,[13] and attracted a predictable
critical volley from Tarasenkov. The first of these was
indeed prefixed by the heading *Iz tsikla "Pam'yati Kuz'my
(sic) Prutkova"*; its title, *Sluzhenie nauke*, points to a
characteristic theme. For the "philosophizing domestic
poet," as Oleynikov's son Aleksandr aptly characterizes
the dominant *persona* of his otherwise rather diverse
poems,[14] is evidently a devotee of versified scientific
enquiry, and he or his creator has almost an obsession
with the smaller and less regarded specimens of animal
life: beetles, cockroaches, flies, fishes. Equally characteristically, the scientific motif is coupled uneasily
with an apparently arbitrary, absurd yet pervasive amorous
theme. Love as a series of postures, some of them alarming, some grotesque, some sentimentally conventional, some
ludicrous is a clear target of Oleynikov's satire in poem
after poem; there is a disconcertingly Gogolian comprehen-
siveness about this exposure of erotic *poshlost'*. Here
are the characteristic opening lines:

      Я описал кузнечика, я описал пчелу,
      Я птиц изобразил в разрезах полагающихся,
      Но где мне силы взять, чтоб описать смолу
      Твоих волос, на голове располагающихся?

      Увы! Не та во мне уж сила,
      Которая девиц, как смерть, косила!
      И я не тот. Я перестал безумствовать и
                                        /пламенеть,
      И прежняя в меня не лезет снедь.

      Давно уж не ночуют утки
      В моем разрушенном желудке...

An even better apostrophe to popular science is provided in
the next poem of this series, *Khvala izobretateliam*. Here
Oleynikov treads precisely the dividing lines between absurdity and sense, inspiration and banality, that it seems
to have been his lasting concern to seek out.

> Хвала изобретателям,
> Подумавшим о мелких и смешных приспособле-
> /ниях, -
> О щипчиках для сахара, о мундштуках для
> /папирос.
> Хвала тому,
> Кто предложил печати ставить в удостовере
> /ниях,
> Кто к чайнику придумал крышечку и нос,
>
> Кто соску первую построил из резины,
> Кто макароны выдумал и манную крупу,
> Кто научил людей болезни изгонять отваром
> /из малины,
> Кто изготовил яд, несущий смерть клопу.

But already some difficulties in the concept of the "modern
Kozma Prutkov" begin to creep in. A splendidly naïve
dithyramb is offered us, but it is by no means clear who,
if anybody, is being mocked, let alone parodied. Certainly not science itself; nor any identifiable (at least to
me) poet or even group of poets, unless—rather distantly
—some of more ecstatic "proletarians" such as Gastev. Is
even the *persona* of the narrator satirized ultimately?
His initial enthusiasm for sugar-tongs and teapots is
clearly ridiculous, and there are characteristic moments
of bathos, achieved usually through the clever juxtaposition of high style and low concepts, which may well evoke
deserved laughter. But, rather curiously, by the end we
are likely to be on the side of the naïve poet, and he has
unquestionably fulfilled a poetic task by expanding our
consciousness of the world in which we live; the things he
said somehow needed pointing out, despite (or because of)
our normally taking them for granted—and if in so doing
he uses absurd and anti-poetic means is this not thoroughly in the spirit of the anti-sentimental, Futurist-
educated generation of the modern movement?

Such questions arise from many of Oleynikov's other poems, often unconnected with the theme of "popular science." Several take, for example, lowly animals as their focus of attention: in *Mukha* a fly is the lost love-object (" Я муху безумно любил / Давно это было, друзья, / Когда еще молод я был, / Когда еще молод был я... О муха, о птичка моя!");

in *Tarakan* a cockroach awaits dissection by zoologists; in *Karas'* a small fish is brought by unwise passion to the cooking-pot. In all of these a certain parodistic intention can be somewhat more readily discerned than in the "scientific" poems, but it seems more often a broad parody, of genres (for example, of the so-called *zhestokiy romans*, itself a semi-parodistic form) and of stylized poetic attitudes, than of any identifiable writers. What is more, a conflict of attitudes is almost always set up in the reader's mind; when false pathos has been cut through by ridicule, the lowly object, fish, insect or indeed poet, retains and involuntarily reveals a genuine pathos. The very physical black humour of several poems (as in *Smert' geroya*, on the death of a beetle) shows disturbing feeling for the reality of violence and the dissolution of the flesh--as well as of the high-flown euphemisms habitually employed in writing about them. Absurd we may condescendingly consider them, but can we really use any other language, and do they not draw attention to reality in the very act of trying to conceal or prettify it?

If, after this admittedly quick and superficial sketch of some of the features of Oleynikov's work, we try to summarize the relationship with Prutkov, a complex and rather interesting picture emerges. It is certainly not enough to say that Oleynikov simply continues the Prutkovian tradition in 20th century terms; the differences are striking and indicative. The Zhemchuzhnikovs and Tolstoy consciously created a consistent and plausible, if exaggerated figure, the necessary *fons et origo* of the poems themselves. Oleynikov spoke from a variety of different *personae*, often unspecified, though one important cycle (*Stikhi tekhnoruka N.*)[15] presents us with a figure of a Soviet-bourgeois philosopher who, though much less fully delineated, stands comparison with his great predecessor in the Tsarist ministry of finances. But while many Prutkov poems are clearly based on originals by, e.g., Benediktov and Fet, or at least parody various writers'

general mannerisms, Oleynikov's targets are less easy to
determine and are perhaps not really "targets" at all.
Like Prutkov, he has a good ear for the high-style, clumsy
archaisms that are hangover from the age of Derzhavin and
earlier; a characteristic genre is the *Poslanie* (missive):
Poslanie, bichuiushchiy noshenie dlinnykh iubok; Poslanie,
odobriaiushchee strizhku volos, etc. But here, of course,
any parodistic effect is no longer aimed at a living target.   As we know, Formalist theory would have parody as a
stage in the discrediting of outworn literary forms; for a
20th century poet to "parody" forms that were outworn a
century before has no polemic purpose, and must fall
rather into the category of stylistic exercise or pastiche.
Do these exercises even have satirical purpose in any normal sense? At first it seems that ridicule of the senten-
tious, sentimental petty-bourgeois outlook of the poetic
"hero" is the chief intention; but very soon laughter dies
on the lips as we realize that neither reader nor poet himself are free from involvement in the object of attack--
which is language itself as much as the attitudes it expresses. An interesting sub-branch of the poetry of
"Tekhnoruk N." is the series of short verses *In a picture*
gallery (Thoughts about Art).[16] Here brief, entirely dead-
pan descriptions, mostly in free verse, of individual
paintings by well-known masters make no overtly humorous
point, but leave us with a sense of the ludicrousness, not
so much of the aesthetic pretentions of (e.g.) Baroque
painterly subject-matter, but of our own aesthetic responses that would define art in everyday terminology. It
is worth noting that certain contemporary poets, such as
the follower of Acmeism Antokolsky, were fond of expressing
experiences from the visual arts in well-polished verse.
Here is a characteristic poem from this sequence (evidently describing the ceiling of Inigo Jones' Banqueting
Hall in London):

> Король Британии сидит на облаке, ногою
>   /левой попирая мир.
> Над ним орел, парящий в воздухе, сжимает
>   /молнии в когтях.
> Два гения - один с огромной чашей,
> Похожею на самовар,
> Другой - с жезлом серебряным в руках -
> Склоняются к ногам непобедимого владыки.
> Внизу вдали идут в цепях закованные
>   /пленники.

For all Oleynikov's differences from his 19th c. predecessor, Soviet commentators frequently use words like
"Prutkovian intonation" about his work, and they are right
to do so. Oleynikov is not so much following the detailed
example of Prutkovianism as trying to identify, and make
modern use of, what he feels to be its essence: and for
that essence both parody and satire in any narrow sense are
incidentals. Dr. Monter rightly makes the point that
Prutkov, too, while taking some actual work as a "jumping-
off point," goes far beyond the "parody of a few lines [or]
even of one poet."[17]   Prutkov, and following him Oleynikov,
jumps into an inspired craziness (where incidentally the
regular metrics of conventional poetry soon begin to break
down) that suggests the "alogism" that was a key concept
for the modernist generation of Malevich and Khlebnikov,
the Formalists and Zabolotsky himself. What Oleynikov
felt may perhaps be formulated best in the well-known remark made by a character in Noel Coward's *Private Lives*:
"Extraordinary how potent cheap music is." Oleynikov felt
the allurement of bad art more strongly than anybody, and
his mixture of revulsion, curiosity and attraction lies at
the basis of his aesthetic. As an editor in the Donbass
he kept a notebook: but it was an unusual notebook, a
notebook of bad verses that would-be contributors had
sent to him, and in which he took a relish that was not
merely patronizing.

I have deliberately avoided discussing other possible
predecessors of Oleynikov in the history of Russian poetry:
an investigation into half-forgotten figures such as
Miatlev and Neelov, the poets of *Iskra* and *Satirikon*, would
be a worthwhile matter for specialist endeavour, but would
deflect this paper from its primary task, which is to set
Oleynikov in the context of his immediate colleagues, in
particular Zabolotsky. However, one further progenitor of
his work must be mentioned, not only because Oleynikov had
a special affection for him, but because he forms an important bridge first between Prutkov and Oleynikov, then
between Oleynikov and his friends. The figure in question
is Dostoevsky's creation in *Besy*, Captain Lebiadkin. The
Captain's uncompleted fable, *Zhil na svete tarakan...*, is
actually taken up and continued, in a series of ever more
harrowing episodes, by Oleynikov himself. Lebiadkin,
though a figure of comedy, is an altogether more unsettling
fictional character than Prutkov, with some of the demonic,
self-destructive energy that memoirists have noted behind

the good-humoured exterior of Oleynikov himself: as
Marshak wrote, "Берегись / Николая Олейникова, /
     Чей девиз - / Никогда не жалей никого!"[18]
Lebiadkin's remarkable and misdirected attempt to quote by
heart Fet's "*Ya prishel k tebe s privetom*... is somehow
both funnier and more destructive of the original than any
straightforward parody could be. Lebiadkin picks up and
develops certain possibilities inherent in Prutkov; and if
Oleynikov is Prutkov's "grandson," Dostoevsky might well
be seen as representing the intermediate generation.

     It is, in fact, this "Lebiadkinism" that seems to lend
some of its odd intonation to the verse of the young
Nikolay Zabolotsky. When the Captain gives voice to his
emotions thus: "Любви пылающей граната / лопнула
     в груди Игната...",
we find Zabolotsky (in 1932) beginning with a similar
initial image of similarly exaggerated apparent inappro-
priateness: "Как бомба в небе разрывается / и
     сотрясает атмосферу / так в человеке начи-
     нается / тоска, нарушив жизни меру..."
But what is significant is that the poem turns out long,
solemn-paced and undoubtedly seriously intended, despite
curious pastiche echoes and exaggerated imagery throughout. Its subject is a study of the reflections on life
and the natural world of an "alienated hero," Lodeynikov,
whose *toska* is expressed ultimately in lofty and philosophic terms. Precisely this nickname, Lodeynikov, had
been given to Oleynikov himself by members of the poetic
circle around him in the late 1920s. But Zabolotsky's
image of his friend is not a portrait--it is stylized, and
as he continued to work on it in the 1940s the abstract
elegiac elements grew stronger, and absurdities of intonation were almost eliminated.

     Other early Zabolotsky poems, from the time when he
was preparing his grotesque city-cycle published in 1929
as *Stolbtsy*, have clear Prutkovian moments. Describing
the motion of a paddle-steamer returning from an excursion
to Kronshtadt, Prutkov ends with a delightfully ambiguous
image:

     Еду я на пароходе,
     Пароходе винтовом;
     Тихо, тихо всё в природе,
     Тихо, тихо всё кругом,
     И, прверхность разрезая
     Темно-синей массы вод,

Мерно крыльями махая,
Быстро мчится пароход.

Zabolotsky's poetic analysis of motion, *Dvizhenie* (1927)
describes a horse-cab trundling into motion with similar
absurdity:

А бедный конь руками машет,
То вытянется, как налим...

but the whole poem is no parodistic or satirical exercise:
it in fact tries to reproduce in words the effect of a
Cubist painting:

"То снова восемь нос сверкают
В его блестящем животе."

But the closest kinship with Oleynikov comes in Zabolotsky's basic poetic concerns: with scientific phenomena
(some of Oleynikov's work may have been intentionally
parodying his friend in this area), with the "architecture"
of fundamental natural phenomena (Oleynikov was incidentally a brilliant self-taught mathematician), with the varieties, and significance of, *poshlost'*. And it would seem
that just as Oleynikov looked for the significant essence
of Prutkov and Lebiadkin, so Zabolotsky in turn looked for
the essence of serious purpose that lay behind Oleynikov's
and Shvarts' humorous, or apparently humorous verse. That
significance seems to have been for him the multiplication
of modes of literary perception, for the purpose of renewing and variegating our apprehension of life and of basic
phenomena. None of the grotesqueries, the witticisms, the
pastiche effects, the sententiousness or parodistic moments
of the early Zabolotsky are ever arbitrary or unmotivated,
and he worked immensely hard to achieve his casual-seeming
effects.

  This astonishing seriousness with which Zabolotsky approached the writing of poetry that could incorporate
grotesque, amusing, parodistic or outrageous moments is
underlined by the curious fate of his own light verse. He
was a master of impromptu epigrammes and versified witticisms, sometimes bordering on the indecently suggestive,
and particularly enjoyed exchanging these with Shvarts and
Oleynikov. He went further in the direction of Oleynikov,
and indeed Prutkov, by creating his own versifying
meshchanin, a *stary aptekar'*. But nearly all Zabolotsky's

light verse is lost, save for remembered or half-remem-
bered fragments: he himself ruthlessly destroyed and disavowed everything this did not match up to an exacting
standard of poetic seriousness that he set himself--in-
cluding much that we should probably consider excellent
literature, and be glad to have today. In other words,
the Prutkovian-Oleynikovian notes sounded in his poetry
are considered as contributing necessarily and seriously
to an ultimate aesthetic effect, which in Zabolotsky's
case was generally on a considerable scale of ambition:
the building-up of a metaphorical, even allegorical picture of basic areas of human experience. It is worth mentioning that, although these observations have been based
on Zabolotsky's early work, say up to 1934, there are often
strong pastiche notes in his later, post-exile work. The
beautiful 1947 poem *Ia trogal listy evkalipta*... takes as
its jumping-off point, I believe, a poem by Nadson (of all
improbable writers),[19] while his last great *poema*-cycle,
Rubruk v Mongolii, has a wealth of jaunty and unexpected
pastiche effects and deliberate anachronisms. But to pursue the development of Zabolotsky's poetry, with its overt
discontinuities and hidden consistency any further, is
another and much longer subject.[20]

Curiously, Oleynikov himself seems also to have under-
estimated the quality of his very funny, but (as we have
seen) more than merely funny, verse. He joined no literary
group. By the mid-1930s he had more or less given up writing poetry; he and Zabolotsky, with two or three others of
their former *Detgiz* colleagues, joined an idiosyncratic,
semi-philosophical discussion group of which records have
been preserved. At the beginning of this the participants
provided lists of all their interests, however heterogen-
eous, which are of considerable importance for our understanding of their perceptions of the world, and which incidentally show quite a degree of spiritual kinship between the two figures we have been discussing.[21] Out of
this period emerged the new, metamorphosed Zabolotsky:
maybe we should have seen a new Oleynikov if his career
had not been forcibly and fatally interrupted in 1937.

There is much that I have not mentioned in this short
sketch, and much concerning Oleynikov and the ramifications
of the modern Prutkovian tradition that awaits scholarly
research. For example, the published and unpublished
sources seldom attach dates to Oleynikov's poems; thus it
is difficult for us to trace his development, though it

would certainly be of interest to know how far his fateful
meeting with the future *Oberiuty* in 1927 affected his manner of writing (as was probably in fact the case). The relationship of his work for children with the "adult" poems
we have been discussing deserves more investigation. And
of course he should be placed in the whole web of inter-
connections in Leningrad literary life of the time, the
other writers--most notably Zoshchenko, but also the other
Oberiuty whom I have not discussed--who combined a grotesquely humorous, parodistic surface texture with deeper
implications, often indeed a note of catastrophism. But
such problems must be left for the future. Meanwhile it
is worth ending with a reminder that, however deserving of
literary-critical or historical analysis Oleynikov may be,
he remains a great humorous writer--whose astonishing,
shocking and very funny poems deserve the spontaneous enjoyment of readers as well as the attentions of a handful
of scholars.

University of Sussex

NOTES

[1]The basic editions are: N. A. Zabolotsky
Stikhotvoreniia i poemy, ed. A. Turkov (*Biblioteka poeta,*
M-L. 1965); *Stikhotvoreniia*, ed. G. Struve and B. Filipoff
(Washington/New York 1965); *Izbrannoe v dvukh tomakh* (M.
1972; the best).
    [2]F. Björling: *Stolbcy by Nikolaj Zabolockij: Analyses*
(Almqvist & Wiksell, Stockholm, 1975), p. 3.
    [3]Republished as appendix to R. R. Milner-Gulland,
"Left Art in Leningrad: the OBERIU Declaration," in *Oxford
Slavonic Papers*, N.S. III (1970); English translation in
G. Gibian, trsl. & ed., *Russia's Lost Literature of the
Absurd* (Cornell U.P., 1971).
    [4]See for example Milner-Gulland, op. cit.; Gibian,
op. cit.; A. Aleksandrov "Oberiu; predvaritelnye zametki,"
in *Československa rusistika* XIII (1968); A. Wolodźko,
"Poeci z Oberiu," in *Slavia Orientalis* XIV (1967); M.
Arndt, "Oberiu," in *Grani* No. 81; A. Aleksandrov, "Ignavia,"
in *Světova Literatura* 1968:6.
    [5]Cf. *Kozma Prutkov, Polnoe sobranie sochiniy*, ed.
B. Ya. Bukhstab (*Biblioteka poeta,* M.-L., 1965).
    [6]B. H. Monter, *Koz'ma Prutkov: the Art of Parody*
(Mouton, the Hague, 1972).

[7] Op. cit., p. 27.

[8] Cf. note 3.

[9] *Kratkaia literaturnaia entsiklopediia* (M. 1968) vol. V.

[10] Cf. several contributions to *My znali Yievgeniia Shvartsa*, ed. S. Tsimbal (L.-M. 1966), for reminiscences of Oleynikov; also A. Dymshits and publications mentioned in notes 10, 11 and 12

[11] I. Bakhterev & A. Razumovsky, "O Nikolae Oleynikove" in *Den'poezii* (Leningrad 1964), p. 154.

[12] A collected edition has recently been published: N. M. Oleynikov *Stikhotvoreniia*, introd. L. S. Fleyshman (K-Presse, Bremen, 1975). The chief earlier publications, all in the Soviet Union, include Bakhterev & Razumovsky, op. cit.; "Dva stikhotvoreniia," in *Den' poezii* (Leningrad 1966), with introduction by the poet's son A. Oleynikov; "Iumoristicheskie stikhi Nikolaia Oleynikova," with article by A. Dymshits in *Voprosy literatury* 1969: 3; Neizvestnye stikhi tekhnoruka N.," in *Voprosy literatury* 1971:3; and the only group of his poems (apart from those for children) to be published in his lifetime: "Sluzhenie nauke. Mukha. Khvala izobretateliam," in *Tridtsat' dney* 1934: 10. There are several accounts of his work in children's literature: see for example, L. Chukovskaya *V laboratorii redaktora* (M. 1960), ch. 7; I. Rakhtanov "Ezh" i "Chizh," in *Detskaya literatura* 1962, and *Rasskazy po pamiati* (2nd. ed., M. 1969); also contributions to *My znali Yevgeniia Shvartsa* (see note 9). The only extensive literary-critical accounts of Oleynikov's work are the introductory articles by Fleyshman and Dymshits (see above).

[13] In *Tridtsat' dney*: see note 12.

[14] In *Den' poezii* (Leningrad 1966): see note 12.

[15] Cf. *Voprosy literatury* 1969: 3 and 1971:3 : see note 12.

[16] In *Voprosy literatury* 1971:3: see note 12

[17] B. H. Monter, op. cit., pp. 116-117.

[18] I. Bakhterev & A. Razumovsky, op. cit., p. 155.

[19] S. Ya. Nadson *Grezy* (1881); in, e.g., *Russkie poety* (M. 1966), vol. III, p. 457.

[20] See R. R. Milner-Gulland, "Zabolotsky and the Reader: Problems of Approach," in *Russian Literature Triquarterly* 8 (Winter 1974), and "Zabolotsky: Philosopher-Poet," in *Soviet Studies* April 1971.

[21] The list compiled by Zabolotsky has been published in R. R. Milner-Gulland, "Zabolotsky: Philosopher-Poet"

(see note 20), p. 602. Oleynikov's list, published here
for the first time, is as follows:

> Меня интересуют: питание, числа, насекомые,
> журналы, стихи, свет, цвета, оптика, занима-
> тельное чтение, женщины, "пифагорейство-лейб-
> ницейство", картинки, устройство жилища, пра-
> вила жизни, опыты без приборов, задачи, рецеп-
> тура, масштабы, мировые положения, знаки,
> спички, рюмки, вилки, ключи и т.п., чернила.
> карандаш и бумага, способы письма, искусство
> разговаривать, взаимоотношения с людьми, гип-
> нотизм, доморощенная философия, люди 20 века,
> скука, проза, кино и фотография, балет, еже-
> дневная запись, природа, "Александрогринов-
> щина", история нашего времени, опыты над са-
> мим собой, математические действия, магнит,
> назначение различных предметов и животных,
> озарение, формы бесконечности, ликвидация
> брезгливости, терпимость, жалость, чистота
> и грязь, виды хвастовства, внутренее стро-
> ение земли, консерватизм, некоторые разго-
> воры с женщинами.

MARXISM AND RUSSIAN FORMALISM

Stanley Mitchell

Bertolt Brecht wrote: "The techniques of Joyce and
Döblin are not simply products of decadence; if one excludes their influence instead of modifying it, one will
simply get the influence of the epigones, namely the
Hemingways. The works of Joyce and Döblin reveal, in an
impressive way, the world-historical contradiction between
the forces and the relations of production. In these
works productive forces are to a certain extent represented. It behoves Socialist writers above all to acquaint themselves with the valuable, highly-developed
technical elements in these documents of despair
(Ausweglosigkeit), for they can see beyond the despair."[1]
In a footnote Brecht lists the following examples of
"highly-developed technical elements": "Interior monologue (Joyce), stylistic alternation (Joyce), dissociation
of elements (Döblin, Dos Passos), associative writing
(Joyce, Döblin), news-montage (Dos Passos), estrangement
(Verfremdung) (Kafka)."
It is in the light of these remarks that I wish to
examine the relationship between Marxism and Russian Formalism. Brecht was one of the few Marxists in his time who
did not reject the bourgeois *avant garde* as merely decadent. And he has a special connection with Russian Formalism: his concept of *Verfremdung* and Shklovsky's *ostranenie*
belong to the same tradition, and it is possible that
through his association with Tretyakov the term was trans-
mitted to him directly.[2]
Brecht's point here is that art does more than express ideology, it develops skills for representing reality. These skills, he argues, correspond to developments
in science and technology. For example, one could corre-
late "interior monologue" with psychoanalysis; "stylistic
alternation," "dissociation of elements," "associative
writing" with the speed and dislocations of the modern
city; the multiple perspectives of a complex and rapidly-
changing society, the technical extensions of perception
provided by the new media of photography, radio, film,
newspaper, etc., with the theory of relativity. "News-

montage" speaks for itself: new methods of communication,
starting with the telegraph.

"Estrangement" (*Verfremdung*) is a little different
from the others. It is an artistic technique designed to
counter the routinization of life in the modern city. By
Verfremdung Brecht means here not the Marxist *Entfremdung*,
which describes a condition, but an active concept of
"making strange" or "defamiliarising." The aim of
Verfremdung, whether Kafka's or Brecht's, is to shock people into recognizing their *Entfremdung*.

It is here that ideology enters. What do you do with
your multiple viewpoints, varying perceptions, estranging
techniques? It is clear that they can be put in the service of different ideologies. They can buttress relativism
or resignation, promote aestheticism, recall people to all
manner of "true selves." Or, as Brecht argues, if the
writer is a Socialist, they can be used to demonstrate
the need for Socialist revolution. Brecht's own use of
Verfremdung illustrates eloquently his advice to Socialist
writers. While Kafka practised the technique to recall men
to their metaphysical condition, Brecht harnessed it to a
philosophy of social and political change: if the world
could be shown to be alterable, then one could discover how
and in which direction to alter it. In his hands
Verfremdung served to reveal the inner workings of society and to unmask the habits and beliefs which disguised
those workings.

We can learn from Brecht how careful a Marxist critic
must be in relating ideology to technique. 'Official'
Marxist criticism, from crude Zhdanov to sophisticated
Lukács, has characteristically identified them, thereby
doing an immense disservice to Marxist aesthetics. By the
Zhdanov critic Joyce's techniques would be considered
purely an expression of his "rotten" outlook (see Radek's
speech at the 1934 Soviet Writers' Congress). The Lukács
critic, more subtly, distinguishes between technique and
form, regarding Joyce's technical devices as a fragmentation of form (here the 'epic' form of the novel). In
mainstream Soviet criticism a superficial treatment of
technique emerged under the head of *masterstvo*, 'craftsman-
ship,' meaning no more than 'polish,' 'economical' writing,
'sense of measure,' etc., which had no relation either to
genuine technical innovation or to ideology.

Brecht linked literary technique with technology as such. To the Lukács critic and to Lukács himself he countered: "One should not expect too much of people who make free with the word form, meaning something different from content or related to content or whatever, but who shy away from the word 'technique' as smacking of something 'mechanical.' Nor should it worry one too much that they quote from the classics (of Marxism) and that the word 'form' occurs there: the classics did not teach the technique of writing novels. And the word mechanical need frighten no-one, so long as it refers to technique; there is a mechanics which has performed great services for mankind and continues to do so - the mechanics of technol ogy."[3]

The concept of form as used by Lukács, Zhdanov or Radek was as conservative in relation to technique as the architecture of Stalin's skyscrapers in relation to Soviet technology. In order to throw a nationalist bridge between past and present, Soviet literature and literary theory in the Stalin period fell victim to the models of the previous century: Socialist Realism was bourgeois realism plus 'optimism.' The 'positive' Socialist here took the place of the 'superfluous man,' or, worse, as in the 'greatest' Soviet novel, *The Quiet Don*, the 'superfluous man' continued to thrive (Grigorii Melekhov).

Form is a more immediately ideological concept than technique. The form of the bourgeois novel, for example, sets an individual or group of individuals at the centre. The plot revolves round them. Brecht observed that the novel "does not stand or fall with 'characters,' above all not with characters of the type that existed in the nineteenth century."[4] On writing novels in the period of "final struggle between the bourgeois and proletarian class" he remarked: "It is absolutely false, that is to say, it leads nowhere, it is not worth the writer's while, to simplify his problems so much that the immense, complicated, actual life-process of human beings" in this age "is reduced to a 'plot,' setting or background for the creation of great individuals."[5]

* * * * *

Today Marxist critics are seeking to recuperate the losses incurred by Stalinist aesthetics. One way has been to resurrect and reappraise the debate between Marxism and Formalism. This has happened principally through attempts to incorporate structuralism into Marxism, structuralism being regarded as the heir to Formalism; secondarily by recapturing and developing the positions of the 'political' or, better, 'politicized' Formalists who joined Mayakovsky's *LEF*.

Marxism has not been the winner in these resurrections. In each case it has been robbed of its core--the base-superstructure relationship or, what is another expression for the same thing, the theory of reflection. Semiology, the political wing of structuralism, sensitive to the 'consciousness industry'[6] of late capitalism and its shaping social power, makes no philosophic distinction between consciousness and reality. Structuralism subsumes literature and society under philosophically equivalent 'systems' or 'components.' In each approach the notion of *communication* replaces that of reflection. Language becomes the methodological *lingua franca* or model for social and cultural analysis. The concept of society is dissolved into systems of codes and signs. In this way the methodological errors of Formalism are repeated and amplified. (The Formalists were indeed more materialist than their heirs, for at least they considered the work of art as a *thing*, which now becomes a structure or, worse, a set of signs.)

What then has Formalism to offer Marxism? Or, how can Marxism incorporate the insights of Formalism without forfeiting its philosophic integrity?

Marxism is a philosophy of change. "The philosophers have only interpreted the world differently; the point, however, is to *change* it." (Marx)[7] What part does a theory of literature play in changing the world? First, it must help us understand literature *ideologically*, that is in terms of an active relationship of superstructure to base. The Marxist theory of reflection is a revolutionary one. Literature like all other forms of consciousness does more than reflect the world, passively. It is the place where, as Marx put it, men become aware of their conflicts and fight them out.[8] Secondly, literature disposes of special forms and techniques. A Marxist theory of literature must also tell us how these relate to consciousness and ideology, which of themselves will not produce a literary device.

It is at this point that a Marxist can approach Formalism. The Formalists restricted the study of literature to the study of literary devices, rejecting every other consideration as extraneous. Even so, they were not

ideologically innocent.   Victor Erlich makes the point
when he contrasts the two most 'formalist' literary-
critical schools of the twentieth century, the Russian
Formalists and their American 'counterparts,' the New
Critics: "The 'New Criticism' developed in a social and
philosophical climate vastly different from that which had
given rise to Russian Formalism or Prague Structuralism.
Hence the wide divergencies in manner and ideological lean-
ings of the two movements.   The typical Formalist was a
radical Bohemian, a rebel against authority, seeking to
avoid a total commitment in favour of the new regime, but
little concerned with the old.   The 'New Critic,' especially his American variant, is more often than not a
conservative intellectual, distrustful of the 'mass-man,'
repelled by industrial civilization, looking back nostalgically toward a more stable society and more binding set
of values.   For Jakobson and Shklovsky, the watchword was
innovation, for Tate and Ransom, tradition.   Anti-
academic in the extreme, the Russian Formalists would have
little use for Ransom's attempt to confine professional
criticism within the walls of *Academia*.   Their esthetic
'purism,' which they eventually renounced, had more to do
with Bohemian extravagance and provocative bravado than
aristocratic aloofness from the *profanum vulgus*."[9]
     The ideology of the Russian Formalists can in general
terms be described as that of petit-bourgeois revolt, very
much in the sense that Trotsky described the ideology of
their 'practical' associates, the Futurists.   It was as
iconoclasts and debunkers that they formed part of the
general revolutionary movement.   They saw the history of
literature as a process of debunking: a new school or
movement developed by parodying its predecessor.   The
Formalists masked their ideology, claiming to attend purely to questions of form.   Yet here they regarded themselves
as "revolutionary."   Tomashevsky wrote: "The impetus administered by the formal method to the contemporary study
of literature was sufficiently significant to merit the
description 'revolutionary.'"[10]
     Even the 'exclusive' attention to form was itself an
ideological choice, as the 'official' Marxists, like
Trotsky and Lunacharsky, were not slow to point out.
Trotsky regarded Formalist disdain for content as a
bourgeois escape from the "hard reality" of the revolution:
"The assertion of complete independence of the aesthetic
'factor' from the influence of social conditions, as is
made by Shklovsky, is an instance of specific hyperbole

whose roots ... lie in social conditions too; it is the
megalomania of aesthetics turning our hard reality on its
head."[11]

In his essay on the Futurists Trotsky shows more
acutely the necessary duality of petit-bourgeois revolt.
And Erlich, in the passage quoted, puts the situation of
the Formalist in a like manner: "The typical Formalist was
a radical Bohemian, a rebel against authority, seeking to
avoid a total commitment in favour of the new regime, but
little concerned with the old." He is an *aesthetic* rebel
in the Romantic tradition (however much he would have ab-
horred such a genealogy): that is, he is anti-bourgeois in
the sense of anti-establishmentarian, while he remains
profoundly bourgeois in his individualism. Bourgeois 'establishment' and Romantic revolt belong together as 'dialectical' poles of the same social order.

Like the Futurists, the Formalists were caught between their 'radical Bohemianism' and commitment to the
new regime. If we take Shklovsky's 'canonical' *Art as a
Device* (1916), we can already detect a split between, as
Jurij Striedter has put it, aesthetics and ethics.[12] On
the one hand Shklovsky affects complete indifference to
the subject-matter of literature. The aim of *ostranenie*
is to refresh the palate, resurrect the 'tangibility' of
things, prolong the moment of aesthetic enjoyment. Yet
the example with which Shklovsky chooses to illustrate his
argument could not be more anti-aesthetic, namely some of
the most unabashedly socially-critical passages in Tolstoy.
What kind of a purely aesthetic thesis is it that explains
the technique of *ostranenie* by means of Tolstoy's attack on
the institution of private property in *Kholstomer*? This
could be Brecht writing rather than an intransigeant Formalist. (As we shall suggest, Brecht reunites the aesthetic and ethical sides of *Art as a Device*--not this work
as such, but in principle--in terms of a social aesthetics,
according to which 'estrangement,' the 'shock of recognition' brings pleasure, not in the 'resurrection of the
word,' but in the unexpected discovery of an alterable
world; pleasure combines with understanding to encourage
a revolutionary attitude of mind.)

Recently, Shklovsky has corrected himself in a
'Brechtian' manner: "I should have asked myself: what were
you proposing to make strange if art did not express reality? The sensation of what did Sterne or Tolstoy wish to
restore?

"The theory of estrangement which has been accepted by many, including Brecht, speaks of art as knowledge, as a means of investigation."[13]

At this late stage, indeed ever since the thirties, it was impossible in the Soviet Union really to restate Formalism in a Brechtian manner, because Brecht conceived of art not merely as a means of knowledge and investigation, but as a form of political *practice*, the results of which were not necessarily predictable. Of the literary bureaucrats in Moscow he wrote: "They are, to put it bluntly, enemies of production. Production makes them uncomfortable. You never know where you are with production; production is the unforseeable. You never know what's going to come out. And they themselves don't want to produce. They want to play the *apparatchik* and exercise control over other people. Every one of their criticisms contains a threat."[14]

The bureaucrats in Moscow treated art, indeed all of the superstructure, in a positivistic manner as an affirmatory reflection of the new socialist society. Although art was called upon to educate the masses, it was put in a dependent and necessarily passive position: it was told *how* to educate. The Soviet Marxists abandoned a revolutionary understanding of reflection.

It was not, therefore—and could not have been—the 'self-correcting' Shklovsky who brought together Formalism and Marxism in a 'Brechtian' manner. This was done, or rather anticipated, by the LEFists who politicized Formalism (including to some extent the younger Shklovsky). The later Shklovsky does not (for whatever reasons) examine his earlier work closely enough. For, as we have seen, he does address himself there to the social motives behind Tolstoy's estrangement-technique. Subsequently, Shklovsky eschewed the 'ethical' implications of *Art as a Device*, becoming aesthetically more purist and intransigent. Paradoxically, the LEFists chose the 'aesthetic' rather than the 'ethical' side of Formalism for politicization.

The paradox is to be explained as follows. The LEFists wished to align themselves with the workers, to see the artist as a worker, a producer. Hence what they fastened on in Formalism was the concern with *making*. Shklovsky had written in *Art as a Device*: "Art is a means of experiencing the making of a thing" (adding "what is made in art is unimportant"). The LEFists shared with the Formalists their rejection of art-as-reflection. (This

was one of Trotsky's charges against the left Futurists.)
They too described art as a thing. In their case it was a
way of subsuming social production and art under the same
term.

The philosophic basis of Formalist aesthetics was a
mechanical-perceptual objectivism that responded to the beginnings of a technological age from the standpoint of the
radical-Bohemian *petite-bourgoisie*. Art, the Formalists
argued, had a habit of becoming 'automatized' and required
to be shocked back into life again. These 'estranging
shocks' were the way in which men refreshed their perceptions. In fact, the modernism of the Formalists, like
that of the Futurists, indeed of most 'modernism,' is
strongly tinged with nostalgia, and in this respect has
more in common with the American New Critics than Professor Erlich admits. As Fredric Jameson has shrewdly remarked, the Formalist emphasis on *making*, on the folktale
and the *skaz*, is *artisanal* in character. The 'impersonal-
ity' of Formalist aesthetics is that of the craft. The
'mechanical' categories of Formalism, even at their most
developed, are fairly simple: device, shift, lever, series,
displacement.

LEF inaugurates the 'industrial' phase of Formalism
or the 'industrialization' of Formalism. Its language
changes from mechanical-perceptual (making, estranging,
experiencing) to 'constructivist' (building, organizing,
constructing, producing). Finally, a split develops in
LEF between the older Formalists (Shklovsky, Brik and the
Futurist Mayakovsky, who associates more closely with them)
and the new 'productionists,' in particular Tretyakov and
Chuzhak, the former wishing to remove 'aesthetics' entirely from their theory and practice, demanding that art
should 'construct' reality directly, without 'aesthetic
interruption,' as he called it. The Formalists had replaced 'reflection' with 'estrangement,' but, Tretyakov
argued, 'estrangement' still remained an aesthetic category, deviating from a direct engagement with reality.

Nevertheless, what united the Formalists and 'productionists' throughout was their conception of reality
as thing and of art as the production of things. The
'productionists' ('constructionists'/constructivists) de-
aestheticized the perceptual side of Formalism, replacing
it with a behaviourist psychology, which regarded the
psyche as a machine to be acted upon and changed (Eisen-
stein is at first strongly representative of this trend
in his LEF article *Montage of Attractions*, but in practice

combines both aestheticism and behaviourism). And they materialized the Formalist notion of thing, which became one with material reality. Inevitably, they ran into an impasse, because no role was left for art at all. Tretyakov finally called for a literature of fact, pure documentary art, reportage.

The common philosophical mistake of both Formalists and productionists/constructivists was to identify consciousness and reality. It was the self-overestimation of people working in the 'higher' spheres of the superstructure. Their motives differed: the productionists/constructivists wished to consider themselves workers pure and simple. But their image of a worker was that of a machine. They were no less *petit-bourgeois* in their revolt and their espousal of Communism, only different: in renouncing aestheticism and bourgeois individualism they sought to efface themselves into workers. Yet, despite their intentions, this was a patronizing and inhuman way of regarding workers. They were visiting their own social-psychological problems on the artistic needs of the proletariat. Trotsky put it aptly: "The call of the Futurists to break with the past, to do away with Pushkin, to liquidate tradition etc., has a meaning insofar as it is addressed to the old literary caste, to the closed-in circle of the intelligentsia. In other words, it has a meaning insofar as the Futurists are busy cutting the cord which binds them to the priests of bourgeois literary tradition.

"But the meaninglessness of this call becomes evident as soon as it is addressed to the proletariat. The working-class does not have to and cannot break with literary tradition, because the working-class is not in the grip of such tradition. The working-class does not know the old literature, it still has to commune with it, it still has to master Pushkin to absorb him, and to overcome him."[15]

'Productionism,' however, has another side which Trotsky (and Lunacharsky) overlooked. It was certainly important to reassert the Marxist theory of reflection. But in the light of the subsequent use of the theory--as a means of confirming the status quo--the Formalist/Futurist emphasis on art as production resumes its relevance, and it is for this reason that Marxists in Western Europe today are trying to recover and re-apply the Formalist heritage. Formalists and Futurists were fighting an academicism in the arts which reappeared under Stalin. What was needed was a revolutionary theory of reflection, but the practice of Stalinism made this impossible.

Production as against reflection meant to the LEFists activity versus passivity. Certainly, their understanding of forms was behaviouristic. The question is: how was this behaviourism used? Brecht too began his Marxist career as a behaviourist.

The LEFists, like the Formalists, shifted their attention from content to form, indeed rejecting the terms altogether in favour of the "construction of material," conceiving language as the material of literature. The ideological aim of this 'construction' was to fashion a new man, a new consciousness. But the technologism of the method inhibited the aim. For the psyche is more than a machine. Like Zhdanov and Lukács, though in a different manner, the LEFists were unable to distinguish between form as technique and form as ideology. But their special sensitivity to form enabled them to lay bare, better than anyone else, the ideologies implicit in formal and stylistic devices. For them ideology started with form rather than with content. Schools of criticism and art had always fought over formal questions--Romantics versus Classicists, for example. But it required a subsequent sociological analysis to uncover the ideological roots of these battles. What the LEFists did, with all the drawbacks of their technologism, was to make explicit the ideological function of form in and for the present.

They did not understand the relationship between content and form dialectically. Tretyakov, for example, could write in a manner characteristic of Formalists and Futurists that innovation begins with the formal breaking of tradition rather than with changes in attitude and outlook. Form (or technique)-determines-content remained the philosophic essence of both Futurism and Formalism. But in the context of revolution this over-emphasis alerted the LEFists to the ideological function of form in new works of literature. In particular, they criticized writing which was revolutionary in theme, but conventional in form. As Arvatov pointed out in his over-combative analysis of Briusov's poetry, characteristically entitled "Counter-revolution in Form" ("Kontrrevolyutsiya formy"), Briusov's choice of metre, syntactical arrangement, metaphor, diction was not merely a formal matter; it sabotaged ideologically, or revealed the reactionary essence of, the ostensibly revolutionary content.[16] Arvatov over-reaches himself because of his militant-formal premise, but the methodological insight is important.

How different is this point of view from that of the 'official' Marxists? We saw how Zhdanov and Lukács, in their different ways, aligned form and ideology. Lukács, for example, attacks left-wing modernists because they use a purportedly 'right-wing' form. The deciding factor here is one's attitude to the relationship between literature and reality. If, like the 'official' Marxists, you think that the role of literature is to reflect reality (and 'mould' your readership ideologically), then you will treat form as merely the articulation of content. If you are a Lukács, you will argue a dialectical relationship between form and content in order to avoid the charge of positivism. (In fact, Lukács produces no more than a 'dialectical' positivism.) If with Brecht you see the role of literature not merely to reflect and 'mould,' but to show reality as alterable, then you will accord a much more combative agency to form. The Lukács approach is gnoseological in the manner of Hegel's aesthetics: i.e., art gives shape to reality in individualized forms. And these forms (genres, types) are confirmations, articulations of given ontological forms--growth, conflict, moments of choice, calling to account, etc. As in Hegel the gnoseology cannot lead to practice, for the emphasis stops short at the *forms of consciousness* through which men fight out their material conflicts: the *combative* element is missing. Form in Lukács and Stalinist aesthetics is, for different reasons, confirmatory.

For Brecht, the Russian Formalists and LEFists, form was always a combative concept. From the beginning the Formalists argued that the aim of art was not to reproduce the 'essence' of reality, but to make you see things differently.

When Lukács criticizes modernist 'fragmentation,' it is on the basis that the world is not in essence fragmented, but only appears so. Accordingly, an ideologically acceptable form will be one which underscores the essential unity and rationality of the world. In other words the applauded work of art will resolve dissonance in the time-honoured Aristotelian fashion. For the 'non-Aristotelian' Brecht it is the register of these dissonances which is important, because they underline uncertainty, conflict, change, and these, though painful, contain hope--or at least they can be used hopefully according to Brecht's notion of 'refunctioning' the insights and techniques of the bourgeois *avant-garde*.

And from a technical point of view the methods used by
the 'modernists' are more 'up-to-date' than those preferred by Lukács and the Zhdanovist aestheticians. As
Brecht put it, the experimental modernists reflect the
'world-historical contradiction' of our time, where the
productive forces outstrip the social relations of production.

The LEFists understood how important it was to match
a revolutionary content with a revolutionary form, and how
a reactionary form could nullify the most revolutionary of
contents. From this point of view, for all their denunci-
ations of 'aesthetics,' they appreciated perfectly the
special powers of the 'aesthetic.'

What is at issue here is the difference between a
gnoseological-confirmatory and a practical-political aesthetics. The gnoseological-confirmatory is interested in
form only from an immanent point of view—the way in which
'content' becomes 'form.' The practical-political is concerned with the effect upon the reader or viewer. Lukács
treats effect only in terms of post-cathartic aftermath,
affecting the receiver's moral personality. The Zhdanovist
understands effect only as 'ideological education,' making
no connection between this and questions of form (unless
it is a matter of 'accessibility').

A practical-political aesthetics must take its start-
ing-point from the Formalists and their successors in LEF.
The vitality, viability and necessity of this tradition
(defects notwithstanding) is shown in a recent study, only
marginally (but very perceptively) concerned with aesthetic questions, Stanley Aronowitz's *False Promises*, a history of American working-class consciousness.

Discussing contemporary Hollywood films and noting
that they "provide little or no space for the audience to
supply their own insights," he observes: "It is not only
the content of the film—the plot and the action—that
limits the participation of the observer. The techniques
of film-making embody these limitations as well.... Unlike the important efforts of Japanese and European film-
makers to fix the camera directly on the action and permit
the scene to work 'itself' out, American films are characterized by rapid camera work and sharp editions whose effect is to segment the action into one-or-two minute time
slots, paralleling the prevailing styles of television
production."[17]

Aronowitz concludes that a film-maker who subordinates action and characters to such a concept of dramatic time "reveals a politics inside technology that is far more insidious than 'reactionary' content." "When viewed from this perspective," he adds, "the film-maker, such as Howard Hawks, who refuses to subordinate art to the requirements of segmented time, becomes more resistant to authoritarianism than the liberal or left-wing film-makers who are concerned with the humanitarian content of film, but have capitulated to techniques that totally reduce the audience to spectators."[18]

In place of the (literally) deformed aesthetics of the "liberal or left-wing film-makers" Aronowitz counsels a Brechtian approach: "without the distantial element in plays or films, the control of communication remains in the hands of those who produce the films. And the immediacy by which the consumption of the film or television show occurs militates against the participation of the audience unless the presentation offers an opportunity for participation in its own structure."[19]

Aronowitz recognizes here exactly what the LEFists discovered: that the 'politics' of artistic technology could be far more insidious than a 'reactionary' content.

Aesthetic *distance* was at the heart of Formalist aesthetics. The aim of *ostranenie* and *exposing the device* was to free the reader from automatic response, from lazy familiarity and habituation. Politically, Formalism was at its best attacking routine and mystification. Some of the LEFists, Levidov, for example, applied the notions of *estrangement* and *exposing the device* to the function of revolution. Social forms, he argued, became routines, protecting themselves by closed-in ideologies which hid their true motivation: it then became necessary, ideologically and politically, to expose the motivation and destroy the routine.[20]

This application, refreshing as it is, suffers from the Formalist dichotomy (and false identification—two sides of the same coin) of consciousness and being. Reality is regarded as a machine which necessarily runs down and rusts and which therefore requires a mechanic to derust it and change its parts. Neither Formalists nor LEFists could understand development *dialectically*, i.e., in terms of the internal self-movement, the internal contradictions, the *praxis* of society. Revolution occurs not by application of change from outside the social process, but by the accumulation and intensification of conflict.

That this internal intensification might need 'external'
guidance in the form of a political party is a secondary
matter. The LEFists put all their emphasis on the external guidance, reducing reality to the notion of 'material'
which required 'organization' and 'construction.'

* * * *

A special issue of LEF was devoted to a study of
Lenin's language, and it was here that the older Formalists, Kazansky, Shklovsky, Eikhenbaum, Tynyanov came into
their own and produced their best *political* work. Their
perceptions remained linguistic and they made no attempt
to transfer the categories of linguistic analysis to society. Nor did they regard language here as a material
reality in its own right. Tynyanov, in particular, established a clear dialectical relationship between language and reality, word and thing. It is fascinating to
see how all the familiar Formalist terms themselves undergo an 'estrangement' and 'displacement' under the pressure
of analyzing Lenin's political language.

Tynyanov deals, for example, with the change of name
of the revolutionary party from *social-democrat* to *Communist*. He remarks: "The change of party name from 'social-
democratic (Bolsheviks)' to 'Communists' was not merely a
terminological demarcation from 'social democracy,' but a
revitalization of meaning.

"Lenin conceived the change of name as a shift
(*sdvig*), a struggle with linguistic routine; the habituation of the old term was not a reason for keeping it, but
for changing it."

Tynyanov quotes Lenin: "The masses have got used to
and the workers 'love' their social-democratic party."

"...this is an argument from routine, sleepiness,
stagnation (*kosnost'*). But we wish to transform the world.

"...And we are afraid of ourselves.

"We prefer the 'familiar,' 'beloved' dirty shirt. It
is time to cast off the dirty shirt and put on a clean
one."[21]

The two concepts with which Tynyanov operates throu-
out his essay are *revitalization* (*ozhivlenie*) and *shift*
(*sdvig*). A word loses its original meaning, in this case
as a result of political misuse and mystification. By
'shifting' the word into a new 'lexical plane,' if necessary changing it, one strips it of what Tynyanov calls
elsewhere its paralyzing 'aureole' (which inhibits

analysis), exposes its function and resurrects its original
meaning.

The notion of *revitalization* is free here of that nostalgia which clings to so much of Formalist thinking, from
Shklovsky's very early *Resurrection of the Word* (1914) to
Eikhenbaum's use of the *skaz*, the oral narrative, as an
'artisanal' premise for the analysis of literature.   The
notion here has been 'politicized.'

This fresh, 'political' concept of revitalization is
given broad historical dimensions by Kazansky.   Noting
Lenin's knowledge of Cicero, he compares Lenin's political
rhetoric with that of classical antiquity.   Of political
language in classical Greece he writes: "In no place and
at no time in the world is it possible to find in the
sphere of political language that exclusive freedom and
direct action of the word which in Athens constituted an
organic and permanent aspect of public affairs an inseparable fact, like air, of political life."[22]

In the light of the Greek example Kazansky argues
that we should resurrect the real meaning of rhetorical
terminology which has become obfuscated and scholastified
by the ideological takeovers of successive ruling classes.
In other words Kazansky calls upon us to restore political
democracy to the use of languge.   In the context of the
early years of the Russian revolution such a programme is
anything but restorationist.

Each of the Formalist critics shows Lenin restoring
democracy to political language, Eikhenbaum analyzing his
'deflation' of Ciceronian rhetoric, Tynyanov describing
his lexical concretization of political generalities like
'freedom,' 'the people' or even 'the dictatorship of the
proletariat.'

It is striking that the Formalists do not go to the
excesses of their 'more political' LEFist associates.
Very carefully they establish and themselves adhere to the
manner in which Lenin relates words to things.   The emphasis is put on the productive-ideological function of language.   Quoting Lenin: "We must be able to measure schemes
against life, and not repeat meaningless words about 'the
dictatorship of the proletariat and peasantry in general,'
Tynyanov comments: "Each word either seizes hold of a
process and therefore runs ahead, anticipating the process,
or lags behind, attaching itself to a particular phase of
the process.   In order that the process should not freeze
in the consciousness and reality appear monochrome through

this prism, it is necessary to test the words, laying bare
their link with things."[23]

Both Eikhenbaum and Shklovsky compare Lenin's style
with the 'deflating,' 'taking-apart' manner of Tolstoy.
Lenin and Tolstoy are regarded as masters of 'exposing the
devices' used by convention and self-concealing ideologies.
Shklovsky recovers here the 'ethical' side of his old article *Art as a Device* and politicizes the 'aesthetic' side,
refining Tynyanov's analysis of the relationship of word to
thing in Lenin. Viewing Lenin's style as a permanent linguistic revolution, he remarks that it "consists in the deflation (*snizhenie*) of the revolutionary phrase, the substi-
tution of everyday language for traditional revolutionary
phraseology. In this respect his basic device comes close
to the style of Lev Tolstoy. Lenin is against nomenclature,
he is always establishing new relationships between words
and their objects, he avoids naming things and fixing the
new name."[24]

Shklovsky argues that Lenin is always bringing new perceptions to bear in his methods of comparison, so that
nothing becomes standardized, neither the reality spoken of
nor the language used: "This style consists in the fact of
change, not of consolidation. When Lenin introduces an
everyday fact, it is not to 'standardize' the everyday, but
to use the everyday in order to change the yardsticks of
comparison.

"He compares the large with the small, using the example of minimal quantity in order to strip language of
its falsity and revitalize it."[25]

The quality of 'petit-bourgeois revolutionism' remains
in Shklovsky's analysis. It is certain that Lenin wishes
to consolidate a new terminology as much as he sought to
destroy or deflate the old, although the new in its turn
would at some point come in for demolition or refreshment.
But Shklovsky's over-emphasis on permanent change expresses
the paradoxically static conception of change common to all
the Formalists. Fredric Jameson rightly remarks: "Shklovsky's doctrine ..., by seeing literary change as a uniform
mechanism the same at all times and all places, no doubt
keeps faith with the existential situation of literary production ..., but at the same time ends up by turning di-
achrony into mere appearance and undermining any genuine
historical awareness of the changing of forms."[26] What
Trotsky says of the inner division of Futurist ideology
applies equally here to the Formalists: "Here lies the
incompatibility of psychological type between the Futurist,

who is a political revolutionist, and the Futurist, who is
a revolutionary innovator of form.... The trouble is not
that Futurism 'denies' the holy traditions of the intelligentsia. On the contrary, it lies in the fact that it does
not feel itself part of the revolutionary tradition."[27]

The old Formalist philosophic idealism and aestheticism express themselves even in Shklovsky's appraisal of
Lenin's comparisons: the example of the everyday serves
to refresh the comparison rather than to 'standardize' the
everyday.

These criticisms apart, two valuable things emerge
from the Formalist analysis of Lenin's language. The
first is a paradigm of literary change which is more political and ideological than anywhere else in their writings.
And it is a paradigm which (implicitly) uses Lenin's own
theory of reflection (itself a restatement and clarifica-
tion of Marx). Shklovsky (with all our reservations) and,
more so, Tynyanov see the relationship between language
and society, words and things, dialectically. Tynyanov
elsewhere, for instance in his essay on *Literary Evolution*,
analyzes literary change as an immanent process linked to
society not by reflection, but by the narrow sociolin-
guistic concept of speech function, which connects the
literary 'system' with its nearest addressee in the social
'system.' Tynyanov's speech-function, along with Eikhenbaum's *skaz*, characterize the 'artisanal' nature of the
Formalists. The more political LEFists, like Levidov or
Chuzhak, collapsing language ('material') and reality,
thought that by changing language you could change society
directly. Both positions are characteristic examples of
vulgar sociology current at the time, the first a 'structuralist,' the second an instrumentalist empiricism.

The second valuable thing to emerge is the revolu-
tionary-political understanding of style. Again the insights suffer from a certain formalization. Comparison,
for instance, is understood only *polemically*: it always
deflates or decanonizes, it never confirms. Nevertheless,
if one removes the formalization and rigidity, there remains an understanding of the revolutionary energy that
is condensed into literary devices. Much later, in his
recent *Tetiva* (1970), Shklovsky remarks: "If in art we
compare a cat with a cat or a flower with a flower, the
artistic form bases itself not merely upon the moment of
this intersection; these moments are detonators of big
explosions (*vzryvy*), entries into consciousness, explorers
(*razvedchiki*) of the new."[28] The title of the book, the

'bowstring,' captures a dialectical conception of imagery:
"The harmony of the bow is the drawn bow, drawn by the
bowstring--unity and contradiction; kinetic energy ready
to become dynamic."[29]

The politicization of Formalism redeems and transforms its intransigent hedonism. The importance of aris-
tic 'estrangement' Shklovsky had written originally, lay in
its increase of aesthetic pleasure. What was perceived or
what was 'made' did not matter: it was the prolongation of
aesthetic enjoyment which characterized the nature of art.
Looking back on the origins of Formalism, Shklovsky relates
the movement to the Revolution. He remarks: "In 1916 the
theory of *ostranenie* appeared. In it I tried to generalize
the means of renewing perception and the way phenomena were
shown. It was all connected with the period, with pain and
inspiration, with wonder about the world."[30]   A very far
cry this from the demonstrative scientism of the original
Formalists. But, as we have already seen, the contradiction is not so complete. We noted that Tomashevsky, perhaps the 'driest' of all the Formalists, wrote at the time
that their researches in 'literary science' were truly
revolutionary. The inspirational element was not far from
their work, flashing out in maximalist assertions. No
mere 'scientistic' movement would have continued to labour
hard at their theories in the freezing tenements of Petrograd and Moscow. Wonder, the desire to see the world in a
new way, fired both Formalists and Futurists. Of the
Futurists Shklovsky aptly remarked: "The poetry of Mayakovsky and Khlebnikov--the painting of the time--wished to see
the world in a new way and to that end changed the very
sound of verse."[31]

The politicization of Russian Formalism is completed
after a long and complex journey in Brecht's *Short Organum
for the Theatre* (1948). Here pleasure and wonder become
the basic constituents of a Marxist aesthetics, drawing
their sustenance not merely from the renewal of perception,
but from insights into the possibilities of changing the
real world, 'laying bare' the mechanisms of social development and surprising people out of received attitudes.

University of Dar-es-Salaam

NOTES

[1] Bertolt Brecht, *Über Realismus*, ed. Werner Hecht (Frankfurt am Main, 1971), p. 116.

[2] Bernhard Reich, *Im Wettlauf mit der Zeit* (Berlin, 1970), pp. 371-2.

[3] Op. cit., p. 54; see also Bertolt Brecht, "Against Georg Lukács," transl. Stuart Hood, *New Left Review* 84 (March-April 1974), p. 46. (My translation differs in some respects.)

[4] Ibid., p. 55.

[5] Ibid., pp. 55-56.

[6] See Hans Magnus Enzensberger's article of this title in *New Left Review* 64 (November-December 1970).

[7] Karl Marx and Frederick Engels, *Selected Works in Two Volumes* (Moscow 1951), vol. 2, p. 367.

[8] Ibid., vol. 1, pp. 362-64.

[9] Victor Erlich, *Russian Formalism: History, Doctrine* (The Hague, Netherlands, 1955), pp. 241-42.

[10] Boris Tomashevsky, *Formal'nyi metod (vmesto nekrologa)*.

[11] Leon Trotsky, *Literature and Revolution* (Paperback: Ann Arbor, Mich., 1969), p. 181.

[12] Jurij Striedter, Introduction to *Texte der Russichen Formalisten* Band 1 *Texte zur allgemeinen Literaturtheorie and zur Theorie der Prosa* (Munich 1969), p. xxiii.

[13] Viktor Shklovsky, *Tetiva* (Moscow 1971), p. 351.

[14] Walter Benjamin, *Understanding Brecht*, trans. Anna Bostock, intro. Stanley Mitchell (London 1973), p. 118.

[15] Leon Trotsky, op. cit., p. 130.

[16] Boris Arvatov, "Kontrrevoliutsiia formy," *LEF* 1 (March 1923).

[17] Stanley Aronowitz, *False Promises: The Shaping of American Working Class Consciousness* (New York, 1970), p. 117.

[18] Ibid., pp. 117-18.

[19] Ibid.

[20] Levidov, *LEF*, II (1923), p. 131.

[21] Iu. Tynyanov, "Slovar' Lenina-Polemista," *LEF* V (1924), p. 102.

[22] B. Kazansky, "Rech' Lenina," *LEF* V (1924), p. 113.

[23] Iu. Tynyanov, "Slovar' Lenina-Polemista," *LEF* V (1924), p. 104.

[24] V. Shklovsky, "Lenin, kak dekanizator," *LEF* V (1974), p. 55.

[25] Ibid., p. 56.

[26] Fredric Jameson, *The Prison House of Language* (Princeton, 1972), p. 59.

[27] Trotsky, op. cit., p. 132

[28] Shklovsky, *Tetiva*, p. 12.

[29] Ibid., p. 50.

[30] Ibid., p. 11.

[31] Ibid.

THE PESSIMISTIC VISION OF THE REVOLUTION IN MIKHAIL SHOLOKHOV'S NOVEL *THE QUIET DON*

Dragan Nedeljković

Sholokhov's manner of treating the theme of revolution reminds us somewhat of Homer's attitude towards the Trojan War. For despite the climate of hatred that reigns in their respective works, both authors are objective in their portrayals, and in both cases we can say that objectivity in no way closes the authors off from human sentiments. In Homer's case, we find that Hector is more humane and more tragic than all the Greek heroes portrayed, including Achilles; and in Sholokhov's case it is evident that Grigori Melekhov is more humane and more tragic than both the "white" and the "red" heroes who are portrayed. Homer's portrayal is certainly more harmonious than Sholokhov's. Not only does poetry always triumph over history, but the forces in conflict depicted by Homer are truly beautifully balanced. In *Quiet Flows the Don*, the victory of poetry over history is far from evident, and the Homeric sense of perfect balance is hardly ever attained. For, where Homer portrays the Greeks and the Trojans equally deeply and equally beautifully, Sholokhov devotes more time and effort to the war that the "whites" are waging against the "reds" than vice-versa.

However, Sholokhov's choice is not gratuitous; rather, he is a born novelist, and as such, his artistic instinct naturally attracts him to a hero and a milieu in which tragic contradictions and fatal misunderstandings are the most complex. As such, the central figure of his novel's principal source of poetry is Grigori Melekhov. Melekhov's dilemma is virtually inextricable: he is incapable of adapting to an epoch which stifles human sentiments and exalts violence in the name of the momentary political interests of a class or a party. Given this, Melekhov can situate himself neither on the 'revolutionary' nor on the 'counter-revolutionary' side. This inability to situate himself in clear and distinct terms is precisely what makes Melekhov a novelistic figure, whose tragic existence is full of adventure and contradiction.

In direct opposition to Melekhov stand characters in Sholokhov's novel who are clearly 'situated': these

characters incarnate either revolutionary faith or old
world interests. From a purely novelistic point of view,
these 'revolutionaries' and 'reactionaries' are inferior
to Melekhov; they lack his abundant poetry and they are
devoid of all profound internal conflict. Their goals
are too clear and too utilitarian to be novelistically
satisfying.

With Grigori Melekhov, Sholokhov gives rise to a
certain form of symbolic realism, which is rich not only
in its poetry, but above all in its 'generalization' of
human experience. This symbolic realism enables Sholokhov
to transform the individual destiny of his hero into an
eternal type or myth. In opposition to this, the secondary characters of Sholokhov's novel are prosaic, and
naturalistically depicted; they only attain the poetic
heights of symbolism in those rare and drastic situations
which demand a complete exteriorization of hidden emotions and contradictions. Grigori Melekhov is constantly
plunged into such drastic 'situations,' and the greatness
of *Quiet Flows the Don* lies in the symbolic realism which
Sholokhov utilizes to depict and explain Melekhov's deep
tragedy. If the naturalism which Sholokhov uses to depict his secondary figures and to describe the vast historical context of his novel is less great, it is nonetheless fully justified and even has a distinct purpose:
it accentuates and brings to the fore the tragic and
poetic humanity of the main hero; Grigori Melekhov.

Indeed, Grigori Melekhov is both the focal point of
the tragedy and its principal source of poetry; he incarnates the triumph of imagination, and as such, he has
no rival within the novel.

In my opinion, it is senseless to compare Sholokhov
to Tolstoy and to maintain as does Bratko Kreft that the
former is an optimist and the latter a pessimist. On the
contrary: *Quiet Flows the Don* is clearly a tragedy, and
what is more, a typical tragedy. The path which was wide
open at the beginning of the novel narrows progressively
as the novel evolves until it is transformed finally into
a total impasse. At the end, as befits all tragedies,
there is no "way out" possible. In *War and Peace*, on the
contrary, life is constantly renewed. Each and every figure that disappears in the novel is replaced, and the epilogue far from being an end: on the contrary gives rise
to a new cycle of heros and happenings. The old Natasha,
the former enchantress who has become indolent and neglected is reassumed progressively by a new and turbulent

little Natasha; little Petia Rostov who has died is replaced and hence renewed by a new little Petia who has
just been born; the spirit of Prince Andrei Bolkonski is
resurrected in the dreams of Nicolas, and so on. In
Sholokhov's novel no such renewals take place; in other
words, there is no victory of life over death. The mar-
vellous transformations which keep appearing in *War and
Peace*, making it a novel rivalled only by life itself,
have absolutely no place in *Quiet Flow the Don*. This is
simply because Sholokhov's is a blatantly pessimistic
novel, whereas *War and Peace* in its power transcends the
categories of pessimism and optimism.

Sholokhov's pessimism is portrayed in a two-fold manner in the novel. On the one hand, we cannot help but
notice that the precarious balance between life and death
always tilts over in favour of death. Are not all the
heroes in *Quiet Flows the Don*--Petia and Daria, Stepan
and Aksinia, Mishka Koshchevoi and Duniashka--childless?
The only couple that has children is Grigori and Natalia;
however, little Poliusha dies prematurely, whereas
Mishatka, the only remaining one, is, as Sholokhov puts
it, "an orphan despite the fact that her father is still
alive." The image that Sholokhov evokes of Grigori carrying his son beneath the 'cold and grey skies' is a sad one
indeed; for Grigori is carrying not the future, but a grim
tragedy. Above him, "the skies are closed," and he is
"alone in an immense world." Described as such, Grigori's
destiny is harsher than Hector's, and Mishatka's more
hopeless than that of Astyanax; for if Astyanax is the son
of Troy's most glorious hero, Mishatka is the son of a
mere "bandit."

If the balance between life and death in *Quiet Flows
the Don* tilts over in favour of death, so does the balance of happiness vs. unhappiness tilt towards the latter.
Grigori's, Nathalie's and Aksinia's lives are, as
Sholokhov puts it, "rich in pain and poor in joy." Indeed, few are the characters in *Quiet Flows the Don* who
truly believe in and are struggling for personal happiness and marital stability. The only two that seem to be
doing so are Natalia and Aksinia, however both of them
will perish in their struggle, after having tasted only a
few morsels of happiness. As for the revolutionaries who
are struggling for new world ideals, they all end up by
sacrificing happiness, subordinating it as they do to the
new and doubtful ideal. As for the masses, they can only
seize fleeting moments of pleasure as death is constantly

wavering above their heads. Their universe is totally devoid of any and all true values, and all norms are abol-
ished by them: within it fathers rape daughters, sons and
mothers kill fathers; women are by definition adultresses
and husbands drunkards. Brothers abuse their sisters, and
noblemen are attracted to peasant girls and vice versa.
Everybody seems to be living in and for the present only,
and in this chaotic universe of violence and infidelity,
of pleasure-seeking and violence, pure love and fidelity
are doomed to ridicule and failure. Even Natalia, the
only defender of moral principles and the only pure creature around, even she is condemned to suffering and death.

Attitudes and human relations such as these are inconceivable in *War and Peace*, where, on the contrary, the
universe depicted is imbued with the ideas of lasting
happiness, family joy and prosperity of future generations. In comparison, the apparent 'joie de vivre' and
vitality of the characters in Sholokhov's novel are pitiful. They only mask, in reality, a deep sense of doom.

Pessimism in *Quiet Flows the Don* is portrayed in yet
another context, the social one. The only Communist in
the novel who remains alive to be able to preside over the
destiny of the village is Mishka Koshchevoi, and he is the
least capable one! Because of this, Grigori's future and
the future of the entire Cossack community is destined to
be a somber one.

The pessimism of *Quiet Flows the Don* is further confirmed by the absurdities which abound: the absurdity of
life which is given only to be destroyed cheaply and prematurely; the absurdity of heroism which borders on crime
and is often nothing but crime itself; the absurdity of
freedom which leads to crime; the absurdity of a revolution which sacrifices the best of its men and confides the
future to the worst of its partisans; the absurdity, finally, of a revolution in which the supreme victim is the
poor plebian with his calloused hands, whose only desire
is to work in peace; the absurdity even of love, which, if
it triumphs, only does so in death. Such was the love of
Grigori's grandfather for his Turkish grandmother, and
such is the love of the pure and unhappy Natalia, and of
the debauched Daria who pays for her sensual ardour with
her life. And so it is for Anna and Bunchuk, even for
that supreme preacher of free love, Aksinia. Nobody is
forgotten by Sholokhov.

If the precarious balance between life and death is
in favour of death, that of happiness and unhappiness in

favour of unhappiness, and that of fidelity and infidelity
in favour of infidelity, where then in *Quiet Flows the Don*
are the conflicting elements at least equally balanced-
out? Alas, only in pain, suffering, crime and death. For
are not the victors and the vanquished both united equally
in death and suffering? A strange sort of justice is here
carried out, one that has as its sole guiding principle an
'eye for an eye' and a 'tooth for a tooth,' except that
here it is pain for pain, blood for blood and death for
death. The images of pain and suffering so impregnate
this work that we soon get the feeling that the endless
promises of a better world are hollow and empty promises
that will never come true. Yes, *Quiet Flows the Don* is
indeed a pessimistic work; it depicts the end of a civilization which is breathing its last: an epoch in history
is closing, and the new era which is opening is full of
uncertainties, to say the least.

Pain, suffering, crime, misery and death are therefore the only elements equally balanced-out within the
novel. In fact, the structural composition of the entire
novel seems to be founded on the equal "balancing-out' of
these elements. Is not the father who has raped his 16-
year old daughter killed, beaten to death by the girl's
mother and brother? And the hideous rape of young Frania,
is it not 'balanced-out' by the atrocious death of
Zharkov, one of the Cossacks who took part in the rape?
And will not Grigori and Aksinia pay for the rest of
their lives for Natalia's humiliation and suffering? Yes,
the macabre justice of death for death and humiliation for
humiliation is inevitably carried out, each and every time.
Kalmykov's death is 'balanced-out' by that of his murderer
Bunchuk; the savage massacre of Chernetsov and his white
officers finds its justification and balance in the equally horrible agony of Podtelkov and his Comrades. Ivan
Alekseevich pays with his life for the death of Petia
Melekhov; and so on ad infinitum. Scenes of torture,
murder and agony deploy themselves before us, one after
another, all equally 'balanced-out' and based on the sinister principle of an 'eye for an eye.'

In order to provide some form of relief from this
suffocating atmosphere, it is indispensable for Sholokhov
to provide his reader with moments of escape into a universe of serenity and freedom. Hence his frequent descriptions of nature, particularly of the steppe. These
descriptions give the reader a moment quite literally to
'take a breath' before being plunged once again into a

universe of horror. Sholokhov also uses the song as a
mode of lyrical relief, the song in his novel playing
much the same role as the chorus in ancient tragedy.
Comic relief is the third method employed by Sholokhov
to distract his reader from the painful atmosphere of destruction and death. Crude jokes and terre à terre laughter are both present in *Quiet Flows the Don*, and they
prove that at least some form of human vitality remains
even within the chaotic universe of suffering and death.

    Quiet Flows the Don is a unique novel for more rea-
sons than one. Above all, it is unique in that it triumphs over crass dogmatism and pitiless despotism. It
does this by way of its artistic truth. Furthermore,
Quiet Flows the Don is a great novel because of its un-
forgettable description of the primitive world of the
peasantry. In its brilliant portrayal of this particular
world, the novel probably has no rival. Sholokhov is indeed a master when he draws his inspiration from the very
roots of society, from society's most backward class. The
limitations are of course evident, but so are the advant-
ages, for Sholokhov finds eternal poetic sources in nature, in the peasantry and in the natural elements: man
struggles for the *earth* just as he does 'for a lover';
water, *fire*, *air* and the *winds*, the animal and the veg-
table worlds--all are depicted by Sholokhov. Indeed,
Quiet Flows the Don is in constant contact with nature's
richness and some of its most poetic and symbolic moments
are tied to nature.

    But once this has been said, we all must admit that
the *real* theme of the novel is not nature, but man: man,
the conscious being who struggles against the natural and
instinctive forces which he carries within himself, and
man, who also struggles against the forces of history and
society. Man's struggles against all these elements is
incarnated in the novel most deeply and most completely
by Grigori Melekhov. Grigori's battle with the elements
is the strongest; his struggle to defend human dignity
and liberty against all the odds, is the most powerful.
His very suffering and remorse make of him an exceptional
figure, one who is not afraid to confront the most essential human problems which most 'common' mortals avoid. In
order to nurture compassion for this remarkable hero,
Sholokhov constantly brings to the fore his purity and
high moral principles, against a background which, as we
have seen, is anything but pure and moral. Sholokhov is
constantly directing our sympathies towards his hero, and

our antipathy towards the other characters in the novel.
This he does through words images, comparisons, metaphors
and symbols, so much so, that the reader's sympathies and
sentiments become Sholokhov's sympathies and sentiments.
For example, if we examine the text carefully we realize
how reserved Sholokhov actually is towards the Bolsheviks,
towards Stockman, Koshchevoi and others, and how attentive
he is to Grigori, how careful he is never to reduce
Grigori's dignity. We find ourselves sympathizing with
Grigori *because of Sholokhov's text,* and not because of
his social or policial inclinations, to which we are somehow almost indifferent. Similarly, it is Sholokhov's
text, his words, metaphors and comparisons, etc., which
prevent us from ever really sympathizing with Stockman,
Bunchuk or Podtelkov, even though their political aspirations are sometimes dearer to us. Sholokhov seems to
have understood one thing well: human sympathy is not
limitless; it has to be economized, and in the case of
Quiet Flows the Don is reserved mainly for the main hero,
for Grigori Melekhov. How exactly does Sholokhov go
about this?

Let us give a concrete example here. We are, in the
novel, within the context of a dramatic situation: the
'Reds' have just murdered a group of Cossacks, without
even having put them on trial, merely because the Cossacks could become, in their eyes, potential enemies of
the new regime being set up. Kotliarov is frightened by
by what he has just witnessed, but all the Bolshevik
Stockman finds to say in such moment is: "Do not shout.
You'll wake up the housekeeper." In other words, Stockman is worried not about the death of a group of men and
about the fate of their families, but rather about
whether the housekeeper's sleep has been interrupted!
This tiny sentence pronounced by Stockman, in the context
of what has happened cannot but shift the reader's sympathies from him. And Sholokhov uses this 'method' to
enhance our sympathies for Grigori, for he makes us understand, from what has passed in the novel, that Grigori
Melekhov, in a similar situation (confronted with the
death of a human being, even an enemy) could never have
reacted like Stockman. The reader feels this, and hence
his sympathy for Grigori and his antipathy for Stockman.
All this is contained in one simple sentence! Other details are naturally accumulated in the novel making
Stockman an unsympathetic character. We are told, for
instance, that his flannel shirt is 'dirty,' and that his

'myopic' eyes are too 'closely set.' Sholokhov never
makes reference to Grigori's 'dirty shirt,' though it is
evident that under the circumstances of war and death,
etc., his shirt is often dirty. The fact that Sholokhov
never mentions Grigori's 'dirty shirt' is not fortuitous.
On the contrary, it is supplementary evidence that Sholokhov is constantly desirous of preserving the unified personality of his hero and the hero's dignity. Even when
Grigori commits misdeeds, for instance, when he avenges
his brother's death, Sholokhov only makes an elusive and
"passing" remark to these misdeeds, as if they were in no
way an intrinsic part of his hero's personality. Similarly, we only see Grigori fighting in combat, i.e., in
heroic circumstances. Is not this because Sholokhov is
purposely avoiding any image of his hero that might tar-
nish him? Could we ever conceive of Grigori ending up
comically like Mishka, with his pants down, being
strapped? Never! Grigori could conceivably end up
hanged or shot, but never with his pants down! Likewise,
it is inconceivable to imagine Grigori pillaging, attacking, killing old and defenseless people, or setting fire
to their homes. Koshchevoi is guilty of all this and
more, and Sholokhov describes his excesses in full detail. Is this not simply because Sholokhov considers
that crime is what fundamentally defines Koshchevoi, and
because he considers that Koshchevoi is an inferior and
basely instinctive human being? All this, of course, dis-
qualifies the image that certain Soviet critics have drawn
up of Mishka, as being a man convinced of the Revolution
and positive in his aspirations, as opposed to the "hesitant" Melekhov. To be sure, Melekhov is "hesitant," but
this only makes him human, and Sholokhov proves throughout his novel that Grigori's humanity, his personality
and fate are what interest him most. It is through
Grigori that Sholokhov is depicting his own humanitarian
ideals, and it is through Grigori that Sholokhov is drawing his latent critique of the milieu of the times.
Grigori is, of course, in many ways, merely a young and
highly simple-minded peasant, and this easily indisposes
and disappoints the reader who is used to noble, complex
and highly intelligent heroes such as Onegin, Pechorin,
Rudin and Prince Andrei Bolkonski, to name only a few.
But our disappointment does not last, for we soon realize
that simple-minded Grigori is in the process of something
vast in the novel; he is in the process of awakening,
'his' day, we feel, is approaching. There is something
symbolic in the fact that we meet up with him for the

first time in the novel at dawn, just as the sun is coming up. Grigori himself is just awakening from a long
sleep, and is still in a semi-somnolent state when we see
him first descending towards the river, coming up the
river in a boat and then disappearing. Where is he going, we ask ourselves? And as everything in this novel
seems to carry a hidden meaning, so does this image of
Grigori rowing his boat on the waves of the agitated
river. He seems almost to be embarking on a long voyage,
the voyage of life. Similar symbols abound in Chapter
III. Here we find Grigori, still in a semi-somnolent
state, leading his horse to the Don River. Grigori suddenly stops in his walk, charmed by the remarkable spectacle of nature, of the sky, the sun, the river and the
steppe. As Sholokhov puts it: "A ray of moonlight spread
out across the Don, like a path upon which no voyager had
yet travelled."

Is this not Grigori's path--this imaginary road upon
no one has yet trod? Alas, it is a path without solid
foundations, a path on which our courageous voyager can
only ultimately succumb.

And so the hero's destiny is evoked from the very
beginning,even if it is in a poetic and sublimated manner. But Sholokhov wants us to keep in mind this image
of the moonlit path which no traveller has yet trodden
upon, because this makes it a unique path, one reserved
only for Grigori. We then will better understand (if we
keep this image in mind) Grigori's uniqueness. Who but
Grigori in the novel jumps to the defence of a young girl
who is being raped? Who but he breaks open the door of a
prison to disperse the jailers? Who but he pursues the
violent and the wicked unflinchingly, even though he is
living in an epoch of extreme violence, in which murder
and pillage are daily events? It is evident that
Sholokhov has bestowed upon his hero all the virtues of
ancient chivalry. It is Grigori, and not a Bolshevik,
who takes up the cause of modest men and their modest
dignity; it is he who opposes the vanity of the men "on
the top," be they nobles, bourgeois, officers or party
functionaries. Finally, it is Grigori, and he alone, who
represents national pride in his provocative disdain of
foreign officers who have come to save his country from
the "Reds." In contrast to him, not one of the Bolsheviks
is ever depicted in a chivalrous role. And therefore,
despite the crimes of circumstance which he has committed,
Grigori is the only really "chivalrous" character in the

novel, the only defender of the ideal. In defending the ideal, he is also defending eternal human values and a certain poetic conception of life. To be sure, Grigori is a solitary figure: the more he defends humanity, the more he is threatened by the revolutionary and counter-revolutionary forces which are both blinded by prosaic transient political interests. Grigori rejects these interests; he looks down upon them—and in this resides his error. But this also constitutes his true and lasting value as a human being.

Even when Sholokov directs his hero towards the Fomin group, we comprehend that he is doing so not to lower his hero, but rather to show us that nothing on earth can destroy Grigori's fundamental sense of dignity. For even within the Fomin group Grigori manages to remain faithful to his ideal, and this is of course possible only because he unconsciously carries this ideal within himself; he has not picked it up in books; it is a very part of his personality and as such, it is inalienable. Sholokhov's message is evident here: individual man counts more than any other factor, even more than the circumstances in which he finds himself. Certain men are weak in favourable conditions, whilst others—exceptional ones like Grigori—remain true to themselves even in the most adverse conditions. If Sholokhov purposely throws Grigori down into the gutter, it is only in order to confirm his human dignity. This is why Grigori doesn't even try to escape from the Fomin group; when Kaparin proposes that he save himself by betraying Fomin, Grigori refuses. Grigori even refuses to wait for amnesty, and we see him returning to his village to see his son without even having measured the consequences of what he has done. Once again, Grigori has remained true to himself: he who has been 'chivalrous' all his life cannot at the end become a simple calculator. Even Grigori's final act is one of chivalry: we seen him abandoning his arms by throwing them into the River Don, this river which has been flowing eternally and which remains an eternal witness to human joys and miseries. We cannot imagine Grigori doing anything else; we cannot imagine him abandoning his arms anywhere else. His final act is a beautiful one: it is the culminating poetic moment of the novel.

Pages and pages have been written to prove that Grigori is representative of a stratum of the prosperous peasantry which is bound to the earth and its traditions, and which is more than hesitant vis-à-vis revolution.

This is only partially true, but it is above all insuf-
ficient to explain Grigori and thus somehow secondary.
Because this schematic view of Grigori completely by-
passes the central, the focal point of Sholokhov's novel,
which remains from beginning to end the human being, the
human person who cannot be reduced to a schema. For as
Marx has said it: man is not only a "sum of social relations"; but the "essential for man is man himself." If
the schema of *Quiet Flows the Don* had been as simple as
many Soviet critics make it out to be, the novel would
never have survived as a work of art. The best proof
that we have that it is indeed a great work of art is
that Sholokhov leaves one question unanswered, the one
which is most important: whose fault was it? Who is to
be condemned? The hero, who refused to submit to the
imperatives of a milieu and an epoch, or society which
took revenge upon a champion of chivalrous spirit by
plunging him into the dirt and grime of existence, into
the troubled waves of those very elements against which
he was revolting? Is this not the eternally suspended
question which Sholokhov leaves us with at the end of his
novel?

University of Belgrade

"BOY GETS TRACTOR" AND ALL THAT: THE PARABLE STRUCTURE OF THE SOVIET NOVEL.

Katerina Clark

I would like to begin with a passage from one of the most popular novels in the Soviet Union. In this novel the action is set in a factory making ball-bearings for Soviet tractors. The hero, Bakhirev, is the factory's chief engineer. In his work Bakhirev has become aware that much of the factory's equipment is obsolescent and drastically needs overhauling if the nation's tractors are to have efficient ball-bearings. When he proposes this to the administration they object on the grounds that an overhaul would be expensive, and hurt their production figures for the Stalin prize awards. Bakhirev knows he will lose his job if he presses the matter too far. But what of the nation's tractors? The precious harvest? The country's economy?

Bakhirev is married, with children, but his wife does not share his concern for the nation's tractors. Worse still--all she really cares about is her social position and material comforts: she even nags him for not going along with the administration. But there is in the factory a certain young Tina who *does* share Bakhirev's concern for the nation's tractors. Bakhirev finds himself spending less and less time at home. He seems to be always at the factory, where he often finds himself talking to Tina-- about the vast perspectives for the future of ball-bearing factories. You can fill in the rest. My passage comes from a section where the author explains how it all happened:

> Curiously, it was a speech of Bakhirev's which
> had brought them together to begin with. At
> one of the rare regional ball-bearing factory
> conferences he had talked about coming develop-
> ments in technology and the lag in factory use
> of new techniques compared with progress in
> science. He had used the occasion as a dry run
> for a speech he intended to deliver at an All-
> Union conference a week or so later. Tina had
> been among the factory's contingent, and next

day had sent him [a note about it]...the note had
caused him to think...he realized he had concentrated on facts and systems to the exclusion of
people as individuals. He revised his speech
notes, shifting the emphasis as Tima had suggested. The result was the most successful presentation he had ever made. It gained him an ovation
and was widely reported. Afterward he telephoned
Tina to thank her. That was when they had started
seeing each other.[1]

This novel was published in 1957. You can tell it is
relatively recent because the author has dispensed with the
sense of decorum which caused writers of the Stalin period
to avoid involving "positive heroes" in adultery. But in
every other respect it meets our expectations of the Soviet
novel, expectations capsulized affectionately as the "boy
gets tractor" syndrome. That is to say, in it the hero
wages battle with the most powerful of careerist bureaucrats and even risks his personal future in the name of
the Socialist tomorrow as represented by the almighty
tractor. And "boy's" love for tractor is shared by "girl"
--and thus boy and girl come to love eachother.
    This novel was written by that well-known Soviet
writer, Arthur Hailey. The above passage comes from his
popular novel *Airport* which was one of the hits of the Soviet literary year 1971 when it appeared in translation in
Inostrannaia literatura. Of course to present it as a
Soviet novel I have had to make several substitutions of
names and so on.[2] But in doing so I was lucky enough to
find a Soviet novel, Galina Nikolaeva's *Battle En Route*
(*Bitva v puti*) of 1957, whose plot parallels that of *Airport* in all the above details except that whereas in *Battle
En Route* you have Bakhirev, the chief engineer at a ball-
bearing factory, and Tina, a minor engineering employee,
in *Airport* you have Mel Bakersfield, the director of a major American airport, and Tanya, a senior official with
the airport staff of an airline company. In both novels
the hero is concerned that unless the physical organization
of his institution keeps pace with modern technology disaster will occur, and both heroes have to fight powerful
careerists in order to implement their ideas. In short,
perhaps Tanya's Russian name was Hailey's clue to the fact
that he was really writing a Soviet novel.
    Battle En Route is no randomly chosen Soviet novel.
At the Fourth Writers' Congress in 1967 it was the only

novel of the fifties to make it into the list of exemplary
novels cited in the official speech on Soviet prose.[3] It
is solid, representative stuff. And of course *Airport* was
a best seller in the U.S.

What does all this mean? That the typical Soviet novel is like Western kitsch? Most Western critics stop short
of saying so, but they come pretty close when they complain,
for instance, that the characters are "stilted and two-
dimensional,"[4] and that the whole production lacks "verisimilitude."[5] Many Western critics use the nineteenth-century novel as their yardstick here and suggest that the
Soviet novel represents a sort of vulgarized, confused and
cliché version of that great predecessor.

Such commentators look at the Soviet novel from a
standpoint which stopped somewhere at the turn of the century: such literary criteria as "verisimilitude" and multi-
dimensionality of character have not been shared by many
of the literary movements of the twentieth century—here we
could think of such obvious examples as the vogue for myth
and the *nouveau roman*. Western critics see the Soviet
novel as a confused array of imperfectly realized elements
from an outdated tradition, but they might entertain the
possibility that it represents a completely new tradition,
as Soviet theorists have claimed. The familiarity of some
of the elements should not delude us: Tynianov and
Shklovskii have suggested that in the bizarre business of
literary evolution a new tradition often arises when a new
mix of forms emerges: the mix itself is new but is made up
of debased and parodied elements from sub-literary genres.[6]
So too with the Soviet novel many of the elements were
hackneyed, but the particular combination of forms was new.

Additionally, some of our most knowledgeable commentators look at the Soviet novel from a Western standpoint.
And here I mean Western not just in the sense that such
commentators cannot share the Soviet novel's ideological
underpinnings. They look at it from the standpoint of a
society where intellectuals create the literary canon. In
the Soviet Union intellectuals do not enjoy that status.
The literary canon is established in some dynamic interaction between the tastes of the people and the tastes and
needs of the political establishment. Intellectuals have a
choice between functioning as auxiliaries to that axis, or
choosing to work outside the canon with concomitant penal-
ties in publishability, material rewards, etc.

So if we were to seek parellels in our Western experience, it seems reasonable that we should go to popular

literature. Of course there are major differences between
modern kitsch and the Soviet novel. The Soviet novel is
intensely political and stolidly pedagogical. Most popular Western novels strive to entertain and if they reflect
a political viewpoint or enlarge the reader's store of
knowledge this is only incidental to their design. It
must be quickly said here, however, that in American literature over recent years--and furthermore in both high-[7]
and low-brow literature--the imparting of information has
become a central function of the work. Indeed, Hailey's
Airport (together with his *Hotel*, *Wheels*, etc.) can be seen
as a significant example of this trend.

But there are more fundamental differences between the
Soviet novel and Western kitsch literature, differences
such that this new Western trend cannot alter their basic
dissimilarity. The fact that the Soviet novel is cast in
novel form should not blind us to its considerable affinities with pre-modern literature. After all, the other
side of the coin stamped "clichéd" could be "formulaic";
the other side of "two-dimensional" and lacking proper
psychological motivation could be "having ritual function." Of course much kitsch is formulaic, but not to the
same degree or in the same way as the Soviet novel.

The best way to get at the differences here is by
looking at the role of the author. Even with the most
highly formulaic types of modern popular literature the
author, if he is to be deemed good or prove successful,
must create his own formulae: in particular, he must create his own hero or hero-type. When we want light reading
matter we will look in the bookstore for "*a* James Bond" or
"*a* Sherlock Holmes"--or we may look for "*a* Dorothy Sayers"
or "*an* Ellery Queen." In the Soviet Union the writer is
not expected to create a new hero. He does not even have
autonomy over his own texts. Many a Soviet writer has been
required to rewrite his novel, the most dramatic example
being the well-known one of Aleksandr Fadeev who, *even
while he was head of the Writers' Union*, was required to
rewrite his best seller *The Young Guard* (*Molodaiagvardiia*)
in 1946. This is because the Soviet writer is not so much
a "creator" but something closer to a "teller." And
Fadeev did not tell it right: he *forgot* that the Party
played the leading role in guiding Komsomol resistance under the German occupation of World War II.[8]

The Soviet writer does not create out of the void,
but within a pre-existing lore. Most tales have already
been told--in marxist-leninist theory, in Party histories,

in official documents and speeches. The writer must retell
them, and use his skills as a "teller" to tell them well--
use his imagination and ingenuity to make them lively,
fresh, and in their own way original. Of course in translating them into novel form the "teller" also has to wrest
the tales from their prosaic beds. Even there he does not
work in isolation, but builds on the *topoi* which have
evolved over time in earlier novels.

It could be said, indeed, that the conventions upon
which the Soviet writer draws in "telling" his tale are
not merely made up of isolated motifs, epithets, etc. Over
time these conventions evolved into a coherent system. A
single general structure emerged, one which was followed by
almost all novelists, regardless of the subject they chose
to write about.

This article will attempt to describe the nature of
that all-purpose structure. But first some preliminary remarks indicating when and where it is operative. Although
the elements which make up the standard structure can be
found in novels of the twenties (and especially in novels
by "proletarian" authors), it was not until the early
thirties that a common structure emerged. In effect, then,
its institutionalization can be associated with stalinism.[9]
However, after Stalin died in 1953 the structure was not
abandoned. Rather it was used as a ready-made system of
signs, a sort of language for discussing the phenomenon of
stalinism. Consequently the novels of the fifties are more
complex in structure than their stalinist predecessors, but
nevertheless represent but a modification of the same basic
structure. Of course since the early sixties Soviet literature has become much more variegated in forms and styles,
and while one still finds novels where some variation on
the old standard structure has been used, it no longer
dominates Soviet literature.

What this common structure means for the Soviet writer
is a completely different tradition of composition from the
Western one. The Soviet writers do not merely tell pre-
existing tales, they also follow pre-existing models. Here
both criticism and official speeches play a major role in
suggesting which literary models novelists should follow
and which they should not. A constant refrain is: "Give
us more novels like X!" And since the kernel of any Soviet
novel is its "positive hero," this injunction very often
appears as: "Give us more heroes like X!" Indeed, my following account of the structure of the Soviet novel is
based on those lists of exemplars supplied in the official

speeches made at the various Writers' Union congresses.
However, the structure has its own logic, and is sufficiently broadly represented in Soviet novels of the thirties
through the early sixties for me to propose it as *the* paradigmatic structure.

The crucial role played by models in the Soviet novel
tradition is but a further way in which the activity of the
Soviet writer approaches that of a pre-modern counterpart.
In thinking of the role of the Soviet writer over these
years, one is reminded of the icon painter.   Thus an obvious place to go in looking for points of comparison with
the Soviet novel would be to the literary counterpart of
the icon, i.e., the saint's life or *zhitie*.   In the degree
to which the Soviet novel represents a formulaic biography
of the primary hero type of the world view (i.e., of marx-
ism-leninism) it could be described as a sort of secular
zhitie.   Unfortunately, most Soviet novels do not take
their reader into the early life--let alone the birth!--
of their positive hero, but if one avoids making a liter-
alist, *topos* by *topos*, comparison, one can find much common ground between the two genres.   A more substantial
difference, however, could be found in comparing the relationship in each case between the hero as champion of the
"world view," and the temporal organization which represents it--i.e., the church for the *zhitie* and the Party or
Soviet government for the Soviet novel: no Soviet hero can
be truly great unless he can be shown to be a strong link
in that mighty organizational chain, whereas the holy man's
mandate for sainthood comes directly from God.

Actually (if somewhat predictably) Soviet criticism
has consistently rejected the possibility of comparing the
Soviet novel with the *zhitie*.   However, prominent theorists of socialist realism--and Gorky in particular--have
proposed another genre of old Russian literature as a
model for the Soviet novel and a source for the positive
hero--the folk-tale. [10]

In truth, one can find in most Soviet novels motifs
of the *zhitie and* of the Russian folk-tale, *and* also of
several other genres of old Russian literature such as the
folk epic or *bylina*, and even the *Igor Tale*.   But there
has been so much eclecticism and lack of consistency in
using the conventions of a particular genre--eclecticism
even within the one novel--that it is difficult to pin
down a single, specific parallel.   A very obvious example
of this eclecticism would be that well-known scene in
Gladkov's 1925 novel *Cement* (*Cement*) where at a town meet-

ing the hero, Gleb, rips open his shirt to show his Civil
War wounds. As he does so, Gleb likens himself to the
"immortal Koshchei" of Russian folk-tale fame, and then invites his audience to come up and touch his wounds to ver-
ify them for themselves, thus invoking the Christ and
doubting Thomas pattern.[11]

Speaking in very general terms, however, it could be
said that the Soviet novel resembles both the *zhitie* and
the folk-tale in that all three have the same type of plot.
This plot might rather loosely be called the quest structure and is found in narratives where the hero sets out to
reach a particular goal, be it acquiring a loved one or a
dominion, reaching a place (it should be noted that all
these goals are commonly found in the folk-tale[12]), or at-
taining a spiritual or psychological state in himself (as
in the *zhitie*). En route he encounters many obstacles
which test his strength and determination, but at the end
he attains his goal. In the Soviet novel the goal is a
complex one, and usually involves all the above dimensions
--love, power, material and spiritual progress and a journey.

But the common motif of the questing hero is not sufficient to establish the Soviet novel's affinities with
early Russian literature. Having gone so far in time,
why confine this search for pre-modern genre parallels to
the Russian borders! One could look at mediaeval European
literature, the *Fürstenspiegel* and other varieties of the
speculum, the heroic epic, English literature under Cromwell, and so on.

One suspects this game of "hunt the genre parallel"
could go on indefinitely. The very wealth of possibilities suggests that the exact triangulation of the Soviet
novel on the graph of genres has not yet been found. To
say that the Soviet novel is an example of the quest
structure is hardly to pinpoint the novel's place on the
graph because that structure represents one of the most
age-old and universal of all plot types.[13] One need
think only of science fiction, adventure kitsch and the
Bildungsroman to realize that the questing hero is still
alive and well in the modern period.

And in fact the Soviet novel does not represent merely
a return to traditional literary forms--for all its many
resemblances to and borrowings from pre-modern genres.
Its particular "mix" of elements is not only new, but also
a considerably more complex one than that of the folk-tale
or *zhitie*, for instance. In a twentieth-century novel it

is not possible to recapture the simplicity and "innocence" of a pre-novel genre. And here I mean not only the
formal purity of the genre, but also the relative simplicity of the relationship between the teller, the tale, his
society and the system of belief which informs the tale.

The Soviet novel has many functions and several layers of complexity. The surface plot normally represents
occasional writing: it celebrates some recent Soviet
achievement or policy decision. Simultaneously, it edu-
cates--the novel tells the readers a little technology,
geography, economics, or whatever. The material presented here varies from book to book. But if (and only if)
all this complexity is distilled to its absolute essence,
the result is a simple structure which can be compared to
a pre-modern genre.

Whichever of the many possible tales a Soviet author
may choose to tell, this tale must itself confirm the
validity of that great tale which is the masterplot of all
others, History. Consequently, all typical Soviet novels
have been constructed as parables. At the level of surface structure we find a slice from the life of an individual hero. He provides a focus through which the novel's various public relations functions are fulfilled.
Thus a Bakhirev (of *Battle En Route*) is similar to a Mel
Bakersfield (of *Airport*) in that, through the events of
Bakhirev's daily life we learn a lot about things on the
order of airport management. The crucial difference between a Bakhirev and a Mel Bakersfield, however, is that
the events of Bakhirev's life simultaneously recapitulate
that more timeless story which is History itself--and
nothing of that order can be found in the life of the
capitalist manager, Bakersfield.

Two modes coexist in the Soviet novel--the realistic
and the symbolic. But the genre is predicated upon the
unity of the two, the "real" providing an existential illustration of the "ideal." The same phenomenon can be
seen in those classical examples of the parable to be
found in the Bible. The noted commentator on the biblical
parable, C. H. Dodd, comments in his book *The Parables of
the Kingdom* (1935):

> There is a reason for this realism of the para-
> bles of Jesus. It arises from a conviction that
> there is no mere analogy, but an inward affinity,
> between the natural order and the spiritual order;
> or as we might put it in the language of the par-

ables themselves, the Kingdom of God is intrinsi-
cally *like* the processes of nature and of the daily
life of men. Jesus therefore did not feel the
need of making up artificial illustrations for
the truths He wished to teach.[14] He found them
ready-made by the Maker of man and nature. That
human life, including the religious life, is a
part of nature is distinctly stated in the well-
known passage beginning "Consider the fowls of
the air...." (Mt. vi. 26-30; Lk. xii, 24-28).
Since nature and super-nature are one order, you
can take any part of that order and find in it
illumination for other parts.[15]

An analogous "affinity" to that between "nature and super-
nature" is a postulate of the Soviet novel. Here, however, the "affinity" is between history--even as found in
"the daily life of men"--and History. This, by the way,
is one reason why so many Soviet novels are based on
actual historical incidents: reality illumines history's
processes and purposes.

Of course to see the Soviet novel as having a parable
structure is to see it as a simple form. Inevitably its
"simplicity" is undermined by both the sheer profusion of
material introduced in the service of the novel's various
public relations functions and by the fact that its
authors live in a complex political and social reality.
For the purposes of this article, however, the structure
will be treated as if pristine.

Unlike the biblical parables, each of which tends to
illumine a different aspect of "super-nature," the Soviet
novel is somewhat obsessive in that particular aspect of
History it chooses to bring out in each individual work.
So close, indeed, are the different accounts of History
illustrated by the lives of the various positive heroes
that it is possible to postulate a single common structure for most Soviet novels. In each case, the account
of History centers around that crucial marxist-leninist
dialectical conflict between "spontaneity" (*stixiinost'*)
and "consciousness" (*soznatel'nost'*).

The Soviet novel is based on a particular view of
history which sees all things as striving to reach out
beyond their original, primitive state known as one of
"spontaneity" to the ultimate stage of development in
Communism. The dynamic force of History is derived from
the dialectical tension between "spontaneity" and the

higher state of "consciousness." The ultimate end of History, Communism, is marked by a resolution of this dialectic in the highest form of "consciousness," one where
"consciousness" is not in conflict with "spontaneity."
Other ways of characterizing this movement include, on the
one hand, a progression from a more arbitrary, spontaneous
and haphazard state to one of complete discipline and control, and, on the other hand, a progression from a state
where actions are determined by individual decisions and
inclinations to one where they become the expression of a
collective judgment and will.[16] In other words, the age-
old problem of the individual and society is resolved in
Communism.

In the Soviet novel this broad historical process is
caught in the life of an individual hero, and the standard
plot used for this purpose is, as I have already indicated,
a variant on that age-old one whereby the questing hero
undergoes a series of trials but ultimately reaches the
goal of his quest. In most Soviet novels the hero's quest
is two-fold, both public and external, and private and inner: the plot is a fusion of the public and private goals.
In *Battle En Route*, for instance, Bakhirev's public goal
is to see to it that his factory turns out sturdy tractors.
And when Bakhirev fights the careerist bureaucrats in the
name of the mighty tractor, these are trials--or in the
words of the title, "battles en route." And when he confronts his chaotic private life, technological breakdowns,
and manpower problems these are trials too. But when
Bakhirev wins through all this his achievement is not
merely that the nation's tractors are purring contentedly
with their strong ball-bearings; he has achieved a major
breakthrough in self-control. This pattern is duplicated,
mutatis mutandis, in almost all Soviet novels so that at
the end not only is the plan fulfilled, the tractors purring, the dam built, the enemy routed, or whatever, but the
hero has forged a new self which can withstand all future
trials. The hero's individual struggle for mastery of
those "spontaneous" impulses within himself stands in for
the resolution of the dialectic in the larger arena of
History.

Of course for the marxist-leninists the "spontaneity"/
"consciousness" dialectic represents not only a general
model for historical development, but also one of the most
thorny practical problems. As the Soviet state became entrenched, it became difficult to reconcile its ultimate
aims in theory with the fact that the state continued to

be governed by a centralist, highly disciplined and hier-
archical ruling party or "vanguard."[17]

In effect, then, the Soviet novel reduces this problem
to more manageable dimensions by locating the *main* focus of
the dialectic in the hero's individual struggles. The
hero's saga of self-mastery leads to his social integration, and this development in the hero's life stands in for
the movement of the nation in time. Furthermore, by adopt-
ing the parable structure, the Soviet novelist avoids the
necessity for justifying his account of the dialectic's
resolution in historical time.

There is a further respect in which it could be said
that the Soviet novel resembles the old parables, a respect
which is vital for elucidating the structure of the Soviet
novel--i.e., the central role which nature plays in the
novel's world. In the above-quoted passage describing the
biblical parable, Dodd listed among the parable's assumptions one "That human life, including the religious life,
is a part of nature..." for "...nature and super-nature are
one order..."[18] And for all its momentous implications in
political terms, the way the hero's progress to consciousness is presented in the Soviet novel makes it but a variant of the age-old metaphor of organic development; there
is a homology between nature and society.

It is a curious fact that the very novels which tell
of twentieth-century man's march into the future the climax
is most often marked by some dramatic reminder of nature's
power (e.g., a flood). In most Soviet novels, regardless
of the setting, the author contrives to bring the elemental
into a large percentage of the action. But even when nature is not represented directly, the struggle with the
elemental is used as the controlling metaphor for the
trials which mark the hero's ritual progress towards "consciousness."

This situation has its own logic, given that the Russian words for both "the elemental" and "spontaneity" are
formed from the same root (i.e., they are *stixiia* and
stixiinost', respectively);[19] in a sense the hero's
tussle with nature's forces stands in for the dialectical
process. I would suggest, however, that nature's presence
in the Soviet novel is so pervasive (whether her presence
be real or metaphorical) that she does not merely perform
a symbolic function. Rather, her role is but one of the
most striking symptoms of the fact that the world of the
Soviet novel is palpably pre-modern in many respects.

In Nikolaeva's *Battle En Route*, for instance, one soon senses the tension between the industrial theme and the village world in which the drama is played out. Ostensibly most of the action takes place on the floor of a large tractor factory situated in Moscow itself, yet somehow elemental forces become the major anagonist from whose hands the heroes must wrest the Soviet tractor. Nikolaeva sets up the opposition rather schematically in the opening pages where she has Bakhirev muse that at the heart of the "ongoing movement" of the nation lies a struggle between "two worlds," "the human and the bestial."[20] As the various factory engineers work to perfect the tractor they see similarities between its parts and the parts of the body, and come to understand their work with the tractor as a struggle to control it for "the human," and not let it fall prey to the dark, irrational forces. Whenever the tractor parts crack and buckle, as they so often do, the engineers perceive this as an "affliction" which has deformed the tractors' bodies, something which has "leapt out of the depths of the earth, mysterious and full of malicious joy."[21]

As this primordial struggle with dark forces goes on its progress is marked not by linear, calendar time, but by the cyclical time of the seasons. Almost every one of the countless sub-chapters opens with a description of nature which frames the events on the factory floor and chronicles the latest seasonal change. The book goes through all four of them in their smallest gradations. And the characters themselves seem to reckon time by the "signs" of nature rather than by dates. For instance, when Bakhirev notes one day that the trees have begun to bud, he reflects that when the buds open the factory director will return from a business trip! And just as nature with her cycles plays such a large part in the hero's world, so does the passage of the generations: at the end of the novel Bakhirev does not get his "girl" (Tina), but he finds consolation not only in the "tractor," but also in his young son as a symbol of the upcoming generations.

Thus in the typical Soviet novel you find a hero who pits himself against elemental (or elemental-like) forces in a series of trials which help him gain sufficient mastery of the self to ensure successful social integration. And once he has completed his ritual progress, he can to look to the next generation which will go through it all again--but this time better. It should come as no surprise, therefore, that a compelling metaphor for the

structure which charts the hero's progression is the rite
of passage of traditional society. In its most defining
expression this rite is of course enacted when a youth of
the tribe goes through a series of trials and, if successful, is initiated into manhood status and becomes a fully-
fledged member of the tribe. The rite has many modern
avatars, used to mark transitions from one stage of life
to the other—for instance graduation cermonies—but
structurally (as distinct from thematically) the Soviet
novel is closer to the rite's more paradigmatic, traditional expressions.

As with the rite of passage, the Soviet novel shows
its hero earning the right to make the passage to a new
order of existence. The novel's plot line charts a dialectical movement in the hero from self-expression to
expression of an extra-personal self. The moment of synthesis or formal *telos* of the novel occurs when the hero
sheds that personal self which is encumbered by the last
vestiges of a bourgeois, individualistic consciousness and
attains the level of the extra-personal (i.e., History).
He dies toward himself as individual and is reborn as a
function of the collective. Thereby he reenacts on a small
scale the great moment of the Revolution. The hero also
resolves in this moment those problematical contradictions
between "spontaneity" and "consciousness," between concern
for one's fellow man and the harsh demands of the Revolution, between the here and now and History.

In traditional versions of the rite the moment of
passage is marked by an initiation ceremony. Something
comparable occurs in the Soviet novel where the hero's
personal breakthrough is invariably attended by a scene in
which he has a man to man encounter with an elder or mentor figure who gives him advice. Since initiation is a
rite of regeneration by succession, the elder figure will
also very commonly hand the initiate some physical object
which symbolizes allegiance to the Revolution—e.g., a
Party card, badge or banner—or the two may be temporarily
linked by some physical object before separating again.
The narrator commonly describes these two elements in the
initiation scene, the giving of advice and symbolic trans-
action, as a "last testament" (*pouchenie*) and "passing
the baton" (*estafeta*), respectively. After this scene
the hero does not see the elder figure again because once
the hero has been initiated he has gained mastery over
life and can control his own destiny.

Although this moment of passage is the structural
pivot of the prototypical Soviet novel, this elder figure
is often not a major character. Being so hallowed a figure few authors allow him to become too familiar to the
reader. Indeed he may appear in the novel only for the
initiation scene itself. Since, however, in this parable-
like structure history and History are one, this character
function is usually assumed by the most senior figure in
the local administrative hierarchy of the place where the
novel is set. And, as if to bring the passage of the generations to its logical conclusion, the elder figure often
leaves his post after the initiation scene (he may be promoted or posted away, retire, fall ill, or even die),
whereupon it is assumed by the initiate (or hero), his
junior in the hierarchy.

It must also be pointed out that the elder/initiate
relationship represents the paradigmatic model for the
Soviet novel. Many actual novels do not confine the number of characters crucially involved in the rite of passage to a mere two. There may be several initiates and/or
several elders, and they may appear in the novel either in
a hierarchy determined by the degree of "consciousness"
each has (for instance, A may play initiate to B as elder,
while B in turn plays initiate to C as elder[23]), or in a
sequence such that no two elders or initiates occupy center stage at any one time.[24]   Another possibility, and one
which was very common in novels of the fifties, is the
presence in the novel of two contenders for the role of
both elder and initiate, one (as soon becomes apparent in
the plot) a "false" and unworthy contender, and the other
patently the "true" elder or initiate, the right person
for the role. Such twinning can be seen in *Battle En
Route* where Bakhirev as "true" initiate has to fight
against that stalinist usurper Valgan (the factory director), while Bakhirev's mentor must until the end of the
novel remain but an office-bearer in the local Obkom, in
the shadow of the "false," stalinist elder the Obkom
secretary.

All these patterns can very readily be reduced to
different variations on the same basic dual model of the
single elder and initiate. Indeed, in doing this one is
assisted by the fact that it is not hard to ascertain who
is a provisional elder and who a provisional initiate
(provisional because only by participating in the initiation scene can a given character realize this potential).
Both roles are very distinctly marked by a whole series

of formulae. The elder figure, for instance, is always
shown to represent some corporeal incarnation of "consciousness." Primarily this fact is conveyed by certain
epithets such as "decisive," "composed," "serious," etc.
The conventionalized image of the hero or initiate, on the
other hand, is of a person of incredible energy and zeal
who is unfortunately torn by his struggle to master an inner turbulence (and here the love plot comes into its own)
and impulsiveness (read "spontaneity"). The initiate's
great desire is to attain that calm and resolution which
so attracts him to the elder.

   The formulae used here are by no means confined to
those which indicate the elder and initiate's respective
relations to the "spontaneity"/"consciousness" dialectic.
The rite of passage structure has a crucial function in
the novel because it motivates the resolution (in the plot)
of the dialectical conflict. Consequently, the hero's and
elder's roles in that rite are underlined in a further set
of conventions: the standard elder figure is cast as a man
of great experience and wisdom, but now very old or ill
while, by contrast, the initiate is passing vigorous, but
immature.

   Thus we in the West have often reduced the Soviet
novel to the formula "Boy gets tractor" with the variable
"plus or minus girl." But in point of fact both the public plot (boy gets tractor) and the love plot (boy gets/
does not get girl) are subordinate to the parable of
quest, struggle, symbolic death and rebirth (i.e., initiation) whereby the life of a Soviet citizen parallels one
stage in the reaching out of History towards Consciousness
in an ascending series of moments of epiphany leading up
to the ultimate leap into Communism.

Wesleyan University
Middletown, Connecticut

NOTES

[1]Arthur Hailey, *Airport* (New York: Bantam, 1969), pp.
31-32.
   [2]The *Airport* text reads:

   Curiously, it was a speech of Mel's which had
   brought them together to begin with. At one
   of the rare interline meetings which airlines

held, he had talked about coming developments
in aviation, and the lag in ground organization
compared with progress in the air. He had used
the occasion as a dry run for a speech he intended to deliver at a national forum a week or
so later. Tanya had been among the Trans America contingent, and next day had sent him one of
her lower case notes:...

   As well as amusing him, the note had caused
him to think. It was true, he realized--he had
concentrated on facts and systems to the exclusion of people as individuals. He revised his
speech notes, shifting the emphasis as Tanya
suggested. The result was the most successful
presentation he had ever made. It gained him
an ovation and was widely reported internation-
ally. Afterward he had telephone Tanya to thank
her. That was when they had started seeing each
other.

[3] G. M. Markov, "Sovremennost' i problemy prosy,"
Chetvertyi s"ezd pisatelei SSSR. Stenograficheskii otchet,
Moscow: Sovetskii pisatel', 1968, p. 17.

[4] Gleb Struve, *Russian Literature Under Lenin and
Stalin* (Norman: University of Oklahoma Press, 1971), p.
133.

[5] Rufus W. Mathewson, *The Positive Hero in Russian
Literature* (New York: Columbia University Press, 1957),
passim.

[6] See Iu. Tynianov, *Arkhaisty i novatory,* Leningrad,
1929, Viktor Shklovskii, *O teorii prozy,* Moscow, 1925.

[7] See Tom Wolfe, "The New Journalism," in Tom Wolfe
(ed.), *The New Journalism* (New York: Harper & Row, 1974),
pp. 3-52.

[8] S. Sheshukov, *Aleksandr Fadeev,* Moscow: Sovetskij
pisatel', 1964, pp. 186-87.

[9] It should be noted that many of the Five Year Plan
novels do not replicate the structure described here.

[10] See his speech to the First Writers' Congress in
1934 (*Pervyi vsesoiuznyi s"ezd pisatelei. Stenograficheskii otchet,* Moscow: Ogiz., 1934, pp. 5-18.

[11] *Novyi mir,* II, no. 2 (1925), p. 81.

[12] Maria-Gabriele Wosien, *The Russian Folk-tale: Some
Structural Aspects* (Munich: Verlag Otto Sagner, 1969),
passim.

[13] See Angus Fletcher, *Allegory The Theory of a Symbolic Mode* (Ithaca: Cornell University Press, 1965), pp. 151-160.

[14] Some might have preferred that I analyzed the Soviet novel as allegory. Actually, the distinction between parable and allegory is a very fraught one, but I find this observation by Dodd to be crucial in my decision to opt for parable. As Edwin Honig says in his book on Allegory entitled *The Dark Conceit: The Making of Allegory* (Evanston, 1969, p. 113): "An allegory starts from the writer's need to create a specific world of fictional reality. Like the divine creator in Genesis, he ordains the reality by designating it according to functions: Let there be light, and there was light...." The double purpose of *making* a reality and making it *mean* something is peculiar to allegory..."

[15] C. H. Dodd, *The Parables of the Kingdom* (London: Nisbet, 1952), pp. 21-22.

[16] V. I. Lenin, "Chto delat'" (1905), *Polnoe sobraniie sochinenii*, v. 6, Moscow: Politicheskaia literatura, 1960, pp. 1-192 (esp. pp. 29-31).

[17] V. I. Lenin, "Gosudarstvo i revoliutsiia" (1917), *Polnoe sobraniie sochinenii*, v. 33, Moscow: Politicheskaia literatura, 1962, pp. 1-120 (esp. p. 91).

[18] (Reference back to the quotation on p. 367) of this text).

[19] Clearly the prominence of nature in the Soviet novel has a great deal to do with the peculiar cultural matrix of both pre- and post-revolutionary Russia. However, it will not be possible to go into this within the scope of this article.

[20] Galina Nikolaeva, *Bitva v puti, Oktiabr'*, XXXIV, no. 3 (1957), p. 13.

[21] op. cit., *Oktiabr'*, XXXIV, no. 4 (1957), pp. 105, 107.

[22] Ibid., p. 102.

[23] As in Valentin Kataev's novel *A Lonely White Sail Gleams* (*Beleet parus odinokii*, 1936).

[24] One can see this in N. Ostrovskii's *How the Steel Was Tempered* (*Kak zakalialas' stal'*, 1934): whenever the hero Pavel Korchagin is absent from center stage for any period of time a temporary substitute initiate appears and likewise every time Pavel moves to a new town or job that new situation produces a fresh elder figure for him.

MANDELSTAM AND PASTERNAK: THE ANTIPODES

Henry Gifford

Nadezhda Mandelstam's memoirs make it necessary to think again about Pasternak, who appears often in her pages. Akhmatova stood very much closer to Osip Mandelstam: 'they were allies in the literal sense of the word.'[1] But both Akhmatova and Mandelstam were constantly aware of Pasternak as a poet who, in spite of many differences, had a good deal in common with them. It is the purpose of this paper to sort out some of the differences--though Nadezhda has already done the essential work here--and to consider in what ways the significance of Pasternak for the western reader may be altered by the achievement of Mandelstam.

Only ten years have passed since the beginning of Mandelstam's full re-emergence with the edition by Struve and Filippov, and the two indispensable volumes by Nadezhda herself. Yet already the belief is growing that he may be the most important Russian poet of his generation, and perhaps of his century; and if this is so, what consequences follow for the reputation of Pasternak? Long before the publicity that came with the Nobel Prize it had been widely assumed--except by the not very numerous votaries of Mandelstam--that Pasternak embodied the best hope for Russian poetry, and that through him lay the road to its renaissance. The formula 'from Pushkin to Pasternak' was convincing, with the added charm of alliteration. For the western world Pasternak stood as the one veritable voice in Russian poetry of this age; or if a second voice could be allowed, it was that of Akhmatova.

Now everything has been changed, and principally by the intervention of Nadezhda. As a critic of contemporary Russian literature she is without peer. This derives above all else from the consistency and sureness of Osip's judgments which she has meditated through a much longer experience than his, testing and refining them. All that she has to say about Pasternak relates of necessity to Osip's achievement, to Osip's conception of what poetry entails for its practitioners, and to his understanding of his own talent. That does not, however, impart the wrong bias to her opinions. They have been deeply considered, and essentially, I think, they are just.

It was difficult for the Mandelstams not to view
Pasternak without a certain uneasiness. Pasternak and Osip
Mandelstam, born within a year of each other, and publishing their first books of verse again within the space of a
year, the sons both of Jewish fathers, combining a wide
knowledge of other literatures and the arts with a very
strong sense of the Russian heritage--were yet so widely
sundered as to deserve the name of antipodes which Nadezhda
has given them in *Hope Against Hope*.[2] Pasternak throughout
the lifetime of Mandelstam could be seen by him to belong,
in a way that Osip never did, to the Soviet literary world.
Nadezhda has pointed out more than once that for the Acmeists there was no encouragement whatsoever from any of the
bodies that sought to direct Soviet literature. Both her
husband and Akhmatova knew that within a very few years of
the October revolution solitude was their lot. Pasternak
could be roped in to Lef for a while; he was able to write
poems such as *The High Malady, Nineteen Five* and *Lieutenant Schmidt*, the two latter of which were approved by
Gorky; and afterwards settled with good grace and with energy to the tasks of translation. None of these things
was possible for Mandelstam, who remained loyal exclusively to the poetic school in which he had grown up, had no
wish to participate in the main movement of Soviet poetry
during the 1920s, and looked on translation for the most
part as a form of drudgery injurious to the creative mind.
While Pasternak flourished, Mandelstam was already an outcast. He showed no envy of Pasternak, but must often have
felt the differences between them after their meetings.

However, it is well here to recall what Nadezhda says
about people who are antipodes to each other. They cannot
be this unless they are 'located at opposite poles of the
same sphere.' The reason that she so often glances across
at Pasternak is not hard to find. Mandelstam and Akhmatova
held his poetry in respect, and they also regarded him as
bound more or less in their own direction.[3] The three
poets had enough in common to ensure that eventually their
paths would converge. Mandelstam recognised the originality of Pasternak, and he wrote most generously of *My Sister
Life* on its appearance in 1922. Nadezhda's motive is not
to establish her husband's superiority over Pasternak, but
she has seen that their careers cannot be taken separately.
These were the two most considerable poets of the time; at
one in their loyalty to the same vocation; and however
various their approach to specific problems in art and
life, by the end Pasternak, as the author of *Doctor*

Zhivago, had gone a long way to meet Mandelstam. Some
differences of outlook were to persist. Yet it makes
sense to read the achievement of either poet in the light
of what the other did.

Mandelstam's poetry, like the critical views that
supported it, is remarkably consistent and shows an unfal-
tering evolution. Pasternak, while much more productive,
lacks that steadiness of purpose. His achievement includes some failure along with a larger variety. The com-
pactness of Mandelstam's work reflects that sense of rec-
titude which he thought so necessary for the poet. Reading him, one is persuaded that to Mandelstam, and so to
Nadezhda, belongs the authority for pronouncing finally
upon other poets. However, what she says about Pasternak
must be interpreted first in relation to the problems confronting her husband. An awareness of these ought to precede the act of judgment upon Pasternak--they make plain
the criterion she has in mind.

Mandelstam is the poet as poet and nothing else. He
objected to what he termed literature--the whole clogging
activity that was promoted by official persons, with its
placemen and hangers on. He resembled Khlebnikov in a
willingness to live by the discipline of poverty for his
art's sake, though he had neither Khlebnikov's naiveté nor
his trance-like self-absorption. The writing of Mandelstam's poetry demanded no accessories--desk, *dacha*, a comfortable way of life, the status of a respected author.
Nor did it necessitate an audience before his eyes: he
addressed himself to the far-off, unknown 'interlocutor'
who some time, somewhere would respond to his poem. It
was a very austere ideal, expressed in strongly disciplined verse. The poet for him has to be a *pravednik*,
since Acmeism, as he understood it, was the 'conscience'
of poetry.[4] A deliberate nomad, Mandelstam would accept
no compromise with those who aimed to regulate poetry and
reward the obedient writer with privileges and a stake in
the world.

About Pasternak, whom she accuses of claiming as by
right the favoured position he thought due to an intellectual and artist, Nadezhda is at times severe. She regards
the domestic yearnings of Pasternak as a weakness. He
wanted too badly to reach an accommodation with the order
that Osip by now altogether distrusted. Pasternak, as she
observes, did not arouse the same suspicions in Soviet
officialdom. 'You know,' Fadeev said to her, 'Pasternak

is not one of us either, but all the same he is a little
closer to us and we can come to terms with him in some
things.'[5] She emphasises above all the Muscovite quality
of Pasternak. 'A Muscovite born and bred,' he belonged
through and through to the city and reflected its manners
in everything, notably in his speech. She seems to regard
this as a triumph of assimilation ('Jewish children who
grew up in Moscow were particularly quick to pick up the
city's accent ...').[6] The Muscovite quality in Pasternak,
which at once amuses and a little perplexes her, does indeed separate him from Mandelstam. It is not only that he
belonged to a different camp in poetry, at first with the
Moscow futurists, and then with Marina Tsvetaeva. Every
student of Russian literature has by now heard more than
enough about the different intellectual climates of Moscow
and St. Petersburg, and their opposed traditions. However, with Pasternak and Mandelstam the antithesis runs to
its fullest depth. More than imaginative sympathies are
involved here--Mandelstam's love of architecture and the
classical poets, or Pasternak's awareness of the steppe
beyond the city, his delight in the Slav rather than the
Mediterranean heritage. His Moscow upbringing enabled
Pasternak to become a social being in a way that Mandelstam would have found impossible. When Fadeev told
Nadezhda that Pasternak was 'a little closer to us,' he
can hardly have meant closer in ideology. But Pasternak
had been accustomed to the artist's life as one led in a
society of fellow-spirits, which had been the life known
to his parents in Moscow. He naturally conceived literature as a profession, and the artist as belonging to an
honoured elite. It was long before he understood that
under the new regime the pursuit of literature had been
compromised beyond recognition.

Yet a common bond did exist. Nadezhda is highly
critical of Pasternak's demand for 'a seat by the columns,'[7] and right in giving it a central importance for
his character. Pasternak could not easily divorce the
ideas of art and privilege; yet he would not trade art to
obtain privilege. In many respects it is now plain that he
put his trust too impulsively and unreflectingly in Soviet
leadership. He was not by temperament one who resists and
keeps apart. The summer of 1917 released in him a creative energy which hallowed the revolution and warmed his
spirit to ecstasy even in the cold and death-dealing years
that followed. Nadezhda greatly admires *My Sister Life*:

> Wonderment at living in this world and being en-
> dowed with the mysterious gift of speech, man's
> finest possession, this surely is the seed from
> which poetry springs, its very foundation. It
> is this that makes *My Sister Life* so remarkable:
> it is a book of knowledge about the world, of
> thanksgiving and joy ...[8]

For all the unlikeness in attitude between Mandelstam and
Pasternak, strangely enough--when we remember the desolation of his years at Voronezh--thanksgiving and joy never
deserted Mandelstam either. Nadezhda tells how even under
the shadow of doom he took extreme pleasure in the smallest things. Like Pasternak he never lost his 'wonderment
at living in this world.' He had, Nadezhda tells, an 'exceptional capacity to live for the moment.'[9]

Pasternak had at first aligned himself with the
Futurists, though his particular group, *Tsentrifuga*, was
less revolutionary than the others (it had begun as something not very easily distinguishable from a Symbolist
circle). More significant perhaps is the dedication of
his third book *My Sister Life* to Lermontov. He did not
want to throw the past overboard, which had been the declared aim of Mayakovsky and his associates in 1912.
Pasternak shared with Mandelstam the sense of a living
European culture, but for him this did not take the form of
nostalgia. Andrey Sinyavsky says in his latest book, that
'Mandelstam lives in history as in the air'; it is his
native element, and he cannot escape from it: 'he treats
it as freely and unaffectedly as Pasternak does nature.'[10]
This attitude, Sinyavsky says, 'made him alien to the
futurist grimaces of the twentieth century.' He was never
in the least attracted by Futurism, but 'amazed' rather by
its 'intellectual poverty.'[11] The historical sense gives
a great dignity to Acmeism, the Russian poetic school which
most nearly evokes the spirit of the Renaissance. Greece
and Rome, Tauris and Colchis, were not radiant presences
for Pasternak's imagination; nor would he be drawn later,
as Mandelstam was, to the Renaissance poets of Italy and
to Dante. Rather grudgingly, towards the end of his life,
Mandelstam asked Nadezhda 'to teach him how to read my
"Englishman"'--Shakespeare.[12] It was jealousy of her interest he could not share that prompted this, rather than
a pressing need such as brought him to Dante. Pasternak,
on the other hand, seems to have sported dolphin-like in
the sea of Shakespeare: it must have been deeply refreshing to him in the heyday of socialist realism. But if he

had admired Gautier and Villon (who surely meant more to
Mandelstam than the other two paragons of the Acmeists,
Shakespeare and Rabelais), and also the classical poets
of Rome, it seems less probable he would have responded
so fully to Shakespeare. His pieties are different from
those of Mandelstam. It is well brought out by Clarence
Brown that in Mandelstam's work 'the epic, heroic world
of Homer is practically never to be found without a leaven
of the domestic, the low, the thoroughly Russian.'[13]   For
Pasternak the domestic is no less important, but he links
it, not with Homer and the classical past, but with the
birchwood and the gulley below the house where they are
putting cloves into pickle.[14]   He could never have ex-
claimed like Mandelstam that nature and Rome are identical ('*Priroda - tot zhe Rim*').[15]

Pasternak is continually aware of the living world
that surrounds the human city with trees, far vistas and
thunderstorms. For him the house opens on to its garden,
the town on to the sky, and the railway explores the
steppe. He has an immediate sense of the circumambient,
whereas Mandelstam sees the human city in time. Nadezhda
criticises Pasternak for not being 'satisfied with the
best that nature could have given him: his lyrical gift,
his "wet and trembling hands."'[16]   This led him to the
pursuit of 'major forms' during the 1920s and eventually
to his novel. The preoccupation with major forms can certainly be explained by the course of Soviet literature
after the revolution. One can also see that a tendency
to expand from the lyrical centre of his genius was natural in Pasternak. The characteristic poem that he writes
early or late sends out ever widening circles of apprehension: it will not stay at home. Thus the major forms ex-
erted a strong pull on his imagination, which could only
fulfil itself spatially. With Mandelstam the need was
different. Condensation, the maturing of insight through
history, a reaching back into the luminous past—these
constitute his mode. The characteristic poem he writes
is stationary in space, but it gathers volume, it solidi-
fies with the weight of associations. Where the process
so manifestly makes for plenitude, he can ignore major
forms. What could they add to the stature of his poetry?

When Pasternak began to speak about writing a novel,
and wanted Mandelstam to do the same, he replied that for
this purpose 'you need either the country estate of a
Tolstoy or the prison experience of a Dostoevsky.'[17]   He
believed that the biography of an individual must form the

starting point for a novel, and the first characters of
fiction had been extraordinary people.[18]　One concludes
from this remark that Tolstoy's freedom in his social
position made him extraordinary, and the prison ordeal
did the same for Dostoevsky.　Lyric poetry, however, does
not depend on 'the fate of the individual in history,'
with which Mandelstam rightly saw the novel to be inti-
mately connected.[19]　Indeed, his own poetry demonstrates
that the individual who has no standing in history, but
becomes merely its victim, nonetheless can express himself
with force undiminished.　And sensing this faculty in himself, not surprisingly he had little confidence in Pasternak's project.

　　　Nadezhda comments that Pasternak 'began to think
about writing a novel at a time when all movement of ideas
had ceased.... It was hence extremely hard for him to col-
lect his thoughts and actually embark on a study of the
times.'　However, 'for a brief moment the war brought
people together again,' and 'this momentarily restored
sense of community' enabled Pasternak to complete his novel.　What he finally wrote had a poignant interest for
her.　'I find it significant that the hero of the novel is
a poet with a biography parallel to the author's, but much
more disastrous.　Pasternak was trying to see what his own
life would have been like if the river had been deflected
into a different course.'[20]　He had in fact caught up with
the realities that faced Mandelstam.　This comparison is
what gives a particular force to Nadezhda's comments on
Doctor Zhivago.　Osip and its fictitious hero have certain
qualities in common, but the differences between them are
crucial.

　　　She sees in the conception of Yury Zhivago once again
proof that Pasternak was clinging to his notion of the
privileged artist.　Mandelstam did not demand 'a seat by
the columns'; but for Pasternak it seemed natural that the
State should look after its artists and place 'a protective wall between the intelligentsia and the people.'　Even
the intelligentsia as he understood it was no more than a
special minority of the class--'those members of it for
whom the Revolution meant the end of gracious living and
the destruction of their peaceful mode of life.'[21]　The
protective wall that Pasternak allows his hero is the work
of Evgraf, whose connection with the highest authorities
of the regime is constantly made clear.　She is not willing to look at this character in any other light.　(The
Rowlands, for instance, take it that Evgraf, from the

Greek *eugraphēs*, 'writing well', 'personifies the Doctor's
poetic inspiration and his guardian spirit.'[22]) Evgraf
represents the beneficent state which here fulfils in a
mysterious way Pasternak's dream. For Nadezhda this is
mere fantasy, and selfish fantasy, just as she maintains
that the first sojourn of Yury and his family at Varykino
is what can 'happen only in fairy tales, or in the imagination of Soviet citizens.'[23]

There is more than a little truth in her reduction of
Evgraf to these terms, and most readers are probably uncomfortable with him. The role of Evgraf is like the role
of coincidence in the novel--an intrusion from outside,
hinting at providential designs. Nadezhda herself has
lived to see her own miracle in the publication of Mandelstam's poetry, against all the odds; but there was no
Evgraf to perform it. She knows how much depended on the
effort and willingness of herself and a few others to take
enormous risks, and how much on mere chance. Like Pasternak she found herself arriving at a sympathy with the
Christian view of the world, which Mandelstam had broadly
accepted, it would seem, from the time he knew Father
Pavel Florensky. But she is wholly unable to share Pasternak's optimism: the Christianity she understands is
that of the lonely witnesses in the concentration camp,
whereas throughout *Doctor Zhivago* the underlying Christian
message spells hope and resurrection. For Nadezhda these
things are not excluded, but far more than Pasternak she
recognises the vacancy of the modern world, and prophesies
disaster.

The situation of Yury and Lara on the second visit
to Varykino, when he realises that their days of freedom
are numbered, might also have been based on that of the
Mandelstams in Voronezh. Nadezhda does not refer to this
episode, but she recognises that for the Pasternak who
wrote it, no less than for her husband, the genuine poet
must be an outcast in Soviet society. How far, we may ask,
does Yury Zhivago, Pasternak's uncompromising artist, correspond to the ideals Mandelstam set himself? Nadezhda
finds fault with a well-known phrase in one of Pasternak's
later poems, 'the aim of creation is self-surrender' (*Tsel'
tvorchestva samootdacha*). She discusses it in her chapter
of *Hope Abandoned* which bears the title of 'Poetic Recognition' and the phrase belongs to a meditation by Pasternak
on the indecency of fame.[24] In the ideas of 'creation'
and 'self-surrender,' or giving oneself, she detects a hidden self-importance. Pasternak in her view as she has

said a page earlier, did sometimes fuss about his own
reputation. He liked to measure himself against contemporaries such as Mandelstam and Akhmatova.[25] Nor is
Zhivago quite free from self-importance, despite his very
real submission to a poetic purpose transcending personality. At his last meeting with Gordon and Dudorov he
longs to tell them that to have lived in his day and to
have known him is their one distinction.[26] Pasternak
finds it hard not to glorify the artist, with his power
of creation and miracle-working (*I tvorchestvo, i
chudotvorstvo*).[27] The artist is for him the human being
at his most developed. Destroy the artist, and you destroy man's highest potential. Pasternak is like Henry
James: the sufferings of those who are most 'finely aware
and richly responsible' engage him beyond those of ordinary men. To Zhivago much may be forgiven--all the confusion and eventual squalor of his personal life--because
he lives only for and through his art.

The poems Mandelstam wrote at Voronezh, when he collected his strength for a last declaration of faith, do
indeed claim that poetry is needed no less than 'light and
the blue air,' than 'bread and the snows of Elbrus.'[28] He
attends to the art more than to the artist, to 'song' and
the integrity of its making. The Voronezh lyrics may fit-
tingly be compared with the poems attributed to Zhivago,
most of which bear the impress of a spirit that foresees
its ordeal and is braced to meet it. Zhivago identifies
himself with Hamlet, the actor upon the stage called on to
play a part he would willingly resign, and also with
Christ, who judges the centuries as they float like a
string of barges out of the darkness.[29] Mandelstam does
not want to exalt the artist in this way: for him the
sense of 'poetic rightness' was very important, but the
poet himself had to submit finally to the people's verdict.[30]

Nadezhda came to understand why Pasternak had under-
taken his novel. It was 'an attempt to determine his own
place in the swift-flowing movement of days....' She
notes that everyday life and the immediate present were
Pasternak's true concern, but he felt also 'a nagging
urge to analyze, to look at things from a distance, to
see them in larger perspective.'[31] This reconciles her
to his novel, though she is obviously impatient with
Pasternak's desire also to write a play, *The Blind Beauty*,
which she dismisses as 'some strange fragments.'[32] It is
fair comment that Pasternak had little dramatic sense.

She criticises the way Markel is made to speak. 'Such a
language never existed, any more than that of his Siberian
grocer's wife.'[33]   Whereas 'in *The Childhood of Luves*
Pasternak was quite clearly able to identify himself with
his adolescent heroine, this power failed him in *Doctor
Zhivago.*   ... The dialogues between Lara and Zhivago are
simply variations on Pasternak's own words.' His success
with   *The Chilhood of Luvers*   proves for her that Pasternak's was a lyrical imagination which needed to find itself partly through the opposite sex, and which had not
the univocal nature that was consistently Mandelstam's.[34]
The major form held such temptations for Pasternak because,
as he often explained in later life, he wanted to transcend the lyric and its restrictions. As he wrote to
Eugene M. Kayden, 'You say I am "first and last a poet, a
lyric poet." Is it really so? And should I feel proud
of being just that?'[35]

Mandelstam never wanted to be more than "just that.'
(His prose writings appeared in the intervals between
bouts of poetic inspiration. Perhaps it was only in *The
Egyptian Stamp*, as Nadezhda suggests, that he yielded
momentarily to the lure of major forms.[36]) His genius is
purely lyrical, but the discipline that one associates
with Acmeism enabled him to concentrate a total vision in
lyric poetry. To do this was impossible for Pasternak,
as indeed it was for Blok and in an earlier age Pushkin.
The gains for Mandelstam in this comparison are evident,
and very little of his poetry shows a dissipation of
strength. It is, of course, futile to attempt a relative
estimate of *Doctor Zhivago* and Mandelstam's poetry of the
1930s. These things are not commensurable. Certainly
Nadezhda, with an eye on her husband's achievement, has
been able to point out some notable weaknesses in Pasternak. But, as she reminds us in the chapter on 'Poetic
Recognition,' poetry is what Pasternak called it, 'a duel
between two nightingales.'[37] The notes of Pasternak and
of Mandelstam are distinct, but they belong to the same
species; and if one of them sings more irresistibly to our
ears in the 1970s, the other too was a nightingale.

University of Bristol

NOTES

[1] N. Mandelstam, *Hope Abandoned* (London, 1974), p. 230; this volume will subsequently be referred to as *H.A.*

[2] N. Mandelstam, *Hope Against Hope* (London, 1971), Ch. 33, p. 149f; this volume will subsequently be referred to as *H.A.H.*

[3] *H.A.*, p. 230.

[4] *H.A.*, p. 42.

[5] *H.A.H.*, p. 152.

[6] *H.A.*, p. 79.

[7] *H.A.H.*, p. 151.

[8] *H.A.*, p. 331.

[9] *Op. cit.*, p. 302.

[10] A. Sinyavsky, *Golos iz khora* (London, 1973), p. 296.

[11] *H.A.*, p. 303.

[12] *Op. cit.*, p. 234.

[13] *Mandelstam* (Cambridge, 1973), p. 254.

[14] 'Bab'e leto', in B. Pasternak, *Stikhotvoreniya i poemy* (Moscow-Leningrad, 1965), p. 433.

[15] *Stikhotvoreniia* (Leningrad, 1973), p. 105.

[16] *H.A.*, p. 344.

[17] *Loc. cit.*

[18] 'Konets romana' (1928), in Mandelstam, *Sobrannye sochinenii* II (2nd edn., New York, 1971), p. 267.

[19] *Sobr. soch.*, p. 267

[20] *H.A.*, pp. 345-6.

[21] *H.A.H.*, p. 153

[22] Mary F. Rowland and Paul Rowland, *Pasternak's 'Doctor Zhivago'* (Carbondale and Edwardsville, Illinois, 1967), p. 107.

[23] *H.A.*, p. 52.

[24] Pasternak, *Stikh. i poemy*, p. 447.

[25] *H.A.*, p. 330.

[26] *Doctor Zhivago*, ch. 15, 7.

[27] 'Avgust'.

[28] Mandelstam, *Stikh.*, p. 189.

[29] 'Gefsimanskiy sad'.

[30] *H.A.*, p. 336.

[31] *Op. cit.*, p. 345.

[32] *Op. cit.*, p. 350.

[33] *Op. cit.*, p. 79.

[34] *Op. cit.*, p. 322.

[35] Pasternak, *Poems*, tr. Eugene M. Kayden (Ann Arbor, 1959), p. vii.

[36] *H.A.*, p. 186.

[37] *Op. cit.*, p. 331.

MANDEL'SHTAM'S CREATIVE PROCESS--IN THE LIGHT OF HIS WIDOW'S MEMOIRS

Donald Rayfield

At intervals, throughout Mandel'shtam's poetry--and continuously in his prose--we can see the poet formulating and reformulating his poetics, looking not so much at the world, or experience, or culture, so much as at the way in which objects become images and symbols, and speech poetic language. There is an inner consistency in Mandel'shtam's creative process: it is always Hellenic in that it looks for an eternally poetic element to be *recognised* in the present, in that it senses an Apollonic force which reduces even the self-confident Acmeist persona into a vessel for a musical power inherent in language: *Ne u menia, ne u tebia, u nikh/Vsia sila okonchaniy rodovykh.* But Mandel'shtam's poetics are constantly restated. They are expressed in terms of various arts: at first, play, then music, then spinning, weaving and encapsulating, finally moulding (*lepit'*). They come under the aegis of different languages, whose musicality Mandel'shtam is trying to extract from Russian and whose culture he is inoculating into his own. French, then Latin dominate *Kamen'*; Greek dominates *Tristia.* The poetry of the nineteen-thirties is infused first with Armenian (the "cat" language), then Italian and, perhaps, as the Keatsian motifs of the poems of spring 1937 suggest, with English. *Chuzhaya rech' mne budet obolochkoy*, Mandel'shtam said to the German language: it applies to all the languages he used, some known, some merely heard.

The poetry, and therefore the poetics, of *Kamen'* and *Tristia* need little interpretation. We can recognise its continuity with lines that flow from Russian symbolism, from the providential thought of Chaadayev and Leont'yev, from ancient Greece. Its use of Petersburg and the Crimea develops the myth of north and south to be found in Pushkin and Tyutchev. But after *Tristia*, the Russian poetic tradition that nurtures Mandel'shtam is more allusive, more complex and more intimate. We can sense without difficulty that a poem such as *Nashedshiy podkovu* (1923), the two cycles *Armenia* (1930-31) and the *Vos'mistishiia* (1932-1935), the essay and poems on Dante (1933-7), the

poem *Fleyty grecheskoy tèta* (or *myata*) *i iota* (1937) are
indeed new stages in Mandel'shtam's poetic thought. But
because the origins and circumstances of these poems are—
or were—only fragmentarily known to us, the poetry of the
thirties, in particular of the Voronezh notebooks, has
seemed an embarrassingly hermetic posthumous addition to
what was once regarded as a complete oeuvre.

Nadezhda Yakovlevna's memoirs—apart from being a
remarkable autobiographical document and a unique record
of the mass psychosis of Stalinism—serve Mandel'shtam's
poetry as no other poet in history has been served. But
then few poets have been married to such an observant
critical intelligence. Through both volumes of her memoirs Nadezhda Yakovlevna has scattered enough facts, insights and hints to make it possible for a reader to approach Mandel'shtam's poetry of the thirties better prepared and better attuned than he has a right to hope.

It is in 1930, Nadezhda Yakovlevna records, that she
"first understood how poetry originates." She understood
that the lines which she wrote down to her husband's dic-
tation were the last stage in a long, laborious process of
perambulation and mumbling, in which the poet's mind
worked only to remove the superfluous and to fill in the
gaps in a product which was not cerebral, but physical.
From this year—which in any case broke a poetic silence
of virtually six years—she begins to observe the ante-
and perinatal stages of the poem, as well as its interpretation of things seen and heard. Thus Nadezhda Yakovlevna
gives us far more valuable information than Table-Talk or
biographical reference-points—valuable though these are:
we can watch the birth of a poem.

One of the most important factors in the conception
of the poem, Nadezhda Yakovlevna shows and the poems confirm, is the poet's recognition of the parallels between
the poetic and the anti-poetic. Thus the Africa-shaped
map of Voronezh province, lit up by light bulbs at the
station, the dense coniferous forests of the Kama, the
sunbaked clay of Armenia or the featureless black earth
of the steppe are all "inimical" to poetry—they imprison
the poet, they blot out the sun, they are formless, sterile, impervious or unmalleable. Yet they enter Mandel'-
shtam's poetry—which had always shunned imagery of forests and earth—because the anti-poetic mirrors the poetic.
Nadezhda Yakovlevna relates her husband's conciliation
with Cherdyn' and Voronezh and we are thus enabled to understand the role they play in his imagery. The Africa-

shape of Voronezh, the nonsense-poetry of its place names
--*Anna, Rossosh' i Gremiach'e*--release it from the bonds
of the everyday; the stinging-fir forests suddenly suggest
to Mandel'shtam the beautiful, structural image of the sap
running to create the rings that mark each year's growth
of the tree. Once he perceives poetic form, a hostile object becomes a fruitful image. Just as the sterile clay
of Armenia suggests to Mandel'shtam that poetry is now
analogous to the intimate art of the potter, instead of
the subtle work of the spinner or weaver, so the steppe
black earth--heavy and sticky to the touch--begins to
take on those qualities of mutability which make poetry
possible.

　　　Mandel'shtam's poetry of the thirties incorporates
new and alien imagery with bewildering speed Nadezhda
Yakovlevna shows what precipitates the process and how a
group--twins or triplets--of poems turns a lightning analogy into a metaphor which retains its symbolic associations for the rest of his life. One example is Mandel'-
shtam's comment when he sees hoof-marks on a dirt road
that the rain has turned to little pools--"that's what
memory is." This casts light on the overtones of
Nashedshiy podkovu written twelve years earlier, where
the horseshoe "contains" in itself all the action, spark
and sound of the galloping horse (an idea that can be
traced through Khlebnikov back to stanza 9 of Pushkin's
Osen'). Now we see how the comment relates to the triad
of poems which link the image of water in hoof-marks--
memory of impressions, residue of dynamic motion--to al-
lied images: the cart whose axle (or axis: *os'*) is out of
true and which erases these marks and splatters the water
--an alien, totalitarian system of thought; the life-giv-
ing image of water, linked to tears and linked to the
leavening image of yeast so important in Mandel'shtam's
poetry of 1922 and of 1936. Given this simple point of
departure, the poem *Drozhzhi mira dorogiye* fits not only
with the other two poems which Nadezhda Yakovlevna identifies as its "triplets," but with a whole series of poems
that link phonetically, by the syllable *os'*, the poet
(Osip), his killer (Iozif Stalin) and the dislodged axis
(*os'*) of culture.

　　　A reader of the Voronezh notebook poems will first of
all perceive that the images are linked not only by visual
and above all tangible similarities, but by a phonetic
grouping of words: words in *os'/us*; heavy "black-earth"
words with chuintantes and sibilants--*ch,zh,z*; musical

(flute and violin) words with the syllables *ol/ul*, and
whispering words, the "cat" sounds of Eastern Armenian
with its plethora of unvoiced plosives, which give rise to
a conspiratorial pattern of *p-t-k*: *On opyt iz lepeta lepit/
I lepet iz opyta p'yot*. An habitue of Khlebnikov will
find nothing strange in this attribution of meaning to individual phonemes; but Mandel'shtam, unlike Khlebnikov,
gave us no key to the semantic nuance of each sound and we
have to seek reassurance of the values of our intuition
from Nadezhda Yakovlevna. She shows, as an open-minded
and patient reader might suspect, that phonetic parallels
between the anti-poetic hostile words and the poetic,
"friendly" words are the most powerful structural force in
Mandel'shtam's late work. Some of these antonymic parallels are well established in Russian poetry: *gubit'/lyubit'*
in Pushkin (Yevgeniy Onegin, ch. 4) and Tyutchev, for in-
stance--they are ironies of rhyme. Mandel'shtam takes the
opposition of *guby*--the creative lips of the poet--and
gubit'--the destructive words of the anti-poetic, the
powers that be, and elevates these rhyming antonyms into a
whole system.

Throughout Mandel'shtam's work, poems are built on a
contrast of chaotic matter--which the poet feels, from the
very beginning, with claustrophobic intensity--and ordered,
ethereal structure. Thus the "sticky pool" of Mandel'-
shtam's Jewishness is contrasted with the classical proportions, the airy stone of Petersburg's architecture; the
Crimea of Wrangel' with the Crimea of the ancient Hellenes;
Leningrad with Petersburg; Armenia after the Persian conquest with independent Armenia; Asia and Europe; Assyria
and Greece; Stalin and the poet; Soviet passport and ra-
tion book with books of verse. Out of such opposing forces
an architectonic structure arises; the poet may be ironical
or may be horrified at the way in which the anti-poetic
apes the poetic or mirrors it, but the negative is as indispensable to his poetry as the positive.

Negative and positive poles are bridged by arcs; and
arcs are perhaps the key image in Mandel'shtam's work.
From his earliest poems--such as *Kazino*, where the arc-
like images of a sail and a bay outside are recreated inside in the ball and green baize of the casino--to his
last, the arc shape and movement is the essence of poetry.
It is there in the rainbow, in the lines of cathedrals, in
the movement of the shuttle on the loom, in the intonation
and shape of a poetic sentence, in the breath and breathing
rhythm of a human being, above all in the lips. The arc is

a straightening of spirals--a symbol of revelation, honesty and truth in poems such as *Royal'* or the elegies for
Andrey Bely.

Nadezhda Yakovlevna traces the development of the
"super-image" of the arc in the Voronezh poetry. She un-
derlines an analogy which is noticeable in Mandel'shtam
from the poem *Vek*, in 1923: the juxtaposition of the
human body with other-wordly imagery of the starry firma-
ment or of musical instruments. This analogy is essential
to symbolism: Mallarmé's *Une dentelle s'abolit* with its
dream of being born from the belly of the lyre, the auto-
genesis of the poet, is perhaps the *locus classicus*. It
is there in Cubist painting and thus in Mayakovsky's *Fleyta
i pozvonochnik*. Mandel'shtam follows Mayakovsky by bringing out the visual and mystical parallel of the flute and
the spine; he follows it in the Voronezh poems with the
parallel of the human brain contained in the dome of the
skull with its starry seams to the universe contained by
the starry arch of the sky.

In the Voronezh poetry Mandel'shtam intensifies this
use of the human body and its life on a cosmic scale. He
had always leant towards this analogy: the body was never
a sensual vessel for him; the first poem to attract wide
attention (in 1909) began *Dano mne telo, chto mne delat' s
nim*. Last poems often answer first poems and the corporeal
imagery of the Voronezh notebooks is perhaps not surprising. What Nadezhda Yakovlevna brings out is the creative
value of Mandel'shtam's illness. The first attacks of
angina, followed by a brief (and in the circumstances perfectly healthy) attack of persecution mania, remained for
Mandel'shtam as an increasing awareness of his own heartbeat, of his breathing, of his postures. The hallucinations he suffered from in Cherdyn' were, it turns out,
only more specific and more morbid forms of poetic revelation. Now the breathlessness, the *pereboi pul'sa*, the
cyanosed lips become not embarrassing or frightening signs
of mortality, but part and parcel of the rhythms of poetry
and its humanity.

Voronezh completed the process of isolation of
Mandel'shtam; it naturally turned him in on himself and
made his poetry more intimate, for he was now his own
collocutor. Friends were dead, exiled, alienated or intim-
idated. New acquaintances--biologists such as Kuzin--gave
to his poetry the extraordinary relativism and philosophical breadth that could in such times come only from natural scientists; but these contacts were shortlived. As

Nadezhda Yakovlevna tells us, Mandel'shtam's circles--in
every sense--were narrowing. It was a process Mandel'shtam
foretells in *K nemetskoy rechi: Zvuk suzilsya*. The only
equal Mandel'shtam was still in touch with, Anna Akhmatova,
records the same narrowing of sound. But for her, narrowing of sound was the condensation of poetry; as Nadezhda
Yakovlevna says, she was diametrically opposite from
Mandel'shtam in that her lips pursed as though to say *net*
when she was creating a poem, while Mandel'shtam's worked
feverishly. Both use the image of sound narrowing, but
for Mandel'shtam it seemed a thanatoid image.

The moving lips that are mentioned so often in the
Voronezh poems are the indomitable force of poetry*: *gub
sheveliashchikhsia otniat' vy ne mogli*. Pacing, mumbling
were Mandel'shtam's birth travail. The lips take on cosmic significance: the poem *Rozhdeniye ulybki* shows the
lips parting in two arcs to smile, as an event that parallels the emergence of a continent from beneath the waves--
an image Mandel'shtam uses on several occasions and which
reminds us of the image of Aphrodite arising from and returning to the sea that occurs in *Kamen'*. The moving lips,
like the continent of Atlantis, may give birth to a new
poem or new world of only limited duration, but the poem
is a momentary conquest over anarchy and therefore, even
when doomed, a positive act. Just as *guby*, lips spawn a
whole family of sound-related images, so their action,
ulybka, the smile, is the source for another group: *ulitka*,
both the snail (negative image) and the helix (positive
arc-like image) is one of the number of words that focus
around the syllable *ul/ol--stvol,viola, shchegol--*in itself a liquid and traditionally melodious syllable and
for Mandel'shtam indissolubly linked with music.

The moving lips, Nadezhda Yakovlevna suggests, go
back to a Sephardic Jew (did he exist or did Mandel'shtam
invent him?) who persisted in composing a sonnet a day
while awaiting for death in an Inquisition dungeon.
Mandel'shtam is said to have brought up this Sephardic
Jew in a conversation with a GPU investigating officer.
Fictional or not, the Jew's moving lips were an example
of all but dumb insubordination for the poet. It was,
after all, an orally composed poem--the lampoon on Stalin--

---

*They not only give utterance, they fight with poetry.
The poet doesn't just blow the Greek flute, he bites it,
he chews it, he tries to make it speak or be silent.

that sealed Mandel'shtam's fate. Moving lips become a
symbol of defiance and a model for the poet faced with
execution which only André Chénier and Osip Mandel'shtam
have ever succeeded in living up to.

   Topot i Shopot is the title of one of Nadezhda
Yakovlevna's chapters: the moving lips are accompanied by
pacing feet. In a poet so urban, so unlike those ramblers
Wordsworth or Pasternak, this comes as a surprise. Perhaps it dates from Armenia--the first "open-air" inspiration for Mandel'shtam, and the place where news of
Mayakovsky's suicide, the first knell of doom for all
poets in Russia, reached him. In Armenia that nervous,
quicksilver movement, which marks Mandel'shtam's last
poetry off from the rest, began. We sense perambulation
not only in the nervous haste and the progression from one
image to another nor just in the powerful motor rhythms of
the Voronezh poems. Images are no longer toyed with, they
move past, approach and recede. The *Conversation on
Dante* develops perambulation to a theory of poetics: in
his Heraclitian vision of poetry, Mandel'shtam sees each
image generating another image "in flight" in a perpetual
motion of images dying as new ones are generated and pro-
pelled. Mandel'shtam's perambulation in itself expresses
that dynamism; it is the pacing of a caged man, not the
tour of a hiker.

   Armenia taught Mandel'shtam to cope with the world
outside Petersburg and outside the Hellenic dreamworld of
the Crimea, to cope with earth. It was Asia, now not just
the deadly "Assyrian" world which he talks of in the
hermetic lyrics of 1921 to 1923 and which he first knew
from Akhmatova's Egyptologist husband, Shileyko. Soviet
Russia was Asiatic in the sense that Tsarist Russia was
European. Cut off from Paris, Rome or Athens, the poet
had to look at Tiflis, Erevan or Samarkand. For some,
such as Mayakovsky and Khlebnikov, this came only too
easily: Mayakovsky's Georgian and Khlebnikov's Tatar can
be heard in the very sounds of their poems. For Mandel'-
shtam it was a terrific step. Armenia altered his whole
poetry: it not only made him pace, it made him whisper and
his poetry is as infused with the Caucasian consonants of
Armenian as Mayakovsky's hyperboles, alliteration and "internal declension" (*bog/beg, boy/bey*) is with Asiatic
poetics.

   Having absorbed Armenia and created the "cat" like
language we hear muttering and spluttering from 1934 to
1937, Mandel'shtam could take in other once alien elements.

Nadezhda Yakovlevna feels that no poetry can be wholly
divorced from folklore and the folk. Mandel'shtam's, up
to the 1930s, certainly seems to be cut off from them.
Like Moscow, the bearded peasantry and the violent mythol-
ogy of folklore are as horrific and anti-poetic as the
forests in which they dwell. But, sailing to Cherdyn'
Mandel'shtam was for the first time in his life brought
into the forests and among the peasants. Trees, we have
seen, gradually become distinguished—Mandel'shtam names
different species for the first time in his work—and
their growth becomes poetic. The peasant with his axe
loses some of the aura of the executioner and begins to
look like a fellow victim. With the folk and the rhythms
of folklore, which Nadezhda Yakovlevna points out in the
blat vocabulary and song rhythms of the poems about
Cherdyn', comes nature. Not only trees, but birds begin
to function as images. It is not the Hellenic swallow
(the medium between the living and the shades in the
ancient world) nor the Roman sparrow, but the goldfinches
of the Voronezh birdmarket that help Mandel'shtam review
himself in his last poems.

The goldfinch, like the peasant, is a victim. Seeing
himself as a victim rather than as a demiurge reconciles
the poet to his fate. Nadezhda Yakovlevna rightly defends
fear as a primary, creative emotion. Fear howls, protests, makes the executioner's job harder, warns poster-
ity. Fear, in Mandel'shtam's case, a nervous haste rather
than a paralytic cringing, is the inspiratory emotion that
Nadezhda Yakovlevna shows we are right to sense behind all
the Voronezh poems. It makes the poem a defensive riposte,
it accelerates the processes of association, it groups the
poems into serried ranks that make the Voronezh poems, as
Nadezhda Yakovlevna says, a book, a complete defence of
culture. Fear accelerates Mandel'shtam's development: the
Italian phase which incorporates Dante and Petrarch, those
guides for living under Guelphs and Ghibellines who help
us to live with more modern holocausts, into his poetry
lasts a mere four years; English poetry, as Nadezhda
Yakovlevna hints on two occasions and as two very Keatsian
poems, *Fleyty grecheskoy*... and *Goncharami velik ostrov
siniy*, confirm, transforms the spring of 1937 into an
affirmation that beauty and imminent death are inextricably
interdependent. The development remains Hellenic: a conception of poetry in which the poet must immolate himself
to survive only in the texture of his verse. Without
Nadezhda Yakovlevna's testimony it would take an uncommon

mind to trace all the disparate tributaries to this
Hellenic stream and to fit each poem to its foetal mem-
brane. Mandel'shtam's poetry resumes almost everything
European poetry has expressed; Nadezhda Yakovlevna's memoirs tell us everything about the physiology of another
person's poetic expression that we can ever know.

Queen Mary College
University of London

BIBLIOGRAPHY

Some of the material for this paper derives from an unpublished study of Mandel'shtam's poetry, which is the source
for a number of articles:

The flight from chaos, European Judaism, winter 1971-72.
A winter in Moscow, Stand, vol. 14, no. 1, 1972.
Deaths and Resurrections, Grosseteste, Summer 1974.
Mandel'shtam's Voronezh poetry, Russian Literature Tri-
    quarterly, No. 11.

SHKLOVSKII AND MANDELSHTAM

Richard Sheldon

For students of Shklovskii, one of the most moving
sections of Nadezhda Mandelshtam's memoirs is the portrait
of Shklovskii's son, Nikita. The Nikita Viktorovich who
appears in *Hope Against Hope*, as part of the chapter entitled "The Shklovskiis," is a boy of about fifteen--a boy
unusually perceptive and human, with a passion for truth
that would not have stood him in good stead during the
late forties and early fifties.

Reading this passage, one inevitably recalls the portrait of Nikita in Shklovskii's book *Third Factory*, where
elements of his life at the age of one are converted by a
proud father into recurrent leit-motifs. We see Nikita as
a precocious baby, playing with his toy elephant, being
amazed by his first look at a horse, reaching forbidden
things on a table by standing on a basket, and marveling
at his father's shiny bald skull, which had been lavishly
endowed with curls just a decade before when it had been
immortalized by Repin.[1]

Nikita, Shklovskii's only son, died during the final
weeks of the war--on February 8, 1945. The people of
Shklovskii's generation lost many sons. The single sons
of Bagritskii, Olesha, Gor'kii and Tsvetaeva died young,
and the sons of Gumilev and Akhmatova, of Esenin spent
years in the camps. The children of those tried during
the late thirties were used to extract confessions in a
way rendered most immediate not by the statistics, but by
Nabokov's brilliant *Bend Sinister* (1947). One understands
why Nadezhda Iakovlevna is glad that she and Mandelshtam
had no children.

The picture of Shklovskii himself that accrues from
the memoirs is more complicated. In fact, there are two
portraits of Viktor Borisovich in the memoirs and they are
contradictory. The portrait in Volume One is essentially
flattering; the portrait in Volume Two is not. I want to
confine myself to an examination of the portrait in Volume
Two, but let me begin by saying a few words about the portrait in Volume One.

The prevalent conception of Shklovskii's career is
that he submitted to the regime on at least two major

occasions during the twenties, with his books *Zoo or Letters Not about Love* (1923) and *Third Factory* (1926), and that he finally capitulated decisively to the regime with his much-discussed article "A Monument to Scientific Error" (1930).[2] By his readiness to compromise and surrender, he supposedly contributed substantially to--or perhaps even caused--the destruction of the Formalist movement. His handiwork completed in 1930, he supposedly has spent the last forty-five years attentively heeding Party dictates and thereby earning the right to publish.[3]

Yet the first volume of the memoirs contains a dozen words that are of sufficient impact to make us question seriously this conception of Shklovskii's career. Nadezhda Iakovlevna tells us, in no uncertain terms, that Shklovskii actively helped her and her husband during the late thirties--at a time when even their most courageous friends avoided them like the plague. That single fact makes no sense whatsoever if everything that we have assumed about Shklovskii--basically, a lavish concern about saving his own skin, whatever the consequences to others--were true.

I believe that if we look more closely at his career, as her new information demands, we will discover that our assumptions about *Zoo* and *Third Factory* are, at best, oversimplified and, in all likelihood, seriously defective. I believe that if we look more closely at "A Monument to Scientific Error," we will see that it is really a mock surrender--a thin conciliatory veneer with a subtle and devious subtext that in fact amounts to a strong defense of Formalism.[4]

The topic at hand, however, is the portrait in Volume Two, which is perhaps best introduced by a discussion of the discrepancy between the two portraits and the probable cause of that discrepancy. In Volume One, Nadezhda Mandelshtam wanted, above all else, to pay tribute to Shklovskii for his help, to which end she restrained ancient resentments. Having paid him that tribute, she allowed those resentments to emerge in Volume Two.

Nadezhda Iakovlevna is, perhaps understandably, harsh toward those of her countrymen who were less than superhuman during the ordeal. For example, she depicts the twenties as merely the first stage of all the woes that were to follow--and blames the people of the twenties for their complacency and lack of vigilance, but nowhere in her account is the name of Zamiatin ever mentioned--not in either volume, yet without that name no accurate measure of that vigilance can ever be taken. Perhaps it is unfair

to expect objectivity. Certainly, Nadezhda Mandelshtam's
memoirs, in some curious way, attain a monumental truthfulness despite this lack of objectivity--and probably
because of it. Still, her approach, especially in Volume
Two, leads her to be unjust toward certain individuals.
The fact remains, that whenever she speaks about Shklovskii and the Formalists in Volume Two, her observations
do not ring true.

The nature of the problem is made quite clear by the
following passage:

> The Formalists studied formal "devices," the
> stylistic aspects of language, and the interplay
> of literary schools--for instance, the conflict
> between traditionalists and innovators. In
> other words, the Formalists thought on the same
> lines as the representatives of official liter-
> ature. The only difference was the degree of
> sophistication, rather than the substance--the
> people promoting the officially recognized line
> were simply barbarians. Poetry may, of course,
> be studied by any means at all, provided it
> yields points of substantive interest, but
> mechanically picking it over with a pair of
> forceps can only produce specious results. It
> is no accident that the Formalists spent so
> much time on Senkovskii and Benediktov. The
> most attractive of their favorite writers was
> Küchelbecker, Pushkin's friend and the subject
> of an enthusiastic study by Tynianov.[5]

To say that the Formalists lingered on Senkovskii and
Benediktov is, of course, a gross exaggeration, as anyone
even slightly familiar with the movement knows. In his
comprehensive study of the movement, Victor Erlich mentions each of them once. He refers to Benediktov only in
his discussion of Tynianov's work on the problem of what
happened to Russian poetry after the death of Pushkin and
he refers to Senkovskii only in a footnote mentioning
Kaverin's 1929 monograph on the man.[6]

What is the ominous hint lurking in Nadezhda
Iakovlevna's statement that the Formalists had good reasons for their overweening interest in Senkovskii and
Benediktov? One need look no further than D. S. Mirsky,
who describes Benediktov as a writer of meretricious poetry who, during the 1830s, was the "idol of all the romantically inclined officials of every rank throughout

Russia." Senkovskii is described by Mirsky as a "fundamentally cynical man, who had no respect for genius, sincerity, or generous emotion. His smart and witty reviews
and critical surveys poured out contempt and obloquy on
all the best authors of the time. His style, flippant,
facile, tasteless, and cheaply humorous, had an immense
influence on the formation of Russian journalese." The
journal edited by Senkovskii, *Library for Reading*, is described by Mirsky as servile and subservient to the authorities.[7]

Abuse of logic, though, becomes most evident when one
examines closely what happens between the first and the
second sentence of the preceding quotation. The first
sentence is a sober, accurate statement about the Formalists. The second sentence begins with the disarming
phrase "In other words," which prepares the reader for a
restatement or amplification of the first sentence. What
we get instead is a non sequitur of considerable magni-
tude--a leap to the incorrect and slanderous conclusion,
then elaborated in the remainder of the quotation, that
the Formalists and the Bolsheviks more or less worked hand
in glove.

In any case, we begin to see that Nadezhda Mandelshtam
has long nursed a deep-seated antipathy for the Formalists
and this suspicion is reinforced by the following comment:

> Survivors of LEF, people who worked with Tairov,
> Meierkhol'd, and Vakhtangov, former students and
> teachers of IFLI and the Zubov Institute, former
> members of the Institute of Red Professors, old
> Marxists, not to mention the Formalists--they
> would all like us to go back to that time when
> they were young men of thirty, so that we might
> once again set out on the road which they then
> opened up for us--this time without deviating
> from it. In other words, they deny responsibility
> for what happened later. But how can they? It
> was, after all, these people of the twenties who
> demolished the old values and invented the for-
> mulas which even now come in so handy to justify
> the unprecedented experiment undertaken by our
> young state: you can't make an omelet without
> breaking eggs. Every new killing was excused on
> the grounds that we were building a remarkable
> "new" world in which there would be no more vio-
> lence, and that no sacrifice was too great for it.

> Nobody noticed that the end had begun to justify
> the means, and then, as always, had gradually
> been lost sight of. It was the people of the
> twenties who first began to make a neat distinc-
> tion between the sheep and the goats, between
> "us" and "them". . . .[8]

Some serious questions must be asked about this passage. First, why does nostalgia for the twenties on the
part of people involved in the movements of that decade
mean that they are denying responsibility for what happened after 1930? Second, were the Formalists really responsible for what happened after 1930? It is to be
doubted. In this paragraph, one notes that the recurrent
phrase "people of the twenties" is being used in a special
way. The category, as used here, excludes Acmeists. It
includes the Formalists and the Bolsheviks--once again,
roughly equating the two. Proceeding in that fashion, we
arrive quickly at the unthinkable conclusion that it was
the Formalists who demolished the old values, who invented
the infamous omelet formula and who were actually responsible for the killing--they and their colleagues, the Bolsheviks. The process by which we arrive at the conclusion
that Shklovskii, Eikhenbaum, Tynianov, Jakobson are not to
be distinguished from the Bolsheviks in their ruthless
disregard for human life is quite simply indefensible. In
both this and the previously discussed passage, the technique is essentially the same: to tar the Bolsheviks and
the Formalists with the same brush. In both passages, the
phrase "In other words" signals a non sequitur of massive
proportions.

Let us examine one final passage with some care:

> In 1932, an evening reading of Mandelshtam's po-
> etry was arranged in the editorial offices of
> *Literary Gazette* . . . . At this reading,
> Shklovskii wavered for a moment in his attitude
> to Mandelshtam, but was immediately called to
> order by Kirsanov, who reminded him of the dis-
> cipline and unity of views expected of members
> of their group [LEF], and Shklovskii at once
> fell into line. The group whose purity was so
> zealously guarded by Kirsanov also included
> Roman Jakobson and the Aragon family.[9]

People familiar with the twenties and thirties will
be jarred by several elements of this paragraph. To begin

with, LEF was not a viable organization in 1932; in any
case, it is difficult to attach to that organization the
phrase "united front," since it was a startlingly hetero-
genous group, riven by internal dissent and factionalism
almost from its very beginning in 1923. Also, the notion
of Shklovskii's being "called to order" by Kirsanov rings
false. Contrary to the general conception of Shklovskii's
activities, he was not meekly following the Party line
during the early thirties, as I will discuss in more detail very shortly. Finally, it is difficult to contend
with the category that is presented in the last sentence.
The Aragon family presumably includes Aragon and his wife
Elsa Triolet, as well as Lily and Osip Brik--perhaps
Maiakovskii, too; but Jacobson, to the best of my knowledge, was never a member of LEF; moreover, Shklovskii and
Jakobson were not even on good terms in 1932.

How can this animosity toward Shklovskii in Volume
Two be explained? It appears to be fairly simple.
Shklovskii was, above all else, a Futurist, a fact which
has always been known but never sufficiently stressed.
His gods, from at least 1910 to the present day, have always been Maiakovskii and Khlebnikov; he shared, even
helped to form, the Futurist attitude toward Acmeism.
Specifically, his own attitude toward the Acmeists may
perhaps best be summarized by saying that he was not particularly interested in them. Apart from an occasional
fleeting remark interspersed in an article on someone or
something else, he has, I believe, never written about
Akhmatova. His reference to her in *A Sentimental Journey*
supplies the information that she had a marble fireplace
in her apartment. In the same book, he observes that
Gumilev is alien to him, though he strongly protests the
fact that he was shot by the Bolsheviks. He also indicates in that book a certain lack of enthusiasm for
Mandelshtam's poems. He found them overburdened with
proper names and archaic Slavonic words--bordering on the
ludicrous. [10]

That lack of enthusiasm is what Nadezhda Iakovlevna
finds difficult to forgive. What she really seems to resent in Shklovskii, despite her genuine gratitude for his
help during the thirties, is the Futurist orientation that
kept him from wholehearted endorsement of Mandelshtam's
poetry. In that respect, then, her memoirs revive the old
disputes between those rival groups of fifty years ago.
The unfairness results from the fact that Nadezhda
Iakovlevna makes Shklovskii's lack of enthusiasm seem to

stem from a slavish obedience to governmental policies.

It will be remembered that Shklovskii has been depicted by Nadezhda Iakovlevna as meekly quenching his own
impulse toward Mandelshtam in order to follow the line
dictated by Kirsanov. In order to gain some perspective
on her protrait of Shklovskii in the early thirties, let
us examine some outside evidence--in particular, the
events of the year 1933, as they affected Shklovskii and
Mandelshtam.

Though Shklovskii is supposed to have renounced once
and for all the pernicious doctrines of Formalism in 1930,
the *Literary Gazette* was rebuked in 1933 for printing
articles of his between 1930 and 1932 that were "too for-
malistically oriented" and the *Large Soviet Encyclopedia*
described Shklovskii's articles of this period as "based
on false concepts of Formalism."[11] His worst offense was
the article "Southwest," published in January, 1933. Here
he spoke in detail about the important school of Russian
writers that had formed over the years as a kind of en-
clave on Ukrainian soil--a school based in the city of
Odessa, which had nurtured such writers as Bagritskii,
Olesha, Lunts, Kataev, II'f and Petrov, Babel', Nikulin
and Sel'vinskii. Particularly characteristic of this
school was its orientation toward the West--its receptiv-
ity to Western influences, which it reworked and brought
into the mainstream of Russian literature. After discussing the salient features of each writer, he expressed
the hope that they would value their distinctiveness,
which promised to be very important in the future development of Russian literature.[12]

This article caused a furor. Three months later, in
April, 1933, Shklovskii printed a retraction, whose peculiar stilted style calls attention to the fact that the
retraction has been forced. He confesses to the following
heresies: that he had exaggerated the influence of the
West on these writers, that he had failed to show that
these men became real writers only after they had reworked
their worldviews after the revolution, that he had been
wrong to treat the Ukrainian and Russian cultures as two
separate entities, rather than as two branches of a single
entity, etc.[13]

It was in the following month--May, 1933--that
Mandelshtam's long prose work "Journey to Armenia" appeared in *Zvezda*.[14] That piece, like Shklovskii's, provoked a major scandal, which resulted, among other things,
in the dismissal of the editor. Nadezhda Iakovlevna views

this prose as the work that sealed Mandelshtam's doom. The
unfavorable reaction to "Journey to Armenia" culminated in
August, when an attack of major proportions was published
in *Pravda*, where it was described as the "prose of a
lackey." The article also observed:

> The Petersburg of cocottes, government offi-
> cials, priests, decadents, mystics, intellectuals
> "seeking God" and a warm place under the wing of
> the old Russian aristocracy is dead and buried.
> But leftovers from the Petersburg period of lit-
> erature, of the old classes and literary move-
> ments, are still alive: V. Shklovskii, O. Mandel-
> shtam, Vaginov, Zabolotskii. It makes no differ-
> ence that some of them have come down directly
> from the past, while others simply continue its
> traditions.[15]

Of special interest here, apart from the virulence of
the attack, is the fact that Shklovskii and Mandelshtam
were singled out and grouped together as the two writers
"leftover from the past"--those most pernicious. There is
no mistaking the ominous warning that is intended.

Two months later, in October, 1933, Shklovskii published a long important article about Mandelshtam in *The
Literary Critic*. The article, entitled "Pathway to the
Net," begins by describing Mandelshtam as a "prekrasnyi
poet"; his work is described as "prekrasnye stikhi."
Shklovskii makes it clear to the reader that the man being
discussed is one of the major Russian poets of his time.
He then turns to Mandelshtam's prose. Here the discussion
is geared to those aspects of the prose most appealing to
the regime. He says, for instance, that in *The Noise of
Time*, Mandelshtam exhibits his contempt for the prerevolutionary way of life, with its serious attempts to imitate
a British education. In discussing *The Egyptian Stamp*, he
points to Mandelshtam's condemnation of the vigilante justice that flourished between the February and the October
revolutions. His main point about both books, which he
clearly admires, is that in them Mandelshtam exposed the
evils of prerevolutionary Russian society.

Finally, Shklovskii broaches the subject of the much-
maligned "Journey to Armenia." The flavor of his discussion may be conveyed by the fact that he describes the
book as a "journey among grammatical forms, libraries,
words and quotations." He reminds the reader once again
of Mandelshtam's stature, when he refers to him as

an   "ogromnyi poet," but he reaches the conclusion that
the "Journey" falls short of the standard set by Mandelshtam's other prose works--basically because it is too
mannered. This criticism, incidentally, is reminiscent of
the reservations that Shklovskii had expressed in *A Sentimental Journey* about Mandelshtam's poetry. The article
concludes, then, with the anecdote from which its title
derives. Mandelshtam speaks in "Journey to Armenia" about
an exhibition of French Impressionists that he had attended
in Sukhumi. After seeing the dazzling paintings, he found
the real sun and real world that it illuminated dull and
blighted--as if "stuffed into a rope net." Shklovskii
concludes by saying: "Paintings are not made for the purpose of compromising the sun. When art becomes mannered
it is actually we who find ourselves in a cage whose mesh
separates us from the world."[16]
    Students of literature are familiar with the literary
genre known as the mock encomium. Those of us who study
twentieth-century Russian literature have learned to recognize a counterpart genre that might be called the mock
condemnation--that Aesopian technique, in other words,
whereby a writer, under the guise of attacking someone,
conveys information that is officially prohibited and essentially positive in nature. Shklovskii's long article
on Mandelshtam is clearly an example of that genre. By
comparison with the attacks that had just been made on
Mandelshtam and his work, this article, though superfici-
ally critical, looms as strong praise. Shklovskii was
evidently attempting to provide an antidote to the official poison being administered by the authorities. His
only recourse was to remind everyone of Mandelshtam's
stature. Furthermore, he was making that attempt at a
time when he had been under unremitting attack for years
and when he had just been explicitly linked with Mandelshtam as an arch-enemy of the new order.
    In conclusion, then, there are two portraits of
Shklovskii in the memoirs and they are indeed contradictory, but Nadezhda Iakovlevna witnessed and shared the
unspeakable ordeal of her husband and no one can complain
if she now views any conditional support of him with bitterness. On the other hand, it is important to understand what she says from the perspective of the ancient
rivalry between the Futurists and the Acmeists.
    When all is said and done, it is the portrait in
Volume One that matters, providing in a few words evidence
for a new conception of Shklovskii's career. It should

not be forgotten that in the nightmare years of the late
thirties, there was but one house in Moscow where such
pariahs as the Mandelshtams could seek shelter--and that
was the house of Viktor and Vasilisa Shklovskii.

Richard Sheldon
Dartmouth College

NOTES

[1]See Viktor B. Shklovskii, *Tret'ia fabrika* (Moscow:
Krug, 1926), especially the chapters entitled "O Krasnom
slonike" and "Detstvo vtoroe."

[2]Viktor B. Shklovskii, *Zoo ili Pis'ma ne o liubvi*
(Berlin: Helikon, 1923). Modified editions were published
in the Soviet Union in 1924, 1929, 1964 and 1966; and an
English translation taking note of the changes was published by Cornell University Press in 1971. The second
book mentioned is *Tret'ia fabrika*, of which an English
translation will be published by Ardis Press in 1976.
The third work is "Pamiatnik nauchnoi oshibke," *Literaturnaia gazeta*, no. 4 (January 27, 1930), 1.

[3]The interpretation sketchily described in this paragraph is essentially that given by Victor Erlich in his
seminal study of Russian Formalism, *Russian Formalism:
History and Doctrine* (The Hague: Mouton & Co., 1955), of
which later editions appeared in 1963 and 1969. An even
more negative view of Shklovskii may be found in D. G. B.
Piper's book *V. A. Kaverin: a Soviet Writer's Response to
the Problem of Commitment* (Pittsburgh: Duquesne University
Press, 1970).

[4]An attempt to present this side of the question is
made in my article "Viktor Shklovskii and the Device of
Ostensible Surrender," *Slavic Review*, Vol. 34, no. 1
(March, 1975).

[5]Nadezhda Mandelshtam, *Hope Abandoned*, trans. Max
Hayward (New York: Atheneum, 1974), p. 304.

[6]Erlich, *Russian Formalism*, pp. 125 and 231.

[7]D. S. Mirsky, *A History of Russian Literature*, ed.
and abr. by Francis J. Whitfield (New York: Alfred A.
Knopf, 1964), pp. 122, 159-160.

[8]Nadezhda Mandelshtam, *Hope Against Hope*, trans.
Max Hayward (New York: Atheneum, 1970), pp. 167-168.

[9]Mandelshtam, *Hope Abandoned*, p. 335.

[10] Viktor B. Shklovskii, *Sentimental'noe puteshestvie* (Berlin: Helikon, 1923). Heavily censored editions were published in the Soviet Union in 1924 and 1929; and an English translation was published by Cornell University Press in 1970. The comments in this paragraph may be found on page 191 and pages 236-238, of the English translation.

[11] See "Usilit' bor'bu s formalizmom," *Literaturnaia gazeta*, no. 17 (April 11, 1933), p. 1, and also the entry on "Formalizm" in *Bol'shoe sovetskoe entsiklopediia* (Moscow, 1933), Vol. LXII, p. 441.

[12] Viktor B. Shklovskii, "Iugo-zapad," *Literaturnaia gazeta*, no. 1 (January 5, 1933), p. 3.

[13] Viktor B. Shklovskii, "Pis'mo v redaktsiiu," *Literaturnaia gazeta*, 20 (April 29, 1933), p. 4.

[14] Osip Mandelshtam, "Puteshestvie v Armeniiu," *Zvezda*, no. 5 (May, 1933), pp. 103-125.

[15] This passage is quoted by Nadezhda Iakovlevna in her discussion of the unfavorable reaction to "Journey to Armenia" (*Hope Abandoned*, pp. 420-422). The attack in question is the article by S. Rozental called "Teni starogo Peterburga," which appeared in *Pravda* on August 30, 1933.

[16] Viktor B. Shklovskii, "Put' k setke," *Literaturnyi kritik*, no. 5 (October, 1933), pp. 113-117.

REASSESSING OVECHKIN

Patricia Carden

Valentin Ovechkin has an established historical importance as the first voice to speak in the "Thaw." His
sketch, "Raionnye budni" ("Daily Life in the District")
published in September, 1952, before the death of Stalin,
created a sensation by its forthright look at the problems of the countryside. Its publication has justly been
called "an act of great civic and artistic daring."[1] So
important did Ovechkin's work become for the subsequent
history of Soviet literature that his name has become attached to a period of literary history and critics now
write of the "Ovechkin era."[2] The writer Troepolsky said
of him, "It was as though he opened up a massive gate that
had until then been closed. A whole pleiad of writers,
each with his own voice, his own style, rushed in behind
him."[3] By opening up the Soviet countryside as a topic
for a new, analytical and observant literature, Ovechkin
gave a new content to the term "narodnost'." Later his
work was eclipsed by the stories of younger writers who
had profited from his example. Ovechkin came to be looked
upon as a writer who "in his practical immediacy quickly
burned out precisely because of the narrowly practical
nature of the questions he raised."[4]

But the announcements of Ovechkin's literary death
turned out to be greatly exaggerated. His stories and
sketches about country life have recently been reprinted
in an edition of 100,000 copies.[5] The posthumous observ-
ance of his seventieth birthday led to the publication of
a number of memoirs and articles calling attention to his
significance. Excerpts from his notebooks were brought
out. This amounts to a modest Ovechkin renaissance.

Twenty years away from the time of Ovechkin's greatest fame in the early 1950s, we are now in a position to
judge his work apart from the political situation that
formed a part of the significance of its original publication. We can now look at the body of work as a whole
and get a sense of what Ovechkin was like as a writer and
what his contribution was to Soviet literature. We are
dealing here with a body of work of remarkable unity and
integrity, atune with the deepest impulses of the writer's

life and original in style.

In the most extended and evocative memoir of Ovechkin Nikolai Atarov recalls arriving on the Kerch front in 1942 to learn that his friend is serving there. To Atarov's excited questions the chauffeur replies, "He's a free lance" (On po vol'nomu naimu).[6] This phrase becomes the theme of Atarov's *povest'* about Ovechkin. The independence that Ovechkin demonstrates before his superiors, the clear negativism of his estimate of the management of the campaign, remind us that a similarly independent spirit, Solzhenitsyn, ended up in prison as the price of independence. As one reads the anecdotes about Ovechkin recounted by Atarov and other friends, one can but wonder that Ovechkin survived the Stalin period without coming to grief. One is forced back to Ehrenburg's explanation that survival was a matter of luck.

The picture that emerges from recent memoirs is of a man of admirable principle and personal force. Reading of him, I recalled Pavel Ivanych from Chekhov's story "Gusev." Pavel Ivanych says of himself:

> Yes, I always tell people the truth to their
> faces. I'm not afraid of any or anything...
> I am protest personified. I see tyranny--I
> protest, I see a triumphant swine--I protest.
> And I cannot be put down, no Spanish Inquisition
> can silence me. No. Cut out my tongue and I
> will protest with gestures. Wall me up in a
> cellar--I will shout so that you will hear me
> half a mile away, or will starve myself to
> death, so that they may have another weight on
> their black consciences. Kill me and I will
> haunt them. All my acquaintances say to me:
> "You are a most insufferable person, Pavel
> Ivanych." I am proud of such a reputation. I
> serve three years in the Far East and I shall
> be remembered there a hundred years. I had rows
> there with everybody. My friends wrote to me
> from Russia: "Don't come back," but here I am
> going back to spite them... Yes.... That's life as
> I understand it. That's what one can call life.

As for Ovechkin, "he couldn't tolerate unprincipled people, vacillators, double-dealers, time-servers, 'manoeuverers.' He absolutely broke off all relations with them, broke off completely, abruptly, at times even rudely, although not without regret."[7] The parallels with Chekhov

are instructive. Ovechkin, like Chekhov, is keenly aware
of the tyranny of petty men, the Sergeant Prishibeevs of
the Soviet world. He is aware of the force of banal evil
when it is multiplied through the efforts or lack of effort of thousands of men who lack spirit or principle. He
says on one occasion that what is required in the countryside are leaders "u kogo serdtse izbolelos'" (whose hearts
are wrenched). The phrase again is strikingly reminiscent
of the language of Chekhov's concerned heroes (see the
words of Ivan Ivanych in "Gooseberries": "Behind the door
of every contented, happy man there ought to be someone
standing with a little hammer and continually reminding
him with a knock that there are unhappy people...").

Nor is this parallel surprising, for Ovechkin came
directly out of the Chekhovian milieu. Like Chekhov, he
grew up in the provincial town of Taganrog. Like Chekhov
his childhood was spent under the heavy hand of a *samodur*
father. Like Chekhov, as a child he had to help support a
large and needy family.[8] But instead of growing up to be
a Chekhov, Ovechkin, a far simpler man, grew up to be a
Chekhovian character, holding to only one of the many possibilities envisaged by Chekhov with his complex sense of
reality.

Yet in his straightforward adherence to principle,
Ovechkin is beyond reproach. Atarov tells two stories illustrating Ovechkin's brave challenge to the powers during
the difficult years of the purges. In 1937 Ovechkin was
expelled from the Party for defending a friend who had been
unjustly accused of being an "enemy of the people." With
characteristic boldness Ovechkin went to Veshenskaia to
appeal to Sholokhov (whom he did not know), not for himself, but for the friend. And in 1940 when Ovechkin had
just been published in the prestigious journal *Krasnaia
nov'*, had come to Moscow in triumph and been received and
acclaimed at a meeting of the Moscow writers' club, he took
advantage of the occasion to go to a functionary in the
Writer's Union to appeal on behalf of another friend. The
functionary responded: "The times are such, Comrade
Ovechkin, that a man can't even believe himself. I say
that to you as an old communist to a young." Ovechkin's
reply as he marched out the door: "I'll never agree to not
believing in a Party comrade."[9]

Ovechkin's love of truth did in fact lead to his downfall at the height of his influence and popularity. Speaking in 1961 at the Kursk Party Congress, he took exception
to the official line which placed the blame for a disas-

trous harvest upon the weather. Ovechkin, as usual, called
attention to the significance of human factors. As a Soviet writer puts it with discreet understatement, "Ovechkin's speech was received very nervously."[10] Ovechkin was
driven from his native Kursk province. A sick and broken
man he took refuge with his two sons in Tashkent, where to
their credit, the Uzbek writers welcomed him and gave him
a pension.

Ovechkin was a difficult, intractable character. The
wary diffidence that he depicts in officials having to deal
with his alter-ego characters must have come directly from
personal experience. But his pugnaciousness is so in-
gratiating that one can also equally believe in the affection and respect that these same characters so naturally
receive. One cannot help smiling fondly upon reading his
outraged letter to the Minister of Communications of the
U.S.S.R., N.D. Psyrtseva, complaining about the length of
time required for an air mail letter to arrive.[11] Pavel
Ivanych, indeed.

The journalism and stories are very much of a piece
with Ovechkin's character. Ovechkin's fullest fame came
on the wave of controversy generated by Pomerantsev's famous article on sincerity. Pomerantsev's praise of
Ovechkin's sketch "Borzov and Martynov" made him a symbolic center of the "new" literature. And yet in fact
many of the qualities that were to be considered so daring
in the cycle *Raionnye budni* are apparent in the earlier
work. Atarov speaks of the "intimacy" of the stories published in *Krasnaia nov'* in 1940, an intimacy that was felt
at the time to be in sharp contrast to other stories about
collective farms.[11] Two of the stories "Oshibka" and
"Praskovya Maksimovna" are centered around the typical
Ovechkin character--a trouble-maker who refuses to go
along and fit in.

Grandfather "Oshibka" ("Mistake") earns his nickname
because he goes about the collective farm starting rows
over the many mistakes that careless or poorly-trained
workers make. His constant harassment and refusal to keep
still become so troublesome that he is finally expelled
from the commune. But the political commissar, hearing
about the case, comes to understand the valuable experience embodied in the old man and prevails upon the commune
to readmit him as a work inspector. The story's freshness
comes from the vivid depiction of the intransigent old
man. The commissar Pavlov strikes up a conversation with
Grandad when he meets him on the street. Grandad, not

knowing who Pavlov is, answers with his customary sarcasm.

> Pavlov asks Grandad: "Well, Grandad, how are things
> going on the kolkhoz?"
> "Smooth as butter," answers Grandad. "They're
> working two shifts."
> "What do you mean, two shifts?"
> "Like this: one group sleeps and the other fans
> the flies."[13]

The same delight in the troublemaker is apparent in
his sketch of the Stakhanovite farm worker Praskovya
Maksimovna. Far from subscribing to Soviet cant about
production, Ovechkin concentrates entirely on the petty
persecutions and hindrances to work that Praskovya
Maksimovna suffers as a result of the envy, ignorance and
resistance to change of the other collective farmers. Her
wit and malice in getting revenge and countering the opposition to her new methods of cultivation are described
with relish.

Ovechkin's popular novella published during World War
II, *Greetings from the Front*, has as its chief character a
"goriachii kapitan" Spivak who first frightens and then
entertains the people in his railway car by his fierce
attacks on a smug opportunist whose favorite excuse for
taking advantage of every situation is "After all, it's
wartime." Spivak, provoked to rage, challenges him:

> "Citizen, I see that you're going to live much
> worse when the war's over."
> "Why?" the passenger looked up.
> "You're going to lose your slogan. You're go-
> ing to lose the ground under your feet."[14]

This concentration on the troublemaker is carried over into
the work that was to make Ovechkin's enduring reputation,
Raionnye budni. The two heroes of that work, Martynov and
Dolgushin, are "uneasy souls" in the nineteenth-century
tradition of the *intelligent*. Even beyond that, the work
is filled with a whole gallery of lesser characters each
of whom is in his own way "protest personified." Perhaps
one of Ovechkin's greatest contributions is his giving
form to the unrest that is felt on every level and in
every sphere in Russian society. Martynov and Dolgushin
seem less and less futile Don Quixote figures and more and
more a part of the mainstream, spokesmen for the very center of public opinion.

Protest is an empty gesture without a program and the body of Ovechkin's work is concerned with setting forth that program. In its general outlines it is clear and straightforward. Its points are these:

1. Devotion to efficiency, modern technology and practical knowledge in the organization of work.

2. Care for the workers' well-being, shown not merely through practical measures but through spontaneous heart-felt acts.

3. Self-sacrificing, modest leadership.

4. General civility.

There is little to object to in these principles and Ovechkin's importance come not from his espousing them, but from the passion and wholeness of his devotion.

What is the special vision of the countryside that animates Ovechkin's work (for the dialogues that compose Ovechkin's sketches are based upon a constant vision that does not change, are attempts to draw that vision together with reality)? The 'narodnost'" of his work rests upon two points: deep love of the land and feeling for its rhythms of rest and fecundity and the ways in which human labor depends upon those rhythms; and a belief in the public life of action and discourse. The dialogues of the stories are tautly stretched between these two points. As Efim Dorosh has observed, a great deal of the country is left out in these stories. In fact, the whole middle is left out--that complex organization of the daily life of the village that joins the tilling of the soil on one hand to the great bureaucratic machine of social organization on the other. It is not that Ovechkin is unknowing of the villagers' needs of life--on the contrary, a fundamental part of his "program" is that Soviet agriculture must be humanitarian, that it exists to serve the people and not they it--yet he feels no need to enlarge descriptively upon that life.

Some mention needs to be made of the reason for his "gap" in Ovechkin's depiction. It is in fact, the blindness of the man who stands inside the frame and is himself part of the picture. As an insider, and Ovechkin naturally and unselfconsciously writes from the position of the insider, he takes many things for granted. The village is not exotic to him and he indulges very little in the kind of ethnographic description of scene and character familiar to us from *The Sportsman's Sketches* and taken up anew by many contemporary writers about village life. As Felix Kuznetsov has pointed out, most of the practitioners of

"derevenskaia proza" are the sons of peasants.[15] But
this has not precluded the adoption by many of these
authors of the role of observer, even outsider. Kuznetsov
points to the difference in attitude between Soloukhin,
who takes an "aesthetic" view of the village and decries
the introduction of radio and television as corrupters of
the cultural heritage, and Yashin who, speaking as an
"insider," shows the meaning to the villagers of having
their lives extended by these instruments of communication
with a larger world.

Ovechkin's attitude is far from Soloukhin's nostalgia. The man who is within the landscape and takes it for
granted does not feel nostalgia for it. Aware of the
weight of the past, his aspirations are nevertheless projected towards the future, towards what is developing and
yet to come. In his notebook he writes: "We live in a
time when the past is regrettably more understandable and
closer to us than the future."[16] Ovechkin's work is permeated with the optimism of the future-oriented man.
Writing in difficult times, he nevertheless praises action
and change, proposes programs. He does not have the paradoxical "gains-losses" view of the present and future
characteristic of writers who followed him like Belov.
Ovechkin "knew the village as no one else among our writers" as his friend Georgii Radov writes in a memoir.[17] He
was, "in love with the [kolkhozes] from the time in the
twenties when he organized a commune." Ovechkin writes as
a committed "new man" who has come up under the Soviet
system, has imbibed the ideals of the Revolution and
thinks in the terms of those ideals.

One striking feature of his writing from within the
frame, being himself a chief part of the picture, is that
he sees the life of the village and the peasant differently from the traditional Russian *intelligent*, standing outside to "liubovat'sia." When his alter ego, Martynov,
goes into the fields and villages he observes with a knowing eye that calls forth the enthusiastic agreement of the
peasants. His expertise, coming from Ovechkin's own involvement and knowledge, is persuasive.

There are moments in the writing that are masterful
in their depiction of the insider's appreciative grasp of
the art of his labor, conveyed in his own vernacular:

> Mikhailo Potapovich stops next to a horse-drawn
> seeder. He squats, attentively examines the
> bolt, pressing one of the plough shares against

the cam of the disc, asks the blacksmith for the
wrench, tries the screw with the wrench. And so
it is. The bolt is threaded left-handed, the
screw is tightened in the direction of the disc's
turning. The first trip down the furrow, the
screw will jam and the disc won't turn.
Mikhailo Potapovich shows the blacksmiths their
mistake. They agree. One runs to the smithy,
brings another bolt and replaces the wrong one
on the spot. But Korzhov doesn't get up. He
sits under the seeder, looks over the plough-
shares, thinks about something.

"Tell the truth," he glances over his shoulder
at the senior blacksmith from the "Red Caucasus,"
Trofim Mironovich Kandeev.
"What do you do when the cam on the disc wears
loose? Do you wrap it with a patch?"
"Well, yes," answers Kandeev.
"A tin one?"
"Yes, tin."
"And the tractors, too?"
"Yes, the tractors, too."
"That's the reason why your rows look like a
road where a bull pissed," said Korzhov and got
up. "You've got ten blacksmiths here and you
didn't think it out for yourselves. A patch
isn't the thing. It will either fold up so that
it jams completely or in two days it will crack
and the disc will be left hanging again.
"There's no other way to do it," said Kandeev.
"You've got to spread the cam."
"How can you spread it when it's steel and
cemented in?"
"You can. Not with a hammer, of course. Easily,
carefully."
"No, you can't," Kandeev said stubbornly.
"It doesn't matter how careful you are, its
going to break into bits."
"You can't?" Take off a disc and let's go into
the smithy."...

Ovechkin's material is of a sort that is easy to pat-
ronize. In his famous story "Borzov and Martynov" the
chief female character, Marya Sergeevna, is a former tractor driver who has the order of Lenin. The characters
argue earnestly about the good of agriculture. Marya

Sergeevna, the wife of the villain Borzov, invites Martynov
to an intimate tête à tête where they discuss--how to get
the lagging collective farms to produce to capacity! The
coincidence of Ovechkin's materials with the novels of
collectivization which were a prominent feature of official Soviet literature of the 1930s and 40s and the
sharply polemical style of his writings have led to the
opinion that his work is simply "Socialist Realism turned
upside down."

Ovechkin's work has been given much more careful and
serious attention by the Soviet critic, Ivan Vinogradov.
In a commemorative article for Ovechkin's sixtieth birthday, published in *Novyi mir* in 1964 and later incorporated
into his book on "derevenskaia proza,"[18] Vinogradov gives
a sensitive explication of the social and political subtleties underlying Ovechkin's point of view as it developed during the course of the publication of his sketches
in the 1950s. Vinogradov's theme is the "put' poznaniia"
or developing consciousness of the life of the people as
expressed in the literature of the 1950s. This emphasis
on cognitive process characterizes his approach to
Ovechkin's work taken separately--he draws for us the
emerging and developing consciousness of the agricultural
problem in the cycle *Raionnye budni*--as well as his approach to village prose as a phenomenon of Soviet intellectual life. He is a sensitive critic and he makes
artistic judgments that are provocative and acute, yet
there remains the possibility of a different kind of examination of the writers covered, an examination that
focuses more intensively on the special forms of individual writers. The developmental or chronological approach
inevitably involves some degree of distortion. This is
apparent in two ways in Vinogradov's analysis of Ovechkin.
The first is that he is in fact trying to unfold into a
linear process an artistic development that took place in
a few brief years and was in fact much folded in upon itself. For example, it seems to Vinogradov that Troepolsky's story "Sosedi" which appeared in 1956 came out "much
later" than the first sketch of "Raionnye budni" which was
published in 1952.[19] The second is that he inadvertently
distorts Ovechkin's own process of development in his attempt to show a clear movement from early writings to
later.[20]

Ovechkin's work has also been obscured by the partisan
criticism of the factions within "village prose." Those
who take a position in favor of technological progress in

the countryside find a rallying point in Ovechkin. Those
who tend towards nostalgia for the values represented by
(or imposed upon) the village life of the past see his
work as passé. The recent interest in Ovechkin's work
comes partly from the renewed virulence of this argument
between the new "Westernizers" and "Slavophiles."[21]

Even those critics who have been sympathetic to
Ovechkin's ideological position or who have admired his
courage have taken the position that there are grave lacks
in his writing when judged from the artistic point of
view. These judgments are based on traditional conceptions of form. For example, it is argued that Ovechkin
fails to distinguish among the voices of his characters,
all of whom are spokesmen for the author's point-of-view.
Efim Dorosh, who has often benefitted from the critics'
comparison of his work to Ovechkin's, suggests that instead of condemning these features of Ovechkin's work, we
might better consider each of these departures from narrative norms as "svoistvo pisatelia."[22]

Every critic grants Ovechkin the significance of his
influence in bringing the genre of the *ocherk* (or sketch)
back into prominence. In the history of Russian literature the ocherk has established two especially strong
traditions for itself: as a means to convey the chaos and
immediacy of war and revolution and as a path to explora-
tion of the alien (to the *intelligentsia* and nobility and
town-bred new classes) life of the countryside. Many of
the works dealing with the countryside (for example, a
number of *The Sportsman's Sketches*) can well claim the
title of short story. There is a substantial critical
literature that attempts to make distinctions between
those works which retain the marks of the *ocherk* as a
specific genre and those works that "violate" its boundaries.[23] Yet when one looks at these works from the thematic
point of view, their likenesses often seem more important
than formal differences.

There is a natural tension in the genre of the *ocherk*
between its primarily didactic and publicistic aims and
the belles-lettristic possibilities inherent in any description. In fact, the chief distinction that gives the
ocherk continuity as a genre seems to be its relationship
to the events it describes rather than any specific demands of form. It is an appropriate form for dealing with
contemporary events whose meaning has not yet emerged on
an historical scale and which are not fully assimilated by
the author into a world view or statement. Often it

represents a working out of significances by the author
and its tone is problematical. Ovechkin often carries on
an implicit dialogue with himself about what values should
be given priority in collective farm life.

The *ocherk* presents itself primarily as a form of
witnessing and thus there is always a witness, a learner,
a seeing "I" who forms the experience for us. This "I"
may intrude to a greater or lesser degree. In the *Sportsman's Sketches*, the center of gravity shifts sharply towards the narrator and his consciousness. Ovechkin at
first appears to be a much more reticent narrator than
Turgenev and intrudes himself very little upon the sketch
in the author's voice. His most common intrusion is precisely to remind the reader that there is a witness to the
events. In "V odnom kolkhoze" the narrator intervenes for
the first time ten pages into the story: "Many times in
another setting I had the opportunity to hear Nazarov's
stories about what had been lived through and accomplished
on the kolkhoz in five years." This intrusion calls our
attention to the fact that such judgments in the story as
"Nazarov's speech was rather dry" come from an eyewitness.
Ovechkin's strong dependence on dialogue as a form of exposition may well be related to his sense of the limitations of the eyewitness narrator as well as to his fine
ear for colloquial speech.

And yet, the reticence of Ovechkin's narrator is deceptive. The author actually intrudes upon the work to a
far greater degree than does Turgenev's narrator, for the
chief characters in Ovechkin's sketches are alter egos of
the author, projections of his own thinking and concerns.
Where Turgenev's narrator is looking at an alien group,
the peasants, and seeking to understand them, the chief
figures in Ovechkin's work are party members and acti-
vists--District Secretaries of the Party, chairmen of
collective farms and managers of Machine Tractor Stations,
who far from being observed from outside, are given the
substance of the author's own thinking and concerns. As
has often been noted, Ovechkin is not really much interested in the "folk" of the countryside except in a general
way, in the mass, as the problem to be considered. (This
is all the more surprising given the clearly humane and
person-centered thrust of his criticism of Soviet agricultural organization.) Ovechkin dramatizes far more directly
than Turgenev the *intelligent's* dilemma of understanding.
His dialogue with himself now occupies the whole of the
work and its processes are limited entirely to the absorp-

tion by his consciousness of the facts and his meditation
upon them.

One curious feature of Ovechkin's form is the process
of "twinning" in the characters. In conventional Socialist realist literature, the form depends on a fairly simple, black-and-white opposition between characters. The
"villains" of Ovechkin's work tend to recede into the
background or if like Borzov, who gave his name to a whole
phenomenon of Soviet life (*borzovshchina*, meaning the
overbearing behavior of functionaries who lose sight of
genuine goals in their desire to carry out directives and
fulfill the plan), they occupy an important place, their
very energy introduces something equivocal into the characterization and leads almost to a grudging respect.
Among the characters who speak for the author, the "twinning" process invariably takes place in which two or more
alter egos emerge, the second a more idealized version of
the first.

This phenomenon is first clearly demonstrated in the
sketch "V odnom kolkhoze" where the District Secretary of
the Party Nazarov and the chairman of the kolkhoz Staro-
dubov are almost identical in their characteristics: both
are heroes of the war, both have refused the *Pobeda* that
they are entitled to in order to use the money for the
general welfare, both are intensely interested in improv-
ing the state of agriculture and so on. These two men, who
should be natural allies and friends, feel a good deal of
unease with each other though they feel mutual respect.
The sketch meditates upon this anomaly, demonstrating
Ovechkin's interest in the subtleties of human psychology.

In *Raionnye budni* Ovechkin prepares a fate for his
chief character that surely must be one of the strangest
fates in literature. The District Party Secretary Martynov, who is the representative of the Ovechkinian virtues
in the first half of the book, is displaced in the latter
half of the book by a new figure, Dolgushin, who possesses
all of Martynov's virtues and is prepared to advance the
same program, but who is superior to Martynov in one critical point, his intense natural interest in the personal
lives and fates of the people of the village. Martynov
cannot help feeling envious of the larger magnanimity of
this new figure and is uneasy with him, but he nevertheless resigns his own position as District Secretary and
proposes Dolgushin for it. It is as though Ovechkin were
concurring with the frequent criticism of his own limited
interest in the daily lives of the villagers. This

intensity of self-examination is one of the most persuasive
features of the book.

The "twinning" in the characters is matched by
Ovechkin's form of exposition which consists for the most
part of long dialogues in which two characters deliver
extended statements to each other. Oftener than not, the
characters are in basic agreement and so the form moves
away from argument and towards contemplation, becomes a way
of enlarging upon the many ramifications of a question.
The work keeps moving, changing, the quest for a better
answer does not come to an end. Perhaps even more significant, the presence in the work of a chorus of voices
echoing and enlarging upon the main theme gives the sense
of an emerging consensus of opinion. Ovechkin himself has
called attention to the choral effect of his plays, "A
play ought to sound like a symphony, like a chorus. Various voices are singing, but one tune."[24] Ovechkin thus
overcomes the impression that his chief figures tend to
give of being embattled loners, fighting for unpopular
positions.

If we are to do justice to Ovechkin's work, a more
precise definition of its formal characteristics needs to
be made. Upon examination the work does turn out to have
formal coherence, though its features are not derived from
either the lyrical or narrative traditions in literature.
Ovechkin's works belong rather to the tradition of oratory
that "catches the rhythm of history, that seizes on a crucial event or phase of action, interprets it, articulates
the emotions concerned with it, or in some means employs a
verbal structure to insulate and conduct the current of
history."[25]

Much of Ovechkin's adult life was spent in the exercise of his own oratorical powers: as a functionary of the
Party, as an agitator among Soviet soldiers during World
War II, and as a constant debater with his friends and acquaintances. Atarov says that Ovechkin's favorite word
was "rugat'sia." He looked forward to coming to Moscow
for extended arguments with his old friends: "Budem
rugat'tsa." "Towards the end of a conversation he became
raptly serious and thought so powerfully and infectiously
that next to him you caught the desire to reflect and in
that he saw the chief significance of his intercourse with
you."[26] Atarov found extensive notes among Ovechkin's
papers for the talks that he made to soldiers at the front:
"As an agitator he knew that you have to know how to begin
the talk with a joke and when you criticize them, then it

has to be jovially:...Or he thought up funny, harmless
surnames: Razdobud'ko, Tsiferblat, Slabchuk..."[27]
    Ovechkin repeatedly criticizes the deadness of offi-
cial oratory.

> A woman was reading a speech page by page halt-
> ing painfully after every word:
>   "Our attainments...are the result of
> stubborn...labor and highlyconscious...relation-
> ships...Exceptionally great attention...is given
> to the nurture...of suckling pigs...The farrow
> is raised...in a clean, dis...infected pen...
> Employing abundant and varied...feed for swine...
> and young ones, creating favorable conditions for
> them, we attained...the result from the sows of
> healthy and viable offspring...Now we set our-
> selves the task...by these means...to raise the
> productivity of livestock management."
>   She even stopped in the places where uplift
> and animation were required. "Having adopted
> living...lively competition, we take on the ob-
> ligation..."
>   At the end of the speech, she mixed the
> pages, lost her place, got upset and left the
> rostrum without finishing the sentence.
>   Martynov got up to announce the intermission.
>   "Is the Party Secretary from the Friendship
> Kolkhoz here?" he asked in a voice that was
> hoarse from a cold.
>   "Here," a man in an officer's overcoat with-
> out shoulder-straps got up in the back row.
>   "Comrade Mostovoi, did you write her speech
> for her?"
>   "Together with the chairman of the kolkhoz."
>   "Well, so you really worked at it! The best
> livestock manager in the district. She made
> your farm into a showplace. She had what it takes
> to do that, but to give a speech here, to tell
> about her work without your crib notes--it appears
> you're afraid she can't manage that? Don't be
> embarrassed about making a bad speech, Comrade
> Goncharova. It's not your fault, it's ours.
> Before I announce the intermission, here's what
> I want to say, comrades." Martynov glanced at
> the instructor of the *oblast'* Party committee who
> was sitting on the rostrum, because he foresaw a
> clash with him. There were long-standing

disagreements with this instructor, Golubkov,
who often came to their district. "Let's make
an agreement: Let anyone who doesn't have anything sensible to say not make speeches here,
taking up everyone's time. We don't need ac-
tivism just for the sake of bookkeeping: 'Such
and such a percentage of those present spoke at
the meeting.' What matters is, what did we
talk about and to what point? Nikolenko here
repeated his address that we had already read
three days ago in the newspaper. The Party
group meets for business-like discussion of
problems and not for speeches for the sake of
speeches..."[28]

Ovechkin does not reject the importance of oratory and official meetings as would many of the younger generation of
writers. He does not turn away from the public life to a
private lyricism. When everyone is weighed under by a
dead official rhetoric, lyricism may appear to be a way to
cleanse the language and restore the moral climate of a
century. But in fact, as Ovechkin realizes, oratory itself needs to be renewed so that there can be genuine public discourse. In the most impish of his sketches, "About
some conferences that have not yet taken place," he proposes that instead of constantly holding conferences for
the exemplary kolkhozes and workers, the Party ought to
hold a conference for the laggards. His peasant spokesman says:

They're always conferring with the frontrunners. But if I went in now and asked to say
a word, you just look, they wouldn't let me
speak. They'd just laugh. They'd say, "Who are
you to get up with the swells. You aren't fit
to get up on that rostrum. Only the frontrunners
are gathered here, famous people..." And what
are we to do, the unknown people? How are we to
get free from our shame? If we aren't fit to
sit together with the frontrunners, then they
could have us get together separately, without
honors, without music, not even in an auditorium,
but maybe somewhere outside of town, in the
woods, and then they could talk with us there.
But let them listen instead of abusing us. We'd
tell them a thing or two! Who knows about our
lives better than we do? Not a single front-

runner worries about us the way we do. They've
already forgotten the time when they got kopeks
for a work-day...[29]

In a brilliant article on style in contemporary Soviet literature, the Soviet critic Marianna Chudakova observes that the resurgence of first-person narrative in
the 1950s and early 60s was related to the reestablishment
of "the sacred right of personal opinion."[30] Perhaps we
can see Ovechkin's most profound contribution to the sense
of "narodnost'" in his desire that there be a national
forum for the people in which their problems can be heard
and given heartfelt attention. One of the living traditions of the language that Soviet literature can draw upon
is precisely its tradition of oratory--not the dead oratory of prepared speeches, but the living oratory of such
natural propagandists and inspired speakers as Ovechkin.
His greater contemporary Solzhenitsyn makes extensive use
of these oratorical possibilities in the language of the
people. Ovechkin's impassioned regard for truth, the tone
and spirit of his works, draws him closer to Solzhenitsyn
stylistically than almost any other writer of the Thaw.
In both writers' works one finds the same central character, the troublemaker who won't be beaten down, who keeps
his spirit intact in the face of the most discouraging
opposition. Such wholeness of being can in itself furnish
an adequate style if the author holds stubbornly to its
essence. Ovechkin had the good sense to find his form and
so the vigor and special quality of his writing continue
to assure him a place in the reader's attention.

Cornell University
Ithaca, New York

NOTES

[1]I. Vinogradov, "Derevenskie ocherki Valentina
Ovechkina," *Novyi mir*, 1964, no. 6, p. 217.
[2]See for example, the article by Felix Kuznetsov,
"Sud'by derevni v prose i kritike," *Novyi mir*, 1973, no. 6,
p. 233.
[3]Quoted by Vladimir Kantorovich, "Delat' pravdu: Valentin Ovechkin i sovremennyi ocherk," *Voprosy literatury*,
1974, no. 6, p. 154.

[4]M. Lobanov, *Muzhestvo chelovechnosti.* Quoted by Kuznetsov, p. 246.

[5]*Gosti v Stukachakh.* Moscow: 1972.

[6]"Dal'naia doroga," *Novyi mir*, no. 9, 1973, p. 109.

[7]Mikhail Kolosov, preface to *Gosti v Stukachakh*, p. 7.

[8]Ibid., p. 8.

[9]Atarov, p. 114.

[10]Vladimir Kantorovich is the first Soviet writer to mention this episode openly in print. "Delat' pravdu...," p. 168.

[11]*Literaturnaia gazeta*, 1960, October 2.

[12]Atarov, p. 112.

[13]*Gosti v Stukachakh*, p. 29.

[14]*Izbrannye proizvedeniia v dvukh tomakh.* Moscow: 1963, p. 21.

[15]"Sud'by derevni...," p. 235.

[16]V. Ovechkin, *Stat'i, dnevniki, pisma.* Moscow: 1972, p. 218.

[17]*Literaturnaia gazeta*, June 26, 1974.

[18]"Derevenskie ocherki Valentina Ovechkina," *Novyi mir*, 1964, no. 6. *V otvete u vremeni: zametiki o derevenskom ocherke piatidesiatykh godov.* Moscow: 1966. Vinogradov's interpretation of Ovechkin has been concurred with in its essential points by Professor Gleb Zekulin, "Aspects of Peasant Life as Portrayed in Contemporary Soviet Literature," *Canadian Slavic Studies*, Winter, 1967.

[19]*V otvete u vremeni*, p. 29.

[20]Ovechkin's just anger at Vinogradov for the oversimplification of his position is discussed in detail by Atarov.

[21]Kuznetsov's 1973 article is a forceful presentation of the "Westernizer" argument and calls attention to the main arguments of his opponents.

[22]"Zametki o literaturnoi kritike," *Znamia*, 1954, no. 11.

[23]For a discussion of this controversy and an attempt to make distinctions see L. Emel'ianov, "Estetika zhanra" in *Geroi sovremennoi literatury*. Moscow-Leningrad: 1963.

[24]*Stat'i, dnevniki, pis'ma*, p. 204.

[25]Northrup Frye, *Anatomy of Criticism.* New York: 1968, p. 310. The category of oratorical forms in Russian literature has not been extensively studied, but there are excellent, isolated pieces of criticism that illuminate it: Eremin's brilliant study of the forms of "krasnorechie" in old Russian literature (*Lektsii po drevnei russkoi literatury*), Tynianov's work on the 18th century ode, and

Bakhtin's work on the "polyphonic" structure of Dostoevsky's novels.

[26] Atarov, p. 134.

[27] Ibid., p. 129.

[28] *Izbrannye proizvedeniia*, vol. 2, p. 144.

[29] *Gosti v Stukachakh*, p. 274.

[30] "Zametki o sovremennoi prozy," *Novyi mir*, 1972,
no. 1.

EFIM DOROSH

Gleb Žekulin

Efim Dorosh[1] and his main work – *The Countryside Diary (DD)*[2] are well known to Soviet readers and often referred to by Soviet critics. However, neither in the S. U. nor in the West, have they received the attention which, in my view, they deserve.[3]

In this short study an attempt will be made to show the originality of *DD* and its uncommonness even in the context of Soviet literature of the late 1950s and the 1960s. Further, the attempt will be made to draw some conclusions as to the author's views of the concept of *narodnost'*, a concept which is of primary importance to every publicly active artist in the S. U., and to assess the impact *DD* made on the Soviet literature contemporary to it. In preparing this paper, I have used extensively Dorosh's post-1953 writings other than those which constitute *DD* and have found them to be of considerable interest both because they complement and, in some cases, explain his *DD*, and because they have a merit of their own.

When in 1956, in the now famous second volume of *Literaturnaia Moskva*, there appeared in the section entitled *Ocherki* Dorosh's "Derevensky dnevnik," there was no indication that this 'sketch' of some 90,000 words represented only the first part of a work which would take the author 15 years and about a quarter of a million words to complete. The first critical reaction, found in general reviews of *Literaturnaia Moskva*, welcomed, on the whole, the appearance of a work which followed, in its own peculiar manner, the example of V. Ovechkin's *Rayonnye budni*. The more thorough reviews, which appeared in the period 1958-62, continued, in general, this view and ranked Dorosh's work—by now, of course, augmented by two to four further installments—among the best created by the group of *'ocherkisty'* consisting of Ovechkin, Troepol'sky, Tendriakov, Soloukhin ("Vladimirskie prosielki"), Yu. Kazakov ("Prokliaty sever"), Fomenko, L. Ivanov, Zalygin, Mozhaev, Nosov and a few others.

But we had to wait for the later articles and studies, particularly by Turkov, Starikova and I. Vinogradov,[4] to

notice that Dorosh's sketches began to be singled out. It
was in V. Lakhshin's article "Tri mery vremeni," published
on the occasion of *Novy Mir*'s recommendation of Dorosh's
sketches up to and including the sixth instalment "Dozhd'
popolam s solntsem" ("DPS")[5] for the Lenin Prize, that *DD*
was described for the first time as a work which contributes, in a quite specific manner, to the knowledge and understanding of Soviet reality.[6] As on another, earlier
occasion,[7] the Lakshin article, by emphasising the uncommon aspects of Dorosh's work, turned out to be the last
thorough, thoughtful and nonconformist analysis of *DD*.
Its last two parts were received in the S. U. with subdued reaction. Even after Dorosh's death the reviews of
the latest edition of *DD*, though praising it in hackneyed
terms, dealt in meaningless generalities and did not attempt to put the by now completed work into any kind of
perspective.[8]

The reasons for such treatment are to be found, I
feel, in the work itself. What began, in 1956, as a
'countryside sketch' (*derevensky ocherk*), that differed
only in its manner of presenting the material from the
growing mass of works of this genre, reached out, with the
publication of "DPS," into the sphere which, by the standing Soviet rules, was forbidden. If the first five parts
of *DD* were at times very critical of the realities of Soviet countryside, and suggested improvements, changes, and
even drastic reforms, they were, still, conceived within
the framework of officially sponsored and supported inves-
tigations of the reasons for the 'retardation' (*otstavanie*)
of agriculture. Other sketch writers, in what seems today
to have been the 'bright Khrushchev years,' were at times
possibly even sharper and more radical in their criticism
of mistakes and mismanagement by, or sheer incompetence of,
those responsible for agriculture. But we do not find
that, because of this, their works were neglected by critics or practically silenced, as was the case with the parts
of *DD* which followed "DPS." What distinguished the latter
from other countryside sketches was its shift in emphasis
from 'what is wrong and, therefore, ought to be corrected'
to 'what kind of values are being destroyed and how.'[9]

The shift became truly a break in the last two instalments of *DD*, "Ivan Fedoseevich ukhodit na pensiiu"
("IFU") and "Piatnadtsat' let spustia" ("PLS") which represent Dorosh's reassessment of the quality of Soviet life
as a whole, not of the backward countrylife alone, and his
attempt to propose a different set of values which would,

perhaps, bring a universal remedy to the peoples of the
U.S.S.R. In this respect, the concluding parts of *DD*
could have been seen by the authorities as having been
written in the spirit of 'dissent.'

    But how and why did the shift to a qualitatively dif-
ferent "diary" occur?
    Dorosh's first visit to Raygorod and its surroundings
was on the request of the newspaper for which he worked.
He "wrote and published a sketch,"[10] and never expected to
go back to these places: this had been a normal journalist's assignment, and the writing of the sketch ("Ivan
Fedoseevich") had been routine work. But "something drew
(him) to the shore of the calm lake Kaovo, to Raygorod
with its old Kremlin, to Uzhbol which stretches itself on
the slope of a hillock, to Lyubogostitsy and Veksa which
stand on the shores of languid rivers rich in fish, to the
ancient Ugozhi..."[11] This 'something' could have been, as
Dorosh remarks, the "unostentatious nature" of the district, or the "smart, quick-witted people who, for almost
a thousand years, have tilled the soil," or "the history
of these settlements which were the most ancient in Russia,
as well as their eventful present day with its economic,
domestic and cultural problems,"[12] or a combination of all
of these. From then on he returned regularly to the district and entered regularly in his diary notes on all
that he saw and heard. These notes grew in number, covered more than the merely observable, began to include
historical references, comparisons, thoughts and feelings,
speculations and meditations. Thus, the peculiar form of
DD was born, the form which he himself called "life in motion."[13]
    Dorosh was lucky that his 'boss' in *Novy Mir*, where,
beginning with its third part--"Dva dnia v Raygorode,"--
his *DD* found its permanent home, was A. T. Tvardovsky; also that he began writing it under Khrushchev's rule. We
now know that Tvardovsky's "personal tragedy" was the
'dekulakization' (*raskulachivanie*),[14] his father and the
whole family having been displaced beyond the Urals, and
that only the future poet, who at the time was studying in
the city, "survived by accident."[15] We also know that
Khrushchev did not, in fact, firmly believe in the collectivisation of agriculture.[16] Thus, in Khrushchev Dorosh
found a political leader who could be expected not to in-
terfere with his searches; in Tvardovsky he found a kindred spirit and a willing helper.[17]

But the March 1965 Plenum of the Central Committee of
the CPSU which denounced Khrushchev's "voluntaristic pro-
ject-making" (voliuntaristskoe prozhektorstvo), coupled
with the new agricultural policies announced at the XXIIIrd
Party Congress which claimed to have solved definitely the
main problems in the countryside, put an end to open criticism of shortcomings in the kolkhozes and sovkhozes. The
'countryside sketch' as it had developed over the previous
13 years or so had outlived, in the official view, its
usefulness and, therefore, practically ceased to exist. In
all fairness, however, it should be noted that by that time
the limited demands, as they had been formulated by the
bulk of writers in this genre, had been satisfied to a
great extent by the official policies. Two of the most
prominent sketch writers, Ovechkin and Dorosh, disagreed
with this view. Ovechkin[18] was hounded for his noncon-
formism and died in disgrace in January 1968, having been
expelled from the Party. Dorosh was more circumspect:
when finally, in January 1969, the next instalment of his
DD--"IFU"--appeared in print, he briefly acknowledged in
the introduction the successes of official measures concerning agriculture. And he could well do this because,
by this time, he was concerned less with the material or
technical specifics in the countryside than with the quality of peasant life and, hence,--in his view--of life in
general in the Soviet Union.

Particular incidents, in "IFU" as in previous instalments, referred to what went wrong in kolkhozes, but the
number of incidents had considerably diminished. We see
Dorosh, as before, protesting vigorously the interference
from outside and from above with the reasonable and sound
decisions made by the experienced and knowledgeable till-
ers of soil, but the points he makes are not belaboured.
The protagonists are shown less in their actions and more
in their behaviour; their ideas and feelings are noticed
and discussed, and their life and its quality are critically assessed. Thus, the old agronomist Nikolai Semio-
novich is seen as a more useful man than new specialists
who have succeeded him not just because his practical
knowledge is incomparably greater, but because he loves
his work and those he works for--the peasants ("IFU,"
pp. 12,13,18,19). Aleksandr Ivanovich, a builder by profession and an amateur gardener for 30 years, is seen as
having been "ennobled" by his hard but loving labours on
the land. When looking at his orchard, the author is reminded of "the oldest mention of work on the land [Gen.

2:8]: 'And the Lord God planted a garden eastward in Eden
...'" ("IFU," p. 33). When looking at the old bookbinder
Maksim Gerasimovich's naturalness and elegance of movements
while he works ("IFU," p. 11), Dorosh thinks of the way
"culture is created" ("IFU," p. 12). The work, its eternal repetitiveness, has formed the bookbinder's habits and
skills as well as his opinions and moral notions (ibid.).
On the other hand, Mikhail Vasilyevich, the man with whom
Dorosh used to stay during his visits to Raygorod, is re-
assessed in this part of *DD* as a Philistine whose materialistic interests and lack of culture are brought into direct
relation with the fact that "he never had a spade" in his
"idle hands" ("IFU," p. 14).

The main protagonist of *DD*, his old friend, the former '*dvadtsatipiatitysiachnik*' Ivan Fedoseevich, the crafty, autocratic, hard-working, enthusiastic, inventive and
successful kolkhoz chairman, respected and loved by the
peasants of Lyubogostitsy, is viewed more critically now
than in the previous instalments. Dorosh tries to understand what the real values which form his outstandingly
strong personality are. His weak points, such as parsi-
moniousness ("IFU," p. 7), vanity (p. 8,14), stubborness
(p. 10) and capriciousness (p. 39) are not glossed over.
But these minor vices do not detract from the image of an
able organiser and great specialist (p. 14,24), whose work
has benefited not only the peasants he led as chairman of
the kolkhoz but the whole country. Ivan Fedoseevich's
greatness is based on the fact that he is, and always has
been, a peasant (p. 7,23-4, 25,39) who has tried all his
life to "change the worker into a 'poet-peasant' [Gleb
Uspensky's expression used by Dorosh] whose existence cannot be separated from the eternally recurrent miracle--the
transformation of seed into fruit which feeds us" (p. 40).

This praise of the cultivator of land is not based on
superficial admiration or idealisation. It rests on the
realisation that it is the peasant's work--the only work
in our days which (as is true for art) cannot be divided
into separate operations performed by separate people (p.
38)--which provides a total satisfaction and creates a
total personality. The peasant's way of life is hard, uncertain as to its immediate success, and not profitable,
but it "feeds the dreams and the moral outlook" (p. 9) of
man. Thus, the land which man cultivates (and Dorosh gen-
eralises his ideas by using, as illustrations, examples
taken from the lives of people who, though they work the
land, are, strictly speaking, non-peasants) is "the source

of physical and moral strength, it develops his mind in a
particular way and gives him ... precious qualities" (p.
33). The land forces the tiller of soil to labour in a
certain manner, and it is the particular quality of this
labour "which fills his existence. The latter, that is,
the fulness of existence, helps the peasant to carry his
burden lightly" (p. 36).

     The last instalment of *DD*--"PLS"--contains the same
ideas about the quality of peasants' life, only expressed
in stronger terms. The elements of nostalgia and sadness,
and even those of pessimism concerning the likelihood of
these correct and proper values surviving the pressures
exercised not so much by educational and technological
advances as by the ideological clamp imposed from above,
become, however, predominant.

     In attempting to summarise now the implied message
which Dorosh incorporates into the last two installments
of his *DD*, I shall try to move from the particular to the
general.
     In Dorosh's view, there should be as little interfer-
ence as possible from outside in the way the peasantry or-
ganises and performs its work. This attitude is justified
by the recognition that the cultivation of land, which
means, predominantly, the production of food, is the primary, the fundamental activity of man on which the human
organisation as a whole, i.e., the society, is based, a
recognition which Dorosh himself acquired slowly through
acquaintance with, and meditation about,[19] the work done
by peasants, and which he wishes his readers to understand
and to make their own. Through their work, the peasants
enable all other members of society to function and to
perform their important and much needed tasks. It does
not matter how numerically important or unimportant the
peasantry is in comparison with other sections of society,
because their work permits them to exist without society,
while society cannot exist without them and their work.
Herein lies the qualitative difference of the peasant's
labour (*trud*) and the worth of the peasant as man.
     Thus, it is the peasant who, through the eternally
recurrent sequence of operations, maintains the continuity
between the past and the future;[20] in whose life "the
natural, economic and moral categories are interwoven so
closely"[21] that they are practically indistinguishable;
and who is the creator of values which, in their totality,

form the tradition and the culture of the people.[22] These
ideas have their more precise and complete expression in
his "Razmyshleniya v Zagorske" ("RZ"),[23] an essay that
could be considered a complement to *DD*.

The aim of "RZ" is the rehabilitation for contemporary readers ("RZ," p. 113) of the group of those outstanding individuals who assembled around St. Sergius of
Radonezh and who, in the second half of the 14th and the
beginning of the 15th century, became the founders of the
new *Rus'* and the forefathers of contemporary Russia.
These veterans of the battle of Kulikovo   - contemporaries of the participants in the War of the Roses - and
originators of what Dorosh, following the example of D. S.
Likhachev, calls the "Russian Pre-Renaissance" (p. 109,
111), all friends or disciples of St. Sergius,[24] laid the
foundation of Russian modern culture based, in addition to
various secondary foreign influences, on "something of our
own, fundamental, forever existing in our land in all
those places where the knots of (future) national culture
were being tied" (p. 105, also 111). They were successful
in their task, but only because these sons of Russian
peasants followed in the footsteps of their fathers who,
with a broad axe in their hands (p. 98[25]) or with a wooden
plough and a sowing pouch (ibid.) prepared by both physical and moral efforts the land and the country for enlightenment. "I remember the words of Kliuchevsky about
the rough preparatory work of civilising which consumes
centuries of stubborn struggle with forests and marshes,
about the fact that after this work has been completed it
becomes necessary, without losing the acquired practical
stamina, to work on one's self and to develop one's mental and moral strength. And I thought to myself that, in
this task of selfperfection which stands perennially before man, it is impossible to manage without the experience contained in the history of a nation, however foreign and naive the moral aims of our forefathers appear to
us today" (p. 120).

Dorosh's main thesis, as expressed in his *DD*, and confirmed by his other works and utterances published in the
1960s, is that the rôle of peasantry as he conceives it,
is not being recognized in present-day Soviet Union. He
maintains that even today the tiller of soil, because of
the influence which the unique kind of work he performs
has on him, is still not only the custodian of old, time-
honoured values and the link between the past and the present of the nation, but also the prime creator of cultural

and moral values: "We forget that they (peasants) are the
people. The people who create language, songs, tales, who
stand up against the enemy, send their sons and daughters
to build cities and factories, to study sciences and art
..."[26]   Dorosh sees in the revolutionary reorganisation of
countryside life, which began with the collectivisation
and goes on at a steadily increasing pace,[27] the destruction of the very base which for so long maintained and
further developed traditions and thus supported the specifically Russian, i.e., national and popular, culture.
The most dangerous 'attack' upon this base is the attempt
to transform the peasant into a worker (*rabochy*) and,
therefore, the unwillingness to see the peasant as more
than a producer of foodstuff.[28]   Thus, Dorosh builds in
his *DD* a definite schema which can be expressed by the
following relation:

peasant work : moral values; culture: national speci-
ficity. His views of the latter concept, known in Russian
under the name of *narodnost'*, is of particular interest.

The term *narodnost'* itself is not used by Dorosh in
his *DD*. I see the reason for this in the fact that, because of the term's use and misuse in official pronouncements, studies of Soviet literary theory and works of literary criticism over the last decades, its meaning has become too confused and vague, not to say meaningless.[29]   But
all through his work he tries, I feel, to define his understanding of this term. It would appear that he is not
satisfied with the usual narrowing of the meaning which
would limit *narodnost'* to *ethnos*, or *demos*, or the fusion
of both (therefore, the usual English translation of
narodnost' as 'national' or 'popular' spirit or character
seems to be, in this case, inadequate). If *ethnos* or
demos, however, were to be considered, in Locke's terms,
as substance, then *narodnost'*, as understood by Dorosh, is
the mode of this substance, its concrete modification. But
narodnost' can be considered only in relation with the
idea of *kul'tura* to which Dorosh in his writings assigns a
primary rôle. In *DD*, *cultura agri* is consistently and em-
phatically equated with *cultura animi*. But *cultura agri*
is dependent upon, and affected by, the traditions developed by the people, in the people and through the people
over a period of a thousand years;[30] hence, *cultura animi*
is similarly affected. *Kul'tura* is, therefore, for Dorosh,
the live memory of the past, it is the continuous productive realisation of the practice and experience of the

people's life in all its aspects--practical as well as intellectual and spiritual--and on all levels. It is process
by which the past is being realised in the present in order
to be passed on, in its renewed form, to the future.[31] The
past's realisation and renewal, in order to be done properly, must be done, Dorosh insists, with the preservation
of "national peculiarities" (*natsional'nye osobennosti*)
("PLS," p. 55), "without depriving (them) of their national singularities (*natsional'noe svoeobrazie*)" (ibid.).
This, then, is *narodnost'* as Dorosh understands this concept and as he incarnates it, on the artistic level, in
Ivan Fedoseevich.

Understood in this manner, *narodnost'*, as the people's guiding principle, does not permit the restoration
of the past in whatever form, nor does it limit the tradition to folklore and old habits and customs. And this is
where Dorosh differs radically both from the so-called
russity of V. Soloukhin type and from the supra-national-
ists (sometimes referred to as national-chauvinists with
fascist tendencies) of *Molodaia gvardiia*'s V. Chalmaev
type. (A thorough description of, and an attempt at
classifying, various nationalistic groups in the 1960s is
given in the important chap. 11 of the forthcoming book by
Prof. Dmitry Pospielovsky of University of Western Ontario. I would disagree only with the mention of Dorosh's
name along with those of various types of neo-Slavophiles
and, specifically, with labelling him a "universalist -
soil - boundist" side by side with the *russit* V. Soloukhin.
If it is necessary to use a composite label - sobriquet for
Dorosh, I would suggest that "cultural - traditionalist -
progressist" would suit him better. The Great-Russian
nationalism of this culturally fully assimilated Jew is an
incidental by-product of his search for a morally responsible and, therefore, dignified way of life). *Narodnost'*
for Dorosh is not, therefore, the jealous preservation of
that which disappears, nor the blind faithfulness to the
prescriptions bequested to descendants by their forefathers
but it is, rather, the constant ingredient of spirituality
which permeates all the realities of the nation's life,
including the most trivial; it is the only firm thread
which joins the nation's past with its present and future.
Under 'normal' conditions, the thread is invisible, hardly
detectable in the continual regular flow of national life.
But if it breaks, then the whole fabric of life, bereft of
its true values, collapses. When this happens, the remedy
is to go back to the primary sources of the tradition and

from there to its reappraisal and re-evaluation in the
light of the tragic mistakes.

And this is what *DD* is all about.

The first five parts represent a thorough and
thoughtful analysis of the collapse of national life, expressed through the appalling material conditions which
the people who live on and by the land have to endure, and
through the moral degradation which this kind of existence
brings about. The selection of these people, rather than
workers, civil servants or members of the intelligentsia
has not been quite accidental. As mentioned earlier, the
impetus could have been provided by the 1953 Khrushchev
speech and by Ovechkin's sketches. From the point of view
of the content and, more generally, of the 'line' taken by
Dorosh in these early sketches, the latter, too, differed
very little from the general run of *derevenskie ocherki* as
they began to appear at the time. Even the increasingly
speculative and meditative character of the work, by which
DD is distinguished, can be seen as resulting from the accidentally adopted form of loose, apparently unconnected
diary entries.[32] However, Dorosh's concern grew as he
realised that the problems which he had been observing and
describing were deeper and more complex than they appeared
to be on the surface.

This realisation found its reflection for the first
time quite clearly in "DPS." The entries dealing with nature and its beauty, with his own and other people's
thoughts about the state of the countryside and the reasons for it, as well as excursions into the historical
past of the region, became more numerous. Perhaps in order to outweigh these 'lyrical asides,' he published,
barely 6 months later, "Poezdka v Lyubogostitsy"--a brief
(7 pages) and very dry and matter-of-fact addition to this
instalment. The form of "DPS" must have worried him, too,
because, to the usual "derevensky dnevnik" or "iz dnevnika"
and the date, he added in the subtitle, rather unexpectedly, "povest'." There seems to be no justification for
this addition, since the form of "DPS," if anything, is
even more disconnected and rambling than in previous parts
of *DD*. Only the fact[33] that Dorosh seems to be more concerned with inquiring into the characters of his protagonists and with understanding them can explain, perhaps,
this use of genre designation.

"IFU" shows a striking difference in the content of
diary entries and, though the form on the surface appears

to be unchanged, a great strengthening of the inner structure of his part of *DD* can be observed. It is possible to
speak, for the first time, about a compositional beginning
and end. The 'case histories' of individuals, which provide the raw material for further treatment, are more coherent and, therefore, more illuminating.[34] Each individual case is concluded by a general statement which under-
lines its relevance today.[35] The first part of "IFU,"
which could be described as laying the groundwork and
which contains, in addition to 'case histories,' an actu-
alised historical reminiscence and a description of the
peasants' relation with the Church in the past and in the
present ("IFU," p. 3-29), is then followed (from about p.
32 to the end of this instalment on p. 41) by a philosophical reflection in which the generalisation is extended to
include every Soviet man and woman. Thus, the last paragraph of "IFU" strikes the reader as a logical, inescap-
able and universally valid conclusion: "The crux of the
matter is that I ... insist on the necessity for everyone
who lives by bread to be fully aware of his direct dependence on the land ..." (p. 41).

It is this philosophical part, which includes the
denomination of the reasons for the lack of quality of
life, both material and spiritual (Dorosh, of course, pre-
fers to use the term "moral"), which, obviously, found
little favour in official circles. Dorosh expected this
kind of reaction. In several places, he makes remarks
which indicate his lack of confidence in his being understood,[36] but he does not give up.[37]

The glimmer of hope, that can still be detected in
"IFU" which covers the year 1961, almost disappears in
"PLS," the concluding instalment covering the year 1967.
The composition of this part of *DD* is as careful as it
was in "IFU." There is also present very prominently a
preoccupation with universal moral problems. But the
material used (the 'case histories') is differently slant-
ed, and from this slant a new, resigned, even dispairing
note--mentioned earlier--is derived. The familiar old
places, described previously as clean, clear, beautiful
and vital, are being seen suddenly as dirty, dark, in dis-
repair and lifeless.[38] Many of the author's friends--pro-
tagonists of *DD*--have died, kolkhozes have been changed
into "state agro-factories," i.e., sovkhozes, a great number of fields have been abandoned, rivers and the lake
have become overgrown and almost dead, but mainly, the
peasant has been separated from his land.[39] The feeling

of nostalgia for the 'natural' ways and means of life as
they have existed in the district and the town of Raygorod
("PLS," p. 58-61) is not alleviated by the knowledge that
the material well-being and comfort of peasants have im-
proved over the last 15 years or so (p. 55) and, using the
example of the changes which have occurred over the centuries in the manner in which countryside houses have been
built (p. 55-6), he shows the inadequacy, inappropriate-
ness and sheer ugliness of alien elements forcibly introduced into today's life. Even the references--very infre-
quent in this part of *DD*--to the favourite protagonist Ivan
Fedoseevich are, in fact, reminiscences about him as he was
and an assessment of him as a peasant.[40]   The author takes
leave of Ivan Fedoseevich, strangely and unexpectedly, by
relating the story of the latter's childhood and adolescence, a story hitherto unknown to the readers.

Thus, the last instalment of *DD* conveys a strong feeling of pessimism as far as the fate of the Soviet peasant
is concerned; of a battle having been lost as regards the
efforts of the author himself. The future seems to be un-
sure, stormy and dangerous: "The thunder can be heard all
around, the lightnings glitter, the storm is somewhere
near" (p. 73). These words, contained in the penultimate
paragraph of "PLS," represent the real ending of *DD*.

The only satisfaction which Dorosh has derived from
writing his *DD* appears to be the knowledge that he was
"able to see that life does not stand still" (PLS," p. 73).
These words, repeated by him as a kind of personal *credo*
in other works,[41] should have been used as an epigraph for
his diary. He started to write *DD* as an honest, objective
observer, and in the process of continuing it he acquired
respect, love and boundless admiration for the people who
were the object of his observations, remarks and meditations. He saw the qualities in these people which deserved
to be preserved and further developed rather than being
slowly and relentlessly destroyed. And in the process of
unfolding--using a manner which he himself defined as
"lyrical prose"[42] -- the disappearing values, the beauty and
the rightness of their lives, he created an important and,
in many ways, a seminal work. The form, which, he felt,
developed naturally because it fitted so well the content,
found no followers. But the ideas and ideals expressed in
DD have found their continuation in the writings of a
group of writers who dominated the open Soviet literature
of the 1960s and who have produced, in the words of a

Soviet critic, "the most serious trend in contemporary
Russian prose."[43]   These writers, following the example
set for them by Dorosh and his *DD*, have tackled the problems connected with "the direct expression of contemporary man's spiritual world, of the character of his intellectual interests and his emotional life"; they were
"afraid of losing their moral entirety"; they described
"the aesthetic and moral entirety of the notions of life
and death"; they rediscovered "the highly spiritual old
peasant culture"; they were determined to see that "the
spiritual heritage of old peasant culture would not disappear from life"; and they wrote works whose "main aspect was moral, whose main worry was about spiritual
values, human justice and about the *transformation of outdated and outlived notions into new ones*"[44] (my emphasis,
G.Ž.) Dorosh followed very closely the work of this
group of writers which consisted of such writers as V.
Astaf'ev, V. Belov, V. Likhonosov, M. Roshchin and V.
Shukshin,[45] and on one occasion wrote an enthusiastic, and
at the same time very thoughtful review of V. Belov's
"Privychnoe delo."[46] His work of fifteen years has not
been in vain.

    I mentioned here the unusualness of the form which
Dorosh adopted for his *DD* and also the fact that this
form developed 'naturally,' almost without a conscious effort on the part of the author. The result was a documentary with strong lyrical, i.e., subjective, overtones
--a genre which was novel and which seemed to answer the
requirements of the times. Perhaps because of its formal
proximity to the 'countryside sketch,' the novelty of *DD*'s
form has not been noticed. Could this be, therefore, an
artistic shortcoming or failure? But where Dorosh has
certainly not failed is in having written his own version
of a contemporary critical 'encyclopaedia of Soviet life.'

                                        University of Toronto

                            NOTES

    [1]See the short bio-bibliographical note, Appendix A.
    [2]*Derevensky dnevnik*, which will be abbreviated hence-
forth in the text as *DD*; the titles of all works published
in Russian will be given in transliteration and not translated; all translations from Russian are mine.

[3] See the selected bibliography, Appendix B.

[4] See App. B. for particulars of these and earlier reviews.

[5] *Novy Mir*, 1964, no. 6, pp. 11-83; henceforth, the abbreviation "DPS" will be used to designate this part of *DD*.

[6] *Novy Mir*, 1966, no. 3, pp. 221-28, partic. p. 221, 224, 226-7.

[7] V. Lakshin, "Ivan Denisovich--ego druz'ia i nedrugi," *Novy Mir*, 1964, no. 1, pp. 223-45.

[8] See, e.g., A. Turkov's review "Zorkaia pamiat'" in *Literaturnaya gazeta*, no. 5, 30 Jan. 1974; this is by the same Turkov who, in his book published in 1962, had interesting things to say about *DD*.

[9] It is this shift in "DPS"which has been noticed by the perceptive Lakshin. It was described and well analysed by Jean Cathals in the valuable introduction to his French translation of this part of *DD*--see App. B for particulars. Cathala wrote his introduction in March 1968, in Moscow, when he was in close contact with Dorosh --see "Zhivoe derevo iskusstva," M. 1970, p. 267.

[10] *Literaturnaya Moskva*, vol. 2, p. 549.

[11] Ibid.

[12] Ibid., p. 550.

[13] "Estestvennost' prozy," *Voprosy literatury*, 1967, no. 2, p. 129.

[14] The Anglicised form of this term has been used, e.g., in the transl. of A. Sakharov's "In Answer to Solzhenitsyn," *The N. Y. Review of Books*, vol. XXI, no. 10 (13 June 1974), pp. 3-6, on p. 3.

[15] See Roy Medvedev, "O knige Solzhenitsyna "Arkhipelag GULag'," *Novy Zhurnal*, no. 115 (June 1974), p. 214.

[16] See "Khrushchev Remembers," transl. and ed. by Strobe Talbott, Little, Brown & Co. (Canada) Ltd, Toronto, vol. 1, 1970 and vol. 2, 1974. In vol. 1 Khrushchev states that kolkhoz is an artificial organisation (p. 387); in vol. 2 he regrets that Stalin won his battle with enemies of collectivisation (p. 107) and asserts that Gomu*ł*ka was correct in resisting collectivisation: as a result, the agriculture in Poland was in good shape (p. 182).

[17] In 1961, in his speech at the XXIInd Congress of the CPSU, Tvardovsky singled out Dorosh; there is a hint in Jean Cathala (p. 10) that Dorosh became member of *Movy Mir* editorial board on Tvardovsky's personal insistence.

[18] For the basic difference in the approaches to countryside problems by Ovechkin and Dorosh see my "Aspects

of Peasant Life As Portrayed in Contemporary Soviet Literature," *Canadian Slavic Studies* I, no. 4 (Winter 1967),
pp. 552-65, partic. pp. 555-8 for Ovechkin and pp. 558-60
for Dorosh.

[19] See, e.g., "IFU," p. 39-40.

[20] See, e.g., "IFU," p. 11. Also "Yestestvennost'
prozy," *op. cit.*, p. 133; "Obrazy Rossii," *Novy Mir*, 1969,
no. 3, pp. 181-208, p. 208; "Zhivoe derevo iskusstva," 2nd
compl. ed., "Iskusstvo," M. 1970, p. 133.

[21] "IFU," p. 24.

[22] Ibid., p. 40-1.

[23] *Novy Mir*, 1967, no. 5, pp. 96-120. Further references, by code and page number, will be made in the text.

[24] A selected list of names, in their Russian forms:
Prince Iuriy Zvenigorodsky (son of Dmitry Donskoy),
Saints Stefan Permsky, Iepifany Premudry, Roman Kirzhatsky,
Andronik Spassky, Mefody Pesnoshsky, Avraamy Gorodetsky,
Fedor Simonovsky, Afanasy Vysotsky, Nil Sorsky, Zosima and
Savvaty Polovetsky, Kirill and Ferapont Belozersky, and,
of course, Saint (*Prepodobny*) Andrey, called Rublev, and
his friend Daniil Cherny.

[25] See also "Zhivoe derevo iskusstva," p. 209, 288.

[26] Ibid., p. 249, also 248.

[27] See, e.g., "IFU," p. 13, 20, 24, 32, 35, 39-40 and
partic. p. 29; "PLS," p. 52, 54, 57, 71.

[28] See, e.g., "Zhivoe derevo iskusstva," p. 247-9,
250, 295.

[29] Particularly noticeable, since the XXth Congress of
the CPSU, is the confusion of concepts *narodnost'* and
partiynost' which have become practically identical and,
therefore, interchangeable in such theoretical works as
those of N. Gey & V. Piskunov, "Estetichesky ideal sovetskoy literatury," ANSSSR, M. 1962, and of V. Ivanov, "O
sushchnosti sotsialisticheskogo realizma," "Khud. lit.,"
M. 1963.

[30] "IFU," p. 40; "PLS," p. 46.

[31] See, e.g., "PLS," p. 54-5, 55-6.

[32] See App. A.

[33] Notice by the interviewer A. Kuznetsov in "Yestestvennost' prozy," p. 131.

[34] E.g., the case of Liuda occupies, with hardly an
interruption, 5 pages (pp. 14-19) and covers a lengthy
period of life of this protagonist, from the 'scandal'
which forces her to leave the old kolkhoz, through a period of 'drifting,' to the seemingly happy ending upon her
becoming the chairwoman of a kolkhoz; the actual conclusion,

however, comes suddenly and in an unexpected form, with the
new chairwoman's angrily resigned stand: "Blushing, Lyuda
articulates with anger: 'Let it be, then... When the cows
will all die, then they'll understand.'" (p. 19).

[35] E.g., the Church passage ends thus: "It seems to me
--I continue to develop my idea--that all this concerns
our today's observations, because the actual life of the
people consists of numerous, often contradictory details
and cannot be compressed into the schema of economico-
political campaigns which are all that some district
leaders find the time to do" ("IFU," p. 29).

[36] "It dawns on me suddenly that my collocutors did
not understand me" ("IFU," p. 9); "For the time being I
do not say anything about these thoughts of mine to my
collocutors" (ibid., p. 14).

[37] "I do not consider, at this moment, the material
side... It is the moral side which interests me" (ibid.,
p. 36); "As I understand now..." (ibid., p. 38); "Do I
have to prove that everything that I am trying to say in
no way contradicts the idea of collective agriculture..?"
(ibid., p. 39).

[38] "PLS," e.g., p. 40, 42, 46, 54, 70.

[39] "The contemporary kolkhoz worker stands in far-
removed and indirect relationship with the soil" ("PLS,"
p. 54).

[40] "Ivan Fedoseevich, as a true peasant, honoured customs and respected traditions" ("PLS," p. 71).

[41] See, e.g., "Yestestvennost' prozy," p. 129, 130.

[42] Ibid., p. 129. Also "Zhivoe derevo iskusstva," p.
253.

[43] V. Gusev in *Literaturnaia gazeta*, 14 Febr. 1968.
See also Ye. Starikova, "Sotsiologichesky aspekt sovremennoy 'derevenskoy prozy,'" *Voprosy literatury*, 1972, no. 7,
pp. 11-35--the most interesting assessment of writings by
authors such as V. Belov, P. Rebrin and V. Likhonosov.
See also my contribution to James R. Millar, ed., *The
Soviet Rural Community*, U. of Ill. Press, Urbana, 1971,
entitled "The Contemporary Countryside in Soviet Literature: A Search for New Values," pp. 376-404, partic. p.
388-403. See also articles in *Voprosy literatury*, 1973,
no. 3, pp. 46-78, by Sh. Galimov, Yu. Galkin, S. Shurtakov
and L. Ivanov in reply to Starikova's article mentioned
above.

[44] All quotations are taken from Starikova, *op. cit.*,
p. 12, 22, 26, 27 (twice) and 28.

[45] For more details on these writers see my contribution to James R. Millar, ed., *op. cit.*
[46] "Zhivoe derevo iskusstva," pp. 287-297.

Appendix A

Biobibliographical note

Yefim Yakovlevich Dorosh (Gol'berg)* was born on the 12/25 Dec. 1908 in Yelisavetgrad (now Kirovograd in Ukr. SSR) in the family of a merchant employee. In the early 1920s he worked in handicraft workshops in Odessa, in 1925 moved to Moscow and attended there the applied arts college where he remained after graduation as a junior instructor. In the period 1928 to 1931 he also studied fine arts and directed various amateur arts groups' activities and co-authored a number of short plays for amateur theatre. In 1932, as an employee of the Fine Arts Section of the RSFSR Commissariat of Public Education, he became instructor in amateur arts activities of the Red Fleet in Kronshtadt. During this period he started to work as a journalist and wrote newspaper and magazine articles, reportages and short stories about life in the navy (collection of short stores *Marshal'skie zviozdy* - 1939 - and *Voyennoe pole* - 1941) and in the kolkhozes (e.g., sketches "Kolkhoznaya osen'" - 1937, - "Velik chelovek" - 1939, "Predsedatel' kolkhoza" - 1940).

During the war he was correspondent on an NKVD-troups newspaper.

After the war, in 1945, Dorosh became member of the CPSU and special correspondent of the *Literaturnaia gazeta* and wrote regularly sketches and short stories, more and more of which were concerned with the countryside, especially kolkhoz, themes. The first collection of these—*Novy sekretar'*—was published in 1948 and was followed by four more, the last one, published in 1954 and entitled simply *Rasskazy*, contained some 22 sketches and stories and is the most complete. Looking at his writings in these genres up to then, one is struck by their ideological orthodoxy, their thematic narrowness and their dependence on models (e.g., frequent appearance in them of the

---

*Biographical data were taken mainly from *Russkie pisateli-prozaiki*, Bibliografichesky ukazatel', vol. 1, L. 1959, pp. 656-68; from *Kratkaia literaturnaia entsyklopediia*, vol. 2, M. 1964, p. 753; and from *Slovník spisovatelů národů SSSR*, Praha, 1966, p. 108.

Sholokhovian Grampa Shchukar's doubles). The style of
these writings is detached, seems to lack any kind of emotional involvement on the part of the author and makes the
reading of the stories unexciting.

What must be seen today as a breaking point in
Dorosh's writing career occurred in 1953 when, after
Khrushchev's speech at the September 1953 Party CC Plenum
on the situation in the countryside, he was sent by *Literaturnaia gazeta* to investigate the latter and report on
it. Dorosh chose the countryside near Rostov-Iaroslav-
sky, better known by its historic predicate Veliky, where
an old friend of his, the successful kolkhoz chairman Ivan
Aleksandrovich Fedoseev, lived. As a result of this first
visit he published in *Ogonyok* (1954, no. 46) the sketch
"Ivan Fedoseevich", followed by "Derevenskie zametki" (*Literaturnaia gazeta*, 27 Oct. 1955). The latter should be
considered as being the beginnings of *Derevensky dnevnik*
which, as Dorosh relates (see "Estestvennost' prozy,"
Voprosy literatury, 1967, no. 2, p. 128), represented at
first simply daily notes made *pro memoria*. Emmanuil
Kazakevich, when collecting materials for *Literaturnaia
Moskva*, read these notes and convinced Dorosh that, after
some editing, they should be printed. When published in
the second volume of *Literaturnaia Moskva* in 1956, the
sketch "Derevensky dnevnik" was a great success. It was
at about that time that Dorosh began to spend half a year
or so living in Moscow and half a year in the Rostov, and
later the Vologda and Radonezh districts.

"Derevensky dnevnik" was quickly followed by
"Dozhdlivoe leto. Iz derevenskogo dnevnika" (*Moskva*,
1958, no. 3, pp. 18-117) and "Dva dnya v Raygorode. Iz
derevenskogo dnevnika" (*Novy Mir*, 1958, no. 7, pp. 3-27).
Three years later "Sukhoe leto. 1960. Ocherk" (*Novy Mir*,
1961, no. 7, pp. 3-51) appeared, followed by "Raygorod v
fevrale. Ocherk" (*Novy Mir*, 1962, no. 10, pp. 9-46) and
"Dozhd' popolam s solntsem. Derevensky dnevnik. 1959.
Povest'" (*Novy Mir*, 1964, no. 6, pp. 11-83) followed almost immediately by "Poezdka v Liubogostitsy. Iz dnevnika"
(*Novy Mir*, 1965, no. 1, pp. 81-7). After a considerable
interval appeared "Ivan Fedoseevich ukhodit na pensiyu.
Derevensky dnevnik. 1961" (*Novy Mir*, 1969, no. 1, pp. 3-41)
and, then, the last instalment "Piatnadtsat' let spustya.
Derevensky dnevnik. 1967" (*Novy Mir*, 1970, no. 9, pp. 39-
73).

Dorosh's thorough acquaintance with the countryside
to the north of Moscow was not, however, his only pursuit

after 1953. More and more, he became involved in the study
of old Russian arts (for which he was educationally and
professionally well prepared), wrote short articles and
reviews of films and books in this field, and became active in the society for the defence of historical monuments ("All-Russian Society for the Protection of Historical Monuments"). Two important essays, "Razmyshlenia v
Zagorske. Iz knigi 'Drevnee riadom s nami'" (*Novy Mir*,
1967, no. 5, pp. 96-120) and "Obrazy Rossii" (*Novy Mir*,
1969, no. 3, pp. 181-208) attest to this interest. The
latter article, along with a great many articles on arts,
and book, film and exhibition reviews, published over the
period 1953 to 1969 in various publications, was included
in the book "Zhivoe derevo iskusstva" (2nd compl. ed.,
M. 1970). Finally, Dorosh' interests extended also to the
craft and art of writing - "Iz zapisnoy knizhky" (*Voprosy
literatury*, 1969, no. 1, pp. 103-16) and "Estestvennost'
prozy" (*Voprosy literatury*, 1967, no. 2, pp. 126-35).

     The esteem Dorosh enjoyed among his peers was ex-
pressed by his appointment in 1967 to the editorial board
of *Novy Mir*, where he remained until June 1970, half a
year longer than his friend A. T. Tvardovsky.
     Dorosh died in 1973.

Appendix B

Selected Bibliography

DD *Derevensky dnevnik*, consisting of:
    "Derevensky dnevnik," *Literaturnaia Moskva. Sbornik
        vtoroy*, Moscow, 1956, pp. 549-626.
    "Dozhdlivoe leto. Iz derevenskogo dnevnika," *Moskva*,
        1958, no. 3, pp. 18-117.
    "Dva dnya v Raygorode. Iz derevenskogo dnevnika,"
        Novy Mir, 1958, no. 7, pp. 3-27.
    "Sukhoe leto. 1960. Ocherk," *Novy Mir*, 1961, no. 7,
        pp. 3-51.
    "Raygorod v fevrale. Ocherk," *Novy Mir*, 1962, no. 10,
        pp. 9-46.
"DPS" "Dozhd' popolam s solntsem. Derevensky dnevnik. 1959.
        Povest'," *Novy Mir*, 1964, no. 6, pp. 11-83.
    "Poezdka v Lyubogostitsy. Iz dnevnika," *Novy Mir*,
        1965, no. 1, pp. 81-7.
"IFU" "Ivan Fedoseevich ukhodit na pensiiu. Derevensky
        dnevnik. 1961," *Novy Mir*, 1969, no. 1, pp. 3-41.
"PLS" "Piatnadtsat' let spustia. Derevensky dnevnik.
        1967," *Novy Mir*, 1970, no. 9, pp. 39-73.

The most complete bibliography (primary and secondary
sources) up to the end of 1958 is contained in *Russkie
sovietskie pisateli-prozaiki*. Bibliografichesky ukazatel',
tom 1. Leningrad, 1959, pp. 656-68.

Books, articles and essays by Dorosh published after 1958:

"Ivan Fedoseevich" (Rasskaz. - Dva dnia v Raygorode. Iz
    derevenskogo dnevnika), "Pravda," M. 1959.
"Chetyre vremeni goda" (Kinopovest'), *Novy Mir*, 1960, no.
    7, pp. 3-79.
"Pochemu ya ne pishu dlia kino," *Iskusstvo kino*, 1962, no.
    4, pp. 76-80.
"Knigi o nashikh predkakh," *Novy Mir*, 1962, no. 10, pp. 9-
    46.
"Chetyre vremeni goda." Povest". "Sov. Pisatel'," M. 1962.
"Moy drug Fedoseev" (O byvshem predsedatele kolkhoza im.
    Kirova, pensionere I. A. Fedoseeve, Rostovsky rayon
    Yaroslavl'skoy oblasti. Ocherk), *Druzhba narodov*, 1963,
    no. 1, pp. 211-19.

"Derevensky dnevnik. Chetyre vremeni goda," "Sov. Pis.,"
    M. 1963.
"Mne dvadtsat' let," *Iskusstvo kino*, 1965, no. 4, pp. 27-
    46.
"Slovo o Rostove Velikom," "Znanie," M. 1965.
"Dozhd' popolam s solntsem" (Sketches: Raygorod v fevrale,
    Sukhoe leto, Dozhd' popolam s solntsem), "Sov. Pis.,"
    M. 1965.
"Tam, za perevalom," in *Yesli ne ty, to kto*? (Sketches),
    "Sov. Rossiya," M. 1965.
"Razmyshleniia v. Zagorske" (Iz knigi "drevnee riadom s
    nami"), *Novy Mir*, 1967, no. 5, pp. 96-120.
"Zhivoe derevo iskusstva" (Russkoe iskusstvo), "Iskusstvo,"
    M. 1967. 2nd, compl. ed., "Iskusstvo" M. 1970.
"Sredniy syn Noia" (O pamiatnike drevnerusskoy arkhitektury
    14-go veka v Tomskom monastyre, Yaroslavl'),
    Dekorativnoe iskusstvo, 1968, no. 7, pp. 4-12.
"Iz zapisnoy knizhki," *Voprosy literatury*, 1969, no. 1,
    pp. 103-16.
"Obrazy Rossii," *Novy Mir*, 1969, no. 3, pp. 181-208.

Miscellaneous articles, reviews:

"Khudozhnik i kniga," *Novy Mir*, 1963, no. 7, pp. 222-28
    (About illustrator N. V. Kuz'min).
"Derevnia na stsene teatra 'Sovremennik'," *Teatr*, 1964,
    no. 2, pp. 11-18. (The play "Bez kresta," an adapta-
    tion of Tendriakov's "Chudotvornaia")
"Opasnost' nazvana ne sovsem tochno," *Iskusstvo kino*, 1964,
    no. 5, pp. 57-61. (Commentary on M. Bleyman's arti-
    cle "Opasno".)
"Mavrina," *Teatr*, 1964, no. 7, pp. 88-90. (On painter
    T. A. Mavrina.)
"Drevnee i velikoe iskusstvo," *Yunost'*, 1965, no. 10, pp.
    79-80. (On Old-Russian painting.)
"Na vystavke Serebryakovoy," *Teatr*, 1965, no. 11, pp.
    104-9.
"Estestvennost' prozy." Besedu vel A. Kuznetsov. *Voprosy
    literatury*, 1967, no. 2, pp. 126-35.
"Rostovsky Kreml'." Fotoal'bom. Tekst Ye. Dorosha.
    Fotografiia I. Gol'berga i G. Zemtsova. "Sov.
    Khudoznik," M. 1967.

Secondary Literature:

Trifonova, T. "Mnogoobrazna, kak zhizn'," *Voprosy litera-
    tury*, 1959, no. 4, pp. 45-65.
Mikhailov, O. "O traktore, o khudozhestvennosti, o tom,
    chto mozhno uvidet' iz okna vagona, i o knizhnom
    zatvornichestve," *Molodaia gvardiia*, 1959, no. 9,
    pp. 191-200.
Kardin, V. "Geroy nashikh dney," *Voprosy literatury*,
    1959, no. 6, pp. 7-27.
Solov'eva, I. "Khorosho idti po zemle...," *Yunost'*, 1959,
    no. 7, pp. 66-70.
Vinogradov, I. "O sovremennom geroe," *Novy Mir*, 1961, no.
    9, pp. 232-54.
Kuznetsov, M. "Novoe v zhizni i literature," *Novy Mir*,
    1961, no. 10, pp. 229-45.
Shekhovtsev, I. "Letopis' kolkhoznoy zhizni," Sibirskie
    ogni, 1962, no. 7, pp. 184-6.
Napolova, T. "Sila pravdy," *Zvezda*, 1962, no. 6, pp. 164-
    72.
Turkov, A. "Poeziya sozidaniya," "Sov. Pis.," M. 1962
    (pp. 217-37).
Kuznetsov, M. "Literatura i stroitel'stvo kommunizma,"
    Literatura v shkole, 1962, no. 2, pp. 8-17.
Starikova, Ye. V. "Poeziia prozy," "Sov. Pis.," M. 1962
    (pp. 152-90).
Shishkina, A. "Na bol'shikh dorogakh i na obochinakh,"
    Neva, 1962, no. 8, pp. 162-70.
Solov'eva, I. "Fedoseev i Ivan Fedoseevich," *Novy Mir*,
    1963, no. 6, pp. 250-3.
Turkov, A. "Razdum'ia nashikh druzey," *Krest'ianka*, 1963,
    no. 2, p. 18.
Vinogradov, I. "Po stranitsam Derevenskogo dnevnika Ye.
    Dorosha," *Novy Mir*, 1965, no. 7, pp. 234-53.
Tvardovsky, A. "Po sluchaiu iubileia," *Novy Mir*, 1965,
    no. 1, pp. 3-18.
Burtin, Yu. Review of Mikhail Alekseev, "Khleb - imia
    sushchestvitel'noe," in *Novy Mir*, 1965, no. 1, pp.
    257-62.
Vinogradov, I. "V otvete u vremeni," "Sov. Pis.," M. 1966.
Lakshin, V. "Tri mery vremeni," *Novy Mir*, 1966, no. 3,
    pp. 234-53.
Shekhovtsev, I. S. "Obraz sel'skogo kommunista-
    rukovoditelya v 'Derevenskom dnevnike' Ye. Dorosha,"
    Uch. zap. Pskovskogo ped. instituta, vyp. 30, 1967,
    pp. 5-13.

Jean Cathala, transl. of Ephim Doroch, "Pluie et soleil,
    suivi de Méditations à Zagorsk," nrf: Gallimard,
    Paris, 1968.   (Contains a very thoughtful introduc-
    tory article by the translator.)
Starikova, Ye.   "Sotsiologichesky aspekt sovremennoy
    'derevenskoy prozy'," *Voprosy literatury*, 1972, no.
    7, pp. 11-35.
Sotsiologichesky aspekt sovremennoy 'derevenskoy prozy',
    Voprosy literatury, 1973, no. 3, pp. 45-78.   Articles
    by: Sh. Galimov, "Khudozhestvennost', sotsiologiya,
    zhizn'" (pp. 46-56); Yu. Galkin, "Derevnia - litera-
    turnaia i podlinnaia" (pp. 56-62); S. Shurtakov,
    "Zhivoy chelovek, a ne obshchiie tsifry" (pp. 62-71);
    L. Ivanov, "Videt' segodniashniy den'" (pp. 71-8).
Turkov, A.   "Zorkaia pamiat'," *Literaturnaia gazeta*, no.
    5 (30 Jan. 1974).

VASILY SHUKSHIN - A CONTEMPORARY SCYTHIAN

Stephen le Fleming

In the first compendium "The Scythians" published by
"The Scythians" in St. Petersburg in 1917, the introductory
article is entitled "The Scythians" and signed "The Scythians." The article begins: "'Scythian.' There is in
this word, in its very sound, the hiss of an arrow, intoxicated with flight, flight measured by the resilience of a
heavy, reliable bow, bent by a daring hand. For the essence of the Scythian is his bow: a combination of the
force of eye and arm, hurling into boundless distances his
blows of strength."[1] The Scythian has the bold energy of
the barbarian according to this romantic myth, which cor-
responds to the deprecatory observations of classical historians, but which must be modified, as popular conceptions of barbarians often must, by the archaeological evidence of their decorative arts, in this case the Scythians'
remarkable gold ornaments, basically representing animals
in movement. The article goes on to contrast the Scythians
with the barbarians whose lands they settled: "People of
the black earth, of gold fallen from the sky, of the plough
and the open steppe, at a furious gallop even the heady
stagnant air fans like a whirlwind your face bent over the
fiery mane. A tribe, its mysterious roots entwined in legend, hurled from the west to the east in a persistent
stream, a victorious stream into the expanses of the
yellow-faced, narrow-eyed barbarian hordes, who gulp their
wine out of skulls." Zamiatin in 1918 offered his vision:
"...a solitary, savage horseman--a Scythian--gallops across
the green steppe, hair streaming in the wind. Where is he
galloping? Nowhere. What for? For no reason. He gal-
lops simply because he is a Scythian, because he has become one with his horse, because he is a centaur, and the
dearest things to him are freedom, solitude, his horse,
the wide expanse of the steppe."[2]
This evocation of the Scythian as a mythical ideal is,
like the various other aspects of the idea which were prop-
agated by Ivanov-Razumnik and others in the years of the
revolution, highly subjective. The word in fact does not
define an ideology or programme in any narrow sense. While

Ivanov-Razumnik, their "chief ideologist" as Professor
Filippov[3] calls him, was politically active at the time,
his many proclamations of Scythianism only loosely correspond to the Left-wing Social-Revolutionary policies he
supported. Filippov conveys the elusiveness of the idea
in his introduction to Kliuev's works: "...on the threshold
of the revolution there was founded not exactly a literary-
philosophical-political society and not exactly a neo-
slavophile--Left Social-Revolutionary movement--the Scythians." He goes on to equate Scythian with "slavophilising
narodnik" and to approve of yet another definition: "B.
Iakobenko[4] called the Scythians 'revolutionary slavophiles'
and this is a completely accurate definition of 'Scythianism.' The Scythians' programme was quite hazy and fluid.
Although the poets did not participate directly in the
composition of the manifestos, programmes and mobilisa-
tions of groups, it was precisely they, in fact, who made
up the soul of 'Scythianism.' For the 'ideological'
speeches of the main inspiration of the 'Scythians,'
Ivanov-Razumnik, consisted of declamation which converted
the poetic images of the literary nucleus of the 'Scythians' into clichés."[5] Ivanov-Razumnik himself is remembered as applauding Esenin's reading of *Inonia* with the
words "Here is genuine revolutionary subjectivism."[6]
     The Scythian impulse is a yearning for the freedom of
open horizons; these seemed to be promised by the February
revolution but: "After the surf an ebbtide of bourgeois
slime slowly came onto the just-cleared horizon, again
obscuring the distant view.... And at street corners the
emboldened crowd, confirmed in its philistinism, has once
again started to mutter, swapping whispered slander and
rumour with knowing winks."[7] Philistinism is not confined
to the old order and it is characteristic of the Scythian
that he may rebel against any system; Ivanov-Razumnik in
a foreword to a collection of his articles published in
1923 uses words almost identical to the introductory
article of the compendium *Skify*: "'Scythian' means the
permanent revolutionariness (for any system, for any 'external order') of those aspirations of the unreconciled
and irreconcilable spirit, a distant reflection of which
has perhaps fallen on the pages of this book."[8] While
sympathising with the professed aims of the bolsheviks,
who replaced the "philistine" socialists, to abolish the
death penalty and stop the war, Ivanov-Razumnik has his
doubts. In his article *Svoe litso*[9] dated October 28th
1917, he says that internal terror has begun and he is

almost certain that war will be used to carry through the
social revolution in Europe. Since neither revolution
satisfies him, he asks what can be done and concludes,
"one must cut oneself off from both sides in order to preserve one's true face."[10]

Ivanov-Razumnik cannot tolerate revolution imposed
socially without a corresponding spiritual change in man.
In his article *Ispytanie v groze i bure*,[11] written as a
foreword to an edition of Blok's "The Twelve" and "The
Scythians" published in Petrograd in 1918, Ivanov-Razumnik
argues the need for a spiritual revolution to accompny the
social revolution, and harks back to Pushkin, Tyutchev and
Solovyov who had evoked a sense of mission, national, religious and spiritual. Whereas for Pushkin, when he wrote
"To the Slanderers of Russia" the threat to national religious and spiritual values came from European revolutionary movements, for Blok Europe is defending the old
world against revolutionary Russia. But Blok goes beyond
the external difference to find the opposition between the
very spirit of Europe, reactionary or revolutionary, and
the spirit of maximalism characteristic of Russia and he
quotes Blok's lines:

> "Yes, we are Scythians! Yes we are Asiatics
> With slanting and hungry eyes!"

"And," says Ivanov-Razumnik, "This spiritual 'hunger' of
Russia and this 'Scythianism" of hers clash irreconcilably
with the restrained and outwardly powerful 'gradualism' of
the old Europe."[12]   New Russia, with its spiritual and social maximalism, faces Europe which calculates and accu-
mulates its strength slowly and surely. The Scythian accepts the Hellenism of European culture. This characteristic is what Dostoevsky called the Russian's *vsechelove-
chnost'*, his universality. One might also add that it is
a quality of the Scythian noted by Pushkin in his poem
K vel'mozhe of 1830, in which he describes Prince Yusupov's
studies in Europe:

> "For a time learning became your idol:
> You withdrew and to your austere feast
> Settling on his shaky three-legged stool came Diderot,
> Now devotee of providence, now sceptic, now atheist,
> And flinging off his wig closed his eyes in rapture
> And prophesied. And modestly over your patient cup
> You harkened to this atheist or deist
> Like an inquisitive Scythian to an Athenian Sophist."

The Scythian's curiosity is not uncritical. It allows him
to make up his own mind and it does not mean that he has
nothing to contribute. For Ivanov-Razumnik, he confronts
the European bourgeois: "If Russia has a mission, then
this is it: to blow apart from within the old world of
Europe with her 'Scythianism,' with her spiritual and
social 'maximalism'--in fact to do the very thing that
the old world once did in the opposite direction with the
spiritual and social maximalism of Christianity. The old
world entered this 'barbarism' and exploded it from within
and then by its nature philistinised Christianity. And
now Russia's mission is to impregnate the 'cultured' old
world with the spirit of maximalism. For only this spiritual maximalism, this 'Scythianism,' can open the way to
the genuine liberation of man which Christianity simply
could not achieve, for Christianity itself 'failed.'"[13]
The old world challenges the revolution with guns and bay-
onets but the Russian Scythian calls to the western
Scythian, in Blok's poem:

> "Come into our peaceful embrace."

"This," suggests Ivanov-Razumnik, "is the call of the
Russian revolution (for 'Scythianism' is revolution) to
world revolution."[14] But while Blok began his poem with
the claim that there were hosts and hosts and hosts of
Scythians who were not afraid of the mere millions of the
West, Zamyatin was quick to point out that Blok had not
made sufficient distinction between the many who adapt,
who make a practical compromise with their ideals and who
appear as victorious in revolution while in fact being
philistines and those few who hold their belief in freedom, accepting it as an unattainable ideal, but who are
victorious on the plane of ideas and who are rebels and
heretics under any regime. "But there will never be
'hosts' of them. The divine course of every true Scythian
is to be 'a stranger in his own land, not in a strange
land,'"[15] says Zamyatin, quoting Remizov.

The writers who best answered the Scythians' aspirations with emotional, un-philistinised, totally committed
responses to the revolution were, in Ivanov-Razumnik's
opinion the peasant poets Kliuev, Esenin and Oreshin. The
reason for this, he decides is "authenticity of experience
--this is the great little thing which gave strength to
the voices of the popular poets during the days of the
revolution. And it is noteworthy that almost all the
'city poets' failed miserably in revolution just as they

had during the war."[16]   It is still impossible to improve
on Professor Filippov's term of 'slavophilising
narodniks,' quoted earlier.

While acknowledging the vagueness of the terms, we
are nevertheless able to recognise the consistency of the
Scythians' claim for the validity of a spontaneous approach
to things.   They reject reasoned calculation just as they
reject compromise or half measures.   They insist that the
individual assert his point of view within the collective:
a natural, popular, even primitive, awareness of right and
wrong and a sense of responsibility towards the collective
would guarantee that people responded as individuals within a collective without coercion by systematisation.

Summarised thus baldly the "Scythian" approach, though
revolutionary in spirit, sounds naïve, if not heretical, in
the context of a disciplined and centrally controlled
social reorganisation such as has been pursued in the Soviet Union over the past half-century.   That a "Scythian"
assertion of individual freedom can survive even a past
policy of internal terror and the more reasoned appeals of
the promise of social justice, peace and relative prosperity of the present is evidenced in the work of the contemporary prose writer Vasily Shukshin, among others.

By collating the information contained in various
volumes and magazine publications and in his obituaries it
is possible to compile a short biography of Shukshin.
Vasily Makarovich Shukshin was born of peasant stock in
1929 in the village of Srostki near Biisk in the Altai
steppe of south central Siberia.   His mother was living
there in 1968, his brother was a truck-driver and his sister a school teacher.   He finished seven-year school in
1943 and at sixteen went to work in the collective farm
after failing in his studies at a motor-technical college,
then worked as a labourer, apprentice painter and scaf-
folder building factories in Kaluga and Vladimir.   He did
his military service from 1949 to 1952 as a radio operator
on a destroyer of the Black Sea Fleet and finished the
ten-year school course as an external student.   From 1953-
1954 he was a teacher of literature and history and then
director of a seven-year evening school for rural youth.
In 1954 he went to Moscow to study at the All-union State
Institute of Cinematography, graduating as a director in
1960 in Mikhail Romm's class.   For four years he lived in
a Moscow hostel without a residence permit.   His acting
career had begun in 1959 in Marlen Khutsiev's film *Dva
Fedora*.   He also played in *My, dvoe muzhchin* scripted by

Anatoly Kuznetsov and a number of other films, but during
a lull when he was offered only unsuitable parts and not
yet offered any films to direct, he wrote some of his early
stories. His first stories were published in *Oktiabr* in
1961 and his first edition of stories, *Sel'skie zhiteli*
came out in 1963. In 1964 he received his Moscow residence
permit and directed the film *Zhivet takoi paren'*, which was
awarded the Grand Prix for children's films in Venice. He
published a novel, *Liubaviny*, "The Lyubavin Family," in
1965 and in 1967 was awarded the Vasilyev Brothers State
Prize for a film he directed the previous year, *Vash syn i
brat*. Two more editions of his stories, *Tam vdali* and
Zemliaki, came out in 1968 and 1970. By 1970 he had acted
in some ten films including *U ozera* which criticised official indifference to the pollution of Lake Baikal, and
Osvobozhdenie, and had directed *Strannye liudi* based on
three of his own stories. He was by then married to the
actress Lida Fedoseeva and had two daughters. He was a
Merited Artist of the RSFSR and had been awarded the Red
Banner of Labour. He had also written the screenplay for
a two-part film of Stenka Razin which he was to direct and
in which he was to play the central rôle. In an interview
in 1974 he confirmed that he was still planning the production of this film but had meanwhile published a novel
based on the screenplay. In 1973 another edition of stories, *Kharaktery*, was published. Over the years some 29 of
his stories were published in *Novy mir*. 1974 saw the success of his film *Kalina krasnaia* which he scripted, directed and starred in. A new edition of his stories, *Besedy
pri iasnoi lune*, appeared and in the summer he was acting
in the film of Sholokhov's *Oni srazhalis' za rodinu*. He
died suddenly on October 2nd 1974.

   Shukshin's stories, like most of his films, present
images of contemporary Russian village life, but, as one
Soviet critic says, "not the village as a whole, rather
that part of it which is most affected by urban culture
and which constitutes fertile ground for migration from
the village to the construction site, to the nearest re-
gional centre or to small towns. It cannot be an accident
that Shukshin's most frequent heroes are village truck-
drivers (they have also featured in his films), a profession new to the village to whom Marx's words about the
'idiocy of rural life' were inapplicable right from the
start."[18] But while recording the villager's desire to
catch up with the modern world he is primarily interested

in character and spiritual values. He avoids a sociological analysis of the village, does not illustrate the workings of agricultural, educational or administrative policies or describe techniques, work schedules or economic
responsibilities. The few officials who appear are either
not considered as officials, or play minor and negative
rôles. Thus Matvei Kazantsev in *Dumy* is seen not as the
collective farm chairman but as an elderly insomniac working out a new outlook on life, and in *Nol'-nol' tselykh*
the sovkhoz pay clerk Sinel'nikov flaunts his authority
over the young Kol'ka Skalkin provoking him to throw a
bottle of ink at him, and though this was deserved, being
sure that there is no legal proof of the verbal abuse
which led to Kol'ka's assault. If anything, a social consciousness coincides in Shukshin's stories with the appearance of forces which destroy the personality. In
Oratorskii priem the long-awaited recognition of a man's
zeal with the award of some authority over his thirteen
fellow peasants leads to a swing towards dictatorship, and
in *Zhena muzha v Parizh provozhala* Kol'ka Paratov, married
to a tailor's daughter, finds he cannot escape his new
bourgeois environment because he is devoted to his own
daughter, and commits suicide. But this social dimension
is a relatively recent intrusion into Shukshin's village
scene. The conflict between town and village, however,
has long been a theme with Shukshin who has consistently
shown us the countryman's superior moral standards and
fortitude, for example in *Kukushkiny slezki* where a young
artist is shamed by being gently rebuffed in an attempted
seduction of a village girl, or in *Tam, vdali*, when the
young man from the village resists the corruption of the
town including the criminal speculation of his wife with
whom he remains infatuated. In *Kapronovaya elka* the sup-
plier from the town, epitomising the Soviet bourgeois,
loses his courage in a blizzard and has to be carried by
two peasants over whom he had previously boasted his superiority. In *Zmeiny iad*, a student from the country is
brought to despair by the indifference and obstructiveness
of the chemists from whom he tries to obtain the medicine
his mother needs. The note of social criticism is incidental to Shukshin's theme of humanity and kindness which
are lost in an urban setting. Shukshin himself claims not
so much to hate the town as to bewail its attraction for
villagers: "It pains me when a sinister silence falls
over a village in the evenings: there is no accordion
calling you, no song to listen to. Cocks crow, but

somehow they don't sound right, they are not part of the
community. There are no fishermen's fires across the
river, there are no shots over the islands and lakes in
the twilight. The shooting and singing have gone. I am
alarmed. They have gone, but where? If another rude
salesgirl has appeared in town (and it does not take her
long to learn) then who has gained? The town? No, the
village has lost. It has lost a worker, a bride, a mother, a preserver of national costumes, an embroiderer...
If a peasant lad after a little training in town draws a
line round himself, becomes smug and ashamed of his rural
relations, then this is patently a loss to humanity."[19]
Rather than analyse social phenomena Shukshin in his stories offers us a gallery of character studies of Russian
collective farmers and rural types which adds up to a
sympathetic overall view of the aspirations of the Soviet
village as well as the fallibility of its individual inhabitants.

But in his novels *Liubaviny*, about an Altai village
during the early twenties, and *Ya prishel dat' vam voliu*,
the novel which followed his screenplay for a film on
Stenka Razin, Shukshin does try to reveal the eternal
qualities of the Russian peasant as a social phenomenon
extending roots into history and independent of the particular conditions of the sixties and seventies which he
describes in his stories. As he said in an interview, to
understand the processes which have taken place in the
Russian peasantry you need to stand back and look at them
from a distance; "then you see the deep, intimate, indis-
soluble bond between Stepan Razin and the Russian peasantry. Razin's movement was not just outlaws from down
the Don, it was a movement fed by the life-blood of the
peasants and paid for with the heads and blood of the
peasants."[20] As with *Liubaviny* it is the personal, spiritual characteristics that concerned Shukshin in Razin:
"who he was, what he was, what sort of person--not on the
outside but in essence, in the depths--this had to be
answered. At a distance of 300 years the figure of Stepan
Razin is much more complex, more three-dimensional, more
contradictory. In his unrestrained passion for freedom
Razin is absolutely contemporary and consonant with our
period. Nevertheless he remains a man of his age and I
have no desire to smooth him out, to drag him into our
times."[21] By this Shukshin presumably meant his retention
of Razin's political immaturity; as the Great Soviet Encyclopedia puts it: "Marxist-Leninist classics have often

indicated the typical features of peasant movements during
the feudal epoch which are fully consistent with the peasant war of 1667-1671: their spontaneous character, dis-
jointedness and localisation of their manifestations. Besides this it was characteristic of peasant uprisings that
the peasants who rebelled were tsarist: they were acting
against the landowners but for the 'good tsar.'" Razin's
movement was, in fact, composed not only of peasants; its
military success depended on the experienced cossacks and
renegade *streltsy* who directed operations and formed the
army's core, as well as Tartar horsemen. But Razin's personality reigns supreme. It is he who expresses what
Shukshin feels is deep down in the Russian peasant soul, a
yearning for release.

The peasants in Shukshin's stories of contemporary
Russia often achieve this sense of release through violence or drink, though on not so grand a scale as Razin.
An alternative might be the village expedition to cut the
hay up in the mountains, which with its nocturnal high
jinks reminded the young policeman in *Liubaviny* of "a
feast-day, but without the vodka and fights."[22]

Shukshin's titles reveal his preference for the characters of peasant radicals--his collections *Sel'skie
zhiteli*, *Zemliaki* and *Kharaktery* as well as his individual
works *Strannye Liudi*, *Chudik*, *Diad'a Ermolai*, *Petia* and so
on. Many titles are snatched from direct speech: *Mil'
pardon, Madam!*, *Moi ziat' ukral mashin drov!*, which are
already evocative of quirky rustics.

Shukshin's method of creating these characters is
that of the actor. He aims to submerge his own presence
and to create a personality, its spiritual values, morality and ideology. In his stories he creates rôles to perform, but on paper, not on stage; the stories are the literary records of a method actor's preparation for self-
identification with a rôle, they are exercises in methodological keep-fit in which narrative has no value beyond
the requirements of characterisation. Unlike a method
actor, however, Shukshin concentrates on one type, the
peasant, and as a peasant by origin himself, he does not
need to invent, for he has the speech of the characters he
"plays" in his own upbringing. His language often contains colloquial words and syntax which merge with the dialogue. (Since no narrator emerges as a distinct consciousness and the stories concentrate on the characters
rather than the action we are not dealing with *skaz*).
Like Blok in "The Twelve," Shukshin enlivens the language

of the streets with popular expressions but not folksy say-
ings. Reflecting his attention to the urban influences on
rural culture he records, as one critic says, "the modification of the Russian language of the village and the intrusion of the urban literary language and sometimes even
of scientific or intellectual language into the very heart
of popular country speech and that of small towns, populated in their turn by recent arrivals from the countryside."[23] Shukshin has confirmed his preference for un-
bookish language and style: "So what is a story then? A
man was walking along a street and saw a friend and told
him for instance of an old woman who had just then round
the corner fallen down in the road and of a lanky bloke
who had roared with laughter, and then immediately felt
ashamed of his idiotic laughter, gone over and helped the
old woman up. And he had even looked round to see if anyone had seen him laughing. That's all. The man starts
his story: 'I'm going along the street just now and I see
an old woman going along. She slipped - crash! And some
lanky bloke didn't half laugh...' That is probably how he
would tell it. Why then when your story writer settles
down to write about the old woman does he have to tell us
what she was before 1917 or spend two pages telling us
what a fine morning it was the day the old woman fell
down. If he had just said: 'The morning was fine and
warm. It was autumn,' the reader would probably remember
a morning like that, warm and autumnal, from his own
life."[24]

By giving his characters the opportunity to reveal
themselves and to provide the logic of their actions he
allows them to take over the narrative, restricting the
author's rôle to scene-setting.

Shukshin does not identify with his characters, he
withholds comment on them, so we can only guess to what
extent he sympathises with his characters. In his subjects Shukshin has chosen peasants who are in themselves
remarkable and original in their aspirations, and there is
a sympathetic irony in the conflict between their environment and these aspirations. There is wit in their expressive language, so there is no need for the authorial irony
or elaborate imagery of Aksenov, for example. Shukshin's
own origins give us some right to suppose his sympathy for
his peasant subjects. This sympathy is manifest in the
extent to which Shukshin allows his characters to persevere
with unorthodox points of view and to retain a moral superiority over representatives of bureaucratic conformity.

In the story *Artist Fedor Grai*,[25] Grai, the village
blacksmith, speaks his lines too quietly and awkwardly for
the producer of the farm's amateur dramatics. Derided at
rehearsals, laughed at by audiences, he plays the "peasant" rôles but baulks not only at bureaucratic words like
sel'khoznauka, nezamedlitel'no and *v sushchnosti govoria*
but more stubbornly still at the non-literary "peasant"
forms *chiavo, kudy, evon, einy*. Incensed by the producer's nagging to speak louder he replaces his first line to
the bureaucratic collective-farm chairman: "How do you do,
Ivan Petrovich. I've come about the social club again,
ahem. You see, Ivan Petrovich, the youth of our village
..." with a surly "When are we going to get a social
club?" followed by a harangue which, while avoiding the
peasant clichés, the dull ungrammatical indicators of peasant speech, contains threat and invective of vivid pic-
turesqueness: "Carve this on your nose, chairman. You can
rot on your stove with your woman as long as you like but
we need the club. We've earned it. We also need a library. You've picked up the idea you can brow-beat us
with papers. I'm not interested in them, these papers.
And I don't want to live my life a fool, either!... You
sit there flapping your eyes like a crow. We would have
got to communism long ago if it weren't for people like
you. You tsarist basket!" Fyodor eventually leaves the
stage of his own club after his simultaneous plea for social improvement for the fictional village of the play and
his revolt against the phoney lines he was to have performed, determined to have no more to do with art. Three
days later he is announced the best actor in twenty rural
districts.

In a more recent story, *P'edestal*,[26] an ex-criminal, a
self-taught painter, a man whose figure, dress, speech and
manners are inelegant, has spent a year on a painting of
suicide, depicting a man aiming a gun at his double. The
picture is appallingly bad but his creative sense is satisfied by it and the ideas it awakens in his mind. He is
not a materialistic man, he had cooperated in counterfeit-
ing money only because his artistic talents were being appreciated by someone. He is happy with his taciturn wife
and has almost the same instinctive willingness to help
that marks Matryona and Solzhenitsyn's other characters
who fall foul of the system. But he is less than respect-
ful about the patrons of his art, both those who order the
café murals and advertising daubs and the public at whom
they are aimed. He is terribly disappointed when a local

professional artist laughs at his beloved painting but he
responds at once to his wife's hysteria when her secret
hopes of a different life once he is recognised as a great
artist are dashed. Though once a criminal, his natural
human qualities have survived and he has begun to think
for himself originally, albeit not intellectually, about
the larger questions of life--suicide, the peace-bomb,
drink and the need to show concern for others.

      In both these stories, as in others depicting self-
educated rural intellectuals, such as *Srezal*[27] and *Shtrikhi
k portretu*,[28] Shukshin's characters reject "official" solu-
tions to work out their own. Their thirst for knowledge is
inspired, except possibly in *Srezal*, by a desire to help
the community. Shukshin, as an *intelligent* from the village himself, must know and sympathise with these impatient
individualists or, to put it another way, "for a number of
writers, in particular V. Shukshin, V. Belov and V. Ras-
putin, the combination of a concrete, accurate and detailed
description of way of life with a profound sense of the
high tension of the spiritual life of the popular masses is
typical."[29]   (Conversely we may suggest that some of
Shukshin's attraction for intellectual readers comes from
his rustic coarseness.) The need to answer the questions
"What is it all for? Why work?" is felt by many of
Shukshin's characters and not always solved, which shows
some originality in a society where answers to such questions are journalists' bread and butter. The truck-driver
Ivan in *V profil' i anfas*, deprived of his licence though
basically a good worker, has time to philosophise, but unlike Efrem Podduev in "Cancer Ward," cannot find anything
with which to "pacify his soul." The nocturnal realisa-
tions of kolkhoz chairman Matvei Riazantsev in *Dumy* that
he had never stopped to think what it was all for because
everything had seemed self-evidently urgent and important
echo faintly the spiritual crisis of Chekhov's professor
in "A Boring Story." One of Shukshin's achievements, a
critic points out, is "to show a character in his realistic confusion without raising him on stilts and at the
same time bring the reader into contact with the poetic
world of the people and the lofty spiritual values of the
time--its humanism, moral firmness and communist convic-
tions."[30]   Shukshin is representative of a generation that
does not have to doubt that socialist values are normal
and natural. The Scythian mentality as defined by Ivanov-
Razumnik was hostile to the organised imposition of a social programme on the innocent populace but now that that

programme has been imposed the population of even the remoter villages of the Soviet Union accept the system that
has emerged as normal and display independence of outlook
within the context of that system. This does not often
result in law-breaking or ideological hostility, though a
casual attitude to bureaucratic formalities does result
from a rugged physical life-style and the necessary self-
sufficiency of the remoter villages. Shukshin's peasants
retain archetypal characteristics originating long before
Soviet ideology was conceived and Shukshin has explored
the historical dimension in his two novels to reveal in
the contemporary scene not Soviet ideology which is familiar to all but the now unfamiliar past. He can take the
ideals of socialism for granted, but the contemporary mis-
fit can only be explained in terms of the admirably re-
bellious but benighted cossacks of Stenka Razin or the im-
placable opponents of social conformity such as Egor
Liubavin, who joins the bandits after a fight with his
father over his right to marry, who kills the bandit leader when he finds him trying to seduce his bride, who kills
her when told that she is unfaithful, who shoots the man
who shot his brother, and who ends up an outlaw fiercely
struggling to survive according to his own concepts of
justice and integrity, sworn to kill the village policeman,
the representative of the new order.

Shukshin's irreverance for cultural niceties reaches
its end-stop in his evocation of the character of Stenka
Razin. First published as a screenplay entitled "I Have
Come to Set you Free"[31] and later expanded into a novel[32]
it recounts Razin's campaign on the Volga and Don starting
with the cossacks' return from a raid on Persia and their
efforts to buy their way back into the Tsar's favour and
past Astrakhan, followed by Razin's anti-boyar campaign
and ending with his inevitable bravely-faced torture and
execution. Only in a dozen short satirical scenes or
takes of the screenplay do we meet the opposition, Tsar
Alexei Mikhailovich and his court, the ruling clique in
Astrakhan and the town's *voevody* or outraged churchmen
intoning anathema on Razin. Shukshin's concern is for the
character of Razin, and his appeal for the cossacks and
peasants who rally to him. And Razin abandons conventions
of human behaviour with a totality that is Scythian, even
bearing in mind the relative ferocity of a seventeenth-
century peasant revolt. His unclearly defined programme
with its overt call for the destruction of the boyars and
his vision of Russia as a land of free cossacks surely

strike a chord with the subjectively revolutionary Scythians of 1918 or so.   There is a Scythian disdain of political considerations as well as humane ones in Razin's apparently thoughtless brutality: his tossing overboard of
the Persian princess (as in the song) and, in the screenplay, the summary beheading of her young brother--both of
them were hostages who could have been exchanged for cossack prisoners and who might have helped him in his tacit
ambition to become tsar by helping to make an ally of the
Shah; but ambition is not supported by calculation.   True,
he is dissuaded from murdering the metropolitan of
Astrakhan by the warning that this would merely create a
martyr for the established order but he promptly sets
about the iconostasis instead, an act of desecration
which, in the novel, almost leads to a split in his forces.
His total dedication to the cause of Russian popular revolt is reflected in his simple military premise that no
one who is hostile to his movement or causes disunity
should be spared.   *Streltsy*, merchants and *voevody* are accordingly massacred, drowned or executed without heed to
considerations of humanity or diplomacy.   Foreign experts,
admired by the Tsar's men, are scorned by Razin.   The pre-
revolutionary past with its social imperfections has been
adequately discredited in Russian and Soviet literature.
What Shukshin is looking for in Razin is the origin of the
rustic individualism in which he clearly delights.

     In his stories Shukshin explores this rustic indi-
vidualism within the familiar settings of the Soviet village.   His characters face ordinary situations which most
people have to react to conventionally or with official
etiquette, but which the conventional person imagines himself capable of confronting with urgent, selfish indifference to rational or ideological considerations.   In
Shukshin's sympathetic treatment of his very human mis-
fits with their tendency to resolve problems by deceit or
by the folk remedies of fists or vodka, with their hearts
of gold and livers of cast iron, we are allowed a sense of
anarchic release, but not total escapism since the system
is not rejected or even challenged.   One of Shukshin's few
statements of total release comes in the story *Dumy* when
an old man remembers being sent as a boy to fetch milk for
his dying brother: "Horse and human merged into one and
flew into the night.   And the night rushed towards them
and struck them in the face with the heavy scent of dew-
damp grass.   A wild delight seized the boy; the blood
flooded to his head and sang.   It was like flying--as if

he had torn himself off the earth and taken to the air.
Nothing was visible anywhere: not the ground, nor the sky,
not even the horse's head--there was only the noise in his
ears, only the huge night world on the move and rushing at
him... His soul was exultant, every fibre in his body vi-
brated. It was a kind of longed-for, rare, instinctive
joy." But this joy is only a childhood memory and even so
was not an irresponsible indulgence, but experienced while
trying to help someone else. As a statement of the Scythian mentality one could hardly do better. A response is
made on a basic human level without reference to lofty
ideals. There is a natural order of things, primitive and
simple, and this includes an awareness of the community,
of the collective, of identity, as well as of independent
decision-making. The individual's self-discovery, the
realisation of social responsibility and strength is the
keynote of Shukshin's more recent stories. His characters discover fulfilment in freedom of action in the common cause. This freedom does not require surrender of all
individual responsibility à la Grand Inquisitor; unlike a
capitulation it preserves the individual's conscious, active choice. He has the right to participate in the community and awakens from a feudal, conscience-less subservience, from a mindless stampede through life. The
realisation that he has lived without genuine involvement,
integrity or purpose and the questioning of motives after
an impulsive action or a whole lifetime of conformity may
come belatedly. If may be provoked by the prospect of
death, as in *Dumy* or *Kak pomiral starik*. In some stories
the awakening does not quite succeed, as in *Okhota zhit'*
where the young criminal on the run finally shoots the old
man who has sheltered him for the night, or *Krepkii muzhik*
in which the hero bulldozes down the village church in
spite of, perhaps because of, everyone's objections; (The
objections of course are not religious--Shukshin takes
materialism for granted). There is, however, a predom-
inance of stories whose theme is regret for past mistakes
and wasted lives, or about impulses to redress a balance
or work for the social good. In their individually recognised social responsibilities Shukshin's characters manifest a fundamental Scythian principle.
     Personal responsibility begins with deciding what is
right and wrong, and Shukshin's rogues with their reliance
on an instinctive sense of justice inevitably come into
conflict with the established law code. Shukshin's treatment remains sympathetic: the hero of *Stepka*, who defaults

from his labour-camp three months before his sentence ex-
pires in order to see his family after tormenting dreams,
is even treated sympathetically by the village policeman
yet, content to have seen his home, he is quite resigned
to serving two more years for his escape. "This world is
pure and bright"[33] admits a Soviet critic. Even the bland
killer of *Okhota zhit'* has admirable qualities: unlike the
intellectual he is pure instinct, he has barbaric energy
and determination to survive and his ruthless consistency
and rejection of compromise are those that Dostoevsky admired in the less social inmates of The House of the Dead.
Literary precursors for the majority of Shukshin's heroes
who are not desperadoes are not easy to find. Gorky's
strong, revolutionary tramps, Chelkash perhaps, recommend
themselves but they stood up for themselves and despised
the masses who conformed to a system that was unjust.
Shukshin's heroes also stand up for themselves, respond
openly and accept no convenient compromise, but their assertion of independently formulated morality leads them
broadly to accept their social duty with and for their
fellow men. Uncoerced, their expression of popular but
independent attitudes and occasional iconoclastic violence mark a reemergence of the Scythian ethos.

Shukshin stated his position as citizen and artist in
1965 when Khutsiev's film *Mne 20 let* was being vigorously
discussed in the Soviet press. Shukshin's first screen
rôle had been in a Khutsiev film and he rallied to his
cause: "I profoundly admire the resoluteness with which
Marlen Khutsiev has attempted to understand the spiritual
life of our young and not so young contemporaries. If
this sounds too arrogant then I can put it another way: I
value his civic conscience, the ability of his soul to
feel other people's anguish.

"We, the living, were never given ready answers on
how best to live. And we do not believe in this--in
ready answers. As a film-goer I am grateful to Marlen
Khutsiev for his latest picture. He probably did not express everything the way it should have been expressed but
he has made me think once again about myself and about how
one should live. Is this not the artist's happiest lot?"[34]

University of Durham

NOTES

[1]*Skify: sbornik pervy* Knigoizdatel'stvo "Skify," SPb. 1917. p. vii.

[2]Ye. Zamiatin "Skify li?" *Mysl'* 1918. No. 1 translated as "Scythians?" in "A Soviet Heretic. Essays by Evgeny Zamiatin," Chicago UP 1970, p. 21.

[3]B. Filippov, "Nikolai Kliuev," introduction to Kliuev's "Sochineniia," Neimanis, 1969, vol. 1, p. 81.

[4]B. Iakobenko, "Izdatel'stvo "Skify" v Berline," *Russkaia Kniga*, No. 1, Berlin, 1921, p. 9.

[5]B. Filippov, ibid., p. 86.

[6]Ilya Ehrenburg, "Men, Years - Life," vol. 2. "First years of Revolution," London, 1962, p. 161.

[7]"Skify," op. cit., p. ix.

[8]Ivanov-Razumnik, "Skifskoe," in *Puti Revoliutsii (stat'i, materialy, vospominaniia)*, Knigoizdatel'stvo "Skify," Berlin, 1923, p. 7. (See also "Skify," op. cit., p. x.)

[9]Ivanov-Razumnik, "Svoe litso," in the 2nd compendium Skify, pp. 78-79.

[10]Ivanov-Razumnik, "Svoe litso," p. 79.

[11]Ivanov-Razumnik, "Ispytanie v groze i bure," in A.A. Blok *Dvenadtsat'*. *Skify*, Sankt-Peterburg, 1918, pp. 3-30.

[12]Ibid., pp. 23-24.

[13]Ibid., p. 24.

[14]Ibid., p. 26.

[15]Zamiatin, op. cit., p. 32.

[16]Ivanov-Razumnik, "Poety i revoliutsia," in *God Revoliutsii. Stat'i 1917 goda*, S-Pb, 1918, p.177.

[17]I. Gummer, "A stepnaia trava pakhnet gorech'iu," *Literaturnaia gazeta*, 1974, no. 25, p. 8.

[18]V. Kantorovich, "Novye tipy, novyi slovar', novye otnosheniia," *Sibirskie ogni*, 1971, no. 9, p. 176.

[19]V. Shukshin, "Voprosy samomu sebe," *Sel'skaia molodezh'*, 1966, no. 11, quoted in V. Iavinsky, "Pisatel', akter, rezhisser," *Altai*, 1968, no. 1, p. 113.

[20]Interview with Shukshin in *Literaturnaia gazeta*, quoted by V. Petelin in "Stepan Razin - lichnost' i obraz," *Volga*, 1972, no. 3, p. 158.

[21]Ibid.

[22]V. Shukshin, "Liubaviny," Moscow, 1965, p. 162.

[23]V. Kantorovich, op. cit., p. 177.

[24]Shukshin in a discussion on the short story in *Literaturnaia Rossiia*, quoted by S. Borovikov in "Kharaktery Vasiliia Shukshina," *Volga*, 1972, no. 1, p. 183. (See

also his answers to a questionnaire on the language of literature in *Voprosy literatury*, 1967, No. 6, pp. 148-150.)

[25] *Moskva*, 1962, No. 4.

[26] *Sel'skaia molodezh'*, 1973, No. 5.

[27] In *Zemliaki* and *Kharaktery*.

[28] *Nash sovremennik*, 1973, No. 9.

[29] Ia. El'sberg, "Vysokoe naprazhenie. Zametki o svoeobrazii literatury v razvitom sotsialisticheskom obshchestve," *Literaturnaia gazeta*, 1973, No. 51, p. 4.

[30] V. Voronov, "*Liki narodnoi zhizni*," M. 1972, p. 294.

[31] "Ya prishel dat' vam voliu. Stsenarii," *Iskusstvo kino*, 1968, No. 5, pp. 143-187 and No. 6, pp. 131-185.

[32] "Ya prishel dat' vam voliu. Roman," *Sibirskie ogni*, 1971, No. 1, pp. 3-95 and No. 2, pp. 3-122.

[33] S. Borovikov, "Kharaktery Vasiliia Shukshina," *Volga*, 1972, No. 1, p. 185.

[34] V. Shukshin in *Iskusstvo kino*, 1965, No. 4, p. 36.

OTHER BOOKS FROM SLAVICA PUBLISHERS, INC.

Henrik Birnbaum: *Common Slavic Progress and Problems in Its Reconstruction*, xi + 436 p., 1975.

Malcolm H. Brown, ed.: *Papers of the Yugoslav-American Seminar on Music*, 208 p., 1970.

Catherine V. Chvany: *On the Syntax of Be-Sentences in Russian*, viii + 311 p., 1975.

Frederick Columbus: *Introductory Workbook in Historical Phonology*, 39 p., 1974.

Dina B. Crockett: *Agreement in Contemporary Standard Russian*, iv + 456 p., 1976.

Charles E. Gribble: *Medieval Slavic Texts, Vol. 1, Old and Middle Russian Texts*, 320 p., 1973.

Charles E. Gribble: *Russian Root List with a Sketch of Russian Word Formation*, 56 p., 1973.

Charles E. Gribble: Словарик русского языка 18-го века, 103 p., 1976.

Charles E. Gribble: *Studies Presented to Professor Roman Jakobson by His Students*, 333 p., 1968.

Raina Katzarova-Kukudova & Kiril Djenev, *Bulgarian Folk Dances*, 174 p., numerous illustrations, 2nd printing 1976 (1st printing, Sofia, 1958).

Demetrius J. Koubourlis, ed.: *Topics in Slavic Phonology*, viii + 270 p., 1974.

Michael K. Launer: *Elementary Russian Syntax*, ix + 140 p., 1974.

Alexander Lipson: *A Russian Course*, Revised edition, 1977.

Kenneth E. Naylor, ed.: *Balkanistica: Occasional Papers in Southeast European Studies; I(1974)*, 189 p., 1975; *II(1975)*, 153 p., 1976.

Vasa D. Mihailovich and Mateja Matejić: *Yugoslav Literature in English A Bibliography of Translations and Criticism (1821-1975)*, ix + 328 p., 1976.

OTHER BOOKS FROM SLAVICA PUBLISHERS, INC,

Hongor Oulanoff: *The Prose Fiction of Veniamin A. Kaverin*, v + 203 p., 1976.

Jan L. Perkowski, ed.: *Vampires of the Slavs* (a collection of readings), 294 p., 1976.

Lester A. Rice: *Hungarian Morphological Irregularities*, 80 p., 1970.

Midhat Ridjanović: *A Synchronic Study of Verbal Aspect in English and Serbo-Croatian*, ix + 147 p., 1976.

David F. Robinson: *Lithuanian Reverse Dictionary*, ix + 209 p., 1976.

Ernest A. Scatton: *Bulgarian Phonology*, xii + 224 p.

William R. Schmalstieg: *Introduction to Old Church Slavic*, 290 p., 1976.

Michael Shapiro: *Aspects of Russian Morphology, A Semiotic Investigation*, 62 p., 1969.

Charles E. Townsend: *Russian Word-Formation, corrected reprint*, xviii + 272 p., 1975.

D. N. Ushakov, ed.: Толковый словарь русского языка, original edition in 4 volumes, Moscow, 1934-1940; reprint (slightly reduced in page size, corrections indicated throughout, 4 volumes bound in 3) 1974.

Victor A. Friedman: *The Grammatical Categories of the Macedonian Indicative*, ca 160 p., 1977.

Jules F. Levin: *Reading Contemporary Russian*, 1977.

Maurice I. Levin: *Russian Declension and Conjugation: A Structural Description with Workbook.* 1977.

Alexander Lipson: *Verb Workbook, revised edition.*

F. V. Mareš: *Hospodine Pomiluj Ny, A Study of the Language, Verse, and Origin of an Old Slavic Hymn*, ca. 190 p., 1977.

Mateja Matejić and Dragan Milivojević: *An Anthology of Medieval Serbian Literature.*